FOOD & WINE
ANNUAL COOKBOOK 2014

FOOD & WINE ANNUAL COOKBOOK 2014

EXECUTIVE EDITOR **Kate Heddings**

EDITOR **Susan Choung**

DESIGNER **Jooyoung Hsu**

FEATURES EDITOR **Michael Endelman**

SENIOR WINE EDITOR **Megan Krigbaum**

COPY EDITOR **Lisa Leventer**

EDITORIAL ASSISTANT **Sarah Kraut**

PRODUCTION MANAGERS
Matt Carson, Amelia Grohman

PHOTO EDITOR **Sara Parks**

FRONT COVER

Mixed Grill with Fresh Tomato-and-Pepper Salsa (recipe, page 207)

PHOTOGRAPHER **Fredrika Stjärne**

STYLIST **Alison Attenborough**

BACK COVER

PHOTOGRAPHER (PASTA AND CHICKEN)
Con Poulos

PHOTOGRAPHER (CAKE) **Johnny Miller**

FOOD & WINE MAGAZINE

SVP/EDITOR IN CHIEF **Dana Cowin**

CREATIVE DIRECTOR **Stephen Scoble**

EXECUTIVE MANAGING EDITOR **Mary Ellen Ward**

EXECUTIVE EDITOR **Pamela Kaufman**

EXECUTIVE FOOD EDITOR **Tina Ujlaki**

EXECUTIVE WINE EDITOR **Ray Isle**

EXECUTIVE DIGITAL EDITOR **Rebecca Bauer**

DEPUTY EDITOR **Christine Quinlan**

FEATURES

FEATURES EDITOR **Michael Endelman**

RESTAURANT EDITOR **Kate Krader**

TRAVEL EDITOR **Gina Hamadey**

SENIOR WINE EDITOR **Megan Krigbaum**

MARKET EDITOR **Suzie Myers**

EDITORIAL ASSISTANTS **Maren Ellingboe, Chelsea Morse, M. Elizabeth Sheldon**

FOOD

DEPUTY EDITOR **Kate Heddings**

TEST KITCHEN SENIOR EDITOR **Kay Chun**

ASSOCIATE EDITOR **Daniel Gritzer**

TEST KITCHEN ASSOCIATE EDITOR **Justin Chapple**

TEST KITCHEN ASSISTANT **Gina Mungiovi**

EDITORIAL ASSISTANT **Julia Heffelfinger**

ART

DESIGN DIRECTOR **Patricia Sanchez**

ASSOCIATE ART DIRECTOR **James Maikowski**

DESIGNER **Bianca Jackson**

PHOTO

DIRECTOR OF PHOTOGRAPHY **Fredrika Stjärne**

PHOTO EDITOR **Sara Parks**

PHOTO ASSISTANT **Tomi Omololu-Lange**

COPY & RESEARCH

SENIOR COPY EDITOR **Ann Lien**

ASSOCIATE RESEARCH EDITOR **Erin Laverty**

ASSISTANT RESEARCH EDITOR **Joseph Harper**

PRODUCTION

PRODUCTION MANAGERS
Matt Carson, Amelia Grohman

PRODUCTION ASSISTANT **Chelsea Schiff**

DIGITAL MEDIA

FEATURES EDITOR **Alex Vallis**

SENIOR EDITOR **Lawrence Marcus**

ASSOCIATE ART DIRECTOR **Jooyoung Hsu**

ASSISTANT EDITOR **Justine Sterling**

EDITORIAL ASSISTANT **Brianna Wippman**

EDITORIAL CONTENT MANAGER
Kerianne Hansen

ASSISTANT TO THE EDITOR IN CHIEF
Jacqueline Westbrook

AMERICAN EXPRESS PUBLISHING, A DIVISION OF TIME INC. AFFLUENT MEDIA GROUP

PRESIDENT/CHIEF EXECUTIVE OFFICER **Ed Kelly**

CHIEF MARKETING OFFICER/PRESIDENT, DIGITAL MEDIA **Mark V. Stanich**

SVP/CHIEF FINANCIAL OFFICER **Paul B. Francis**

VPS/GENERAL MANAGERS
Frank Bland, Keith Strohmeier

VP, BOOKS & PRODUCTS/PUBLISHER **Marshall Corey**

DIRECTOR, BOOK PROGRAMS **Bruce Spanier**

SENIOR MARKETING MANAGER, BRANDED BOOKS
Eric Lucie

DIRECTOR OF FULFILLMENT & PREMIUM VALUE
Philip Black

MANAGER OF CUSTOMER SERVICE & PRODUCT FULFILLMENT **Betsy Wilson**

DIRECTOR OF FINANCE **Thomas Noonan**

ASSOCIATE BUSINESS MANAGER **Uma Mahabir**

VP, OPERATIONS **Tracy Kelliher**

OPERATIONS DIRECTOR **Anthony White**

SENIOR MANAGER, CONTRACTS & RIGHTS
Jeniqua Moore

FOOD&WINE

ANNUAL COOKBOOK 2014

AN ENTIRE YEAR OF RECIPES

FOOD&WINE
BOOKS

American Express Publishing,
a division of Time Inc. Affluent Media Group, New York

MARINATED SKIRT STEAK
TACOS, PAGE 198

CONTENTS

SKILLET PORK CHOPS WITH
WARM ESCAROLE CAESAR, PAGE 176

MARINATED SKIRT STEAK
TACOS, PAGE 198

FOOD&WINE
ANNUAL
COOKBOOK 2014

AN ENTIRE YEAR OF RECIPES

FOOD&WINE
BOOKS

American Express Publishing,
a division of Time Inc. Affluent Media Group, New York

FOREWORD

EVERY YEAR WE TEST THOUSANDS OF RECIPES in our kitchen, tucked away on the ninth floor of a nondescript building in midtown Manhattan. The testing allows our amazing cooks to make the recipes, which we then taste and discuss and debate. (A recent quinoa salad was especially divisive.) Everyone scribbles on a comment sheet, offering suggestions on how to improve the dish—except when we hit on a winner. Then it's all raves; those recipes become our staff favorites.

Over the year, we name roughly 200 staff favorites, and some of our readers cook only those recipes—you'll see those dishes throughout this book marked with yellow dots next to the titles. Here, a few to get you started:

Cucumber-Fennel Salad with Herbed Goat Yogurt, P. 56. From chef Tom Colicchio, this is an outrageously tasty recipe with a super-simple four-ingredient dressing. "I love how tangy and crunchy this is," one editor wrote on the comment sheet.

Grilled Pork with Coconut Rice and Lemongrass Sambal, P. 180. Chef Suzanne Goin's all-in-one meal (the recipe includes bok choy as a side) is deceptively easy. Editor comment: "The herbs, the heat, the aromatics—they all come together so well."

Cherry-Almond Clafoutis, P. 316. Pastry chef Belinda Leong smartly adds almond flour to the batter to lighten the texture and add flavor. "This is the best version of a clafoutis we've ever had," one editor exclaimed.

We encourage you to try all our staff favorites, and also to find your own favorites among the 700 recipes in the book—grab your marker and start making dots!

Editor in Chief
FOOD & WINE

Executive Editor
FOOD & WINE Cookbooks

Fashion designer Erin Fetherston hosts a chic dinner at her Manhattan apartment, serving updated party food by chef Michael White of The Butterfly.

Opposite: recipe, page 12.

ARTICHOKE DIP WITH CRISPY SHALLOTS

HORS
D'OEUVRES
& STARTERS

Árbol Chile Salsa

TOTAL: 35 MIN PLUS CHILLING
MAKES 1 CUP ● ● ●

¼ teaspoon cumin seeds
5 allspice berries
2 whole cloves
1½ teaspoons dried Mexican oregano
2 tablespoons sesame seeds
2 tablespoons raw *pepitas*
  (pumpkin seeds)
1 ounce dried árbol chiles (about
  50 chiles), stemmed and seeded
1 cup apple cider vinegar
2 large garlic cloves
1½ teaspoons sugar
1½ teaspoons kosher salt

1. In a mortar or spice grinder, combine the cumin seeds, allspice berries, cloves and oregano; finely grind. Transfer to a blender.
2. In a small skillet, toast the sesame seeds over moderate heat, stirring, until golden, 3 to 5 minutes. Transfer the seeds to the blender. Add the pumpkin seeds to the skillet and toast over moderate heat, tossing occasionally, until golden, 3 to 5 minutes. Transfer the pumpkin seeds to the blender.
3. Add the chiles, vinegar, garlic, sugar and salt to the blender and puree until smooth. Funnel the salsa into a glass jar or bottle and chill before serving. —*Alex Stupak*
MAKE AHEAD The salsa can be covered and refrigerated for at least 3 months.

Habanero Salsa

ACTIVE: 40 MIN; TOTAL: 1 HR 45 MIN
PLUS CHILLING • MAKES 1¾ CUPS ● ● ●

20 red or orange habanero chiles
1 medium white onion, thinly sliced
1 teaspoon finely grated orange zest,
  plus ½ cup fresh orange juice
¾ teaspoon finely grated lime zest,
  plus 2 tablespoons fresh lime juice
1 cup apple cider vinegar
1 teaspoon dried Mexican oregano
2 tablespoons extra-virgin olive oil
2 teaspoons kosher salt
1½ teaspoons sugar

1. Preheat the oven to 375°. Spread the habaneros and onion in a single layer on a large rimmed baking sheet. Roast for about 30 minutes, stirring once, until the chiles and onion are soft and barely browned in spots. Let cool completely.
2. Wearing gloves, carefully remove and discard the stems and seeds from the habaneros and transfer the chiles to a blender. Add the onion, orange and lime zests and juices, vinegar, oregano and ½ cup of water and puree until smooth.
3. In a saucepan, heat the oil. Carefully add the puree and bring to a simmer. Cook over moderately low heat, stirring occasionally, until reduced to 1¾ cups, about 30 minutes. Stir in the salt and sugar and let cool completely. Funnel the salsa into glass jars or bottles and chill before serving. —*Alex Stupak*
MAKE AHEAD The habanero salsa can be refrigerated for at least 3 months.
BEER Brisk, hoppy kölsch: Captain Lawrence.

Mayan Pumpkin-Seed Dip

TOTAL: 25 MIN
MAKES 1¼ CUPS ● ● ●

5 ounces raw *pepitas* (pumpkin
  seeds; about 1 cup)
2 tablespoons canola oil
½ cup finely chopped shallots
1 large jalapeño—stemmed, seeded
  and finely chopped
3 garlic cloves, minced
Kosher salt
¼ cup lightly packed parsley
¼ cup lightly packed cilantro
2 tablespoons fresh lime juice
1 tablespoon extra-virgin olive oil
¼ teaspoon finely grated orange zest
Tortilla chips, for serving

1. In a large skillet, toast the pumpkin seeds over moderate heat, tossing occasionally, until lightly golden, about 5 minutes. Transfer to a food processor.
2. In the same skillet, heat the canola oil until shimmering. Add the shallots, jalapeño, garlic and a generous pinch of salt and cook over moderate heat, stirring occasionally, until softened, about 5 minutes. Transfer the mixture to the food processor and let cool.
3. Add the parsley, cilantro, lime juice, olive oil, orange zest and ¼ cup of water to the food processor; puree until nearly smooth. Season with salt. Transfer the *sikil pak* to a bowl and serve with tortilla chips.
—*Mike Isabella*
MAKE AHEAD The *sikil pak* dip can be refrigerated for up to 3 days. Bring to room temperature before serving.

Smoked-Chile-and-Mango Guacamole

TOTAL: 20 MIN
MAKES 2½ CUPS ● ●

1 tablespoon extra-virgin olive oil
2 plum tomatoes,
  cut into ¼-inch dice
1 shallot, finely chopped
2 dried chipotle chiles, stems
  discarded and chiles finely crushed
Kosher salt
2 Hass avocados—halved,
  pitted and diced
½ cup finely chopped white onion
1 serrano chile, minced
3 tablespoons fresh lime juice
½ mango, cut into ¼-inch dice
  (½ cup)
1 cup lightly packed cilantro, finely
  chopped, plus whole cilantro leaves
  for garnish
Tortilla chips, for serving

1. In a medium skillet, heat the olive oil. Stir in half of the diced tomatoes and add the shallot, chipotles and a generous pinch of salt. Cook over moderate heat, stirring occasionally, until the chiles are softened, about 5 minutes. Scrape the mixture into a large bowl and let cool completely.
2. Add the avocados, onion, serrano chile, lime juice and the remaining diced tomato to the bowl and stir gently. Gently fold in the diced mango and chopped cilantro and season with salt. Garnish the guacamole with cilantro leaves and serve with tortilla chips.
—*Steve Menter*

● HEALTHY ● MAKE AHEAD ● VEGETARIAN ● STAFF FAVORITE

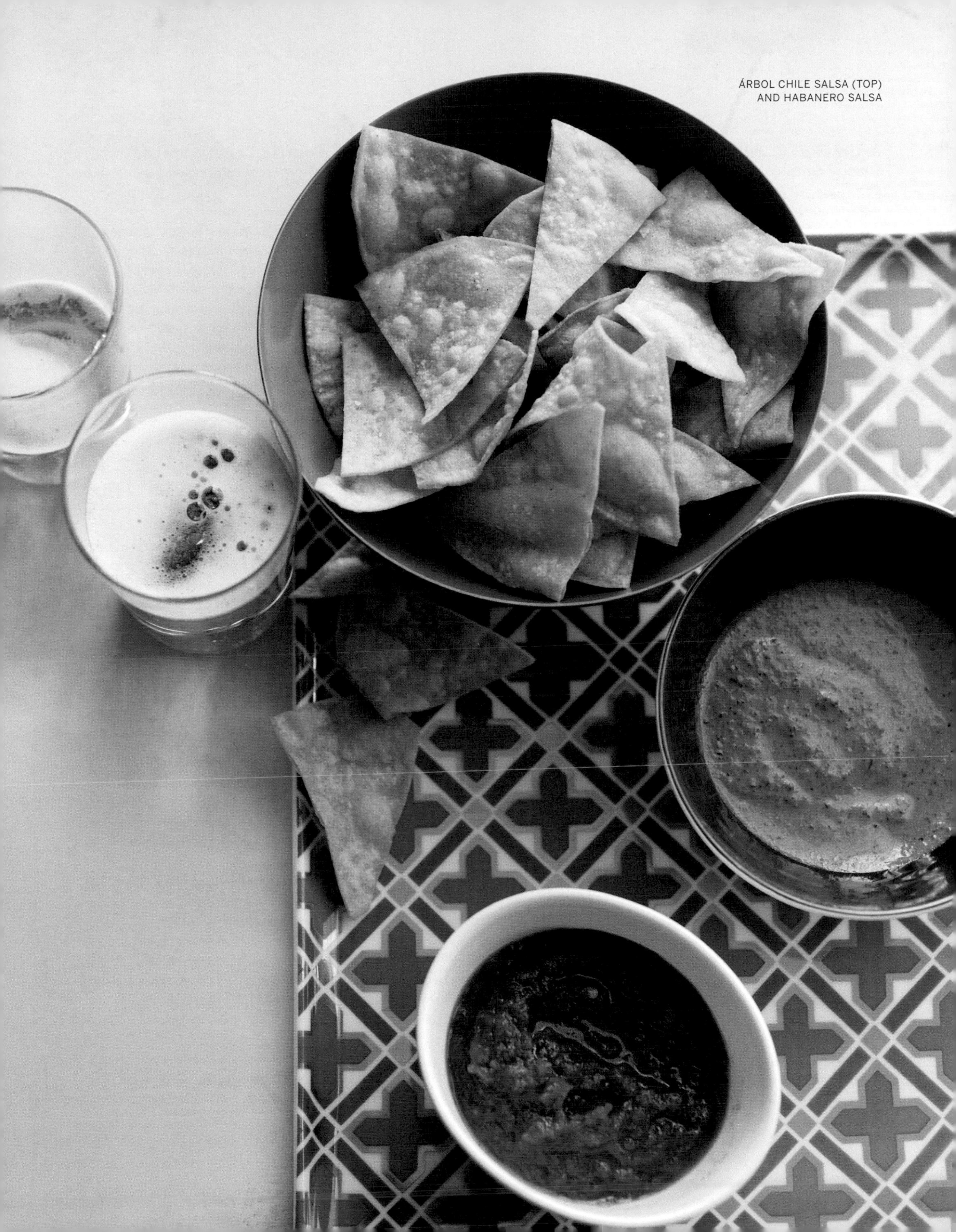

ÁRBOL CHILE SALSA (TOP)
AND HABANERO SALSA

Artichoke Dip with Crispy Shallots

📷 PAGE 9

ACTIVE: 30 MIN; TOTAL: 1 HR

8 SERVINGS ● ●

- 2 tablespoons extra-virgin olive oil, plus more for frying
- 2 large shallots—1 minced, 1 thinly sliced
- 2 garlic cloves, minced

One 9-ounce package frozen artichoke hearts, thawed and drained

- ¼ cup dry white wine
- 8 ounces cream cheese, softened
- 1 cup shredded Gruyère cheese (3 ounces)
- 2 tablespoons finely chopped parsley
- 1½ tablespoons fresh lemon juice
- 1 teaspoon Tabasco
- ½ cup plus 2 tablespoons freshly grated Parmigiano-Reggiano cheese

Kosher salt and freshly ground pepper

- ¼ cup panko (Japanese bread crumbs)

Toast points and assorted crudités, such as blanched broccoli or romanesco florets, red bell pepper strips and fennel wedges, for serving

1. Preheat the oven to 400°. In a medium skillet, heat the 2 tablespoons of olive oil until shimmering. Add the minced shallot and garlic and cook over moderately low heat, stirring occasionally, until softened, about 5 minutes. Add the artichokes and cook over moderate heat, stirring occasionally, until heated through, about 5 minutes. Add the wine and simmer until most of the liquid has evaporated, about 3 minutes; let the mixture cool.

2. In a medium bowl, combine the cream cheese with the Gruyère, parsley, lemon juice, Tabasco and ½ cup of the Parmigiano. Fold in the artichoke mixture and season the dip with salt and pepper. Scrape into a shallow 3-cup baking dish and smooth the surface. Sprinkle the panko and remaining 2 tablespoons of Parmigiano on top. Bake for about 20 minutes, until heated through and lightly golden on top.

3. Meanwhile, in a small skillet, heat ¼ inch of olive oil until shimmering. Add the sliced shallot and fry over moderate heat, stirring, until golden and crisp, about 5 minutes. Using a slotted spoon, transfer the fried shallot to paper towels to drain and cool. Sprinkle the fried shallot on top of the artichoke dip and serve with toast points and crudités. —*Michael White*

MAKE AHEAD The unbaked dip can be refrigerated overnight; the fried shallot can be kept at room temperature. Bring the dip to room temperature before baking.

WINE Lively, creamy Champagne: NV Piper-Heidsieck Brut.

Creamy Cheese and Green Herb Spread

⏱ TOTAL: 15 MIN

6 TO 8 SERVINGS ● ●

This fresh cheese spread, called *cervelle de canut,* is a specialty of Lyon, France; the name means "silk worker's brain." The dish is a popular starter at London's Brawn restaurant, where chef Owen Kenworthy makes it with herbs, cider vinegar and walnut oil.

- 1 pound *fromage blanc,* quark or pureed cottage cheese
- 2 tablespoons minced shallot
- 2 tablespoons chopped chives
- 1 tablespoon chopped tarragon
- 1 tablespoon apple cider vinegar
- 1 tablespoon walnut oil

Kosher salt and freshly ground pepper

Extra-virgin olive oil, for drizzling

Grilled sourdough bread, for serving

In a medium bowl, whisk the cheese with the shallot, chives, tarragon, vinegar and walnut oil and season with salt and pepper. Drizzle the spread with olive oil and serve with grilled sourdough bread. —*Owen Kenworthy*

MAKE AHEAD The herbed cheese can be refrigerated overnight.

WINE Apple-scented Loire sparkling wine: 2011 Thierry Puzelat Pétillant Naturel.

Paprika Cheese Spread

⏱ TOTAL: 15 MIN • MAKES 3 CUPS ● ●

- 1 pound farmer cheese
- 1 stick unsalted butter, softened
- ½ cup crème fraîche
- 1 tablespoon Dijon mustard
- ¼ teaspoon hot Hungarian paprika
- 2 teaspoons sweet Hungarian paprika, plus more for garnish
- 1 teaspoon caraway seeds
- 2 tablespoons minced scallions
- 2 teaspoons drained small capers

Salt and freshly ground pepper

In a food processor, combine the cheese, butter, crème fraîche, mustard, hot paprika, the 2 teaspoons of sweet paprika and the caraway and process to a coarse spread. Add the scallions and capers and pulse to combine. Scrape the spread into a bowl and season with salt and pepper. Sprinkle with sweet paprika and serve. —*Sarah Copeland*

SERVE WITH Sliced brown bread, radishes and cucumbers.

WINE Fresh, citrusy sparkling wine: NV Caposaldo Prosecco.

Olive Bagna Cauda

📷 PAGE 367

⏱ TOTAL: 20 MIN • MAKES 1 CUP ● ●

Bagna cauda is a warm Italian olive oil dip that's normally made with anchovies. This vegan version gets its richness from oil-cured olives. It's delectable over raw tomatoes, with grilled vegetables or tossed with hot pasta.

- 4 ounces oil-cured black olives, pitted (1 cup)
- 1 tablespoon capers
- 1 teaspoon chopped thyme
- 1 teaspoon sherry vinegar
- ½ teaspoon crushed red pepper
- ¾ cup extra-virgin olive oil

In a food processor, pulse all of the ingredients until smooth. Transfer to a saucepan and cook over moderate heat just until the oil begins to separate, 5 minutes. Scrape into a bowl and serve warm. —*Richard Landau*

● HEALTHY ● MAKE AHEAD ● VEGETARIAN ● STAFF FAVORITE

The Farmer's Plate

TOTAL: 1 HR • 6 SERVINGS ● ●

L.A. chef Suzanne Goin's appetizer plate is completely vegetarian yet rich and satisfying. She describes it as "a vegetable antipasto through a Southern California lens."

CHICKPEA PUREE

- 2 cups canned chickpeas, rinsed and drained
- 1 tablespoon tahini
- 1 garlic clove, crushed
- ½ teaspoon cayenne pepper
- ¼ teaspoon ground cumin
- ½ cup extra-virgin olive oil
- Kosher salt and freshly ground black pepper

MUHAMMARA

- ⅔ cup walnuts
- ⅛ teaspoon ground cumin
- ¼ cup plus 2 tablespoons extra-virgin olive oil
- Half of a ¼-inch-thick slice of whole wheat bread
- ¾ cup drained piquillo peppers
- ½ teaspoon pomegranate molasses (optional)
- ½ teaspoon fresh lemon juice
- ¼ teaspoon kosher salt, plus more for seasoning
- Pinch of cayenne pepper
- Freshly ground black pepper
- 6 ounces burrata cheese or buffalo mozzarella, cut into 6 equal pieces, for serving
- Grilled peasant bread and roasted vegetables, such as carrots, fennel and red onions, for serving

1. MAKE THE CHICKPEA PUREE In a food processor, pulse the chickpeas, tahini, garlic, cayenne and cumin until finely chopped. With the machine on, drizzle in the oil and puree until smooth. Transfer to a bowl; season with salt and pepper. Wipe out the processor.

2. MAKE THE MUHAMMARA Preheat the oven to 375°. Toast the walnuts in a pie plate for 5 to 7 minutes, until lightly golden and fragrant. Let cool completely, then transfer the walnuts to the food processor.

3. Meanwhile, in a small skillet, toast the ground cumin over moderately low heat, stirring, until fragrant, about 2 minutes. Scrape the cumin into the processor. Heat 2 tablespoons of the olive oil in the skillet. Add the bread and cook until golden and crisp on both sides, 3 to 4 minutes. Tear the bread into small pieces and add it to the processor. Add the piquillos, pomegranate molasses, lemon juice, ¼ teaspoon of salt and the cayenne pepper. With the machine on, drizzle in the remaining ¼ cup of olive oil and 1 tablespoon of water and puree until smooth. Season the *muhammara* with salt and black pepper. Transfer to a bowl.

4. Serve the chickpea puree and *muhammara* with burrata, grilled bread and roasted vegetables. —*Suzanne Goin*

MAKE AHEAD The chickpea puree and *muhammara* can be covered and refrigerated for up to 2 days. Let both return to room temperature before serving.

WINE Fruity southern French red blend: 2010 Château de la Liquière Faugères.

Warm Ricotta with Roasted Grapes

ACTIVE: 35 MIN; TOTAL: 2 HR
8 SERVINGS ● ●

GRAPES

- 2 cups seedless red grapes
- ½ large shallot, thinly sliced lengthwise
- 1 tablespoon extra-virgin olive oil
- ¼ teaspoon kosher salt
- Freshly ground black pepper

BAKED RICOTTA

- 1 pound fresh ricotta cheese
- 2 teaspoons unsalted butter, softened, for greasing
- ¼ cup freshly grated Parmigiano-Reggiano cheese
- 1 large egg
- 1 teaspoon thyme leaves, chopped, plus whole thyme leaves for garnish
- 2 teaspoons finely grated lemon zest
- Kosher salt and freshly ground black pepper

1. PREPARE THE GRAPES Preheat the oven to 425°. Stem and wash the grapes well and pat dry. In a medium bowl, toss the grapes with the shallot, olive oil and salt; season with pepper. Spread the grapes on a small rimmed baking sheet and roast for 10 minutes, stirring once. Continue roasting for another 5 to 7 minutes, until most of the grapes have burst and their juices thicken; watch carefully to make sure that the juices do not burn. Scrape the grapes into a bowl and let them cool to room temperature, about 30 minutes.

2. MEANWHILE, PREPARE THE RICOTTA Reduce the oven temperature to 350°. If the ricotta seems wet, drain it in a sieve lined with paper towels to remove excess moisture. Butter a 2-cup soufflé dish. Fold an 18-inch-long sheet of parchment paper in half lengthwise and trim to a 4-inch width. Wrap the parchment around the inside of the soufflé dish to form a collar that extends 2 inches above the rim; secure the collar by tucking one end into the fold of the other to prevent overflow.

3. In a medium bowl, mix the drained ricotta with the Parmigiano-Reggiano, egg, chopped thyme and lemon zest until the mixture is combined and smooth; season with salt and pepper. Spread the cheese mixture in the prepared soufflé dish. Set the dish on a baking sheet and bake for about 50 minutes, until the center is barely set and the top is nicely browned. Remove the dish from the oven and let it stand for 10 minutes, then remove the parchment collar. Let the baked ricotta cool another 30 minutes.

4. Turn the baked ricotta out onto a small plate, then use a second plate to turn it right side up. Transfer the cheese to a serving plate and top with the grapes. Garnish with thyme and serve warm or at room temperature. —*Susan Spungen*

VARIATION To garnish the ricotta simply, roast a cluster of grapes in a 500° oven for about 8 minutes.

SERVE WITH Spungen's Homemade Wheat Crackers (recipe on following page).

WINE Cherry-scented Lambrusco: NV Cleto Chiarli Grasparossa di Castelvetro Amabile.

Butternut Squash and Tahini-Yogurt Dip

ACTIVE: 40 MIN; TOTAL: 1 HR 15 MIN
MAKES 2½ CUPS ● ● ◉

Sweet from squash, tangy from yogurt and nutty from tahini, this silky dip is a great alternative to hummus.

- 1 head of garlic
- 3 tablespoons plus 1 teaspoon extra-virgin olive oil, plus more for drizzling
- One 1½-pound butternut squash, peeled and cut into 1½-inch pieces
- Kosher salt and freshly ground black pepper
- 2 tablespoons pumpkin seeds
- ½ cup plain fat-free Greek yogurt
- ¼ cup tahini paste
- 3 tablespoons fresh lemon juice
- Pinch of cayenne pepper

1. Preheat the oven to 425°. Cut 1 inch off the top of the garlic head and place the head on a piece of foil; drizzle with 1 tablespoon of the olive oil and wrap it tightly. On a large baking sheet, toss the squash with 2 tablespoons of the olive oil and season with salt and black pepper. Set the garlic on the oven rack. Roast the squash for 35 to 40 minutes, turning occasionally, until tender and golden brown. Roast the garlic for about 1 hour, until completely soft. Let cool.

2. Meanwhile, in a small nonstick skillet, heat the remaining 1 teaspoon of olive oil. Add the pumpkin seeds and cook, stirring, until lightly golden and starting to pop, 3 minutes. Transfer the seeds to a paper towel–lined plate and season with salt.

3. Scrape the roasted squash into a food processor. Squeeze the garlic cloves from their skins into the processor. Add the yogurt, tahini, lemon juice and cayenne pepper. Puree until smooth, adding a little water if the dip is too thick. Season with salt and black pepper. Transfer the dip to a serving bowl and drizzle with olive oil. Top with the toasted pumpkin seeds and serve.
—*Susan Spungen*

SERVE WITH Warm roasted vegetables, such as beets and parsnips.
MAKE AHEAD The dip can be covered and refrigerated overnight. Bring to room temperature before serving.

Homemade Wheat Crackers

ACTIVE: 30 MIN; TOTAL: 1 HR 15 MIN
PLUS COOLING • 8 SERVINGS ● ◉ ◉

These thin, super-crisp crackers from cookbook author Susan Spungen are excellent with her warm ricotta (on the previous page) or any soft cheese.

- 1½ cups all-purpose flour
- ½ cup whole-wheat flour
- 2 tablespoons sugar
- ½ teaspoon kosher salt, plus more for sprinkling
- 4 tablespoons cold unsalted butter
- ½ to ¾ cup whole milk
- 1 egg white, lightly beaten

1. Preheat the oven to 400°. In a food processor, combine the flours, sugar and ½ teaspoon of salt and pulse for 15 seconds. Add the butter and pulse for another 15 seconds, until a coarse meal forms. Add ½ cup of milk and pulse until the dough just comes together, about 30 seconds; add the extra ¼ cup of milk if necessary. Gather the dough into a ball and wrap in plastic. Refrigerate for 15 minutes.

2. Line 2 baking sheets with parchment paper and divide the chilled dough into 4 even pieces. Dust a work surface and rolling pin with flour. Roll out 2 pieces of the dough as thinly as possible into 13-by-8-inch oblong rectangles. Transfer to the prepared baking sheets. Prick the dough all over with a fork. Brush lightly with some of the egg white and sprinkle with salt. Bake the crackers in the center of the oven for 14 minutes, until golden brown and crisp; shift the sheets halfway through baking. Transfer the crackers to a rack; let cool for 15 minutes. Repeat with the remaining dough. Break the crackers into shards or serve whole. —*Susan Spungen*
MAKE AHEAD The crackers can be stored in an airtight container for up to 2 days.

Ember-Roasted Baba Ghanoush

ACTIVE: 45 MIN; TOTAL: 1 HR 15 MIN
6 SERVINGS ● ● ◉

- 3½ pounds eggplants (about 4 medium eggplants), pierced all over
- 2 medium onions, unpeeled
- 2 tablespoons extra-virgin olive oil, plus more for drizzling
- ¼ cup pine nuts
- 2 tablespoons rosemary leaves
- 1 tablespoon thyme leaves
- 1 garlic clove, minced
- 2 teaspoons fresh lemon juice
- Kosher salt and freshly ground pepper
- Grilled country bread, for serving

1. Light a hardwood charcoal fire. When the coals are hot, create a bed of embers and set the eggplants and onions directly on it. Cook, turning occasionally, until the eggplants and onions are tender but not falling apart, about 15 minutes for the eggplants and 25 minutes for the onions. Transfer the vegetables to a baking sheet to cool, brushing off any embers.

2. Meanwhile, in a medium cast-iron skillet, heat 1 tablespoon of the oil. Add the pine nuts; toast over moderately high heat, stirring, until golden, about 5 minutes. Transfer to a plate. Add the rosemary and thyme to the skillet; cook over moderately high heat, stirring, until fragrant and just crisp, about 3 minutes. Transfer the herbs to another plate and let cool. Coarsely chop the herbs.

3. Slit open each eggplant and scoop the flesh into a food processor; discard the skins. Peel and quarter the onions and add to the processor; discard the skins. Add the pine nuts to the processor and puree until smooth.

4. Wipe out the skillet and heat the remaining 1 tablespoon of oil in it. Add the baba ghanoush and cook over moderate heat, stirring, until thickened, 6 minutes. Scrape into a serving bowl and let cool slightly. Stir in the garlic, lemon juice and chopped herbs; season with salt and pepper. Drizzle with olive oil and serve warm with grilled country bread.
—*Michael Chiarello*

● HEALTHY ● MAKE AHEAD ◉ VEGETARIAN ● STAFF FAVORITE

BUTTERNUT SQUASH AND
TAHINI–YOGURT DIP

Tangy Sun-Dried Tomato and Olive Dip

⏱ ACTIVE: 20 MIN; TOTAL: 40 MIN
8 TO 10 SERVINGS ● ● ●

4   ounces sun-dried tomatoes
    (not oil-packed), about 1½ cups
4   ounces pitted kalamata olives
1   tablespoon drained capers
2   garlic cloves, smashed
1   slice of white sandwich bread, torn
½   teaspoon crushed red pepper
2   tablespoons balsamic vinegar
2   tablespoons red wine vinegar
1   teaspoon dried oregano
½   cup extra-virgin olive oil
Breadsticks and assorted crudités,
    such as fennel wedges, baby
    carrots, radishes, celery sticks and
    endive spears, for serving

1. In a small bowl, soak the tomatoes in hot water until softened, about 20 minutes; drain.
2. In a food processor, combined the softened tomatoes, olives, capers, garlic, bread, red pepper, balsamic and red wine vinegars and oregano and puree to a chunky paste. With the machine on, add the oil and process to a fine paste. Add ¼ cup of warm water and process until slightly creamy. Scrape into a bowl and serve with the crudités.
—*Michael White*
MAKE AHEAD The dip can be refrigerated for up to 3 days.

Black Olive Tapenade with Figs and Mint

⏱ TOTAL: 15 MIN
MAKES ABOUT 1½ CUPS ● ● ●

¾   cup pitted oil-cured black olives
¾   cup pitted kalamata olives
6   small dried figs, coarsely chopped
2   tablespoons capers, rinsed
2   small garlic cloves, crushed
¼   cup packed mint leaves
4   anchovy fillets
¼   cup extra-virgin olive oil
Kosher salt and freshly ground pepper
Bagel chips, for serving

1. In a food processor, pulse the olives, figs, capers, garlic, mint, anchovies and olive oil until the tapenade is thick and somewhat chunky. Season with salt and pepper.
2. Transfer the tapenade to a bowl, cover and refrigerate until chilled. Serve with bagel chips. —*Jacques Pépin*

Creamy Eggplant and White Bean Spread

ACTIVE: 15 MIN; TOTAL: 1 HR
MAKES 3 CUPS ● ●

Pureed with hazelnut oil, garlic and thick yogurt, this silky eastern European roasted-eggplant spread is like a nutty baba ghanoush. It's especially good served the traditional way: on toasted rye bread with thinly sliced red onion.

2   large eggplants (1½ pounds each)
2   medium garlic cloves
Sea salt
½   cup drained canned white beans
¼   cup plain whole-milk Greek yogurt
2   tablespoons extra-virgin olive oil
2   tablespoons mayonnaise
1   teaspoon hazelnut oil
1   tablespoon fresh lemon juice
Freshly ground black pepper
Hot Hungarian paprika
¼   cup chopped flat-leaf parsley

1. Preheat the oven to 450°. Set the eggplants on a baking sheet and poke them all over with a knife tip. Roast for 40 to 45 minutes, until very soft. Let cool slightly.
2. Scrape the eggplant flesh into a food processor; discard the skins. Using the side of a chef's knife, mash the garlic to a paste with a generous pinch of salt. Scrape the garlic paste into the food processor. Add the beans, yogurt, olive oil, mayonnaise, hazelnut oil and lemon juice. Pulse to a coarse puree, scrape into a bowl and season with salt, pepper and paprika. Stir in the parsley and serve. —*Sarah Copeland*
SERVE WITH Toasted peasant bread, thinly sliced red onion and squash blossoms.
MAKE AHEAD The eggplant spread can be refrigerated for up to 3 days.

Bacon-Wrapped Cherry Peppers

⏱ TOTAL: 30 MIN • 4 TO 6 SERVINGS ●

Colby Garrelts, the chef at Bluestem in Kansas City, Missouri, makes these genius hors d'oeuvres with just three ingredients. The peppers can be prepped ahead of time, then popped in the oven just before guests arrive.

6   jarred hot cherry peppers—
    halved through the stem, seeded,
    drained and patted dry
⅓   cup cream cheese, softened
12 thin bacon slices (6 ounces)

1. Preheat the oven to 350°. Stuff each cherry pepper half with a heaping teaspoon of cream cheese and wrap with a slice of bacon; secure with a toothpick.
2. Arrange the stuffed peppers in a large ovenproof skillet and cook over moderate heat, turning, until the bacon is browned, 12 to 15 minutes. Transfer the skillet to the oven and bake for about 5 minutes, until the bacon is crisp and the cream cheese is hot. Serve the stuffed cherry peppers warm.
—*Colby Garrelts*

Okra Double Dippers

⏱ TOTAL: 10 MIN • 6 TO 8 SERVINGS ● ●

The okra here gets not one but two coatings: Dip first in miso mayo, then add crunch with sesame seeds or heat with fresh chiles.

1   pound okra
½   cup mayonnaise
2   tablespoons white miso
    (also called *shiro* miso)
Black and white sesame seeds and thinly
    sliced fresh red chiles, for dipping

1. In a large pot of salted boiling water, blanch the okra until bright green, about 30 seconds; drain well. Transfer the okra to a baking sheet and refrigerate until it has cooled slightly.
2. In a small bowl, mix the mayonnaise with the miso. Put the sesame seeds and chiles in 2 small bowls. To eat, dip the okra spears in the miso mayonnaise, then in the toppings.
—*Kay Chun*

● HEALTHY ● MAKE AHEAD ● VEGETARIAN ● STAFF FAVORITE

Chicken Liver Mousse with Red-Wine-Glazed Prunes

TOTAL: 1 HR PLUS 9 HR CHILLING
MAKES 2½ CUPS ●

For this luscious mousse, chef Aaron Barnett of St. Jack in Portland, Oregon, cooks chicken livers in brandy and honey; the wine-glazed prunes he serves alongside are so good, you'll want to double the recipe.

- 1 pound chicken livers, trimmed
- 2 cups whole milk
- 1 cup pitted prunes
- ⅓ cup red wine
- 2 tablespoons fresh orange juice
- 1 tablespoon fresh lemon juice
- 1 tablespoon sugar
- ¼ cup vegetable oil
- ¼ cup finely chopped onion
- 1 garlic clove, finely chopped
Salt and freshly ground black pepper
- 2 tablespoons honey
- ¼ cup plus 1 tablespoon brandy
- 1 cup heavy cream
- 1 medium baguette, cut into ¼-inch slices and toasted

1. In a medium bowl, cover the livers with the milk and refrigerate for at least 5 hours or overnight.

2. In a small saucepan, combine the prunes with the red wine, orange juice, lemon juice and sugar and simmer, stirring occasionally, until the liquid has reduced to a thick syrup, about 6 minutes. Let cool and refrigerate.

3. In another small saucepan, heat 1 tablespoon of the oil over moderate heat. Add the onion and garlic and cook until softened, about 4 minutes.

4. Drain the livers, pat dry with paper towels and season with salt and pepper. In a large, heavy skillet, heat the remaining 3 tablespoons of oil until shimmering. Add the livers and cook over high heat until well browned, about 1 minute per side. Add the onion-garlic mixture along with the honey and ¼ cup of the brandy and light carefully with a long match. Cook the livers until the flames die out and the brandy has reduced to a glaze, about 3 minutes.

5. Scrape the hot livers into a food processor. Add the cream and blend until smooth. Blend in the remaining 1 tablespoon of brandy; season with salt and pepper. Strain the mousse through a fine sieve into a bowl, then pack into a serving bowl; press plastic wrap directly onto the surface. Refrigerate for at least 4 hours or overnight. Serve with the toasts and prunes. —*Aaron Barnett*
WINE Bright-berried Gamay Noir from Beaujolais: 2012 Clos de la Roilette Fleurie.

Smoked Whitefish Brandade

TOTAL: 45 MIN • MAKES 1½ CUPS ●

- 1½ cups whole milk
- 7 garlic cloves, crushed
- ½ teaspoon fine sea salt
- 1 medium Yukon Gold potato, peeled and sliced ¼ inch thick
- 3 bay leaves
- 1 thyme sprig
- 5 ounces skinless, boneless smoked whitefish
- ¼ cup extra-virgin olive oil, plus more for drizzling
- 1 cup freshly grated Parmigiano-Reggiano cheese (3 ounces)
Grilled bread, for serving

1. In a saucepan, simmer the milk with the garlic, salt, potato, bay leaves and thyme, covered, until the potato is tender, 15 minutes. Remove from the heat and add the whitefish; let stand for 5 minutes. Fine-strain the mixture, reserving the milk; discard the herbs.

2. Preheat the broiler. In a food processor, blend the fish, potato and garlic, adding the reserved milk 1 tablespoon at a time, until a thick puree forms. Blend in the ¼ cup of olive oil in a thin stream. Add ¾ cup of the grated cheese and pulse just until incorporated.

3. Grease a 2½- to 3-cup baking dish. Spread the whitefish brandade in the dish; drizzle with oil. Top with the remaining cheese. Broil the brandade 6 inches from the heat until golden, 10 minutes. Serve with grilled bread. —*Amy Thielen*
WINE Zesty Michigan Riesling: 2011 Left Foot Charley Dry Riesling.

Prosciutto-Wrapped Asparagus with Lemony Bread Crumbs

TOTAL: 35 MIN • 6 SERVINGS ●

Napa chef Michael Chiarello grills these asparagus twice: the first time on their own, the second time right before serving, after they've been wrapped in prosciutto.

- 1 pound thin asparagus
- 1 tablespoon extra-virgin olive oil, plus more for brushing
Kosher salt and freshly ground pepper
- ¼ cup plain dry bread crumbs or panko
- 1 garlic clove, minced
- 1 tablespoon freshly grated Parmigiano-Reggiano cheese
- 1 tablespoon finely chopped flat-leaf parsley
- 1 teaspoon finely grated lemon zest
- 12 thin slices of prosciutto

1. Light a hardwood charcoal fire. Brush the asparagus with olive oil and season with salt and pepper. Grill the asparagus over moderately high heat, turning, until lightly charred and almost tender, about 4 minutes. Transfer to a plate and let cool.

2. Meanwhile, in a small cast-iron skillet on the grill, heat the 1 tablespoon of olive oil. Add the bread crumbs and garlic and cook over moderately high heat, stirring, until the crumbs are golden and crisp, about 4 minutes. Remove the skillet from the heat and let cool slightly, then stir in the Parmigiano-Reggiano, parsley and lemon zest; season with salt and pepper.

3. Divide the asparagus into 6 even piles. On a work surface, arrange the prosciutto slices in 6 pairs, overlapping them slightly. Set an asparagus pile on each prosciutto pair and roll up into tight bundles.

4. Grill the asparagus bundles over moderately high heat, turning, until the asparagus are tender and the prosciutto is crisp, about 4 minutes. Transfer to a platter or plates. Sprinkle the lemony bread crumbs on top and serve. —*Michael Chiarello*
WINE Bubbly, fruity Prosecco: NV Riondo Spago Nero.

● HEALTHY   ● MAKE AHEAD   ○ VEGETARIAN   ● STAFF FAVORITE

Sausage-Stuffed Peppadew Peppers

⏱ TOTAL: 40 MIN

MAKES 2 DOZEN STUFFED PEPPERS ●

Vegetable cooking spray
1 tablespoon extra-virgin olive oil
4 ounces cremini mushrooms, minced
2 anchovy fillets, drained and minced
3 ounces hot Italian sausage, casings removed
2 garlic cloves, finely chopped
½ teaspoon thyme leaves, chopped
Kosher salt and freshly ground pepper
One 14-ounce jar peppadew peppers, drained

1. Preheat the oven to 400°. Lightly grease a 9-by-13-inch baking dish with cooking spray.
2. In a skillet, heat the oil. Add the mushrooms and anchovies and cook over moderate heat, stirring occasionally, until the mushrooms are golden, 5 minutes. Stir in the sausage, garlic and thyme; cook, breaking up the sausage, until no trace of pink remains, 5 minutes. Season with salt and pepper. Let cool slightly.
3. Stuff each peppadew with about 1 teaspoon of the filling; arrange in the dish. Bake for about 10 minutes, until the peppadews are hot. Serve warm. *—Kay Chun*

Sausage-and-Apple Stuffing Bites

ACTIVE: 35 MIN; TOTAL: 1 HR

MAKES 2 DOZEN MINI MUFFINS ●

Vegetable cooking spray
4 ounces white country bread, cut into ½-inch cubes (3 cups)
¼ cup extra-virgin olive oil
Kosher salt and freshly ground pepper
2 tablespoons unsalted butter
⅔ cup finely chopped onion
⅔ cup finely chopped celery
½ pound sweet Italian sausage, casings removed
6 garlic cloves, finely chopped
¾ teaspoon dried sage
1 small Granny Smith apple, peeled and finely chopped
4 large eggs, beaten
2 tablespoons chicken broth

1. Preheat the oven to 350°. Grease two 12-cup mini-muffin pans with cooking spray.
2. On a baking sheet, toss the bread cubes with 2 tablespoons of the olive oil and season with salt and freshly ground pepper. Bake for about 10 minutes, until toasted. Transfer the croutons to a bowl.
3. Meanwhile, in a large skillet, melt the butter in the remaining 2 tablespoons of oil. Add the onion and celery and cook over moderately high heat, stirring occasionally, until golden, about 5 minutes. Add the sausage, garlic and sage and cook, stirring and breaking up the meat, until no trace of pink remains, 5 minutes. Mix the sausage, apple, eggs and broth into the croutons; season with salt and pepper. Let stand for 5 minutes.
4. Pack the stuffing into the prepared muffin cups and bake for 20 to 25 minutes, until golden. Transfer to a rack and let stand for 5 minutes. Loosen the muffins with a sharp paring knife and lift them out. Serve warm. *—Kay Chun*

MAKE AHEAD The muffins can be refrigerated overnight in the pans. Rewarm for 10 to 15 minutes in a 350° oven before serving.

INGREDIENT TIP: CURED MEATS FROM SALUMI SPECIALISTS

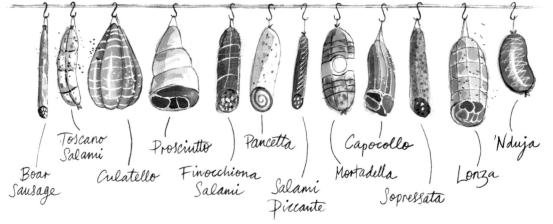

Boar Sausage · Toscano Salami · Culatello · Proscuitto · Finocchiona Salami · Pancetta · Salami Piccante · Capocollo · Mortadella · Sopressata · Lonza · 'Nduja

BOCCALONE, SAN FRANCISCO Chef Chris Cosentino's shop has portable *"salumi* cones" and a mail-order club. *boccalone.com.*

THE BUTCHER SHOP, BOSTON A butcher shop, *salumeria* and wine bar from chef Barbara Lynch. *thebutchershop boston.com.*

PUBLICAN QUALITY MEATS, CHICAGO This butcher shop, market and café is from star chef Paul Kahan. *publican qualitymeats.com.*

RED APRON, WASHINGTON, DC A farmers' market favorite now has three new shops in DC. *redapron butchery.com.*

SALUMERIA ROSI PARMACOTTO, NEW YORK CITY Chef Cesare Casella sells domestic and imported *salumi. salumeriarosi.com.*

SALUMI, SEATTLE Armandino Batali (Mario Batali's father) runs this iconic Pioneer Square shop. *salumi curedmeats.com.*

Squash Fritters and Fried Sage
⏱ TOTAL: 45 MIN • 8 SERVINGS ●

Vegetable or peanut oil, for frying
1½ cups all-purpose flour
1½ cups seltzer or club soda, chilled
Kosher salt
1½ pounds kabocha squash or sugar
   pumpkin—peeled, seeded and cut
   into ⅛-inch-thick wedges
½ cup sage leaves
Flaky sea salt and lemon wedges,
   for serving

1. In a large saucepan, heat 1 inch of oil to 360°. In a bowl, whisk the flour and 1¼ cups of the seltzer until smooth and the consistency of sour cream; add more seltzer if the batter is too thick. Season with salt.
2. Working in 3 or 4 batches, dip the squash and some of the sage in the batter; let excess batter drip back into the bowl. Carefully add the battered squash and sage, and some uncoated sage leaves, to the hot oil. Fry over moderately high heat, turning, until lightly golden and crisp, 3 to 5 minutes. Using tongs, transfer the fried squash and sage to paper towels to drain. Season with sea salt and serve right away, with lemon wedges. —*Richard Betts*
WINE Lively rosé from Sonoma: 2012 Vaughn Duffy.

Salmon Caviar Sushi Bites
⏱ TOTAL: 10 MIN • MAKES 3 DOZEN
HORS D'OEUVRES ●

4 ounces cream cheese, softened
1 teaspoon prepared wasabi
1 tablespoon finely shredded nori
36 mixed rice crackers
¼ cup salmon caviar

In a bowl, stir the softened cream cheese with the wasabi and nori. Transfer the mixture to a small sturdy plastic bag and snip off one corner. Pipe a small mound onto each rice cracker and top with a small dollop of the caviar. Serve right away.
—*Grace Parisi*

Potato and Mozzarella Croquettes
ACTIVE: 50 MIN; TOTAL: 1 HR 50 MIN
4 SERVINGS ● ●
These light and cheesy potato croquettes are dipped in a mustard-garlic egg wash and breaded twice before frying. The payoff is a flavorful, crisp crust for the soft potato-and-cheese filling.

1 pound baking potatoes,
   peeled and cut into large chunks
Kosher salt
6 ounces fresh mozzarella,
   cut into ⅓-inch dice
2 tablespoons finely chopped
   flat-leaf parsley
Freshly ground pepper
2 tablespoons extra-virgin olive oil
2 medium tomatoes (¾ pound),
   cut into 1-inch pieces
2 tablespoons finely chopped basil
1 cup plain dry bread crumbs
3 large eggs
1 tablespoon Dijon mustard
2 garlic cloves, minced
Vegetable oil, for frying

1. In a saucepan, cover the potatoes with cold water. Bring to a boil, add a generous pinch of salt and simmer over moderate heat until tender, 20 minutes. Drain and let cool. Pass the potatoes through a ricer into a large bowl. Stir in the mozzarella and parsley and season with salt and pepper. Shape the mixture into 8 oval croquettes and transfer to a plate. Cover and refrigerate until firm, 30 minutes.
2. Meanwhile, in a saucepan, heat the olive oil. Add the tomatoes and cook over moderate heat, stirring, until softened and saucy, 8 minutes. Stir in the basil; season with salt and pepper. Transfer to a bowl; keep warm.
3. Spread the bread crumbs in a shallow bowl. In another shallow bowl, beat the eggs with the mustard, garlic and a pinch each of salt and pepper. Dredge the croquettes in the bread crumbs, tapping off the excess. Dip the croquettes in the beaten egg mixture to coat, then dredge again in the bread crumbs, pressing lightly to help the crumbs adhere.

4. In a large saucepan, heat 1 inch of vegetable oil to 350°. Working in 2 batches, fry the croquettes, turning, until golden and crisp, about 3 minutes per batch. Transfer to paper towels to drain. Serve with the tomato sauce.
—*Marcelo Betancourt*
WINE Crisp Italian sparkling wine: NV Sorelle Bronca Extra Dry Prosecco.

Grilled-Beef Summer Rolls
⏱ TOTAL: 40 MIN • MAKES 12 ROLLS ● ●
For this easy, vegetable-packed riff on Vietnamese summer rolls, chilled leftover steak (or deli roast beef) is swapped in for the usual shrimp-and-pork filling.

1½ ounces rice vermicelli
Twelve 8-inch round rice paper wrappers
¼ cup chopped basil leaves
¼ cup cilantro leaves
¼ cup mint leaves
1 large carrot, finely shredded
2 Persian cucumbers, cut into long
   matchsticks
6 ounces very thinly sliced leftover
   Grilled Rib Eye (page 196) or deli
   roast beef
2 tablespoons fresh lime juice
2 tablespoons Asian fish sauce
2 tablespoons sugar
1 teaspoon minced garlic
1 teaspoon Sriracha

1. Soak the rice vermicelli in boiling water until opaque and softened, 10 minutes. Drain, rinse and squeeze dry.
2. Fill a medium skillet with hot water. Soak 3 rice paper wrappers at a time in the water for 30 seconds, until just pliable. Transfer to a work surface and blot dry. Top each wrapper with some noodles, herbs, carrot, cucumber and beef. Tightly roll up the wrappers around the filling, tucking in the sides as you roll. Repeat with the remaining fillings.
3. In a bowl, stir together the lime juice, fish sauce, sugar, garlic, Sriracha and 2 tablespoons of water. Serve the rolls with the dipping sauce. —*Tim McKee*
WINE Light, chilled Italian red: 2011 Le Vigne di Zamo Refosco.

● HEALTHY ● MAKE AHEAD ● VEGETARIAN ● STAFF FAVORITE

GRILLED-BEEF
SUMMER ROLLS

DIY SOUP DUMPLINGS

The entire recipe takes about 7 hours, but each component can be ready in under 2. Makes about 4 dozen dumplings.

Dim sum master **JOE NG** reveals the secret to getting the soup inside the dumpling: Set the rich stock with gelatin before folding it into the dumpling skin along with the ground-meat filling.

STEP 1 MAKE THE JELLIED STOCK

One 3-pound chicken, quartered
1 pound boneless pork shoulder, sliced 1 inch thick
Eight ¼-inch-thick slices of fresh ginger
2 scallions, halved
1 large carrot, thinly sliced
2 quarts low-sodium chicken broth
3 envelopes unflavored gelatin

1. In a large, deep pot, combine the chicken, pork, ginger, scallions, carrot and broth with 1 quart of water and bring to a boil. Reduce the heat and simmer until the chicken is cooked through, about 30 minutes. Remove the chicken and, when it is cool enough, pull the meat from the bones. Return the bones to the pot and simmer until the broth is very flavorful and reduced to 6 cups, 1½ hours longer; strain the stock and skim the fat from the surface. Reserve the chicken meat and pork for another use.
2. In a small bowl, combine the gelatin with ⅓ cup of cold water and let stand for 5 minutes. Whisk the softened gelatin into 3 cups of the hot stock until melted. (Reserve the remaining stock for another use.) Pour the gelatinized stock into a 2-quart glass or ceramic baking dish and refrigerate until firm, at least 3 hours or overnight.
MAKE AHEAD The jellied stock can be refrigerated in an airtight container for up to 3 days.

STEP 2 MAKE THE PORK-AND-CRAB FILLING

4 dried shiitake mushrooms
Boiling water
¾ pound ground pork shoulder
¼ cup Asian crab paste (optional; see Note)
½ cup finely chopped chives
2 tablespoons potato starch
2 tablespoons toasted sesame oil
1½ tablespoons dark soy sauce
1½ tablespoons mushroom soy sauce, such as Healthy Boy (see Note)
1 tablespoon sugar
1 teaspoon finely chopped peeled fresh ginger
¾ teaspoon salt
½ teaspoon freshly ground white pepper
3 cups Jellied Stock (recipe above)

1. In a small bowl, cover the dried mushrooms with boiling water and soak until softened, about 20 minutes. Drain, squeezing out any excess liquid; discard the stems. Finely chop the caps and transfer to the bowl of a standing mixer fitted with the paddle. Add the pork, crab paste, chives, potato starch, sesame oil, dark and mushroom soy sauces, sugar, ginger, salt and white pepper. Beat at medium speed until thoroughly combined, about 5 minutes.
2. In a food processor, pulse the Jellied Stock until chopped; beat into the pork mixture at medium speed until light and fluffy, 5 minutes.
NOTE Crab paste (a concentrated condiment) and mushroom soy sauce are available at Asian markets and online at *amazon.com*.

SAFETY TIP *To avoid burning your mouth, place the soup dumpling on a spoon and carefully bite a hole in the top to let the steam out.*

PORK-AND-CRAB SOUP DUMPLING

STEP 3 MAKE THE DOUGH

4½ cups all-purpose flour, plus more for dusting
1½ cups bread flour
Boiling water
Large pinch of saffron threads, crumbled
1 tablespoon fine sea salt

1. In a medium bowl, stir ½ cup of the all-purpose flour with ½ cup of the bread flour and ½ cup of boiling water until combined. Turn the hot-water dough out onto a work surface and knead until fairly smooth, about 5 minutes.
2. In a glass measuring cup, combine 2 cups of room-temperature water with the saffron threads and let it stand for 5 minutes. In the bowl of a standing mixer fitted with the dough hook, blend the remaining 4 cups of all-purpose flour and 1 cup of bread flour with the sea salt. Add the saffron water and beat at medium speed until a smooth dough forms, about 5 minutes. Add the hot-water dough and beat at medium speed until incorporated, about 5 minutes longer. Turn the dough out onto a work surface and knead it into a smooth ball. Wrap the dough in plastic and let it stand at room temperature for 30 minutes or refrigerate overnight.

STEP 4 FORM & STEAM THE DUMPLINGS

The soup dumplings can be steamed fresh, right after forming. Alternatively, freeze uncooked dumplings on a baking sheet, seal in a plastic bag and freeze for up to 2 weeks. Steam the unthawed dumplings until cooked, about 10 minutes.

1. Cut the dough into 4 pieces. Working with 1 piece at a time and keeping the rest covered, roll the piece of dough into a 1-inch-thick rope. Pinch or cut the rope into ¾-inch pieces and roll them into balls. Then, using a small dowel, glass bottle or Chinese-style rolling pin, roll each piece of dough into a thin 3½-inch round, dusting with flour as necessary. Lightly dust the rounds with flour, transfer them to a floured baking sheet and cover with a damp towel to keep them from drying out. Repeat with the remaining dough. You should have about 4 dozen rounds.

2. Line 2 baking sheets with wax paper and dust lightly with flour. Working with 1 dough round at a time and keeping the rest covered,

spoon a well-rounded tablespoon of the filling onto the center of the round. Using your fingers, pinch and pleat the dough around the filling, leaving a tiny steam vent at the top; transfer to the baking sheet and garnish with a goji berry (optional). Repeat with the remaining dough and filling.

3. Fill a pot with 2 inches of water and bring to a boil. Arrange the dumplings in a bamboo steamer basket in batches, leaving at least 1 inch between them. Cover and steam the dumplings over the boiling water until the dough is shiny and the filling is soupy, about 5 minutes. Serve with the dipping sauce (see below) while you steam the remaining dumplings.

ROLL OUT & FILL THE WRAPPERS

1 FORM ROPES Divide the dough into quarters and, working with 1 piece at a time, roll into 1-inch-thick ropes.

2 MAKE BALLS Pinch or cut each rope into ¾-inch pieces and roll into balls.

3 ROLL OUT ROUNDS Using a dowel or glass bottle, roll each ball into an even circle.

4 FORM WRAPPERS Continue rolling out the dough, rotating it as you go, to form a thin 3½-inch round.

5 ADD FILLING Using a small offset spatula, spoon or butter knife, spoon a well-rounded tablespoon of the filling onto the center of each dough round.

6 FORM DUMPLINGS Carefully pinch and pleat the wrapper, using your thumb to tamp down the filling as you go; leave a tiny steam vent at the top.

7 STEAM Fill a steamer basket with the soup dumplings, leaving plenty of space between them to allow for expansion as they cook.

ROLLING SHORTCUT While Ng's method yields the best results, an easier way is to flatten the dough in a pasta machine and stamp out rounds with a 3½-inch biscuit cutter.

DIPPING SAUCE Mix ¼ cup Chinese black vinegar with 1 tablespoon julienned ginger. Drizzle on each dumpling before eating.

Shrimp and Shiitake Gyoza

TOTAL: 1 HR • MAKES ABOUT 50 GYOZA ●

At Lucky Belly in Honolulu, chef Jesse Cruz serves these juicy, pan-fried dumplings with *ponzu* (a citrus-soy dipping sauce) and an edamame-avocado puree. But the gyoza are also delicious on their own, or with a small bowl of unadulterated soy sauce.

¼ cup plus 1 tablespoon vegetable oil
4 ounces shiitake mushrooms, stems discarded and caps thinly sliced
4 ounces asparagus, thinly sliced crosswise
1 medium shallot, sliced
1 pound shelled and deveined shrimp
4 tablespoons oyster sauce
2 tablespoons chopped cilantro
1 scallion, finely chopped
½ teaspoon kosher salt
One 10- to 12-ounce package gyoza wrappers

1. In a skillet, heat 1 tablespoon of the oil. Stir-fry the shiitake, asparagus and shallot over high heat until softened, about 8 minutes. Transfer to a bowl to cool. In a food processor, pulse half of the shrimp until smooth. Coarsely chop the remaining shrimp. Add all of the shrimp to the vegetables with the oyster sauce, cilantro, scallion and salt.

2. Working in batches, lightly brush the edges of the gyoza wrappers with water. Spoon a scant tablespoon of the filling in the center of each wrapper and fold in half, pressing to seal. Arrange the gyoza on a wax paper–lined baking sheet, seam side up, and cover with a damp paper towel.

3. Divide the remaining ¼ cup of oil between 2 large nonstick skillets. Arrange the gyoza in the skillets seam side up in 2 concentric circles without touching. Cook over high heat until the bottoms are lightly browned, 2 minutes. Add ½ cup of water to each skillet, cover and cook until the water has evaporated and the dumplings are cooked through, about 5 minutes. Uncover the skillets and cook until the gyoza bottoms are browned and crisp, about 1 minute. Transfer the gyoza to a plate and serve. —*Jesse Cruz*

Spicy Uni-Lardo Sushi in Lettuce Cups

⏱ **TOTAL: 45 MIN**

MAKES 2 DOZEN BITE-SIZE CUPS

These lettuce cups are filled with surprising ingredients: crisped sushi rice wrapped in paper-thin sheets of lardo (Italian cured pork fat) and topped with fresh *uni* (sea urchin).

¾ cup short-grain Japanese rice
1 tablespoon *tobanjan* (see Note)
1 teaspoon red chile oil
⅛ teaspoon minced fresh ginger
⅛ teaspoon Chinese black vinegar
½ teaspoon sugar
¼ teaspoon mirin
¼ teaspoon rice vinegar
¼ teaspoon kosher salt
2 heads of butter lettuce (about 1 pound), 24 smallest leaves reserved
½ teaspoon vegetable oil
24 paper-thin slices of lardo (see Note)
24 lobes of sea urchin (6 ounces; see Note)
Thinly sliced scallions, for garnish

1. Cook the rice in a rice cooker according to the manufacturer's instructions. Alternatively, in a small saucepan, combine the rice with 1 cup of cold water and bring to a boil over high heat. Cover and simmer over low heat until the water is absorbed, 15 minutes. Remove from the heat and let stand, covered, for 10 minutes. Transfer 1 cup of the cooked rice to a small bowl; reserve the rest for another use.

2. In a bowl, stir the *tobanjan,* chile oil, ginger and black vinegar with 1 tablespoon of water. In another bowl, combine the sugar, mirin, rice vinegar and salt and sprinkle it over the cup of cooked rice; mix well. Form the rice into 24 loosely packed ½-inch balls.

3. Arrange the 24 lettuce leaves on a platter. In a large nonstick skillet, heat the oil. Add the rice balls and cook over moderately low heat, turning, until crispy all over, 6 minutes. Wrap a slice of lardo around each warm rice ball and set in a lettuce cup. Top each with a lobe of sea urchin and dab with the *tobanjan* sauce. Garnish with scallions and serve. —*Sang Yoon*

NOTE *Tobanjan* (spicy, fermented broad-bean paste, also sold as *doubanjiang*) is available at Asian food stores. Lardo is available at specialty and Italian food stores. Look for *uni* (sea urchin) at Japanese markets.

WINE Fragrant, minerally Blanc de Blancs Champagne: NV Delamotte Brut.

Cold Tofu with Chestnuts in Apple Dashi

⏱ **TOTAL: 20 MIN • 4 SERVINGS** ● ●

This light and elegant no-cook dish features custardy silken tofu in an ultra-refreshing broth. Star chef David Chang uses umami-packed *shiro* dashi, a bottled Japanese stock, as the savory base for the broth, stirring in Fuji apple juice for just the right amount of sweetness.

2 cups Fuji apple juice (see Note)
3 tablespoons *shiro* dashi (see Note)
2 tablespoons soy sauce
½ tablespoon sherry vinegar
½ tablespoon untoasted sesame oil
One 12-ounce package soft silken tofu, drained and sliced
2 cooked chestnuts, thinly sliced
Light green frisée leaves and wasabi oil (see Note), for garnish

In a small bowl, whisk the apple juice with the *shiro* dashi, soy sauce, sherry vinegar and sesame oil. Arrange the tofu slices in shallow bowls. Top with the chestnuts and frisée. Pour the apple dashi around the tofu. (Reserve any remaining apple dashi for another use.) Drizzle each bowl with a few drops of wasabi oil and serve.
—*David Chang*

NOTE Fuji apple juice is available at supermarkets and juice bars, or you can make your own. *Shiro* dashi is a stock made with soy sauce, white soy, bonito flakes and seaweed. *Shiro* dashi and wasabi oil are both available at Japanese and Korean markets.

WINE Full-bodied, apple-scented orange wine: 2010 Monastero Suore Cistercensi Coenobium Rusticum.

Ricotta Crostini with Pickled Ramps and Crisp Pancetta

ACTIVE: 40 MIN; TOTAL: 2 HR 45 MIN
10 TO 12 SERVINGS ●

- 2 teaspoons coriander seeds
- 1 cup apple cider vinegar
- 2 tablespoons sugar
- 2 bay leaves
- 1 teaspoon crushed red pepper

Kosher salt

- 8 ramps or scallions, white and light green parts only, cut into 1-inch pieces
- 3 garlic cloves, crushed
- 1½ cups fresh ricotta cheese
- 3 tablespoons extra-virgin olive oil, plus more for brushing

Freshly ground black pepper

- ½ pound pancetta, cut into ½-by-¼-inch pieces

Ten ½-inch-thick slices of ciabatta, cut into 2-by-2-inch squares

1. In a saucepan, toast the coriander seeds over moderate heat until fragrant, 1 minute. Add the vinegar, sugar, bay leaves, crushed red pepper and 2 tablespoons of salt. Bring just to a boil, stirring to dissolve the sugar and salt. Remove the brine from the heat and add the ramps and garlic. Let stand at room temperature for 2 hours. Drain the ramps, reserving 3 tablespoons of the brine.

2. In a bowl, mix the ricotta with the 3 tablespoons of oil. Season with salt and pepper.

3. In a skillet, cook the pancetta over moderate heat, stirring, until browned and just crisp, 8 to 10 minutes. Remove from the heat and add the reserved 3 tablespoons of brine, scraping up any browned bits in the pan.

4. Preheat the broiler and set a rack 8 inches from the heat. Brush the bread with oil and arrange in a single layer on a large rimmed baking sheet. Broil until golden, 1 minute per side. Spread half of each crostini with the ricotta and top with the pickled ramps, pancetta and any pan juices, then serve. —*Ryan Hardy*

WINE Bright, fruit-forward Grüner Veltliner: 2010 Kuenhof Veltliner.

Stilton and Burst Cherry Tomato Crostini

ACTIVE: 30 MIN; TOTAL: 1 HR
MAKES 2 DOZEN CROSTINI ● ●

Roasting cherry tomatoes until they burst makes them succulent and sweet; combining them with salty Stilton cheese on toast makes for a quick and tasty starter.

Two 10-ounce containers cherry tomatoes

- 3 tablespoons extra-virgin olive oil, plus more for brushing
- 1½ teaspoons sugar

Kosher salt and freshly ground black pepper

- 1 tablespoon unsalted butter
- 3 small onions, halved and sliced ¼ inch thick

Twenty-four ⅓-inch-thick slices of baguette

- 6 ounces Stilton cheese, crumbled

1. Preheat the oven to 400°. In a 9-by-13-inch baking dish, toss the tomatoes with 2 tablespoons of the olive oil and 1 teaspoon of the sugar; season with salt and pepper. Roast for 35 to 40 minutes, shaking the dish occasionally, until the tomatoes start to burst and are lightly browned. Leave the oven on.

2. Meanwhile, in a large skillet, melt the butter in the remaining 1 tablespoon of oil. Add the onions and the remaining ½ teaspoon of sugar; season with salt and pepper. Cook over moderately high heat, stirring occasionally, until the onions start to brown, about 12 minutes. Reduce the heat to moderately low and cook, stirring occasionally, until the onions are very soft, 20 to 25 minutes longer.

3. Brush the baguette slices with olive oil and arrange on a large baking sheet. Bake for about 12 minutes, until lightly golden but still chewy; let cool slightly. To serve, top the crostini with the cheese, onions, tomatoes and any accumulated tomato juices.
—*Susan Spungen*

MAKE AHEAD The roasted tomatoes and caramelized onions can be refrigerated separately overnight. Bring to room temperature before serving.

Crispy Polenta Bites with Arugula Tapenade

TOTAL: 10 MIN • 8 SERVINGS ● ● ●

One 16-ounce log of prepared polenta, at room temperature

- ½ cup panko (Japanese bread crumbs)
- 3 tablespoons olive oil
- 2 teaspoons fresh lemon juice
- ½ cup finely chopped arugula
- 2 tablespoons chopped olives

Kosher salt and ground black pepper

- 3 radishes, very thinly sliced

1. Trim the polenta's rounded edges to create a rectangle; halve lengthwise. Spread the panko on a plate. Press both sides of the polenta in the panko to coat. In a nonstick skillet, heat 1 tablespoon of the oil. Cook the polenta until crispy, 2 to 3 minutes per side; add 1 tablespoon of the oil after flipping.

2. Meanwhile, in a bowl, mix the remaining 1 tablespoon of oil with the lemon juice, arugula and olives. Season the arugula tapenade with salt and black pepper and toss.

3. Cut the polenta into 16 pieces, top with the radishes and arugula tapenade, then serve. —*Kay Chun*

ALMOST-INSTANT HORS D'OEUVRES

GREEK SHRIMP DIP Stir tzatziki (Greek cucumber-yogurt sauce) with chopped cooked shrimp and serve with warm pita.

SNACK MIX Toss toasted, salted pumpkin seeds with popped sorghum or Pop'd Kerns (*popdkerns.com*).

OYSTER BUNS Fill refrigerated biscuit dough (from a tube) with smoked oysters, form into buns and bake.

WHITE BEAN DIP Blend canned white beans with pesto and lemon juice and serve with celery and sliced fennel.

Piquillo Pepper and White Anchovy Toasts

⏱ **TOTAL: 10 MIN**
MAKES 1 DOZEN TOASTS ● ●

Six ½-inch-thick slices cut from a round
    loaf of country bread
Extra-virgin olive oil, for brushing
¼ cup black olive tapenade or spread
12 piquillo peppers (from a 9.8-ounce
    jar)—drained, halved lengthwise and
    patted dry
12 white anchovies (*boquerones*)

1. Preheat the broiler. Brush the bread slices
on both sides with olive oil and arrange on
a large rimmed baking sheet. Broil 8 inches
from the heat, turning once, until golden but
still chewy in the center, about 2 minutes.
2. Top the toasts with the tapenade, piquillo
peppers and anchovies. Cut the toasts in
half crosswise and serve. —*Felip Llufriu*
WINE Ripe, fruit-forward sparkling rosé: NV
Freixenet Cordon Rosado Brut.

PB&J Canapés

⏱ **TOTAL: 25 MIN • 6 SERVINGS** ● ● ●

16 green grapes, peeled
 1 teaspoon minced tarragon
¼ teaspoon Blis Elixir vinegar
    (see Note)
Freshly ground pepper
12 thin baguette slices
 1 tablespoon roasted peanut oil
Maldon salt, for serving

1. Preheat the oven to 325°. In a small bowl,
using a fork, crush the peeled grapes. Stir
in the minced tarragon and vinegar. Season
with pepper.
2. Brush the baguette slices with the oil and
toast in the oven for 8 to 10 minutes, until
crisp. Top the toasts with the grapes, sprinkle
with Maldon salt and serve.
—*Grant Achatz*
NOTE Blis Elixir is a brand of aged sherry
vinegar. It's available at *blisgourmet.com*.
WINE Strawberry-scented sparkling rosé:
NV Scharffenberger Brut Excellence.

Open-Face Four-Cheese Quesadillas

⏱ **TOTAL: 45 MIN • 4 SERVINGS** ○
At El Toro Blanco in Manhattan, chef Josh
Capon elevates the quesadilla by topping it
with roasted poblanos and tomatoes as well
as a mix of four cheeses.

 4 plum tomatoes, quartered
    lengthwise
 3 large poblano chiles
Four 10-inch flour tortillas
Extra-virgin olive oil, for brushing
 3 ounces *asadero* (see Note) or
    Monterey Jack cheese, coarsely
    shredded (about 1 cup)
 3 ounces Oaxaca cheese (see Note)
    or mozzarella, coarsely shredded
    (about 1 cup)
 3 ounces Manchego cheese,
    coarsely grated (about 1 cup)
 2 ounces Cotija cheese (see Note),
    finely grated (½ cup)
 2 tablespoons finely chopped
    fresh oregano
Kosher salt

1. Preheat the broiler and set a rack about
6 inches from the heat. Line a rimmed baking
sheet with parchment paper and spread the
tomatoes and poblanos on it. Broil for 4 to
5 minutes, turning the tomatoes once, until
softened and charred in spots. Transfer the
tomatoes to a work surface. Broil the poblanos for 4 to 7 minutes longer, turning occasionally, until they are charred all over.
2. Let the tomatoes and poblanos cool.
Coarsely chop the tomatoes; peel, seed and
stem the chiles, then thinly slice them crosswise. Leave the broiler on.
3. Preheat a cast-iron griddle or large, heavy
skillet. Brush the tortillas with olive oil. Toast
the tortillas on the hot griddle, turning once,
until browned in spots and crisp, 4 minutes.
4. In a bowl, toss together the *asadero*,
Oaxaca and Manchego cheeses. Arrange
2 tortillas on each of 2 large rimmed baking
sheets. Sprinkle the cheese mixture over the
tortillas, covering the entire surface. Scatter
the tomatoes and poblanos over the cheese.

Top each tortilla with 2 tablespoons of the
Cotija and ½ tablespoon of the oregano and
season lightly with salt.
5. Broil the quesadillas one sheet at a time
about 6 inches from the heat until the cheese
is just melted, 3 to 4 minutes. Transfer the
quesadillas to a work surface, cut into wedges
and serve while you broil the second batch.
—*Josh Capon*
NOTE *Asadero* (also known as *queso quesadilla*) and Oaxaca are great cheeses for melting. Cotija is a white, dry, crumbly cheese.
All of the cheeses are available at Mexican
markets and online at *igourmet.com*.
BEER Malty Mexican lager: Dos Equis Amber.

Creamed-Kale Toasts

⏱ **TOTAL: 40 MIN**
MAKES 2 DOZEN TOASTS ● ● ○

 1 pound Tuscan kale, stems discarded
 2 tablespoons unsalted butter
 2 garlic cloves, minced
Pinch of crushed red pepper
 1 cup heavy cream
½ cup freshly grated Parmigiano-
    Reggiano cheese
Kosher salt and freshly ground
    black pepper
Twenty-four ½-inch-thick slices of
    baguette, oiled and toasted

1. In a large saucepan of salted boiling water,
blanch the kale until just tender, 3 to 5 minutes. Drain, let cool slightly, then finely chop.
2. Preheat the broiler. In a large skillet, melt
the butter. Add the garlic; cook over moderate
heat, stirring, until just starting to brown,
2 minutes. Add the kale and crushed red pepper and cook for 2 minutes, tossing. Add the
cream; bring just to a boil. Simmer over moderately low heat, stirring, until the cream has
thickened, 5 minutes. Stir in ¼ cup of the
cheese; season with salt and black pepper.
3. Spoon the kale on the toasts and sprinkle
with the remaining ¼ cup of cheese. Broil
for about 2 minutes, rotating the pan as
necessary, until the cheese is just melted
and the kale is hot. Serve right away.
—*Maria Helm Sinskey*

● HEALTHY ● MAKE AHEAD ○ VEGETARIAN ● STAFF FAVORITE

PIQUILLO PEPPER AND
WHITE ANCHOVY TOASTS

Creamed Kale and Mushroom Toasts

⏱ TOTAL: 45 MIN • 8 SERVINGS ●●

¾ pound kale—tough stems and
inner ribs removed, leaves
coarsely chopped
Sixteen ½-inch-thick slices of brioche
6 tablespoons unsalted butter
½ cup minced shallots
1 garlic clove, minced
1 teaspoon coarsely chopped
thyme
¾ pound mixed mushrooms,
such as cremini, oyster
and shiitake, stemmed and
thinly sliced
1 tablespoon dry sherry
½ cup heavy cream
Salt and freshly ground pepper
1 tablespoon chopped
flat-leaf parsley

1. Bring a large saucepan of water to a boil. Add the kale and cook until just tender, about 2 minutes. Drain, pressing out the excess water.
2. Using a 1½-inch round cookie or biscuit cutter, punch out 32 rounds from the brioche slices (you can save the scraps to toast and grind for bread crumbs). In a large skillet, melt 2 tablespoons of the butter. Add half of the brioche rounds and toast over low heat, turning once, until golden, 3 minutes. Transfer the rounds to a work surface. Wipe out the skillet. Add 2 more tablespoons of butter and let it melt. Add the remaining brioche rounds and toast.
3. Wipe out the skillet and melt the remaining 2 tablespoons of butter in it. Add the shallots, garlic and thyme and cook over moderate heat, stirring, until softened, about 4 minutes. Add the mushrooms and cook until just tender, about 5 minutes. Add the kale and cook, stirring, for 2 minutes. Add the sherry and cook until evaporated. Add the cream, season with salt and pepper and cook until thickened, about 5 minutes. Stir in the parsley. Spoon the mixture onto the toasts and serve warm. —Michael White

Spiced-Ham-and-Cheese Toasts

ACTIVE: 30 MIN; TOTAL: 1 HR
MAKES 2 DOZEN TOASTS

2 tablespoons rendered bacon fat
or unsalted butter
1 medium onion, chopped
2 tablespoons minced sage
¼ teaspoon ground cloves
¼ teaspoon cayenne pepper
2 cups finely diced smoked ham
½ pound cream cheese,
at room temperature
½ cup shredded sharp cheddar cheese
4 scallions—2 thinly sliced,
2 julienned
2 tablespoons Dijon mustard
1 teaspoon apple cider vinegar
6 slices of firm white bread or
pain de mie, crusts removed
2 tablespoons unsalted butter, melted
Kosher salt

1. Heat the bacon fat in a large, heavy skillet. Add the onion, sage, cloves and cayenne and cook over moderate heat, stirring occasionally, until the onion is softened but not browned, 6 to 8 minutes. Add the ham and cook, stirring occasionally, for 2 minutes. Remove the skillet from the heat; let the mixture cool to room temperature.
2. In a food processor, combine the ham mixture with the cream cheese, cheddar cheese, sliced scallions, mustard and vinegar and pulse until the mixture resembles the texture of a rustic country pâté.
3. Preheat the oven to 400°. Brush the bread slices with the melted butter and sprinkle with salt. Using a sharp knife, cut each slice of bread into 4 triangles. Transfer the bread triangles to a baking sheet and bake for about 5 minutes, until golden.
4. Spread some of the spiced ham mixture on each toast triangle and bake for about 10 minutes, until browned in spots. Garnish the toasts with the julienned scallions and serve. —Lauren Kiino

WINE Juicy, berry-rich California red blend: NV Modern House Wines Here's To You.

Sweet Corn Pancakes with Mt. Tam Cheese

⏱ TOTAL: 35 MIN • 4 TO 6 SERVINGS ●

These corn pancakes are from Stuart Brioza, the chef at State Bird Provisions in San Francisco and an F&W Best New Chef 2003. They're puffy in the center and crispy at the edges, with lots of crunchy corn inside and melted cheese on top. Brioza loves Mt. Tam, a triple-cream cow-milk cheese from California's Cowgirl Creamery; St. André is delicious here, too.

3 large ears of corn, shucked
1 large egg, lightly beaten
1½ cups all-purpose flour
1½ teaspoons salt
1 teaspoon baking powder
½ cup finely chopped scallions
¼ cup canola oil, plus more as needed
2 ounces Cowgirl Creamery
Mt. Tam or other triple-cream
cheese, such as St. André,
cut into ½-inch wedges
Freshly ground black pepper

1. In a large saucepan of salted boiling water, cook the corn until crisp-tender, 3 to 5 minutes. Transfer the corn to a plate and let cool completely, then cut the kernels off the cobs.
2. In a large bowl, beat the egg with 1¼ cups of water. Sift the flour, salt and baking powder over the egg and whisk until a batter forms. Stir in the corn kernels and scallions.
3. In a large nonstick skillet, heat the ¼ cup of canola oil until shimmering. Spoon a scant ¼ cup of the batter into the skillet for each pancake and cook over moderate heat until browned on the bottom, 1 to 2 minutes. Flip the pancakes and top each with a piece of cheese. Cook until the cheese just starts to melt and the pancakes are cooked through, about 2 minutes longer. Transfer the pancakes to a platter and season with black pepper. Serve warm. —Stuart Brioza

MAKE AHEAD The pancake batter can be refrigerated overnight. Stir in the corn and scallions just before cooking.

WINE Ripe, full-bodied California Chardonnay: 2011 St. Francis Sonoma County.

● HEALTHY ● MAKE AHEAD ● VEGETARIAN ● STAFF FAVORITE

Mini Calzones Stuffed with Pepperoni, Pesto and Ricotta

ACTIVE: 1 HR 15 MIN; TOTAL: 3 HR 30 MIN
MAKES 16 MINI CALZONES ●

Star chef Mario Batali thinks that everyone should learn to make pizza dough, but he understands the convenience of buying it from your local pizza place. Either way, keep extra dough in your freezer to make calzones or pizzas any time you like.

DOUGH

- ¼ cup dry white wine
- 1 tablespoon honey
- 1 envelope active dry yeast
- 1 teaspoon kosher salt
- 1 tablespoon extra-virgin olive oil, plus more for brushing
- 3 cups all-purpose flour, plus more for dusting

FILLING

- 1 cup fresh ricotta cheese
- 4 to 6 ounces thinly sliced pepperoni
- ¼ cup prepared basil pesto
- 1 large egg lightly beaten with 1 teaspoon of water

Olive oil, for frying

1. MAKE THE DOUGH In a large bowl, stir the wine, honey and yeast with ¾ cup of warm water until the yeast is dissolved. Let stand until foamy, 5 minutes. Stir in the salt and the 1 tablespoon of olive oil. Add 1 cup of the flour and stir until a loose batter forms. Stir in the remaining 2 cups of flour until almost completely incorporated. Turn the dough out onto a work surface with any remaining flour and knead until the flour is incorporated and the dough is smooth and silky, 7 minutes. Transfer the dough to a large, lightly oiled bowl; brush all over with olive oil. Cover with plastic wrap and let rise in a warm place until doubled in bulk, 1 hour and 30 minutes.

2. Scrape the dough out onto a lightly floured work surface and cut into 16 equal pieces. Roll the pieces into balls and transfer to a baking sheet. Cover loosely with plastic wrap and let stand for 15 minutes.

3. FILL THE CALZONES Working with 1 ball of dough at a time, roll it out on a lightly floured work surface to a 4-inch round, a scant ⅛ inch thick. Spoon 1 tablespoon of the ricotta on one half of the round, then top with 2 to 4 pepperoni slices and a heaping ½ teaspoon of the pesto. Fold the dough over to form a half-moon and press the edge to seal tightly. Crimp the edge with a fork or pinch at intervals to make pleats. Transfer the calzone to a baking sheet and brush with the egg wash. Repeat with the remaining dough and filling to make the remaining calzones.

4. Preheat the oven to 325°. In a large saucepan, heat 1½ inches of oil to 350°. Fry 4 calzones at a time, turning once, until browned and crisp, 3 to 4 minutes. Drain the calzones on paper towels and keep warm in the oven while you fry the rest. Serve hot.
—*Mario Batali*

MAKE AHEAD The stuffed calzones can be prepared through Step 3 and frozen for up to 1 month. Let the calzones return to room temperature before frying.

WINE Refreshing sparkling wine: 2009 Contadi Castaldi Franciacorta Rosé.

Flaky Beef Empanadas

ACTIVE: 1 HR 15 MIN; TOTAL: 3 HR 30 MIN
PLUS OVERNIGHT CHILLING
MAKES 16 EMPANADAS ●

FILLING

- 6 tablespoons unsalted butter
- ¼ cup plus 2 tablespoons rendered lard (see Note)
- 1¼ pounds beef chuck, cut into ¼-inch dice

Kosher salt and freshly ground black pepper

- 1 large white onion, finely chopped
- 2 bay leaves
- ¾ cup finely chopped scallions
- 2 teaspoons ground cumin
- 1½ teaspoons crushed red pepper

DOUGH

- 1 cup water
- 1 stick unsalted butter, cut into ½-inch pieces
- 1 tablespoon kosher salt
- 3¼ cups all-purpose flour

Oil, for greasing

1. MAKE THE FILLING In a very large skillet, melt 4 tablespoons of the butter in ¼ cup of the lard. Add the beef, season with a generous pinch each of salt and pepper and cook over high heat, stirring, until browned and any liquid has evaporated, 8 minutes. Transfer to a bowl along with any fat in the skillet.

2. In the same skillet, melt the remaining 2 tablespoons of butter in the remaining 2 tablespoons of lard. Add the onion, bay leaves and a generous pinch each of salt and pepper and cook over moderate heat, stirring, until the onion is soft and golden, 10 minutes. Discard the bay leaves. Scrape the onion and any fat over the meat and let cool slightly. Stir in the scallions, cumin and red pepper; season with salt and black pepper. Refrigerate overnight.

3. MAKE THE DOUGH In a small saucepan, bring the water, butter and salt to a simmer. When the butter is melted, pour the mixture into a large bowl and let cool to room temperature. Add the flour and stir until the dough comes together. On a lightly floured work surface, gently knead the dough until almost smooth but still slightly tacky, with some streaks of butter. Divide the dough into 2 pieces, wrap them in plastic and refrigerate until firm, at least 1 hour or overnight.

4. Preheat the oven to 400° and oil 2 large baking sheets. Work with 1 piece of dough at a time: On a generously floured work surface, roll out the dough ⅛ inch thick. Using a 5-inch round plate as a guide, cut out 8 rounds of dough. Moisten the edge of the dough rounds with water. Mound 1½ packed tablespoons of the beef filling on one half of each round and fold the dough over to form half-moons; press the edge to seal. Pinch the edge at intervals to make pleats or crimp with the tines of a fork. Repeat with the remaining piece of dough to form 8 more empanadas.

5. Place the empanadas on the baking sheets; bake in the upper and lower thirds of the oven for 35 minutes, shifting the pans once halfway through, until browned. Serve warm or at room temperature. —*Santiago Garat*

NOTE Rendered lard is available at farmers' markets and specialty butcher shops.

WINE Spiced, dark-berried Argentinean Malbec: 2011 Don Miguel Gascón Malbec.

Red Potato and Apple Galette

ACTIVE: 50 MIN; TOTAL: 2 HR 30 MIN
MAKES ONE 11-BY-15-INCH GALETTE ● ● ●

The flaky, buttery crust of this easy appetizer forms the base for the following two galettes as well. Here, it's perfectly complemented by the decadent crème fraîche and tangy apple topping. Serve the tart on its own or, for a fun presentation, cut it into squares to mix and match with the Spinach and Artichoke Galette and Pigs on a Blanket.

The Ultimate Savory Pie Crust dough
 (recipe follows)
½ cup crème fraîche
¼ cup grated Pecorino Romano
 cheese
 1 medium red potato, very thinly
 sliced, preferably on a mandoline
 1 Granny Smith apple—halved, cored
 and very thinly sliced, preferably on
 a mandoline
Melted unsalted butter, for brushing
 1 teaspoon thyme leaves
Kosher salt and freshly ground
 black pepper
 1 large egg beaten with 1 tablespoon
 of water

1. Preheat the oven to 450°. Line a large baking sheet with parchment paper. On a lightly floured work surface, roll out the dough to a 12-by-16-inch rectangle, then transfer it to the lined baking sheet. Fold the dough edge over itself to form a ½-inch border all around and pinch the corners together. Refrigerate until firm.

2. Spread the crème fraîche and pecorino cheese over the dough; top with overlapping slices of the potato and apple in rows. Brush the potato and apple slices with the melted butter, sprinkle with the thyme leaves and season with salt and freshly ground pepper. Brush the edges of the dough with the egg wash.

3. Bake the galette in the bottom third of the oven for 25 minutes, or until the edges are slightly puffed. Cut into squares and serve warm or at room temperature.
—*Justin Chapple*

THE ULTIMATE SAVORY PIE CRUST

ACTIVE: 10 MIN; TOTAL: 1 HR 10 MIN
MAKES ONE 11-BY-15-INCH CRUST ● ●

1¾ cups all-purpose flour
Kosher salt and freshly ground pepper
 1 stick plus 2 tablespoons cold
 unsalted butter, cut into cubes
⅓ cup ice water

In a food processor, pulse the flour with 1 teaspoon of salt and ¼ teaspoon of pepper. Add the butter and pulse until the mixture resembles coarse meal, with some pea-size pieces of butter still visible. Sprinkle the ice water over the mixture and pulse until the dough just starts to come together; you should still see small pieces of butter. Scrape the dough out onto a work surface, gather up any crumbs and pat into an 8-inch square. Wrap in plastic and refrigerate until well chilled, about 1 hour or up to 2 days. —*JC*

Spinach and Artichoke Galette

ACTIVE: 45 MIN; TOTAL: 2 HR 30 MIN
MAKES ONE 11-BY-15-INCH GALETTE ● ●

The Ultimate Savory Pie Crust dough
 (recipe above)
½ cup crème fraîche
½ garlic clove, finely grated
½ teaspoon hot sauce
½ teaspoon finely grated lemon zest
Salt and freshly ground pepper
 1 cup shredded Manchego cheese
 5 ounces frozen chopped spinach,
 thawed and squeezed dry
One 14-ounce can artichoke hearts—
 drained, quartered and patted dry
 1 large egg beaten with 1 tablespoon
 of water
Thinly sliced scallions, for garnish

1. Preheat the oven to 450°. Line a large baking sheet with parchment paper. On a lightly floured surface, roll out the dough to a 12-by-16-inch rectangle; transfer to the baking sheet. Fold the dough edge over itself to form a ½-inch border all around and pinch the corners together. Refrigerate until firm.

2. In a bowl, mix the crème fraîche, garlic, hot sauce and lemon zest; season with salt and pepper. Spread the mixture over the dough, then top with the cheese, spinach and artichokes. Brush the edges of the dough with the egg wash.

3. Bake the galette in the bottom third of the oven for about 25 minutes, until the edges are slightly puffed. Cut into squares, garnish with sliced scallions and serve warm.
—*Justin Chapple*

Pigs on a Blanket

ACTIVE: 45 MIN; TOTAL: 2 HR 30 MIN
MAKES ONE 11-BY-15-INCH GALETTE

This recipe reimagines a classic party appetizer with chorizo and sauerkraut.

The Ultimate Savory Pie Crust dough
 (recipe above left)
¼ cup crème fraîche
¼ cup spicy brown mustard,
 plus more for serving
½ cup drained sauerkraut,
 plus more for serving
 1 large egg beaten with 1 tablespoon
 of water
 3 ounces Spanish chorizo, cut into
 1¼-by-¼-inch matchsticks
Snipped chives, for garnish

1. Preheat the oven to 450°. Line a large baking sheet with parchment paper. On a lightly floured surface, roll out the dough to a 12-by-16-inch rectangle; transfer to the baking sheet. Fold the dough edge over itself to form a ½-inch border all around and pinch the corners together. Refrigerate until firm.

2. In a bowl, whisk the crème fraîche with the mustard. Spread the mixture over the dough, then sprinkle with the sauerkraut. Brush the dough edges with the egg wash.

3. Bake the galette in the bottom third of the oven for 10 minutes. Scatter the chorizo evenly over the galette and bake for 15 minutes longer, until the edges are slightly puffed. Cut the galette into squares and garnish with chives. Serve with spicy brown mustard and sauerkraut.
—*Justin Chapple*

● HEALTHY ● MAKE AHEAD ● VEGETARIAN ● STAFF FAVORITE

PIGS ON A BLANKET, SPINACH AND ARTICHOKE
GALETTE, RED POTATO AND APPLE GALETTE

Sheep-Cheese Soufflés

ACTIVE: 45 MIN; TOTAL: 1 HR 15 MIN
6 SERVINGS ● ●

- 2 tablespoons unsalted butter, plus more for greasing
- 2 tablespoons all-purpose flour, plus more for dusting
- ¼ cup minced shallots
- 1¾ cups whole milk
- 1 teaspoon kosher salt
- Pinch of piment d'Espelette or other red chile powder
- Freshly ground black pepper
- 6 ounces Ossau-Iraty Brebis cheese or other semi-firm sheep-milk cheese, grated on the large holes of a box grater (2½ cups)
- 4 large eggs, separated
- 4 large egg whites

1. Preheat the oven to 400°. Butter and flour six 1½-cup ramekins.

2. In a medium saucepan, melt the 2 tablespoons of butter. Add the minced shallots and cook over moderate heat, stirring constantly, until they are softened, about 2 minutes. Add the 2 tablespoons of flour and cook, whisking constantly, for 30 seconds. While whisking, add the milk in a slow, steady stream, then whisk in the salt and piment d'Espelette; season with freshly ground black pepper. Cook over moderate heat, whisking, until the mixture comes to a simmer and is slightly thickened, about 5 minutes. Remove the saucepan from the heat and stir in the grated sheep-milk cheese until it is melted.

3. Transfer the soufflé base to a large bowl and let cool slightly. Whisk in the egg yolks, one at a time, until incorporated and no streaks remain. Let cool to room temperature, about 15 minutes.

4. In a large stainless steel bowl, using an electric mixer, beat all of the egg whites at high speed until firm peaks form. Fold one-third of the whites into the soufflé base to lighten it, then fold in the remaining whites until no streaks remain.

5. Spoon the soufflé base into the prepared ramekins, filling each one about three-fourths full. Bake the soufflés for 12 to 13 minutes, until puffed, just set and golden on top. Serve immediately. —*Jaime Davis*

Mini Spinach-Feta Pies

ACTIVE: 30 MIN; TOTAL: 50 MIN
MAKES 1 DOZEN MINI PIES ● ●

- 10 ounces curly spinach, stems discarded
- 3 tablespoons minced yellow onion
- 2½ tablespoons crumbled feta cheese
- Heaping ¼ teaspoon ground allspice
- 1 tablespoon extra-virgin olive oil
- 1 teaspoon fresh lemon juice
- Kosher salt and freshly ground pepper
- One 14-ounce package all-butter puff pastry, thawed
- 1 large egg, beaten
- Sesame seeds, for garnish

1. In a large saucepan of salted boiling water, blanch the spinach for 30 seconds. Drain and rinse under cool water. Squeeze out as much water as possible from the spinach. Chop the spinach and transfer it to a medium bowl. Add the onion, feta, allspice, olive oil and lemon juice, season with salt and pepper and mix well.

2. Line a baking sheet with parchment paper. On a lightly floured work surface, using a lightly floured rolling pin, roll out the puff pastry ⅛ inch thick. Using a 3½-inch round biscuit cutter, cut out 12 rounds; transfer them to the prepared baking sheet. Working with one round at a time, brush the edge with some of the beaten egg, then mound about 1 tablespoon of the spinach filling in the center. Bring three sides of the dough together in the center to form a triangle and pinch to seal. Repeat with the remaining pastry rounds, egg wash and spinach filling.

3. Brush the pastries all over with the beaten egg and sprinkle with the sesame seeds. Bake for 18 to 20 minutes, until the pastry is puffed and golden. Serve. —*Kay Chun*
WINE Delicate French sparkling wine: NV Parigot Crémant de Bourgogne.

Artichokes Two Ways, with Bresaola

TOTAL: 1 HR 20 MIN • 6 SERVINGS ●

- 6 large artichokes
- 2 lemons—1 halved, 1 thinly sliced
- 3 garlic cloves, thinly sliced
- ½ teaspoon crushed red pepper
- ½ cup dry white wine
- ½ cup plus 2 tablespoons extra-virgin olive oil, plus more for drizzling
- ⅔ cup chopped mint
- Sea salt and freshly ground pepper
- ¼ cup thinly sliced red onion
- ¼ cup fresh lemon juice
- ½ teaspoon finely grated orange zest
- ½ teaspoon finely grated lemon zest
- 8 very fresh baby artichokes
- 24 thin slices of *bresaola* (4 ounces)

1. Work with 1 large artichoke at a time: Cut off all but 2 inches of the leaves. Discard the dark outer leaves; trim the bottom and stem. Quarter the bottom; scrape out the hairy choke. Rub the quarters with 1 lemon half; squeeze the juice from the half into a bowl of water. Add the artichoke quarters. Repeat with the remaining large artichokes and lemon half.

2. In a saucepan, combine the lemon slices, garlic, red pepper, wine and ½ cup each of oil, mint and water. Arrange the artichoke quarters in the saucepan; season with salt and pepper. Bring to a boil, cover and simmer over moderately low heat until just tender, 25 minutes. Let cool to room temperature.

3. In a small bowl, toss the red onion with 2 tablespoons of the lemon juice; let stand for 10 minutes. In another bowl, whisk the remaining 2 tablespoons each of oil and lemon juice with the citrus zests.

4. Remove the dark outer leaves from the baby artichokes and trim the stems. Using a mandoline, thinly shave the artichokes and toss with the lemon dressing. Drain the onion and add to the shaved artichokes with the remaining mint. Season with salt and pepper.

5. Arrange the *bresaola* on a platter. Using a slotted spoon, spread the cooked artichokes on the *bresaola*. Top with the artichoke salad and a drizzle of oil and serve. —*Mario Batali*

● HEALTHY ● MAKE AHEAD ● VEGETARIAN ● STAFF FAVORITE

Curried Crab and Watermelon Salad with Arugula

:) TOTAL: 35 MIN • 4 SERVINGS ● ●

Master chef Daniel Boulud was one of the early innovators who paired sweet, crisp watermelon with savory seafood. This easy, sophisticated first course has since become a classic combination.

3 tablespoons extra-virgin olive oil
2 tablespoons finely chopped Granny Smith apple
1 tablespoon finely chopped onion
1½ teaspoons mild curry powder
Pinch of saffron threads, crumbled
½ cup mayonnaise
1 tablespoon finely chopped cilantro
1 tablespoon finely chopped mint
Salt and freshly ground black pepper
1 pound jumbo lump crabmeat
Four ½-inch-thick half-round watermelon slices from a large watermelon, rind removed
2 tablespoons plus 1 teaspoon fresh lime juice
5 ounces arugula

1. In a saucepan, heat 1 tablespoon of the oil until shimmering. Add the apple, onion, curry powder and saffron and cook over moderate heat until the onion is softened, about 5 minutes. Remove from the heat and stir in 1 teaspoon of water; let cool.
2. Scrape the mixture into a mini food processor, add the mayonnaise and process. Transfer the mayonnaise to a bowl and add the cilantro and mint. Season with salt and pepper, then fold in the crabmeat.
3. Cut each slice of watermelon into 2 triangles and transfer to 4 plates. Season with salt and pepper and sprinkle each plate with 1 teaspoon of lime juice. Mound the crab salad on the watermelon. In another bowl, toss the arugula with the remaining 1 tablespoon of lime juice and the remaining 2 tablespoons of oil and season with salt and pepper. Arrange the arugula on the plates and serve. —Daniel Boulud
WINE Dry, fruit-forward Provençal rosé: 2012 Château Montaud.

Double-Baked Three-Cheese Soufflés

ACTIVE: 1 HR; TOTAL: 2 HR
12 SERVINGS ● ○ ○

4 tablespoons unsalted butter, plus more for the ramekins
¼ cup all-purpose flour, plus more for the ramekins
1 cup milk
2½ cups heavy cream
4 ounces mild goat cheese, crumbled
10 large egg yolks, lightly beaten
2 ounces Roquefort cheese, crumbled
1½ cups freshly grated Gruyère cheese (4 ounces)
Salt and freshly ground white pepper
8 large egg whites

1. Preheat the oven to 350°. Butter and flour twelve ⅓-cup ramekins, tapping out any excess flour. In a medium saucepan, melt the 4 tablespoons of butter over moderate heat. Whisk in the ¼ cup of flour until smooth. Gradually whisk in the milk and 1 cup of the heavy cream until smooth; bring to a boil, whisking, then reduce the heat to low and simmer, whisking, for 5 minutes. Remove from the heat and stir in the goat cheese. Scrape the sauce into a bowl and let cool to room temperature, stirring occasionally.
2. Beat the egg yolks into the sauce. Stir in the Roquefort and ½ cup of the Gruyère. Season with salt and white pepper.
3. In a large stainless steel bowl, beat the egg whites with a pinch of salt until almost firm. Using a large rubber spatula, fold one-third of the beaten whites into the cheese sauce, then fold in the remaining egg whites just until blended. Gently spoon the soufflé mixture into the prepared ramekins, filling them three-fourths full. Set the ramekins on a rimmed baking sheet. Run your thumb around the rim of each ramekin to clean the inside.
4. Bake the soufflés for 25 minutes, or until risen and golden but not quite set in the center. Let cool, then invert the soufflés onto a large ovenproof platter or individual dishes.
5. Raise the oven temperature to 400°. Pour 2 tablespoons of the remaining heavy cream over each soufflé and sprinkle them with the remaining 1 cup of Gruyère. Bake the soufflés for 8 to 10 minutes, or until puffed and golden brown. If baking the soufflés on a platter, use a flat spatula to transfer them with their cream to plates, then serve. —Jeremiah Tower
MAKE AHEAD The unmolded baked soufflés can be refrigerated overnight. Bring to room temperature before proceeding.
WINE Lively, luxurious Champagne: NV Christian Etienne Brut.

Tuna Ceviche with Avocado and Cilantro

ACTIVE: 30 MIN; TOTAL: 1 HR 45 MIN
6 SERVINGS ● ●

1 pound sushi-grade tuna, sliced ¼ inch thick
1 small red onion, halved and thinly sliced
¾ cup fresh lime juice
1 teaspoon freshly ground pepper
1 large Hass avocado, cut into ⅓-inch dice
¼ cup coarsely chopped cilantro, plus cilantro leaves for garnish
Salt

1. Line a baking sheet with plastic wrap. Arrange the tuna slices in a single layer on the baking sheet and freeze until fairly firm, about 15 minutes.
2. Stack the slices of tuna. Using a very sharp chef's knife, cut the tuna into neat ¼-inch cubes. Transfer the cubed tuna to a medium glass or ceramic bowl and stir in the red onion, lime juice and pepper. Cover the tuna with plastic wrap and refrigerate for 1 hour, stirring gently with a plastic spatula every 15 to 20 minutes (the tuna will change color slightly).
3. Just before serving, gently fold in the avocado and chopped cilantro; season with salt. Transfer the ceviche to a serving bowl or individual glasses. Garnish with cilantro leaves and serve. —Rick Bayless
SERVE WITH Tortilla chips.
WINE Bright Spanish white: 2011 Bodegas Naia Las Brisas.

Spiced Shrimp with Tomato Salsa and Avocado Dip

TOTAL: 40 MIN PLUS 2 HR MACERATING
10 SERVINGS ● ●

A dusting of ground fennel and mustard seeds gives these sautéed shrimp an intriguing South Asian flavor.

TOMATO SALSA

2 cups yellow cherry tomatoes, halved
⅓ cup finely diced onion
⅓ cup finely diced peeled jicama
¼ cup finely chopped cilantro
1 jalapeño, seeded and minced
2 tablespoons fresh lime juice
1 large garlic clove, minced
¼ teaspoon cumin seeds
Kosher salt

AVOCADO DIP

2 Hass avocados, pitted and peeled
½ cup lightly packed cilantro leaves
6 large basil leaves
2½ tablespoons fresh lime juice
Kosher salt

SHRIMP

2 pounds shrimp, shelled and deveined
¾ teaspoon ground fennel seeds
¾ teaspoon ground mustard seeds
½ teaspoon crushed red pepper
3 tablespoons vegetable oil
Kosher salt

1. MAKE THE SALSA In a bowl, toss all of the salsa ingredients together; season with salt. Let stand at room temperature for 2 hours.
2. MAKE THE DIP In a food processor, combine the avocados, cilantro, basil and lime juice and puree. Season with salt. Scrape the dip into a bowl and refrigerate until chilled.
3. PREPARE THE SHRIMP In a bowl, toss the shrimp with the fennel, mustard, red pepper and 1 tablespoon of the oil; season with salt.
4. In a skillet, heat 1 tablespoon of the oil. Add half of the shrimp; cook over moderately high heat, turning once, until just cooked, 3 minutes. Transfer to a platter. Wipe out the skillet and repeat with the remaining oil and shrimp. Serve with the salsa and dip. —*Bill Kim*
WINE White peach–scented Sauvignon Blanc: 2012 Trinchero Mary's Vineyard.

Scallop Rosettes with Avocado and Creamed Tandoori Chayote

⏱ **TOTAL: 45 MIN • 8 SERVINGS** ●

2 medium tomatillos, husked
1 Hass avocado, coarsely chopped
2 tablespoons fresh lime juice
5 tablespoons extra-virgin olive oil, plus more for brushing
1 tablespoon chopped pickled cherry peppers, plus slices for garnish
Salt and freshly ground white pepper
2 chayotes—halved lengthwise and pitted; 3 halves cut into ¼-inch dice, 1 half shaved on a mandoline
1 teaspoon tandoori seasoning (available at *penzeys.com*)
½ cup heavy cream
½ cup low-sodium chicken broth
2 tablespoons chopped parsley, plus parsley leaves for garnish
8 jumbo sea scallops, thinly sliced crosswise

1. Preheat the oven to 400°. In a blender, puree the tomatillos, avocado and lime juice. With the machine on, add 3 tablespoons of the oil. Transfer to a bowl; fold in the chopped peppers. Season with salt and white pepper.
2. In a large skillet, heat the remaining 2 tablespoons of oil. Add the diced chayote and tandoori seasoning and season with salt and white pepper. Cook over moderate heat, stirring, for 2 minutes. Add the cream and broth and simmer over low heat until the chayote is tender and coated in a thick sauce, about 5 minutes longer. Stir in the chopped parsley.
3. Cut eight 6-inch squares of parchment and lightly brush them with oil, then place on a large baking sheet. Arrange 1 sliced scallop in a rosette on each piece of parchment and season with salt and white pepper. Bake for 5 minutes, just until the scallops are white.
4. Spoon the chayote onto plates and top with a dollop of the tomatillo-avocado puree. Slide the scallop rosettes over the puree. Garnish with parsley leaves, cherry pepper slices and shaved chayote and serve. —*Daniel Boulud*
WINE Minerally, fresh strawberry–scented rosé: 2012 Gothic.

Smoked Sturgeon with Caviar and Everything Bagel Crumbs

⏱ **TOTAL: 45 MIN • 4 SERVINGS**

This simplified take on chef Daniel Humm's whimsical appetizer at Manhattan's Eleven Madison Park combines store-bought smoked sturgeon, rye crackers, toasted bagel bits and domestic hackleback caviar.

½ everything bagel—bread scooped out and discarded, crust finely diced
¼ cup extra-virgin olive oil
Kosher salt and freshly ground pepper
4 quail eggs
One 1-ounce jar hackleback or other black caviar
3 tablespoons cream cheese
1 tablespoon white balsamic vinegar
1 head of Bibb lettuce, torn into bite-size pieces
½ pound smoked sturgeon, thickly sliced
¼ cup sliced pickled cocktail onions
Rye crisps and dill pickles, for serving

1. Preheat the oven to 350°. In a pie plate, toss the bagel dice with 1 tablespoon of the oil and season with salt and pepper. Toast for about 10 minutes, until golden; let cool.
2. In a small saucepan of salted boiling water, cook the quail eggs for 2 minutes. Transfer the eggs to a bowl of ice water to cool. Peel the eggs and halve them lengthwise.
3. Using a ceramic or plastic spoon, scrape the caviar into a small bowl; wipe the jar clean. Spread the cream cheese into the empty caviar jar. Spread the caviar over the cream cheese in an even layer to cover it completely.
4. In a small bowl, whisk the vinegar with the remaining 3 tablespoons of olive oil and season with salt. In a large bowl, toss the lettuce and dressing and season with salt. Arrange the smoked sturgeon on 4 plates. Mound the salad alongside the fish. Arrange the sliced onions and quail eggs on the salads and sprinkle the bagel crumbs on top. Serve with the caviar cream cheese, rye crisps and pickles. —*Daniel Humm*
WINE Crisp, green apple–inflected sparkling wine: NV Zardetto Brut Prosecco.

● HEALTHY ● MAKE AHEAD ● VEGETARIAN ● STAFF FAVORITE

SPICED SHRIMP WITH TOMATO
SALSA AND AVOCADO DIP

Gravlax-Style Salmon Tartare with Dill Oil

TOTAL: 40 MIN PLUS 8 HR CURING
6 SERVINGS ● ●

For this variation on classic salmon gravlax, food writer Anya von Bremzen cuts the fish into small cubes before adding salt and sugar, so it cures quickly—overnight instead of over several days. She serves the tartare as an hors d'oeuvre with blini.

¾ pound skinless salmon fillet, cut into ¼-inch dice
1 teaspoon finely grated lemon zest
1 tablespoon sugar
2 teaspoons sea salt, plus more for seasoning
½ teaspoon smoked salt
1 cup lightly packed dill, thick stems discarded
½ cup canola oil
1 ice cube
1 Persian cucumber, finely diced (1 cup)
2 red radishes, halved and thinly sliced
1 tablespoon vodka, preferably lemon vodka
1 tablespoon extra-virgin olive oil
Quick Buckwheat Blini (recipe follows), for serving

1. In a medium bowl, toss the salmon with the lemon zest, sugar, 2 teaspoons of sea salt and the smoked salt. Cover the fish with plastic wrap and refrigerate for at least 8 hours or overnight.
2. Meanwhile, in a blender, combine the dill, canola oil and ice cube and puree until nearly smooth. Strain the dill oil through a fine sieve into a glass bottle or bowl, pressing gently on the solids.
3. Stir the cucumber, radishes, vodka and olive oil into the salmon and lightly season the tartare with sea salt. Serve the tartare with blini and a drizzle of the dill oil.
—Anya von Bremzen
WINE Bright, citrusy white: 2012 Condes de Albarei Salneval Albariño.

Quick Buckwheat Blini

ACTIVE: 45 MIN; TOTAL: 1 HR
MAKES ABOUT 40 BLINI ● ● ●

Called *oladyi* or *blinchiki* (the diminutive of blini) in Russian, these mini blini get their nutty flavor from buckwheat flour. They require no rising, so this recipe is ideal for making a big batch quickly.

1½ cups buttermilk
¾ cup all-purpose flour
½ cup buckwheat flour
2 large eggs
3 tablespoons unsalted butter, melted
1 tablespoon sugar
1 teaspoon salt
½ teaspoon baking powder
¼ teaspoon baking soda
½ cup seltzer or club soda
Canola oil, for brushing

1. In a food processor, combine all of the ingredients except the seltzer and oil and puree until smooth. Scrape the batter into a large bowl and let stand for 15 minutes.
2. Whisk ⅓ cup of the seltzer into the batter; it should have the consistency of pancake batter; add a bit more seltzer if the batter is too thick.
3. Heat a large nonstick skillet or griddle over moderate heat until very hot. Brush with oil. Spoon tablespoon-size mounds of batter into the hot skillet and cook until bubbles form on the surface and the blini are browned on the bottom, about 1 minute. Flip the blini and cook for 30 seconds longer. Transfer the blini to a baking sheet. Brush the skillet with oil as needed and repeat with the remaining batter, layering the cooked blini on the baking sheet. Serve the blini warm or at room temperature.
—Anya von Bremzen
SERVE WITH Gravlax-Style Salmon Tartare with Dill Oil (recipe at left), salmon roe, sour cream, smoked fish, such as salmon and sable, or fruit jam.
MAKE AHEAD The blini can be stored in an airtight container overnight; serve warm or at room temperature.

Happy Pancakes

TOTAL: 1 HR
MAKES ABOUT 10 PANCAKES ●

The name says it all for these thin, crackly starters from Vietnamese-food expert and former F&W Test Kitchen supervisor Marcia Kiesel. The pancakes—studded with pork, shrimp and mushrooms and folded around raw bean sprouts—represent everything we love about Southeast Asian cuisine: They're simultaneously hot and crisp, cold and juicy, and invigoratingly aromatic.

DIPPING SAUCE
2 Thai red chiles or 1 medium jalapeño, thickly sliced
2 medium garlic cloves, thickly sliced
2 tablespoons sugar
2 tablespoons Asian fish sauce
2 tablespoons fresh lime juice
PANCAKES
1¾ cups rice flour
¼ teaspoon turmeric
1 scallion, thinly sliced
¾ cup plus 3 tablespoons vegetable oil
1 pound boneless pork loin, cut crosswise into very thin slices
½ pound medium shrimp, shelled and deveined
½ small onion, thinly sliced
10 medium mushrooms, sliced
Salt and freshly ground pepper
2½ cups mung bean sprouts

1. MAKE THE DIPPING SAUCE In a mortar, pound the chiles, garlic and sugar to a paste. Stir in the fish sauce, lime juice and 2 tablespoons of water.
2. MAKE THE PANCAKES In a bowl, whisk together the rice flour and 2 cups of cold water. Mix in the turmeric and scallion.
3. In a large nonstick skillet, heat 1½ tablespoons of the vegetable oil over high heat. Add 3 slices of pork, 3 shrimp and a few slices of onion and mushroom. Season with ⅛ teaspoon each of salt and pepper. Cook for 1 minute. Stir the rice flour mixture again and ladle ⅓ cup into the pan; tilt the pan to evenly distribute the batter. Cover and cook until

● HEALTHY ● MAKE AHEAD ● VEGETARIAN ● STAFF FAVORITE

the sides of the pancake turn deep brown and curl up, 5 minutes. Scatter ¼ cup of the bean sprouts over the pancake, fold it in half and slide it onto a warm platter. Keep warm in a low oven while you repeat with the remaining ingredients. Serve the pancakes warm, with the dipping sauce on the side. —*Marcia Kiesel*

WINE Zesty Grüner Veltliner: 2011 Forstreiter Grooner.

Chicken-Fried Chicken Livers

TOTAL: 45 MIN PLUS OVERNIGHT MARINATING • 6 SERVINGS

James Holmes, the chef at Lucy's Fried Chicken in Austin, soaks livers in buttermilk, soy and hot sauce to temper the gaminess and make them extra-delicious. The smoky chipotle mayo is a perfect dipping sauce.

3½ cups buttermilk
⅓ cup Louisiana-style hot sauce, such as Crystal
1½ tablespoons soy sauce
1 pound chicken livers, trimmed
½ cup mayonnaise
1 small chipotle chile in adobo, seeded and minced, plus 1 tablespoon adobo sauce
3 cups all-purpose flour
3 large eggs
2 teaspoons cayenne pepper
2 teaspoons ground black pepper
1½ teaspoons ground cumin
1 teaspoon garlic salt
Canola oil, for frying
Kosher salt

1. In a large bowl, whisk 2 cups of the buttermilk with the hot sauce and soy sauce. Add the chicken livers and turn to coat. Cover and refrigerate overnight.

2. In a small bowl, whisk the mayonnaise, chipotle and adobo sauce; refrigerate.

3. Set a rack over a baking sheet. Spread 1½ cups of the flour in a shallow bowl. In another shallow bowl, beat the eggs with the remaining 1½ cups of buttermilk. In a third shallow bowl, mix the remaining 1½ cups of flour, the cayenne, black pepper, cumin and garlic salt.

4. Remove the livers from the buttermilk, then dredge them in the plain flour. Dip the livers in the egg mixture, then dredge in the seasoned flour. Transfer to the rack.

5. In a large saucepan, heat 2 inches of oil to 350°. Set another rack over a rimmed baking sheet. Add half of the livers to the hot oil and fry over moderately high heat, turning once, until barely pink inside, 3 to 5 minutes. Transfer to the clean rack and season lightly with salt. Repeat with the remaining livers. Serve hot, with the chipotle mayonnaise.
—*James Holmes*

WINE Earthy red Burgundy: 2010 Michel Gros Hautes Côtes de Nuits.

Hand-Chopped Spiced Beef Tartare

⏲ **TOTAL: 30 MIN • 6 SERVINGS** ●

Fast and easy to make ahead, this exceptional beef tartare is prepared with super-flavorful hanger steak that's hand-chopped with fresh rosemary and the mildly spicy Basque pepper piment d'Espelette. Be sure to use the freshest, best-quality beef from your butcher.

1½ pounds hanger steak—trimmed of all sinew and fat, chilled
2 teaspoons finely chopped rosemary
Pinch of piment d'Espelette (see Note)
Kosher salt and freshly ground pepper
2 tablespoons extra-virgin olive oil
1 tablespoon fresh lemon juice
Grilled sourdough bread, for serving

On a cutting board, slice the steak into very thin strips. Stack the strips and cut into fine cubes. Add the chopped rosemary and piment d'Espelette and chop together until the meat is minced. Season with salt and pepper and transfer to a bowl. Stir in the olive oil and lemon juice; serve with grilled sourdough bread. —*Owen Kenworthy*

NOTE Piment d'Espelette, a mildly spicy, ground red pepper, is available at specialty food shops and *zingermans.com*.

MAKE AHEAD The chopped beef can be refrigerated for up to 4 hours.

WINE Light-bodied, fruit-forward red: 2012 Château Cambon Beaujolais.

Korean Flapjacks

⏲ **TOTAL: 30 MIN • MAKES 9 PANCAKES** ●

Korean restaurants make seafood pancakes without leavening for a crispy, chewy texture. This multiculti revamp uses a batter with baking soda for much fluffier pancakes.

4 ounces shelled and deveined medium shrimp
4 ounces cleaned small squid— tentacles halved, bodies sliced into ¼-inch-thick rings
1½ cups plus 2 tablespoons all-purpose flour
1 teaspoon kosher salt
1 teaspoon baking powder
½ teaspoon baking soda
1½ cups whole milk
2 large eggs, beaten
Canola oil, for frying
Toasted sesame oil, for frying
1 cup kimchi, drained and chopped

1. In a medium saucepan of salted boiling water, cook the shrimp until almost white throughout, 2 minutes. Using a slotted spoon, transfer the shrimp to a bowl of ice water. Add the squid to the saucepan and cook until white, 30 seconds; drain and transfer to the ice water. Drain the seafood and pat dry; cut the shrimp into ½-inch pieces.

2. In a large bowl, whisk the flour with the salt, baking powder and baking soda. Add the milk and eggs and whisk until smooth. Fold in the shrimp and squid.

3. In a large nonstick skillet, heat 1 tablespoon each of the canola and sesame oils. For each flapjack, ladle ¼ cup of the batter into the skillet, leaving space between them. Scatter some kimchi on top, pressing gently, and cook over moderate heat until bubbles start to appear on the surface and the edges are golden, about 3 minutes. Flip the flapjacks, add another tablespoon of canola oil to the skillet and cook until golden and crisp on the bottom, about 3 minutes longer. Transfer to a plate and repeat with the remaining batter.
—*John Gorham*

WINE Spritzy, citrusy Portuguese white: 2012 Casa do Valle Vinho Verde.

Chicken Wings with Angry Sauce

TOTAL: 50 MIN • 8 TO 10 SERVINGS ●

This Korean-inspired recipe is fiery and a little bit sweet. Lisa Shin, co-owner of Wing Wings in San Francisco, also uses the versatile sauce as a marinade for pork and a dip for cucumber spears.

6 pounds chicken wings (about 24), tips discarded and wings split
¼ cup canola oil
Kosher salt and freshly ground pepper
⅓ cup *gochujang* (Korean chile paste; see Note)
2 tablespoons *gochugaru* (Korean chile powder; see Note)
2 tablespoons sugar
1 tablespoon toasted sesame oil
1 tablespoon water
2 teaspoons unseasoned rice vinegar
2 teaspoons soy sauce
2 teaspoons minced peeled fresh ginger
1 teaspoon minced garlic
Sesame seeds and thinly sliced scallions, for garnish

1. Preheat the oven to 450°. Line 2 large rimmed baking sheets with foil and coat with nonstick cooking spray. In a large bowl, toss the wings with the canola oil and season with salt and pepper. Transfer the wings, skin side up, to the prepared baking sheets and roast them for about 45 minutes, until they are cooked through and crisp.

2. Meanwhile, in another large bowl, whisk all of the remaining ingredients except the garnishes with a pinch of freshly ground pepper.

3. Add the crispy wings to the chile sauce, toss to coat and garnish with the sesame seeds and scallions. Serve hot. —*Lisa Shin*

NOTE Korean chile paste and powder are available at *hmart.com.*

MAKE AHEAD The sauce can be refrigerated overnight. Bring to room temperature before tossing with the wings.

BEER Malty brown ale: Avery Brewing Company Ellie's Brown.

Chicken Wings with Fragrant Herb Sauce

TOTAL: 50 MIN • 8 TO 10 SERVINGS

Instead of being deep-fried, these wings are blast-roasted so they crisp up without using any additional fat. The sauce is herby and fresh, with a vibrant, peppery heat tamed by honey. The sauce would also be great with fish or steak.

6 pounds chicken wings (about 24), tips discarded and wings split
¼ cup plus 3 tablespoons canola oil
Kosher salt and freshly ground black pepper
½ cup lightly packed parsley leaves
4 scallions, white and light green parts only, chopped
1 jalapeño—halved lengthwise, stemmed and seeded
2 tablespoons apple cider vinegar
1 tablespoon honey
1 teaspoon minced peeled fresh ginger
1 garlic clove, crushed
½ habanero pepper, stemmed and seeded
½ teaspoon finely chopped thyme leaves
¼ teaspoon finely grated orange zest
Pinch of freshly grated nutmeg

1. Preheat the oven to 450°. Line 2 large rimmed baking sheets with aluminum foil and coat them with nonstick cooking spray. In a large bowl, toss the chicken wings with ¼ cup of the canola oil and season them with salt and pepper. Transfer the wings, skin side up, to the prepared baking sheets and roast for about 45 minutes, until they are cooked through and crisp.

2. Meanwhile, in a food processor or blender, combine all of the remaining ingredients with the remaining 3 tablespoons of oil and puree until nearly smooth. Season the green sauce with salt and pepper and transfer to a large bowl.

3. Add the crispy wings to the green sauce and toss well to coat. Transfer to a platter and serve hot. —*Lisa Shin*

MAKE AHEAD The herb sauce can be made up to 3 hours ahead.

WINE Vibrant Sauvignon Blanc from New Zealand: 2012 Mount Nelson.

Sticky Miso Chicken Wings

ACTIVE: 15 MIN; TOTAL: 1 HR
6 SERVINGS ●

Miso and fish sauce give these irresistible sweet-sour wings a savory earthiness, while lime juice and ginger add zing.

12 chicken wings, tips discarded and wings split
2 tablespoons canola oil
Salt and freshly ground black pepper
⅓ cup *shiro* miso (light yellow)
2 teaspoons fresh lime juice
1 teaspoon finely grated peeled fresh ginger
1 teaspoon Asian fish sauce
1 Thai bird chile, minced
3 tablespoons turbinado or light brown sugar
Cilantro leaves, for garnish
Lime wedges, for serving

1. Preheat the oven to 400°. In a large bowl, toss the chicken wings with the oil and season lightly with salt and pepper. Transfer the wings to a rack set over a baking sheet. Bake for about 40 minutes, turning the wings halfway through, until they are golden, crispy and cooked through.

2. Meanwhile, in a small saucepan, combine the *shiro* miso with the lime juice, ginger, fish sauce, chile and sugar. Add 3 tablespoons of water and cook over moderately low heat, whisking frequently, until the sugar is dissolved and the glaze is smooth and slightly thickened.

3. Brush the glaze all over the wings and bake for about 10 minutes longer, until the wings are golden brown and sticky. Transfer the wings to a platter, garnish with cilantro and serve with lime wedges.
—*Kay Chun*

WINE Juicy, cherry-scented Pinot Noir: 2009 Chalone Monterey.

CHICKEN WINGS WITH ANGRY SAUCE (TOP)
AND CHICKEN WINGS WITH FRAGRANT HERB SAUCE

Stockholm-based food bloggers
David Frenkiel and Luise Vindahl
(with their daughter, Elsa) of
Green Kitchen Stories prepare
healthy, ingenious salads
with their fresh-produce haul.
Opposite: recipe, page 58.
SUMMER VEGETABLE "CEVICHE"

FIRST
& MAIN
COURSE
SALADS

Creamy Caesar Salad with Torn Croutons

ACTIVE: 25 MIN; TOTAL: 1 HR
6 SERVINGS ●

½ pound day-old rustic Italian bread, crusts discarded and bread torn into bite-size pieces
10 anchovy fillets, plus more for garnish
¼ cup red wine vinegar
3 tablespoons Dijon mustard
2 garlic cloves
1 large egg
1 cup vegetable oil
⅓ cup freshly grated Parmigiano-Reggiano cheese, plus finely shredded cheese for serving
Kosher salt and freshly ground pepper
18 ounces Little Gem lettuce, leaves separated and chilled

1. Preheat the oven to 400°. Spread the bread pieces on a rimmed baking sheet and bake for about 12 minutes, until golden and crisp; let the croutons cool.

2. Meanwhile, in a food processor, combine the 10 anchovy fillets with the vinegar, mustard and garlic and puree until smooth. Add the egg and pulse until just incorporated. With the machine on, gradually drizzle in the vegetable oil until emulsified. Scrape the dressing into a bowl and stir in the ⅓ cup of grated cheese. Season with salt and pepper. Cover the dressing with plastic wrap and refrigerate until well chilled and thickened, at least 30 minutes.

3. In a very large bowl, toss the chilled lettuce leaves with half of the dressing, gently rubbing the dressing onto the leaves with your hands. (Save the remaining dressing for another salad or to serve with grilled chicken.) Arrange the dressed lettuce on a platter; scatter the croutons on top. Garnish with anchovy fillets and serve right away, passing shredded Parmigiano at the table. —*April Bloomfield*

MAKE AHEAD The Caesar dressing can be refrigerated for up to 2 days.

WINE Medium-bodied Bordeaux blanc: 2012 Château de Bonhoste.

Heirloom Lettuces with Benne Seed Dressing

ACTIVE: 30 MIN; TOTAL: 1 HR
8 SERVINGS ● ●

At Two Boroughs Larder in Charleston, South Carolina, the ingredients are Southern, but the influences are global. Here, chef Josh Keeler makes a dressing with toasted benne seeds (a regional sesame variety), giving it a Middle Eastern, tahini-like flavor.

½ cup plus 1 tablespoon benne (sesame) seeds (2½ ounces)
½ teaspoon finely grated lemon zest
¼ cup fresh lemon juice
½ cup plus 1 tablespoon extra-virgin olive oil
Kosher salt and freshly ground white pepper
1 tablespoon unsalted butter
½ cup panko (Japanese bread crumbs)
2 pounds heirloom lettuces, torn into bite-size pieces

1. Preheat the oven to 375°. Spread the benne seeds on a baking sheet and bake for about 45 minutes, stirring once, until browned and fragrant. Transfer ½ cup of the seeds to a mini food processor and let cool; reserve the remaining 1 tablespoon of seeds for garnish. Add the lemon zest, lemon juice and ¼ cup of cold water to the food processor and puree until a paste forms. With the machine on, drizzle in ½ cup of the olive oil. Season the benne seed dressing with salt and freshly ground white pepper.

2. In a medium skillet, melt the butter in the remaining 1 tablespoon of olive oil. Add the panko and cook over moderate heat, stirring occasionally, until golden, about 5 minutes. Season with salt and white pepper; let cool completely.

3. In a large bowl, toss the lettuce leaves with the dressing and season lightly with salt. Sprinkle the toasted panko on top, garnish with the reserved 1 tablespoon of toasted benne seeds and serve right away. —*Josh Keeler*

MAKE AHEAD The dressing can be refrigerated overnight.

Bitter-Greens Salad with Melted Cheese

☉ TOTAL: 30 MIN • 4 SERVINGS ● ●

Chef Joshua McFadden creates edgy yet satisfying Italian dishes at Ava Gene's in Portland, Oregon. The menu includes this clever salad; McFadden heats it briefly before serving so the greens wilt and the cheese melts over them.

½ cup hazelnuts
3 tablespoons red wine vinegar
¼ cup extra-virgin olive oil
Kosher salt and freshly ground black pepper
1 large head of radicchio (¾ pound), cored and coarsely shredded
5 ounces baby arugula
4 ounces semi-firm Italian cheese, such as Crucolo (see Note) or Pecorino Toscano, thinly shaved
Saba (see Note) or balsamic vinegar, for drizzling

1. Preheat the oven to 350°. Spread the hazelnuts in a pie plate and toast them until their skins start to wrinkle, about 10 minutes. Let the hazelnuts cool, then rub them together in a clean kitchen towel to remove the skins. Coarsely chop the hazelnuts. Leave the oven on.

2. In a large bowl, whisk the red wine vinegar with the olive oil and season with salt and pepper. Add the radicchio and arugula and toss well. Mound the salad on ovenproof plates and top with the shaved cheese. Arrange the plates on trays and warm the salads in the oven for about 1 minute, until the cheese is just melted. Sprinkle the toasted hazelnuts on top. Drizzle a little *saba* over the salads and serve right away. —*Joshua McFadden*

NOTE Crucolo is a semi-firm cow-milk cheese characterized by a deep, rich and buttery flavor. Made by a single producer at the Rifugio Crucolo in the Trentino region of northern Italy, it is available at *dipaloselects.com. Saba,* the Italian condiment made from reduced grape must, is available at specialty food stores and online at *igourmet.com.*

● HEALTHY ● MAKE AHEAD ● VEGETARIAN ● STAFF FAVORITE

CREAMY CAESAR SALAD
WITH TORN CROUTONS

Butter Lettuce Salad with Persimmons and Radishes

TOTAL: 30 MIN • 8 SERVINGS ● ●

Star sommelier Richard Betts makes his colorful salad with pretty orange Fuyu persimmons, sliced radishes and red scallions. The richness of the salad dressing helps it pair well with wine.

¼ cup plus 2 tablespoons pumpkin seed oil

3 tablespoons sherry vinegar

Kosher salt and freshly ground pepper

Two 10-ounce heads of butter lettuce, leaves torn into bite-size pieces

2 Fuyu persimmons, cut into wedges

1½ cups thinly sliced radishes

1 cup thinly sliced red scallions or red onion

1. In a small bowl, whisk the pumpkin seed oil with the vinegar; season with salt and freshly ground pepper.

2. In a large bowl, toss the lettuce with the persimmons, radishes and scallions. Serve the salad, passing the dressing at the table. —*Richard Betts*

WINE Fruit-forward Sonoma Sauvignon Blanc: 2012 Hanna.

SALAD DRESSING TIP

Who says a vinaigrette has to be made with oil? Gabriel Rucker, chef at Le Pigeon in Portland, Oregon, uses brown butter instead to create a warm version that revolutionizes the way we dress lightly cooked vegetables and warm, mustardy potato salads.

Green Salad with Smoky Barbecue Vinaigrette

TOTAL: 30 MIN • 6 SERVINGS ●

CROUTONS

8 ounces thinly sliced corn bread, cut into 2-inch squares

Vegetable oil spray

½ cup freshly grated Parmigiano-Reggiano cheese

SALAD

¼ cup smoky barbecue sauce

¼ cup extra-virgin olive oil

2 tablespoons fresh lemon juice

1 tablespoon honey

Salt and freshly ground pepper

1 bunch of arugula, leaves torn

1 bunch of watercress, stemmed

1 head of treviso or radicchio, torn

1 head of escarole, light green and yellow inner leaves only, torn

1 small shallot, very thinly sliced

2 ounces shaved Parmigiano-Reggiano cheese (about 1½ cups)

1. MAKE THE CROUTONS Arrange the corn bread on a work surface and spray with vegetable oil. Sprinkle half of the grated Parmesan cheese on top and press to help it adhere. Carefully flip the corn bread and repeat with the remaining Parmesan.

2. Spray a large nonstick skillet with vegetable oil and arrange the corn bread squares in the skillet in a single layer. Cook over moderate heat, turning once, until the cheese is browned, 2 to 3 minutes. Let the croutons cool until crisp, then tear into chunks.

3. MAKE THE SALAD In a large bowl, whisk the barbecue sauce with the olive oil, lemon juice and honey; season with salt and pepper. Add the greens and shallot and toss. Add the corn bread croutons and Parmesan shavings, toss gently and serve. —*Grace Parisi*

MAKE AHEAD The corn bread croutons and barbecue vinaigrette can be refrigerated separately overnight. Recrisp the croutons in a 300° oven before serving.

WINE Lively, raspberry-inflected rosé: 2012 J.M. Raffault Chinon Rosé.

Garden Salad with Shanagarry Cream Dressing

ACTIVE: 30 MIN; TOTAL: 1 HR 15 MIN

6 SERVINGS ●

This salad is from Rachel Allen of the Ballymaloe Cookery School in Ireland. The tangy-sweet dressing is named after the small village next to the school.

2 medium golden beets

Olive oil, for brushing

Kosher salt

4 large eggs

½ cup heavy cream

1 tablespoon apple cider vinegar

1 teaspoon dry mustard powder

1 teaspoon dark brown sugar

1 small head of Bibb lettuce, leaves torn into bite-size pieces

2 cups lightly packed baby arugula

2 medium tomatoes, cut into wedges

½ English cucumber, halved lengthwise and thinly sliced crosswise

4 thinly sliced radishes

2 thinly sliced scallions

2 tablespoons chopped parsley

1. Preheat the oven to 375°. Brush the beets with oil and season with salt. Wrap the beets in foil and bake for 1 hour, until tender when pierced with a knife. Let cool slightly, then peel and cut into ½-inch wedges.

2. In a saucepan, cover the eggs with water and bring to a vigorous boil. Cover the saucepan, remove from the heat and let stand for 10 minutes. Drain and shake the pan to crack the eggs, then cool under cold running water and peel. Quarter 2 of the eggs lengthwise. Halve the remaining 2 eggs and scoop out the yolks. Press the 2 yolks through a fine sieve into a bowl. Finely chop the 2 egg whites.

3. Whisk the cream into the egg yolks until smooth, then whisk in the vinegar, mustard powder and brown sugar. Stir in half of the chopped egg whites and season with salt.

4. Pile the greens on a platter. Arrange the beets, tomatoes, cucumber, radishes and quartered eggs on top. Garnish with the scallions, parsley and remaining egg whites; serve with the dressing. —*Rachel Allen*

● HEALTHY ● MAKE AHEAD ● VEGETARIAN ● STAFF FAVORITE

Roasted Romaine with Pine Nut Vinaigrette

⏲ TOTAL: 30 MIN • 4 SERVINGS ● ● ●

At Refectorio at LeDomaine, a restaurant in an abbey-turned-wine-estate in the Ribera del Duero region of Spain, chef Pablo Montero creates a warm, deeply savory dressing with pine nuts, sun-dried tomatoes and black olives to spoon over roasted romaine hearts.

- 2 tablespoons balsamic vinegar
- 3 oil-packed sun-dried tomatoes, drained and minced
- 1 tablespoon minced kalamata or other black olives
- ¼ cup extra-virgin olive oil, plus more for brushing
- 2 large romaine hearts
- ⅓ cup pine nuts

Kosher salt

Shaved Pico Melero (see Note) or Manchego cheese, for serving

Flaky sea salt, such as Maldon, for sprinkling

1. Preheat the oven to 425°. In a medium bowl, whisk the balsamic vinegar with the minced sun-dried tomatoes and olives and the ¼ cup of olive oil.

2. Brush the romaine hearts all over with olive oil and arrange them on a rimmed baking sheet. Spread the pine nuts in a pie plate. Roast the romaine hearts and pine nuts for about 13 minutes, tossing the nuts occasionally, until the lettuce is browned in spots and the nuts are golden.

3. In a mortar, finely crush the pine nuts. Stir into the vinaigrette and season with kosher salt. Transfer the romaine hearts to a work surface. Cut the hearts in half lengthwise, transfer to a platter and spoon the vinaigrette on top. Scatter shaved cheese over the romaine and sprinkle with sea salt. Serve right away. —*Pablo Montero*

NOTE Pico Melero is a buttery and complex firm sheep-milk cheese from Spain with a spicy bite and sherry-like finish. It is available online at *igourmet.com*.

WINE Ripe, green apple–inflected Spanish white: 2012 Protos Verdejo.

Winter Salad with Avocado, Pomegranate and Almonds

⏲ TOTAL: 30 MIN • 8 SERVINGS ● ● ●

"Lettuce is one of my favorite foods—people laugh at me because of it," says jewelry and tabletop designer Cathy Waterman. She loves to eat the greens tossed in a vinaigrette made with preserved lemons. "They add brightness to so many things," she says. Waterman preserves her own lemons with salt for six months, but you can simply substitute store-bought preserved lemons.

- ¼ cup Champagne vinegar
- 2 tablespoons minced shallot
- 1 tablespoon minced preserved lemon peel (see Note)
- 1 tablespoon Dijon mustard
- ½ teaspoon kosher salt
- ⅔ cup extra-virgin olive oil
- 18 ounces Little Gem or romaine lettuce (about 16 cups), torn into bite-size pieces
- 1 Hass avocado—halved, pitted and thinly sliced lengthwise
- 1 fennel bulb—halved lengthwise, cored and very thinly sliced
- ½ cup marcona almonds
- ½ cup pomegranate seeds

Maldon salt, for sprinkling

Freshly ground pepper

1. In a medium bowl, whisk the vinegar, shallot, preserved lemon, mustard and kosher salt. Whisk in the olive oil in a steady stream until blended.

2. In a large bowl, toss the lettuce, avocado, fennel and ¼ cup each of the almonds and pomegranate seeds. Toss with ½ cup of the preserved-lemon vinaigrette. Transfer the salad to a serving bowl or platter and garnish with the remaining almonds and pomegranate seeds. Sprinkle with Maldon salt and season with freshly ground pepper. Serve with the remaining vinaigrette at the table. —*Cathy Waterman*

NOTE Preserved lemons are available at specialty food shops and *kalustyans.com*.

WINE Citrusy Chilean Sauvignon Blanc: 2011 Casa Marin Cipreses Vineyard.

Antipasto Salad with Green Olive Tapenade

⏲ TOTAL: 25 MIN • 8 SERVINGS ●

Nancy Silverton has shown her mastery of Italian food at L.A.'s Osteria Mozza and Pizzeria Mozza, getting the biggest flavor from the simplest ingredients. She does just that with this dish, which reinterprets the creamy, spicy, tangy and salty components of a typical antipasto platter as a crisp salad.

- 3 tablespoons green olive tapenade from a jar
- ¼ cup peperoncini—stemmed, seeded and finely chopped
- ½ cup extra-virgin olive oil
- 1½ cups bocconcini (about 9 ounces)
- 1 tablespoon plus 1 teaspoon fresh lemon juice
- 1 tablespoon plus 1 teaspoon red wine vinegar
- 1 tablespoon plus 1 teaspoon minced garlic
- 1 teaspoon dried oregano

Salt and freshly ground pepper

- 1 small head of iceberg lettuce, halved, cored and finely shredded (4 cups)
- 6 ounces thinly sliced Genoa salami, cut into thin strips (1½ cups)
- 6 small basil leaves
- ½ cup green olives, such as Picholine

1. In a medium bowl, mix the green olive tapenade with the peperoncini and ¼ cup of the oil. Add the bocconcini and toss.

2. In a small bowl, whisk the lemon juice with the vinegar, garlic and oregano. Whisk in the remaining ¼ cup of olive oil and season the dressing with salt and pepper.

3. In a large bowl, combine the lettuce and salami. Add the marinated bocconcini and half of the dressing and toss well. Transfer the antipasto salad to a platter. Top with the basil and olives. Drizzle the remaining dressing around the salad and serve. —*Nancy Silverton*

WINE Frothy, berry-scented Lambrusco: NV Venturini Baldini Lambrusco dell'Emilia.

Kale Caesar with Rye Croutons and Farro

⏱ TOTAL: 30 MIN • 6 SERVINGS ● ●

This reimagined Caesar salad substitutes two kinds of kale for romaine lettuce, rye bread cubes for the usual croutons and silken tofu for raw egg in the garlicky dressing.

Kosher salt
⅓ cup farro
2 tablespoons extra-virgin olive oil
One 1-inch-thick slice of rye bread, cut into 1-inch cubes
12 ounces Tuscan kale, stems discarded and leaves shredded
8 ounces red or green kale, stems discarded and leaves torn
6 ounces silken tofu, drained
5 oil-packed anchovy fillets, drained and chopped
½ teaspoon finely grated garlic
1 teaspoon Dijon mustard
2 tablespoons grapeseed or canola oil
¼ cup freshly grated Parmigiano-Reggiano cheese
Freshly ground pepper

1. Bring a small saucepan of salted water to a boil. Add the farro and cook until tender, 20 to 25 minutes. Drain, then transfer the farro to a bowl of ice water to cool. Drain again.
2. Meanwhile, in a large skillet, heat the olive oil. Add the rye bread and cook over moderate heat until crisp and golden, 7 to 9 minutes. Season the croutons with salt and transfer to a plate to cool.
3. In a large bowl, toss all of the kale. In a food processor, puree the tofu, anchovies, garlic and mustard. With the machine on, drizzle in the grapeseed oil and 2 tablespoons of water. Add 2 tablespoons of the cheese and puree. Season with salt and pepper. Add the dressing to the kale and toss; season with salt and pepper. Transfer to a platter or plates. Top with the farro, rye croutons and the remaining 2 tablespoons of cheese and serve. —Kay Chun

WINE Fresh, citrusy Sauvignon Blanc: 2010 Chateau L'Escart Comtesse Bordeaux Blanc.

Kale Salad with Ricotta Salata, Pine Nuts and Anchovies

⏱ TOTAL: 30 MIN • 6 SERVINGS ●

Los Angeles chef Nancy Silverton is well-known for the obsessive attention she pays to her salads. The key to her kale salad is layering the greens, nuts, cheese and white anchovies so that there's something delicious in every forkful.

¼ cup pine nuts
1 small shallot, minced
Finely grated zest of 1 lemon
¼ cup freshly squeezed lemon juice
1 tablespoon Champagne or white wine vinegar
1 garlic clove, grated
Pinch of crushed red pepper
½ cup extra-virgin olive oil
3 ounces *ricotta salata* cheese, coarsely shredded (¾ cup)
Kosher salt and freshly ground black pepper
1 bunch of kale, preferably Tuscan (6 ounces), stemmed and leaves torn into bite-size pieces (8 cups)
8 marinated *alici* (white anchovies), drained

1. In a small skillet, toast the pine nuts over moderately low heat, stirring frequently, until light golden, about 10 minutes. Transfer to a small bowl.
2. In a medium bowl, combine the shallot, lemon zest, lemon juice, vinegar, garlic and crushed red pepper. Whisk in the olive oil until emulsified. Stir in ½ cup of the *ricotta salata* and season the dressing with salt and black pepper.
3. In a large bowl, toss the kale with half of the dressing; add more dressing if desired. Transfer half of the kale to a serving platter and top with half of the remaining *ricotta salata*, 4 anchovies and half of the pine nuts. Repeat the layering with the remaining kale, *ricotta salata*, anchovies and pine nuts and serve. —Nancy Silverton

WINE Lively, brisk northern Italian Pinot Grigio: 2012 Tiefenbrunner.

Escarole with Pickled Butternut Squash

⏱ TOTAL: 45 MIN
8 SERVINGS ● ● ○ ○

Quick-pickling raw butternut squash in cider vinegar, sugar and salt makes it tart and crunchy. Chef Gabriel Rucker of Le Pigeon and Little Bird in Portland, Oregon, tosses the pickled squash with pleasantly bitter greens and a creamy, garlicky sage dressing.

1 cup plus 2 tablespoons apple cider vinegar
2 tablespoons sugar
Kosher salt
3 ounces butternut squash, peeled and cut into ¼-inch dice (½ cup)
1 large egg yolk or 3 tablespoons mayonnaise
1 tablespoon freshly grated Parmigiano-Reggiano cheese
6 large sage leaves
1 garlic clove
1 teaspoon fresh lemon juice
⅓ cup canola oil
Freshly ground pepper
1 head of escarole (12 ounces), inner yellow and light green leaves only, torn into bite-size pieces

1. In a medium saucepan, combine 1 cup of the apple cider vinegar with the sugar, 1 tablespoon of salt and ¼ cup of water and bring to a boil. Add the diced squash and let cool to room temperature. Drain the pickled squash.
2. Meanwhile, in a food processor, combine the egg yolk with the cheese, sage, garlic, lemon juice and the remaining 2 tablespoons of vinegar. With the machine on, drizzle in the oil until emulsified. Season the dressing with salt and pepper.
3. In a large bowl, toss the escarole with the dressing and season with salt. Arrange the greens on plates, top with the pickled squash and serve. —Gabriel Rucker

MAKE AHEAD The drained pickled squash and the dressing can be refrigerated for up to 2 days.

● HEALTHY ● MAKE AHEAD ● VEGETARIAN ● STAFF FAVORITE

Kale Caesar with Bacon and Eggs

TOTAL: 1 HR • 16 SERVINGS

1½ pounds green kale, stems discarded
    and leaves torn into bite-size pieces
1 pound Tuscan kale, stems discarded
    and leaves torn into bite-size pieces
½ cup fresh lemon juice
Kosher salt
1 pound sliced bacon
1 pound day-old rustic Italian bread,
    crusts discarded and bread cut into
    bite-size pieces
Two 2-ounce cans anchovy fillets,
    drained
4 large egg yolks (see Note)
1 tablespoon Dijon mustard
½ teaspoon dried oregano
½ teaspoon finely grated lemon zest
1½ cups canola oil
½ cup extra-virgin olive oil
1 cup freshly grated Parmigiano-
    Reggiano cheese (4 ounces)
Freshly ground black pepper
1 large romaine heart, chopped
8 large hard-boiled eggs, quartered

1. Preheat the oven to 400°. In a very large serving bowl, toss the kale with ¼ cup of the lemon juice and 1 teaspoon of kosher salt. Using your hands, massage the lemon juice and salt into the kale to soften it. Let the kale stand for 30 minutes, until tender.
2. Meanwhile, lay the bacon slices on a large rimmed baking sheet and bake for 12 minutes, until crisp. Transfer the bacon to paper towels to drain, then cut into 1-inch pieces.
3. Spread the bread on another large rimmed baking sheet and toast for about 12 minutes, until crisp. Let the croutons cool.
4. In a food processor, combine the anchovies, egg yolks, Dijon mustard, oregano and lemon zest with ¼ cup of water and the remaining ¼ cup of lemon juice and puree. With the machine on, slowly drizzle in the canola oil and olive oil until the dressing is thick. Transfer the dressing to a medium bowl, stir in the grated Parmigiano-Reggiano cheese and season with salt and pepper.

5. Add the romaine, bacon and croutons to the kale and toss with 1½ cups of the dressing; season with salt and pepper. Add the eggs and toss gently. Serve with any extra dressing at the table. —*Nicholas Wilber*
NOTE To make the dressing without raw eggs, omit the egg yolks and substitute 1½ cups of mayonnaise for the canola oil.
WINE Minerally, medium-bodied Italian white: 2012 Bisci Verdicchio di Matelica.

Lemony Escarole Salad with Peaches and Feta

◔ TOTAL: 30 MIN
6 TO 8 SERVINGS ● ●

¼ cup plus 1 tablespoon
    extra-virgin olive oil
¾ teaspoon finely grated lemon zest
¼ cup fresh lemon juice
1 garlic clove, finely grated
Pinch of sugar
Kosher salt and freshly ground pepper
2 medium heads of escarole,
    inner light green and white leaves
    only, torn into bite-size pieces
2 large peaches—halved,
    pitted and thinly sliced
2 cups yellow cherry tomatoes,
    halved
2 Persian cucumbers, thinly sliced
    crosswise
½ small red onion, halved and sliced
6 ounces feta cheese, crumbled
    (about 1½ cups)
Ground sumac (see Note) and/or dried
    oregano, for garnish (optional)

1. In a large bowl, whisk the olive oil with the lemon zest, lemon juice, garlic and sugar. Season the dressing with salt and pepper and let stand for 10 minutes.
2. Add the escarole, peaches, tomatoes, cucumbers and onion to the dressing and toss well. Season the salad with salt and pepper and transfer to a serving platter. Scatter the feta on top, sprinkle with the sumac and serve. —*Anya von Bremzen*
NOTE Sumac, a fruity, tart Middle Eastern spice, is available at *kalustyans.com*.

Chicory Salad with Pickled Quince and Pomegranate

ACTIVE: 40 MIN; TOTAL: 2 HR
10 SERVINGS ● ● ●

Eight ¼-inch-thick slices of peeled
    fresh ginger
3 whole cloves
1 small star anise pod
1 bay leaf
2 quinces—peeled, halved, cored and
    sliced ½ inch thick, peels and cores
    reserved
1 cup white wine vinegar
⅔ cup sugar
1 cup hazelnuts
1 medium shallot, minced (¼ cup)
⅓ cup Moscato vinegar (see Note)
1 tablespoon red wine vinegar
⅔ cup extra-virgin olive oil
1 teaspoon hazelnut oil
Salt and freshly ground pepper
1¾ pounds mixed chicories, such as
    endives, radicchio and escarole
    hearts, torn into bite-size pieces
    (16 cups)
1 cup pomegranate seeds
    (from 1 large pomegranate)
2 tablespoons pomegranate molasses

1. Preheat the oven to 350°. Tie the ginger, cloves, star anise, bay leaf and the reserved quince peels and cores in a cheesecloth bundle. In a large saucepan, combine the white wine vinegar with the sugar and 1½ cups of water and add the cheesecloth bundle; bring to a boil. Add the quince slices and simmer, partially covered, until tender, about 1 hour. Let cool completely. Using a slotted spoon, transfer the quince slices to a plate and refrigerate until chilled.
2. Meanwhile, spread the hazelnuts in a pie plate and toast until the skins blister, about 14 minutes. Rub the hazelnuts together in a clean kitchen towel to remove the skins. Coarsely chop the hazelnuts.
3. In a bowl, combine the shallot with the Moscato vinegar and red wine vinegar; let stand for 15 minutes. Whisk in the olive and hazelnut oils. Season with salt and pepper.

● HEALTHY ● MAKE AHEAD ● VEGETARIAN ● STAFF FAVORITE

4. In a large bowl, toss the chicories with the pomegranate seeds, toasted hazelnuts and pickled quince slices. Add half of the vinaigrette and toss well. Drizzle the pomegranate molasses over the salad, season with salt and pepper and toss again. Serve right away, passing the remaining vinaigrette at the table. —*Michael Tusk*

NOTE Moscato vinegar, made from fragrant Moscato wine grapes, is available at specialty food stores and *formaggiokitchen.com*.

Escarole Salad with Apples, Blue Cheese and Pecans

TOTAL: 45 MIN

10 TO 12 SERVINGS ● ● ●

- 6 ounces pecans, coarsely chopped (1½ cups)
- 3 tablespoons apple cider vinegar
- 1 tablespoon minced shallot
- 1 teaspoon Dijon mustard
- 1 teaspoon sugar
- ¼ cup canola oil
- 2 tablespoons extra-virgin olive oil

Kosher salt and freshly ground pepper

One 1½-pound head of escarole—dark green leaves discarded, remaining leaves torn into bite-size pieces

- 5 celery ribs, halved lengthwise and thinly sliced crosswise
- 2 Pink Lady or Honeycrisp apples—halved, cored and sliced ⅛ inch thick
- ½ pound Point Reyes or Maytag blue cheese, crumbled (2¼ cups)

1. Preheat the oven to 375° and spread the pecans in a pie plate. Bake for 10 to 12 minutes, until lightly browned. Let cool.

2. Meanwhile, in a large bowl, whisk the vinegar with the shallot, mustard and sugar; let stand for 10 minutes. Whisk in both oils and season with salt and pepper.

3. Add the escarole, celery, apples and toasted pecans to the vinaigrette and toss to coat thoroughly. Season the salad with salt and pepper and transfer to a platter. Scatter the crumbled blue cheese on top and serve. —*Maria Helm Sinskey*

Warm Castelfranco with Vin Cotto and Blu di Bufala

TOTAL: 20 MIN • 4 SERVINGS ●

Carlo Mirarchi helped pioneer the concept of the chef-driven Brooklyn restaurant, starting with Roberta's in Bushwick and followed by the Michelin-starred Blanca, which he opened next door. Here, his simple and magical combination of ingredients includes *vin cotto* (aged vinegar), the superb blue cheese *blu di bufala* and Castelfranco (a mild radicchio). It's a very Italian dish, but Mirarchi gives it a personal imprint by adding Asian fish sauce to the dressing.

- 2 heads of Castelfranco (see Note) or radicchio, trimmed and leaves separated
- 5 tablespoons extra-virgin olive oil
- 2 teaspoons Asian fish sauce
- 2 teaspoons freshly squeezed lemon juice, plus 4 lemon wedges for serving
- 1 teaspoon white balsamic vinegar, plus more to taste
- 3 ounces *blu di bufala* or Gorgonzola *piccante* cheese, crumbled

Vin cotto or aged balsamic vinegar, for drizzling

1. In a large bowl, combine the Castelfranco leaves with 3 tablespoons of the olive oil, the fish sauce and lemon juice; toss to coat the leaves.

2. In a large skillet, heat the remaining 2 tablespoons of olive oil until shimmering. Add the Castelfranco and cook over moderately high heat, stirring, until it is golden in spots and just wilted, about 2 minutes. Stir in the white balsamic vinegar.

3. Transfer the Castelfranco to plates and top with the cheese. Drizzle with the *vin cotto* and serve with lemon wedges. —*Carlo Mirarchi*

NOTE Castelfranco, a mild member of the radicchio family, has pale yellow or green leaves with red speckles. Look for it at specialty or farmers' markets.

WINE Light-bodied Dolcetto d'Alba: 2012 Francesco Rinaldi & Figli Roussot.

Roasted Fennel Salad with Bagna Cauda Dressing

ACTIVE: 30 MIN; TOTAL: 1 HR

4 SERVINGS ●

- ¼ cup walnuts
- 2 medium fennel bulbs (2 pounds), halved and sliced ¼ inch thick
- ½ cup plus 2 tablespoons extra-virgin olive oil

Sea salt and freshly ground pepper

- 1 pound fingerling potatoes, halved

One 2-ounce can anchovy fillets, drained

- 2 tablespoons drained capers
- 2 garlic cloves, crushed
- 2 teaspoons finely grated lemon zest
- 2 tablespoons fresh lemon juice
- 1 tablespoon unsalted butter, melted and cooled
- 1 large head of radicchio, shredded
- 2 heads of Belgian endive, thinly sliced

1. Preheat the oven to 425°. In a pie plate, toast the walnuts for about 5 minutes, until golden, and coarsely chop.

2. Line 2 baking sheets with parchment paper. On one baking sheet, toss the fennel with 1 tablespoon of the olive oil; season with salt and pepper. Place the potatoes on the second baking sheet and toss with 1 tablespoon of the olive oil; season with salt and pepper. Turn the potatoes cut side down. Roast the fennel and potatoes for about 30 minutes, rotating the pans halfway through, until the vegetables are golden and tender.

3. Meanwhile, in a mini food processor, pulse the anchovies with the capers, garlic, lemon zest and lemon juice until finely chopped. With the machine on, drizzle in the cooled butter and the remaining ½ cup of olive oil and puree until smooth. Season the dressing with salt and pepper.

4. In a large bowl, combine the fennel and potatoes with the radicchio, endives and three-fourths of the dressing; season with salt and pepper. Transfer the salad to a platter and garnish with the walnuts. Serve the remaining dressing on the side. —*Phoebe Lapine*

Raw and Charred Zucchini Salad

⏱ TOTAL: 45 MIN • 8 SERVINGS ●

Trey Foshee, chef at George's at the Cove in La Jolla, California, tops this salad with a savory crumble of pine nuts, chile and garlic.

2 cups diced crustless country bread
3 garlic cloves, halved
½ cup extra-virgin olive oil, plus more for the grill
1 ancho chile, stemmed and seeded
½ cup pine nuts, toasted
Salt and freshly ground pepper
2½ pounds mixed zucchini and yellow summer squash
1 cup loosely packed mint leaves, torn
1 cup loosely packed flat-leaf parsley
1 pint grape tomatoes, halved
1 teaspoon finely grated lemon zest
2 tablespoons fresh lemon juice
5 ounces feta, crumbled (1 cup)

1. Preheat the oven to 325°. On a baking sheet, toss the bread and garlic with 2 tablespoons of the olive oil. Bake for 20 minutes, until the bread is lightly golden; transfer to a bowl and crush.

2. In a microwave-safe bowl, cover the ancho with water and microwave for 1 minute. Let stand for 5 minutes. Scrape the ancho flesh from the skin and add to the bread along with the pine nuts; mash until moist crumbs form. Season with salt and pepper.

3. Light a grill and oil the grate or preheat a grill pan. Using a wide vegetable peeler, thinly slice one-third of the zucchini and summer squash into ribbons and refrigerate. Cut the rest into ¼-inch rounds and transfer to a large bowl; toss with 3 tablespoons of the oil. Season with salt and pepper. Grill over high heat until lightly charred, 5 minutes; return to the bowl. Add the ribbons, mint, parsley and tomatoes and toss.

4. In a bowl, whisk the lemon zest and juice with the remaining oil; season with salt and pepper. Toss the dressing with the salad. Add the feta and toss again. Sprinkle with the pine nut crumbs and serve. —*Trey Foshee*
WINE Fruit-forward rosé: 2012 Librandi Cirò.

Roasted Squash Salad with Bitter Greens and Cheese

ACTIVE: 45 MIN; TOTAL: 1 HR 45 MIN
8 SERVINGS ● ● ●

Scott Boggs, the farmer-turned-chef at Rose Bakery in Manhattan, serves this salad with the rich, salty Toussaint cheese made at Sprout Creek Farm (*sproutcreekfarm.org*) in Dutchess County, New York. The salad is equally fabulous with Parmigiano-Reggiano.

2 pounds thin-skinned winter squash, such as acorn, buttercup or kabocha—washed well, halved lengthwise, seeded and sliced crosswise ¾ inch thick
¼ cup plus 2 tablespoons extra-virgin olive oil
1 tablespoon finely chopped flat-leaf parsley
1 teaspoon finely chopped marjoram
½ teaspoon finely chopped thyme
Kosher salt and freshly ground black pepper
2 tablespoons maple sugar (see Note)
2 tablespoons red wine vinegar
1 small shallot, minced
10 ounces bitter salad greens, such as baby arugula, frisée and Belgian endive (about 16 cups)
Shaved hard cheese, such as Toussaint or Parmigiano-Reggiano, for serving

1. Preheat the oven to 375°. On a rimmed baking sheet, toss the squash wedges with 2 tablespoons of the olive oil and the parsley, marjoram and thyme. Season with salt and pepper and spread the squash in a single layer. Roast for 20 to 25 minutes, turning once, until just softened. Sprinkle 1 tablespoon of the maple sugar over the squash and roast for 15 minutes longer, until the sugar just starts to caramelize. Turn the squash over, sprinkle with the remaining 1 tablespoon of maple sugar and roast for 15 minutes longer, until the pieces are tender and golden. Let cool.

2. In a large bowl, whisk the vinegar with the shallot and remaining ¼ cup of olive oil. Add the greens, toss to coat and season with salt and pepper. Transfer the greens to plates or a platter and arrange the squash on top. Shave hard cheese over the salad and serve. —*Scott Boggs*
NOTE Granulated maple sugar, which is made from reduced maple syrup, is available at specialty food stores and online at *crownmaple.com*.

Spinach and Edamame Salad with Basil and Asian Dressing

TOTAL: 30 MIN PLUS 2 HR MARINATING
10 SERVINGS ●

Fish sauce, lime juice and lemongrass make such a delicious dressing that it's easy to forget how healthy this salad is.

¼ cup Asian fish sauce
3 tablespoons distilled white vinegar
3 tablespoons sugar
½ teaspoon finely grated lime zest
3 tablespoons fresh lime juice
2 tablespoons extra-virgin olive oil
1 tablespoon minced fresh lemongrass (tender inner bulb only)
1 teaspoon *sambal oelek*
1 Thai chile, minced
1 medium garlic clove, minced
2 cups frozen shelled edamame (12 ounces)
10 radishes, thinly sliced
10 ounces baby spinach
½ cup torn basil leaves

1. In a medium bowl, whisk the fish sauce with the vinegar, sugar, lime zest, lime juice, olive oil, lemongrass, *sambal oelek*, Thai chile and garlic. Let the dressing stand at room temperature for 2 hours.

2. Meanwhile, in a saucepan of salted boiling water, blanch the edamame until crisp-tender, 2 minutes. Drain and cool under running water, then spread on a plate and blot dry.

3. In a large bowl, combine the edamame with the radishes, spinach and basil. Add the lemongrass dressing and toss well. Serve right away. —*Bill Kim*

RAW AND CHARRED
ZUCCHINI SALAD

Fresh Snow Pea Salad with Pancetta and Pecorino

⏱ **TOTAL: 35 MIN**
6 TO 8 SERVINGS ● ●

This terrific summer salad from chef Daniel Humm of Eleven Madison Park in Manhattan is crisp and lemony, with bits of meaty pancetta and lots of fresh mint. Since the snow peas are raw, it's best to buy super-fresh ones—they will be more tender.

1	pound snow peas—strings removed, pods sliced on the diagonal ¼ inch wide
¼	cup plus 1 tablespoon extra-virgin olive oil
4	ounces thickly sliced pancetta, cut into ¼-inch dice
½	small white onion, finely chopped
2	tablespoons fresh lemon juice
½	teaspoon lemon oil (see Note)

Kosher salt and freshly ground black pepper
½ cup mint leaves, torn
2 ounces Pecorino Sardo cheese

1. Soak the snow peas in a medium bowl of ice water for 10 minutes.

2. Meanwhile, in a medium skillet, heat 1 tablespoon of the olive oil. Add the pancetta and cook over moderate heat until lightly browned and the fat has rendered, about 5 minutes. Spoon off all but 1 tablespoon of the fat in the skillet. Add the onion and cook, stirring occasionally, until softened, about 5 minutes.

3. Drain the snow peas and pat dry. In a medium bowl, whisk the remaining ¼ cup of olive oil with the lemon juice and lemon oil and season with salt and pepper. Add the snow peas, pancetta, onion and half of the mint and season with salt and pepper; toss well. Garnish with the remaining mint, shave the pecorino on top and serve. —*Daniel Humm*

NOTE Olive oil pressed or infused with lemon is available at specialty food stores and most supermarkets.

WINE Lively, light-bodied Sicilian white: 2011 Tami Grillo.

Spring Peas and Greens with Cacio e Pepe Dressing

⏱ **TOTAL: 45 MIN • 4 SERVINGS** ●

The classic Italian pasta dish *cacio e pepe* (cheese and pepper) is made with Pecorino Romano, a tangy aged sheep-milk cheese, and lots of freshly ground black pepper. F&W's Kay Chun channels those flavors into a buttermilk dressing to toss with spring vegetables and wedges of creamy avocado.

1	large egg yolk
3	tablespoons buttermilk
1	small garlic clove, finely grated
½	cup extra-virgin olive oil
3	tablespoons finely grated Parmigiano-Reggiano cheese, plus more for garnish
¾	teaspoon coarsely cracked black peppercorns

Kosher salt
2 pounds fava beans, shelled (2 cups)
2 cups fresh or thawed frozen peas
4 cups spring greens, such as pea tendrils or baby arugula (2 ounces)
1 Hass avocado, peeled and cut into thin wedges

1. In a food processor, pulse the egg yolk with the buttermilk and garlic. With the machine on, drizzle in the olive oil until incorporated. Add the 3 tablespoons of cheese and the peppercorns and puree until smooth. Season the dressing with salt.

2. Bring a large pot of salted water to a boil. Fill a bowl with ice water. Boil the favas until just tender, 3 to 4 minutes. Using a slotted spoon, transfer the fava beans to the ice bath. Add the peas to the pot and cook until tender, about 5 to 7 minutes for fresh and about 1 minute for frozen. Drain and transfer to the ice bath. Drain the favas and peas. Pinch the favas out of their skins.

3. In a bowl, toss the favas, peas and greens. Add some dressing, season with salt and toss. Arrange the avocado on plates and top with the salad. Garnish with grated cheese and serve. —*Kay Chun*

WINE Zesty Italian white: 2011 Kris Pinot Grigio delle Venezie.

Radish Salad with Pumpkin Seeds and Pumpkin Oil

⏱ **TOTAL: 30 MIN • 4 SERVINGS** ● ●

The secret to this salad is pumpkin seed oil, an Austrian staple made from roasted pumpkin seeds. It gives radishes a heartier flavor, while the toasted pumpkin seeds on top add an appealing extra crunch.

¼	cup raw pumpkin seeds
2	tablespoons plus ¼ teaspoon canola oil

Kosher salt
2 tablespoons apple cider vinegar
Freshly ground black pepper
½ pound radishes, very thinly sliced on a mandoline
2 tablespoons finely chopped mixed herbs, such as parsley, chives, dill and chervil
1 tablespoon roasted pumpkin seed oil (see Note)
2 cups mixed microgreens, such as pea tendrils or baby arugula (about 1 ounce)

1. Preheat the oven to 350°. Spread the pumpkin seeds in a pie plate and toast for about 5 minutes, until lightly golden. Transfer the seeds to a small bowl; add ¼ teaspoon of the canola oil, season with salt and toss.

2. Meanwhile, in another small bowl, whisk the cider vinegar with the remaining 2 tablespoons of canola oil; season the vinaigrette with salt and pepper.

3. In a medium bowl, toss the radishes with 2 tablespoons of the vinaigrette. Arrange the radishes on plates or a platter. Sprinkle the herbs and the toasted pumpkin seeds on top and drizzle with the pumpkin seed oil. Toss the microgreens with the remaining vinaigrette. Top the radish salad with the microgreens and serve. —*Christopher Israel*

NOTE Pumpkin seed oil is available at specialty food shops; one that's made in the US is available at *wholeheartedfoods.com*.

WINE Delicate *feinherb*-style Riesling from Germany: 2011 Günther Steinmetz Brauneberger Juffer Kabinett.

● HEALTHY ● MAKE AHEAD ● VEGETARIAN ● STAFF FAVORITE

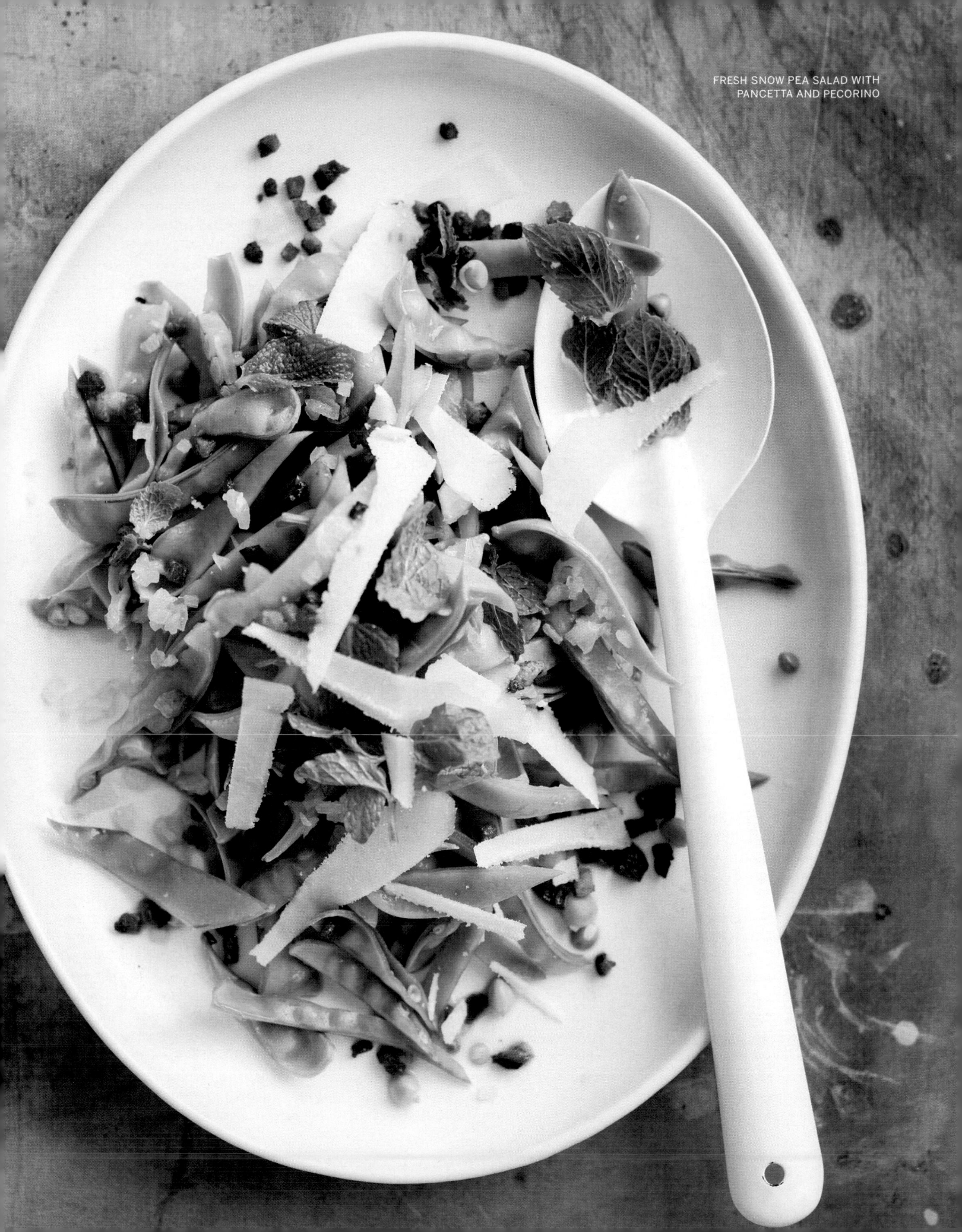

FRESH SNOW PEA SALAD WITH
PANCETTA AND PECORINO

Thai-Style Radish and Watermelon Salad

◷ TOTAL: 30 MIN
8 TO 10 SERVINGS ● ●

¼ cup plus 2 tablespoons
    fresh lime juice
1 tablespoon Asian fish sauce
1 tablespoon *sambal oelek* or
    other Asian chile sauce
2 teaspoons finely grated fresh ginger
Kosher salt and freshly ground pepper
One 5-pound watermelon—rind and
    seeds removed, flesh cut into
    1½-inch chunks (8 cups)
12 radishes, very thinly sliced
8 scallions, thinly sliced
2 fresh hot red chiles, such as Holland
    or cayenne, thinly sliced crosswise
¾ cup lightly packed mint leaves,
    coarsely chopped
¾ cup lightly packed
    Thai basil leaves, torn

In a large bowl, whisk the lime juice with the
fish sauce, *sambal oelek* and ginger. Season
the dressing with salt and freshly ground
pepper. Add the watermelon, radishes, scallions and red chiles and toss well. Fold in the
mint and Thai basil, season with salt and
freshly ground pepper and serve right away.
—*Tom Colicchio*
WINE Fragrant Provençal rosé: 2012 Triennes.

Cucumber-Radish Salad with Crème Fraîche, Dill and Mint

ACTIVE: 20 MIN; TOTAL: 1 HR 45 MIN
6 TO 8 SERVINGS ● ● ●

1½ pounds small cucumbers,
    peeled if the skin is thick
Sea salt
3 large radishes, thinly sliced
    (½ cup)
1 small garlic clove, finely grated
2 tablespoons white wine vinegar
8 ounces crème fraîche (about 1 cup)
2 tablespoons chopped dill
Freshly ground pepper
Shredded mint leaves, for garnish

Slice most of the cucumbers ¼ inch thick;
cut the rest into spears. In a colander, season
the cucumbers with salt, top with a small
plate and let stand for 1 hour. Press gently to
remove some of the liquid; rinse the cucumbers quickly in cold water. Pat dry and transfer to a bowl. Add the radishes, garlic, vinegar,
crème fraîche and dill; season with pepper.
Refrigerate for 30 minutes, until chilled. Garnish with mint and serve. —*Sarah Copeland*

Cucumber and Radish Salad with Burrata

◷ ACTIVE: 15 MIN; TOTAL: 45 MIN
4 SERVINGS ●

3 Kirby cucumbers, cut into
    ½-inch pieces
3 garlic cloves, lightly crushed
1 small dried red chile, crushed
½ teaspoon sugar
Kosher salt
2 tablespoons fresh lime juice
¼ cup extra-virgin olive oil
4 radishes, thinly sliced
1 cup mixed herbs, such as cilantro,
    parsley, basil, tarragon and chives
Freshly ground black pepper
One 8-ounce piece of burrata or fresh
    buffalo mozzarella, quartered

1. In a large resealable plastic bag, combine
the cucumbers, garlic, chile, sugar, ½ teaspoon of salt and 1 tablespoon of the lime
juice. Seal and shake the bag, squeezing
slightly to mash the cucumbers and release
the juices. Let stand at room temperature
for 30 minutes.
2. Drain the cucumbers, reserving 2 tablespoons of the cucumber juice. Discard the
garlic and chile. In a medium bowl, whisk the
cucumber juice with the remaining 1 tablespoon of lime juice and 2 tablespoons of the
oil. Add the cucumbers, radishes and herbs
and season the salad with salt and pepper.
3. Arrange the salad on plates. Place a piece
of burrata or buffalo mozzarella alongside
each serving, drizzle with the remaining 2
tablespoons of oil and serve. —*Kay Chun*
WINE Bright, citrusy rosé: 2012 Apaltagua.

Japanese Cucumber Salad with Sesame-Miso Dressing

◷ TOTAL: 30 MIN • 6 SERVINGS ● ● ●
Two types of miso form the base of the
dressing in this salad: rich, malty brown rice
miso and the milder white miso. Firm, super-
crunchy Kirby, Japanese or Persian cucumbers, which have few seeds, are best here.

⅓ cup Japanese sesame paste
    or tahini
3 tablespoons brown rice miso
    (see Note)
3 tablespoons white miso
    (see Note)
3 tablespoons mirin
2 tablespoons rice vinegar
1 teaspoon toasted sesame oil
⅓ cup pine nuts
12 ounces Japanese, Persian
    or Kirby cucumbers, halved
    lengthwise and sliced crosswise
    ¾ inch thick
Kosher salt
1 tablespoon fresh lemon juice
1 tablespoon extra-virgin olive oil
2 tablespoons toasted
    sesame seeds

1. In a blender or food processor, blend the
sesame paste, brown rice and white misos,
mirin, vinegar and sesame oil until smooth.
Transfer the miso dressing to a jar and refrigerate until chilled, at least 15 minutes.
2. Meanwhile, in a small skillet, toast the pine
nuts over moderate heat, shaking the pan,
until the nuts are golden, about 5 minutes.
Transfer to a plate and let cool.
3. In a medium bowl, sprinkle the cucumbers
with salt and refrigerate for 10 minutes. Add
the lemon juice, olive oil and ¼ cup of the
miso dressing (reserve the rest for another
use) and toss well. Garnish with the pine
nuts and sesame seeds and serve.
—*Matt Abergel*
NOTE Brown rice miso and white miso are
both available at Japanese markets, health
food stores and *amazon.com*.
MAKE AHEAD The miso dressing can be
refrigerated for up to 1 week.

● HEALTHY ● MAKE AHEAD ● VEGETARIAN ● STAFF FAVORITE

THAI-STYLE RADISH AND
WATERMELON SALAD

Cucumber-Fennel Salad with Herbed Goat Yogurt

⏱ TOTAL: 30 MIN
8 TO 10 SERVINGS ● ● ●

Star chef and *Top Chef* head judge Tom Colicchio's supremely simple salad features an herb-packed dressing made with goat yogurt—a superbly tangy and slightly funky alternative to conventional cow-milk yogurt.

1 cup plain whole-milk goat yogurt
3 tablespoons white wine vinegar
½ cup chopped flat-leaf parsley
¼ cup snipped chives
Kosher salt and freshly ground pepper
4 English cucumbers—halved lengthwise, seeded and thinly sliced on the diagonal
2 fennel bulbs—halved lengthwise, cored and very thinly sliced
7 small celery ribs, thinly sliced crosswise
1 cup thinly sliced scallions, preferably red

In a large bowl, whisk the goat yogurt with the white wine vinegar, parsley and chives. Season the dressing with salt and pepper. Fold in the sliced cucumbers, fennel, celery and scallions, season the salad with salt and pepper and serve. —*Tom Colicchio*

Watermelon and Charred-Tomato Salad

⏱ TOTAL: 30 MIN • 6 TO 8 SERVINGS ● ●

The trick to this salad is searing the tomatoes on one side only so they're fresh and smoky at the same time.

4 plum tomatoes, halved lengthwise
Extra-virgin olive oil, for brushing
2 pounds seedless watermelon—rind removed, flesh cut into ½-inch dice
1 English cucumber—halved, seeded and cut into ½-inch dice
3 tablespoons fresh lime juice
½ teaspoon crushed red pepper
½ cup chopped cilantro
Kosher salt

1. Light a grill or preheat a grill pan; oil the grill grate. Brush the tomatoes with olive oil and grill cut side down over high heat until charred, about 4 minutes. Transfer to a plate and let cool completely. Cut the tomatoes into ½-inch dice.
2. In a large bowl, toss the tomatoes with the watermelon, cucumber, lime juice and crushed red pepper. Stir in the cilantro, season with salt and serve at once.
—*Tim Byres*

Heirloom Tomatoes with Anchovies and Red Chiles

⏱ TOTAL: 20 MIN • 6 SERVINGS

This lovely salad from London's Brawn restaurant requires sweet, juicy tomatoes. "It's all about the way one cuts the tomato: a badly cut one is not as appetizing," says chef Owen Kenworthy, who favors slices and wedges made with a very sharp knife. To punch up the tomatoes, he adds salty anchovies, briny capers and spicy chiles. The salad is great as an appetizer or served alongside grilled steak or pork.

2¼ pounds mixed heirloom tomatoes, cut into thick slices or chunks
¼ cup extra-virgin olive oil
2 tablespoons minced shallot
1½ tablespoons fresh lemon juice
1 tablespoon minced hot fresh red chile, such as Holland or cayenne
2 teaspoons salt-packed capers, rinsed well and drained
2 large anchovy fillets, minced
½ teaspoon finely chopped oregano
Kosher salt and freshly ground black pepper

1. Arrange the tomatoes on a platter.
2. In a small bowl, whisk together the olive oil, minced shallot, fresh lemon juice, minced chile, capers, anchovies and oregano; season the dressing with salt and freshly ground pepper. Drizzle the dressing over the tomatoes and serve. —*Owen Kenworthy*
MAKE AHEAD The dressing can be refrigerated overnight. Bring to room temperature before serving.

Grilled Leeks with Leek-Tomato Salad and Citrus Dressing

⏱ TOTAL: 45 MIN • 4 SERVINGS ● ●

For this warm summer salad, Tara Duggan, author of *Root-to-Stalk Cooking,* uses the whole leek—grilling the bottoms in large chunks and braising the sliced tops.

2 large leeks, roots trimmed
Extra-virgin olive oil
Salt
½ teaspoon finely grated lime zest
½ teaspoon finely grated tangerine or orange zest
2 tablespoons fresh lime juice
2 tablespoons fresh tangerine juice
1 tablespoon soy sauce
Pinch of crushed red pepper
½ cup fresh corn kernels
1 cup mixed heirloom cherry tomatoes, halved

1. Light a grill or preheat a grill pan. Separate the dark green leek tops from the white and tender green parts. Halve the leek bottoms; run under cold water to remove any grit. Slice the dark green leek tops crosswise ½ inch wide, discarding the top inch, and wash well. You should have about 8 cups of the tops.
2. Pat the halved leeks dry. Brush with olive oil and season with salt. Grill over moderate heat, covered with a lid or a bowl and turning occasionally, until tender, 18 minutes.
3. Meanwhile, in a small bowl, whisk the citrus zests with the citrus juices, soy sauce and 2 tablespoons of oil.
4. In a skillet, heat 2 more tablespoons of oil with the crushed red pepper. Add the leek tops and cook over high heat, stirring, until softened, 6 minutes. Add the corn and cook for 2 minutes, stirring. Add half of the dressing and cook until evaporated. Scrape into a bowl and let cool slightly. Stir in the tomatoes.
5. Arrange the grilled leeks on plates and drizzle with the remaining dressing. Spoon the leek-tomato salad on top and serve warm. —*Tara Duggan*
MAKE AHEAD The salad and grilled leeks can be refrigerated separately overnight and rewarmed before serving.

Fresh Fig Salad with Feta and Blistered Jalapeños

⏱ **TOTAL: 45 MIN**
4 TO 6 SERVINGS ● ● ●

This salad is a fig lover's feast: Plump, juicy figs are grilled with sugar until caramelized, then paired with a quick sweet-spicy fig jam spiked with red wine and ancho chile.

- 1 ancho chile, stemmed and seeded
- 1 cup dry red wine
- 12 dried Black Mission figs, halved lengthwise
- ¼ cup packed dark brown sugar
- ⅓ cup granulated sugar
- 6 large fresh Black Mission figs, halved lengthwise
- 4 shallots, cut through the root into ¼-inch wedges
- 4 jalapeños, seeded and julienned
- 1 tablespoon extra-virgin olive oil
Kosher salt and freshly ground pepper
- 2 ounces feta cheese, crumbled (½ cup)
Cilantro leaves and crushed pink peppercorns, for garnish
Lime wedges, for serving

1. In a medium saucepan, toast the ancho chile over moderate heat, turning, until fragrant and charred in spots, about 2 minutes. Remove from the heat and let cool slightly.
2. Add the wine, dried figs, dark brown sugar and ¼ cup of water to the saucepan with the chile and bring to a boil. Cover and simmer over moderately low heat until the chile and figs are tender, about 20 minutes. Transfer to a food processor and let cool slightly. Pulse until a chunky puree forms. Scrape the fig jam into a bowl.
3. Light a grill or preheat a grill pan. Set a mesh or perforated pan on the grill. Spread the granulated sugar in a pie plate. Dip the cut sides of the fresh figs in the sugar and grill over high heat until caramelized on 1 side only but still firm, 1 to 2 minutes. Transfer the caramelized figs to a plate.
4. In a medium bowl, toss the shallots and jalapeños with the olive oil; season with salt and freshly ground pepper. Add the shallots and jalapeños to the mesh or perforated pan and grill over high heat, tossing, until lightly charred and softened, 6 minutes. Transfer the vegetables to a plate.
5. Spoon 1 or 2 tablespoons of the fig jam onto plates and arrange the shallots, jalapeños, caramelized figs and crumbled feta around it. Garnish the salad with cilantro leaves and crushed pink peppercorns and serve with lime wedges.
—*Tim Byres*

MAKE AHEAD The fig jam can be refrigerated for up to 1 week. Bring to room temperature before serving.

Double-Apple and Brussels Sprout Slaw

⏱ **TOTAL: 30 MIN • 10 SERVINGS** ● ● ●

In her light, zippy version of coleslaw, F&W Test Kitchen senior editor Kay Chun swaps brussels sprouts for cabbage and combines them with a mix of sweet and tart apples. Instead of the usual mayonnaise, she tosses the slaw in a gingery yogurt dressing.

- ½ cup plus 2 tablespoons plain fat-free Greek yogurt
- ½ cup extra-virgin olive oil
- 3 tablespoons raw unfiltered apple cider vinegar
- 2 tablespoons very finely grated peeled fresh ginger
Kosher salt and freshly ground pepper
- 2 Granny Smith apples—peeled, cored and julienned
- 2 Fuji apples—peeled, cored and julienned
- ½ pound brussels sprouts, finely shredded
- 2 tablespoons chopped chives

1. In a small bowl, whisk the yogurt with the olive oil, vinegar and ginger and season with salt and pepper.
2. In a large bowl, combine the apples, brussels sprouts and chives. Add the dressing and toss to coat. Season the slaw with salt and pepper and serve. —*Kay Chun*
MAKE AHEAD The slaw can be refrigerated overnight.

Brussels Sprout Slaw with Hazelnuts and Pomegranate

⏱ **TOTAL: 30 MIN • 8 SERVINGS** ● ●

- 1 cup hazelnuts
- 2 tablespoons hazelnut oil
- 2 tablespoons extra-virgin olive oil
- 2 tablespoons red wine vinegar
- 2 teaspoons Dijon mustard
- 1 teaspoon finely grated lemon zest
- 1 tablespoon fresh lemon juice
Salt and freshly ground pepper
- 1 pound brussels sprouts, shredded
Seeds from 1 pomegranate (¾ cup)
- 1 loose cup shaved Parmigiano-Reggiano cheese (2 ounces)

1. Preheat the oven to 350°. In a pie plate, toast the hazelnuts until the skins blister, about 15 minutes. Transfer the nuts to a clean kitchen towel and let cool, then rub to remove the skins. Coarsely chop the nuts.
2. In a large bowl, whisk the hazelnut oil with the olive oil, vinegar, mustard, lemon zest and lemon juice and season with salt and pepper. Add the shredded brussels sprouts, pomegranate seeds and shaved cheese and toss well. Sprinkle the chopped hazelnuts on top and serve right away. —*Michael White*

TOP U.S. BALSAMIC

"This Nebraskan vinegar is Italian-level good." *$45; georgepaulvinegar.com.*
—*Clayton Chapman, chef at The Grey Plume, Omaha*

Vegetable Rainbow Salad

ACTIVE: 1 HR; TOTAL: 4 HR

6 SERVINGS ● ● ● ●

This salad brilliantly combines some of the most exciting food trends of 2013 in one amazing recipe—quick-pickled vegetables, uncommon produce, ancient grains and a cross-cultural dressing that includes miso and chipotle chile in adobo. If ingredients like lime radishes and baby orange cauliflower aren't available at your farmers' market, use equal quantities of similar vegetables.

6   purple pearl onions,
     root ends trimmed
6   small red radishes, tops trimmed
     to ⅓ inch and radishes halved
     lengthwise
2   small lime radishes,
     sliced ¼ inch thick
1   medium watermelon radish,
     halved lengthwise and sliced
     crosswise ¼ inch thick
1   cup unseasoned rice vinegar
2   tablespoons sugar
Kosher salt
10 baby beets of varying colors
     (about 6 ounces), scrubbed
5   medium carrots of varying colors
     (about 6 ounces), tops trimmed
3   tablespoons extra-virgin olive oil
1   small purple sweet potato
     (about 4 ounces)
½   cup vegetable oil, plus
     more for rubbing
3   heads of baby orange cauliflower
     (6 ounces total), cut into
     ¾-inch florets
½   small head of Romanesco broccoli
     (about ⅔ pound), cut into ¾-inch
     florets
1   small chipotle chile in adobo
1   tablespoon yellow miso paste
1   tablespoon honey
4   cups escarole (from about
     2 heads)—tender white and
     light green leaves only, cut
     into bite-size pieces
1   cup pea shoots
½   cup cooked black quinoa

1. In a small saucepan of salted boiling water, blanch the pearl onions for 3 minutes. Drain the onions and cool them under running water. Slip off the skins and pack the onions into a small heatproof jar. Pack each type of radish into separate small heatproof jars. In the same saucepan, combine ¾ cup of the rice vinegar with the sugar, 2 tablespoons of salt and 1 cup of water and bring to a boil. Pour the hot brine over the jarred onions and radishes and let stand at room temperature for 3 hours.

2. Preheat the oven to 400°. Place the beets and carrots on 2 separate sheets of foil and drizzle them with 2 tablespoons of the olive oil. Fold up the edges of the foil sheets to make two sealed packets. Rub the sweet potato with vegetable oil, prick it all over with a fork and set it on a sheet of foil. In a medium baking dish, toss the cauliflower and broccoli florets with the remaining 1 tablespoon of olive oil. Roast the cauliflower and broccoli for about 12 minutes, the sweet potato for about 30 minutes and the carrots and beets for about 35 minutes, until they are all tender. Let the roasted vegetables cool slightly.

3. Using paper towels, rub off the beet and carrot skins; quarter the beets and halve the carrots. Peel the sweet potato and cut it into ½-inch-thick rounds.

4. In a mini food processor or blender, puree the chipotle with the miso paste, honey and the remaining ¼ cup of rice vinegar. With the machine on, add the ½ cup of vegetable oil in a thin stream and process until emulsified. Season the dressing with salt.

5. Drain the pickled vegetables. Slice the pearl onions ¼ inch thick. In a serving bowl, combine the pickled and roasted vegetables with the escarole, pea shoots and cooked black quinoa. Add ¼ cup of the dressing and toss gently. Serve the salad right away, passing the remaining dressing on the side. —Grace Parisi

MAKE AHEAD The pickles and roasted vegetables can be stored in the refrigerator separately overnight.

WINE Zesty Italian white: 2011 Jankara Vermentino di Gallura.

Summer Vegetable "Ceviche"

📷 PAGE 41

ACTIVE: 30 MIN; TOTAL: 2 HR 30 MIN

8 SERVINGS ● ● ● ●

For this perfect summer salad, bloggers David Frenkiel and Luise Vindahl of Green Kitchen Stories (greenkitchenstories.com) marinate fresh corn, shelling beans, tomatoes and nectarines in a bright lime juice dressing just like other cooks would prepare fish for ceviche. In the winter, they give sprouts the ceviche treatment.

1   cup fresh baby lima beans
     (from about 1½ pounds in the pod)
     or other shelling bean
1   teaspoon finely grated lime zest
⅓   cup fresh lime juice
¼   cup extra-virgin olive oil
1   scallion, thinly sliced
1   jalapeño, seeded and thinly sliced
1   small shallot, thinly sliced
Sea salt
1½ cups fresh corn kernels
     (from 2 ears)
2   nectarines, cut into thin wedges
1   Hass avocado, cut into
     ½-inch cubes
1   large orange bell pepper,
     finely julienned
1   pint heirloom cherry tomatoes,
     halved
½   cup coarsely chopped cilantro

1. In a small saucepan of salted boiling water, cook the lima beans until tender, about 10 minutes. Drain and rinse under cold water.

2. In a large bowl, whisk the lime zest and juice with the olive oil, scallion, jalapeño and shallot; season the dressing with salt. Gently fold in the lima beans, corn, nectarines, avocado, orange pepper and tomatoes. Refrigerate the "ceviche" for at least 2 hours. Fold in the cilantro just before serving and serve the "ceviche" chilled. —David Frenkiel and Luise Vindahl

MAKE AHEAD The salad can be refrigerated for up to 8 hours.

WINE Tropical-fruity South African Sauvignon Blanc: 2012 Southern Right.

● HEALTHY ● MAKE AHEAD ● VEGETARIAN ● STAFF FAVORITE

VEGETABLE RAINBOW SALAD

Roasted Carrot and Avocado Salad with Citrus Dressing

TOTAL: 50 MIN • 6 SERVINGS ● ● ●

Combining roasted carrots with a cumin dressing isn't a particularly novel idea; nor is pairing raw avocado with citrus. But until we tried this recipe from British megachef Jamie Oliver, we'd never thought to put all of those things together. (Variations on the combination have since popped up on menus across the country.) This salad exemplifies what Oliver does so well: bringing together familiar ingredients in unfamiliar yet incredible ways.

- 1 pound medium carrots
- 2 teaspoons cumin seeds
- 1 fresh árbol chile or other small red chile

Kosher salt and freshly ground pepper

- 2 garlic cloves
- 1 teaspoon thyme leaves
- ⅓ cup plus 2 tablespoons extra-virgin olive oil
- 3 tablespoons red wine vinegar
- 1 orange, halved
- 1 lemon, halved

Four ½-inch-thick slices of ciabatta bread

- 3 Hass avocados—pitted, peeled and cut into 6 wedges each
- 8 ounces assorted greens, such as watercress, spinach or mesclun
- 2 cups baby arugula
- 2 tablespoons unsalted roasted sunflower seeds
- 1 tablespoon roasted sesame seeds
- 1 tablespoon poppy seeds
- 3 tablespoons low-fat sour cream mixed with 1 tablespoon water

1. Preheat the oven to 375°. Bring a deep skillet of salted water to a boil. Add the carrots and simmer, covered, over moderately low heat until crisp-tender, 10 minutes. Drain and transfer the carrots to a large roasting pan.
2. In a mortar, crush the cumin seeds, árbol chile, ½ teaspoon of salt and ¼ teaspoon of pepper. Add the garlic and thyme and pound into a paste. Stir in 2 tablespoons of the oil and 2 tablespoons of the vinegar.

3. Pour the cumin dressing over the carrots and toss well. Add the orange and lemon halves to the roasting pan, cut side down. Roast for about 25 minutes, until the carrots are tender.
4. Meanwhile, toast the ciabatta until the edges are golden brown. Tear the bread into bite-size pieces and, in a large bowl, gently toss with the avocados, greens and arugula. In a small bowl, combine the sunflower, sesame and poppy seeds.
5. Using tongs, squeeze the hot orange and lemon halves into a measuring cup until you have about ⅓ cup of juice. Whisk in the remaining 1 tablespoon of red wine vinegar and ⅓ cup of olive oil and season with salt and pepper. Add the warm carrots to the large bowl along with the citrus dressing and toss to coat. Transfer the salad to plates and drizzle with the sour cream. Sprinkle the salad with the seed mixture and serve.
—Jamie Oliver

Hearts of Palm and Avocado Salad

TOTAL: 20 MIN • 4 SERVINGS ● ●

Hearts of palm, which are popular in Latin and Brazilian cooking, are tangy and tender, with a pleasant crunch. Here, they're tossed with creamy avocado and a mayonnaise dressing, resulting in a salad that might taste a bit rich but is really quite healthy.

- 1 cup yellow cherry tomatoes, halved
- ½ small sweet onion, cut into thin slivers

Two 14-ounce cans hearts of palm, drained and sliced ½ inch thick

- 1 Hass avocado, cut into ½-inch pieces
- ¼ cup coarsely chopped flat-leaf parsley
- ½ teaspoon finely grated lime zest
- 2 tablespoons freshly squeezed lime juice
- 2 tablespoons mayonnaise
- 2 tablespoons canola oil

Salt and freshly ground pepper

1. In a medium bowl, toss the halved cherry tomatoes with the sweet onion slivers, sliced hearts of palm, avocado pieces and chopped parsley.
2. In a small bowl, whisk the lime zest and lime juice with the mayonnaise and oil; season the dressing with salt and pepper.
3. Pour the dressing over the salad, toss gently and serve right away.
—Grace Parisi

WINE Lemony California Sauvignon Blanc: 2012 Teira Woods Vineyard.

Broccoli Carpaccio with Grapes and Watercress

TOTAL: 30 MIN • 4 SERVINGS ● ● ●

For this vegetarian play on carpaccio, broccoli is very thinly sliced and topped with crunchy pine nuts, juicy grapes and a sweet-tangy honey-mustard dressing.

- ⅓ cup pine nuts
- ½ teaspoon fine sea salt
- ½ cup plain yogurt
- 2 tablespoons Dijon mustard
- 1 tablespoon honey
- 1 very fresh head of broccoli (12 ounces)—cut into large florets, stem peeled and reserved
- 1 cup seedless green grapes, halved
- ½ cup golden raisins
- 2 ounces small watercress sprigs or pea shoots

1. In a small skillet, sprinkle the pine nuts with the sea salt and toast over moderately low heat, shaking the skillet occasionally, until golden, 7 to 8 minutes.
2. Meanwhile, in a small bowl, combine the yogurt with the mustard and honey.
3. Using a sharp knife or the slicing blade in a food processor, very thinly slice the broccoli florets and stem. Arrange the broccoli in a single layer on 4 plates. Top with the grapes, raisins and watercress and drizzle with the dressing. Garnish the carpaccio with the pine nuts and serve.
—David Frenkiel and Luise Vindahl

WINE Lively, minerally northern Italian white: 2012 Abbazia di Novacella Kerner.

● HEALTHY ● MAKE AHEAD ● VEGETARIAN ● STAFF FAVORITE

BROCCOLI CARPACCIO WITH
GRAPES AND WATERCRESS

Roasted Beets with Hazelnuts and Goat Cheese

ACTIVE: 45 MIN; TOTAL: 2 HR 15 MIN
16 TO 20 SERVINGS ● ●

5½ pounds medium beets (about 20)
1¼ cups extra-virgin olive oil
 6 garlic cloves, crushed
 2 tablespoons thyme leaves
Kosher salt and freshly ground
    black pepper
 1 cup hazelnuts
½ cup fresh lemon juice
 1 shallot, minced
 1 tablespoon Dijon mustard
½ cup chopped chives or scallions
Shaved aged goat cheese, like Midnight
    Moon or Garrotxa, for serving

1. Preheat the oven to 375°. In a large roasting pan, toss the beets with ¼ cup of the oil and the garlic and thyme; season with salt and pepper. Cover tightly with foil and roast for about 1 hour and 15 minutes, until the beets are tender. Let cool, then peel the beets and cut them into different-sized wedges, chunks and slices.

2. Meanwhile, spread the hazelnuts in a pie plate and bake for about 12 minutes, until fragrant. Transfer the nuts to a kitchen towel and let cool slightly, then rub them together in the towel to remove the skins. Coarsely chop the nuts.

3. In a medium bowl, whisk the lemon juice with the shallot and mustard and let stand for about 10 minutes. Gradually whisk in the remaining 1 cup of olive oil and season the dressing with salt and pepper.

4. In a large bowl, toss the beets with half of the dressing and season with salt and pepper. Arrange the beets on a platter and sprinkle the chives and hazelnuts on top. Scatter shaved goat cheese over the salad and serve, passing the additional dressing and cheese at the table. —Nicholas Wilber

MAKE AHEAD The roasted beets can be refrigerated for up to 2 days. Bring to room temperature before proceeding. The lemon-shallot dressing can be refrigerated for up to 2 days.

Beet, Avocado and Arugula Salad

ACTIVE: 25 MIN; TOTAL: 1 HR 25 MIN
4 TO 6 SERVINGS ●

This salad manages to be both hearty and light, combining strong flavors (beets, arugula, cheese) in a bracing lemon dressing.

1½ pounds medium beets
 ¼ cup plus 1 tablespoon
    extra-virgin olive oil
Kosher salt
 ¼ cup pine nuts
 1 whole lemon
 ½ teaspoon finely grated lemon zest
 2 tablespoons fresh lemon juice
Freshly ground black pepper
 2 Hass avocados, peeled and
    cut into 1-inch pieces
 4 cups lightly packed baby arugula
 4 ounces Spanish Caña de Cabra,
    coarsely crumbled, or semi-firm
    aged goat cheese, shaved (1 cup)

1. Preheat the oven to 375°. In a small baking dish, rub the beets all over with 1 tablespoon of the oil; season with salt. Add ¼ cup of water, cover with foil and bake for about 1 hour, until the beets are tender. Uncover the dish and let the beets cool slightly. Peel the beets and cut them into 1-inch wedges.

2. Meanwhile, spread the pine nuts in a pie plate and bake for about 7 minutes, until golden. Let cool completely.

3. Using a sharp knife, peel the lemon, removing all of the bitter white pith. Cut in between the membranes to release the sections; cut the sections into small pieces. In a small bowl, whisk the zest and juice with the remaining ¼ cup of oil; season with salt and pepper. Stir in the lemon pieces.

4. In a large bowl, toss the avocados and arugula with half of the dressing and season lightly with salt and pepper. Transfer to plates. In the same bowl, toss the beets with the remaining dressing. Spoon the beets over the salads, top with the toasted pine nuts and cheese and serve. —Nancy Oakes

WINE Elegant, floral Provençal rosé: 2012 Bieler Père et Fils Coteaux d'Aix-en-Provence.

Double-Beet Salad with Radicchio and Blue Cheese

ACTIVE: 30 MIN; TOTAL: 1 HR
6 SERVINGS ● ●

Chef Deborah Madison, author of Vegetable Literacy, turns a classic beet-and-walnut salad into something surprising by serving the beets two ways: grated raw and pan-seared.

 ⅔ cup walnuts (2 ounces)
3½ tablespoons walnut oil
Smoked sea salt
 3 medium golden beets (about
    1¾ pounds), 1 peeled and
    shredded on a box grater
 2 tablespoons extra-virgin olive oil
1½ tablespoons minced shallot
1½ tablespoons Banyuls or
    balsamic vinegar
Freshly ground pepper
 1 large head of radicchio,
    cored and shredded
 2 ounces Maytag blue cheese,
    crumbled

1. Preheat the oven to 350°. Spread out the walnuts on a pie plate and toast for 8 minutes, until golden. Toss the walnuts with ½ tablespoon of the walnut oil and a pinch of smoked salt and let them cool.

2. Cut the 2 unpeeled beets into 8 wedges each. Set a steamer basket over 2 inches of boiling water. Add the beets, cover and steam until tender, 25 minutes. Let cool slightly, then rub off the skins. Slice ¼ inch thick.

3. In a skillet, heat ½ tablespoon of the olive oil until shimmering. Add the steamed beets and cook over high heat until blistered in spots, about 3 minutes. Transfer to a plate.

4. In a bowl, whisk the shallot, vinegar and remaining 3 tablespoons of walnut oil and 1½ tablespoons of olive oil. Season the dressing with smoked salt and pepper.

5. In a bowl, toss the shredded beet with the radicchio and half of the dressing. Mound the salad on a platter. In the same bowl, toss the cooked beets with the remaining dressing, season with smoked salt and pepper and arrange around the salad. Top with the walnuts and blue cheese. —Deborah Madison

● HEALTHY ● MAKE AHEAD ● VEGETARIAN ● STAFF FAVORITE

Golden Beet Carpaccio with Pickled Mustard Seeds

ACTIVE: 30 MIN; TOTAL: 1 HR 30 MIN

4 SERVINGS ● ●

At Social in Charleston, South Carolina, chef Jesse Sutton's beet salad features tender, baked golden beets topped with a sweet-tart dressing that combines Dijon mustard, horseradish and tarragon vinegar. Social's owner and wine director, Brad Ball, likes to pair the sweet beets with semisweet Riesling. "I don't have a scholarly analysis for the pairing of Riesling and mustardy things, but it works," says Ball.

Four 6-ounce golden beets
Extra-virgin olive oil
Sea salt and freshly ground pepper
3 tablespoons white balsamic vinegar
2 tablespoons yellow mustard seeds
1 tablespoon sugar
1½ tablespoons tarragon vinegar
1 tablespoon Dijon mustard
1 tablespoon prepared horseradish
Arugula leaves, snipped chives and
   minced red onion, for garnish

1. Preheat the oven to 375°. On a large sheet of heavy-duty foil, toss the beets with oil and season with salt and pepper. Wrap the beets in the foil and bake for about 1 hour, until tender when pierced. Let the beets cool slightly, then peel and let cool completely. Slice the beets crosswise ⅛ inch thick.

2. Meanwhile, in a small saucepan, combine ⅓ cup of water with the balsamic vinegar, mustard seeds, sugar and a pinch of salt and bring to a boil. Simmer over moderately low heat, stirring occasionally, until the seeds are nearly tender and most of the liquid is absorbed, about 12 minutes; let cool.

3. In a small bowl, whisk the tarragon vinegar with the Dijon mustard, horseradish and 3 tablespoons of olive oil. Season the vinaigrette with salt and pepper.

4. Arrange the beet slices on 4 plates or a platter, season with salt and pepper and drizzle with the horseradish dressing. Dollop the pickled mustard seeds on top; if the pickling liquid seems too thick, stir in water

1 teaspoon at a time before dolloping. Garnish the beets with arugula leaves, snipped chives and minced red onion and serve.
—Jesse Sutton

MAKE AHEAD The dressing can be refrigerated overnight.

WINE Semisweet Finger Lakes Riesling: 2012 Hermann J. Wiemer Late Harvest.

White Anchovy and Grilled Radicchio Bread Salad

🕒 **TOTAL: 45 MIN • 8 SERVINGS** ● ●

Grilled radicchio, flavorful white anchovies, ginger and soy sauce make for a fun twist on traditional panzanella.

½ cup extra-virgin olive oil,
   plus more for brushing
5 garlic cloves
6 ounces rustic Italian bread,
   torn into 1½-inch pieces
Kosher salt and freshly ground pepper
1 large head of radicchio,
   quartered through the core
2 teaspoons honey,
   plus more for drizzling
¼ cup white verjus (see Note)
1 teaspoon soy sauce
1 jalapeño, seeded and minced
1½ tablespoons minced fresh ginger
1 tablespoon minced preserved
   lemon rind (optional; see Note)
   or 1 teaspoon grated lemon zest
3 plum tomatoes, cut into ¾-inch dice
2 roasted red bell peppers,
   cut into ¾-inch dice
1 English cucumber—halved
   lengthwise, seeded and sliced
   crosswise ¼ inch thick
4 scallions, thinly sliced
2 celery ribs, thinly sliced crosswise,
   plus ½ cup celery leaves
3 ounces white anchovy fillets
   (*alici* or *boquerones*), cut into
   ¾-inch pieces (see Note)
1 cup lightly packed flat-leaf parsley

1. Preheat the oven to 350°. In a blender, blend the ½ cup of olive oil with the garlic until smooth. On a rimmed baking sheet,

toss the bread with the garlic oil and season with salt and pepper. Spread the bread in a single layer and bake for about 15 minutes, stirring once, until golden and barely crisp. Let cool completely.

2. Meanwhile, light a grill or preheat a grill pan. Brush the cut sides of the radicchio with olive oil and drizzle with a little honey. Grill the radicchio cut side down over high heat, turning once, until charred and just starting to soften, about 3 minutes. Let cool completely, then cut into 1-inch pieces; discard the cores.

3. In a large bowl, whisk the 2 teaspoons of honey with the verjus, soy sauce, jalapeño, ginger and preserved lemon, if using. Add the tomatoes, roasted red peppers, cucumber, scallions, sliced celery and celery leaves and toss well. Stir in the croutons, grilled radicchio, anchovies and parsley and season with salt and pepper. Serve right away.
—Tim Byres

NOTE Verjus is the juice of unripened grapes. It's often used as a substitute for vinegar. Preserved lemon is a condiment used primarily in Indian and North African cooking. Both are available at specialty food shops. White anchovy fillets are available in the deli section of specialty food shops.

WINE Robust Australian rosé: 2011 Robert Oatley Rosé of Sangiovese.

LEMON SHORTCUT

Instead of salting lemons for months to make Moroccan preserved lemons, L.A. chef Jeff Cerciello cures thin lemon slices in salt, sugar and olive oil for just 4 hours.

Seared-Tuna Niçoise Salad with Sesame and Miso Dressing

TOTAL: 1 HR 30 MIN • 6 SERVINGS ●

The classic Niçoise salad is reimagined here with Japanese flavors and served with sheets of crispy nori (dried seaweed) so guests can assemble their own hand rolls.

- 6 large eggs
- ¼ cup mirin
- ¼ cup soy sauce
- ½ pound thin green beans, trimmed
- 1 pound baby potatoes
- 1 pound tuna steak, ¾ inch thick

Salt

- 2 tablespoons toasted sesame oil
- ¼ cup light miso
- ¼ cup rice vinegar
- ¼ cup mayonnaise
- ¼ cup plus 2 tablespoons vegetable oil
- 5 ounces tatsoi, baby spinach or mesclun greens
- 1 cup cherry tomatoes, quartered
- 6 small radishes, thinly sliced
- 1 red bell pepper, thinly sliced
- 1 Hass avocado, thinly sliced

Black sesame seeds, for garnish

- 18 large sheets seasoned nori (see Note)

In this pair of small, stackable bowls, one has a little spout, making it perfect for sauces or dressings. *$30; teroforma.com.*

1. In a saucepan, cover the eggs with cold water and bring to a boil. Cover and let stand off the heat for 10 minutes. Drain and shake the eggs to crack the shells. Fill the saucepan with cold water and ice; let the eggs cool. Peel the eggs and transfer them to a resealable plastic bag. Add the mirin and soy sauce and refrigerate for 30 minutes or overnight.

2. Bring a large pot of salted water to a boil and fill a bowl with ice water. Boil the green beans until crisp-tender, about 3 minutes. Using a slotted spoon, transfer the beans to the ice water, then drain and pat them dry. Add the potatoes to the boiling water and cook until tender, about 12 minutes. Drain and add the potatoes to the ice water to cool slightly. Peel the potatoes and slice them ⅓ inch thick.

3. Preheat a grill pan. Season the tuna with salt; rub with the sesame oil. Grill the tuna over high heat for 3 minutes, turning once, for medium-rare. Let stand for 5 minutes, then slice the tuna.

4. In a mini food processor, combine the miso, vinegar and mayonnaise. Slowly add the vegetable oil and process the dressing until it is creamy.

5. Drain the eggs and halve them. On a large platter, arrange the greens, vegetables, eggs and tuna. Sprinkle with sesame seeds. Pass the nori sheets and dressing at the table. —*Grace Parisi*

NOTE Seasoned nori, dried seaweed roasted with sesame oil and salt, is available at Japanese and most Asian markets.

WINE Lively, green apple–scented Spanish white: 2011 Shaya Old Vines Verdejo.

Potato and Green Bean Salad with Nori Tartare

**ACTIVE: 30 MIN; TOTAL: 1 HR 45 MIN
6 SERVINGS** ● ● ●

This salad is by Clotilde Dusoulier, creator of the popular food blog Chocolate & Zucchini (*chocolateandzucchini.com*). It's a clever vegan take on surf and turf: The nori is the surf, the potatoes and green beans the turf. The nori "tartare," which is adapted from Dusoulier's book *The French Market Cookbook,* is also delicious as a dip for crackers.

- ¾ cup shredded nori (8 grams; see Note)
- 1 garlic clove, minced
- 2 tablespoons finely chopped shallot
- 2 tablespoons fresh lemon juice
- 1 tablespoon drained capers
- ¼ cup plus 1 tablespoon extra-virgin olive oil
- 1 tablespoon walnut oil

Salt and freshly ground pepper

- 1½ pounds baby potatoes, halved or quartered if large
- ¾ pound haricots verts, cut into 1-inch lengths
- 1 Hass avocado, cut into ½-inch chunks

1. In a medium bowl, cover the nori with 1 cup of cold water and let stand for 30 minutes. Transfer to a fine sieve to drain, lightly pressing to remove excess water.

2. Meanwhile, in a mini food processor, combine the garlic, shallot and lemon juice and let stand for 15 minutes. Add the nori, capers, 3 tablespoons of the olive oil and the walnut oil and pulse to a fine paste. Season with salt and pepper. Transfer the "tartare" to a jar and refrigerate for at least 1 hour.

3. In a steamer basket set over 2 inches of boiling water, steam the potatoes until tender, 12 minutes; transfer the potatoes to a bowl. Add the haricots verts to the steamer and steam until crisp-tender, 5 minutes. Add the beans to the potatoes, then fold in the nori "tartare" and the remaining 2 tablespoons of olive oil. Season the salad with salt and pepper. Gently fold in the avocado and serve warm. —*Clotilde Dusoulier*

NOTE Shredded nori (*kizami nori* in Japanese) is dried seaweed that has been cut into fine ribbons. Often used to top noodles or rice dishes, shredded nori is available for purchase at Japanese markets, health food stores and *amazon.com*. Alternatively, you can purchase full sheets of nori and use clean kitchen shears to cut them into very thin 2-inch-long strands.

MAKE AHEAD The "tartare" can be refrigerated for up to 3 days. Bring to room temperature before using.

● HEALTHY ● MAKE AHEAD ○ VEGETARIAN ● STAFF FAVORITE

SEARED-TUNA NIÇOISE SALAD
WITH SESAME AND MISO DRESSING

Southern Cobb Salad with Roasted Sweet Onion Dressing

TOTAL: 1 HR 15 MIN • 4 TO 6 SERVINGS

DRESSING

- 6 unpeeled garlic cloves
- 2 Vidalia onions (1½ pounds), peeled and quartered through the core
- 1¼ cups vegetable oil, plus more for brushing
- ½ cup apple cider vinegar
- ¼ cup fresh lemon juice

Kosher salt and freshly ground pepper

SALAD

- 10 lightly packed cups mixed lettuces (8 ounces)

Kosher salt and freshly ground pepper

- 2 cups shredded cooked chicken
- 1 cup cooked fresh or thawed frozen corn kernels
- 1 cup buckwheat or radish sprouts
- 4 ounces blue cheese, crumbled (1 cup)
- ½ cup crumbled cooked bacon
- 1 Hass avocado, peeled and diced
- 1 medium tomato, diced
- ½ cup toasted pecans, chopped
- 2 hard-cooked eggs, peeled and sliced lengthwise

1. MAKE THE DRESSING Preheat the oven to 425°. Wrap the garlic cloves in foil and set on a rimmed baking sheet. Brush the onions with oil and arrange on the baking sheet. Bake for about 1 hour, until the onions and garlic are lightly charred and soft. Let cool.
2. Peel the garlic and transfer the cloves to a blender. Add the onions, cider vinegar and lemon juice and puree until smooth. With the blender on, gradually add the 1¼ cups of vegetable oil until incorporated. Season the dressing with salt and pepper.
3. MAKE THE SALAD In a large bowl, toss the lettuces with ½ cup of the dressing; season with salt and pepper. Transfer to a platter. Arrange the remaining ingredients on top and serve, passing the remaining dressing at the table. —*Shaun Doty*
WINE Medium-bodied Sauvignon Blanc: 2012 Domaine Cherrier Père & Fils Sancerre.

Squash, Apple and Warm Lentil Salad

ACTIVE: 30 MIN; TOTAL: 1 HR
16 SERVINGS ● ●

- ¼ cup plus 2 tablespoons extra-virgin olive oil, plus more for drizzling
- 1 medium shallot, minced
- 3 garlic cloves, minced
- 2 cups French green lentils (14 ounces), rinsed
- 3 thyme sprigs
- 3 tablespoons fresh lemon juice
- 2 tablespoons chopped chives, plus more for garnish

Kosher salt and freshly ground black pepper

- 6 tablespoons unsalted butter, melted
- ¾ teaspoon cinnamon
- ½ teaspoon freshly grated nutmeg
- ⅛ teaspoon ground cloves
- 2 medium acorn squash (3 pounds)—scrubbed, halved, seeded and cut into ½-inch-thick wedges
- 1 Golden Delicious apple—quartered, cored and sliced ¼ inch thick
- ½ small head of radicchio, leaves torn into small pieces

Parsley sprigs, for garnish

1. In a large saucepan, heat 2 tablespoons of the olive oil. Add the shallot and cook over moderate heat, stirring, until lightly golden, about 5 minutes. Add the garlic and cook, stirring, until fragrant, 2 minutes. Stir in the lentils, thyme and 3 cups of water and bring to a boil. Cover and simmer over low heat until the lentils are tender and all of the liquid has been absorbed, about 30 minutes. Discard the thyme sprigs. Transfer the lentils to a medium bowl and let cool slightly. Stir in the lemon juice, 2 tablespoons of chives and remaining ¼ cup of olive oil; season with salt and pepper.
2. Meanwhile, preheat the oven to 400°. In a small bowl, whisk the butter with the cinnamon, nutmeg and cloves; season with salt and pepper.

3. In a large bowl, toss the squash with 5 tablespoons of the spiced butter and season with salt and pepper. Arrange the squash on 2 baking sheets and roast for 10 minutes. In the same bowl, toss the apple with the remaining 1 tablespoon of spiced butter. Turn the squash wedges and add the apples to the baking sheets. Roast for about 10 minutes longer, until the squash and apples are tender and golden.
4. Arrange the squash, apples and radicchio on a platter. Spoon the lentils on top and drizzle with olive oil. Garnish with parsley and chives and serve. —*Nicholas Wilber*
MAKE AHEAD The squash and apples can be roasted up to 6 hours ahead and kept, covered, at room temperature. The lentils can be refrigerated overnight.
WINE Full-bodied white blend from California: 2011 Pine Ridge Chenin Blanc Viognier.

Layered Chicken Salad with Coriander-Yogurt Dressing

TOTAL: 30 MIN • 4 SERVINGS ●

- ¼ cup plus 2 tablespoons plain fat-free Greek yogurt
- 1 tablespoon chopped dill
- 1½ teaspoons coriander seeds, crushed
- ¼ cup plus 2 tablespoons extra-virgin olive oil

Kosher salt and freshly ground pepper

- 4 roasted red bell peppers from a jar, drained and sliced ¼ inch thick
- 1 pound mixed tomatoes, chopped
- 2 Hass avocados, diced

One 3½- to 4-pound rotisserie chicken, meat shredded (4 cups)

- 1 cup mixed fresh herbs, such as parsley, basil, tarragon and dill

1. In a bowl, combine the yogurt, dill, coriander and 3 tablespoons of water; whisk until smooth. Whisk in the oil in a steady stream. Season the dressing with salt and pepper.
2. Layer the remaining ingredients in 4 jars. Serve the salads with the yogurt dressing. —*Kay Chun*
WINE Lively, strawberry-inflected rosé: 2012 Birichino Vin Gris.

● HEALTHY ● MAKE AHEAD ● VEGETARIAN ● STAFF FAVORITE

LAYERED CHICKEN SALAD WITH
CORIANDER-YOGURT DRESSING

Cookbook author Anya von Bremzen and her mother reinvent the soups, salads and other dishes of their native Russia.

Opposite: recipe, page 70.
BORSCHTPACHO

SILKY TORTILLA SOUP

A Bouillabaisse of All Things Green from the Garden

TOTAL: 2 HR • 4 SERVINGS ● ●

Like the classic Provençal seafood stew, this lovely vegetarian version of bouillabaisse is laced with saffron and fennel.

    4 baby artichokes
    ½ lemon
    3 tablespoons unsalted butter
    1 tablespoon extra-virgin olive oil
    1 leek, white and light green parts
       only, thinly sliced crosswise
    1 large Yukon Gold potato, peeled and
       cut into ¾-inch pieces
    1 medium fennel bulb, cut through
       the core into ½-inch wedges
    1 medium spring onion, cut into
       ¾-inch pieces, or 4 scallions, cut
       into 1-inch lengths
    ½ teaspoon finely chopped thyme
Kosher salt
    6 cups Vegetable Bouillabaisse Broth
       (recipe follows)
Pinch of saffron threads
    4 baby turnips, halved lengthwise, or 2
       small turnips, cut into ¾-inch pieces
    3 plum tomatoes, seeded and diced
    1 medium zucchini, cut into large dice
    8 asparagus, cut into 2-inch lengths
    2 tablespoons Pernod
Freshly ground pepper
Classic Aioli, Nettle Salsa (recipes
       follow) and grilled bread, for serving

1. Working with 1 artichoke at a time, pull off the dark outer leaves. Cut off the top fourth of the artichoke and peel and trim the stem. Halve the artichoke and scrape out the hairy choke. Rub the artichoke all over with lemon. Repeat with the remaining artichokes.
2. In a saucepan, melt 1 tablespoon of the butter in the oil. Add the leek, potato, fennel, spring onion, thyme and a generous pinch of salt. Cook over moderate heat, stirring, until the vegetables are barely softened, 7 minutes. Add the broth and saffron and bring to a boil. Stir in the turnips and artichokes; simmer over moderately low heat, stirring, until the vegetables are tender, 7 minutes.

3. Add the tomatoes, zucchini and asparagus to the broth and simmer until the asparagus is crisp-tender, 3 to 5 minutes. Stir in the Pernod and the remaining 2 tablespoons of butter and season with salt and freshly ground pepper. Serve the bouillabaisse in bowls with Classic Aioli, Nettle Salsa and grilled bread. —*Daniel DeLong*
WINE Lively, medium-bodied California Sauvignon Blanc: 2012 Long Meadow Ranch.

VEGETABLE BOUILLABAISSE BROTH

TOTAL: 1 HR

MAKES ABOUT 6 CUPS ● ● ●

    3 tablespoons extra-virgin olive oil
    1 onion, coarsely chopped
Stalks and fronds from 1 fennel bulb,
       chopped
    1 large Yukon Gold potato,
       peeled and chopped
    2 celery ribs, chopped
   10 unpeeled garlic cloves, crushed
Green tops from 1 large leek, chopped
    1 plum tomato, chopped
One 1-inch piece of peeled fresh ginger,
       finely chopped
    1 teaspoon ground coriander
    1 teaspoon ground fennel seeds
    ½ star anise pod, crushed
    1 bay leaf
   1½ cups dry white wine
    1 teaspoon kosher salt
Pinch of crushed red pepper

1. In a large pot, heat 1 tablespoon of the olive oil until shimmering. Add the onion, fennel, potato, celery, garlic, leek tops, tomato and ginger and cook over moderate heat, stirring occasionally, until softened, 10 minutes.
2. Scrape the vegetables to one side of the saucepan and add the remaining 2 tablespoons of oil to the opposite side. Add the coriander, fennel seeds, star anise and bay leaf to the oil and cook, stirring, until fragrant, about 1 minute. Stir in the wine, salt, crushed red pepper and 8 cups of water and bring to a boil. Simmer over moderately low heat, stirring occasionally, until the vegetables are very tender, 20 to 25 minutes.

3. Strain the broth through a sieve into a clean saucepan, pressing the vegetables to extract the liquid. Discard the vegetables. —*DD*

CLASSIC AIOLI

TOTAL: 10 MIN

MAKES ABOUT 1 CUP ● ●

Serve leftover aioli in sandwiches or on fish.

    3 small garlic cloves, finely grated
Kosher salt
    1 large egg yolk
    1 teaspoon fresh lemon juice
    ¾ cup extra-virgin olive oil
    ¼ cup vegetable oil
Freshly ground pepper

1. On a work surface, using the flat side of a chef's knife, smash the garlic with a generous pinch of salt into a paste; scrape into a bowl.
2. Whisk the egg yolk, lemon juice and 1 teaspoon of water into the garlic paste. Whisk in the olive oil, a few drops at a time, until the aioli starts to thicken. Add the remaining olive oil in a very thin stream, whisking constantly. Slowly whisk in the vegetable oil; season the aioli with salt and pepper and serve. —*DD*

NETTLE SALSA

TOTAL: 20 MIN • MAKES ¾ CUP ● ●

Nettles—wild greens often sold at farmers' markets—have a deep, earthy flavor. Because raw nettles can irritate bare skin, handle them with gloves; once cooked, they lose their sting. The salsa is also delicious over pasta.

    5 ounces nettles or baby spinach
    1 shallot, finely chopped
    ½ garlic clove, minced
    ½ teaspoon finely grated lemon zest
   1½ teaspoons fresh lemon juice
    ½ cup extra-virgin olive oil
Kosher salt and freshly ground
       black pepper

1. Prepare an ice bath. In a large saucepan of salted boiling water, blanch the nettles until tender, about 2 minutes. Using a slotted spoon, transfer the nettles to the ice bath to cool. Drain and squeeze dry, then chop.

● HEALTHY   ● MAKE AHEAD   ● VEGETARIAN   ● STAFF FAVORITE

2. In a food processor, combine the nettles, shallot, garlic, lemon zest and lemon juice; puree to a paste. Add the olive oil and puree until nearly smooth. Season with salt and pepper and scrape the salsa into a bowl. —DD

Fennel Avgolemono

⏱ **TOTAL: 45 MIN • 4 SERVINGS** ● ● ○ ○

This velvety, richly flavored fennel soup has no cream; the exquisite texture comes from swirls of beaten eggs.

- 3 tablespoons extra-virgin olive oil
- 1 medium onion, finely chopped
- 2 fennel bulbs (2 pounds)—trimmed, fronds chopped and bulbs thinly sliced (about 6 cups)

Kosher salt and freshly ground pepper
- 1 tablespoon unsalted butter
- 2 large eggs
- 2 tablespoons freshly squeezed lemon juice

1. In a large saucepan, heat 2 tablespoons of the olive oil. Add the onion and all but 1 cup of the sliced fennel, season with salt and pepper and cook over moderately low heat, stirring frequently, until softened but not browned, about 10 minutes. Add 6 cups of water and bring to a boil. Cover partially and simmer the soup until the fennel is very tender, about 15 minutes.

2. Meanwhile, in a small skillet, melt the butter in the remaining 1 tablespoon of olive oil. Add the remaining sliced fennel and season with salt and pepper. Cook over moderately high heat, stirring occasionally, until the fennel is tender and lightly caramelized, about 5 minutes. Keep warm.

3. Puree the soup in a blender in 2 batches. Wipe out the saucepan.

4. In a medium bowl, beat the eggs with the lemon juice. Whisking constantly, slowly drizzle 2 cups of the hot soup into the eggs. Return all of the soup to the saucepan and stir over moderately low heat just until thickened, about 2 minutes. Season with salt and pepper. Ladle the soup into bowls, top with the caramelized fennel and chopped fennel fronds and serve. —Kay Chun

Cream of Leek and Potato Soup

ACTIVE: 30 MIN; TOTAL: 1 HR 15 MIN
MAKES 10 CUPS ● ● ○

This smooth pureed soup may sound like an Escoffier classic, but its taste is purely Tuscan. Chef Lauren Kiino of San Francisco's Il Cane Rosso is a believer in whole-vegetable cooking. Here, she uses more of the leek greens than any French chef would tolerate, for tons of gentle leek flavor. Kiino does stir in a little crème fraîche. "But," she insists, "the Italian spirit is still the same."

- 4 tablespoons unsalted butter
- 3 medium leeks, white and light green parts only, thinly sliced
- 2 medium onions, halved and thinly sliced

Kosher salt
- ¼ cup dry vermouth
- ¼ cup dry white wine
- 1 pound Yukon Gold potatoes, peeled and cut into 1-inch cubes
- ½ cup crème fraîche or sour cream
- 1 tablespoon minced chives and freshly ground pepper, for garnish

1. Melt the butter in a large saucepan. Add the leeks, onions and 2 teaspoons of salt and cook over moderate heat, stirring occasionally, until softened, about 10 minutes. Stir in the vermouth and wine and boil until nearly evaporated, about 5 minutes. Add the potatoes and 8 cups of water and bring to a boil. Simmer over moderate heat until the potatoes are very tender, about 35 minutes.

2. Working in batches, puree the soup in a blender until very smooth. Return the soup to the pan. Add the crème fraîche and bring just to a simmer over moderate heat, stirring occasionally. Season with salt. Ladle the soup into bowls, garnish with the chives and pepper and serve. —Lauren Kiino

MAKE AHEAD The pureed soup can be refrigerated for up to 2 days. Add the crème fraîche and reheat just before serving.

WINE Full-bodied, minerally white Burgundy: 2011 Jean-Marc Brocard Vieilles Vignes Chablis.

French Onion Soup with Whole-Grain Cheese Toast

TOTAL: 1 HR • 4 SERVINGS ● ●

Instead of covering French onion soup with a hunk of bread and a thick layer of gooey cheese, food blogger Phoebe Lapine melts a little grated Gruyère over whole-grain toast and floats it on the tasty broth. The stealth ingredient in this healthy soup is soy sauce.

- 1 tablespoon extra-virgin olive oil
- 2 large onions, halved and thinly sliced

Kosher salt
- ¼ cup dry white wine
- 1 tablespoon soy sauce
- 6 cups beef stock or low-sodium broth

Four ½-inch-thick slices of whole-grain baguette
- ¼ cup shredded Gruyère cheese

1. In a large enameled cast-iron casserole, heat the oil until shimmering. Add the onions and cook over moderate heat, stirring occasionally, until the onions are softened and just starting to brown, about 7 minutes. Add a generous pinch of salt and cook over moderately low heat, stirring occasionally, until the onions are soft and golden, 25 to 30 minutes.

2. Add the wine and soy sauce to the casserole and cook over moderate heat until evaporated, scraping up any browned bits from the bottom, about 3 minutes. Add the stock and bring to a boil. Simmer over moderately low heat, stirring occasionally, until the onion broth is well flavored and slightly reduced, about 10 minutes. Season the soup with salt.

3. Preheat the broiler. Arrange the bread slices on a baking sheet and top each piece with 1 tablespoon of the cheese. Broil 6 inches from the heat until the cheese is melted and just starting to brown, about 2 minutes. To serve, ladle the soup into bowls and top with the cheese toasts. —Phoebe Lapine

MAKE AHEAD The recipe can be prepared through Step 2 and refrigerated for up to 2 days. Reheat gently.

Chicken Vermicelli Soup

ACTIVE: 40 MIN; TOTAL: 3 HR

6 SERVINGS ● ● ●

About 5 pounds skinless chicken backs,
      necks and wings
   2 ears of corn, kernels cut off and
      cobs reserved
   2 scallions, cut in half
One 2-inch piece of fresh ginger,
      chopped
   2 large garlic cloves
Kosher salt
   8 ounces dry rice vermicelli
   2 teaspoons vegetable oil
Two 6-ounce skinless, boneless
      chicken breast halves
   ¼ cup Asian fish sauce
Small Thai or sweet basil leaves
      and thinly sliced Thai chiles,
      for garnish

1. In a large pot, combine the chicken parts
with the corn cobs, scallions, ginger, garlic,
2½ teaspoons of salt and 4 quarts of water
and bring just to a boil. Simmer over moderately low heat, skimming the surface, until
the stock is flavorful, about 2 hours.
2. Meanwhile, in a large saucepan of salted
boiling water, cook the vermicelli until al
dente, about 2 minutes. Drain and cool under
running water. Transfer the vermicelli to a
bowl and toss with the oil to prevent sticking.
3. Strain the stock into the large saucepan.
You should have about 2½ quarts of stock;
add water if needed.
4. Add the chicken breasts to the saucepan
and return the stock just to a boil. Remove
the saucepan from the heat, cover and let
stand until the chicken is just cooked through,
about 20 minutes. Using tongs, transfer the
chicken to a plate; let cool slightly, then shred.
5. Add the corn kernels to the stock and
bring just to a boil. Simmer over moderate
heat until the corn is crisp-tender, about
3 minutes. Stir in the shredded chicken and
the fish sauce and season with salt. To serve,
fill bowls with the vermicelli and ladle the
soup on top. Garnish with basil leaves and
Thai chiles and serve. —*Kuniko Yagi*

Thai Coconut Seafood Soup

☼ TOTAL: 15 MIN • 6 SERVINGS

One 14-ounce can unsweetened
      coconut milk
One 8-ounce bottle clam juice
   1 jalapeño, seeded and thinly sliced
   1 tablespoon Asian fish sauce
   1 tablespoon green Thai curry paste
Pinch of sugar
   ¾ pound shelled and deveined
      medium shrimp
   ½ pound sea scallops, quartered
   2 scallions, thinly sliced
   ¼ cup each of chopped mint,
      basil and cilantro
Lime wedges and steamed rice,
      for serving

In a large pot, combine the coconut milk
with the clam juice, jalapeño, fish sauce,
curry paste, sugar and ¼ cup of water and
bring to a boil. Simmer for 2 minutes. Add
the shrimp, scallops and scallions and cook
until the shrimp and scallops are just white
throughout, about 2 minutes. Stir the mint,
basil and cilantro into the soup and serve
with lime wedges and steamed rice.
—*Grace Parisi*

WINE Tangy Austrian Grüner Veltliner: 2012
Fritsch Windspiel.

Easy Dashi

ACTIVE: 20 MIN; TOTAL: 50 MIN

MAKES 7 CUPS ● ●

This dashi (Japanese kelp-and-bonito stock)
delivers an intensely savory broth. Make it at
the last minute, right before using.

  16 grams kombu (dried kelp),
      about two 6-by-1-inch strips,
      wiped with a damp towel
8½ cups cold filtered water
  60 grams bonito shavings
      (about 3 lightly packed cups)

1. In a large saucepan, combine the kombu
with 8 cups of the water and let stand at
room temperature until the kombu starts
to soften, about 30 minutes.

2. Bring the water to a bare simmer over
moderate heat; tiny bubbles will form on
the bottom of the saucepan. Remove from
the heat and discard the kombu. Add the
remaining ½ cup of cold water to the saucepan, then add the bonito shavings and bring
just to a simmer. Immediately strain the
dashi through a fine sieve and use right away.
—*Daniel Duane*

Matzoh Balls in Brodo

ACTIVE: 20 MIN; TOTAL: 1 HR

4 SERVINGS ● ● ●

These bite-size matzoh balls are light and
fluffy, with a delicious Italian spin—they're
made with ricotta and Parmigiano-Reggiano
cheese, then simmered in a garlicky vegetable broth.

   1 large egg
   2 tablespoons fresh ricotta cheese
   2 tablespoons freshly grated
      Parmigiano-Reggiano cheese, plus
      more for garnish
   1 tablespoon extra-virgin olive oil
   ⅛ teaspoon kosher salt
   ⅛ teaspoon freshly ground pepper
   ¼ cup matzoh meal
   6 cups vegetable stock or
      low-sodium broth
   2 garlic cloves, lightly crushed
   1 small carrot, thinly sliced
Tarragon leaves, for garnish

1. In a medium bowl, whisk the egg. Whisk in
the ricotta cheese, Parmigiano-Reggiano
cheese, olive oil, salt and pepper. Stir in the
matzoh meal. Let stand at room temperature
for about 10 minutes, then gently form the
mixture into 1-teaspoon-size balls.
2. In a medium saucepan, bring the vegetable
stock to a boil with the garlic. Add the matzoh
balls, cover and simmer over moderate heat
for about 10 minutes. Add the carrot, cover
and simmer until the carrot is tender and
the matzoh balls are puffed and light, about
10 minutes longer. Ladle the matzoh balls and
brodo into bowls. Garnish each bowl with
tarragon and grated Parmigiano-Reggiano
cheese and serve. —*Kay Chun*

CHICKEN VERMICELLI SOUP

Porcini and Chestnut Soup
ACTIVE: 30 MIN; TOTAL: 1 HR 30 MIN
10 SERVINGS ● ●

- 1 ounce dried porcini mushrooms
- 4 cups boiling water
- 4 tablespoons unsalted butter
- 1 pound white button mushrooms, thinly sliced
- 2 medium leeks, white and tender green parts only, thinly sliced
- 1 carrot, thinly sliced
- 1 celery rib, thinly sliced
- 1 teaspoon minced rosemary
- 1½ cups peeled roasted vacuum-packed chestnuts
- 3 cups chicken stock
- Salt and freshly ground pepper
- 1 cup heavy cream
- 2 tablespoons extra-virgin olive oil
- 4 ounces fresh porcini or cremini mushrooms, thinly sliced

1. In a heatproof bowl, soak the dried porcini in the boiling water until softened, 20 minutes. Remove the mushrooms. Strain the liquid into a bowl through a sieve lined with a moistened paper towel. Rinse the porcini to remove any remaining grit and finely chop.
2. In a saucepan, melt the butter. Add the chopped porcini, button mushrooms, leeks, carrot, celery and rosemary and cook over moderate heat, stirring occasionally, until the vegetables are browned, 15 minutes. Add the chestnuts and stock and scrape up any browned bits stuck to the bottom of the pot. Add 3 cups of the strained porcini soaking liquid and season with salt and pepper. Bring the soup to a boil and simmer over moderate heat until the chestnuts are very tender, 30 minutes. Add the cream and let cool slightly. Puree in a blender in batches and keep warm.
3. In a skillet, heat the oil. Add the sliced porcini, season with salt and pepper and cook over moderately high heat until lightly browned, 6 minutes. Ladle the soup into bowls and garnish with the sautéed porcini.
—*Michael Tusk*
WINE Lean, cool-climate Italian Pinot Noir: 2011 Franz Haas Pinot Nero.

Cabbage Velouté with Poached Pears and Croutons
ACTIVE: 1 HR 30 MIN; TOTAL: 2 HR
6 SERVINGS ● ○ ○

When Christopher Kostow makes this soup at The Restaurant at Meadowood in St. Helena, California, he uses cabbage juice to amplify the flavor, but it's also great made with vegetable stock.

- One 375-milliliter bottle Sauternes
- 1¼ cups sugar
- 1 small cinnamon stick
- 1½ teaspoons caraway seeds
- Kosher salt
- 2 Asian pears, peeled and halved lengthwise
- Two ½-inch-thick slices of pumpernickel bread, cut into ½-inch cubes
- 2 tablespoons extra-virgin olive oil
- 6 tablespoons unsalted butter
- 2 pounds napa cabbage—halved, cored and thinly sliced
- 1 cup vegetable stock
- 1 cup crème fraîche
- Julienned Savoy or napa cabbage, finely diced Gruyère cheese and mustard-seed oil (see Note), for garnish

1. Preheat the oven to 350°. In a medium saucepan, combine the Sauternes, sugar, cinnamon stick, caraway, a pinch of salt and 2¾ cups of water. Bring just to a boil, stirring to dissolve the sugar. Add the Asian pear halves, cover and poach over moderately low heat, turning occasionally, until barely tender, 25 to 30 minutes. Remove from the heat and let cool completely. Core the pears and cut them into 12 wedges each. Return the pear wedges to the poaching liquid.
2. Meanwhile, on a rimmed baking sheet, toss the bread cubes with the olive oil and season with salt. Bake for about 10 minutes, until just crisp; let cool.
3. In a large saucepan, melt the butter. Add the napa cabbage and a generous pinch of salt and cook over moderately high heat, stirring occasionally, until wilted, 12 minutes. Add the vegetable stock and 6 cups of water and bring to a boil. Simmer over moderately

high heat, stirring occasionally, until the cabbage is very tender, 10 to 12 minutes.
4. Working in batches, puree the cabbage soup with the crème fraîche in a blender until smooth. Strain the soup through a fine sieve into a clean saucepan. Bring the soup just to a boil and simmer over moderate heat, stirring often, until reduced to 8 cups, about 7 minutes. Season the soup with salt.
5. Ladle the soup into shallow bowls. Using a slotted spoon, add the poached pears to the bowls. (The poached pear liquid can be served with sparkling water as a spritzer.) Garnish with the pumpernickel croutons, julienned cabbage and diced Gruyère, drizzle with mustard-seed oil and serve.
—*Christopher Kostow*
NOTE Mustard-seed oil is available at specialty food stores and *farawayfoods.com*.
MAKE AHEAD The poached pears and pureed soup can be refrigerated separately overnight. Let the pears return to room temperature and reheat the soup gently before serving.
WINE Vibrant, full-bodied white Burgundy: 2012 Louis Jadot Pouilly-Fuissé.

Bean-Sausage Soup with Sautéed Spring Greens
⏱ TOTAL: 35 MIN • 6 SERVINGS ●

- 1 teaspoon extra-virgin olive oil, plus more for drizzling
- 4 ounces andouille sausage, halved lengthwise and sliced crosswise ¼ inch thick
- One 15-ounce can butter beans, drained and rinsed
- 5 cups low-sodium chicken broth
- Sautéed Spring Greens with Bacon and Mustard Seeds (page 224)
- 1 cup cooked rice, bulgur or quinoa

In a medium pot, heat the 1 teaspoon of olive oil. Add the andouille and cook over moderate heat until browned, about 5 minutes. Add the beans, broth and greens and bring to a boil. Simmer for 5 minutes, then stir in the grains and cook until heated through. Serve in deep bowls, drizzled with olive oil.
—*Grace Parisi*

Three-Greens Soup with Sausage and Potatoes

ACTIVE: 30 MIN; TOTAL: 1 HR
4 TO 6 SERVINGS ● ●

To add a little heat to this hearty soup, consider making it with spicy Italian sausage.

- 3 tablespoons extra-virgin olive oil
- ½ pound Italian sausage, casings removed
- ½ pound baby white potatoes, sliced ¼ inch thick
- 2 shallots, thinly sliced
- 3 garlic cloves, thinly sliced
- 10 ounces curly spinach, thick stems discarded
- ½ pound kale, stems discarded and leaves coarsely chopped

Salt and freshly ground pepper
One 28-ounce can whole tomatoes, crushed

- 6 cups chicken stock or low-sodium broth
- 2 basil sprigs, plus chopped basil for garnish
- 4 ounces escarole, leaves torn (4 cups)

1. In a large pot, heat 1 tablespoon of the olive oil. Add the sausage and cook over moderately high heat, breaking up the clumps, until browned, 5 to 7 minutes. Transfer the sausage to a paper towel–lined plate.
2. Add the remaining 2 tablespoons of olive oil to the pot along with the potatoes, shallots and garlic. Cook over moderate heat, stirring, until the shallots are softened, about 3 minutes. Add the spinach and kale, season with salt and pepper and cook, stirring, until wilted. Add the tomatoes and their juices, the broth and the basil sprigs and bring to a boil. Partially cover and simmer until the greens and potatoes are tender and the soup is thickened, about 25 minutes.
3. Discard the basil sprigs. Stir in the escarole and sausage and season with salt and pepper. Ladle the soup into bowls, garnish with chopped basil and serve right away. —*Kay Chun*
SERVE WITH Crusty bread.

Spaghetti Squash Soup with Wild Mushrooms

⏱ TOTAL: 45 MIN • 4 TO 6 SERVINGS ● ●

This quick soup highlights fall's best flavors. For a fun twist, it uses strands of spaghetti squash like noodles.

- 1 pound spaghetti squash, halved and seeded
- 3 tablespoons extra-virgin olive oil

Kosher salt and freshly ground pepper

- 2 tablespoons unsalted butter
- 1 medium onion, finely chopped
- 1¼ pounds mixed wild mushrooms, such as king oyster and hen-of-the-woods (maitake), stems discarded and mushrooms coarsely chopped
- 3 garlic cloves, finely chopped
- 2 quarts low-sodium chicken broth
- 1 sage sprig
- 1 cup ditalini pasta
- ¼ cup freshly grated Parmigiano-Reggiano cheese, plus more for serving
- 2 tablespoons snipped chives

1. Preheat the oven to 425°. Rub the cut sides of the squash with 1 tablespoon of the olive oil and season with salt and pepper. Place the squash cut side down on a baking sheet and roast for 30 minutes, until tender. Using a fork, scrape the squash strands into bowls and keep warm.
2. Meanwhile, in a large pot, melt the butter in the remaining 2 tablespoons of oil. Add the onion and cook over moderate heat, stirring, until golden, 5 minutes. Add the mushrooms and garlic and cook, stirring, until the mushrooms are golden, 7 to 8 minutes. Add the broth and sage, season with salt and pepper and bring to a boil. Add the pasta and cook until al dente, 9 to 10 minutes. Discard the sage sprig; stir in the ¼ cup of cheese.
3. Ladle the soup over the squash, garnish with the chives and serve with grated cheese. —*Kay Chun*

MAKE AHEAD The soup and squash strands can be refrigerated separately for up to 3 days. Reheat the soup gently before serving.

Spicy Crab Bisque

ACTIVE: 40 MIN; TOTAL: 1 HR 10 MIN
12 SERVINGS ● ●

- 4 tablespoons unsalted butter
- 1 small white onion, finely chopped
- 6 celery ribs, finely chopped
- 6 scallions, thinly sliced
- 2 bay leaves
- ¼ cup all-purpose flour
- 5 cups low-sodium chicken broth
- 2 tablespoons Mashed Roasted Garlic (page 262)
- 3 cups whole milk
- 2 tablespoons dry sherry
- 1 tablespoon ketchup
- 1 teaspoon tomato paste
- ¼ teaspoon sweet smoked paprika
- ⅛ teaspoon cayenne pepper

Pinch of ground cloves
Pinch of ground mace
Pinch of freshly grated nutmeg

- 1 cup heavy cream
- ½ to 1 tablespoon Tabasco

Salt and freshly ground black pepper

- 2 pounds jumbo lump crab or Dungeness crabmeat

Oyster crackers, for serving

1. In a large soup pot, melt the butter. Add the onion, celery, scallions and bay leaves and cook over moderate heat until softened, 5 minutes. Stir in the flour and cook, stirring, for 2 minutes. Gradually whisk in the chicken broth and bring to a boil. Simmer, stirring occasionally, until the broth is thickened and the vegetables are very tender, 15 minutes.
2. Add the garlic and milk; bring to a simmer. Stir in the sherry, ketchup, tomato paste, paprika, cayenne, cloves, mace, nutmeg, cream and Tabasco and bring to a simmer. Season with salt and black pepper, then add the crab; simmer until hot. Discard the bay leaves. Serve the bisque with oyster crackers. —*Tanya Holland*

MAKE AHEAD The bisque can be refrigerated without the crab for up to 3 days. Reheat gently; add the crab just before serving.
WINE Ripe, fruit-forward California Chardonnay: 2011 Cuvaison Estate.

Chicken-and-Shrimp Wonton Soup with Lemongrass Broth

TOTAL: 1 HR 30 MIN

4 TO 6 SERVINGS ● ● ●

Chef Paul Liebrandt of The Elm in Brooklyn, New York, reinterprets classic wonton soup. "They don't use a huge amount of lemongrass in traditional Hong Kong cooking; it's a Southeast Asian ingredient," he says. "But it adds great aroma and it's a nice twist."

CHICKEN BROTH

- 1 tablespoon peanut or canola oil
- 1 pound chicken breasts on the bone, skin discarded
- ½ pound spareribs or baby back ribs, cut into single ribs
- 8 green cardamom pods
- 3 black cardamom pods (optional; see Note)
- ½ tablespoon black peppercorns
- ½ tablespoon Sichuan peppercorns (see Note)
- 2 star anise pods
- 10 cups water
- 1 fresh lemongrass stalk, tender white inner bulb only, chopped

One 1½-inch piece of fresh ginger, peeled and thickly sliced

- 3 cilantro sprigs
- 2 scallions, halved
- 3 tablespoons soy sauce

WONTONS

- 3 ounces shelled and deveined shrimp, minced
- 2 ounces skinless, boneless chicken breast, minced
- 2 garlic cloves, minced
- 2 tablespoons minced shallot
- 1 tablespoon soy sauce
- 1 tablespoon honey
- ½ teaspoon toasted Asian sesame oil, plus 1 tablespoon for garnish
- 1 red Thai chile, seeded and minced
- 1 teaspoon minced cilantro, plus 1 tablespoon small leaves for garnish

Pinch of fine sea salt

- 12 square wonton wrappers
- 1 scallion, white and light green parts only, thinly sliced, for garnish

1. MAKE THE BROTH In a pot, heat the oil. Add the chicken and spareribs and cook over moderate heat, turning occasionally, until lightly browned, 5 minutes. Add the cardamom pods, peppercorns and star anise and cook, stirring, for 1 minute. Add all of the remaining broth ingredients and bring to a boil. Simmer over moderately low heat, skimming off the fat, until the broth is reduced to 6 cups and very fragrant, 40 minutes. Strain the broth through a cheesecloth-lined sieve into a large saucepan; skim off any fat.

2. MAKE THE WONTONS In a bowl, combine all of the ingredients except the wrappers and garnishes. Arrange 4 wrappers on a surface; keep the remaining ones covered with a damp paper towel. Brush the wrapper edges with water. Place 2 teaspoons of the filling in the center of each wrapper. Bring all 4 corners of each wrapper together and twist the top gently to form into purses. Press the edges to seal. Transfer the wontons to a plate. Repeat with the remaining wrappers and filling; cover with plastic wrap.

3. Bring the strained broth to a boil. Add the wontons and simmer over moderate heat until cooked through, about 3 minutes. Spoon the wontons into bowls and ladle the broth over. Garnish the soup with the sesame oil, cilantro leaves and sliced scallion and serve. —*Paul Liebrandt*

NOTE Black cardamom and Sichuan peppercorns are available at *penzeys.com*.

MAKE AHEAD The wontons can be refrigerated for up to 8 hours. The broth can be refrigerated for up to 3 days or frozen for 1 month.

Smoky Oyster Chowder with Bacon, Rosemary and Fennel

ACTIVE: 45 MIN; TOTAL: 1 HR 30 MIN

8 TO 10 SERVINGS ● ●

This velvety chowder from chef Dylan Fultineer of Rappahannock in Richmond, Virginia, is thickened with a classic flour-and-butter roux. He packs it with plump oysters and tender fingerling potatoes, and adds a kick of heat from dried red chiles. For extra flavor, he uses bacon from Benton's Smoky Mountain Country Hams in Tennessee, which is famous for its intense smokiness.

- 4 ounces smoky bacon, such as Benton's (*bentonscountry hams2.com*), cut into 1-by-¼-inch matchsticks
- 1 tablespoon chopped rosemary
- 2 dried red chiles, stemmed and broken
- 4 small celery ribs, finely chopped
- 1 large onion, finely chopped
- 1 fennel bulb, finely chopped
- 2 quarts fish stock or 1 quart bottled clam juice and 1 quart water
- 1 stick unsalted butter
- ½ cup all-purpose flour
- 1 pound fingerling potatoes, cut into ½-inch rounds

1½ cups heavy cream

Salt and freshly ground pepper

- 1 pint freshly shucked oysters with their liquor

Tabasco, for serving

1. In a large pot, cook the bacon over moderately high heat, stirring, until browned, 5 minutes. Transfer the bacon to a paper towel–lined plate to drain. Pour off all but 2 tablespoons of the bacon fat in the pot. Add the rosemary and chiles and cook for 1 minute. Add the celery, onion and fennel and cook over moderately low heat, stirring occasionally, until softened, 10 minutes. Add the fish stock and bring to a simmer.

2. In a medium saucepan, melt the butter. Add the flour and cook over moderate heat, stirring, until the roux is the color of peanut butter, about 5 minutes. Scrape the roux into the soup and bring to a boil. Add the potatoes and simmer until tender and the soup has thickened, about 10 minutes. Stir in the cream, season with salt and pepper and return to a simmer.

3. Add the oysters and bacon to the soup and simmer until the oysters are just cooked, 3 minutes. Spoon the chowder into bowls and serve with Tabasco. —*Dylan Fultineer*

MAKE AHEAD The recipe can be prepared through Step 2 and refrigerated overnight. Return to a simmer before proceeding.

WINE Zippy Muscadet from the Loire Valley: 2011 Michel Delhommeau Cuvée Harmonie.

● HEALTHY   ● MAKE AHEAD   ○ VEGETARIAN   ● STAFF FAVORITE

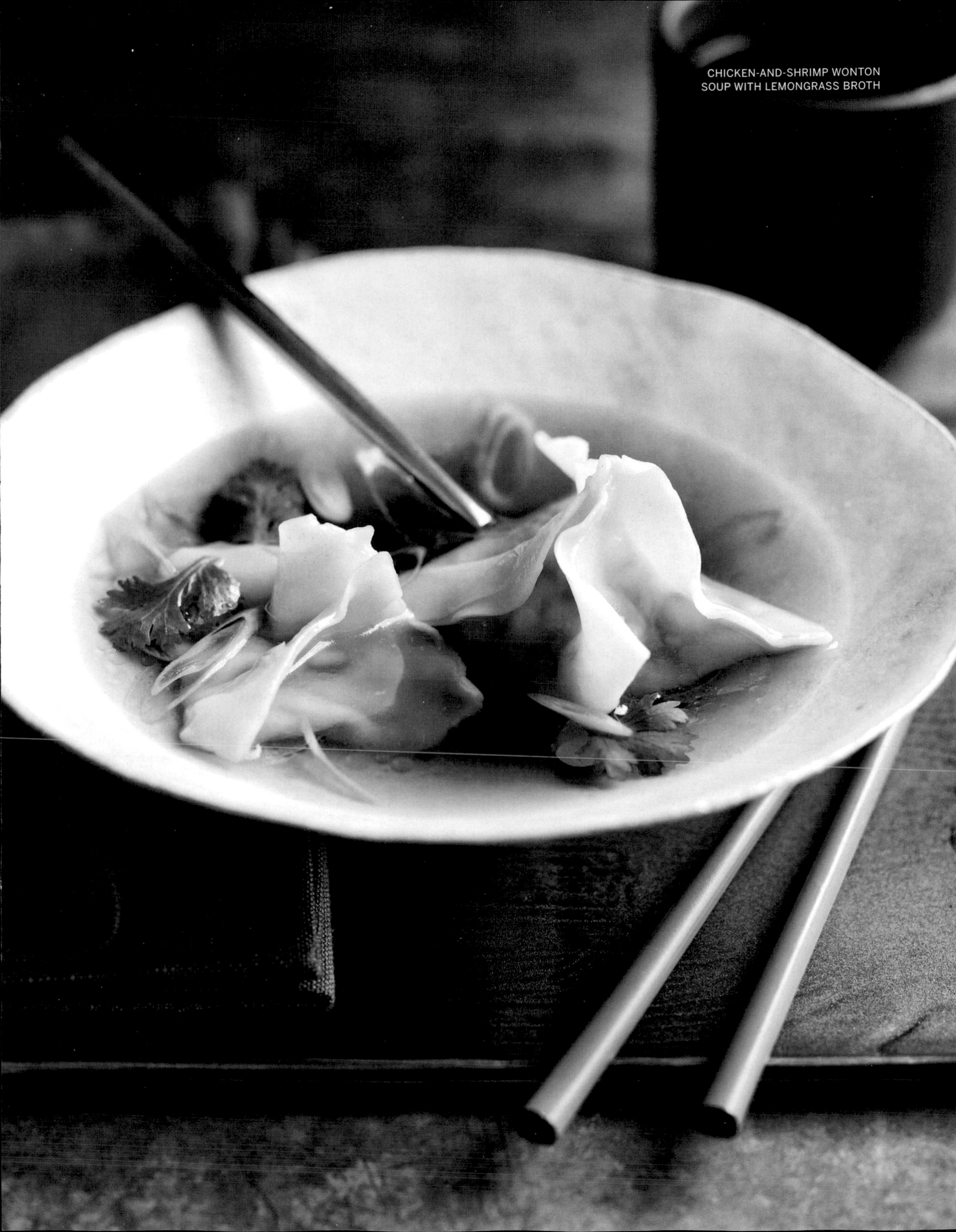

CHICKEN-AND-SHRIMP WONTON
SOUP WITH LEMONGRASS BROTH

Wild Mushroom Goulash

ACTIVE: 45 MIN; TOTAL: 2 HR

6 TO 8 SERVINGS ● ● ◐

This vegetarian goulash contains a lot of sweet paprika, which lends a warm, heady flavor. For the best results, be sure to open a fresh container.

¼ cup extra-virgin olive oil
2 medium onions, coarsely chopped
1 pound Hungarian wax peppers or Italian frying peppers—cored, seeded and chopped
1½ pounds wild mushrooms, cut into 1-inch pieces
1½ pounds cremini or white button mushrooms, quartered
Salt and freshly ground pepper
4 garlic cloves, smashed
1 teaspoon caraway seeds
¼ cup sweet Hungarian paprika
1 tablespoon hot Hungarian paprika
One 28-ounce can diced tomatoes
2 medium Yukon Gold potatoes, peeled and cut into 1-inch pieces
1 pound zucchini, cut into 1-inch pieces
6 cups vegetable broth
2 bay leaves
2 tablespoons fresh bread crumbs
Sour cream and chopped parsley, for serving

1. In a large enameled cast-iron casserole, heat the oil. Add the onions and peppers and cook over moderate heat, stirring, until softened, about 6 minutes. Add all of the mushrooms, season with salt and pepper and cook until browned, about 10 minutes.
2. Using the side of a chef's knife, mash the garlic to a paste with the caraway seeds and a generous pinch of salt; scrape into the casserole. Stir in both paprikas, the tomatoes, potatoes and zucchini. Add the broth and bay leaves, season with salt and pepper and bring to a boil. Cover and cook over low heat until the stew is richly flavored, about 1 hour.
3. Stir the bread crumbs into the stew and cook until slightly thickened, about 10 minutes. Serve with sour cream and parsley. —*Sarah Copeland*

SERVE WITH Copeland's Hungarian Potato Dumplings (page 108).
MAKE AHEAD The goulash can be refrigerated for up to 3 days.
WINE Earthy, red-berried Pinot Noir: 2011 Heron Monterey County.

Chicken Goulash with Biscuit Dumplings

⏱ **TOTAL: 45 MIN • 4 SERVINGS** ●

Creamy chicken stew and biscuits baked together is the ideal meal in a pot. This version is unforgettable: The gravy is boldly spiced, and the biscuits are unbelievably moist and tender thanks to chicken stock and sour cream in the batter.

2 pounds skinless, boneless chicken thighs, cut into 2-inch pieces
Salt and freshly ground pepper
1½ cups all-purpose flour, plus more for dusting
5 tablespoons cold unsalted butter, cut into tablespoons
2 tablespoons extra-virgin olive oil
2 teaspoons baking powder
2½ cups chicken stock
1 cup sour cream
1 large white onion, finely chopped
1 red bell pepper, finely diced
2 garlic cloves, minced
2 tablespoons hot Hungarian paprika
¾ teaspoon caraway seeds
1 teaspoon thyme leaves

1. Preheat the oven to 425°. Season the chicken with salt and pepper; dust lightly with flour. In a deep ovenproof skillet, melt 1 tablespoon of the butter in the olive oil. Add the chicken and cook over high heat, turning once, until browned, 7 minutes. Using a slotted spoon, transfer the chicken to a plate.
2. Meanwhile, in a food processor, pulse the 1½ cups of flour with the baking powder, ½ teaspoon of salt and ¼ teaspoon of pepper. Pulse in the remaining 4 tablespoons of butter until the mixture resembles coarse meal. Whisk ½ cup of the stock with ½ cup of the sour cream and drizzle over the dry ingredients; pulse until a dough forms.

3. Add the onion, bell pepper and garlic to the skillet and cook over high heat, stirring occasionally, until softened, 3 minutes. Return the chicken to the skillet. Stir in the paprika and caraway and cook for 30 seconds. Add the remaining 2 cups of chicken stock and ½ cup of sour cream and stir until smooth. Add the thyme and bring to a boil.
4. Scoop twelve 3-tablespoon-size mounds of biscuit dough over the chicken. Transfer the skillet to the oven and bake for about 20 minutes, until the sauce is bubbling and the biscuits are cooked. Turn on the broiler and broil for about 2 minutes, until the biscuits are golden. Serve the goulash in bowls, spooning the biscuits on top. —*Grace Parisi*
WINE Medium-bodied Cabernet Franc: 2011 Thierry Germain Domaine Des Roches Neuves Saumur Champigny Rouge.

Creamy Reuben Chowder with Rye Croutons

⏱ **TOTAL: 40 MIN • 6 SERVINGS** ● ●

1 tablespoon unsalted butter
1 large onion, very thinly sliced
¾ pound smoked ham, diced
¾ pound andouille sausage, halved lengthwise and sliced ½ inch thick
1½ tablespoons all-purpose flour
4 cups low-sodium chicken broth
1 pound sauerkraut—drained, rinsed and squeezed dry (1½ cups)
¼ cup crème fraîche
¼ cup snipped chives
6 slices of rye bread, cubed and toasted
Prepared horseradish, for serving

In a large enameled cast-iron casserole, melt the butter. Add the onion, cover and cook over moderate heat, stirring, until softened, about 5 minutes. Add the ham and sausage and cook uncovered, stirring, until lightly browned, about 5 minutes. Stir in the flour. Add the broth and sauerkraut and bring to a boil. Simmer over low heat for 15 minutes. Stir in the crème fraîche and chives. Serve in deep bowls with the rye croutons and horseradish. —*Grace Parisi*

● HEALTHY ● MAKE AHEAD ● VEGETARIAN ● STAFF FAVORITE

Crab and Oyster Gumbo

ACTIVE: 30 MIN; TOTAL: 1 HR 30 MIN
8 SERVINGS ●

This sensational seafood-packed gumbo comes from TV personality and F&W contributor Andrew Zimmern. It's terrific in its simplicity, with a foolproof roux (the mix of fat and flour that is the basis for all gumbos) that requires just 15 minutes of stirring instead of the usual hour.

½ cup all-purpose flour
½ cup vegetable oil
1 pound andouille sausage, sliced ¼ inch thick
3 celery ribs, cut into ½-inch dice
1 onion, cut into ½-inch dice
1 red bell pepper, cut into ½-inch dice
1 habanero chile, minced and most seeds discarded
3 garlic cloves, minced
½ pound okra, sliced ¼ inch thick
2 teaspoons dried thyme
1 bay leaf
3 tablespoons filé powder (see Note)
5 cups chicken stock
3 cups bottled clam juice
3 tablespoons Worcestershire sauce
3 large tomatoes, finely chopped
1 pound lump crabmeat, picked over
24 shucked oysters with their liquor
Salt and freshly ground pepper

1. In a pot, stir the flour and oil until smooth. Cook over moderate heat, stirring often, until the roux turns a rich brown color, 15 minutes. Add the andouille, celery, onion, bell pepper, habanero, garlic, okra, thyme, bay leaf and half of the filé powder and cook over moderate heat, stirring, until the onion is translucent. Add the stock, clam juice, Worcestershire and tomatoes; bring to a boil. Reduce the heat to low and simmer for 1 hour, stirring.
2. Stir in the remaining filé powder; add the crab, oysters and their liquor. Season with salt and pepper; simmer gently for 1 minute to just cook the oysters. —Andrew Zimmern
NOTE Filé powder is used as a thickener. Look for it in the spice section of supermarkets.
BEER Malty New Orleans lager: Abita Amber.

Senegalese-Style Seafood Gumbo

⊙ TOTAL: 45 MIN • 6 SERVINGS ●

Inspired by his time in Senegal, South Carolina chef Sean Brock created this delicious, untraditional gumbo using dende (palm) oil, dried shrimp and fish sauce.

Two 1-pound red snappers—
    cleaned, filleted, skinned
    and coarsely chopped, heads
    and bones reserved
1 quart chicken stock or
    low-sodium broth
1 onion, chopped
¾ pound okra, thinly sliced
    and smashed in a mortar
    and pestle
Two 3-ounce cans smoked oysters
10 small dried shrimp
    (see Note)
6 garlic cloves, thinly sliced
3 dried cayenne or árbol chiles
3 tablespoons Asian fish sauce
18 large head-on shrimp
    (about 2¼ pounds)
½ cup palm oil (see Note)
½ pound jumbo lump crabmeat
Kosher salt
Steamed rice, for serving

1. In a pot, combine the fish heads and bones with the stock, onion and 8 cups of water and bring to a boil. Reduce the heat to low and simmer for 20 minutes, skimming off any foam from the surface. Strain the broth into a large bowl.
2. Wipe out the pot and return the broth to it. Add the okra, oysters, dried shrimp, garlic, chiles and fish sauce and bring to a simmer. Cook over moderately low heat for 10 minutes, stirring occasionally. Add the snapper fillets, shrimp and palm oil and simmer until the fish and shrimp are just cooked through, about 4 minutes. Stir in the crab and cook for 1 minute, until heated through. Season with salt. Serve with rice. —Sean Brock
NOTE Dried shrimp are available at Asian markets. Palm oil (also known as dende oil) comes from the fruit of the African oil palm.

It adds a rich flavor and red color to this gumbo. Look for it at specialty food shops and online at amazon.com.
BEER Slightly sweet brown ale: Wolaver's.

Senegalese Okra Stew

⊙ TOTAL: 45 MIN • 4 SERVINGS ● ● ○

This vegan stew is surprisingly rich and satisfying. Its creamy texture comes from the cashew butter that's stirred in at the end.

2 tablespoons vegetable oil
1 small sweet onion, sliced
1 tablespoon minced peeled fresh ginger
2 garlic cloves, minced
1 habanero, seeded and minced
1 tablespoon ground cumin
½ teaspoon ground turmeric
1½ cups ½-inch cubed
    butternut squash
Salt
3½ cups low-sodium vegetable broth
¾ pound okra, trimmed and sliced crosswise ¾ inch thick
¼ cup cashew butter
Cilantro leaves, for garnish

1. In a large, heavy pot, heat the vegetable oil. Add the onion, ginger and garlic and cook over moderate heat, stirring occasionally, until softened, 5 to 6 minutes. Add the habanero, cumin and turmeric and cook, stirring, for 2 minutes. Add the butternut squash, season with salt and cook, stirring, until the squash is coated with the seasonings in the pan. Add 3 cups of the vegetable broth and bring to a boil. Simmer over moderately low heat, stirring occasionally, until the butternut squash is nearly tender, 5 to 6 minutes. Stir in the okra and cook until tender, about 3 minutes.
2. In a bowl, whisk the cashew butter with the remaining ½ cup of vegetable broth. Stir the mixture into the stew and simmer for 5 minutes. Serve the okra stew in deep bowls, garnished with cilantro leaves. —Grace Parisi
MAKE AHEAD The stew can be refrigerated overnight.

Ed's Portuguese Fish Stew

ACTIVE: 45 MIN; TOTAL: 1 HR 30 MIN
6 SERVINGS

At Connie & Ted's, his L.A. spot modeled on a New England seafood shack, chef Michael Cimarusti offers this flavorful stew named after his Portuguese uncle. It's loaded with clams, mussels and cod as well as chunks of smoky, mildly hot Portuguese sausage.

- 5 Anaheim chiles or Italian frying peppers
- ¼ cup extra-virgin olive oil
- ½ pound *linguiça* sausage, quartered lengthwise and sliced crosswise ¼ inch thick (see Note)
- 1 large onion, finely chopped
- 6 garlic cloves, minced
- 2 thyme sprigs
- 2 bay leaves
- ½ teaspoon crushed red pepper

Kosher salt and freshly ground black pepper
- ½ cup dry white wine
- 3 cups bottled clam juice or fish stock
- 1½ pounds unpeeled new potatoes, halved
- 4 medium tomatoes (1¼ pounds)— halved, seeded and chopped
- 1 pound Manila or littleneck clams, scrubbed
- 2 pounds skinless cod fillets, cut into 1-inch pieces
- 1 pound mussels, scrubbed and debearded

Finely chopped cilantro and parsley, for garnish

1. Roast the Anaheim chiles directly over a gas flame or under a preheated broiler, turning, until charred all over. Let cool. Peel, seed and stem the chiles, then coarsely chop them.
2. In a large saucepan, heat the olive oil until shimmering. Add the sausage and cook over moderate heat, stirring, just until the fat starts to render, about 3 minutes. Add the chopped roasted chiles, onion, garlic, thyme, bay leaves, crushed red pepper and a generous pinch each of salt and black pepper.

Cook, stirring occasionally, until the vegetables are softened, about 5 minutes. Stir in the wine and simmer over moderately low heat until slightly reduced, about 3 minutes. Stir in the clam juice, potatoes and tomatoes. Cover the saucepan and cook over low heat, stirring occasionally, until the potatoes are just tender, about 25 minutes.
3. Add the clams to the saucepan, cover and cook over moderately low heat for 3 minutes. Gently stir in the cod and mussels, cover and cook until the clams and mussels have opened and the cod is just white throughout, about 10 minutes; discard any shellfish that haven't opened. Season with salt and black pepper. Ladle the fish stew into shallow bowls and garnish with cilantro and parsley. Serve. —*Michael Cimarusti*

SERVE WITH Crusty bread.

NOTE *Linguiça* is a smoky Portuguese cured sausage widely available at specialty food markets. Andouille sausage can be used as an alternative.

WINE Citrusy Albariño from Spain's coastal Rías Baixas region: 2011 Fefiñanes.

Gumbo z'Herbes

ACTIVE: 1 HR; TOTAL: 3 HR
8 TO 10 SERVINGS ● ●

New Orleans cooks traditionally make this smothered greens dish without meat for Good Friday. California chef David Kinch, however, prepares his gumbo z'herbes with lots of pork, as well as eight different kinds of greens, including carrot tops.

GREENS
- ½ pound mustard greens, stemmed
- ½ pound collard greens, stemmed
- ½ pound turnip greens or kale, stemmed
- ½ pound spinach, stemmed
- 1 cup carrot-top greens
- 1 bunch of watercress
- ¼ head of iceberg lettuce
- ¾ pound green cabbage
- 1 medium white onion, chopped
- 6 garlic cloves, chopped
- 4 scallions, chopped
- 2 tablespoons all-purpose flour

PORK
- 1½ pounds trimmed boneless pork shoulder, cut into 1-inch pieces

Kosher salt and freshly ground black pepper

Cayenne pepper
- 1 pound hot andouille sausage, cut into ½-inch rounds
- ½ pound smoked ham, cut into ½-inch pieces
- 1½ teaspoons chopped thyme
- 1½ teaspoons filé powder (see Note)

Hot sauce and apple cider vinegar, for serving

1. PREPARE THE GREENS Coarsely chop all of the greens and add them to a very large pot along with the chopped onion, garlic and scallions. Add 2 quarts of water and bring to a boil. Cover partially and simmer over moderate heat until the greens are very tender and lose their bright color, about 30 minutes. Using a slotted spoon, scoop the greens into a food processor along with the flour and coarsely puree.

2. PREPARE THE PORK Return the broth in the pot to a boil and add the pork shoulder pieces. Season with salt, freshly ground black pepper and cayenne pepper. Simmer over low heat, partially covered, for about 30 minutes. Add the andouille sausage, smoked ham, thyme and pureed greens and simmer, partially covered, for 1 hour. Stir the filé powder into the gumbo z'herbes and serve with hot sauce and apple cider vinegar. —*David Kinch*

SERVE WITH Bowls of steamed rice.

NOTE Filé powder (also called gumbo filé) is made from ground dried sassafras leaves. Used both to flavor and thicken the gumbo, it has a distinctive earthy flavor. It is available in the spice section of some supermarkets and online at *amazon.com*.

MAKE AHEAD The gumbo can be refrigerated for up to 5 days.

WINE Full-bodied, herbal southern French Cabernet Franc: 2011 Domaine Laroque Cité de Carcassonne.

● HEALTHY ● MAKE AHEAD ● VEGETARIAN ● STAFF FAVORITE

ED'S PORTUGUESE FISH STEW

Short Rib Stew with Caramelized Kimchi

ACTIVE: 45 MIN; TOTAL: 3 HR 30 MIN
8 TO 10 SERVINGS ● ●

½ cup low-sodium soy sauce
3 tablespoons chopped garlic
1 tablespoon minced fresh ginger
1 small Asian pear, grated (¼ cup)
1 teaspoon freshly ground pepper
2 scallions, thinly sliced, plus more for serving
¼ cup toasted sesame oil
6 pounds English-cut beef short ribs (twelve 4-by-2-by-2-inch pieces)
2 tablespoons canola oil
1 small onion, finely chopped
1 quart low-sodium chicken broth
1 large daikon, peeled and cut into 1½-inch chunks
4 large carrots, peeled and cut into 1-inch chunks
2 baking potatoes (1½ pounds), peeled and cut into 1-inch chunks
2 cups (12 ounces) chopped napa cabbage kimchi
4 radishes, thinly sliced

1. In a large bowl, whisk the soy sauce, garlic, ginger, pear, pepper, 2 sliced scallions and 2 tablespoons of the sesame oil. Add the ribs, turn to coat and let stand at room temperature for 30 minutes or refrigerate overnight, stirring occasionally.
2. Heat the canola oil in a large Dutch oven or enameled cast-iron casserole. Lift half of the ribs from the marinade, brushing off the solids, and sear over moderately high heat until browned on all sides, 5 minutes. Transfer to a baking sheet and repeat with the remaining ribs; reserve the marinade separately.
3. Add the onion and 2 tablespoons of water to the pot and cook for 2 minutes, stirring to release the browned bits on the bottom. Return the ribs and any accumulated juices to the pot. Add the reserved marinade, broth and 6 cups of water; bring to a boil. Cover and simmer over moderately low heat for 1 hour, skimming occasionally. Uncover and simmer for 1 hour, stirring and skimming occasionally.

4. Add the daikon, carrots and potatoes to the stew and simmer briskly until the meat is very tender, the vegetables are tender and the sauce is thickened, 30 minutes longer.
5. Meanwhile, in a medium nonstick skillet, heat 1 tablespoon of the sesame oil over moderately high heat. Add half of the kimchi and cook, turning occasionally, until golden and lightly caramelized. Transfer to a plate. Repeat with the remaining sesame oil and kimchi.
6. Serve the stew topped with the kimchi and radishes and garnished with sliced scallions.
—Kay Chun

SERVE WITH White or brown rice.

WINE Generous, fruit-forward Garnacha: 2010 The Show.

Short Rib Stew Banh Mi with Quick Pickles and Fresh Herbs
TOTAL: 30 MIN
MAKES 4 SANDWICHES

2 Kirby cucumbers, sliced ¼ inch thick
1 small red onion, thinly sliced
2 cups distilled white vinegar
½ tablespoon sugar
Kosher salt
4 cups leftover Short Rib Stew (2 pieces of meat and 1½ cups of vegetables; recipe at left)
2 tablespoons mayonnaise
Freshly ground pepper
1 baguette, halved lengthwise
½ cup basil leaves
1 cup small cilantro sprigs

1. Place the cucumbers and red onion separately in 2 small bowls. In a small saucepan, combine ½ cup of water with the vinegar, sugar and 1 tablespoon of salt; stir over moderate heat just until the sugar dissolves. Pour the brine over the cucumbers and onion and let stand at room temperature for 30 minutes, stirring occasionally; drain the pickles.
2. Meanwhile, thinly slice the leftover meat from the beef stew. Lightly rinse the leftover vegetables and pat dry. In a food processor, combine the vegetables and mayonnaise and puree. Season with salt and pepper.

3. Spread the vegetable mayo on the bottom half of the baguette. Top with the pickles, meat and herbs. Top with the other baguette half, cut into 4 sandwiches and serve.
—Kay Chun

BEER Crisp, palate-refreshing pilsner: Victory Prima Pils.

Short Rib Bourguignon
TOTAL: 5 HR PLUS 2 DAYS MARINATING AND CHILLING • 10 SERVINGS ●

5 pounds trimmed boneless beef short ribs, cut into 2½-inch pieces
9 carrots—5 cut into 2-inch pieces, 4 cut into 1-inch rounds
5 celery ribs, cut into 2-inch pieces
5 medium onions, quartered
10 garlic cloves
One 750-milliliter bottle dry red wine
Salt and freshly ground pepper
¼ cup extra-virgin olive oil
6 cups beef stock
1 pound meaty slab bacon—half cut into 2-inch pieces, half cut into ¼-inch-thick lardons
3 bay leaves tied with 15 thyme sprigs
2 pounds stemmed button mushrooms
Chopped flat-leaf parsley, for garnish

1. In a 2-gallon resealable plastic bag, combine the beef, 2-inch carrot pieces, celery, onions, garlic and wine; refrigerate overnight.
2. Preheat the oven to 300°. Strain the beef and vegetables over a bowl; reserve the wine. Separate the meat from the vegetables. Pat the meat dry and season with salt and pepper. In a large enameled cast-iron casserole, heat the olive oil. In batches, sear the meat over high heat until browned on all sides, 30 minutes; transfer the meat to a bowl as you go.
3. Reduce the heat to moderate, add the marinated vegetables and cook until softened, 8 minutes. Add the reserved wine, stock, large bacon pieces, herb bundle and meat along with any juices; bring to a simmer.
4. Braise the stew in the oven for 3½ hours, until the meat is tender. Using a slotted spoon, transfer the meat and bacon to a bowl. Strain the liquid, discarding the solids.

● HEALTHY ● MAKE AHEAD ● VEGETARIAN ● STAFF FAVORITE

5. Wipe out the casserole. Add the lardons; crisp over moderately high heat, 10 minutes; transfer to paper towels. In batches, cook the mushrooms until golden, 8 minutes per batch. Add them to the meat.

6. Add the carrot rounds and braising liquid to the pot and simmer until the liquid is reduced by one-third. Add the meat, bacon, lardons and mushrooms; simmer until the sauce reduces slightly. Season with salt and pepper and let cool. Refrigerate overnight.

7. Skim the fat from the stew and reheat. Garnish with parsley and serve. —*Aaron Barnett*
WINE Concentrated, berry-rich Beaujolais: 2011 Guy Breton Morgon.

Beef Stew in Red Wine Sauce

ACTIVE: 1 HR; TOTAL: 2 HR 40 MIN
4 SERVINGS ● ●

Master chef Jacques Pépin relies strictly on robust red wine for his stew's deep flavor.

- 1 tablespoon unsalted butter
- 2 tablespoons olive oil
- 2 pounds trimmed beef flatiron steak or chuck, cut into 8 pieces
- Salt and freshly ground black pepper
- 1 cup finely chopped onion
- 1 tablespoon finely chopped garlic
- 1 tablespoon all-purpose flour
- One 750-milliliter bottle dry red wine
- 2 bay leaves
- 1 thyme sprig
- One 5-ounce piece of pancetta
- 15 pearl onions, peeled
- 15 cremini mushrooms
- 15 baby carrots, peeled
- Sugar
- Chopped fresh parsley, for garnish

1. Preheat the oven to 350°. In a large enameled cast-iron casserole, melt the butter in 1 tablespoon of the olive oil. Arrange the meat in the casserole in a single layer and season with salt and pepper. Cook over moderately high heat, turning occasionally, until browned on all sides, 8 minutes. Add the chopped onion and garlic and cook over moderate heat, stirring occasionally, until the onion is softened, 5 minutes. Add the flour and stir to coat the meat with it. Add the wine, bay leaves and thyme, season with salt and pepper and bring to a boil, stirring to dissolve any brown bits stuck to the bottom of the pot.

2. Cover the casserole and transfer it to the oven. Cook the stew for 1½ hours, until the meat is very tender and the sauce is flavorful.

3. Meanwhile, in a saucepan, cover the pancetta with 2 cups of water and bring to a boil. Reduce the heat and simmer for 30 minutes. Drain the pancetta and slice it ½ inch thick, then cut the slices into 1-inch-wide lardons.

4. In a large skillet, combine the pancetta, pearl onions, mushrooms and carrots. Add the remaining 1 tablespoon of olive oil, ¼ cup of water and a large pinch each of sugar, salt and pepper. Bring to a boil, cover and simmer until almost all of the water has evaporated, 15 minutes. Uncover and cook over high heat, tossing, until the vegetables are tender and nicely browned, about 4 minutes.

5. To serve, stir some of the vegetables and lardons into the stew and scatter the rest on top as a garnish. Top with a little chopped parsley and serve. —*Jacques Pépin*
WINE Robust, dark-fruited Cabernet Sauvignon: 2011 Ramsay North Coast.

Penang Beef Curry

ACTIVE: 25 MIN; TOTAL: 1 HR 30 MIN
4 TO 6 SERVINGS ● ●

BRAISED BEEF
- One 2-inch piece of peeled fresh ginger, thinly sliced
- 5 cilantro stems
- 3 garlic cloves
- 1 teaspoon whole black peppercorns
- 1 teaspoon whole cloves
- 1 star anise pod
- 3 tablespoons soy sauce
- 1 tablespoon black soy sauce (see Note) or ¾ teaspoon soy sauce mixed with ¼ teaspoon molasses
- 2 teaspoons crushed rock sugar or turbinado sugar
- Kosher salt
- 2 pounds hanger steak, cut into 1-inch cubes

PENANG CURRY
- 2 tablespoons vegetable oil
- 1½ tablespoons Penang or red curry paste (see Note)
- 1 cup unsweetened coconut milk
- 1 tablespoon Asian fish sauce
- 1½ tablespoons freshly squeezed lime juice
- 2 teaspoons sugar
- Kosher salt
- Cilantro leaves, for garnish

1. PREPARE THE BRAISED BEEF Wrap the ginger, cilantro stems, garlic, peppercorns, cloves and star anise in a cheesecloth bundle and tie with kitchen string. In a large saucepan, combine 3 quarts of water with the spice bundle, both soy sauces, rock sugar and ½ teaspoon of salt and bring to a boil. Add the steak cubes and simmer over moderately low heat, stirring occasionally, until the meat is tender, about 1 hour. Using a slotted spoon, transfer the meat to a plate. Discard the spice bundle and reserve the spiced broth for another use.

2. MEANWHILE, MAKE THE CURRY In a large, deep skillet, heat the vegetable oil until shimmering. Add the curry paste and fry over moderately high heat, stirring, until the paste is fragrant and the oil is bright red, about 2 minutes. Add the coconut milk, fish sauce, lime juice and sugar and bring just to a simmer.

3. Add the steak cubes to the curry sauce and simmer over moderate heat, stirring occasionally, until the sauce is slightly reduced, about 5 minutes. Season with salt. Ladle the beef curry into bowls and garnish with cilantro. Serve right away.
—*Bank Atcharawan*

SERVE WITH Steamed white rice and lime wedges.

NOTE Black soy sauce and Penang curry paste are available at Asian markets and online at *kalustyans.com.*

MAKE AHEAD The beef curry can be covered and refrigerated for up to 2 days. Reheat gently before serving.

WINE Steely, citrusy Australian Riesling: 2012 Frankland Estate Isolation Ridge.

Lamb Shank Posole

ACTIVE: 1 HR; TOTAL: 3 HR 30 MIN
8 SERVINGS ● ● ●

¼ cup canola oil
8 lamb shanks (about 8 pounds)
Kosher salt and freshly ground pepper
1 head of garlic, halved crosswise
1 large red onion, diced
3 celery ribs, diced
2 medium carrots, diced
One 2-inch cinnamon stick
2 tablespoons chopped oregano
2 teaspoons ground cumin
8 dried guajillo chiles, stemmed,
   4 chopped
3 quarts chicken stock
¼ cup extra-virgin olive oil
1 teaspoon ground coriander
Two 15-ounce cans hominy,
   rinsed and drained
One 15-ounce can pinto beans,
   rinsed and drained
2 tablespoons fresh lime juice

1. Preheat the oven to 375°. In a large enameled cast-iron casserole, heat 2 tablespoons of the canola oil. Season the lamb shanks with salt and pepper. Add 4 shanks to the casserole; cook over moderately high heat, turning, until browned all over, 7 to 8 minutes; transfer to a baking sheet. Repeat with the remaining canola oil and lamb shanks.
2. Add the garlic and half each of the onion, celery and carrots to the casserole; cook, stirring, until golden, 5 minutes. Stir in the cinnamon, oregano, 1 teaspoon of the cumin and the chopped chiles. Add the lamb and any juices. Add the chicken stock and bring to a boil. Cover and braise in the oven for about 2 hours, until the lamb is very tender.
3. Meanwhile, in a heatproof bowl, cover the whole chiles with 2 cups of boiling water; soak for 30 minutes. Transfer the chiles and 1 cup of the soaking liquid to a blender; puree.
4. Transfer the lamb shanks to a baking sheet and loosely tent them with aluminum foil. Strain the broth into a large bowl, discarding the solids. Skim the fat from the surface of the broth. Wipe out the casserole.

5. Heat the olive oil in the casserole. Add the remaining onion, celery and carrots; cook over moderate heat, stirring occasionally, until golden, about 5 minutes. Stir in the chile puree, the coriander, hominy, pinto beans and the remaining 1 teaspoon of cumin and cook for about 2 minutes. Add the strained broth and simmer for about 10 minutes. Stir in the lime juice and season the posole with salt and pepper. Add the lamb shanks to the casserole and cook just until heated through. Serve the posole in bowls. —*Hugh Acheson*
SERVE WITH Cilantro, avocado and lime.
WINE Medium-bodied Garnacha: 2011 Bodegas Nekeas El Chaparral de Vega Sindoa.

Portuguese Beef Stew with Ruby Port

ACTIVE: 30 MIN; TOTAL: 3 HR
6 SERVINGS ●

2 tablespoons extra-virgin olive oil
3 pounds well-trimmed boneless beef
   short ribs, cut into 1½-inch pieces
Salt and freshly ground pepper
2 large Spanish onions,
   very thinly sliced
3 carrots, cut into ½-inch chunks
1 cup ruby port
1½ cups dry red wine

1. In a large enameled cast-iron casserole, heat the oil until shimmering. Season the beef generously with salt and pepper; add half to the pan. Cook over moderately high heat, turning occasionally, until browned all over, 8 minutes. Using a slotted spoon, transfer to a large plate; brown the remaining meat.
2. Return all of the meat to the casserole. Add the onions, cover and cook over moderately high heat, stirring occasionally, until softened, 5 minutes. Add the carrots and cook until crisp-tender, 5 minutes longer. Add the port and simmer until evaporated. Add the red wine and reduce the heat to low. Cover tightly and cook until the meat is very tender, about 2 hours. Spoon off the fat and serve the stew right away. —*Dirk Niepoort*
WINE Rich, berry-inflected Douro red blend: 2009 Niepoort Vertente.

Three-Chile Beef Chili

ACTIVE: 45 MIN; TOTAL: 3 HR
8 TO 10 SERVINGS ●

2 ancho chiles
2 dried New Mexico chiles
3 dried chipotle chiles
1 tablespoon coriander seeds, toasted
1 teaspoon each of cumin seeds and
   yellow mustard seeds, toasted
1 teaspoon dried thyme
2 whole garlic cloves, plus
   1 tablespoon minced garlic
Three 14.5-ounce cans peeled whole
   tomatoes, drained
2 tablespoons canola oil
2 pounds ground beef
1 large onion, diced
6 ounces meaty bacon, diced (1 cup)
6 cups chicken stock
2 cups stout beer
2 cups brewed coffee
½ cup crushed tortilla chips
8 cilantro sprigs, coarsely chopped
Kosher salt
Three 15-ounce cans pinto beans,
   rinsed and drained

1. In a heatproof bowl, cover the chiles with boiling water and let stand until softened, 15 minutes; drain. Stem and seed the chiles and transfer to a blender. Add the coriander, cumin, mustard seeds, thyme, garlic cloves and one-third of the tomatoes; puree.
2. In a large enameled cast-iron casserole, heat the oil. Add half of the ground beef and brown over moderately high heat, about 2 minutes. Transfer the meat to a plate. Repeat with the remaining ground beef.
3. Add the onion and bacon to the pot; cook until the onion is golden. Add the minced garlic; cook for 1 minute. Add the beef and chile puree; cook, stirring, for 2 minutes. Add the stock, beer, coffee, chips, cilantro and remaining tomatoes; season with salt. Bring to a boil, cover and simmer over moderate heat for 1 hour. Add the beans; cook uncovered for 1 hour. Season with salt. —*Tony Maws*
SERVE WITH Sour cream, grated cheddar and tortilla chips.

● HEALTHY ● MAKE AHEAD ● VEGETARIAN ● STAFF FAVORITE

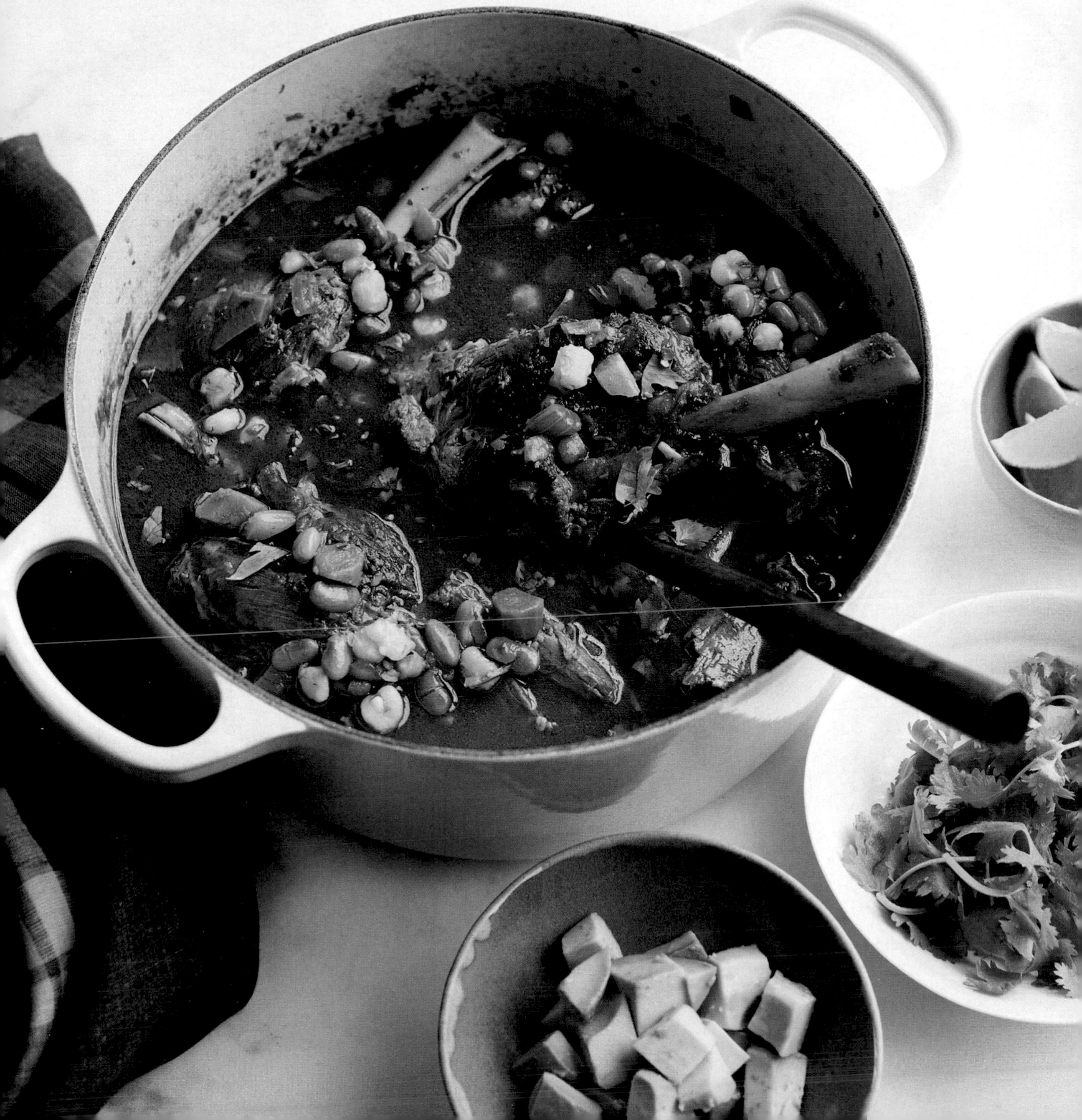

TV host Jimmy Fallon gets a private pasta-making tutorial from Italian cooking guru Mario Batali.

Opposite: recipe, page 109.

FETTUCCINE WITH SPICY
SAUSAGE AND CABBAGE RIBBONS

PASTA & NOODLES

Bucatini with Clams and Red Peppers

⏱ **TOTAL: 45 MIN • 6 SERVINGS** ●

This riff on pasta with clams features strips of roasted pepper and toasted walnuts along with Middle Eastern flavors like pomegranate molasses and cumin.

⅓ cup walnuts
2 large red bell peppers
6 tablespoons extra-virgin olive oil, plus more for drizzling
2 large garlic cloves, minced
1½ pounds plum tomatoes, peeled and coarsely chopped
1 teaspoon ground cumin
1 teaspoon smoked paprika
¼ cup fresh orange juice
1 tablespoon pomegranate molasses
32 littleneck clams, scrubbed
1 pound bucatini
¼ cup chopped mint
¼ cup chopped flat-leaf parsley
¼ cup chopped basil
Salt

1. Preheat the oven to 350°. Spread the walnuts in a pie plate and toast for about 12 minutes, until golden. Let the nuts cool, then coarsely chop them.
2. Roast the peppers over a gas flame or under a broiler until blackened all over. Transfer to a bowl, cover and let cool. Peel and seed the peppers, then cut into very thin strips.
3. In a very large, deep skillet, heat the 6 tablespoons of olive oil. Add the garlic and cook over moderate heat, stirring, until fragrant, 30 seconds. Add the peppers, tomatoes, cumin and paprika and cook until the tomatoes are softened and just beginning to break down, 3 minutes. Add the orange juice and molasses and bring to a boil. Add the clams, cover and cook over high heat, shaking the pan occasionally, until the shells have opened, 6 minutes. Discard any unopened clams.
4. Meanwhile, in a large pot of salted boiling water, cook the bucatini until al dente. Drain the pasta and reserve ½ cup of the water. Return the pasta to the pot. Pour the clams,

vegetables and sauce over the pasta and cook, stirring, for 1 minute; add some of the reserved pasta water if it seems dry. Add the herbs and walnuts, season lightly with salt and toss gently. Transfer to wide bowls, drizzle with olive oil and serve. —*Jody Adams*
WINE Briny, fresh Vermentino: 2011 Argiolas Costamolino.

Sauce-Simmered Spaghetti al Pomodoro

⏱ **TOTAL: 30 MIN**

4 FIRST-COURSE SERVINGS ● ○

After parboiling spaghetti, chef Sarah Grueneberg of Chicago's Spiaggia finishes cooking the pasta right in the tomato sauce, infusing it with flavor.

¼ cup extra-virgin olive oil, plus more for drizzling
2 garlic cloves, thinly sliced
Pinch of crushed red pepper
One 28-ounce can peeled San Marzano tomatoes, pureed until smooth
Salt
½ pound spaghetti
1 basil sprig, plus torn basil leaves for garnish
Freshly grated Parmigiano-Reggiano cheese, for serving

1. In a large, deep skillet, heat the ¼ cup of olive oil. Add the garlic and crushed red pepper and cook over moderate heat, stirring, until the garlic is golden, about 1 minute. Add the tomato puree, season with salt and simmer the sauce until thickened, 15 minutes.
2. Meanwhile, bring a large pot of salted water to a boil. Add the spaghetti; cook until pliable but still hard in the center, about 5 minutes. Drain, reserving 1½ cups of the water.
3. Add the spaghetti, cooking water and basil sprig to the tomato sauce and cook over moderately low heat, stirring gently, until the pasta is al dente and the sauce is thickened and clings to the strands, 8 minutes longer. Discard the basil sprig. Transfer the spaghetti to bowls. Drizzle with olive oil and garnish with basil leaves. Serve with grated cheese. —*Sarah Grueneberg*

All'Amatriciana with Extra Umami

⏱ **TOTAL: 30 MIN • 6 SERVINGS** ●

Classic pasta all'amatriciana features a spicy tomato sauce studded with bits of *guanciale* (Italian cured pork jowl). Here the sauce includes anchovies, making it extra-savory.

3 tablespoons extra-virgin olive oil
3 ounces *guanciale* or pancetta, finely diced (see Note)
½ medium onion, thinly sliced
2 teaspoons minced anchovy fillet
1 large garlic clove, minced
One 14.5-ounce can crushed San Marzano tomatoes
1 pound spaghetti
½ cup torn basil leaves
1 teaspoon crushed red pepper
½ cup freshly grated Pecorino Romano cheese, plus more for serving
Kosher salt and freshly ground black pepper

1. In a large, deep skillet, heat the olive oil. Add the *guanciale* and cook over moderate heat, stirring, until opaque, about 3 minutes. Add the onion, anchovy and garlic and cook over moderately low heat, stirring occasionally, until the onion is softened, about 5 minutes. Add the tomatoes and cook until hot, about 2 minutes.
2. In a large pot of salted boiling water, cook the spaghetti until pliable but still hard in the center, about 5 minutes. Drain the pasta, reserving 2 cups of the cooking water.
3. Add the pasta and cooking water to the sauce and cook until the pasta is al dente; add more water if the sauce gets too thick. Remove the skillet from the heat and stir in the basil, crushed red pepper and the ½ cup of Pecorino Romano. Season with salt and black pepper, transfer to bowls and serve, passing more cheese at the table. —*Sarah Grueneberg*
NOTE *Guanciale,* cured pork jowl, is available at Italian markets, butcher shops and online at *formaggiokitchen.com*.
WINE Spicy, bright, cherry-scented Chianti Classico: 2009 Marchesi Antinori Pèppoli.

● HEALTHY ● MAKE AHEAD ○ VEGETARIAN ● STAFF FAVORITE

BUCATINI WITH CLAMS
AND RED PEPPERS

Fresh Chile Puttanesca

⏱ TOTAL: 40 MIN • 6 SERVINGS ● ●

Swapping in green olives and fresh chile for the usual black olives and crushed red pepper creates an especially vibrant puttanesca.

¼ cup extra-virgin olive oil, plus more for drizzling
3 ounces green olives, such as Castelvetrano, pitted and chopped (½ cup)
1 tablespoon plus 1 teaspoon drained capers, chopped
One 2-ounce can anchovy fillets in oil, drained and chopped
1 Fresno chile or jalapeño, seeded and minced
2 garlic cloves, thinly sliced
½ cup chopped oil-packed sun-dried tomatoes
½ cup canned crushed San Marzano tomatoes
¼ cup sliced almonds
1 cup dry white wine
1 pound spaghetti
¼ cup chopped flat-leaf parsley
¼ cup torn basil leaves
½ teaspoon finely grated lemon zest
1 tablespoon freshly squeezed lemon juice

1. In a large, deep pot, heat the ¼ cup of olive oil. Add the olives, capers, anchovies, chile and garlic and cook over moderately high heat until sizzling. Add the sun-dried and crushed tomatoes and the almonds and cook for 1 minute. Add the wine and cook until reduced by half, about 7 minutes.
2. Meanwhile, in a large pot of salted boiling water, cook the pasta until pliable but still hard in the center, about 5 minutes. Drain, reserving 3 cups of water.
3. Add the spaghetti and the reserved cooking water to the sauce and cook until the pasta is al dente. Stir in the parsley, basil, lemon zest and lemon juice and serve in bowls with a drizzle of olive oil.
—*Sarah Grueneberg*
WINE Vibrant, medium-bodied Barbera d'Asti: 2012 Elio Perrone Tasmorcan.

Pasta with Tomato and Black Olive Sauce

TOTAL: 1 HR • 8 SERVINGS ●

5 tablespoons extra-virgin olive oil
1 small white onion, finely chopped
5 garlic cloves, finely chopped
7 oil-packed anchovy fillets, drained and chopped
2 carrots, peeled and cut into ¼-inch dice
2 celery ribs, cut into ¼-inch dice
2 zucchini, cut into ¼-inch dice
1 eggplant, cut into ¼-inch dice
1 summer squash, cut into ¼-inch dice
¾ teaspoon crushed red pepper
Kosher salt and freshly ground pepper
½ cup dry white wine
5 plum tomatoes, cut into ¼-inch dice
½ cup pitted black olives, coarsely chopped
10 fresh basil leaves
1 pound strozzapreti or other pasta
Freshly shaved Parmigiano-Reggiano cheese, for serving

1. In a large pot, heat 2 tablespoons of the olive oil. Add the onion, garlic and anchovies and cook over moderate heat, stirring occasionally, until starting to soften, 5 minutes. Stir in the carrots and celery and cook, stirring occasionally, until softened, 7 to 8 minutes. Add the zucchini, eggplant, summer squash, crushed red pepper and the remaining 3 tablespoons of oil; season with salt and pepper. Cook, stirring occasionally, until the vegetables are softened, 15 minutes. Add the wine and simmer for 2 minutes. Add the tomatoes, olives and basil and cook, stirring, for 10 minutes. Season with salt and pepper.
2. In a large pot of salted boiling water, cook the pasta until al dente. Drain, reserving ½ cup of the cooking water. Add the pasta and cooking water to the vegetables, season with salt and pepper and cook over moderate heat, tossing. Transfer to a bowl, top with cheese and serve. —*Barbara Lynch*
WINE Earthy, medium-bodied Chianti Classico: 2009 La Maialina.

Mushroom Bolognese

TOTAL: 1 HR • 8 SERVINGS ● ●

Using two kinds of mushrooms—king oyster and dried porcini—adds a meaty punch to this vegetarian twist on classic Bolognese.

1 small onion, coarsely chopped
1 medium carrot, coarsely chopped
1 celery rib, coarsely chopped
1 medium parsnip, chopped
½ small turnip, coarsely chopped
1 pound king oyster mushrooms
¼ cup extra-virgin olive oil
Kosher salt and freshly ground black pepper
1 ounce dried porcini mushrooms
½ cup dry red wine
1 small Parmigiano-Reggiano cheese rind, plus ¼ cup freshly grated Parmigiano-Reggiano
Pinch of crushed red pepper
¼ cup heavy cream
1 teaspoon minced rosemary
1½ pounds spaghetti, cooked until al dente and kept warm
4 tablespoons unsalted butter

1. In a food processor, pulse the onion, carrot, celery, parsnip, turnip and king oysters until finely chopped. In a large pot, heat the oil. Add the chopped vegetables, season with salt and black pepper and cook over moderate heat until softened, 20 minutes.
2. In a bowl, cover the porcini with 1½ cups of boiling water; let stand until softened. Drain, reserving 1 cup of the water. Rinse and chop the porcini, add to the vegetables and cook until fragrant, 10 minutes. Add the wine, cheese rind and red pepper; cook until the wine evaporates. Add the reserved porcini water, cover partially and cook over low heat, stirring occasionally, until thick, 25 minutes. Add the heavy cream, rosemary and ¼ cup of grated Parmigiano-Reggiano and simmer for 5 minutes. Discard the rind.
3. Add the warm pasta, butter and 1 cup of water to the sauce and toss, stirring until the pasta is well coated. Serve right away.
—*Sarah Grueneberg*
WINE Savory, spicy Nero d'Avola: 2012 Calea.

● HEALTHY ● MAKE AHEAD ● VEGETARIAN ● STAFF FAVORITE

Spring Pasta with Blistered Cherry Tomatoes

ACTIVE: 45 MIN; TOTAL: 1 HR
6 SERVINGS ○ ●

- 2 bunches of Broccolini (1¼ pounds), thick stems halved lengthwise
- 1 garlic clove, sliced
- ¼ cup plus 2 tablespoons extra-virgin olive oil
- Flaky sea salt and freshly ground pepper
- 2 pounds yellow and red cherry tomatoes
- 6 scallions, white and tender green parts only, cut into 1-inch lengths
- 1 bunch of asparagus, cut into 1½-inch lengths
- 1 pound mafaldine or other curly, wide noodles
- 2 tablespoons unsalted butter
- Large pinch of crushed red pepper
- ¼ cup chopped flat-leaf parsley
- About ½ cup shaved *ricotta salata* cheese, for garnish

1. Preheat the oven to 425°. In a bowl, toss the Broccolini and garlic with ¼ cup of the olive oil and season with sea salt and pepper; spread on a rimmed baking sheet. In another bowl, toss the tomatoes with the remaining 2 tablespoons of olive oil, ½ tablespoon of sea salt and 1 teaspoon of pepper and spread on a rimmed baking sheet. Roast the vegetables for about 25 minutes, until the Broccolini is tender and charred in spots and the tomatoes are very juicy but not broken down.
2. Meanwhile, in a large pot of salted boiling water, cook the scallions until just softened, 1 minute. Using a slotted spoon, transfer to a bowl. Add the asparagus to the pot; cook until just crisp-tender, about 2 minutes. With the slotted spoon, transfer to the bowl.
3. Add the pasta to the boiling water and cook until just al dente. Drain, reserving ½ cup of the pasta cooking water.
4. Return the pasta to the pot and add the roasted Broccolini, scallions, asparagus, butter, crushed red pepper and half of the parsley. Add the reserved pasta water and cook until the pasta is al dente. Gently fold

in the roasted tomatoes and any juices and season with sea salt and pepper. Garnish with the shaved cheese and the remaining parsley and serve right away. —*Mario Batali*
WINE Crisp Italian white: 2011 Bastianich Adriatico Friulano.

Tomato and Almond Pesto

TOTAL: 15 MIN • MAKES 1½ CUPS ○ ● ○

- ¼ cup extra-virgin olive oil
- ½ cup blanched slivered almonds
- 1 cup cherry tomatoes
- 2 large garlic cloves, minced
- 1 packed cup basil leaves
- Salt and freshly ground black pepper

In a large skillet, heat 2 tablespoons of the oil. Add the almonds and toast over high heat, shaking the pan, until lightly browned, 2 minutes. Add the tomatoes and cook until the skins just begin to brown, 2 minutes longer. Let cool, then transfer to a food processor. Add the garlic, basil and remaining 2 tablespoons of oil; pulse until the almonds are chopped. Add ¼ cup of water and process to a chunky puree. Season with salt and pepper and serve. —*Richard Landau*
SERVE WITH Pasta or grilled vegetables.

Sweet Potato and Tomato Pasta Sauce

TOTAL: 30 MIN
MAKES 3 CUPS ● ● ○ ○

- 1 large sweet potato (1 pound), peeled and cut into 2-inch pieces
- 1 large tomato (8 ounces), chopped
- ¼ cup heavy cream
- 2 tablespoons extra-virgin olive oil
- Kosher salt and freshly ground pepper

Put the sweet potato in a large saucepan with enough water to cover by 2 inches. Boil until tender, about 20 minutes. Drain and transfer the sweet potato to a blender. Add the tomato, cream, olive oil and ½ cup of water and puree. Season the sauce with salt and pepper and serve hot. —*Kay Chun*
SERVE WITH Spaghetti.

Whole-Wheat Pappardelle with Arugula Pesto and Corn

TOTAL: 40 MIN
4 FIRST-COURSE SERVINGS

- 2 cups loosely packed wild arugula (about 1 ounce), plus more arugula for garnish
- 1 medium garlic clove, chopped
- 2 tablespoons toasted sliced almonds
- ¼ cup extra-virgin olive oil
- Salt
- ½ pound dried whole-wheat pappardelle (see Note)
- 3 ounces pancetta, sliced ⅛ inch thick and cut into ½-inch strips
- ½ cup finely chopped onion
- Kernels cut from 2 ears of corn (1 cup)
- 2 tablespoons unsalted butter
- Freshly grated Parmigiano-Reggiano cheese, for serving

1. In a pot of salted boiling water, blanch the 2 cups of arugula for 30 seconds. Using tongs, transfer the arugula to a colander and rinse under cold water. Squeeze the arugula dry and transfer to a blender. Add the garlic and almonds and pulse until finely chopped. With the blender on, gradually add the olive oil in a slow, steady stream; season with salt.
2. Add the pappardelle to the boiling water and cook until it is al dente. Drain, reserving ½ cup of the pasta water.
3. Meanwhile, in a large skillet, cook the pancetta over moderate heat, stirring, until browned, 5 minutes. Spoon off most of the fat. Add the onion to the skillet and cook until translucent, 5 minutes. Add the corn and cook until crisp-tender, 1 to 2 minutes.
4. Add the pasta, reserved pasta water, pesto and butter to the skillet and cook, tossing, until the pasta is hot and evenly coated. Season with salt and transfer to a bowl. Garnish the pasta with arugula and serve, passing grated cheese at the table.
—*Jonah Rhodehamel*
NOTE Dried whole-wheat pappardelle is available at *markethallfoods.com*.
WINE Ripe, full-bodied white: 2012 J. Lohr Estates Riverstone Chardonnay.

Fusilli with Shrimp and Lemon Butter

:D **TOTAL: 30 MIN • 4 SERVINGS**

If he's not making his own fresh gluten-free pasta at Le Virtù in Philadelphia, chef Joe Cicala uses the excellent dried corn pasta produced by Rustichella d'Abruzzo. Because of its deep corn flavor, he pairs the pasta with foods that are typically delicious served with polenta, like shrimp.

½ pound short corn pasta, such as fusilli or rigatoni
2 tablespoons fresh lemon juice, plus 1 teaspoon finely grated lemon zest
½ pound rock shrimp or peeled and deveined medium shrimp
6 tablespoons unsalted butter, cubed
Kosher salt and freshly ground pepper
Finely grated *bottarga,* preferably mullet, for sprinkling (optional; see Note)

1. In a large saucepan of salted boiling water, cook the pasta until al dente.
2. While the pasta is cooking, carefully scoop ¼ cup of the cooking water into a large, deep skillet. Add the lemon juice and zest. Arrange the shrimp and butter in the skillet in an even layer and season lightly with salt and freshly ground pepper. Bring to a simmer over moderate heat and cook, stirring gently, until the butter is melted and the shrimp are nearly cooked through, about 4 minutes.
3. Drain the pasta, reserving another ¼ cup of the cooking water; add the pasta to the skillet. Cook over moderate heat, tossing and adding some of the reserved cooking water if needed, until the pasta is well coated and the shrimp are white throughout, 1 minute. Season with salt and pepper. Transfer to bowls, grate *bottarga* over the top and serve. —*Joe Cicala*
NOTE Bottarga is the roe of tuna or mullet that has been salted, pressed and dried; it can be grated or shaved paper-thin. It is available at specialty food stores and online at *gourmetsardinia.com* and *gustiamo.com.*
WINE Crisp, zesty Vermentino: 2011 Casamatta Bianco.

Squid Ink Pasta with Asparagus

:D **TOTAL: 30 MIN • 6 SERVINGS**

The squid ink in the pasta adds mostly color, not flavor, so using any other long noodle in this dish would be fine.

½ cup extra-virgin olive oil
½ pound shallots, thinly sliced
1½ pounds thin asparagus—tips reserved, spears cut into pieces
1 garlic clove, thinly sliced
1 teaspoon crushed red pepper
Salt
¼ cup dry white wine
1 tablespoon Champagne vinegar
1 pound squid ink linguine or tagliatelle
½ cup crème fraîche
2 tablespoons snipped chives
2 tablespoons chopped parsley
1 tablespoon chopped tarragon
¼ cup fine dry bread crumbs
Freshly grated Parmigiano-Reggiano cheese, for serving

1. In a very large, deep skillet, heat ¼ cup plus 2 tablespoons of the oil. Add the shallots and cook over moderate heat, stirring, until softened, 8 minutes. Add the asparagus spears, garlic and crushed red pepper, season with salt and cook until the asparagus is crisp-tender, 3 minutes. Add the wine and vinegar and cook until nearly evaporated, 2 minutes.
2. Meanwhile, in a pot of salted boiling water, cook the pasta until al dente. Drain, reserving ¼ cup of the cooking water. Add the pasta, cooking water, crème fraîche, chives, parsley and tarragon to the skillet. Keep warm.
3. In a medium skillet, heat 1 tablespoon of the oil. Add the asparagus tips, season with salt and cook over high heat until crisp-tender, 3 minutes. Add to the pasta and toss.
4. In the medium skillet, heat the remaining 1 tablespoon of oil. Add the bread crumbs and cook over moderate heat, stirring, until golden. Sprinkle over the pasta and serve, passing grated cheese at the table. —*Terrence Gallivan and Seth Siegel-Gardner*
WINE Lively Oregon Pinot Gris: 2011 Montinore Estate.

Casarecce with Spicy Skate and Snap Peas

:D **TOTAL: 30 MIN • 4 SERVINGS**

At Perla in Manhattan, chef Michael Toscano serves his perfect fresh pastas with untraditional sauces. Here, he tosses a scroll-shaped pasta known as casarecce (fusilli is a good alternative) with skate so that some of the fish breaks down into lovely shreds.

½ to 1 teaspoon seeded and minced habanero chile
1 teaspoon Champagne vinegar
¼ teaspoon sugar
1 pound skinless skate fillet, cut into 1-inch pieces
¼ cup plus 2 tablespoons extra-virgin olive oil, plus more for drizzling
2 tablespoons fresh lemon juice
Kosher salt and freshly ground pepper
½ pound casarecce pasta
1 garlic clove, minced
½ pound sugar snap peas, thinly sliced crosswise
3 tablespoons unsalted butter, cut into cubes

1. In a small bowl, combine the habanero, vinegar and sugar. In a medium bowl, toss the skate with ¼ cup of the olive oil and the lemon juice and season with salt and pepper.
2. In a large saucepan of salted boiling water, cook the pasta until al dente. Drain the pasta, reserving ½ cup of the cooking water.
3. Meanwhile, in a large, deep skillet, add the habanero mixture, garlic and remaining 2 tablespoons of oil; warm over moderate heat until fragrant, 2 minutes. Spread out the skate in the skillet and cook over moderate heat, without stirring, until nearly white, 4 minutes.
4. Gently fold in the sugar snap peas, butter and ¼ cup of the pasta cooking water and cook until the peas are crisp-tender, 3 minutes. Fold in the pasta until it is coated; add more pasta cooking water if the pasta seems dry. Season with salt and pepper. Transfer the pasta to bowls, drizzle with olive oil and serve. —*Michael Toscano*
WINE Citrusy New Zealand Sauvignon Blanc: 2011 Matua Valley.

● HEALTHY ● MAKE AHEAD ○ VEGETARIAN ● STAFF FAVORITE

FUSILLI WITH SHRIMP
AND LEMON BUTTER

Spaghetti with Clams and Crispy Bread Crumbs

🕐 TOTAL: 30 MIN • 6 SERVINGS ●

¼ cup panko (Japanese bread crumbs)
¼ cup plus 1 tablespoon extra-virgin
    olive oil, plus more for drizzling
Kosher salt and freshly ground
    black pepper
2 large garlic cloves, thinly sliced
3 dozen Manila clams or cockles,
    scrubbed
1 cup dry white wine
1 pound spaghetti
1 teaspoon finely grated lemon zest
3 tablespoons fresh lemon juice
2½ tablespoons finely grated mullet
    bottarga (optional; see Note on
    page 96)
1 teaspoon crushed red pepper
2 tablespoons finely chopped thyme
2 tablespoons finely chopped
    rosemary
2 tablespoons finely chopped parsley

1. In a medium skillet, combine the panko with 1 tablespoon of the olive oil and toast over moderate heat, tossing, until golden, about 3 minutes. Season with salt and black pepper and transfer to a small bowl.
2. In a large, deep skillet, heat the remaining ¼ cup of oil. Add the garlic and cook over moderate heat until fragrant, about 1 minute. Add the clams and wine and simmer over moderately high heat until the wine is slightly reduced and the clams just start to open, about 4 minutes.
3. Meanwhile, in a large pot of salted boiling water, cook the pasta until al dente. Drain, reserving ½ cup of the cooking water. Add the pasta, cooking water, lemon zest and juice, *bottarga*, red pepper and herbs to the clams; toss over moderately high heat until the pasta is well coated and the clams are completely open, 2 minutes. Discard any clams that do not open. Season with salt and black pepper; drizzle with olive oil. Sprinkle with the toasted panko and serve. —*Sarah Grueneberg*
WINE Herb-scented white from Liguria: 2010 Bisson ü Pastine Bianchetta.

Cavatelli with Roasted Broccoli Rabe and Harissa

🕐 TOTAL: 35 MIN • 6 SERVINGS ● ●

1¼ pounds broccoli rabe, ends trimmed
¼ cup extra-virgin olive oil
Salt and freshly ground pepper
6 garlic cloves, thinly sliced
1 Fresno or jalapeño chile,
    seeded and thinly sliced
2 teaspoons harissa
½ teaspoon sweet smoked paprika
1 pound cavatelli
Freshly grated Parmigiano-Reggiano
    cheese
½ cup packed mint leaves, chopped
½ cup packed parsley leaves, chopped

1. Preheat the oven to 425°. In a bowl, toss the broccoli rabe with 2 tablespoons of the oil and season with salt and pepper. Arrange the broccoli rabe on 2 baking sheets and roast for 15 minutes, until crisp-tender, then chop.
2. In a deep skillet, heat the remaining 2 tablespoons of oil. Add the garlic, chile and harissa and cook over moderate heat, stirring, for 2 minutes. Add the broccoli rabe and smoked paprika and cook until tender, 2 minutes.
3. Meanwhile, in a large pot of salted boiling water, cook the pasta until al dente; drain, reserving 1 cup of the cooking water. Add the pasta, cooking water and ¼ cup of Parmigiano to the skillet and cook, stirring, until the pasta is coated in a thick sauce, 2 minutes. Stir in the herbs and serve with more cheese. —*Michael Natkin*
WINE Bright, citrusy white: 2012 Loimer Lois Grüner Veltliner.

Orecchiette with Scallions and Pistachio Pesto

🕐 TOTAL: 30 MIN • 6 SERVINGS ● ●
Maverick New York City chefs Frank Falcinelli and Frank Castronovo are known for making phenomenal versions of super-simple dishes at their Frankies Spuntino restaurants. Their pesto has a key ingredient that makes it stand out: Sicily's famous pistachio nuts, which are sweet, fruity and almost shockingly bright green.

7 ounces shelled, roasted, unsalted
    pistachios (1½ cups)
½ cup extra-virgin olive oil
2 tablespoons chopped mint
1 garlic clove, minced
½ cup finely shredded pecorino
    cheese, plus more for serving
2 scallions, cut into 2-inch lengths
    and julienned
Salt
1 pound orecchiette

1. In a food processor, chop the pistachios. Add the olive oil, mint and garlic and pulse to combine. Transfer to a bowl, stir in the ½ cup of pecorino cheese and the scallions and season the pesto with salt.
2. In a large pot of salted boiling water, cook the pasta until al dente; drain, reserving ½ cup of the cooking water. Return the pasta to the pot. Add the cooking water and the pesto and cook over low heat, tossing, until coated. Serve, passing more cheese at the table.
—*Frank Castronovo and Frank Falcinelli*
WINE Brisk, minerally Italian white: 2011 Alois Lageder Riff Pinot Grigio.

Pasta with Sautéed Spring Greens

🕐 TOTAL: 30 MIN • 4 SERVINGS

¾ pound rotini
1 garlic clove, minced
2 tablespoons extra-virgin olive oil
¼ cup plus 2 tablespoons crème
    fraîche or heavy cream
Sautéed Spring Greens with Bacon and
    Mustard Seeds (page 224)
¼ cup freshly grated Parmigiano-
    Reggiano cheese

1. In a large pot of salted boiling water, cook the pasta until al dente. Drain, reserving ½ cup of the cooking water.
2. In a large skillet, cook the garlic in the olive oil over moderate heat until fragrant, about 30 seconds. Add the pasta, crème fraîche, greens and the reserved pasta water. Cook, tossing, for 2 minutes. Stir in the cheese and serve. —*Grace Parisi*

● HEALTHY ● MAKE AHEAD ● VEGETARIAN ● STAFF FAVORITE

CAVATELLI WITH ROASTED
BROCCOLI RABE AND HARISSA

Toasted Fazzoletti with Chanterelles and Hazelnuts

ACTIVE: 1 HR 40 MIN; TOTAL: 6 HR
6 SERVINGS ●

Pugliese peasants used to make pasta from burned wheat. Now, chefs are toasting flour to give pasta a rich, nutty flavor. Chef Chris Pandel of Balena in Chicago creates fazzoletti (handkerchief-like pasta squares) and serves them with butter-sautéed chanterelles.

½ cup hazelnuts
6 tablespoons unsalted butter
1 pound chanterelle mushrooms, thickly sliced
Salt and freshly ground black pepper
1 large shallot, minced
1 tablespoon chopped thyme
Pinch of crushed red pepper
2 tablespoons sherry vinegar
1 cup chicken stock
¾ pound Fresh Toasted Fazzoletti (recipe follows)
¼ cup snipped chives

1. Preheat the oven to 375°. Spread the hazelnuts in a pie plate and toast them for 12 minutes, until the skins split and the nuts are fragrant. Transfer the nuts to a clean kitchen towel and rub off the skins. Coarsely chop the nuts.
2. Meanwhile, in a large, deep skillet, cook 4 tablespoons of the unsalted butter over moderate heat until lightly browned, about 3 minutes. Add the chanterelles, season with salt and black pepper and cook over high heat, stirring occasionally, until all of the liquid has evaporated and the mushrooms are golden, about 8 minutes. Add the shallot, thyme and crushed red pepper and cook over moderately high heat for about 5 minutes, stirring. Add the sherry vinegar and cook until evaporated, scraping up any browned bits from the bottom of the skillet. Add the stock and simmer until reduced by half, about 10 minutes. Season with salt and freshly ground black pepper.
3. In a large pot of salted boiling water, cook the fazzoletti until al dente. Drain and add the pasta to the skillet along with the remaining

2 tablespoons of butter. Cook over moderate heat, stirring, until the pasta is coated with butter, about 2 minutes. Stir in the chives and serve in shallow bowls, garnishing with the toasted hazelnuts. —*Chris Pandel*
WINE Earthy, fruit-forward Barbera from California: 2010 Sobon Estate.

FRESH TOASTED FAZZOLETTI

ACTIVE: 45 MIN; TOTAL: 4 HR 30 MIN
MAKES 1½ POUNDS OF PASTA ● ●

3 cups durum wheat flour (see Note), plus more for dusting
5 large eggs
⅓ cup milk
1 teaspoon kosher salt

1. Preheat the oven to 375°. Spread 1 cup of the flour on a baking sheet and toast for about 30 minutes, stirring once, until fragrant and honey-colored. Let the flour cool.
2. In a food processor, combine the toasted flour with the remaining 2 cups of flour and pulse. With the machine on, add the eggs, milk and salt and blend until the dough comes together; turn out onto a floured work surface and knead 2 or 3 times to form a soft, supple dough. Wrap the dough in plastic and let stand at room temperature for 2 hours.
3. Cut the dough into 4 pieces. Using a pasta machine on the thickest setting, run 1 piece of dough through the machine, dusting with flour. Fold the dough in thirds and run it through the machine at the same setting. Continue to run the dough on successively thinner settings until you are one setting from the thinnest. Dust the dough with flour and drape over a floured work surface while you repeat with the remaining dough. Cut the pasta into 2-inch squares and dust lightly with flour. Let the squares stand at room temperature for 1 hour, tossing occasionally. —*CP*
NOTE Durum, a high-protein flour, is available at *kingarthurflour.com*.
MAKE AHEAD The uncooked fazzoletti can be spread out on a baking sheet and frozen, then transferred to a resealable plastic bag and frozen for up to 1 month. Cook the pasta squares without thawing.

Fideos with Chorizo and Chickpeas

⏱ TOTAL: 45 MIN • 6 SERVINGS

Fideos are thin, often toasted noodles that are cooked in stock for *fideuá*, a Spanish dish that resembles paella. This recipe instead uses broken pieces of spaghettini and quick flavor boosters (Spanish chorizo, jarred roasted red peppers, green olives and Cotija cheese) to create a fast and tasty one-pot meal, any night of the week.

¼ cup extra-virgin olive oil, plus more for drizzling
¾ pound spaghettini, broken into 1-inch pieces
5 ounces Spanish chorizo, thinly sliced
1 small sweet onion, thinly sliced
One 15-ounce can chickpeas, drained
1 cup jarred marinated roasted red peppers, drained and thinly sliced
½ cup dry white wine
1 cup canned tomato sauce
1 quart low-sodium chicken broth
Salt and freshly ground black pepper
½ cup sliced green olives
½ cup crumbled Cotija or farmers' cheese (2 ounces), optional

1. In a large, deep skillet, heat the ¼ cup of olive oil. Add the broken spaghettini and cook over moderate heat, stirring frequently, until the pasta is golden, about 5 minutes. Transfer the pasta to a plate. Add the sliced chorizo and onion to the skillet and cook over moderately high heat, stirring occasionally, until the chorizo is browned and the onion is softened, about 7 minutes. Return the pasta to the skillet and stir in the chickpeas and sliced roasted peppers. Add the white wine and cook until evaporated, about 2 minutes.
2. In a very large measuring cup or pitcher, combine the tomato sauce with the chicken broth and season the mixture lightly with salt and black pepper. Add the tomato-broth mixture to the pasta 1 cup at a time, stirring over moderate heat until it is almost

completely absorbed before adding more. Once all of the chicken broth mixture has been absorbed, cover the skillet and let it stand off the heat for 10 minutes. Stir in the green olives and Cotija cheese, drizzle with olive oil and serve right away.
—*Grace Parisi*

WINE Fruit-forward, medium-bodied Spanish white: 2011 Ipsum Verdejo.

Farro Pasta with Chicken Scarti and Borlotti Beans

ACTIVE: 1 HR; TOTAL: 1 HR 30 MIN
6 SERVINGS

Farro is an ancient type of wheat that gives pasta a firm bite and sweet, grainy flavor. At Sotto in Los Angeles, chefs Steve Samson and Zach Pollack pair farro pasta with hearty, rustic sauces. This one gets richness from quickly sautéed chicken livers (the *scarti*, or leftovers, from chicken) and deep flavor from porcini mushrooms and Marsala wine.

- ¼ cup dried porcini mushrooms, broken
- 1 cup boiling water
- ¼ cup plus 2 tablespoons extra-virgin olive oil, plus more for drizzling
- 1 pound skinless, boneless chicken thighs, minced
- Salt and freshly ground pepper
- 1 medium onion, finely chopped
- 2 carrots, finely chopped
- 2 celery ribs, finely chopped
- 1 teaspoon finely chopped rosemary
- 1 teaspoon finely chopped sage
- 1 cup chicken stock
- One 15-ounce can borlotti or cranberry beans, drained and rinsed
- 2 teaspoons chopped marjoram
- 1 pound chicken livers, trimmed and cut into ½-inch pieces
- ¼ cup Marsala or dry sherry
- 1 pound farro pasta, such as pizzichi, casarecce or fusilli (see Note)
- ¼ cup freshly grated Parmigiano-Reggiano cheese, plus more for serving

1. In a heatproof cup, soak the dried porcini mushrooms in the boiling water until softened, about 15 minutes. Using a slotted spoon, transfer the porcini to a strainer and rinse off any grit. Finely chop the porcini, reserving the soaking liquid.

2. In a large, deep skillet, heat ¼ cup of the olive oil. Add the minced chicken thighs, season with salt and pepper and cook over high heat, stirring, until browned in spots, about 6 minutes. Add the chopped porcini mushrooms along with the onion, carrots, celery, rosemary and sage. Cook over moderately high heat, stirring occasionally, until the vegetables are crisp-tender, about 5 minutes. Reduce the heat to low and cook until tender, about 7 minutes longer.

3. Gradually add the porcini soaking liquid to the vegetables, stopping before you reach the grit at the bottom. Add the chicken stock and bring to a boil. Simmer over low heat for 10 minutes. Add the borlotti beans and simmer until they are very soft, about 5 minutes, then stir in the marjoram.

4. In a large nonstick skillet, heat the remaining 2 tablespoons of olive oil until shimmering. Season the chicken livers with salt and pepper, add them to the skillet and cook over high heat until they are browned on the bottom, about 3 minutes. Stir and cook until just pink within, about 2 minutes longer. Add the Marsala and cook until nearly evaporated, about 1 minute. Scrape the chicken liver mixture into the skillet with the chicken and beans and keep warm.

5. Meanwhile, in a large pot of salted boiling water, cook the farro pasta until al dente. Drain, reserving ½ cup of the cooking water. Add the pasta and cooking water to the skillet along with the ¼ cup of Parmigiano-Reggiano cheese and toss. Cook over low heat, tossing, until the pasta is thoroughly coated with the sauce, about 2 minutes longer. Serve the pasta in bowls, drizzled with olive oil and sprinkled with Parmigiano.
—*Steve Samson and Zach Pollack*

NOTE Farro pasta is available at specialty food shops and *igourmet.com*.

WINE Juicy, fruit-forward Italian red: 2010 Renato Ratti Colombe Dolcetto.

PASTA TOPPERS

TOASTED CHORIZO BREAD CRUMBS In a food processor, mince 2 ounces sliced dried chorizo and 1 garlic clove. In a skillet, heat 2 tablespoons olive oil. Add the chorizo mixture; cook over moderate heat until sizzling, 30 seconds. Stir in 1 cup panko; cook, stirring, until toasted, 2 to 3 minutes. Season with salt and pepper. Sprinkle over pasta with clams or mac and cheese.

THYME-FRICO CRUMBLE Preheat the oven to 375°. In a bowl, combine 1 cup freshly grated Parmigiano-Reggiano, 1 tablespoon thyme leaves and 1 teaspoon coarsely ground pepper; spread out in a 10-inch ovenproof nonstick skillet. Bake until the cheese is golden and nutty, about 8 minutes. Slide the frico onto a plate and let cool. Coarsely crumble over pasta.

FRIED CAPERS AND SAGE In a medium skillet, heat ½ cup extra-virgin olive oil. Add ¼ cup drained and patted-dry capers, 2 tablespoons small sage leaves and ¼ teaspoon crushed red pepper; cook over moderate heat, stirring, until the capers open and are lightly browned, 4 to 5 minutes. Transfer to paper towels to drain and let cool. Sprinkle over buttered noodles.

ANCHOVY-PARMESAN BUTTER In a bowl, combine 1 stick softened unsalted butter, ¼ cup freshly grated Parmigiano, 1 teaspoon anchovy paste and ½ teaspoon each coarsely ground pepper and grated lemon zest. Serve over plain hot pasta.

OLIVE-PISTACHIO RELISH In a bowl, combine ½ cup chopped pitted green Sicilian olives, ½ cup chopped roasted pistachios, 2 tablespoons chopped Peppadew peppers, 1 teaspoon chopped rosemary and ¼ cup extra-virgin olive oil. Serve over pasta with mild white fish.
—*Grace Parisi*

Pasta with Abruzzi-Style Lamb Sauce

ACTIVE: 30 MIN; TOTAL: 50 MIN

4 TO 6 SERVINGS ●

The late Marcella Hazan was an F&W contributing editor who helped redefine her native Italian cuisine for a generation of Americans. In the recipe here, from her cookbook *Marcella Cucina*, it's the deep, intense flavor of lamb—cut into small pieces rather than ground—that sets the sauce apart from other classic meat sauces.

- 1 tablespoon extra-virgin olive oil
- ¼ cup chopped onion
- 2 ounces thinly sliced pancetta, finely chopped
- 1 tablespoon chopped rosemary
- ½ pound boneless lamb shoulder, cut into very fine dice

Coarse salt and freshly ground black pepper

- ½ cup dry white wine

One 28-ounce can Italian plum tomatoes, coarsely chopped, with their juices

- 1 pound penne or maccheroncini
- ⅓ cup freshly grated Pecorino Romano cheese, plus more for serving

1. In a large skillet, head the olive oil. Add the onion and cook over moderately high heat, stirring frequently, until the onion is pale gold. Add the pancetta and rosemary and cook, stirring occasionally, until the pancetta fat is rendered; the pancetta should remain soft. Add the lamb and cook until browned, about 5 minutes. Season with salt and pepper and stir. Add the wine and simmer until evaporated, about 10 minutes. Add the tomatoes and simmer gently, stirring from time to time, until the fat begins to separate from the sauce, about 15 minutes.

2. Meanwhile, fill a large pot with 4 quarts of water and bring to a boil. Add 1½ tablespoons of coarse salt, cover and return to a boil. Add the pasta to the pot and stir rapidly with a wooden spoon. Cover and bring back to a boil. Uncover and cook the pasta, stirring frequently, until it is al dente.

3. Drain the pasta and immediately transfer it to a warmed bowl. Toss with the lamb sauce and the ⅓ cup of grated cheese. Serve at once, passing additional cheese at the table.
—*Marcella Hazan*

WINE Lively, red cherry–scented Montepulciano d'Abruzzo: 2010 Masciarelli.

Fresh Pasta with Pork Shoulder and Cocoa Sugo

ACTIVE: 45 MIN; TOTAL: 3 HR 30 MIN

6 SERVINGS ●

In traditional Italian recipes like this one, a little unsweetened cocoa powder deepens the savory flavor of a meaty sauce *(sugo)*.

- ¼ cup extra-virgin olive oil
- 2 pounds trimmed boneless pork shoulder, cut into 4 slices

Salt and freshly ground black pepper

- 1 large Spanish onion, finely chopped
- 4 medium carrots, finely chopped
- 4 celery ribs, finely chopped
- 3 garlic cloves, finely chopped
- 1½ tablespoons minced rosemary
- 1½ tablespoons minced sage
- 2 tablespoons unsweetened cocoa powder
- 2 tablespoons tomato paste
- 1 cup dry white wine
- 1 quart chicken stock
- 2 tablespoons chopped mint
- 1 tablespoon chopped parsley

Pinch of crushed red pepper

- 3 tablespoons unsalted butter
- 1 pound fresh tonnarelli or linguine

Freshly grated Pecorino Romano cheese, for serving

1. Preheat the oven to 350°. In a large enameled cast-iron casserole, heat the oil. Season the pork with salt and black pepper and brown over moderately high heat, turning once, about 10 minutes. Transfer to a plate.

2. Reduce the heat to moderate. Add the onion, carrots, celery, garlic, rosemary and sage to the casserole and cook for 1 minute. Stir in the cocoa powder and cook until the vegetables are softened, 5 minutes. Add the tomato paste and cook, stirring, for 2 minutes. Add the wine and cook, scraping up any browned bits from the bottom of the pot, until reduced by half, about 5 minutes. Add the chicken stock and bring to a boil.

3. Return the pork to the casserole, nestling it into the liquid. Cover and braise in the oven until very tender, about 2½ hours.

4. Remove the meat and pull it into large shreds, discarding any fat. Transfer the braising liquid and vegetables to a blender and puree until smooth. Return the meat and sauce to the pot and stir in the mint, parsley, crushed red pepper and butter.

5. Meanwhile, in a large pot of salted boiling water, cook the pasta until al dente. Drain and add the pasta to the sauce, tossing over low heat until nicely coated, about 2 minutes. Serve the pasta in bowls, passing grated Pecorino Romano at the table.
—*Vic Casanova*

MAKE AHEAD The pork-cocoa *sugo* can be refrigerated for up to 5 days.

WINE Ripe, fruit-forward red from Sicily: 2011 Tami Nero d'Avola.

Saffron Orzo

◠ **TOTAL: 15 MIN • 6 SERVINGS**

The classic accompaniment to osso buco is saffron risotto. This simple alternative from star chef Mario Batali has just four ingredients and takes only 15 minutes to prepare.

- 2 cups chicken stock

Kosher salt

Generous pinch of saffron threads

- 1½ cups orzo (about 10 ounces)
- 1 tablespoon extra-virgin olive oil

Freshly ground pepper

In a large skillet, bring the stock to a boil with a generous pinch of salt. Remove from the heat, add the saffron and let steep for 5 minutes. Return the chicken stock just to a boil. Add the orzo and cook over moderate heat, stirring occasionally, until the orzo is al dente and the stock has been absorbed, about 8 minutes. Remove from the heat, stir in the oil, season with salt and pepper and serve.
—*Mario Batali*

● HEALTHY ● MAKE AHEAD ● VEGETARIAN ● STAFF FAVORITE

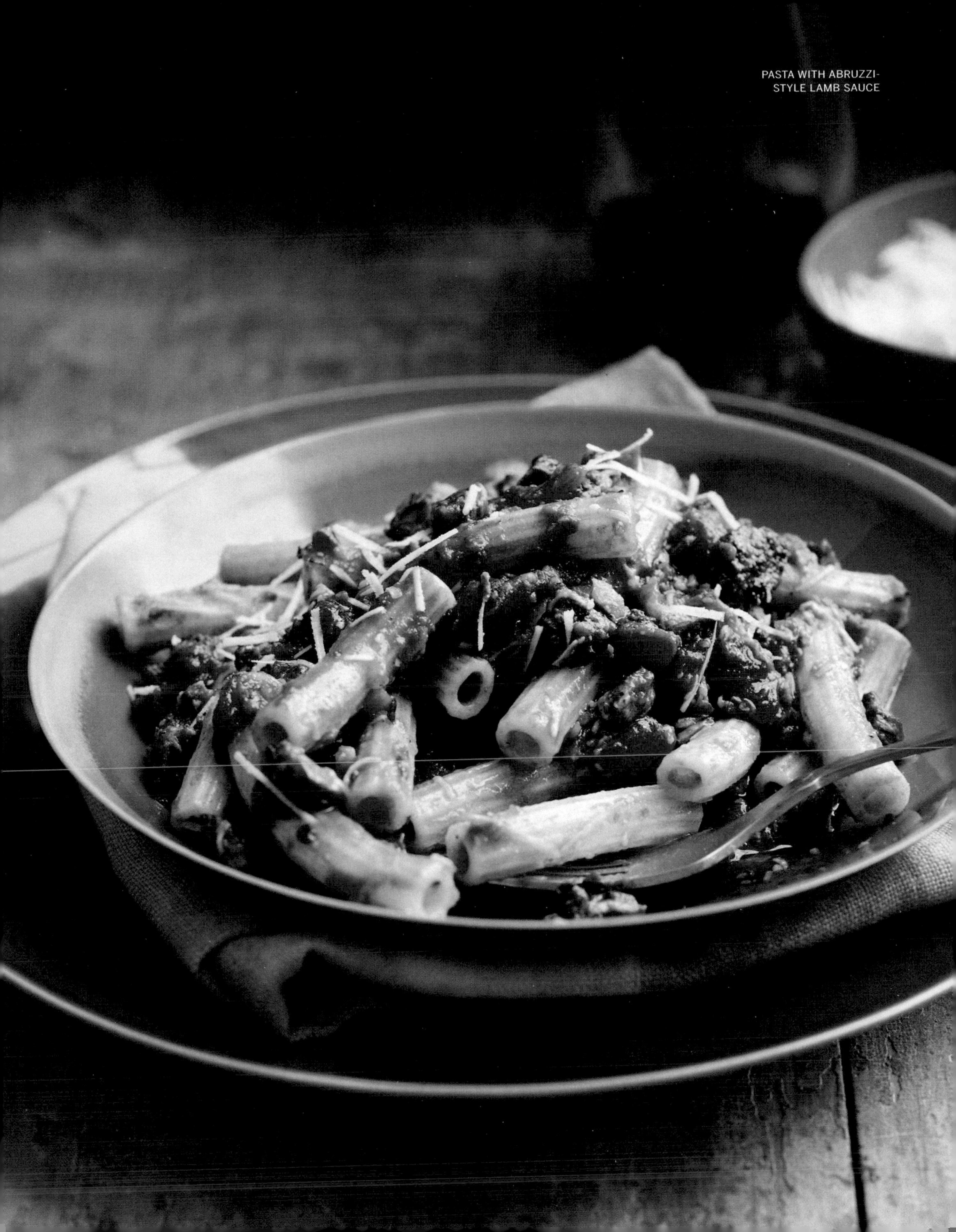

PASTA WITH ABRUZZI-
STYLE LAMB SAUCE

Baked Shells with Cauliflower and Taleggio

ACTIVE: 30 MIN; TOTAL: 1 HR
6 SERVINGS ● ● ●

Salt
1 medium head of cauliflower (1¾ pounds), cut into 1-inch florets
1 tablespoon unsalted butter
3 tablespoons extra-virgin olive oil
1 small onion, finely chopped
2 garlic cloves, minced
2 teaspoons minced rosemary
Freshly ground pepper
½ cup dry white wine
1½ cups heavy cream
1½ cups freshly grated Parmigiano-Reggiano cheese (6 ounces)
½ pound Taleggio cheese—rind discarded, cheese cubed
1 pound large shells, such as conchiglioni
¼ cup dry bread crumbs

1. Preheat the oven to 450°. Bring a large pot of salted water to a boil and fill a large bowl with cold water. Boil the cauliflower until tender, 5 minutes. Using a slotted spoon, transfer the cauliflower to the cold water and let cool slightly. Drain and pat dry; keep the cooking water hot.
2. In a large, deep skillet, melt the butter in the olive oil. Add the onion, garlic and rosemary, season with salt and pepper and cook over moderate heat until softened, about 3 minutes. Add the cauliflower and cook over moderate heat, stirring occasionally, until browned in spots, about 8 minutes. Add the wine and boil until evaporated. Remove the skillet from the heat and stir in the cream, 1 cup of the Parmigiano and the Taleggio.
3. Return the water to a boil and add the pasta. Cook until al dente. Drain the pasta and return it to the pot. Scrape the cauliflower and cheese sauce into the pasta and toss well. Spread half of the pasta into a 3-quart baking dish and top with 2 tablespoons of the bread crumbs. Top with the remaining pasta, 2 tablespoons of bread crumbs and ½ cup of Parmigiano.

4. Bake the pasta for about 20 minutes, until the sauce is bubbling and the top is golden and crisp. Let stand for 10 minutes before serving. —*Dario Barbone and Renato Sardo*
MAKE AHEAD The unbaked assembled pasta dish can be covered and refrigerated overnight. Return the pasta to room temperature before baking.
WINE Robust, dark-berried California Cabernet Sauvignon: 2010 Louis M. Martini Sonoma County.

Stovetop Mac and Cheese

⊙ TOTAL: 30 MIN • 6 SERVINGS ●

1 tablespoon unsalted butter
1 medium onion, finely chopped
1½ teaspoons tomato paste
½ teaspoon chopped thyme
2 cups half-and-half
Salt and freshly ground pepper
3 cups elbow macaroni (12 ounces)
4 ounces each of Gruyère, sharp white cheddar and imported Fontina cheese, shredded
¼ cup freshly grated Parmigiano-Reggiano cheese
2 tablespoons panko bread crumbs

1. Preheat the broiler and position a rack 8 inches from the heat. Put a kettle of water on to boil. In a large, deep ovenproof skillet, melt the butter. Add the onion and cook over moderate heat, stirring frequently, until softened, 5 minutes. Add the tomato paste and thyme and cook for 1 minute. Whisk in the half-and-half and 2 cups of hot water and bring to a simmer. Season with salt and pepper. Add the macaroni and cook over moderately low heat, stirring frequently, until the pasta is al dente, about 8 minutes. Stir in ¼ cup of boiling water along with the Gruyère, cheddar and Fontina. Cover and let stand off the heat for 2 minutes, until the cheese is melted. Season with pepper and stir once or twice.
2. In a bowl, combine the Parmigiano and panko and sprinkle it over the pasta. Broil for 2 minutes or until golden. Serve. —*Grace Parisi*

Cheesy Baked Pasta with Sweet Potatoes and Radicchio

ACTIVE: 1 HR; TOTAL: 2 HR
6 SERVINGS ●

This indulgent, family-style recipe is adapted from *The A.O.C. Cookbook* by Suzanne Goin, the chef at A.O.C. and Lucques in Los Angeles. The dish is her tribute to the spectacular baked pastas at Al Forno in Providence, where Goin worked while attending Brown University. She uses thick, tubular torchio pasta (macaroni in the shape of a torch), but rigatoni is a good substitute.

2 tablespoons unsalted butter, plus more for the dish
1½ pounds sweet potatoes, peeled and cut into 1½-inch pieces
⅓ cup extra-virgin olive oil
2 teaspoons thyme leaves
Kosher salt and freshly ground pepper
1 pound torchio (see Note) or rigatoni pasta
2½ cups milk
2 tablespoons all-purpose flour
1 cup shredded and packed imported Fontina cheese (5 ounces)
1 pound Cantal cheese (see Note) or other Swiss-style cheese—¾ pound cut into 1-inch cubes, ¼ pound shredded
¾ cup packed freshly grated Parmigiano-Reggiano cheese
Pinch of freshly grated nutmeg
½ cup heavy cream
1 large head of radicchio, sliced 1 inch thick
¾ teaspoon minced rosemary
4 ounces pecans, chopped (¾ cup)
Slivered flat-leaf parsley, for garnish

1. Preheat the oven to 400°. Lightly butter a 9-by-13-inch baking dish. On a large rimmed baking sheet, toss the sweet potatoes with ¼ cup of the olive oil, the thyme and 1 teaspoon of salt; season with pepper. Roast the sweet potatoes for about 20 minutes, stirring occasionally, until tender.

2. Meanwhile, cook the pasta in a pot of salted boiling water until almost al dente, 5 minutes for torchio and 10 minutes for rigatoni. Drain the pasta, rinse it under cold water and return it to the pot.

3. In a small saucepan, bring the milk just to a simmer. In a medium saucepan, melt the 2 tablespoons of butter. Add the flour and cook over moderately low heat, whisking frequently, until it is lightly golden, about 3 minutes. Whisk in the hot milk in 3 additions until incorporated. Cook over moderate heat, whisking frequently, until thickened, 10 to 15 minutes. Stir in the Fontina, the shredded Cantal, ¼ cup of the Parmigiano-Reggiano and the nutmeg until the cheeses are melted. Stir in the heavy cream and season with salt and pepper. Stir the cheese sauce into the pasta.

4. In a medium bowl, toss the radicchio slices with the rosemary, the remaining olive oil and ½ teaspoon of salt. Season with pepper and toss, then add to the pasta and mix well. Spread half of the pasta mixture in the prepared baking dish. Tuck in half each of the sweet potatoes, cubed Cantal cheese and chopped pecans. Repeat with the remaining pasta, sweet potatoes, Cantal and pecans. Sprinkle the remaining ½ cup of Parmigiano-Reggiano on top.

5. Cover the baking dish with aluminum foil and bake for 10 minutes. Uncover and bake for about 10 minutes longer, until the cheese is melted and the pasta is tender. Let the baked pasta stand for 15 minutes. Garnish with the slivered parsley and serve.
—*Suzanne Goin*

NOTE Torchio pasta is available at specialty food shops and *amazon.com*. Cantal cheese is a mild, semi-firm cheese from the Cantal region of France. One of the oldest cheeses in France, it has a nutty, buttery flavor and wonderful creamy consistency when melted. It is available at specialty cheese shops and *igourmet.com*.

MAKE AHEAD The unbaked pasta can be refrigerated overnight. Bring to room temperature before baking.

WINE Lean, red-fruited Sicilian red: 2011 Tenuta delle Terre Nere Etna Rosso.

Creamy Tuna Noodle Cazuela
⏱ **TOTAL: 40 MIN • 4 SERVINGS OR 4 INDIVIDUAL GRATINS** ●

Jarred piquillo peppers and canned tuna imported from Spain add an Iberian twist to the classic American tuna casserole, making it more elegant but keeping it as simple and quick as the original.

- 12 ounces farfalle pasta
- 4 tablespoons unsalted butter
- 1 medium onion, finely chopped
- 2 tablespoons all-purpose flour
- 3 cups whole milk or half-and-half
- 1½ cups frozen baby peas
- ¾ cup piquillo peppers, sliced (6 ounces)
- ½ cup freshly grated Parmigiano-Reggiano cheese
- One 6-ounce can or jar solid white tuna in oil, preferably Spanish, drained and flaked
- Salt and freshly ground pepper
- ½ cup panko (Japanese bread crumbs)

1. Preheat the oven to 450°. Cook the pasta in a large pot of salted boiling water until al dente. Drain.

2. Meanwhile, in a large saucepan, melt 3 tablespoons of the butter. Add the onion and cook over high heat, stirring, until softened, about 3 minutes. Add the flour and cook, stirring, for 1 minute. Add the milk and bring to a boil. Cook the sauce over moderate heat, stirring occasionally, until thickened, about 3 minutes.

3. Add the pasta, peas, piquillo peppers, Parmigiano and tuna to the saucepan and season with salt and pepper. Transfer the mixture to a large baking dish, a *cazuela* (casserole dish) or 4 individual gratin dishes.

4. In a small skillet, melt the remaining 1 tablespoon of butter. Add the panko and cook over moderate heat, stirring, until golden, about 1 minute. Sprinkle the panko over the casserole and bake for 10 minutes (5 minutes for individual gratins), or until bubbling. Serve right away. —*Grace Parisi*

WINE Crisp, medium-bodied Languedoc white: 2011 Sasha Lichine La Poule Blanche.

Baked Eggplant Parmesan Penne
TOTAL: 1 HR • 6 SERVINGS ● ●

Served over pasta, this deconstructed take on Eggplant Parmesan swaps the usual fried eggplant for a lighter sautéed version.

- 2 tablespoons extra-virgin olive oil
- 1 large sweet onion, finely chopped
- Kosher salt
- One 1¼ pound eggplant, cut into ½-inch dice
- 4 garlic cloves, minced
- ¼ teaspoon crushed red pepper
- 3 cups marinara sauce
- 1 pound penne rigate
- ½ cup lightly packed basil, torn
- Freshly ground black pepper
- 4 ounces fresh mozzarella, diced
- ¼ cup freshly grated Parmigiano-Reggiano cheese
- ¼ cup panko (Japanese bread crumbs)

1. In a large saucepan, heat the olive oil until shimmering. Add the onion and a generous pinch of salt and cook over moderate heat, stirring occasionally, until the onion is softened. Add the eggplant and ¼ cup of water and cook, stirring, until the eggplant is tender, about 10 minutes. Add the garlic and crushed red pepper and cook, stirring, until fragrant, 2 minutes. Stir in the marinara sauce and cook until hot, scraping up any browned bits from the bottom, about 4 minutes.

2. Preheat the broiler and position the rack 8 inches from the heat. In a large saucepan of salted boiling water, cook the penne until al dente. Drain the pasta, reserving ½ cup of the cooking water. Stir the pasta, cooking water and basil into the sauce and season with salt and black pepper.

3. Transfer the pasta to a 9-by-13-inch baking dish. Scatter the diced mozzarella on top, followed by the grated Parmigiano and the panko. Broil the pasta for about 4 minutes, until the cheese is melted and the panko is lightly browned. Serve hot.
—*Phoebe Lapine*

WINE Purple, effusive Dolcetto d'Alba: 2011 Cascina Fontana.

Spinach Gnocchi with Shaved Ricotta Salata

TOTAL: 1 HR • 6 SERVINGS ●

For his tender spinach gnocchi, Philadelphia chef Marc Vetri uses Grana Padano cheese rather than the traditional ricotta, making them more intensely flavorful. Different varieties of spinach will yield different quantities of puree. This recipe was tested using fresh curly spinach from the farmers' market. If you are using baby spinach, or trimmed, packaged spinach, you will need about 1 pound rather than the 2½ pounds called for below.

2½ pounds fresh spinach, stemmed
½ cup freshly grated Grana Padano cheese (1 ounce)
2 large eggs, lightly beaten
½ cup plain fine dry bread crumbs
¼ teaspoon freshly grated nutmeg
Kosher salt and freshly ground pepper
1¼ cups all-purpose flour, plus more for dusting
6 tablespoons unsalted butter
Freshly grated Parmigiano-Reggiano cheese and shaved *ricotta salata* cheese, for serving

1. In a large pot of salted boiling water, blanch the spinach until tender, about 4 minutes. Drain, reserving ½ cup of the cooking liquid. Cool the spinach in a bowl of ice water, then drain and squeeze dry. Wipe out the pot, fill with water and bring to a gentle simmer.

2. Meanwhile, transfer the spinach to a food processor. Add 3 tablespoons of the reserved cooking liquid and puree until very smooth. You should have 1 cup of puree; add more cooking liquid if needed.

3. Scrape the spinach puree into a large bowl and mix in the grated Grana Padano cheese, eggs, bread crumbs, nutmeg, ¾ teaspoon of salt and ¼ teaspoon of pepper. Stir in ¼ cup of the flour to form a soft dough.

4. Spread the remaining 1 cup of flour in a pie plate and dust a large rimmed baking sheet with flour. Gently roll the gnocchi dough into 1-inch balls. Carefully roll the gnocchi in the flour, shake off the excess and transfer to the prepared baking sheet.

5. Add salt to the simmering water. Add half of the gnocchi to the pot and cook until they rise to the surface, then simmer until cooked through, about 3 minutes (about 5 minutes total cooking time). Using a slotted spoon, transfer the gnocchi to a platter. Cover loosely with foil. Repeat with the remaining gnocchi.

6. In a skillet, cook the butter over moderate heat until golden, about 2 minutes. Spoon the brown butter over the gnocchi. Top with Parmigiano and *ricotta salata* and serve.
—*Marc Vetri*

WINE Juicy, bright, unoaked Chardonnay: 2011 De Forville.

Beet Gnocchi with Walnut-Sage Butter

**ACTIVE: 1 HR; TOTAL: 2 HR 45 MIN
8 SERVINGS** ●

While doing research for her forthcoming book on gnocchi, Portland, Oregon, chef Jenn Louis discovered these sweet, earthy beet gnocchi in northwestern Italy. She adds beet puree to mashed potatoes, which turns the pasta a beautiful magenta color.

2 pounds medium beets, scrubbed
Extra-virgin olive oil, for brushing
Kosher salt and freshly ground pepper
1 cup fresh ricotta (8 ounces)
1 large egg, lightly beaten
Pinch of nutmeg, preferably freshly grated
¾ cup freshly grated Parmigiano-Reggiano cheese (3 ounces), plus more for serving
3 cups all-purpose flour, plus more for dusting
½ cup coarsely chopped walnuts
1½ sticks unsalted butter, cubed
16 small sage leaves
1 tablespoon fresh lemon juice

1. Preheat the oven to 375°. In a 9-inch square baking dish, brush the beets with olive oil and season with salt and pepper. Add ¼ cup of water to the baking dish and cover tightly with foil. Bake the beets for about 1 hour, until tender. Uncover the dish and let the beets cool completely.

2. Peel the beets; cut them into 1-inch pieces. Transfer to a food processor and puree.

3. In the bowl of a standing mixer fitted with the paddle, combine 1½ cups of the beet puree (reserve any remaining puree for another use) with the ricotta, egg, nutmeg, the ¾ cup of Parmigiano and 1 tablespoon of salt and mix at low speed until combined. Using a rubber spatula, scrape down the side of the bowl. Sprinkle on the 3 cups of flour and mix at low speed until the dough just comes together, about 1 minute.

4. Scrape the dough onto a lightly floured work surface and knead gently just until smooth but still slightly sticky. Cover the dough with plastic wrap and let stand at room temperature for 30 minutes.

5. Line a baking sheet with wax paper and generously dust with flour. Cut the gnocchi dough into 10 pieces and roll each piece into a ½-inch-thick rope. Cut the ropes into ½-inch pieces and transfer the gnocchi to the prepared baking sheet.

6. Lightly oil another baking sheet. In a large, deep skillet of simmering salted water, cook one-fourth of the gnocchi until they rise to the surface, then simmer for 1 minute longer, or until they are cooked through. Using a slotted spoon, transfer the gnocchi to the oiled baking sheet. Repeat with the remaining uncooked gnocchi.

7. In a very large skillet, toast the chopped walnuts over moderate heat, tossing, until golden and fragrant, 3 to 5 minutes. Transfer to a plate and let cool.

8. Add the butter to the skillet and cook until golden brown, 2 to 3 minutes. Add the sage; cook for 20 seconds, then stir in the lemon juice. Add the gnocchi and cook for 1 minute, tossing gently. Season with salt and transfer the gnocchi to plates. Sprinkle the walnuts on top and serve, passing grated cheese at the table. —*Jenn Louis*

MAKE AHEAD The gnocchi can be prepared through Step 5 and frozen on the baking sheet, then transferred to a resealable plastic bag and frozen for up to 1 month. Cook without thawing.

WINE Full-bodied white: 2011 Louis Jadot Mâcon Villages.

● HEALTHY ● MAKE AHEAD ● VEGETARIAN ● STAFF FAVORITE

SPINACH GNOCCHI WITH
SHAVED RICOTTA SALATA

Potato Gnocchi with Mushroom Ragù

ACTIVE: 1 HR 15 MIN; TOTAL: 2 HR 15 MIN
8 SERVINGS ●

Master Sommelier Richard Betts is an avid mushroom forager: "Mushrooms are a great expression of *terroir,* just like wine is." Using a recipe from Jennifer Biesty, a contestant on *Top Chef,* he sautés a mix of wild mushrooms with garlic to top his plump, intensely potatoey gnocchi.

GNOCCHI

Four 10-ounce baking potatoes
  2 tablespoons unsalted butter, melted
  1 large egg, lightly beaten
  1 large egg yolk, lightly beaten
1½ teaspoons kosher salt
  ½ teaspoon freshly ground pepper
Pinch of freshly grated nutmeg
  ½ cup freshly grated Parmigiano-Reggiano cheese, plus more for serving
1¼ cups all-purpose flour, plus more for dusting

MUSHROOM RAGÙ

  2 tablespoons unsalted butter
  ¼ cup extra-virgin olive oil
1½ pounds mixed wild mushrooms, such as porcini, morels, oyster and hen-of-the-woods, quartered if large
Salt and freshly ground pepper
  2 shallots, minced
  2 garlic cloves, minced
  1 teaspoon finely chopped thyme
  ½ cup dry white wine
  ¼ cup chicken stock

1. MAKE THE GNOCCHI Preheat the oven to 375°. On a rimmed baking sheet, bake the potatoes for 1 hour, until tender; let cool slightly. Peel the potatoes and pass them through a ricer into a bowl. Stir in the butter, egg, egg yolk, salt, pepper, nutmeg and ½ cup of cheese and let cool.

2. Lightly dust a baking sheet with flour. Sprinkle the 1¼ cups of flour over the potato mixture and gently knead until the flour is almost incorporated. Scrape the dough onto a floured work surface and gently knead until smooth. Divide the gnocchi dough into 4 equal pieces. Roll out 1 piece of the dough into a ¾-inch-thick rope. Cut the rope into 1-inch pieces and transfer the gnocchi to the prepared baking sheet. Repeat with the remaining 3 pieces of dough. Roll each gnocchi against the tines of a fork or gnocchi paddle to make ridges. Cover the gnocchi with plastic wrap and refrigerate until they are firm, about 20 minutes.

3. MEANWHILE, MAKE THE MUSHROOM RAGÙ In a very large skillet, melt 1 tablespoon of the butter in 2 tablespoons of the olive oil. Add half of the mushrooms and season with salt and pepper. Cook over moderately high heat, stirring, until the mushrooms are tender and just browned, about 7 minutes. Add half each of the shallots, garlic and thyme and cook until fragrant, about 3 minutes. Transfer the mushroom mixture to a bowl. In the skillet, melt the remaining 1 tablespoon of butter in the remaining 2 tablespoons of oil and repeat with the remaining mushrooms, shallots, garlic and thyme. Return all of the mushrooms to the skillet. Stir in the white wine and cook until it is nearly evaporated, about 2 minutes. Add the chicken stock and season the mushroom ragù with salt and pepper; keep warm over low heat.

4. Bring a large pot of salted water to a boil. Add half of the gnocchi and simmer over moderately high heat until they rise to the surface, then simmer until cooked through, about 2 minutes longer. Using a slotted spoon, transfer the gnocchi to warm bowls or a platter. Cook the remaining gnocchi. Spoon the mushroom ragù over the gnocchi and serve, passing freshly grated Parmigiano-Reggiano cheese at the table.
—*Richard Betts and Jennifer Biesty*

MAKE AHEAD The uncooked gnocchi can be prepared through Step 2 and frozen on the baking sheet, then transferred to a resealable plastic bag and frozen for up to 2 weeks. Cook without thawing. The mushroom ragù can be refrigerated overnight; add a little water when reheating.

WINE Concentrated, balanced California Syrah: 2011 Copain Tous Ensemble Syrah.

Hungarian Potato Dumplings

ACTIVE: 35 MIN; TOTAL: 1 HR 35 MIN
6 SERVINGS ● ●

Cookbook author Sarah Copeland spends every summer in the Bakony Hills of Hungary, two hours from Budapest. However, she strays from Hungarian tradition and makes these round potato dumplings smaller than usual to ensure that they are light, tender and just a little chewy, like a more rustic gnocchi. They're perfect for serving with Copeland's saucy Wild Mushroom Goulash (page 82) or other stews.

Four 10-ounce baking potatoes
  2 large egg yolks
1¾ cups all-purpose flour, plus more for dusting
  3 tablespoons finely grated Parmigiano-Reggiano cheese
1½ teaspoons sea salt
Extra-virgin olive oil, for drizzling
Chopped parsley and flaky sea salt, such as Maldon, for sprinkling

1. Preheat the oven to 400°. Using a fork, pierce the potatoes all over and wrap them in foil. Bake the potatoes for about 1 hour, until tender; let cool slightly.

2. Peel the warm potatoes and pass them through a ricer into a large bowl. Using your hands, gently mix in the egg yolks. Sprinkle the 1¾ cups of flour, the cheese and sea salt on top and gently stir them in with your hands. Scrape the dough onto a lightly floured surface and knead gently until smooth.

3. Gently roll the potato dough into 1½-inch balls and transfer to a wax paper–lined baking sheet. In a large saucepan of salted simmering water, simmer half of the dumplings until they are cooked through, 7 to 8 minutes. Using a slotted spoon, transfer the dumplings to a large shallow bowl and drizzle with oil. Repeat with the remaining dumplings. Sprinkle the dumplings with chopped parsley and flaky sea salt and serve. —*Sarah Copeland*

MAKE AHEAD The uncooked dumplings can be frozen on the baking sheet, then transferred to a resealable plastic bag and frozen for up to 2 weeks. Cook without thawing.

● HEALTHY ● MAKE AHEAD ● VEGETARIAN ● STAFF FAVORITE

Fettuccine with Spicy Sausage and Cabbage Ribbons

📷 PAGE 91

ACTIVE: 30 MIN; TOTAL: 1 HR

6 SERVINGS

This pasta is star chef Mario Batali's ode to his friend Jimmy Fallon's Irish heritage; it combines blanched cabbage strips with crumbled sausage. The cabbage cooking water does triple duty: Batali uses it to boil the pasta, then adds a little of it to the sauce.

- 1 pound green cabbage (½ medium head), cut into ½-inch-wide ribbons
- ¼ cup extra-virgin olive oil
- 1 medium red onion, finely chopped

Kosher salt

- 1 pound spicy Italian sausage— casings discarded, meat crumbled
- 2 cups Mario Batali's Essential Tomato Sauce (page 364) or jarred tomato sauce
- 1 pound fettuccine

Freshly grated Pecorino Romano cheese, for serving

1. In a large pot of salted boiling water, blanch the cabbage until just tender, 4 to 5 minutes. Using a slotted spoon, transfer the cabbage to a colander. Cool the cabbage under running water and drain well.

2. In a large skillet, heat the oil until shimmering. Add the onion and a generous pinch of salt; cook over moderate heat, stirring, until softened, 7 minutes. Add the sausage and cook, stirring, until no pink remains, 7 minutes. Stir in the tomato sauce and cabbage. Cover and simmer over moderately low heat, stirring, until the cabbage is tender, 15 minutes.

3. Return the cabbage cooking water to a boil. Add the fettuccine; cook until just barely al dente. Drain the pasta, reserving ¼ cup of the cooking water. Add the pasta and reserved cooking water to the sauce. Cook over moderate heat, tossing, until the pasta is coated and al dente, about 2 minutes. Transfer the pasta to shallow bowls, sprinkle cheese on top and serve. —*Mario Batali*

WINE Light-bodied northern Italian red: 2010 St. Michael-Eppan Lagrein.

Italian Ramen

ACTIVE: 45 MIN; TOTAL: 3 HR

6 SERVINGS ●

One 3-pound chicken, cut into quarters
- 2 white onions, quartered
- 4 large carrots—2 cut into large chunks, 2 cut into fine matchsticks
- 4 celery ribs, cut into large chunks
- 4 thyme sprigs
- 2 rosemary sprigs
- 2 basil sprigs, plus basil leaves for garnish

Salt

- 6 large eggs
- ½ pound angel hair pasta

Asian chile oil, for serving

1. Preheat the oven to 500°. Arrange the chicken in a roasting pan and roast until the skin is lightly browned, about 20 minutes.

2. Transfer the chicken and any juices to a soup pot. Add the onions, carrot chunks, celery and herb sprigs. Add 4 quarts of water and bring to a boil. Simmer over moderate heat until the chicken is cooked, about 30 minutes. Using tongs, remove the chicken from the broth and let cool slightly.

3. Remove the meat from the bones, pull into shreds and reserve; discard the skin. Return the bones to the pot; simmer until the broth is reduced to 8 cups, about 1½ hours. Strain the broth, discard the solids and skim off the fat. Season the broth with salt; keep warm.

4. Bring a large pot of salted water to a boil and fill a large bowl with cold water. Add the eggs to the boiling water and cook for 5 minutes. Using a slotted spoon, transfer the eggs to the bowl of cold water for 2 minutes. Crack the shells and peel the eggs.

5. Return the water to a boil and add the pasta. Cook until al dente. Drain and divide the pasta among 6 large soup bowls. Top with the chicken, carrot matchsticks and soft-boiled eggs. Ladle the hot broth on top, garnish with basil leaves and serve, passing chile oil at the table. —*Gerard Craft*

WINE Herbal white: 2011 Cà Adua Gavi.

Late-Night Japanese Noodles

🕐 **TOTAL: 20 MIN • 4 SERVINGS** ● ●

"I love instant ramen. But when I use it, I throw out the seasoning packet," says *Top Chef* Season 9 winner Paul Qui of Qui restaurant in Austin. Instead, he uses the noodles to make his version of Japanese *mentaiko* spaghetti. This creamy, silky pasta gets salty pops of flavor from fish roe. Qui uses spicy marinated pollock roe, but cod roe, trout roe or even caviar would be tasty, too.

- ¼ cup mayonnaise, preferably Kewpie (see Note)
- 3 tablespoons *mentaiko* (see Note)
- 2 teaspoons spicy sesame oil

Two 3-ounce packets dried *yakisoba* or instant ramen noodles, flavoring packets discarded

- 1½ cups low-sodium chicken broth
- 1 tablespoon grapeseed oil

One 7-ounce package enoki mushrooms, bottom halves discarded and top halves coarsely chopped

- 2 large scallions, thinly sliced
- 4 shiso leaves, stemmed and finely shredded (see Note)
- 1 large sheet seasoned nori, shredded

1. In a bowl, gently stir the mayonnaise with the *mentaiko,* sesame oil and ½ cup of water.

2. In a large, deep skillet, combine the noodles with the chicken broth and bring to a boil. Cover and cook over moderately high heat until the noodles are softened and the broth is nearly absorbed, about 3 minutes. Add the grapeseed oil, then stir in the mushrooms and scallions and cook, stirring occasionally, until the broth is completely absorbed and the scallions are softened, about 2 minutes. Stir in the *mentaiko* sauce and cook, tossing, just until the noodles are evenly coated. Garnish with the shiso and nori and serve. —*Paul Qui*

NOTE Look for Kewpie mayonnaise (made with rice vinegar, and very popular in Japan), *mentaiko* (spicy marinated pollock roe) and fresh shiso leaves at Asian markets.

BEER Mild, refreshing lager: Samuel Adams Boston Lager.

DIY RAMEN: CHILE-EGGPLANT MAZEMEN

Total: 5 hr • 8 servings

Tokyo ramen master **IVAN ORKIN** takes a labor-intensive approach to ramen; the broth recipe alone fills five pages in his new cookbook, *Ivan Ramen.* The most manageable—and still inspiring—recipe for the home cook is his *mazemen,* a drier style of ramen. Because the broth is a less critical component, basic chicken stock mixed with instant dashi achieves excellent results. The main project, then, is preparing Orkin's wonderful noodles, with three different kinds of flour, and making toppings like roasted pork belly and a chile-eggplant version of a Latin *sofrito.*

A BALANCED BOWL
Orkin pairs the taste, texture, elasticity and shape of each noodle to the broth or sauce.

THE MEAT

Pork Belly

ACTIVE: 10 MIN; TOTAL: 3 HR 10 MIN

Not only does Orkin serve his ramen with pork belly, he also renders pork fat to dress the noodles so they're luscious and slippery. "I have a philosophy about how to eat ramen," Orkin says. "You need to be able to slurp it."

One 2-pound piece of skinless
    meaty pork belly
1 tablespoon canola oil
Kosher salt and freshly ground
    black pepper
3 cups chicken stock or
    low-sodium broth

Preheat the oven to 425°. Rub the pork belly on both sides with the oil, season with salt and pepper and set it on a rack in a medium roasting pan. Add the stock to the pan, cover and roast the pork for about 2½ hours, until very tender. Let the pork rest for 30 minutes. Strain the rendered fat through a cheese-cloth-lined sieve into a bowl (the stock will have evaporated). Cut the pork into ½-inch-thick slices and keep warm.

MAKE AHEAD The pork belly and its rendered fat can be refrigerated for up to 3 days.

THE SEASONING

Shoyu Tare

TOTAL: 30 MIN

Tare—a mixture of ingredients like *shoyu* (soy sauce), sake and mirin—is the main seasoning in ramen.

⅓ cup canola oil
1 large onion, minced
3 tablespoons minced peeled
    fresh ginger
2 teaspoons minced garlic
⅔ cup reduced-sodium soy sauce
½ cup dry sake
½ cup mirin
2 cups chicken stock or
    low-sodium broth
1 tablespoon instant dashi,
    such as Ajinomoto Hon Dashi

Heat the oil in a saucepan. Add the onion and cook, stirring, until softened, 5 minutes. Add the ginger and garlic and cook, stirring, until lightly caramelized, 10 minutes. Add the soy sauce, sake and mirin and bring to a boil; simmer for 2 minutes. Add the stock and dashi and simmer for 3 minutes. Keep warm.

MAKE AHEAD The *shoyu tare* can be refrigerated for up to 3 days.

THE CONDIMENT

Chile-Eggplant Sofrito

ACTIVE: 25 MIN; TOTAL: 2 HR 40 MIN

Borrowing from Latin American, Italian and Spanish cooking, Orkin tops his ramen with *sofrito:* onions and other vegetables sautéed in oil until almost melting.

1 cup canola oil
1 large onion, minced (2 cups)
½ small eggplant, minced (1½ cups)
2 medium tomatoes, minced
    (1¼ cups)
2½ teaspoons chipotle chile powder
Kosher salt

In a large saucepan, heat the oil. Add the onion and eggplant and cook over low heat, stirring occasionally, until the vegetables are very soft, about 1 hour. Add the tomatoes and cook, stirring occasionally, until they have almost melted, about 1 hour. Stir in the chipotle powder and cook for 15 minutes longer; season with salt. Transfer the *sofrito* to a bowl and let cool to room temperature. Drain the *sofrito* in a sieve; discard the oil or reserve it for another use.

MAKE AHEAD The chile-eggplant *sofrito* can be refrigerated in its oil for up to 3 days.

THE NOODLES

Toasted Rye Noodles

ACTIVE: 1 HR 45 MIN; TOTAL: 3 HR 15 MIN

In Japan, cooks use *kansui* (an alkaline solution) to give ramen noodles their springy texture; here, Orkin substitutes baking soda that's been baked to increase its potency. This dough may seem too dry at first, but adding extra water will result in noodles that are too soft.

20 grams (1 tablespoon plus ¾ teaspoon) baking soda
70 grams (¼ cup plus 2½ tablespoons) rye flour
620 grams (4 cups) bread flour
300 grams (2 cups) cake flour
13 grams (1½ tablespoons) kosher salt
430 milliliters (2 cups plus 2 tablespoons) cool water
Cornstarch, for dusting

1. Preheat the oven to 275°. In a small ovenproof skillet lined with aluminum foil, spread the baking soda in an even layer. Bake for 1 hour. Let cool.

2. Meanwhile, in a nonstick skillet, toast the rye flour over moderately low heat, stirring, until fragrant, 4 minutes. Scrape the toasted rye flour into the bowl of a standing electric mixer fitted with the dough hook. Add the bread flour and cake flour. In a bowl, stir the baked baking soda and salt with the water until dissolved. With the mixer at low speed, blend the baking soda solution into the flour in three additions. Mix, scraping down the bowl, until the dough starts to come together. At medium speed, knead the dough until it forms a shaggy ball, 10 minutes. Cover the bowl with plastic wrap and let stand at room temperature for 30 minutes.

3. Pat the dough into a disk and cut into 8 equal pieces. Work with 1 piece at a time and keep the rest covered with a damp kitchen towel: Flatten the dough to about ¼ inch thick. Roll the dough through a pasta machine at the widest setting. Fold the dough in thirds, like a letter, and roll it again at the widest setting. Repeat this folding and rolling about three more times, until the dough is smooth and elastic. Roll the dough through successively narrower settings, two times per setting without folding, until the sheet of dough is ¹⁄₁₆ inch thick. Cut the sheet of dough into roughly 1-foot lengths and transfer them to a baking sheet or work surface lightly dusted with cornstarch. Lightly dust the pasta sheets with cornstarch and cover with a dry kitchen towel. Repeat with the remaining dough, slightly overlapping the pasta sheets on the baking sheet.

4. Run each sheet of pasta through the spaghetti cutter. Gently toss the noodles with cornstarch and spread them on a baking sheet or work surface in a single layer in 8 even portions (about 5 ounces each).

NOODLES, STEP-BY-STEP

1 TOAST Bake the baking soda in a 275° oven and dissolve in water. Toast the rye flour over moderately low heat; combine with the bread and cake flours.

2 BLEND Gradually add the baking soda solution to the flour mixture. Knead into a rough ball and cover the bowl with plastic wrap.

3 FORM Let the dough rest until it has softened and relaxed, then form it into a disk.

4 DIVIDE Cut the disk into 8 equal pieces; cover them with a damp towel.

5 ROLL OUT Roll the dough into ¹⁄₁₆-inch-thick sheets.

6 CUT Make the noodles and toss with cornstarch.

ASSEMBLE THE RAMEN

Pour ⅓ cup of the warm *shoyu tare* and 1 teaspoon of the reserved rendered pork fat into a bowl. Boil one portion of noodles in unsalted water just until al dente, 1 minute. (You can cook up to 4 portions together.) Drain the noodles and add to the bowl. Top with ¼ cup of the *sofrito* and a slice of pork belly. Garnish with scallions and a dusting of chipotle powder.

Thai Seafood Noodle Salad

ACTIVE: 45 MIN; TOTAL: 1 HR

6 SERVINGS ● ● ●

- 6 ounces rice vermicelli
- 2 red Thai chiles, thinly sliced
- 2 garlic cloves, thinly sliced
- ¼ cup sugar
- ½ cup fresh lime juice
- ⅓ cup Asian fish sauce
- 2 tablespoons boiling water
- ½ pound medium shrimp, shelled and deveined
- ½ pound bay scallops
- ½ pound small squid, bodies cut into ½-inch rings and tentacles halved
- 3 plum tomatoes, seeded and diced
- 1 cup bean sprouts
- 1 cup mint leaves
- ½ small red onion, thinly sliced
- ½ cup salted roasted peanuts
- 6 butter lettuce leaves, for serving

Cilantro leaves, for garnish

1. In a medium bowl, cover the vermicelli with cold water and soak for 30 minutes.
2. Meanwhile, in a mortar, pound the Thai chiles and garlic to a paste with 1 tablespoon of the sugar. Add the lime juice, fish sauce, boiling water and the remaining 3 tablespoons of sugar and pound until the sugar dissolves. Let the dressing stand at room temperature for 30 minutes.
3. Bring a large saucepan of water to a boil. Fill a bowl with ice water. Add the shrimp to the boiling water; cook until white throughout and curled, 2 to 3 minutes. Using a slotted spoon, transfer to the ice water. Add the scallops to the boiling water; cook until white and firm, 2 to 3 minutes. Transfer the scallops to the ice water. Add the squid to the boiling water; cook just until firm, about 45 seconds. Transfer the squid to the ice water. Drain all of the seafood and pat dry.
4. Bring a fresh saucepan of water to a boil and refill the bowl with ice water. Drain the vermicelli, add to the boiling water and cook just until al dente, 1 minute. Drain and transfer to the ice water. Drain again and pat dry. Cut the vermicelli into 3-inch lengths.

5. In a bowl, toss the seafood, vermicelli, tomatoes, bean sprouts, mint, onion, peanuts and dressing. Arrange the lettuce on a platter; fill with the seafood salad. Garnish with cilantro and serve. —*Anya von Bremzen*
WINE Citrusy, off-dry Washington state Riesling: 2011 Eroica.

Vietnamese Chicken-Noodle Salad

TOTAL: 50 MIN • 4 SERVINGS
This salad of cool rice noodles, shredded leftover chicken and fresh herbs is a one-dish meal that's easy to assemble.

- ¾ cup sesame seeds
- ¾ cup canola oil
- 3 tablespoons fresh lime juice, plus lime wedges for serving
- 3 tablespoons Asian fish sauce
- 2 garlic cloves, crushed
- 2 tablespoons minced fresh ginger

Kosher salt and freshly ground pepper

- ½ pound rice vermicelli
- 4 pieces leftover Oven-Fried Chicken by the Bucket (page 164) or store-bought oven-fried chicken—bones and skin discarded, meat shredded (about 3 cups)
- 2 celery ribs, thinly sliced
- 1 carrot, shredded
- 2 cups mixed herbs, such as cilantro, basil and mint

1. Preheat the oven to 350°. Spread the sesame seeds on a rimmed baking sheet and toast for about 5 minutes, until golden. Transfer to a food processor. Add the oil, lime juice, fish sauce, garlic, ginger and 3 tablespoons of water and puree until smooth. Season the sesame sauce with salt and pepper.
2. In a large heatproof bowl, soak the noodles in boiling water until tender, 5 minutes. Drain and rinse under cold running water; drain well. In another large bowl, combine the chicken, celery, carrot, herbs and two-thirds of the sesame sauce. Season with salt and pepper and toss. Top the noodles with the chicken salad and serve with lime wedges and the remaining sauce. —*Kay Chun*

Soba Noodle Salad with Pesto and Grilled Eggplant

TOTAL: 1 HR • 10 SERVINGS ● ●
"Buckwheat and basil actually work really well together," says Chicago chef Bill Kim about this unlikely match-up of Japanese and Mediterranean flavors.

- 1 pound Asian eggplant, sliced crosswise ½ inch thick
- 1 cup extra-virgin olive oil, plus more for brushing and tossing

Kosher salt

- ½ cup pine nuts
- 2 cups basil leaves
- 4 medium garlic cloves, chopped
- 1 tablespoon soy sauce
- ½ pound buckwheat soba noodles
- 1 cup cherry tomatoes, halved
- 6 large radishes, cut into thin wedges through the stem
- ½ English cucumber—halved lengthwise, seeded and thinly sliced crosswise
- 1 cup mint leaves, torn if large

1. Light a grill or preheat a grill pan. Brush the eggplant with olive oil and season with salt. Grill over moderate heat, turning once, until tender and lightly charred, 6 minutes. Transfer the eggplant to a plate and let cool completely, then cut into ¾-inch pieces.
2. In a small skillet, toast the pine nuts over moderate heat, tossing, until golden, about 4 minutes; transfer to a plate and let cool.
3. In a food processor, combine the pine nuts, basil and garlic; pulse until finely chopped. With the machine on, add the 1 cup of olive oil in a steady stream. Add the soy sauce and pulse to blend. Season the pesto with salt.
4. In a large saucepan of salted boiling water, cook the soba noodles until al dente, about 4 minutes. Rinse the noodles under cold water, then drain and pat dry.
5. In a large bowl, toss the soba noodles with the pesto until coated. Add the grilled eggplant, the tomatoes, radishes, cucumber and ¾ cup of the mint leaves; toss well. Season the salad with salt, sprinkle the remaining ¼ cup of mint on top and serve. —*Bill Kim*

● HEALTHY ● MAKE AHEAD ● VEGETARIAN ● STAFF FAVORITE

SOBA NOODLE SALAD WITH
PESTO AND GRILLED EGGPLANT

Drunken Noodles

⏱ **TOTAL: 45 MIN • 4 SERVINGS** ●

A popular street food in Thailand, drunken noodles (*pad kee mao*) are made with broad rice noodles, tofu, chiles and Thai basil—the recipe contains no alcohol. One theory suggests that the super-fiery noodles got their name because they are great to snack on with drinks.

Vegetable oil
7 ounces firm tofu, cubed and dried
½ cup chicken stock
1 tablespoon oyster sauce
1 tablespoon Asian fish sauce
1½ teaspoons roasted red chile paste (see Note)
1 teaspoon black soy sauce (see Note) or ¾ teaspoon soy sauce sweetened with ¼ teaspoon molasses
½ teaspoon sugar
½ red bell pepper, seeded and sliced
½ large jalapeño, seeded and sliced
2 garlic cloves, minced
1 red Thai bird chile, minced
½ pound pad thai rice noodles, cooked and cut in half crosswise
Thai basil leaves
Lime wedges, for serving

1. In a medium nonstick skillet, heat ¼ inch of oil. Add the tofu; cook over moderately high heat, turning, until crisp, 5 minutes. Drain.
2. In a bowl, whisk the stock, oyster sauce, fish sauce, chile paste, soy sauce and sugar.
3. In a large skillet, heat 2 tablespoons of oil. Add the bell pepper, jalapeño, garlic and Thai chile and stir-fry over high heat until fragrant, 2 minutes. Add the noodles and stir-fry until browned, 4 minutes. Add the sauce and toss over moderately high heat until absorbed. Fold in 1 cup of basil and the tofu. Garnish with more basil and serve with lime wedges.
—*Bank Atcharawan*

NOTE Roasted red chile paste and black soy sauce are available at most Asian markets and online at *kalustyans.com*.

WINE Moderately sweet German Riesling: 2012 Leitz Rüdesheimer Klosterlay Kabinett.

Stir-Fried Noodles with Roast Pork

⏱ **TOTAL: 35 MIN • 4 TO 5 SERVINGS** ●

These quick, easy Chinese noodles are savory and chewy, with a bit of heat. You can make them with leftovers from Asian-Brined Pork Loin (page 176) or other roast pork. If Chinese noodles aren't available, fresh linguine is a good substitute.

5 dried shiitake mushrooms
12 ounces fresh Chinese noodles or linguine
¼ cup chicken broth
3 tablespoons soy sauce
1½ teaspoons unseasoned rice vinegar
1 teaspoon toasted sesame oil
1 teaspoon Chinese chile-garlic sauce
Pinch of sugar
3 tablespoons vegetable oil
1 tablespoon minced ginger
2 scallions, thinly sliced, plus more for garnish
½ pound leftover Asian-Brined Pork Loin (page 176) or other roast pork, cut into thin strips
Sliced fresh hot red chiles, for garnish

1. In a microwave-safe bowl, cover the shiitake with water and microwave at high power for 2 minutes. Let stand until plump, about 10 minutes. Drain, rinse and pat dry. Thinly slice the mushrooms.
2. In a saucepan of boiling water, cook the noodles until al dente, 3 minutes; drain and rinse the noodles. In a bowl, combine the broth, soy sauce, vinegar, sesame oil, chile-garlic sauce and sugar.
3. In a large nonstick skillet, heat the vegetable oil. Add the ginger and shiitake and cook over high heat, stirring, for 3 minutes. Add the noodles and scallions and stir-fry until lightly browned, 5 minutes. Add the pork and sauce and cook over moderate heat, tossing, until the sauce is absorbed, 3 minutes. Transfer the noodles to a platter, garnish with scallions and chiles and serve.
—*Grace Parisi*

WINE Slightly sweet white: 2010 Montinore Almost Dry Riesling.

Lo Mein with Mushrooms and Snow Peas

⏱ **TOTAL: 30 MIN • 4 SERVINGS** ●

Shiitake mushrooms add heft to this lo mein, a healthy revamp of the Chinese takeout staple. You can add shredded chicken to make the dish even more substantial.

½ cup low-sodium chicken broth
3 tablespoons low-sodium soy sauce
2 tablespoons Chinese oyster sauce
½ teaspoon toasted sesame oil
1 teaspoon Chinese chile-garlic sauce, plus more for serving
12 ounces fresh linguine or spaghetti
¼ cup vegetable oil
½ pound shiitake mushrooms, stems discarded and caps thinly sliced
1 tablespoon minced peeled fresh ginger
1 garlic clove, minced
6 ounces snow peas, trimmed
3 scallions, julienned

1. Bring a large saucepan of water to a boil. In a small bowl, combine the chicken broth with the soy sauce, oyster sauce, sesame oil and the 1 teaspoon of chile sauce. Add the linguine to the boiling water and cook until al dente, about 3 minutes. Drain and rinse the linguine briefly.
2. In a large nonstick skillet, heat the vegetable oil. Add the mushrooms and cook over high heat, stirring occasionally, until tender and browned, about 5 minutes. Add the ginger and garlic and cook until fragrant, about 1 minute. Add the linguine and snow peas and cook, stirring and tossing occasionally, until the snow peas are barely cooked, about 2 minutes. Stir the sauce and add it to the skillet along with the scallions. Cook, stirring occasionally, until the sauce is absorbed and the noodles are browned in spots, about 5 minutes. Serve right away, passing more chile sauce on the side.
—*Grace Parisi*

WINE Bright, cranberry-inflected Beaujolais: 2011 Domaine des Terres Dorées L'Ancien.

● HEALTHY ● MAKE AHEAD ● VEGETARIAN ● STAFF FAVORITE

LO MEIN WITH
MUSHROOMS AND
SNOW PEAS

Chef David Kinch (second from right) entertains friends in his hometown of New Orleans with his Cal-Med take on Creole seafood.

Opposite: recipe, page 134.

BARBECUE SHRIMP BAGNA CAUDA

FISH & SHELLFISH

Barely Cooked Salmon with Pea-Wasabi Puree and Yuzu Butter Sauce

⏱ TOTAL: 45 MIN • 4 SERVINGS ●

For this beautiful, delicate dish, star chef Eric Ripert gently poaches the fresh salmon fillets for just a few minutes, yielding perfectly rare, incredibly silky fish.

1½ cups fresh or thawed frozen peas
 1 tablespoon plus 1 teaspoon
   wasabi paste
Fine sea salt and freshly ground
   white pepper
 2 sticks cold unsalted butter,
   cut into tablespoons
 1 teaspoon finely grated yuzu zest
   or lime zest
 1 tablespoon yuzu juice (see Note)
Pinch of piment d'Espelette
Eight 3-ounce skinless wild Alaskan
   salmon fillets
 4 ounces salmon roe (⅓ cup)
 2 ounces smoked salmon, diced
   (¼ cup)
 2 tablespoons finely diced celery
 2 teaspoons finely chopped chervil

1. In a medium saucepan of boiling water, cook the peas until just tender, 5 to 7 minutes. Drain and transfer to a blender. Add the wasabi paste and 6 tablespoons of water and puree until smooth. Season with salt and white pepper. Strain the puree through a fine sieve into a small bowl, cover and keep warm. Discard the solids.

2. In the same saucepan, bring ½ cup of water to a boil. Whisk in the butter, 1 tablespoon at a time, until fully incorporated. Whisk in the yuzu zest, yuzu juice and piment d'Espelette. Season the sauce with salt and white pepper and keep warm.

3. Line a baking sheet with paper towels. In a large skillet, bring 1 cup of lightly salted water to a boil. Season the salmon fillets with salt and white pepper. Place the salmon in the skillet and reduce the heat to low. Cover and cook at a gentle simmer just until the fish is warm to the touch, about 3 minutes. Drain the fish on the prepared baking sheet.

4. Spoon the pea-wasabi puree onto plates and top with the salmon fillets. Drizzle the yuzu butter sauce over the salmon and garnish with the roe, smoked salmon, celery and chervil. Serve immediately. —*Eric Ripert*

NOTE If fresh yuzu isn't available, look for bottled yuzu juice at Japanese markets.

WINE Fragrant, lemony Grüner Veltliner: 2012 Hirsch Veltliner #1.

Whole Wild Salmon Fillet with Mustard Sauce

ACTIVE: 25 MIN; TOTAL: 2 HR 30 MIN
16 TO 20 SERVINGS ●

1¼ cups extra-virgin olive oil
 1 large shallot, thinly sliced
 ¼ cup chopped dill
Kosher salt and freshly ground pepper
One 4¼-pound wild king salmon fillet
   with skin
 ½ cup sour cream
 ¼ cup whole-grain mustard
 ¼ teaspoon finely grated lemon zest
 ¼ cup fresh lemon juice
 2 tablespoons Champagne vinegar

1. In a bowl, whisk 1 cup of the oil with the shallot and dill; season with salt and pepper. Pour two-thirds of the marinade onto a rimmed baking sheet; add the salmon skin side up. Spread the remaining marinade over the skin. Cover. Refrigerate for 2 to 4 hours.

2. Meanwhile, in a medium bowl, whisk the sour cream with the mustard, lemon zest, lemon juice, vinegar and remaining ¼ cup of oil; season with salt and pepper. Refrigerate the sauce until chilled, about 15 minutes.

3. Preheat the broiler and position a rack 6 inches from the heat. Scrape the marinade off the salmon and transfer it skin side down to another large rimmed baking sheet. Season with salt and pepper; broil for about 12 minutes, until an instant-read thermometer inserted in the thickest part of the fillet registers 125°. Let the salmon rest for 10 minutes, then transfer it to a platter. Serve with the mustard sauce. —*Nicholas Wilber*

WINE Full-bodied, oaked Chardonnay: 2011 Buehler Russian River.

Poached Salmon with Minted Yogurt Sauce

⏱ TOTAL: 40 MIN • 6 SERVINGS ●

The clever use of tahini (sesame seed paste) here gives this herbed yogurt sauce an instant Middle Eastern flavor.

YOGURT SAUCE
 1 cup plain whole-milk yogurt
 ¼ cup tahini
 ¼ cup packed mint leaves
 2 tablespoons packed parsley leaves
 1 tablespoon extra-virgin olive oil
 1 teaspoon finely grated lemon zest
 ½ tablespoon fresh lemon juice
Kosher salt
SALMON
 2 cups dry white wine
10 parsley sprigs
10 dill sprigs, plus more for garnish
 1 tablespoon whole black
   peppercorns
 1 lemon slice
Six 6-ounce salmon fillets with skin
Kosher salt
Boiled potatoes, for serving

1. MAKE THE YOGURT SAUCE In a blender, combine all of the ingredients and season with salt. Puree until smooth. Transfer the sauce to a bowl and refrigerate.

2. PREPARE THE SALMON In a deep skillet wide enough to fit the salmon fillets in a single layer, combine the wine, parsley, dill, peppercorns, lemon slice and 2 cups of water. Bring to a boil. Season the salmon fillets with salt and add them to the skillet in a single layer. Cover and poach over moderately low heat until the salmon is just cooked through, about 8 minutes.

3. Using a slotted spoon, transfer the salmon to a work surface. Remove and discard the salmon skin. Transfer the fillets to plates and drizzle with some of the yogurt sauce. Garnish with dill and serve with potatoes. —*Renee Erickson*

MAKE AHEAD The minted yogurt sauce can be refrigerated for up to 2 days.

WINE Citrusy Sauvignon Blanc from Chile: 2012 Tibalí Reserva.

● HEALTHY ● MAKE AHEAD ● VEGETARIAN ● STAFF FAVORITE

WHOLE WILD SALMON FILLET
WITH MUSTARD SAUCE

Halibut with Turnip Mash in Mushroom-Kombu Broth
TOTAL: 1 HR 15 MIN • 4 SERVINGS ●

- 2 tablespoons vegetable oil
- 1 pound white button mushrooms, cut into chunks, plus 4 whole white button mushrooms for garnish
- ¼ pound shallots, coarsely chopped
- 3 ounces dried kombu (kelp)
- 3 tablespoons olive oil
- 1½ pounds turnips, peeled and diced
- 5 tablespoons unsalted butter
- Kosher salt
- 2½ teaspoons fresh lemon juice
- Four 5- to 6-ounce skinless halibut fillets
- ½ teaspoon finely grated lemon zest
- ¼ teaspoon crushed red pepper
- ½ cup dry white wine
- 1 baby white turnip, for garnish

1. Preheat the oven to 300°. In a large saucepan, heat the vegetable oil. Add the mushroom chunks and shallots and cook over moderately high heat, stirring occasionally, until well browned, about 10 minutes. Add 6 cups of water and the dried kombu and bring to a boil over high heat. Simmer the mushroom broth over moderate heat for 20 minutes. Strain the broth, discarding the solids. Measure out 1 cup of broth and reserve the rest for another use.

2. In a medium saucepan, heat 2 tablespoons of the olive oil. Add the diced turnips and cook over moderately high heat, stirring occasionally, until golden brown, 8 minutes. Add 2 cups of water, 1 tablespoon of the butter and 1 teaspoon of salt. Cover and bring to a boil. Reduce the heat to moderate and cook the turnips until they are very tender, about 20 minutes. Uncover and boil to reduce any liquid to a glaze. Coarsely mash the turnips with a spoon and season them with 1 teaspoon of the lemon juice.

3. In a medium shallow baking dish, sprinkle the fish with the lemon zest, crushed red pepper and ½ teaspoon of salt. Add the wine and remaining 1 tablespoon of olive oil and bake the fish for 16 to 20 minutes, until just cooked through.

4. In a small skillet, bring the reserved 1 cup of broth to a simmer. Remove from the heat and gradually whisk in the remaining 4 tablespoons of butter until incorporated. Whisk in ½ teaspoon of the lemon juice and season the sauce with salt.

5. Using a mandoline, slice the baby turnip paper-thin into a bowl. Add the remaining 1 teaspoon of lemon juice and toss. Mound the turnip mash in shallow bowls and top with the halibut and sauce. Scatter the turnip slices over the halibut. Using a mandoline, thinly slice the whole mushrooms on top and serve. —*Ignacio Mattos*

WINE Mineral-driven rosé Champagne: NV Billecart-Salmon Brut Rosé.

Salmon and Corn Mixed Grill
TOTAL: 30 MIN • 4 SERVINGS

- 1 tablespoon ground caraway seeds
- ½ teaspoon ground white pepper
- Kosher salt
- 5 ears of corn, husked
- Vegetable oil, for brushing
- 1 stick unsalted butter, softened
- 2 tablespoons chopped dill
- One 2-pound center-cut salmon fillet with skin

1. Light a grill or preheat a grill pan. In a small bowl, mix the caraway seeds with the white pepper and 1 tablespoon of kosher salt.

2. Brush the corn with oil and grill over high heat, turning, until lightly charred, 5 minutes. Wrap 4 ears in foil to keep warm. Cut the kernels from the remaining cob and transfer to a mini food processor. Let cool slightly. Add the butter, dill and 1 tablespoon of the caraway salt and pulse until blended. Scrape the butter into a bowl; refrigerate for 5 minutes.

3. Brush the salmon fillets all over with oil and rub with the remaining caraway salt. Grill the salmon skin side down until the skin is browned and crisp, 4 minutes. Turn the salmon and grill until almost cooked through, 4 minutes longer. Top with the compound butter; serve with the corn. —*Grace Parisi*

WINE Tropical fruit–scented, full-bodied white: 2012 Yalumba Y Series Viognier.

Halibut with Orange-Miso Sauce and Fennel Salad
TOTAL: 45 MIN • 4 SERVINGS ●

- 1½ cups fresh orange juice
- 1½ teaspoons red miso
- 1½ teaspoons fresh lime juice
- 1½ teaspoons minced peeled fresh ginger
- 1½ teaspoons minced shallot
- ½ teaspoon *togarashi* (Japanese spice blend; see Note)
- ¼ cup plus 1 tablespoon extra-virgin olive oil
- Sea salt and freshly ground pepper
- 2 tablespoons softened unsalted butter, plus more for greasing
- Four 6-ounce skinless halibut fillets, about ¾ inch thick
- 1 medium fennel bulb—halved lengthwise, cored and thinly shaved on a mandoline
- 12 cherry tomatoes, halved

1. Preheat the oven to 400°. In a medium saucepan, bring the orange juice to a boil. Simmer over moderate heat, stirring, until reduced to ¾ cup, 8 minutes. Whisk in the miso, lime juice, ginger, shallot and *togarashi*. Cook for 1 minute, then remove from the heat; gradually whisk in ¼ cup of the olive oil. Season the sauce with salt and pepper and keep warm over very low heat.

2. Butter a large ceramic baking dish. Season the fillets with salt and pepper and arrange them in the dish. Gently rub the fish with the 2 tablespoons of butter. Add ¼ cup of water to the dish; bake for 8 to 10 minutes, until the fish is just cooked through.

3. Meanwhile, in a medium bowl, toss the fennel and tomatoes with the remaining 1 tablespoon of olive oil. Season the salad with salt and pepper.

4. Transfer the fish to plates and mound the fennel salad alongside. Drizzle the fish with the sauce and serve. —*Eric Ripert*

NOTE *Togarashi* is available in the Asian section of many supermarkets and at Japanese markets, and online at *amazon.com*.

WINE Dry, spicy Alsace Riesling: 2011 Hugel.

● HEALTHY ● MAKE AHEAD ● VEGETARIAN ● STAFF FAVORITE

SALMON AND CORN MIXED GRILL

Crisp Branzino Fillets with Zucchini and Fresh Tomato Jus

TOTAL: 1 HR
8 FIRST-COURSE SERVINGS ●
This elegant recipe features Morrocan-spiced fish in a delicate tomato broth.

- 2 **pounds large beefsteak tomatoes, chopped**
- ¼ **cup sliced red onion**
- 1 **garlic clove**
- 1 **thyme sprig**
- 1 **mint sprig**
- 1 **parsley sprig**
- ½ **teaspoon coriander seeds**
- **Salt and freshly ground pepper**
- ½ **cup extra-virgin olive oil**
- 2 **medium zucchini, thickly sliced**
- **Eight 3-ounce branzino fillets with skin, pin bones removed**
- **Lemon zest strips, for serving**

1. Puree the tomatoes in a blender. Strain the juice into a medium saucepan, pressing lightly on the solids; you should have about 2 cups. Add the onion, garlic, thyme, mint, parsley and coriander seeds and bring to a boil. Simmer over moderate heat until reduced to 1 cup, about 6 minutes. Strain the jus into a small saucepan, season with salt and pepper and keep warm.

BETTER THAN SASHIMI

Boston chef Tim Cushman marinates thin salmon slices in a citrus-soy dressing for 1 minute, then spoons a smoking-hot sesame-and-grapeseed-oil blend on top right before serving, barely cooking the fish.

2. In a large nonstick skillet, heat ¼ cup of the oil. Season the zucchini with salt and pepper; cook over high heat until lightly browned and tender, 4 minutes. Transfer the zucchini to plates. Wipe out the skillet.

3. Add 2 tablespoons of the olive oil to the skillet and the remaining 2 tablespoons to another large nonstick skillet. Season the fish with salt and pepper and add to the skillets, skin side down. Using a large spatula, press the fish lightly to sear the skin for a few seconds. Cook over high heat until the skin is very crisp and browned, about 5 minutes. Carefully flip the fillets and cook for 1 minute longer, until the flesh flakes when pierced with a fork. Place the fish over the zucchini, skin side up, and spoon the warm tomato jus all around. Garnish with lemon zest and serve right away. —*Mourad Lahlou*
WINE Bright, bold, citrusy California Sauvignon Blanc: 2011 Firestone.

Salt-Baked Branzino with Zucchini Pistou

ACTIVE: 1 HR; TOTAL: 2 HR 30 MIN
4 SERVINGS ● ●
Legendary chef Thomas Keller cooks whole fish in a salt crust to keep it moist, then serves it with lemony marinated tomatoes and a chunky zucchini-basil *pistou*—Provence's version of pesto.

- ¾ **pound cherry tomatoes, preferably heirloom**
- 1 **tablespoon minced shallot**
- ½ **cup extra-virgin olive oil**
- 4 **teaspoons fresh lemon juice**
- **Sea salt and freshly ground pepper**
- 6 **large egg whites (about ¾ cup), lightly beaten**
- 7 **cups kosher salt (about 2½ pounds), plus more for seasoning**
- ¼ **cup ground fennel seeds**
- 2 **branzino (about 1¼ pounds each), cleaned**
- 1¼ **pounds zucchini**
- 2 **garlic cloves, thinly sliced**
- ½ **cup basil leaves, plus more for garnish**

1. Bring a medium saucepan of water to a boil and fill a bowl with ice water. Using a sharp paring knife, score an "X" on the bottoms of the tomatoes and blanch them in the boiling water for 5 seconds; drain immediately and chill in the ice water. Drain again. Peel the tomatoes. In a small bowl, toss the tomatoes with the shallot, 2 tablespoons of the olive oil and 2 teaspoons of the lemon juice and season with sea salt and pepper. Refrigerate the tomatoes.

2. Preheat the oven to 400°. In a large bowl, stir the egg whites with the 7 cups of kosher salt, the ground fennel and ¾ cup of water until the mixture resembles moist sand. Spread a scant ½-inch-thick layer of the salt in an oval baking dish large enough to hold both fish. Pat the salt into a neat oval and place the fish on top, belly to belly. Pack the remaining salt on top of and around the two fish. Poke a hole into the crust at the thickest part of the fish, behind the heads. Bake for 25 to 30 minutes, until an instant-read thermometer inserted in the hole registers 135°. Transfer the baking dish to a warm place and let the fish rest for 10 minutes.

3. Meanwhile, quarter the zucchini lengthwise and cut out the seedy parts; discard or save for making soup later. Cut the zucchini into 2-inch lengths.

4. In a small saucepan, combine the zucchini with the remaining 6 tablespoons of olive oil and the garlic and bring to a simmer over high heat. Add the ½ cup of basil leaves and cook for 1 minute. Transfer the zucchini to a blender. Add the remaining 2 teaspoons of lemon juice and 1 teaspoon of kosher salt and pulse to a chunky puree.

5. Run a serrated knife horizontally around the salt mound and carefully remove the top crust. Transfer the fish to a work surface and fillet them, removing the skin. Transfer to plates. Spoon the zucchini *pistou* around the fish and garnish with the cherry tomatoes. Drizzle some of the tomato marinade on top and garnish with basil leaves. Serve.
—*Thomas Keller*
WINE Minerally, medium-bodied southern French white: 2012 Domaine Houchart Côtes de Provence.

● HEALTHY   ● MAKE AHEAD   ● VEGETARIAN   ● STAFF FAVORITE

CRISP BRANZINO FILLET WITH
ZUCCHINI AND FRESH TOMATO JUS

Crispy Fish with Sweet-and-Sour Sauce

TOTAL: 30 MIN • 4 SERVINGS ●

- 1 cup low-sodium chicken broth
- ¼ cup low-sodium soy sauce
- 3 tablespoons unseasoned rice vinegar
- 2 tablespoons ketchup
- 2 tablespoons sugar
- 1 tablespoon Shaoxing (Chinese cooking wine) or sherry
- 1 tablespoon cornstarch
- 1 teaspoon Chinese chile-garlic sauce
- 3 tablespoons canola oil
- 1½ tablespoons minced peeled ginger
- 2 large garlic cloves, minced
- Four 4- to 5-ounce branzino, striped bass or trout fillets with skin
- 2 scallions, thinly sliced on the bias
- Steamed rice, for serving

1. In a small bowl, whisk the broth, soy sauce, vinegar, ketchup, sugar, wine, cornstarch and chile sauce. In a small saucepan, heat 1 tablespoon of the oil. Add the ginger and garlic and cook over high heat, stirring, just until fragrant, 1 minute. Whisk the sauce mixture, then add it to the pan. Simmer until the sauce is thickened and glossy, 5 minutes. Keep warm over low heat.

2. In a large nonstick skillet, heat the remaining 2 tablespoons of oil until shimmering. Add the fish, skin side down, and press lightly with a spatula to sear the skin for 10 seconds for each fillet. Cook undisturbed over high heat until the fillets are browned and crispy at the edges and just barely opaque on top, about 5 minutes. Flip the fish and cook just until cooked through, about 1 minute longer. Transfer the fish skin side up to plates. Spoon the sweet-and-sour sauce on top, garnish with the scallions and serve with rice. —*Grace Parisi*

NOTE If using striped bass fillets, cook the fish slightly longer.

MAKE AHEAD The sweet-and-sour sauce can be refrigerated overnight.

WINE Lively, citrusy German Riesling: 2011 S.A. Prüm Prüm Blue.

Marinated Poached Fresh Tuna with Caper and Anchovy Sauce

ACTIVE: 30 MIN; TOTAL: 7 HR 15 MIN
PLUS OVERNIGHT MARINATING
4 SERVINGS ● ● ●

- 1 celery rib, chopped
- 1 medium carrot, chopped
- ½ medium onion, chopped
- ¼ cup wine vinegar
- Salt
- One 1-pound yellowfin tuna steak, 1 inch thick
- 1 teaspoon finely chopped garlic
- 3 flat anchovy fillets, finely chopped
- 2 tablespoons finely chopped capers
- ¼ cup fresh lemon juice
- ⅓ cup extra-virgin olive oil
- 1 teaspoon mustard
- Freshly ground pepper

1. In a deep skillet, combine the celery, carrot, onion and vinegar with a pinch of salt and cover with 1½ inches of water. Turn the heat to moderately high, cover and boil for 10 minutes. Add the tuna; when the water in the skillet returns to a boil, adjust the heat to moderately low so that the water simmers gently. Cover and cook the tuna until it is just pink in the center, 5 to 8 minutes.

2. Meanwhile, in a bowl, combine the garlic, anchovies and capers with the lemon juice, olive oil and mustard. Season with salt and pepper and beat with a fork to combine.

3. Remove the tuna from the skillet and pat dry. Slice it ½ inch thick. Choose a deep glass or ceramic dish that will hold the tuna in a single layer. Lightly spread some of the caper and anchovy sauce over the bottom of the dish. Add the tuna slices, laying them flat, and cover with the remaining sauce, spreading it evenly. Cover the dish with plastic wrap; let stand at room temperature for 6 hours, then refrigerate overnight. Bring to cool room temperature before serving. —*Marcella Hazan*

WINE Bright, medium-bodied Sauvignon Blanc: 2011 Hedges CMS.

Oil-Poached Tuna with Fennel and Orange

ACTIVE: 30 MIN; TOTAL: 45 MIN
4 SERVINGS

This clever one-pot recipe starts with poaching fennel, shallots and orange zest in extra-virgin olive oil, then cooking tuna steak in that aromatic oil. The result: incredibly moist and flavorful fish.

- One 1-pound tuna steak, 1 inch thick
- Salt and freshly ground pepper
- 1½ cups extra-virgin olive oil
- 1½ cups canola oil
- 2 fennel bulbs—halved, cored and very thinly sliced (about 5 cups), fronds reserved for garnish
- 2 large shallots, very thinly sliced (about 2 cups)
- 4 small dried red chiles
- Six 1-inch-wide strips of orange zest, preferably organic
- 1 bay leaf
- 2 tablespoons fresh lemon juice
- 2 tablespoons chopped parsley
- 1 blood orange, peeled and thinly sliced

1. Season the tuna with salt and pepper and let stand at room temperature for 10 minutes. In a large saucepan, combine the oils with the sliced fennel, shallots, chiles, orange zest and bay leaf and bring to a boil. Reduce the heat to moderate and simmer until the fennel and shallots are softened, about 10 minutes. Add the tuna to the saucepan and simmer until nearly cooked through and the fennel is tender, about 7 minutes. Transfer the tuna to a plate and let cool slightly.

2. Strain the oil into a heatproof cup. Discard the bay leaf, chiles and orange zest. Shake out as much oil from the fennel and shallots as possible; transfer to a bowl. Return the oil to the saucepan and heat to moderately high. Add one-third of the cooked fennel and shallots and fry, stirring, until golden and crispy, about 5 minutes. Using a slotted spoon, strain the crisp fennel and shallots and drain on paper towels. Season with salt.

● HEALTHY ● MAKE AHEAD ● VEGETARIAN ● STAFF FAVORITE

CRISP BRANZINO FILLET WITH
ZUCCHINI AND FRESH TOMATO JUS

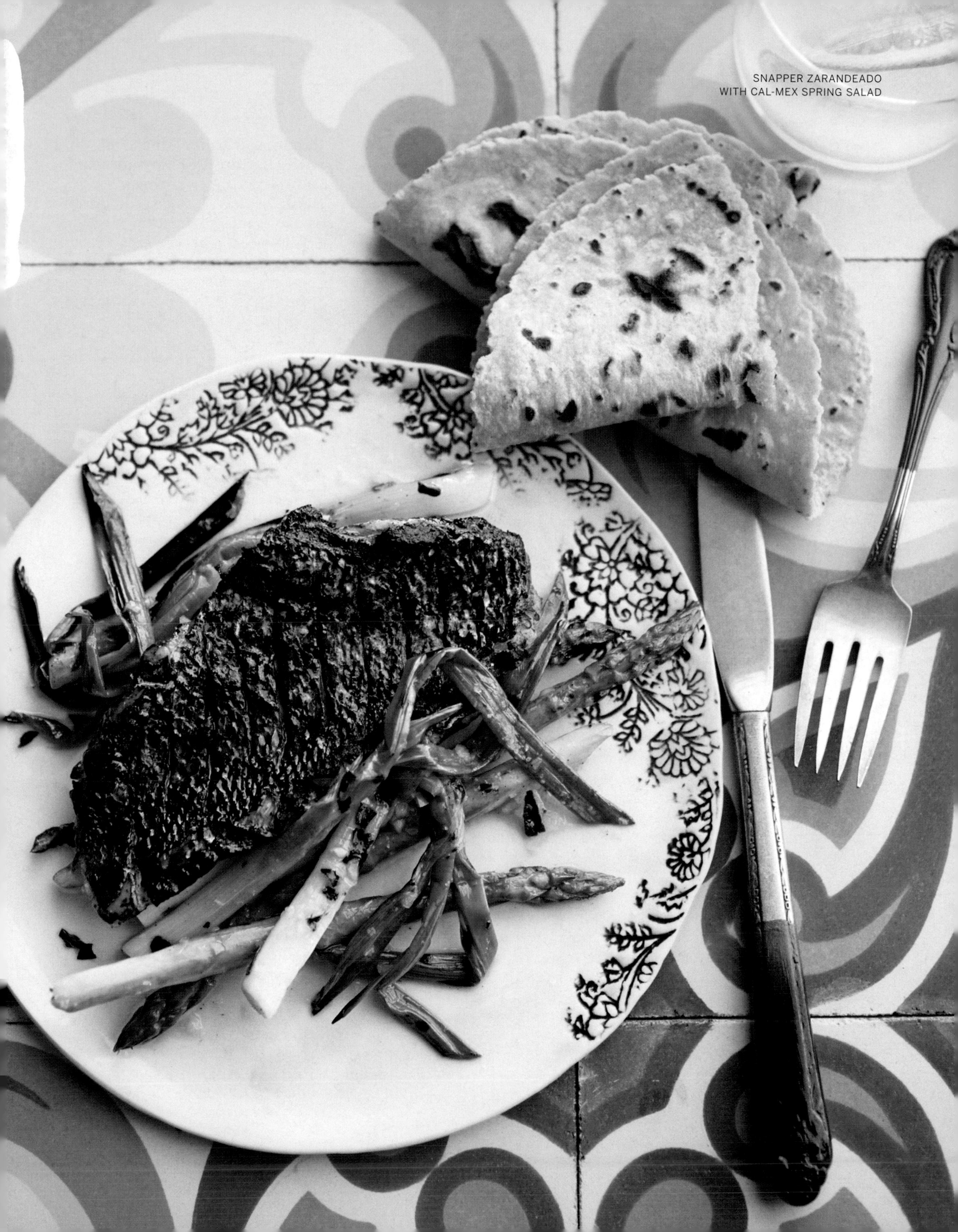

SNAPPER ZARANDEADO
WITH CAL-MEX SPRING SALAD

Thai Catfish Salad (Laap Pla Duk)

TOTAL: 1 HR • 6 SERVINGS ● ●

At Little Serow in Washington, DC, chef Johnny Monis serves this vibrant grilled catfish salad with a bowl of raw vegetables to balance the searing heat of the spicy lime dressing. "You want a really deep char on the catfish skin," says Monis, who recommends wild salmon as an alternative.

Three 1-pound whole catfish—cleaned, heads discarded (see Note)
3 tablespoons Asian fish sauce, plus more for brushing
3 tablespoons fresh lime juice
¾ teaspoon palm sugar or light brown sugar
1¼ teaspoons Thai chile powder or other hot chile powder, like cayenne
2 medium shallots, thinly sliced
½ cup thinly sliced scallions
¼ cup chopped cilantro
¼ cup chopped mint
2 tablespoons chopped dill
Roasted rice powder (see Note)
Radishes, cabbage wedges, cucumber slices, lime wedges and cilantro, mint and dill sprigs, for serving

1. Light a grill and oil the grates. Using a sharp knife, cut 3 shallow slits on each side of the fish and brush with fish sauce; grill over moderate heat, turning once, until white throughout and the skin is crisp, 17 to 20 minutes. Transfer the fish to a baking sheet and let cool.
2. Meanwhile, in a small bowl, whisk the lime juice with the palm sugar, chile powder and the 3 tablespoons of fish sauce.
3. Remove the skin and meat from the catfish; discard the bones. Pinch the meat into small pieces and transfer to a bowl. Chop the skin into small pieces and add to the bowl with the shallots, scallions and chopped cilantro, mint and dill. Add the lime dressing and toss well. Transfer the salad to a platter and sprinkle with roasted rice powder. Serve with vegetables, lime wedges and herbs and pass any remaining roasted rice powder at the table. —*Johnny Monis*

NOTE You can substitute 1 pound skin-on catfish or wild salmon fillets for the whole fish; adjust the grilling time. Roasted rice powder is available at Asian markets, but it can be made at home: In a small skillet, toast ¼ cup raw sticky rice over moderate heat, stirring, until golden, about 12 minutes; transfer to a spice grinder and let cool, then grind to a powder. Store in an airtight container for up to 2 months.
WINE Juicy, citrusy, off-dry Riesling: 2011 St. Urbans-Hof Urban.

Cod with Potatoes and Salsa Verde

TOTAL: 50 MIN • 4 SERVINGS

¼ cup extra-virgin olive oil, plus more for frying
¾ pound small golden new potatoes, thinly sliced
½ large onion, thinly sliced
Sea salt
3 garlic cloves, crushed
1½ pounds cod fillet, cut into 2-inch pieces
½ cup finely chopped parsley

1. In a large skillet, warm ⅓ inch of oil over moderate heat. Add the potatoes, onion and a generous pinch of salt and cook, stirring occasionally, until browned, about 20 minutes. Using a slotted spoon, transfer the potatoes and onion to 4 bowls; keep warm.
2. Strain the oil through a fine sieve into a heatproof bowl, then return it to the skillet. Add the garlic and cook over moderately low heat until golden, about 5 minutes. Discard the garlic. Add the cod to the skillet and cook, turning once, until just white throughout, about 7 minutes. Using a slotted spoon, add the cod to the potatoes.
3. Pour off all but ⅓ cup of the oil from the skillet; let cool slightly. Stir in the ¼ cup of oil and ¼ cup of water; bring to a simmer over moderate heat. Stir in the parsley and season with salt. Spoon the salsa verde over the fish and potatoes and serve. —*Francis Paniego*
WINE Lively rosé from Spain: 2012 Cune Rioja Rosado.

Rosemary-Grilled Mackerel with Mustard-Dill Mayonnaise

☺ **TOTAL: 25 MIN • 4 SERVINGS**

In the summer, Rachel Allen's sons, Joshua and Lucca, fish for mackerel off the rocks near Ballymaloe House, the family's country hotel in Ireland. Rachel has become an expert at preparing the fish. "It has a strong flavor that is not shy," she says, "so it goes well with other strong flavors, like mustard and dill."

MUSTARD-DILL MAYONNAISE
1 large egg yolk
2 tablespoons Dijon mustard
1 tablespoon white wine vinegar
1 teaspoon superfine sugar
½ cup sunflower oil
1 tablespoon finely chopped dill
Kosher salt and freshly ground pepper
ROSEMARY-GRILLED MACKEREL
¼ cup extra-virgin olive oil
2 garlic cloves, minced
3 tablespoons minced rosemary
½ teaspoon finely grated lemon zest
Four 6- to 7-ounce Boston or Spanish mackerel fillets
Kosher salt and freshly ground pepper

1. MAKE THE MAYONNAISE In a medium bowl, whisk the egg yolk with the Dijon mustard, white wine vinegar and sugar. Gradually whisk in the sunflower oil. Stir in the chopped dill and season the mayonnaise with salt and freshly ground pepper.
2. GRILL THE MACKEREL Light a grill or preheat a grill pan. In a small bowl, whisk the olive oil with the garlic, rosemary and lemon zest. Brush the mixture all over the mackerel fillets; season with salt and pepper.
3. Grill the fillets skin side down over high heat until the skin is nicely charred, about 2 minutes. Turn the fillets and grill until just cooked through, about 2 minutes longer. Serve the mackerel with the mustard-dill mayonnaise. —*Rachel Allen*
NOTE Instead of making the mayonnaise from scratch, you can mix ½ cup prepared mayonnaise with the mustard, sugar and dill.
WINE Minerally, dry Alsace Riesling: 2011 Domaine Weinbach Cuvée Théo.

● HEALTHY ● MAKE AHEAD ○ VEGETARIAN ● STAFF FAVORITE

Mixed Pantry Pan Roast

⏱ ACTIVE: 10 MIN; TOTAL: 40 MIN
4 SERVINGS ●

When cooking in the winter, former F&W Test Kitchen senior editor Grace Parisi relies on a pantry stocked with high-quality jars and cans. "Like a chef wandering the stalls of a farmers' market, I'm inspired by what I find in the corners of my cupboard," she says. This one-pan supper combines a number of standard shelf-stable pantry staples—like oil-packed sun-dried tomatoes, tinned smoked sardines and hearts of palm—in a healthy, tasty all-in-one meal.

1 pound fingerling potatoes,
   halved lengthwise
1 medium sweet onion,
   coarsely chopped
4 garlic cloves, thickly sliced
½ teaspoon crushed red pepper
¼ cup extra-virgin olive oil
Salt
½ cup oil-packed, sun-dried tomatoes,
   drained and coarsely chopped
1 lemon, very thinly sliced
   and seeded
One 14-ounce can hearts of palm—
   drained, hearts cut into
   1-inch pieces
Two 4- to 5-ounce cans oil-packed
   smoked sardines, drained

1. Preheat the oven to 450°. In a large bowl, toss the potatoes with the onion, garlic, crushed red pepper and olive oil and season with salt. Spread the potato mixture in a large glass or ceramic baking dish. Add the sun-dried tomatoes and lemon slices to the bowl and toss with any remaining oil from the tomatoes. Scatter the sun-dried tomatoes and lemon slices over the potatoes.
2. Bake for about 25 minutes, or until the potatoes are tender. Stir in the hearts of palm and roast for 5 minutes longer. Add the sardines and roast for about 1 minute longer, just until heated through. Serve the pan roast right away. —*Grace Parisi*
WINE Citrusy, minerally Italian white: 2011 Zuani Vigne Collio Bianco.

Sautéed Shrimp with Gremolata and Spiced Butter

⏱ TOTAL: 30 MIN • 4 SERVINGS

These large, sweet head-on shrimp are sautéed in a butter that's flavored with a mix of spices, including mace. An ingredient usually used in baking, it adds gentle heat to the shrimp. The leftover butter is great with roasted fish, chicken or vegetables.

SPICED BUTTER
½ tablespoon Madeira
½ tablespoon freshly squeezed
   lemon juice
1¼ teaspoons ground mace
1 teaspoon piment d'Espelette
Kosher salt
1 stick unsalted butter,
   at room temperature
GREMOLATA AND SHRIMP
⅓ cup finely chopped flat-leaf parsley
½ tablespoon minced lemon zest
½ teaspoon minced garlic
12 large head-on shrimp (about 1½
   pounds)—heads and tails left on,
   bodies shelled and deveined
Kosher salt and freshly ground pepper
¼ cup extra-virgin olive oil
2 tablespoons fresh lemon juice

1. MAKE THE SPICED BUTTER In a small bowl, combine the Madeira, lemon juice, mace, piment d'Espelette and 1½ teaspoons of salt; mix well. Let the spice mixture stand at room temperature for 10 minutes, then mix in the butter.
2. PREPARE THE GREMOLATA AND SHRIMP In a small bowl, combine the parsley, lemon zest and garlic. Season the shrimp with salt and pepper. In a large skillet, heat 2 tablespoons of the olive oil. Add half of the shrimp and cook over moderately high heat, turning once, until golden brown and just cooked through, 2 to 3 minutes per side. Add 2 tablespoons of the spiced butter to the skillet and cook until lightly browned; add 1 tablespoon of the lemon juice and toss to coat the shrimp in the sauce. Using tongs, transfer the shrimp to a serving platter. Strain the butter sauce through a sieve into a small

bowl. Repeat with the remaining olive oil, shrimp and lemon juice and 2 more tablespoons of the butter. Season the butter sauce with salt and drizzle it over the shrimp. Top with the gremolata and serve.
—*Owen Kenworthy*
MAKE AHEAD The spiced butter can be refrigerated for up to 1 week or frozen for up to 1 month.
WINE Fragrant, full-bodied white: 2011 Triennes Sainte Fleur Viognier.

Mexican Shrimp-and-Avocado Salad with Tortilla Chips

⏱ TOTAL: 30 MIN • 6 SERVINGS ● ●

This recipe is loosely based on *fattoush*, a Middle Eastern salad in which toasted pita is moistened by other ingredients, like tomatoes and cucumbers. Here, tortilla chips soak up the delicious salad juices.

1 pound shelled and deveined
   medium shrimp
2 romaine hearts, coarsely shredded
2 cups cherry tomatoes, halved
1 small seedless cucumber, diced
½ cup coarsely chopped cilantro
1 Hass avocado, diced
4 ounces tortilla chips (about 4 cups)
2 tablespoons reduced-fat sour cream
2 tablespoons reduced-fat
   mayonnaise
2 tablespoons fresh lime juice
½ teaspoon finely grated lime zest
Salt and freshly ground pepper

1. Bring a saucepan of salted water to a boil. Fill a bowl with ice water. Blanch the shrimp just until white throughout, 3 minutes. Drain and chill the shrimp in the ice water, then drain again and pat dry. Transfer the shrimp to a large bowl. Add the romaine, tomatoes, cucumber, cilantro, avocado and tortilla chips.
2. In a small bowl, whisk the sour cream with the mayonnaise, lime juice and lime zest and season with salt and pepper. Pour the dressing over the salad and gently toss to coat. Serve right away. —*Grace Parisi*
WINE Zesty, tropical South African Sauvignon Blanc: 2012 Indaba.

Barbecue Shrimp Bagna Cauda with Crudités

📷 PAGE 117

ACTIVE: 45 MIN; TOTAL: 1 HR
8 SERVINGS

New Orleans–style "barbecue" shrimp is made with Creole seasoning, Worcestershire sauce, beer and butter, but California chef David Kinch switches out those flavors here for a warm garlicky Italian anchovy sauce known as bagna cauda. No actual barbecuing is involved in either version.

1 head of broccoli (1½ pounds), cut into 1-inch florets
1 head of cauliflower (1½ pounds), cut into 1-inch florets
1 fennel bulb (1 pound)—halved lengthwise, cored and cut into thin strips
8 medium fingerling potatoes
8 garlic cloves, finely grated or minced
8 oil-packed anchovy fillets, chopped
2 sticks unsalted butter
1½ cups pure olive oil
1 tablespoon coarsely ground black pepper
3 rosemary sprigs
16 large unpeeled head-on shrimp
4 scallions, cut into 3-inch lengths
Crusty bread, for serving

1. Bring a large pot of salted water to a boil and fill a large bowl with ice water. Blanch the broccoli and cauliflower until crisp-tender, 3 minutes. Using a slotted spoon, transfer the vegetables to the ice water. Add the fennel to the pot and blanch for 1 minute; transfer to the ice water. Add the potatoes to the pot and cook until tender, 10 minutes; transfer to the ice water. Drain the vegetables and pat dry. Cut the potatoes in half lengthwise.
2. On a surface, using the flat side of a chef's knife, mash the garlic and anchovies to a paste; scrape into a large, deep skillet. Add the butter, oil, black pepper and rosemary; bring to a simmer over moderate heat. Nestle the shrimp into the bagna cauda and cook,

turning once, until just pink in spots. Cover and simmer until the shrimp are pink all over, 3 minutes longer. Remove from the heat.
3. Arrange the vegetables, scallions and bread on a platter. Using a slotted spoon, transfer the shrimp to another platter. Pour some of the bagna cauda sauce over the shrimp and the rest into a wide bowl. Serve right away, with plenty of napkins.
—*David Kinch*

WINE Floral rosé from the south of France: 2012 Château Montaud Côtes de Provence.

Chile Shrimp with Butter Beans and Lemony Couscous

⏱ **TOTAL: 10 MIN • 4 SERVINGS**

A tangy, caper-studded couscous with butter beans and lemon juice makes a delicious base for quickly sautéed spicy shrimp.

⅔ cup couscous
3 tablespoons extra-virgin olive oil
1 pound shelled and deveined medium shrimp
½ teaspoon crushed red pepper
2 tablespoons unsalted butter
One 15-ounce can butter beans, rinsed and drained
2 tablespoons capers
1½ tablespoons fresh lemon juice
1 tablespoon chopped parsley
Kosher salt and freshly ground pepper

1. In a large heatproof bowl, stir the couscous with ¾ cup of boiling water. Cover with a lid and steam for 5 minutes. Fluff with a fork.
2. Meanwhile, in a nonstick skillet, heat 2 tablespoons of the oil. Add the shrimp and crushed red pepper and cook over moderately high heat until golden, 2 to 3 minutes; transfer to a plate. Add the butter to the skillet, then add the beans, capers and lemon juice and cook, stirring, for 2 minutes.
3. Fold the bean mixture, parsley and remaining 1 tablespoon of olive oil into the couscous; season with salt and pepper. Serve, topped with the shrimp. —*Kay Chun*

WINE Zippy, medium-bodied Spanish white: 2011 Telmo Rodriguez Basa.

Grilled Shrimp with Miso Butter

⏱ **TOTAL: 30 MIN • 4 SERVINGS**

"I love mixing miso and butter together," says Boston chef Jamie Bissonnette. "If you spread that miso-flavored butter on toast, people always love it and ask, 'What *is* this?'" Bissonnette also transforms the butter into a sauce for grilled shrimp.

1 stick unsalted butter, softened
2 tablespoons white miso
½ teaspoon finely grated lemon zest
1 tablespoon fresh lemon juice
1 tablespoon thinly sliced scallion, plus more for garnish
1 pound shelled and deveined large shrimp
2 tablespoons canola oil
1 large garlic clove, minced
1 teaspoon Korean chile powder (*gochugaru*) or other chile powder
1 teaspoon kosher salt
1½ teaspoons pickled mustard seeds from a jar of pickles

1. In a food processor, combine the butter with the miso, lemon zest and lemon juice and puree until smooth. Add the 1 tablespoon of scallion and pulse just until incorporated. Scrape the miso butter into a large bowl and set aside.
2. In another large bowl, toss the shrimp with the oil, garlic, chile powder and salt and let stand for 10 minutes.
3. Light a grill or preheat a grill pan. Grill the shrimp over high heat, turning once, until just cooked through, about 4 minutes. Immediately add the shrimp to the miso butter and toss until well coated. Garnish the shrimp with scallions and the pickled mustard seeds and serve.
—*Jamie Bissonnette*

SERVE WITH Grilled scallions and steamed white or brown rice.

MAKE AHEAD The miso butter can be refrigerated in an airtight container for up to 3 days or frozen for up to 1 month.

WINE Full-bodied Spanish white with good acidity: 2011 Vevi Verdejo.

● HEALTHY ● MAKE AHEAD ● VEGETARIAN ● STAFF FAVORITE

CHILE SHRIMP WITH BUTTER BEANS
AND LEMONY COUSCOUS

Ale-Poached Shrimp with Saffron Sauce

⏱ **TOTAL: 45 MIN • 4 SERVINGS**

American cooks, especially Southern ones, love to steam or boil shrimp in beer—usually the cheap, watery kind. Here, Luca Cerato, the chef at CitaBiunda brewery in the Piedmont region of Italy, poaches shrimp in the brewery's juniper-and-chamomile-spiced Belgian-style blond ale. The shrimp are so richly flavored that they need little enhancement beyond the blanched asparagus and saffron-cream sauce he serves with them. (They would also be great served chilled, with cocktail sauce.)

- 1 tablespoon unsalted butter
- 1 tablespoon extra-virgin olive oil
- 2 scallions, white and light green parts only, thinly sliced
- 2 cups heavy cream
- 2 cups vegetable stock or low-sodium broth
- Pinch of saffron threads
- Kosher salt and freshly ground black pepper
- Two 12-ounce bottles Belgian-style blond ale, such as Leffe
- 1¼ pounds shelled and deveined large shrimp, tails left on
- 1 pound thick asparagus—woody ends trimmed, tips halved lengthwise and stalks thinly sliced crosswise

1. In a medium saucepan, melt the butter in the extra-virgin olive oil. Add the scallions and cook over moderate heat until softened, about 2 minutes. Add the heavy cream, vegetable stock and saffron and bring just to a boil. Simmer over moderately low heat, stirring occasionally, until the sauce is reduced to 1¾ cups, about 15 minutes. Strain the sauce through a fine sieve into a small saucepan and season with salt and pepper. Keep the saffron sauce warm over low heat, stirring occasionally.

2. Meanwhile, in a large, deep saucepan, bring the ale just to a simmer. Add the shrimp and poach over moderate heat until they are just cooked through, about 3 minutes. Using a slotted spoon, transfer the shrimp to a plate, pat dry and season with salt and pepper.

3. In a medium saucepan of salted boiling water, blanch the asparagus pieces until they are crisp-tender, about 2 minutes. Using a slotted spoon, transfer the asparagus to paper towels to drain.

4. Spoon the saffron sauce into shallow bowls, top with the blanched asparagus and poached shrimp and serve right away.
—*Luca Cerato*

MAKE AHEAD The saffron sauce can be refrigerated overnight and gently reheated before serving; add a little water or vegetable stock, if necessary.

BEER Belgian-style blond ale: CitaBiunda Mary.

Prosciutto-Wrapped Shrimp with Bourbon Barbecue Sauce

TOTAL: 1 HR • MAKES 24 SHRIMP ● ●

Chef Lauren Kiino of Il Cane Rosso in San Francisco's Ferry Building created this recipe after thinking about retro dishes like angels on horseback (bacon-wrapped oysters). "Prosciutto is more delicate than bacon, but it gets a nice crispness," she says. "And the barbecue sauce helps the prosciutto stick to the shrimp."

BARBECUE SAUCE

- 1 tablespoon extra-virgin olive oil
- 1 medium onion, halved and thinly sliced
- 1 teaspoon chopped rosemary leaves
- 1 teaspoon chopped garlic
- 2 tablespoons bourbon
- 2 tablespoons brown sugar
- 1 tablespoon Dijon mustard
- 1 tablespoon apple cider vinegar
- ½ cup prepared barbecue sauce, preferably a less sweet brand, such as Stubb's Original Bar-B-Q Sauce
- Dash of Worcestershire sauce
- Dash of hot sauce
- Salt and freshly ground black pepper

SHRIMP

- 24 extra-large shrimp, shelled and deveined
- 1 tablespoon extra-virgin olive oil
- Salt and freshly ground black pepper
- 12 slices of prosciutto, halved lengthwise
- 2 tablespoons chopped flat-leaf parsley
- Lime wedges, for serving

1. MAKE THE BARBECUE SAUCE In a medium skillet, heat the olive oil. Add the onion and rosemary and cook over moderate heat, stirring occasionally, until the onion begins to brown, about 6 minutes. Add the garlic and cook until softened and fragrant, about 5 minutes. Stir in the bourbon, brown sugar, Dijon mustard, apple cider vinegar, prepared barbecue sauce, Worcestershire and hot sauce; season with salt and pepper. Transfer to a food processor and puree the barbecue sauce until smooth. Transfer the sauce to a bowl.

2. PREPARE THE SHRIMP Preheat the oven to 400°. In a medium bowl, toss the shrimp with the olive oil and season them with salt and pepper. Wrap each shrimp in a half slice of prosciutto and transfer to a large rimmed baking sheet. Brush the shrimp with some of the bourbon barbecue sauce and arrange them 1 inch apart. Roast the prosciutto-wrapped shrimp for 5 minutes. Turn the shrimp over, brush with more bourbon barbecue sauce and roast for about 5 minutes longer, until the shrimp are firm and white throughout and the bourbon barbecue sauce is shiny. Transfer the shrimp to a platter and sprinkle with the chopped parsley. Serve with lime wedges and any remaining bourbon barbecue sauce for dipping. —*Lauren Kiino*

MAKE AHEAD The bourbon barbecue sauce can be refrigerated for 3 days. Let it come to room temperature before serving. The prosciutto-wrapped shrimp can be refrigerated for 8 hours before roasting.

WINE Ripe, fruit-forward Pinot Grigio: 2011 Swanson Vineyards.

● HEALTHY   ● MAKE AHEAD   ● VEGETARIAN   ● STAFF FAVORITE

Mexico City Shrimp with Chipotle Mojo

ACTIVE: 30 MIN; TOTAL: 1 HR 10 MIN
6 SERVINGS ●

Rick Bayless of Chicago's Frontera Grill first discovered *mojo* at a street stall in Mexico City about 30 years ago. "I loved its slow-roasted, caramelly flavor," the star chef says about the classic Latin garlic sauce. Here, he spikes it with smoky chipotle chile and lime juice to season shrimp, but he also likes to use *mojo* to flavor vegetables, chicken and even, sometimes, popcorn.

2 heads of garlic (about 26 cloves), cloves peeled and crushed
1½ cups extra-virgin olive oil
Kosher salt
¼ cup fresh lime juice
1 chipotle in adobo sauce, seeded and minced
2 pounds medium shrimp—shelled and deveined, tails left on
Freshly ground pepper
Chopped cilantro, for garnish
Lime wedges, for serving

1. Preheat the oven to 325°. In a 4-cup ceramic baking dish, combine the crushed garlic and olive oil with a pinch of salt. Put the dish on a cookie sheet and bake for about 30 minutes, until the garlic is tender and just starting to brown. Stir in the lime juice and bake for about 15 minutes more, until the garlic is golden and very soft. Let the mixture cool slightly.

2. Pour the garlic and oil into a small sauce-pan. Using a fork, mash the garlic against the side of the pan and stir to incorporate the oil; the sauce may look like it has sepa-rated. Add the chipotle, season with salt and keep the *mojo* warm.

3. In a large skillet, heat 2 tablespoons of the garlicky oil from the *mojo* until shimmering. Add half of the shrimp and a generous pinch each of salt and pepper and cook over moderately high heat, turning once, until golden and just cooked through, about 3 minutes. Transfer the shrimp to a platter. Repeat with 2 more tablespoons of

the garlicky oil and the remaining shrimp. Top the shrimp with more *mojo* and garnish with chopped cilantro. Serve with lime wedges, passing the remaining garlic *mojo* at the table. —*Rick Bayless*

SERVE WITH White rice or crusty bread.
MAKE AHEAD The garlic *mojo* can be refrig-erated for up to 1 week. Reheat the sauce gently before using.
WINE Crisp, berry-inflected French rosé: 2012 VRAC.

Scallops with Fennel Grenobloise

TOTAL: 15 MIN • 2 SERVINGS ●

Ready in just 15 minutes, these plump seared scallops are perfect with thin slices of fennel in a buttery lemon-caper sauce—a French preparation known as *grenobloise*.

2 tablespoons extra-virgin olive oil
1 pound sea scallops
Kosher salt and freshly ground pepper
2 tablespoons unsalted butter
1 medium fennel bulb—trimmed, halved and thinly sliced, fronds reserved for garnish
2 tablespoons drained capers
2 tablespoons fresh lemon juice, plus lemon wedges for serving
2 tablespoons chopped flat-leaf parsley

1. In a large nonstick skillet, heat the olive oil. Season the scallops with salt and pepper and cook over moderately high heat until golden brown on the bottom, 2 to 3 minutes. Turn the scallops and cook until just opaque throughout, 2 to 3 minutes longer. Transfer to a platter and keep warm.

2. Melt the butter in the skillet. Add the sliced fennel and capers and cook over high heat, stirring, until the fennel is crisp-tender and lightly golden, 2 minutes. Stir in the lemon juice and parsley and season with salt and pepper. Spoon the fennel around the scal-lops and garnish with chopped fennel fronds. Serve with lemon wedges. —*Kay Chun*
WINE Bright Spanish white: 2012 Martin-sancho Verdejo.

Smoky Shrimp Purloo

ACTIVE: 30 MIN; TOTAL: 1 HR
6 SERVINGS ●

A classic one-pot rice-and-meat dish, purloo is "the low-country cousin to jambalaya," explains South Carolina chef Sean Brock. He cooks the rice until crispy on the bottom, then uses it as a garnish.

18 large head-on shrimp (about 2¼ pounds)—shelled and deveined, heads and shells reserved
2 tablespoons peanut oil
¼ cup drained smoked baby clams (from one 3-ounce can)
1 cup finely chopped onion
3 garlic cloves, thinly sliced
1½ cups Carolina Gold rice (10 ounces; available at *ansonmills.com*)
4 ounces smoked trout or catfish, skinned and flaked
2 fresh bay leaves or 1 dry bay leaf
Kosher salt

1. In a pot, bring 4 cups of water to a boil. Add the shrimp heads and shells and sim-mer for 20 minutes, skimming off any foam from the surface. Strain the shrimp broth into a bowl and keep warm. Discard the heads and shells.

2. In a large enameled cast-iron casserole, heat the peanut oil. Add the clams and cook over moderate heat, stirring, until golden and fragrant, 2 minutes. Add the onion and garlic and cook, stirring, until the onion starts to soften, about 2 minutes. Stir in the rice, then stir in the trout and bay leaves and season with salt. Add enough of the shrimp broth to cover the rice (about 2½ cups) and bring to a boil. Reduce the heat to low, cover and cook until the rice is just tender, 20 minutes.

3. Lay the shrimp on the rice in a single layer. Cover and cook until the shrimp are cooked through, 6 minutes. Discard the bay leaves.

4. Spoon the rice and shrimp onto plates. Scrape up the crunchy rice crust on the bot-tom of the casserole, spoon some over the shrimp and serve. —*Sean Brock*
BEER Crisp, refreshing lager: Anchor Cali-fornia Lager.

Shrimp Tacos with Tomatillo Salsa

ACTIVE: 35 MIN; TOTAL: 1 HR 30 MIN
4 SERVINGS ●

½ pound tomatillos—husked, rinsed and quartered
½ small onion, quartered
1 jalapeño, seeded and chopped
3 garlic cloves
Kosher salt and freshly ground black pepper
¼ cup finely chopped cilantro
2 celery ribs, thinly sliced crosswise
1 tablespoon fresh lime juice
1¼ pounds medium shrimp (about 36), shelled and deveined
Twelve 6-inch bamboo skewers, soaked in water for 30 minutes
Extra-virgin olive oil, for brushing
12 corn tortillas, warmed
Shredded green cabbage and parsley leaves, for serving

1. In a medium saucepan, combine the tomatillos, onion, jalapeño and garlic with 1 cup of water and bring to a boil. Simmer over moderate heat until the vegetables are softened, about 8 minutes. Using a slotted spoon, transfer the vegetables to a blender.
2. Boil the cooking liquid until reduced to ¼ cup, then add it to the blender and let cool completely. Puree the vegetables and season with salt and pepper. Transfer to a bowl, stir in the chopped cilantro and refrigerate the salsa until chilled, about 45 minutes.
3. Meanwhile, in a bowl, toss the celery with the lime juice; season with salt and pepper.
4. Light a grill or preheat a grill pan; oil the grill grate. Thread 3 shrimp onto each skewer. Brush the shrimp with olive oil and season with salt and pepper. Grill over high heat, turning once, until lightly charred and cooked through, about 4 minutes. Remove the shrimp from the skewers and transfer to a platter. Serve the shrimp with the salsa, celery salad, warm tortillas, cabbage and parsley leaves so guests can assemble their own tacos. —*Tim Byres*
BEER Cooling Mexican lager: Dos Equis.

Scallops with Blood Orange, Fennel and Pistachios

⏱ TOTAL: 45 MIN
10 FIRST-COURSE SERVINGS ● ●

The flavors of Sicily are alive in this festive blood orange salad topped with seared sea scallops, briny green olives and fried capers.

2 small fennel bulbs—halved, cored and very thinly shaved on a mandoline
2 blood oranges, plus 6 tablespoons fresh blood orange juice
¾ cup extra-virgin olive oil
Salt and freshly ground pepper
10 large sea scallops
1 teaspoon fennel pollen
2 tablespoons unsalted butter
2 tablespoons brined capers, drained and patted dry
¼ cup sliced green olives
¼ cup unsalted roasted pistachios, coarsely chopped

1. In a large bowl, soak the fennel in ice water. Peel the blood oranges with a sharp knife, being sure to remove all of the bitter white pith. Working over a bowl, cut in between the membranes to release the sections.
2. In a medium bowl, whisk the 6 tablespoons of blood orange juice with ¼ cup of the olive oil and season with salt and pepper. Drain the fennel and pat dry. Add it to the dressing and toss to coat. Mound the salad on 10 plates.
3. In a large skillet, heat the remaining ½ cup of oil until shimmering. Season the scallops with salt and pepper and rub with the fennel pollen. Add the scallops to the skillet and cook over high heat until browned on the bottom, about 3 minutes. Add the butter and capers to the skillet. Turn the scallops over and cook just until white throughout, 2 minutes longer. Set the scallops on the fennel salads.
4. Cook the capers, basting them with the fat in the pan, until browned and crisp, 2 minutes. Scatter the capers, olives, pistachios and orange sections all around the salads and serve. —*Michael Tusk*
WINE Light, lemony white from Sicily: 2012 Tasca d'Almerita Regaleali Bianco.

Mussels with Riesling, Citrus and Saffron

TOTAL: 50 MIN
8 FIRST-COURSE SERVINGS

Chef Mourad Lahlou garnishes steamed mussels with brioche toasts and black olives—"an earthy flavor that makes a nice contrast with the flavors of the sea," he says.

2 navel oranges
1 Ruby Red grapefruit
1¼ cups Riesling
4 thyme sprigs
2 garlic cloves
4 pounds mussels, scrubbed and debearded
½ teaspoon saffron threads, crumbled
½ teaspoon finely grated orange zest
½ cup heavy cream
2 tablespoons unsalted butter
Toasted brioche croutons (see Note), sliced pitted Moroccan olives and pea shoots, for garnish

1. Using a sharp knife, peel the oranges and grapefruit, removing all of the bitter white pith. Cut in between the membranes and release the sections into a bowl. Coarsely chop the sections and return to the bowl.
2. In a large pot, combine the Riesling, thyme and garlic with 1 cup of water; bring to a boil. Add the mussels, cover and cook until the shells open, about 5 minutes. Transfer the mussels to a bowl and remove them from the shells. Discard any mussels that do not open.
3. Strain the broth and return it to the pot. Add the saffron and orange zest and boil until the broth is reduced to 2 cups, about 8 minutes. Add the cream and simmer until thickened, about 5 minutes. Add the butter and swirl until melted. Add the mussels.
4. Spoon the mussels and broth into bowls. Garnish with the citrus, croutons, olives and pea shoots and serve. —*Mourad Lahlou*
NOTE To make the croutons, cut 1-inch slices of brioche into cubes and transfer to a baking sheet. Bake in a 350° oven for 10 minutes, or until toasted.
WINE Zesty Riesling from Australia: 2011 Kilikanoon Mort's Block.

● HEALTHY ● MAKE AHEAD ○ VEGETARIAN ● STAFF FAVORITE

SHRIMP TACOS WITH
TOMATILLO SALSA

Mussels with White Beans and Chorizo

⏱ TOTAL: 10 MIN • 2 TO 4 SERVINGS

- ¼ cup plus 2 tablespoons extra-virgin olive oil
- 1 garlic clove, thinly sliced
- 2 ounces dried chorizo, diced
- 10 cherry tomatoes, halved
- Pinch of crushed red pepper
- Salt and freshly ground black pepper
- One 15-ounce can cannellini beans, drained
- 2 pounds mussels, scrubbed and debearded
- Chopped parsley and grilled bread, for serving

In a large, deep skillet, combine the olive oil with the garlic and chorizo and cook over high heat for 1 minute. Add the cherry tomatoes and crushed red pepper, season with salt and black pepper and cook for 1 minute. Add the beans, mussels and ½ cup of water, cover and cook over high heat until the mussel shells open, about 3 minutes; discard any mussels that don't open. Transfer the mussels, beans, tomatoes and chorizo to deep bowls, sprinkle with parsley and serve with grilled bread. —*Michael Schlow*
WINE Citrusy, slightly herbal Sauvignon Blanc: 2011 Benziger.

EQUIPMENT TIP

You can insert this CuizineToolz basket into any 6- to 8-quart stockpot to steam shellfish, then lift it out of the pot to get at the delicious broth. *$35; amazon.com.*

Moules Farcies

⏱ TOTAL: 45 MIN

8 HORS D'OEUVRE SERVINGS

As the founder of the Petite Pêche & Co. travel company, Danika Boyle arranges culinary tours of France and Tuscany as well as cooking classes in Austin. Many of the recipes she teaches are fairly classic, like these broiled mussels with a crispy bread crumb topping. With just a few ingredients, they are a perfect fast hors d'oeuvre.

- ½ cup crushed panko bread crumbs
- ½ cup plus 2 tablespoons extra-virgin olive oil
- Sea salt
- ¼ cup minced flat-leaf parsley
- ¼ cup freshly grated Parmigiano-Reggiano cheese
- 2 large garlic cloves, minced
- 2 pounds large mussels, scrubbed and debearded
- 1 cup dry white wine

1. In a small skillet, toast the panko over moderate heat, stirring, until lightly golden, 2 minutes; transfer the crumbs to a bowl. Stir in 1 tablespoon of the olive oil and season with salt.
2. In another bowl, combine the parsley with the cheese and half of the garlic. Stir in the ½ cup of oil and season the pesto with salt.
3. In a large, deep skillet or pot, stir the mussels over high heat for 2 minutes. Add the remaining garlic and 2 tablespoons of olive oil and cook for 1 minute. Add the white wine, cover with a tight-fitting lid and cook just until the mussels open, 3 minutes. Drain the mussels and let cool on a baking sheet. Loosen the mussels in their shells and discard the empty half shells.
4. Preheat the broiler; position a rack about 8 inches from the heat. Spoon the parsley pesto over the mussels and sprinkle with the toasted panko. Broil until the crumbs are golden, about 6 minutes, shifting the pan for even browning, then serve. —*Danika Boyle*
WINE Fragrant, medium-bodied French white: 2012 Domaine Houchart Côtes de Provence Blanc.

Steamed Mussels with Tarragon

⏱ TOTAL: 45 MIN

8 FIRST-COURSE SERVINGS ● ●

One of the first recipes that *Top Chef* head judge Tom Colicchio learned to cook, when he was about 13, was a version of these steamed mussels, packed with fresh tomatoes and fragrant tarragon.

- 1½ pounds tomatoes, cored
- ¼ cup extra-virgin olive oil, plus more for drizzling
- 2 large shallots, thinly sliced
- 1 cup dry white wine
- 4 pounds mussels, scrubbed and debearded
- 3 tablespoons white wine vinegar
- 2 tablespoons *sambal oelek* or other Asian chile sauce
- 3 tablespoons finely chopped tarragon, plus whole tarragon leaves for garnish
- Kosher salt and freshly ground pepper
- Crusty bread, for serving

1. In a large saucepan of boiling water, blanch the tomatoes until the skins just start to wrinkle, about 45 seconds. Drain and transfer to a bowl of ice water to cool. Peel the tomatoes and coarsely chop them.
2. In the large saucepan, heat the ¼ cup of olive oil until shimmering. Add the shallots and cook over moderate heat until softened, 4 minutes. Add the wine and bring to a boil, then stir in the mussels. Cover and steam until they just start to open, 3 minutes. Stir in the tomatoes, cover and cook, shaking the pan, until the mussels are open, 3 to 5 minutes longer; discard any that don't open. Stir in the white wine vinegar, *sambal oelek* and chopped tarragon and season with salt and pepper. Pile the mussels and tomatoes in a large serving bowl and pour in the juices from the pan. Drizzle generously with olive oil, garnish with tarragon leaves and serve with crusty bread. —*Tom Colicchio*
WINE Minerally Sauvignon Blanc from France's Burgundy region: 2012 Jean-Marc Brocard Saint-Bris.

● HEALTHY ● MAKE AHEAD ● VEGETARIAN ● STAFF FAVORITE

MUSSELS WITH WHITE
BEANS AND CHORIZO

Pan-Roasted Clams with Bacon, Bourbon and Jalapeño

⏱ **TOTAL: 45 MIN**

4 FIRST-COURSE SERVINGS

For this riff on a popular mussels dish served at Holeman & Finch in Atlanta, chef Linton Hopkins swaps in local Sapelo Island clams. Easier-to-find littleneck clams also work well in the recipe.

One 3-ounce slab of smoked bacon,
    cut into ½-inch dice (½ cup)
¼ cup minced shallots
2 tablespoons minced garlic
2 dozen littleneck clams—
    scrubbed, soaked in cold water
    for 15 minutes and drained
¼ cup bourbon
¼ cup bottled clam juice
¼ cup heavy cream
2 jalapeños, thinly sliced
    into rounds
2 tablespoons minced
    flat-leaf parsley
2 tablespoons unsalted butter
Crusty bread, for serving

1. In a large, deep skillet, cook the diced smoked bacon over moderately low heat, stirring occasionally, until the fat has rendered and the bacon has browned, about 10 minutes. With a slotted spoon, transfer the bacon to a plate.

2. Add the shallots and garlic to the skillet and cook over moderately low heat, stirring occasionally, until softened, about 3 minutes. Stir in the clams and bourbon and simmer over moderate heat until the bourbon has almost evaporated, 2 to 3 minutes. Add the clam juice, cover and cook until the clams open, 5 to 7 minutes. Discard any clams that do not open.

3. Transfer the clams to shallow bowls. Add the heavy cream, jalapeños, parsley and bacon to the skillet and simmer for 2 minutes. Swirl in the butter. Pour the sauce over the clams and serve with crusty bread.
—Linton Hopkins

WINE Vibrant, slightly oaky white: 2011 Belondrade y Lurton Rueda Superior.

Grilled Oysters with Chorizo Butter

⏱ **TOTAL: 45 MIN • MAKES 18 OYSTERS** ●

No shucking necessary for these oysters from chef David Kinch of Manresa in Los Gatos, California: The grill does the work here. Once the oysters open, all you do is top them with some of Kinch's smoky, tangy chorizo butter. Despite the butter, spice and pork, the dish is surprisingly light. "That's the lime juice and lime zest," says Kinch. "They bring the dish into harmony."

4 ounces fresh Mexican chorizo,
    casings removed
1½ sticks unsalted butter,
    cut into ½-inch cubes
2 tablespoons freshly squeezed
    lime juice
Salt
18 Louisiana or other medium
    to large oysters, scrubbed
Cilantro leaves and finely grated
    lime zest, for garnish

1. In a medium skillet, cook the chorizo over moderate heat, stirring and breaking it up with a spoon, until lightly browned, about 8 minutes. Scrape the chorizo into a bowl and let cool, then break it into small clumps.

2. Add 1 tablespoon of water to the skillet and simmer over low heat. Add the butter to the skillet a few cubes at a time, whisking constantly until melted before adding more. Stir in the chorizo and lime juice and season with salt. Keep the chorizo butter warm over very low heat.

3. Light a grill. Place the oysters on the grill, flat side up. Grill over high heat until the shells open slightly. Discard any oysters that do not open. Carefully transfer the oysters to a platter and, using kitchen gloves or a mitt, remove the top shell. Spoon the chorizo butter onto the oysters and garnish each with a cilantro leaf and lime zest. Serve right away.
—David Kinch

SERVE WITH Thick slices of good-quality grilled sourdough bread.

WINE Minerally Chablis: 2011 Domaine Christian Moreau Père & Fils.

Fire-Grilled Oysters with Green Garlic and Pastis Butter

ACTIVE 20 MIN; TOTAL 50 MIN

MAKES 2 DOZEN OYSTERS ●

Through his nine restaurants and the John Besh Foundation, chef John Besh is an ardent supporter of southern Louisiana ingredients and culinary traditions. For this dish, he recommends large, plump oyster varieties like those from the Gulf Coast. The mingling of oyster juices with butter, herbs, chile and pastis makes these oysters irresistibly slurpable.

2 sticks unsalted butter,
    at room temperature
¼ cup minced green garlic
    or scallions
1 teaspoon chopped chives
1 teaspoon chopped thyme
1 teaspoon crushed red pepper
1 teaspoon fresh lemon juice
2 tablespoons pastis or Pernod
    (see Note)
2 dozen freshly shucked
    oysters on the half shell

1. In a medium bowl, blend the butter with the green garlic, chives, thyme, crushed red pepper, lemon juice and pastis. Spoon the butter onto a sheet of plastic wrap, roll it into a log and twist the ends to seal. Refrigerate the pastis butter until firm, about 30 minutes.

2. Light a grill. Arrange the shucked oysters on a perforated grill pan and top each with a ¼-inch-thick slice of the pastis butter. Grill the oysters over high heat just until the liquor is bubbling around the edges and the butter has melted, about 3 minutes. Serve the oysters hot. *—John Besh*

NOTE Pastis is an anise-flavored French spirit that turns cloudy when mixed with water. Pernod is a French producer of a liqueur made from the essential oils of star anise and fennel combined with herbs, spices and a neutral spirit.

MAKE AHEAD The pastis butter can be refrigerated for up to 1 week.

WINE Crisp, focused Spanish white: 2011 Lagar de Costa Rías Baixas Albariño.

Pan-Seared Octopus with Italian Vegetable Salad

ACTIVE: 45 MIN; TOTAL: 2 HR 30 MIN
4 FIRST-COURSE SERVINGS ● ●

¼ cup plus 2 tablespoons
  extra-virgin olive oil
One 2½-pound octopus—cleaned,
  head and tentacles separated
6 garlic cloves
1 tablespoon plus 1 teaspoon
  crushed red pepper
One 750-milliliter bottle dry white wine,
  such as Sauvignon Blanc
2 tablespoons red wine vinegar
2 tablespoons fresh lemon juice
1½ teaspoons dried oregano
1 fennel bulb—halved lengthwise,
  cored and thinly sliced
1 medium carrot, thinly sliced
  crosswise
½ small red onion, thinly sliced
3 scallions, thinly sliced
  on the diagonal
One 15-ounce can chickpeas,
  rinsed and drained
Kosher salt
½ cup lightly packed parsley leaves
4 large radicchio leaves
Fennel fronds, for garnish (optional)

1. In a large enameled cast-iron casserole, heat 2 tablespoons of the oil. Add the octopus and cook over moderately high heat, turning, until lightly browned all over, 2 to 3 minutes. Transfer to a plate. Add the garlic to the casserole and cook over moderate heat, stirring, until lightly browned, 2 minutes. Add the crushed red pepper and cook, stirring, until fragrant, 20 seconds. Carefully add the white wine and bring to a boil. Return the octopus to the casserole; if necessary, add up to 1 cup of water to cover the octopus. Cover the casserole and braise over moderately low heat until very tender, about 1 hour and 30 minutes. Transfer the octopus to a plate and let cool completely.
2. Meanwhile, in a large bowl, whisk the red wine vinegar with the lemon juice, oregano and 2 tablespoons of the olive oil. Add the fennel, carrot, onion, scallions, chickpeas and a generous pinch of salt and mix well. Let stand for 30 minutes or up to 4 hours, stirring occasionally. Stir in the parsley and season the salad with salt.
3. Using a paper towel, wipe the purple skin off the octopus tentacles, leaving the suckers intact. Cut the tentacles in half lengthwise, then cut them into 3-inch lengths. Cut the head into 1½-inch pieces.
4. In a large skillet, heat the remaining 2 tablespoons of olive oil. Add the octopus cut side down and cook over moderately high heat until well browned on the bottom, about 1 minute. Turn the octopus and cook for 20 seconds longer. Transfer the seared octopus to a paper towel–lined plate and season lightly with salt. Transfer the octopus to plates. Fill the radicchio leaves with the Italian salad and set beside the octopus. Garnish with fennel fronds and serve.
—*Vinny Dotolo and Jon Shook*
MAKE AHEAD The braised octopus can be refrigerated for up to 3 days.
WINE Citrusy, full-bodied Italian white: 2012 Feudi di San Gregorio Falanghina.

Crab Salad with Mint Oil

🕑 **TOTAL: 20 MIN • 4 TO 6 SERVINGS** ●

½ cup lightly packed mint leaves
¾ cup plus 2 tablespoons
  extra-virgin olive oil
Kosher salt
One 15-ounce can Great Northern beans
  or other canned white beans,
  rinsed and drained
¼ cup minced red onion
1 teaspoon minced rosemary
1 teaspoon minced marjoram
1 teaspoon finely grated lemon zest
2½ tablespoons fresh lemon juice
Freshly ground pepper
1 pound lump crabmeat, picked over

1. In a saucepan of salted boiling water, blanch the mint for 30 seconds. Transfer to a bowl of ice water; drain well and squeeze dry. Transfer the mint to a blender and puree with ¾ cup of the olive oil and a pinch of salt.
2. In a bowl, toss the beans with the onion, herbs, lemon zest and juice and remaining 2 tablespoons of oil. Season with salt and pepper. Fold in the crab. Drizzle the salad with the mint oil and serve. —*Mario Batali*
WINE Mineral-driven northern Italian white: 2012 Terlano Pinot Bianco.

Fresh Crab Escabèche

ACTIVE: 30 MIN; TOTAL: 4 HR 30 MIN
8 TO 10 SERVINGS ●

1 teaspoon coriander seeds
1 teaspoon fennel seeds
½ teaspoon cumin seeds
1½ cups pure olive oil
1 medium onion, thinly sliced
1 large shallot, thinly sliced
1 red bell pepper, thinly sliced
2 garlic cloves, thinly sliced
1 large carrot, cut into
  fine matchsticks
3 tablespoons sherry vinegar
½ teaspoon chopped thyme
Small pinch of saffron threads
Salt
1½ pounds jumbo lump crabmeat,
  picked over
3 tablespoons chopped
  flat-leaf parsley

1. In a large saucepan, toast the coriander, fennel and cumin seeds over moderate heat until fragrant, about 1 minute. Transfer the seeds to a plate and let cool. Finely grind the spices and return them to the saucepan. Add the olive oil, onion, shallot, bell pepper, garlic, carrot and sherry vinegar and bring to a gentle simmer over moderately low heat. Cook until the bell pepper is crisp-tender, about 8 minutes. Add the thyme and saffron and season with salt. Let cool.
2. Put the crabmeat and parsley in a large bowl and pour the *escabèche* mixture on top. Gently toss, being careful not to break up the crab. Refrigerate until chilled, at least 4 hours or overnight. Serve. —*David Kinch*
SERVE WITH Crusty bread.
WINE Tangy, medium-bodied Sauvignon Blanc: 2012 St. Supéry Napa Valley Estate.

Braised Squid with Chermoula, Olives and Pine Nuts

ACTIVE: 40 MIN; TOTAL: 2 HR
4 SERVINGS ● ●

According to Moroccan chef Mourad Lahlou, *chermoula* (a garlicky, herb-packed sauce) is essentially the salsa verde of Morocco. His version here has an abundance of fresh parsley and cilantro. "This dish has the flavors and spices of Morocco, but it's much brighter," he says.

SQUID

1	cup pine nuts (6 ounces)
3	pounds cleaned squid, bodies and tentacles left whole
8	dried árbol chiles
12	large garlic cloves, peeled
24	thyme sprigs
2	tablespoons whole black peppercorns

Kosher salt

4	cups pure olive oil
2	cups pitted green olives (12 ounces), coarsely chopped

CHERMOULA

1½	cups flat-leaf parsley leaves
1½	cups tender cilantro stems
3	garlic cloves
½	teaspoon ground coriander
½	teaspoon freshly ground black pepper
½	teaspoon ground cumin
⅛	teaspoon cayenne
¾	cup extra-virgin olive oil
½	tablespoon chopped preserved lemon peel (see Note)

Kosher salt

1. Preheat the oven to 300°. Spread the pine nuts in a pie plate and toast them for about 10 minutes, until golden. Let the pine nuts cool.
2. BRAISE THE SQUID In a large, deep oven-proof skillet, toss the squid with the dried chiles, garlic cloves, thyme, peppercorns and a generous pinch of salt and let stand for 10 minutes. Add the olive oil and bake for about 1 hour and 10 minutes, until the squid is very tender. Let the squid cool in the oil.

3. Transfer the squid to a cutting board. Cut the bodies into rings and halve the tentacles. Transfer the squid to a large bowl and toss with the toasted pine nuts and the green olives. Discard the oil.
4. MEANWHILE, MAKE THE CHERMOULA In a blender, combine the parsley leaves with the cilantro stems, garlic cloves, ground coriander, black pepper, cumin and cayenne and pulse to chop the herbs. With the machine on, gradually pour in the olive oil and puree until smooth. Add the preserved lemon peel and pulse once or twice to chop. Add the *chermoula* to the squid, season with salt and toss to coat. Serve the squid warm or at room temperature. —*Mourad Lahlou*
NOTE Preserved lemon peel is available at specialty markets and *amazon.com*.
MAKE AHEAD The cooked squid can be refrigerated in the oil overnight. Bring to room temperature before proceeding.
WINE Fragrant, floral Rhône-style white: 2010 d'Arenberg The Hermit Crab.

Charred Squid with Beans and Meyer Lemon

ACTIVE: 35 MIN; TOTAL: 1 HR 30 MIN
PLUS OVERNIGHT SOAKING
4 SERVINGS ●

½	pound large dried white beans, such as gigante, soaked overnight and drained

Kosher salt

3	celery ribs, thinly sliced diagonally
2	tablespoons white wine vinegar
1	cup flat-leaf parsley leaves
6	tablespoons extra-virgin olive oil

Freshly ground black pepper

1½	pounds cleaned small squid bodies and tentacles
2	Meyer lemons, 1½ thinly sliced

1. In a medium saucepan, cover the white beans with 2 inches of water and bring to a boil. Simmer the beans until tender, 35 to 45 minutes. Remove the saucepan from the heat and stir in 1½ teaspoons of salt. Let stand for 20 minutes, then drain the beans and let them cool.

2. In a medium bowl, toss the beans, celery, vinegar, and parsley with ¼ cup of the olive oil. Season with salt and pepper.
3. In a large bowl, season the squid with salt. In a large cast-iron skillet, heat the remaining 2 tablespoons of oil. In batches, cook the squid over high heat, stirring occasionally, until browned in spots and just cooked, 1 to 2 minutes per batch.
4. Squeeze the lemon half over the beans and toss; mound on plates and top with the squid and lemon slices; serve. —*Ignacio Mattos*
WINE Ripe, earthy Loire Valley sparkling rosé: NV François Pinon Touraine Brut Rosé.

Squid with Burst Cherry Tomatoes

⏱ TOTAL: 30 MIN
8 TO 10 SERVINGS ● ●

In summer, most people don't bother to cook tomatoes. But chef Tom Colicchio likes to see what flavors he can bring out. "I was just messing around with cherry tomatoes, and I decided to cook them with garlic until they burst open," he says. The result: extravagantly juicy tomatoes with amped-up flavor. Colicchio cooks squid in the sauce but says you can also serve it with pasta.

⅓	cup extra-virgin olive oil
2½	pounds mixed cherry tomatoes
2	large garlic cloves, minced

Kosher salt and freshly ground pepper

1½	pounds small squid—cleaned, bodies cut into ⅓-inch rings and tentacles halved
1½	tablespoons white wine vinegar
1	cup lightly packed small basil leaves

In a large, deep skillet, heat the oil. Add the tomatoes, garlic and a pinch each of salt and pepper. Cook over moderate heat, stirring, until the tomatoes just start to blister, 4 minutes. Stir in the squid and cook over moderately low heat, stirring, until the squid turns opaque, 5 minutes. Stir in the vinegar and basil. Season with salt and pepper and serve. —*Tom Colicchio*
WINE Mineral-driven, berried rosé from Provence: 2012 Hecht & Bannier.

● HEALTHY ● MAKE AHEAD ○ VEGETARIAN ● STAFF FAVORITE

SQUID WITH BURST
CHERRY TOMATOES

Chef Paul Qui preps a late-night meal of Filipino-style chicken and other Asian-inflected dishes at his home kitchen in Austin.

Opposite: recipe, page 148.

ADOBO CHICKEN
WITH BACON AND BAY LEAVES

CHICKEN, TURKEY & OTHER BIRDS

Quick Chicken Kiev

⏱ TOTAL: 40 MIN • 4 SERVINGS

To make a classic chicken Kiev, Ukrainian cooks pound cutlets flat, roll them around a log of herb butter, then bread and fry them. In this streamlined recipe, a pocket cut into the breast holds the butter.

Four 6-ounce skinless, boneless chicken
    breast halves, lightly pounded to an
    even thickness
Salt and freshly ground pepper
  1 stick unsalted butter, softened
  2 tablespoons finely chopped dill
  2 tablespoons finely chopped chives
All-purpose flour, for dusting
  3 large eggs, beaten
1½ cups panko bread crumbs, crushed
  2 tablespoons extra-virgin olive oil,
    plus more for frying
  1 tablespoon fresh lemon juice
  1 large bunch of arugula, stemmed

1. Carefully slice a pocket into the side of each chicken breast and season with salt and pepper. In a small bowl, blend the butter with the dill and chives and season with salt and pepper. Spoon half of the herb butter into the pockets and pinch closed.
2. Dredge the chicken in flour, tapping off the excess. Put the eggs and bread crumbs in 2 separate shallow bowls; season with salt and pepper. Dip the chicken in the eggs and then in the bread crumbs, sealing the pockets; dab any open spots with egg and sprinkle with bread crumbs to seal. Place the chicken on a baking sheet and freeze for 5 minutes.
3. In a large skillet, heat ½ inch of olive oil until shimmering. Add the chicken and fry over moderate heat, turning once or twice, until golden and cooked through, 8 minutes.
4. In a large bowl, whisk the 2 tablespoons of olive oil with the lemon juice and season with salt and pepper. Add the arugula and toss. Transfer the chicken to plates and top with the remaining herb butter. Serve the arugula salad alongside. —*Grace Parisi*
WINE Green apple–scented, full-bodied Rhône white: 2011 M. Chapoutier Belleruche Blanc.

Adobo Chicken with Bacon and Bay Leaves

📷 PAGE 147

ACTIVE: 30 MIN; TOTAL: 1 HR
6 SERVINGS ● ●

In the traditional Filipino dish adobo, chicken thighs stew in vinegar and soy sauce. If you can find coconut vinegar—made from the sap of the coconut tree—it's delicious here.

  3 ounces thick-cut bacon,
    cut into ¼-inch matchsticks
  6 large chicken thighs
    (about 8 ounces each)
Salt and freshly ground black pepper
  6 garlic cloves, minced
  1 large shallot, thinly sliced
 ¼ cup plus 2 tablespoons coconut
    vinegar or cider vinegar (see Note)
  3 cups low-sodium chicken broth
1½ tablespoons Asian fish sauce
1½ tablespoons *shiro* shoyu
    (white soy sauce; see Note)
  6 bay leaves
Pinch of cayenne pepper

1. In a large, deep skillet, cook the bacon over moderate heat until browned, 3 minutes. Transfer the bacon to a plate, leaving the fat in the skillet. Season the chicken lightly with salt and black pepper and add it to the skillet, skin side up. Cook over moderately low heat, turning once, until browned all over, 12 minutes. Transfer the chicken to a plate.
2. Spoon off all but 2 tablespoons of the fat from the skillet. Add the garlic and shallot and cook over low heat, stirring, until softened, about 3 minutes. Add the vinegar and cook until reduced by half, scraping up any bits stuck to the pan, about 2 minutes. Add the broth, fish sauce, *shiro* shoyu, bay leaves and cayenne and bring to a simmer.
3. Return the chicken and bacon to the skillet and cook over moderately low heat, turning once or twice, until the chicken is cooked through and the sauce is reduced by half, about 30 minutes. Discard the bay leaves, spoon off the excess fat and serve.
—*Paul Qui*
SERVE WITH Qui's Ginger Rice (page 254).

NOTE Coconut vinegar and *shiro* shoyu can be found at Asian markets and online at *amazon.com*.
MAKE AHEAD The adobo chicken can be refrigerated overnight or frozen for 2 weeks.
WINE Earthy, brambly Pinot Noir: 2011 Banshee Sonoma County.

Citrusy Chicken Tenders

ACTIVE: 30 MIN; TOTAL: 2 HR 30 MIN
4 SERVINGS

In this flavorful revamp of *pollo fritto per Chanukah* (fried chicken for Hanukkah), chef Sergio Durando of Le Baladin pub in Piedmont, Italy, marinates thin chicken strips in white ale and citrus juices, then fries them up until they're golden and crisp. He serves the chicken tenders with warm marinara sauce for dipping.

  1 large egg
  1 cup white ale, such as Baladin Isaac
  2 teaspoons each of finely grated
    lemon, lime and orange zests
 ¼ cup fresh orange juice
  3 tablespoons fresh lemon juice
  2 tablespoons fresh lime juice
  1 teaspoon finely chopped thyme
Kosher salt and freshly ground pepper
  1 pound skinless, boneless chicken
    breast halves, cut into ½-inch strips
1½ cups plain dry bread crumbs
Canola or vegetable oil, for frying
Warm marinara sauce, for serving

1. In a large bowl, whisk the egg, ale, citrus zests and juices and thyme. Season with a generous pinch of salt and pepper. Add the chicken, cover and refrigerate for 2 to 4 hours.
2. Set a rack on a baking sheet. Put the bread crumbs in a shallow dish. Working with one strip at a time, remove the chicken from the marinade, dredge it in the bread crumbs and transfer to the rack.
3. In a large, deep skillet, heat 1 inch of oil to 350°. Working in batches, fry the chicken until golden and cooked through, 5 minutes. Drain on paper towels and sprinkle with salt. Serve with warm marinara sauce. —*Sergio Durando*
BEER Belgian-style white ale: Baladin Isaac.

● HEALTHY ● MAKE AHEAD ● VEGETARIAN ● STAFF FAVORITE

CITRUSY CHICKEN TENDERS

Classic Chicken Teriyaki

:) **TOTAL: 30 MIN • 4 SERVINGS** ●

This chicken teriyaki—the best ever from legendary chef Nobu Matsuhisa—is incredibly easy to prepare at home. It calls for lean chicken breasts, but boneless chicken thighs would be wonderful too.

- 1 **cup chicken stock or low-sodium broth**
- ⅓ **cup low-sodium soy sauce**
- ⅓ **cup sugar**
- 2 **tablespoons mirin**
- 2 **tablespoons sake**

Four 6-ounce skinless, boneless chicken breasts, lightly pounded

Kosher salt and freshly ground pepper

- 2 **tablespoons canola oil**
- 2 **large Italian frying peppers, cut into ½-inch strips**

Steamed short-grain rice, for serving

1. In a medium saucepan, combine the chicken stock, soy sauce, sugar, mirin and sake and bring to a boil over high heat, stirring to dissolve the sugar. Reduce the heat to moderate; simmer the sauce until syrupy and reduced to ½ cup, about 20 minutes.

2. Meanwhile, season the chicken with salt and freshly ground pepper. In a large nonstick skillet, heat 1 tablespoon of the canola oil. Add the chicken and cook over moderately high heat, turning once, until browned on both sides and cooked through, 8 to 9 minutes. Transfer the chicken to a plate and let stand for 5 minutes.

3. Wipe out the skillet. Add the remaining 1 tablespoon of canola oil and heat until shimmering. Add the pepper strips and cook over high heat, stirring occasionally, until crisp-tender and lightly charred, about 3 minutes. Transfer the peppers to plates. Slice the chicken breasts crosswise and transfer to the plates. Drizzle the teriyaki sauce over the chicken and serve with rice.

—Nobu Matsuhisa

MAKE AHEAD The teriyaki sauce can be refrigerated for up to 1 month.

WINE Juicy, raspberry-rich Grenache: 2012 Bonny Doon Clos de Gilroy.

Panko-Crusted Chicken Tenders with Kohlrabi Slaw

ACTIVE: 40 MIN; TOTAL: 1 HR 40 MIN 6 SERVINGS

At GBD in Washington, DC, chef Kyle Bailey marinates chicken tenders in a mix of sweet and savory herbs and spices, giving this childhood favorite a sophisticated edge. Panko-breaded and fried, these are the ultimate homemade chicken fingers: juicy, flavorful and exceptionally crispy.

- ½ **cup soy sauce**
- ½ **cup apple cider vinegar**
- 1 **small onion, halved and thinly sliced**
- 5 **garlic cloves, crushed**
- 2 **teaspoons crushed red pepper**
- 1 **teaspoon finely chopped thyme leaves**
- 1 **teaspoon cinnamon**
- ¼ **teaspoon freshly grated nutmeg**
- 2½ **teaspoons garlic powder**
- 2 **pounds chicken tenders**
- 3 **cups panko (Japanese bread crumbs)**
- 1½ **teaspoons kosher salt**
- 1½ **teaspoons onion powder**
- 1½ **teaspoons freshly ground black pepper**
- 3 **large egg whites**

Canola oil, for frying

Kohlrabi Slaw (recipe follows), for serving

1. In a large resealable plastic bag, combine the soy sauce with the cider vinegar, onion, crushed garlic, crushed red pepper, thyme, cinnamon, nutmeg and 1 teaspoon of the garlic powder. Add the chicken tenders, seal the plastic bag and turn to coat the chicken pieces. Let the chicken marinate at room temperature for 1 hour.

2. Meanwhile, in a food processor, combine the panko with the salt, onion powder, black pepper and the remaining 1½ teaspoons of garlic powder and pulse until the panko is finely ground. Transfer the seasoned crumbs to a pie plate. In another pie plate, beat the egg whites until foamy.

3. Remove the chicken tenders from the marinade, scraping off any solids. Pat the chicken tenders dry with paper towels and transfer them to a wax paper–lined baking sheet. Dip the tenders in the egg whites, letting the excess drip back into the pie plate, then dredge them in the seasoned crumbs. Transfer the chicken tenders to the baking sheet.

4. Set a rack over another baking sheet. In a large skillet, heat ⅓ inch of canola oil until shimmering. Working in two batches, fry the chicken tenders over moderately high heat, turning once, until they are well browned and crisp, about 7 minutes per batch. Transfer the panko-crusted tenders to the rack to drain. Serve with Kohlrabi Slaw.

—Kyle Bailey

WINE Spice-inflected Sonoma Chardonnay: 2011 Fogdog.

KOHLRABI SLAW

ACTIVE: 20 MIN; TOTAL: 1 HR 20 MIN 6 SERVINGS ● ● ●

- ⅓ **cup mayonnaise**
- 3 **tablespoons canola oil**
- 3 **tablespoons apple cider vinegar**
- 2 **tablespoons whole-grain mustard**
- ¾ **teaspoon sugar**
- ¾ **teaspoon celery seeds**

Kosher salt and freshly ground black pepper

- 2 **pounds purple and/or green kohlrabi, peeled and coarsely shredded on a box grater**
- 1 **cup shredded green cabbage**
- 1 **medium celery rib, thinly sliced crosswise**

In a large bowl, whisk the mayonnaise with the canola oil, vinegar, mustard, sugar, celery seeds, 1½ teaspoons of salt and ¾ teaspoon of pepper. Add the kohlrabi, cabbage and celery and toss well. Cover and refrigerate for 1 hour. Season the slaw with salt and pepper and serve. *—KB*

MAKE AHEAD The kohlrabi slaw can be refrigerated overnight.

● HEALTHY ● MAKE AHEAD ○ VEGETARIAN ● STAFF FAVORITE

CLASSIC CHICKEN TERIYAKI

Spicy Stir-Fried Cucumbers with Shredded Chicken

◔ TOTAL: 30 MIN • 4 SERVINGS ●

12 ounces skinless, boneless chicken
   breast cutlets, pounded ⅛ inch
   thick and very thinly sliced
   crosswise
5 garlic cloves, smashed
1 tablespoon finely chopped
   peeled fresh ginger
1 teaspoon baking soda
Kosher salt and freshly ground pepper
¼ cup distilled white vinegar
1 teaspoon sugar
3 tablespoons canola oil
12 dried red chiles, such as
   árbol chiles—10 left whole,
   2 stemmed and crumbled
1 pound seedless cucumbers,
   preferably Persian, cut into
   1½-inch pieces
1 serrano chile, thinly sliced
¼ cup chopped cilantro sprigs
Lemon wedges and steamed rice,
   for serving

1. In a medium bowl, toss the chicken with half of the garlic and ginger and the baking soda; season with salt and pepper. In a small bowl, stir the vinegar with the sugar and ¼ cup of water.
2. In a large skillet, heat 2 tablespoons of the oil until shimmering. Add the chicken and stir-fry over moderately high heat until the chicken is almost cooked through, 2 minutes; transfer the chicken to a plate. Add the remaining 1 tablespoon of oil to the skillet along with the whole and crumbled dried chiles, cucumbers, vinegar mixture and the remaining garlic and ginger; season with salt and pepper. Stir-fry over moderate heat until the cucumbers are softened and most of the liquid has evaporated, 3 minutes. Add the chicken and serrano; stir-fry until the chicken is cooked through, 1 minute. Stir in the cilantro and season with salt and pepper. Serve with lemon wedges and rice. —*Kay Chun*
WINE Fruity, full-bodied white from Oregon: 2012 Seven Hills Pinot Gris.

Za'atar-Roasted Chicken Breasts

TOTAL: 1 HR • 4 SERVINGS ●
Za'atar, the Middle Eastern spice mix made with sesame seeds, sumac, oregano and thyme, flavors both the chicken and the cooling yogurt sauce served on the side.

2 tablespoons sesame seeds
2 tablespoons dried oregano
1 tablespoon chopped thyme
½ cup plain fat-free Greek yogurt
Kosher salt and freshly ground pepper
Two 8-ounce bone-in chicken
   breast halves
¼ cup extra-virgin olive oil
¾ pound Persian or seedless
   cucumbers, thinly sliced
1 large romaine lettuce heart
   (12 ounces), chopped
1 tablespoon fresh lemon juice
2 teaspoons sumac (see Note)
Warm pita bread, for serving

1. Preheat the oven to 425°. In a small bowl, combine the sesame seeds, oregano and thyme. In another small bowl, stir 1 tablespoon of the herb mix with the yogurt and season with salt and pepper.
2. On a foil-lined baking sheet, rub the chicken with 2 tablespoons of the olive oil; season with salt and pepper. Roast for 30 minutes, until the skin is golden and crisp. Sprinkle with the remaining herb mix and roast for 10 minutes longer, until the chicken is cooked through. Let the chicken rest for 5 minutes, then carve the breasts off the bone and thinly slice them against the grain.
3. In a large bowl, toss the cucumbers and romaine with the lemon juice, sumac and the remaining 2 tablespoons of olive oil; season with salt and pepper. Transfer the salad to a large platter and top with the chicken. Serve with the za'atar yogurt and warm pita. —*Kay Chun*
NOTE Sumac, a tart and tangy spice made from ground sumac berries, is available at specialty stores and online at *penzeys.com*.
WINE Lively, creamy Chardonnay: 2011 St. Francis Wild Oak.

Spiced Chicken with Coconut-Caramel Sauce and Citrus Salad

ACTIVE: 40 MIN; TOTAL: 1 HR 20 MIN
4 SERVINGS ●
Bora Bora's tropical climate inspired star chef Jean-Georges Vongerichten's chicken with caramel-infused coconut milk sauce.

¼ cup plus 2 teaspoons sugar
1½ teaspoons ground coriander
1½ teaspoons ground cumin
½ teaspoon turmeric
½ teaspoon freshly ground pepper
Cayenne pepper
4 boneless chicken breast halves
   with skin
½ cup unsweetened coconut milk
2 tablespoons Asian fish sauce
1 Thai green chile, minced
Salt
1 grapefruit and 1 lime—peeled,
   sectioned and diced
1 cup diced fresh pineapple
Extra-virgin olive oil
2 tablespoons thinly sliced cilantro
Fleur de sel, for garnish

1. In a bowl, mix 2 teaspoons of the sugar with the coriander, cumin, turmeric, pepper and ½ teaspoon of cayenne. Rub the spices on the chicken, cover and refrigerate for 1 hour.
2. Meanwhile, in a saucepan, mix the remaining ¼ cup of sugar with 2 tablespoons of water; bring to a boil. Simmer until an amber caramel forms, 10 minutes. Off the heat, stir in the coconut milk until the caramel dissolves. Add the fish sauce and chile; let stand for 5 minutes, strain and season with salt.
3. In a medium bowl, gently toss the fruits with a pinch each of salt and cayenne.
4. Light a grill. Rub the chicken with olive oil and season with salt. Grill over moderate heat, turning once, until the skin is charred and the chicken is white throughout, 12 minutes. Transfer to plates along with the fruit salad and sauce. Drizzle with olive oil, sprinkle with the cilantro and fleur de sel and serve.
—*Jean-Georges Vongerichten*
WINE Citrusy, ripe Alsace Pinot Blanc: 2011 Domaines Schlumberger Les Princes Abbés.

● HEALTHY ● MAKE AHEAD ● VEGETARIAN ● STAFF FAVORITE

Chicken-and-Mushroom Fricassee

⏲ **TOTAL: 30 MIN • 4 SERVINGS** ●

Writer Joy Manning creates a chicken stew that tastes slow-cooked even though it's ready in a half hour. Her secret in keeping it light: using just a little cream.

    1   tablespoon grapeseed oil
Four 8-ounce skinless, boneless chicken
        breasts, pounded to an even
        thickness
Kosher salt and freshly ground pepper
    2   teaspoons unsalted butter
    1   medium shallot, minced
    2   pounds cremini or white button
        mushrooms, thinly sliced
    2   tablespoons all-purpose flour
   ½   cup dry white wine
    1   cup chicken stock or
        low-sodium broth
    2   tablespoons minced tarragon
  1½   tablespoons heavy cream

1. In a large nonstick skillet, heat the oil. Season the chicken with salt and pepper, add to the skillet and cook over moderately high heat, turning once, until browned, about 3 minutes per side; transfer to a plate.
2. Add the butter, shallot and mushrooms to the skillet, season with salt and pepper and cook, stirring frequently, until the mushrooms begin to brown, about 12 minutes. Stir in the flour and cook until it smells lightly toasty, about 1 minute.
3. Add the wine, stock and chicken to the skillet. Cover and simmer over moderate heat until the chicken is cooked through, about 5 minutes. Transfer the chicken to a platter.
4. Increase the heat to moderately high and simmer the sauce until slightly reduced, about 5 minutes. Remove the skillet from the heat and stir in the tarragon and cream. Spoon the sauce and mushrooms over the chicken breasts and serve immediately.
—Joy Manning

VARIATION Swap out the mushrooms with leeks for a different flavor profile.
WINE Concentrated, elegant white Burgundy: 2010 Pierre Morey Meursault.

Chicken Meatball and Shishito Yakitori

ACTIVE: 45 MIN; TOTAL: 1 HR
6 FIRST-COURSE SERVINGS ● ● ●

Known as *tsukune,* these juicy Japanese meatballs are grilled on skewers with mild green shishito peppers (available at Japanese and farmers' markets).

   ¼   cup reduced-sodium soy sauce
    2   tablespoons mirin
    5   garlic cloves—2 crushed, 3 minced
One 2-inch piece of ginger, thinly sliced,
        plus 1½ tablespoons minced ginger
    1   teaspoon sugar
    4   white button mushrooms, chopped
  2½   pounds skinless, boneless chicken
        thighs, chopped into ¼-inch pieces
   ¼   cup plus 1 tablespoon *shiro*
        (white) miso
    2   tablespoons untoasted sesame oil,
        plus more for brushing
    3   scallions, minced
   ⅛   teaspoon kosher salt
   ¾   teaspoon freshly ground black
        pepper
   12   shishito peppers

1. In a small saucepan, combine the soy sauce, mirin, crushed garlic cloves, sliced ginger and sugar. Cook over moderate heat until slightly reduced, about 5 minutes.
2. Meanwhile, in a food processor, pulse the mushrooms until minced; transfer to a bowl. Pulse the chicken until very finely chopped; add to the bowl. Add the miso, 2 tablespoons of oil, the scallions, minced garlic and ginger, salt and pepper to the chicken and mushrooms and mix well.
3. In a small nonstick skillet, cook one-third of the chicken mixture over moderate heat, stirring, just until the meat is no longer pink, 2 minutes. Let cool slightly, then mix the cooked chicken back into the raw mixture until blended.
4. Form the meat into twelve ¼-cup oval patties, about ¾ inch thick. Thread 2 meatballs and 2 shishito peppers onto each of 6 skewers. Transfer the skewers to a baking sheet and refrigerate for at least 15 minutes.

5. Light a grill or preheat a grill pan; oil the grate. Brush the meatballs and peppers with oil and grill, turning once and basting with the sauce, until lightly charred and cooked through, 4 minutes per side. Serve warm.
—Kay Chun

WINE Fragrant, fruit-forward Pinot Noir from Chile: 2011 Tres Palacios Reserva.

Chicken Thigh Yakitori

⏲ **TOTAL: 30 MIN • 4 FIRST-COURSE SERVINGS** ● ●

These sweet, charred chicken skewers make a terrific appetizer or passed hors d'oeuvre.

   ⅓   cup mild *tare* sauce (see Note)
    3   tablespoons tamari
  1½   tablespoons prepared wasabi paste
    4   skinless, boneless chicken thighs
        (about 5 ounces each)
    3   scallions, white and tender green
        parts only, cut into 1-inch lengths
Extra-virgin olive oil
Salt

1. In a small bowl, whisk the *tare* sauce with the tamari and wasabi.
2. Trim the chicken thighs of visible fat and cut into 1-inch pieces. Thread 2 pieces of chicken onto a skewer, followed by 1 piece of scallion and 2 more pieces of chicken. Repeat to skewer the remaining chicken and scallions. You should have 8 skewers.
3. Light a grill or preheat a grill pan. Brush the yakitori with olive oil and season with salt. Grill over high heat, turning once, until lightly browned and nearly cooked through, about 5 minutes. Brush the yakitori generously with the *tare* glaze and grill, turning and brushing them, until mahogany-colored, about 2 minutes longer. Serve right away.
—Matt Abergel

NOTE *Tare* is a Japanese dipping and basting sauce made primarily from soy sauce. It is available at Japanese markets and online at *amazon.com.*

MAKE AHEAD The *tare* glaze can be refrigerated for up to 1 week.

WINE Light-bodied Valpolicella from Italy's Veneto region: 2009 Masi Campofiorin.

Coq au Riesling

ACTIVE: 45 MIN; TOTAL: 1 HR 30 MIN
4 TO 6 SERVINGS ● ●

4   pounds chicken legs, split
Kosher salt and freshly ground pepper
¼   cup canola oil
1   medium onion, chopped
1   medium carrot, chopped
1   celery rib, chopped
2   medium shallots, chopped
1½   cups dry Riesling
1½   cups chicken stock
4   thyme sprigs
2   tablespoons unsalted butter
2   tablespoons extra-virgin olive oil
1   pound mixed mushrooms, sliced
½   cup crème fraîche
2   teaspoons fresh lemon juice
Finely chopped tarragon, for garnish

1. Preheat the oven to 300°. Season the chicken with salt and pepper. In a large enameled cast-iron casserole, heat 2 tablespoons of the canola oil. Add half of the chicken and cook over moderately high heat, turning, until browned, 8 minutes. Transfer to a plate. Cook the remaining chicken, then pour off the fat and wipe out the casserole.
2. Heat the remaining 2 tablespoons of canola oil in the casserole. Add the onion, carrot, celery and shallots and cook over moderate heat, stirring, until the vegetables are softened and lightly browned, 8 minutes. Add the wine and simmer for 1 minute, scraping up the browned bits from the pot. Add the chicken stock and thyme and bring to a boil.
3. Nestle the chicken in the casserole; cover and braise in the oven for 1 hour, until tender.
4. Meanwhile, in a very large skillet, melt the butter in the olive oil. Add the mushrooms and cook over high heat, without stirring, until well browned, 5 minutes. Season the mushrooms with salt and pepper and cook, stirring, until tender, 3 to 5 minutes; transfer to a plate.
5. Transfer the chicken to a plate. Strain the braising liquid through a fine sieve into a heatproof bowl, pressing on the solids; skim off the fat. Return the braising liquid to the casserole and boil until reduced to 1½ cups,

3 to 5 minutes. Whisk in the crème fraîche and lemon juice and season with salt and pepper. Add the mushrooms and chicken to the sauce and simmer for 3 minutes. Garnish with tarragon and serve. —*Christopher Israel*
WINE Rich but dry Riesling from Austria's Wachau region: 2011 Prager Achleiten.

Chicken Salad with Tahini-Yogurt Dressing

⏲ **TOTAL: 40 MIN • 6 SERVINGS** ●

1   cup whole-milk Greek yogurt
2   tablespoons fresh lime juice
2   garlic cloves, minced
2   teaspoons tahini
½   teaspoon ground turmeric
1   tablespoon extra-virgin olive oil, plus more for brushing
1   English cucumber, peeled and finely diced
½   cup lightly packed mint, minced
Kosher salt and freshly ground pepper
2¼   pounds skinless, boneless chicken thighs
Chipotle chile powder
Thinly sliced scallions, for garnish

1. In a medium bowl, whisk the yogurt, lime juice, garlic, tahini, turmeric and 1 tablespoon of olive oil. Fold in the cucumber and mint and season with salt and pepper.
2. Light a grill or preheat a grill pan. Generously brush the chicken thighs with olive oil and season with salt, pepper and chipotle chile powder. Grill the chicken over moderately high heat, turning occasionally, until lightly charred outside and cooked through, 8 to 10 minutes. Transfer the chicken to a carving board and let rest for 5 minutes.
3. Cut the chicken into bite-size pieces and transfer them to a large bowl. Add half of the cucumber yogurt and toss well. Season with salt and pepper. Transfer the chicken to plates, garnish with sliced scallions and serve, passing the remaining cucumber yogurt at the table. —*Jamie Bissonnette*
SERVE WITH Warm flatbread or rice.
WINE Bright Greek Moscofilero: 2012 Gaia Notios White.

Filipino Chicken Adobo Skewers

ACTIVE: 30 MIN; TOTAL: 1 HR 30 MIN
16 TO 20 FIRST-COURSE SERVINGS ●

4   pounds skinless, boneless chicken thighs
1   cup low-sodium soy sauce
6   garlic cloves, crushed
One 1-inch piece of peeled fresh ginger, thinly sliced
2   bay leaves
1   tablespoon black peppercorns
1   tablespoon light brown sugar
¾   cup unseasoned rice wine vinegar
¼   cup canola oil
Thinly sliced scallions, for garnish

1. In a large saucepan, combine the chicken thighs with the soy sauce, garlic, ginger, bay leaves, peppercorns, light brown sugar and 4 cups of water and bring just to a boil. Simmer over moderate heat until the chicken is just cooked, about 15 minutes. Add the vinegar and simmer until the chicken is very tender, about 10 minutes longer.
2. Transfer the chicken to a plate. Strain the braising liquid into a heatproof bowl, then return it to the saucepan. Discard the solids. Boil the braising liquid over moderately high heat, stirring occasionally, until the adobo sauce is syrupy, 25 to 30 minutes.
3. Meanwhile, cut the chicken into bite-size pieces. In a large skillet, heat 2 tablespoons of the oil until shimmering. Add half of the chicken and cook over moderately high heat, turning once, until browned and crisp, about 3 minutes. Transfer the pieces to a plate and repeat with the remaining oil and chicken.
4. To serve, thread the crispy chicken pieces onto 6-inch skewers and arrange on a serving platter. Drizzle the adobo sauce over the chicken skewers and garnish with scallions before serving. —*Susan Spungen*
MAKE AHEAD The recipe can be prepared through Step 2 and refrigerated overnight. Rewarm the sauce and bring the chicken to room temperature before proceeding.
WINE Lively, fruit-forward Riesling from Oregon: 2012 Argyle Nuthouse.

Spiced Chicken Thighs with Fava Puree and Yogurt

TOTAL: 1 HR 15 MIN PLUS 4 HR
MARINATING • 4 SERVINGS ● ●

½ cup olive oil
5 garlic cloves, smashed
1½ tablespoons coriander seeds
1 tablespoon cumin seeds
1 teaspoon grated lemon zest
Kosher salt and freshly ground pepper
Eight 6-ounce bone-in chicken thighs
    with skin
½ pound dried split fava beans
¼ cup tahini
2½ tablespoons fresh lemon juice
1 small red onion, halved and sliced
½ cup golden raisins, soaked in hot
    water for 30 minutes and drained
¼ cup pine nuts
8 cilantro sprigs, torn
Splash of white wine vinegar
½ cup plain Greek yogurt

1. In a large bowl, whisk ¼ cup of the oil with the garlic, coriander, cumin, lemon zest, 1½ teaspoons of salt and ¾ teaspoon of pepper. Add the chicken and turn to coat; cover and refrigerate for 4 hours or overnight.
2. In a medium saucepan, cover the fava beans with 2 inches of water; boil until the beans begin to fall apart, 40 minutes. Drain the fava beans, reserving the cooking liquid.
3. In a blender, puree the favas with ⅓ cup of the reserved cooking liquid, the tahini, 1 teaspoon of salt and the remaining ¼ cup of olive oil. Keep the hummus warm.
4. Preheat the oven to 450°. Heat a large cast-iron skillet. Turn the chicken in the marinade and scrape off any solids; add to the skillet skin side down. Cook over moderately high heat until the skin is golden brown. Turn the chicken over, transfer the skillet to the oven and roast for 15 minutes, until the juices run clear. Remove from the oven and drizzle with 1 tablespoon of the lemon juice.
5. In a medium bowl, toss the onion, raisins, pine nuts, cilantro and vinegar with the remaining 1½ tablespoons of lemon juice. Season with salt and pepper. Mound the hummus on plates and spoon on the yogurt. Arrange the chicken on top, skin side up, followed by the salad, then serve. —*Ignacio Mattos*
WINE Bright, lightly spicy rosé cava: NV Canals Canals Rosat Reserva.

Smoked Chicken Drumsticks with Coriander

ACTIVE: 30 MIN; TOTAL: 1 HR 30 MIN PLUS
OVERNIGHT MARINATING • 4 SERVINGS

¾ cup dark brown sugar
¼ cup plus 2 tablespoons
    Dijon mustard
1½ tablespoons ground coriander
1 jalapeño, seeded and minced
Kosher salt and freshly ground pepper
Twelve 4-ounce chicken drumsticks
2 cups hardwood chips, such as
    hickory or applewood, soaked in
    water for 1 hour and drained

1. In a medium bowl, stir the brown sugar with the mustard, coriander and jalapeño and season with salt and pepper. Scrape the mixture into a large resealable plastic bag. Add the chicken drumsticks and turn to coat. Seal the bag, pressing out the air; refrigerate the chicken overnight.
2. Light a grill and oil the grate. Remove the chicken from the marinade and season with salt and pepper. Grill the chicken over moderately high heat, turning occasionally, until browned all over, 10 to 12 minutes. Transfer the chicken to a plate.
3. Wrap the soaked wood chips in a double layer of foil and poke holes in the top of the packet. Remove the grill grate. Turn the heat off on half of the grill or rake the coals to one side. Set the wood chip packet directly on the coals or flames and replace the grill grate. When the chips are smoking, return the chicken to the grill over indirect heat. Cover the grill and smoke the chicken until an instant-read thermometer inserted in the thickest part of the drumsticks registers 165°, about 30 minutes. Transfer the chicken to a platter and serve. —*Tim Byres*
WINE Sweet-berried Pinot Noir from California's Russian River Valley: 2011 Freeman.

Roast Chicken with Walnut Pesto

ACTIVE: 35 MIN; TOTAL: 1 HR 15 MIN
16 TO 20 SERVINGS ●

CHICKEN
Three 3½-pound chickens,
    cut into 8 pieces each
½ cup extra-virgin olive oil
16 garlic cloves, crushed
2 lemons, scrubbed and cut into
    8 wedges each
2 tablespoons chopped thyme
Kosher salt and freshly ground pepper
PESTO
2 cups walnuts
6 cups lightly packed basil leaves
1 large garlic clove
1 cup freshly grated Parmigiano-
    Reggiano cheese
3 tablespoons fresh lemon juice
1 cup extra-virgin olive oil
Kosher salt and freshly ground pepper

1. ROAST THE CHICKEN Preheat the oven to 425°. In a very large bowl, toss the chicken with the olive oil, garlic, lemon and thyme and season generously with salt and pepper. Arrange the chicken pieces skin side up on 2 large rimmed baking sheets and scatter the garlic and lemon around them.
2. Roast the chicken in the upper and lower thirds of the oven for about 45 minutes, rotating the pans halfway through, until an instant-read thermometer inserted in the thighs registers 165°. Transfer the chicken to a platter and let rest for 10 minutes.
3. MEANWHILE, MAKE THE PESTO Spread the walnuts on a baking sheet and bake for about 12 minutes, until golden and fragrant. Transfer to a food processor and let cool.
4. Add the basil and garlic to the food processor and pulse until finely chopped. Add the cheese and lemon juice; pulse until combined. With the machine on, add the oil until incorporated. Season the pesto with salt and pepper and transfer to a bowl. Serve the chicken with the walnut pesto. —*Nicholas Wilber*
WINE Fruit-forward Pinot Noir: 2011 Patz & Hall Sonoma Coast.

● HEALTHY ● MAKE AHEAD ● VEGETARIAN ● STAFF FAVORITE

Tea-Brined and Double-Fried Hot Chicken

ACTIVE: 1 HR; TOTAL: 1 HR 30 MIN PLUS 24 HR BRINING • 4 SERVINGS ●

8 cups sweetened brewed tea
½ cup kosher salt, plus more for seasoning
10 thyme sprigs
1 head of garlic, halved crosswise, plus 3 garlic cloves
½ lemon, thinly sliced
4 chicken drumsticks
4 chicken thighs
3 tablespoons *gochujang* (see Note)
3 tablespoons sorghum molasses
1 tablespoon cayenne pepper
½ cup lard or 1 stick unsalted butter, softened
Canola oil, for frying
1½ cups all-purpose flour
½ cup Wondra flour
1½ tablespoons cornstarch
About 1 cup seltzer or club soda

1. In a large saucepan, bring 4 cups of the sweet tea just to a boil. Add the ½ cup of kosher salt and stir until dissolved. Add the thyme, halved garlic head, lemon slices and the remaining 4 cups of sweet tea and let cool completely, then refrigerate until well chilled, about 45 minutes.
2. Add the chicken to the brine, cover and refrigerate for 24 to 48 hours.
3. Remove the chicken from the brine and pat dry with paper towels. Let stand at room temperature for 30 minutes.
4. Meanwhile, in a food processor, combine the 3 garlic cloves with the *gochujang*, molasses and cayenne and puree until a paste forms. Add the lard and puree until smooth. Season with salt. Scrape the mixture into a very large bowl.
5. In a large saucepan, heat 3 inches of oil until it reaches 350° on a candy thermometer. Set a rack over a rimmed baking sheet. Spread 1 cup of the all-purpose flour in a pie plate. In a bowl, whisk the remaining ½ cup of all-purpose flour with the Wondra flour,

cornstarch and a generous pinch of salt. Whisk in ¾ cup of seltzer until a thick batter forms; add more seltzer if needed.
6. Dredge 4 of the chicken pieces in the flour, tap off the excess and transfer to the rack. Dip 1 piece of chicken at a time in the batter, let the excess drip back into the bowl and add the chicken to the hot oil. Fry the chicken at 350°, turning occasionally, until pale golden and crisp, 8 minutes; return the chicken to the rack. Repeat with the remaining chicken.
7. Return the first 4 pieces of chicken to the hot oil and fry at 350° until golden and an instant-read thermometer inserted in the thickest part registers 165°, 8 to 10 minutes. Drain on paper towels. Repeat with the remaining 4 pieces of chicken.
8. Add all of the fried chicken to the *gochujang* mixture and toss to coat. Transfer the chicken to a platter and serve right away. —*Erik Anderson and Josh Habiger*

NOTE *Gochujang*, Korean chile paste, is available at Asian markets.
WINE Ripe peach–scented German Riesling: 2011 Gunderloch Jean-Baptiste Kabinett.

Mexican Skillet Corn with Chicken and Cilantro

TOTAL: 15 MIN • 4 SERVINGS

2 tablespoons olive oil
½ cup minced onion
3 garlic cloves, smashed
3 cups fresh corn
3 cups diced grilled chicken from Mixed Grill with Roasted-Garlic-and-Pepper Salsa (page 188) or other grilled chicken
1 jalapeño, chopped
¼ cup chopped cilantro
3 tablespoons sour cream
2 tablespoons fresh lime juice
Salt and freshly ground pepper
Grated *queso fresco,* for serving

1. In a large skillet, heat the oil. Add the onion, garlic and corn; cook over moderately high heat until the onion is golden, 5 minutes. Stir in the chicken, jalapeño, cilantro, sour cream and lime juice; season with salt and pepper.

2. Transfer the chicken and corn mixture to a large bowl, top with *queso fresco* and serve right away. —*Kay Chun*

Tarragon Chicken with Spring Greens

TOTAL: 1 HR • 4 SERVINGS ●

2 tablespoons unsalted butter
1 tablespoon canola oil
Eight 6-ounce chicken thighs
Salt and freshly ground pepper
5 ounces baby arugula, cut into ribbons
1 head of romaine lettuce, cut into ribbons
1 bunch of watercress— thick stems discarded, the rest coarsely chopped
1 leek, halved lengthwise and thinly sliced crosswise
3 tablespoons minced tarragon
1 teaspoon caraway seeds
¾ cup dry white wine
½ cup low-sodium chicken broth
4 ounces crème fraîche

1. Preheat the oven to 425°. In a large, deep ovenproof skillet, melt the butter in the canola oil over high heat. Season the chicken thighs with salt and pepper and cook skin side up until browned, about 8 minutes. Transfer the chicken to a platter; pour off most of the fat in the skillet.
2. Add the arugula, romaine, watercress, leek, tarragon and caraway seeds to the skillet and cook, tossing, until the greens are slightly wilted, 2 minutes. Add the wine and bring to a boil. Cook until reduced by half, 5 minutes. Stir in the broth and crème fraîche.
3. Nestle the chicken into the greens, skin side up. Transfer the skillet to the middle of the oven and roast for 30 minutes, until the chicken is cooked through. Turn on the broiler and broil the chicken for about 5 minutes, until the skin is golden. Serve. —*Grace Parisi*

SERVE WITH Steamed rice.
WINE Lively Spanish white: 2011 Ermita de Nieve Verdejo.

Tandoori Chicken Drumsticks with Cilantro-Shallot Relish

ACTIVE: 30 MIN; TOTAL: 1 HR 15 MIN
4 SERVINGS ● ●

Rubbing chicken drumsticks with Indian-spiced yogurt before roasting yields tender meat and super-crispy skin.

- 1 tablespoon sweet paprika
- 1 tablespoon garam masala
- 1 tablespoon ground cumin
- 1 tablespoon ground coriander
- ½ teaspoon ground turmeric
- 1 tablespoon finely grated peeled fresh ginger
- 4 garlic cloves, minced
- ¼ cup plain fat-free Greek yogurt
- 1 tablespoon fresh lemon juice
- ½ cup canola oil
- Kosher salt and freshly ground pepper
- 12 chicken drumsticks (4¼ pounds)
- ¾ cup coarsely chopped cilantro
- 1 small shallot, minced
- 3 tablespoons distilled white vinegar

1. Preheat the oven to 450°. Set a rack on each of 2 large baking sheets. In a small skillet, toast the paprika, garam masala, cumin, coriander and turmeric over moderately low heat, stirring, until fragrant, about 2 minutes. Transfer the spices to a medium bowl and let cool slightly. Stir in the ginger, garlic, yogurt, lemon juice and 2 tablespoons of the oil and season with salt and pepper.

2. Make 2 or 3 slashes in each drumstick. In a large bowl, toss the chicken with 2 tablespoons of the canola oil and season with salt and pepper. Add the spiced yogurt and rub it onto the chicken. Arrange the chicken on the racks, leaving 2 inches between the pieces. Roast for 45 minutes, turning occasionally, until the chicken is golden brown and cooked through. Light the broiler and broil the chicken 6 inches from the heat for about 5 minutes, until lightly charred and crisp.

3. In a bowl, stir the cilantro, shallot, vinegar and the remaining ¼ cup of oil; season with salt. Serve with the chicken. —*Kay Chun*
WINE Bright, fruit-forward Pinot Noir: 2011 Au Bon Climat Santa Barbara County.

Lola's Roast Chicken with Sambal Chimichurri

ACTIVE: 35 MIN; TOTAL: 1 HR 30 MIN
PLUS OVERNIGHT MARINATING
10 TO 12 SERVINGS ●

Chicago chef Bill Kim got the recipe for this roast chicken bathed in a tangy, garlic-laden Puerto Rican–style marinade from his mother-in-law, Lola.

CHICKEN
- 1 cup vegetable oil
- ¾ cup distilled white vinegar
- 9 garlic cloves, minced
- ⅓ cup oregano leaves, finely chopped
- 3 tablespoons sweet paprika
- 3 tablespoons chile powder
- 1 tablespoon curry powder
- Kosher salt
- Three 3½-pound chickens

CHIMICHURRI
- 2 cups parsley leaves
- ½ cup cilantro leaves
- 1 garlic clove, smashed
- 1 cup vegetable oil
- ½ cup distilled white vinegar
- 1 tablespoon each of *sambal oelek* (Indonesian chile paste), mirin, fresh lemon juice and fresh oregano
- Kosher salt

1. PREPARE THE CHICKEN In a bowl, whisk the oil, vinegar, garlic, oregano, paprika, chile powder, curry and 3 tablespoons of salt. Arrange the chickens in a dish and pour the marinade over the chickens, rubbing it all over the birds. Cover and refrigerate overnight.

2. Preheat the oven to 400°. Set a rack on a rimmed baking sheet lined with foil. Remove the chickens from the marinade, scraping off any excess. Twist the wings of the chickens behind the backs and tie the legs together with kitchen string. Lightly season the chickens with salt and arrange them on the rack.

3. Roast the chickens for about 1 hour, until an instant-read thermometer inserted in the inner thigh reaches 160°, rotating the baking sheet halfway through. Transfer the chickens to a carving board and let rest for 10 minutes.

4. MAKE THE CHIMICHURRI In a food processor, combine the parsley, cilantro and garlic and pulse until finely chopped. Add the oil, vinegar, *sambal,* mirin, lemon juice and oregano and pulse to combine. Season with salt and transfer the chimichurri to a bowl.

5. Cut each chicken into 8 pieces and serve with the chimichurri sauce. —*Bill Kim*
WINE Fruit-forward, full-bodied white: 2012 Planeta La Segreta Bianco.

Filipino Grilled Chicken

TOTAL: 1 HR 30 MIN PLUS OVERNIGHT
MARINATING • 8 SERVINGS ●

- 3 cups water
- 1 cup coconut vinegar or apple cider vinegar
- ½ cup fresh lemon juice
- ½ cup tamari or soy sauce
- ¼ cup Asian fish sauce
- 10 garlic cloves, crushed
- 2 tablespoons sugar
- 1 tablespoon crushed red pepper
- 1 tablespoon black peppercorns
- 5 star anise pods
- 5 bay leaves
- Two 3½-pound chickens, cut into 8 pieces each
- Canola oil, for brushing
- Kosher salt and freshly ground pepper

1. In a large, sturdy resealable plastic bag, combine all of the ingredients except the oil, salt and pepper. Shake to evenly distribute the chicken and adobo marinade; seal the bag, pressing out the air. Refrigerate overnight.

2. Remove the chicken from the marinade. Pat the chicken dry and let stand at room temperature for 30 minutes.

3. Meanwhile, light a grill. Brush the chicken with oil and season with salt and black pepper. Grill over moderate heat, turning occasionally, until lightly charred and an instant-read thermometer inserted in the thickest parts registers 165°, about 30 minutes. Transfer the chicken to a platter and let rest for 10 minutes before serving. —*Kristine Subido*
WINE Fruit-forward California Grenache: 2011 Birichino VV.

● HEALTHY ● MAKE AHEAD ● VEGETARIAN ● STAFF FAVORITE

FILIPINO GRILLED CHICKEN

Uncle Boon's Thai Roast Chicken

ACTIVE: 40 MIN; TOTAL: 4 HR 30 MIN
PLUS 8 HR BRINING • 2 TO 4 SERVINGS

At Uncle Boon's in Manhattan, chef Matt Danzer brines whole chickens, then rubs them with a combination of coconut cream and kaffir lime before roasting to create their signature golden, crackly skin.

1 tablespoon coriander seeds
1 tablespoon whole black peppercorns
⅓ cup granulated coconut palm sugar or brown sugar, like Sugar in the Raw
¼ cup Asian fish sauce
6 garlic cloves, peeled and crushed
10 kaffir lime leaves (see Note)
¼ cup kosher salt, plus more for seasoning
One 3-pound chicken
½ cup unsweetened coconut cream (see Note)
Freshly ground black pepper

1. In a large saucepan, toast the coriander seeds and black peppercorns over moderate heat, shaking the pan, until they are fragrant, about 1 minute. Remove the saucepan from the heat and let the spices cool slightly. Add 2½ quarts of water, the palm sugar, fish sauce, garlic, 8 of the kaffir lime leaves and the ¼ cup of salt to the saucepan and bring just to a simmer. Stir to dissolve the sugar and salt. Remove the pan from the heat and let the brine cool completely. Add the chicken to the brine, cover and refrigerate for 8 hours or overnight.

2. Set a wire rack on a large baking sheet. Remove the chicken from the brine and pat it dry with paper towels. Put the chicken on the rack and refrigerate it, uncovered, for 2 hours to dry out the skin.

3. Preheat the oven to 400°. In a food processor, pulse the coconut cream with the remaining 2 kaffir lime leaves until the mixture has green flakes. Rub the chicken all over with the coconut cream and let stand at room temperature for 45 minutes.

4. Season the chicken lightly with salt and pepper and roast for about 1 hour, until an instant-read thermometer inserted in the inner thigh registers 165°. Transfer the chicken to a board and let rest for 10 minutes, then carve the chicken and serve.
—Matt Danzer

NOTE Kaffir lime leaves are available at some Asian markets and at *amazon.com*. Coconut cream is the thick, rich cream that rises to the surface of unsweetened coconut milk. Look for it at specialty food shops.
WINE Full-bodied, off-dry Riesling from Germany: 2011 J.J. Prüm Kabinett.

Herb-Butter Roast Chicken with Tuscan-Style Bread Salad

ACTIVE: 1 HR 30 MIN; TOTAL: 2 HR 45 MIN
PLUS 4 HR MARINATING
10 TO 12 SERVINGS

Four 3½-pound chickens, halved, backbones discarded
Kosher salt and freshly ground pepper
½ cup plus 2 tablespoons extra-virgin olive oil
4 tablespoons unsalted butter, cut into 16 cubes
8 thyme sprigs
8 small rosemary sprigs
8 unpeeled garlic cloves
½ pound crusty Italian bread, such as ciabatta, torn into 1-inch pieces
½ pound chicken livers—trimmed, rinsed and patted dry
2 fennel bulbs, cut through the core into ½-inch wedges
8 small scallions, cut into 2-inch lengths (2 cups)
¼ cup lightly packed sage leaves
One 1-pound head of escarole, white and light green leaves only, torn into bite-size pieces (about 12 cups)
8 anchovy fillets, cut into ½-inch pieces
1½ tablespoons capers, rinsed and chopped
⅓ cup apple cider vinegar
1 cup shaved Parmigiano-Reggiano cheese

1. On a work surface, cut the wings off the chickens at the second joint, leaving the drumettes attached to the breasts. Transfer the wingettes to a bowl and refrigerate. Season the chickens with salt and pepper and arrange them skin side up on 2 large rimmed baking sheets. Cover with plastic wrap and refrigerate for at least 4 hours or overnight.

2. Drizzle 2 tablespoons of the olive oil over the chickens and top each half with 2 cubes of the butter. Scatter the thyme, rosemary and garlic over the chickens; let them return to room temperature.

3. Meanwhile, preheat the oven to 400°. On a large rimmed baking sheet, toss the bread with ¼ cup of the oil; season with salt and pepper. Bake for 10 minutes, until golden but still slightly chewy. Transfer to a large bowl. Increase the oven temperature to 425°.

4. In a very large ovenproof skillet, heat 1 tablespoon of the oil until shimmering. Add the chicken livers and cook over moderately high heat, turning occasionally, until well browned and barely pink inside, 3 to 5 minutes. Transfer to a plate to cool, then cut into ½-inch pieces and add to the bread.

5. Heat 1 tablespoon of oil in the skillet. Add the wingettes and cook over moderately high heat until golden on the bottom, about 4 minutes. Add the fennel, scallions, sage and a generous pinch each of salt and pepper. Transfer the skillet to the oven. Roast, stirring once, until the fennel is tender and the wingettes are cooked through, 30 minutes. Let cool slightly, then remove the meat from the wingettes; discard the skin and bones. Transfer the chicken and vegetables to the bowl with the bread.

6. Roast the chickens in the upper and lower thirds of the oven for 40 to 45 minutes, until an instant-read thermometer inserted in a thigh registers 165°; switch the pans halfway through roasting. Let rest for 10 minutes.

7. Add the escarole, anchovies, capers, vinegar and the remaining 2 tablespoons of oil to the bowl with the bread. Fold in ½ cup of the cheese shavings and season the bread salad with salt and pepper; toss well. Transfer the bread salad to a platter and scatter the remaining ½ cup of cheese shavings on top.

● HEALTHY   ● MAKE AHEAD   ● VEGETARIAN   ● STAFF FAVORITE

8. Cut the chicken halves into two pieces, arrange on another platter and serve with the bread salad. —*Ryan Hardy*

WINE Vibrant, light-bodied Sicilian red: 2008 Fattorie Romeo del Castello Vigo.

"Ode to Zuni" Roast Chicken with Fennel Panzanella

ACTIVE: 1 HR; TOTAL: 2 HR PLUS
2 HR MARINATING • 4 SERVINGS ●

When L.A. chef Suzanne Goin makes this homage to the legendary chicken at Zuni Café in San Francisco, she confits the chicken in duck fat. For this simplified version, she roasts the bird with just a little duck fat.

- 1 tablespoon chopped rosemary, plus 1 rosemary sprig
- 1 tablespoon chopped sage
- 2 tablespoons thyme leaves
- Kosher salt
- One 4-pound chicken
- ½ pound country white bread, torn into 1½-inch pieces (4 cups)
- 1 cup plus 3 tablespoons extra-virgin olive oil
- 2 tablespoons duck fat or olive oil
- 2 tablespoons minced shallot
- 2 tablespoons fresh lemon juice
- 1 Meyer lemon
- ½ cup pitted and coarsely chopped Castelvetrano olives (3 ounces)
- 2 tablespoons chopped flat-leaf parsley
- Freshly ground pepper
- 2 árbol chiles, crumbled
- 1 large fennel bulb, cored and cut into ½-inch dice
- 1 small red onion, cut into ½-inch dice
- ¼ cup thinly sliced garlic
- 1 tablespoon white wine vinegar
- ¼ cup low-sodium chicken broth
- 1 small head of escarole, leaves torn

1. In a small bowl, combine the chopped rosemary and sage with 1 tablespoon of the thyme and 1½ tablespoons of salt. Rub the herb mixture all over the chicken and let stand at room temperature for 2 hours.

2. Preheat the oven to 375°. On a baking sheet, toss the bread with 3 tablespoons of the olive oil and spread it out in a single layer. Toast for 12 to 15 minutes, until lightly golden. Transfer to a large bowl and let cool.

3. Increase the oven temperature to 450°. Brush most of the herb mixture off the chicken. Set the chicken on a rack set over a baking sheet and rub all over with the duck fat. Roast for about 50 minutes, until golden and an instant-read thermometer inserted in the thickest part of the thigh registers 165°. Let the chicken rest for 15 minutes, then cut into pieces.

4. Meanwhile, in a medium bowl, combine the shallot with the lemon juice and a pinch of salt and let stand for 5 minutes. Trim the ends from the Meyer lemon and slice it ⅛ inch thick. Stack the slices and cut them into ⅛-inch-thick matchsticks, then cut into ⅛-inch dice; you should have ¼ cup. Add the diced Meyer lemon to the shallot mixture and stir in the chopped olives, flat-leaf parsley and 6 tablespoons of the olive oil. Season the salsa with salt and pepper.

5. In a large skillet, heat ½ cup of the olive oil. Add the rosemary sprig and crumbled chiles and cook over moderate heat, stirring, until fragrant, about 1 minute. Add the fennel, red onion, garlic, the remaining 1 tablespoon of thyme and 1 teaspoon of salt and cook, stirring occasionally, until the vegetables are softened and lightly golden in spots, about 5 minutes. Stir in the white wine vinegar and cook for 1 minute. Add the chicken broth and bring to a boil. Pour the onion-fennel mixture over the croutons and mix well.

6. Heat the remaining 2 tablespoons of olive oil in the skillet. Add the escarole and season with salt and black pepper. Cook over moderate heat, stirring, just until wilted, about 2 minutes.

7. Spread half of the panzanella on a large serving platter and top with half of the escarole; repeat with the remaining panzanella and escarole. Arrange the chicken on the salad and spoon the lemon salsa on top. —*Suzanne Goin*

WINE Cassis-and-sage-scented Napa Cabernet Franc: 2010 Lang & Reed.

Five-Herb Grilled Chicken with Green Aioli

TOTAL: 1 HR PLUS 4 HR MARINATING
10 TO 12 SERVINGS ●

A fresh herb pesto does double duty here: in the chicken marinade and in the sauce.

- Three 3½- to 4-pound chickens, quartered (see Note)
- ½ cup packed flat-leaf parsley leaves
- ½ cup packed basil leaves
- ½ cup snipped chives
- 2 tablespoons minced jalapeño
- 1 tablespoon minced thyme
- 1 tablespoon minced rosemary
- 1 tablespoon minced garlic
- Kosher salt
- 1 cup extra-virgin olive oil, plus more for the grill
- 1 cup mayonnaise
- 1½ tablespoons fresh lemon juice

1. Using a sharp knife, score each piece of chicken 2 or 3 times through the skin. Transfer the chicken to a large bowl.

2. In a food processor, combine the parsley, basil, chives, jalapeño, thyme, rosemary, garlic and 1 tablespoon of salt; pulse until the herbs are finely chopped. With the machine on, add the 1 cup of olive oil in a steady stream.

3. Pour all but ½ cup of the marinade over the chicken and turn to coat; rub the marinade into the gashes. Refrigerate the chicken for at least 4 hours or overnight. Add the mayonnaise and lemon juice to the remaining marinade in the processor and pulse until bright green. Scrape the green aioli into a small bowl and refrigerate.

4. Light a grill and oil the grates. Grill the chicken over moderate heat, turning occasionally, until lightly charred and an instant-read thermometer inserted in the inner thigh registers 168°, about 35 minutes. Serve the chicken with the green aioli. —*Grace Parisi*

NOTE You can use 4 pounds skinless, boneless chicken breasts instead. Pound them lightly before marinating and grill over high heat for about 12 minutes.

WINE Lemony southern French white: 2011 Domaine Félines Jourdan Picpoul de Pinet.

Julia's Favorite Roast Chicken

ACTIVE: 30 MIN; TOTAL: 2 HR 15 MIN

4 SERVINGS ●

While people usually associate Julia Child with complex French dishes, many of her recipes as an F&W contributor, such as this roast chicken, weren't complicated at all. Julia seasoned the bird inside and out by packing sautéed vegetables, lemon slices and fresh herbs into the cavity, then rubbing the skin all over with butter.

2½ tablespoons unsalted butter
⅓ cup each of finely diced carrots, onion and celery
1 teaspoon dried thyme, savory or mixed herbs, or 2 fresh thyme or savory sprigs
One 3½- to 4-pound chicken
Salt and freshly ground pepper
Parsley stems and celery leaves
Six ⅛-inch-thick lemon slices
½ cup each of sliced onion and carrot
1 tablespoon fresh lemon juice
¾ cup chicken stock or broth

1. Preheat the oven to 425°. Melt 1 tablespoon of the butter in a skillet. Add the diced carrots, onion and celery and cook over moderate heat until softened. Stir in the herbs.

2. Wash the chicken rapidly inside and out with hot water and pat thoroughly dry. For easier carving, cut out and discard the wishbone. Pull the neck skin up over the breast and secure it to the back with a toothpick. Salt and pepper the cavity and spoon in the cooked vegetables, a handful of parsley stems and celery leaves and the lemon slices. Massage the chicken all over with 1 tablespoon of the butter, then truss it. Alternatively, tie the ends of the drumsticks together and tuck the wings under the body.

3. Choose a flameproof roasting pan that is about 1 inch larger than the chicken. Salt the chicken all over and set it breast up on a rack in the pan. (Thoroughly wash all surfaces and utensils that have been in contact with the raw chicken.)

4. Roast the chicken in the oven for about 1 hour and 15 minutes, as follows:

AT 15 MINUTES Brush the chicken with the remaining ½ tablespoon of butter. Scatter the sliced onion and carrot all around. Reduce the oven temperature to 350°.

AT 45 MINUTES Brush the lemon juice over the chicken. If necessary, add ½ cup of water to the vegetables to prevent burning.

AT 60 MINUTES Baste with the pan juices. Test for doneness: The drumsticks should move easily in their sockets; their flesh should feel somewhat soft. If not, continue roasting, basting and testing every 7 to 8 minutes, until an instant-read thermometer registers 165°.

5. Spear the chicken through the shoulders; lift to drain; if the last of the juices run clear yellow, the chicken is done. Let rest on a carving board for 15 minutes; discard the string.

6. Spoon all but 1 tablespoon of fat from the juices in the pan. Add the stock and boil until lightly syrupy, 5 minutes. Strain; you will have just enough to bathe each serving with a fragrant spoonful. —*Julia Child*

WINE Minerally, full-bodied French white: 2008 Domaine de Montcy Cour-Cheverny.

Roast Squab Breast with Two-Grain Porridge

ACTIVE: 1 HR; TOTAL: 3 HR

6 SERVINGS ●

If you're not sure how to remove the squab breasts, ask your butcher to do it for you. The rest of the recipe is easy.

Three 1-pound squabs
2 tablespoons grapeseed oil
1 large onion, chopped
1 fennel bulb—halved, cored and chopped
¼ cup dry red wine
1 Bosc pear—peeled, halved, cored and coarsely chopped
1 teaspoon whole black peppercorns
1 thyme sprig
1 bay leaf
1 cup heavy cream
Salt
4 cups boiling water
½ cup bulgur
¾ cup farro
Freshly ground pepper

1. Preheat the oven to 400°. Using a sharp knife, cut the breasts off the squabs and transfer to a plate, cover with plastic and refrigerate. In a small roasting pan, roast the carcasses for about 30 minutes, until golden. Turn off the oven.

2. In a large pot, heat 1 tablespoon of the grapeseed oil. Add the chopped onion and fennel and cook over moderate heat, stirring occasionally, until tender and lightly browned, about 15 minutes. Add the wine and cook until evaporated. Add the pear, peppercorns, thyme sprig, bay leaf and roast squab carcasses, along with any fat in the pan. Add 8 cups of room-temperature water and bring to a boil. Simmer over moderate heat, skimming, until the stock has reduced by half, about 1½ hours. Strain the stock into a large saucepan and simmer over moderate heat until it is reduced to 1 cup, about 30 minutes.

3. Meanwhile, in a small saucepan, simmer the cream until reduced to ½ cup, about 15 minutes. Whisk the cream into the reduced stock and season with salt; keep warm.

4. In a large heatproof bowl, pour the boiling water over the bulgur; cover and let stand until tender, about 30 minutes. In a large saucepan of salted boiling water, cook the farro until al dente, about 30 minutes. Drain the farro and bulgur, shaking out excess water.

5. Add the farro and bulgur to the cream-stock mixture and cook over moderate heat until thick and porridge-like, about 5 minutes. Season the porridge with salt and pepper and keep warm.

6. Reheat the oven to 400°. Season the squab breasts with salt and pepper. In a large ovenproof skillet, heat the remaining 1 tablespoon of grapeseed oil until shimmering. Add the breasts, skin side down, and cook over high heat until lightly browned, about 2 minutes. Flip the breasts over and roast in the oven for about 4 minutes for medium meat. Transfer the breasts to a cutting board and let rest for 5 minutes. Slice the breasts and serve with the two-grain porridge. —*Johnny Spero*

SERVE WITH Roasted sunchokes or carrots.

WINE Earthy, spicy Sangiovese: 2010 Rocca di Montegrossi Chianti Classico.

● HEALTHY ● MAKE AHEAD ● VEGETARIAN ● STAFF FAVORITE

Oven-Fried Chicken by the Bucket

ACTIVE: 20 MIN; TOTAL: 1 HR
MAKES 16 PIECES ●

Rolling chicken pieces in crushed potato chips before baking simulates a deep-fried crust. Thick-cut potato chips in this crust stay more crispy than the standard kind. Salt-and-pepper is delicious here, but any flavor works beautifully—even barbecue.

Canola oil spray
1¼ cups all-purpose flour
Kosher salt and freshly ground pepper
1 cup whole milk
1 tablespoon Dijon mustard
Two 8½-ounce bags kettle-style potato chips, finely crushed
Four 6-ounce boneless chicken breasts with skin, halved crosswise
4 bone-in chicken thighs (1½ pounds)
4 chicken drumsticks (1 pound)

1. Preheat the oven to 400° and arrange the racks in the upper and lower thirds. Spray 2 wire racks with canola oil and set them over 2 rimmed baking sheets.
2. Place 1 cup of the flour in a medium bowl and season with salt and pepper. In another medium bowl, whisk the milk with the mustard and season with salt and pepper. In a large bowl, stir the crushed potato chips with the remaining ¼ cup of flour.
3. Season the chicken pieces with salt and pepper, then dust with the flour, tapping off any excess. Dip the pieces in the milk, then coat in the crushed potato chips, pressing to help them adhere. Transfer the chicken breasts to one baking sheet and the thighs and drumsticks to the second one. Spray the chicken all over with canola oil.
4. Bake the thighs and drumsticks on the upper rack of the oven for 20 minutes. Transfer to the lower rack. Place the chicken breasts on the upper rack. Bake all of the chicken for about 20 minutes longer, until golden and cooked through. Season with salt and serve. —*Kay Chun*
BEER Crisp, brightly hoppy pilsner from California: North Coast Scrimshaw.

Spice-Rubbed Roast Chicken with Two Sauces

📷 BACK COVER

ACTIVE: 25 MIN; TOTAL: 2 HR
2 TO 4 SERVINGS ●

At Bantam + Biddy in Atlanta, chef Shaun Doty serves rotisserie chickens with sauces like smoky *piri piri* and Dominican *wasakaka*, made with onion, chiles and herbs.

2 tablespoons extra-virgin olive oil
1 garlic clove, minced
1 teaspoon finely grated lemon zest
1 tablespoon fresh lemon juice
1 tablespoon minced rosemary
1 tablespoon ground fennel seeds
1 tablespoon freshly ground pepper
One 3½-pound chicken, chilled
Kosher salt
Wasakaka Sauce and Piri Piri Sauce (recipes follow), for serving

1. In a bowl, whisk the oil, garlic, lemon zest and juice, rosemary, fennel seeds and pepper. Rub the mixture all over the chicken, inside and out. Let come to room temperature.
2. Preheat the oven to 400°. Twist the wings of the chicken behind the back and tie the legs together; set breast side up in a roasting pan. Season all over with salt. Roast until the juices run clear when an inner thigh is pierced, 55 minutes. Transfer to a carving board; let rest 10 minutes. Cut into 8 pieces and serve with the two sauces. —*Shaun Doty*
WINE Bright white Burgundy: 2010 Dominique Cornin Pouilly-Fuissé.

WASAKAKA SAUCE
⏲ **TOTAL: 25 MIN**
MAKES 1½ CUPS ● ● ○

⅓ cup fresh lime juice
½ cup extra-virgin olive oil
¼ cup minced garlic
¼ cup minced red onion
3 fresh red chiles—stemmed, seeded and thinly sliced crosswise
2 tablespoons finely chopped parsley
2 tablespoons finely chopped oregano
Kosher salt and freshly ground pepper

In a small saucepan, combine the lime juice with ¼ cup of water and bring to a boil. Remove from the heat and stir in the remaining ingredients. Let the sauce cool before serving. —*SD*

PIRI PIRI SAUCE
ACTIVE: 30 MIN; TOTAL: 1 HR 30 MIN
MAKES ABOUT 1¼ CUPS ● ○

2 tablespoons extra-virgin olive oil
1 large red bell pepper, seeded and finely chopped
½ onion, finely chopped
3 fresh red chiles, such as cayenne—stemmed, seeded and finely chopped
3 Thai chiles, finely chopped
3 garlic cloves, minced
1 tablespoon sweet smoked paprika
2 tablespoons red wine vinegar
1 tablespoon fresh lemon juice
Kosher salt and freshly ground pepper

1. In a large skillet, heat the oil until shimmering. Add the bell pepper, onion, cayenne and Thai chiles, garlic and paprika; cook over moderate heat, stirring occasionally, until the vegetables are softened, 12 minutes.
2. Scrape the mixture into a blender and let cool slightly. Add the vinegar, lemon juice and ¼ cup of water and puree until almost smooth. Season the sauce with salt and pepper and transfer to a bowl. Let stand at room temperature for 1 hour before serving. —*SD*

The Ultimate Southern Fried Chicken

⏲ **TOTAL: 45 MIN • 4 SERVINGS** ●

6 large eggs
Kosher salt
3 cups all-purpose flour
½ cup cornstarch
1½ tablespoons garlic powder
1 teaspoon paprika
1 teaspoon crushed red pepper
Freshly ground black pepper
One 3½-pound chicken, cut into 8 pieces
Vegetable oil, for frying

1. In a large bowl, beat the eggs with a pinch of salt. In another large bowl, whisk the flour with the cornstarch, garlic powder, paprika, crushed red pepper, 2½ tablespoons of salt and 1 teaspoon of black pepper.

2. Pat the chicken pieces dry. Line a baking sheet with wax paper. Season the chicken with salt and pepper and dredge in the seasoned flour. Dip the coated chicken in the egg, then dredge again in the seasoned flour and transfer to the baking sheet.

3. In a large cast-iron skillet, heat ¾ inch of oil to 360°. Set a rack over another baking sheet. Fry half of the chicken over moderate heat, turning occasionally, until golden brown and an instant-read thermometer inserted nearest the bone registers 165°, about 15 minutes. Transfer to the rack. Repeat with the remaining chicken. Serve right away.
—Shaun Doty

WINE Minerally nonvintage Champagne: NV Christian Etienne Champagne Brut.

Spiced Chicken Dosas

TOTAL: 30 MIN • 4 SERVINGS

These wraps, based on dosas (Indian-style stuffed crêpes), are seasoned with cumin and coriander and served with curry yogurt. Prepared with leftover Oven-Fried Chicken by the Bucket (or other fried chicken), they make a quick lunch.

- 1 cup plain fat-free Greek yogurt
- 1 teaspoon Madras curry powder
- 2 tablespoons canola oil
- 1 medium red onion, chopped
- 3 zucchini (about 1 pound), diced
- 3 garlic cloves, minced
- 2 teaspoons minced fresh ginger
- 1 teaspoon cumin seeds, crushed
- ½ teaspoon coriander seeds, crushed
- 3 cups shredded leftover Oven-Fried Chicken by the Bucket (recipe at far left) or other fried chicken

Kosher salt and freshly ground black pepper
- 4 lavash wraps or flour tortillas

1. In a small bowl, stir the yogurt with the curry powder.

2. In a large nonstick skillet, heat the oil. Add the onion and zucchini and cook over moderate heat until golden, about 10 minutes. Add the garlic, ginger, cumin and coriander and cook for 3 minutes. Stir in the chicken and season the filling with salt and pepper.

3. Spoon the filling in the center of the lavash and top with some of the curry yogurt. Roll up and serve with any extra yogurt sauce on the side. —Kay Chun

BEER Fragrant, hoppy pale ale: Captain Lawrence Freshchester.

Slow-Cooked Duck with Green Olives and Herbes de Provence

ACTIVE: 45 MIN; TOTAL: 3 HR 45 MIN

2 TO 4 SERVINGS ● ●

This is the most forgiving and delicious duck recipe you'll ever find. By slow-cooking duck with aromatics until it's as tasty and tender as confit, then broiling it until the skin is shatter-crisp, Mediterranean food expert Paula Wolfert manages to play to all of the bird's strengths. If you're feeling lazy, you can simply serve the duck with the strained pan juices and forgo the stock and olive sauce altogether. Just be sure to have the butcher cut the duck for you—that's the only step that can be tricky.

- 2 large onions, coarsely chopped
- ¼ cup plus 2 teaspoons coarsely chopped flat-leaf parsley
- 1 tablespoon plus 1 teaspoon chopped thyme
- 8 garlic cloves, halved
- 2 bay leaves
- 1 large celery rib, sliced ¼ inch thick

One 5½-pound duck, halved, with backbone, neck and wing tips removed and reserved

Kosher salt and freshly ground pepper

Herbes de Provence
- 1 tablespoon tomato paste
- ½ cup dry white wine
- 1 cup chicken stock, preferably homemade

Pinch of sugar
- 1½ cups pitted French green olives, rinsed

1. Preheat the oven to 475°. In a small roasting pan, spread half of the chopped onions, ¼ cup of the parsley, 1 tablespoon of the thyme and the garlic, bay leaves and celery. Prick the duck skin all over with a fork and rub the duck with 2 teaspoons of salt, 1 teaspoon of pepper and 1 teaspoon of herbes de Provence. Set the duck halves on the vegetables, cut side down, and roast for 10 minutes. Prick the duck skin again, cover the pan with foil and reduce the oven temperature to 275°. Roast the duck for about 3 hours longer, until the meat is very tender and most of the fat has rendered.

2. Meanwhile, in a large skillet, cook the backbone, neck and wing tips over low heat until well browned all over. Add the remaining chopped onions and cook over moderate heat until browned, about 4 minutes. Pour off the fat from the skillet and add the tomato paste. Cook, stirring, until it begins to brown, about 3 minutes. Add the white wine and bring to a boil. Add 3 cups of water, the chicken stock and sugar and simmer until the stock is reduced to 1 cup, about 1 hour. Strain the stock and skim the fat from the surface.

3. When the duck is tender, transfer the halves to a work surface. Halve each half; remove any vegetables, pockets of fat and loose bones. Transfer the duck pieces to a rimmed baking sheet, skin side up.

4. Strain the juices from the roasting pan into a saucepan and skim off the fat; boil the strained juices until reduced to ¼ cup. Add the strained stock and the olives to the saucepan and simmer for 10 minutes. Season the sauce with salt, pepper and herbes de Provence.

5. Preheat the broiler. Season the duck with herbes de Provence, salt and pepper. Broil 10 inches from the heat for about 5 minutes, or until the duck is hot and the skin is crisp. Spoon the sauce onto a platter and set the duck on top. Sprinkle with the remaining 2 teaspoons of chopped parsley and 1 teaspoon of thyme and serve.
—Paula Wolfert

WINE Herbal, dense Provençal red: 2009 Le Galantin Bandol Rouge.

Four-Spice Duck Breasts with Carrots

TOTAL: 1 HR • 8 SERVINGS ●

People think duck is intimidating to cook, but this recipe is very simple. To make it even easier, substitute five-spice powder for the coriander, cinnamon, star anise and cumin.

CARROTS

- 2 pounds medium carrots, preferably mixed colors, halved lengthwise
- 3 tablespoons extra-virgin olive oil
- 1 tablespoon coriander seeds, finely crushed
- 1 teaspoon ground cumin

Kosher salt and freshly ground pepper

DUCK

- 1 teaspoon coriander seeds
- 1 teaspoon cinnamon
- 1 star anise pod
- ½ teaspoon cumin seeds

Four 10-ounce Muscovy duck breast halves, excess fat removed and skin scored

Kosher salt and freshly ground pepper

1. PREPARE THE CARROTS Preheat the oven to 400°. On 2 large rimmed baking sheets, toss the carrots with the olive oil, coriander and cumin. Season with salt and pepper and roast for about 25 minutes, until crisp-tender; keep warm. Leave the oven on.

2. PREPARE THE DUCK In a skillet, toast the coriander, cinnamon, star anise and cumin over moderate heat, shaking the skillet, until fragrant, 2 minutes. Transfer the spices to a grinder and let cool, then grind to a powder.

3. Season the duck breasts with salt and pepper; rub all over with the spice mix. Heat a large cast-iron skillet. Add the duck, skin side down. Cook over moderate heat, spooning off the fat, until golden and just crisp, about 7 minutes. Turn the duck skin side up. Transfer the skillet to the oven and roast the duck for about 7 minutes, until medium-rare within. Transfer the duck breasts to a carving board; let rest for 5 minutes. Thinly slice crosswise and serve with the carrots. —*Richard Betts*

WINE Spice-inflected Bordeaux: 2010 Saint Glinglin Saint-Émilion Grand Cru.

Tandoori Marinated Quail

TOTAL: 45 MIN PLUS OVERNIGHT MARINATING • 4 SERVINGS ●

These grilled quail are seasoned with a super-quick spiced-yogurt marinade.

- 1 cup plain whole-milk Greek yogurt
- 2 tablespoons fresh lemon juice
- 2 tablespoons fresh lime juice
- 1 tablespoon finely grated peeled fresh ginger
- 2 garlic cloves, finely grated
- 1 tablespoon hot paprika
- 2 teaspoons ground coriander
- 2 teaspoons ground cumin
- 1 teaspoon ground turmeric
- 3 tablespoons minced cilantro, plus cilantro leaves for garnish

Kosher salt

Vegetable oil

- 8 partially boned quail, halved lengthwise

Freshly ground pepper

1. In a medium bowl, whisk the yogurt with the lemon juice, lime juice, ginger, garlic, hot paprika, coriander, cumin, turmeric, minced cilantro, 2 teaspoons of salt and 1 tablespoon of oil. Transfer the marinade to a very large resealable plastic bag and add the quail. Seal the bag, pressing out the air, and turn to coat. Refrigerate the quail for at least 8 hours or overnight.

2. Remove the quail from the marinade and let stand at room temperature for 30 minutes.

3. Light a grill and oil the grates. Lightly season the quail with salt and pepper and grill over moderately high heat, turning once, until the breast meat is barely pink, 8 to 10 minutes. Transfer the quail to a platter, garnish with cilantro leaves and serve. —*Tetsu Yahagi*

VARIATION Marinate eight 6- to 8-ounce whole chicken legs overnight. Grill over moderate heat, turning occasionally, until cooked through, 35 to 40 minutes.

SERVE WITH Indian lime pickles, available at Indian markets.

WINE Moderately sweet Riesling from Oregon: 2012 Trisaetum Ribbon Ridge.

Soy-Ginger-Lacquered Cornish Hens

ACTIVE: 1 HR; TOTAL: 2 HR 45 MIN PLUS 8 HR MARINATING • 10 TO 12 SERVINGS

Serving elegant Asian-inspired Cornish hens allows guests to have their own small bird.

- 4 cups mirin (32 ounces)
- 2 cups soy sauce (16 ounces)
- 8 scallions, thinly sliced
- ¼ cup minced peeled fresh ginger
- 1½ tablespoons minced garlic
- 1½ tablespoons toasted sesame oil
- 1½ tablespoons kosher salt

Ten to twelve 1-pound Cornish hens, legs tied together with kitchen twine

1. In a large bowl, whisk together all of the ingredients except the Cornish hens. Put the hens in 3 large resealable plastic bags and pour in the marinade. Seal the bags, pressing out the air, and turn to thoroughly coat the hens. Transfer the bags to a small roasting pan or large rimmed baking sheet and refrigerate for at least 8 hours or overnight, turning the bags occasionally.

2. Let the hens stand at room temperature for 30 minutes. Preheat the oven to 425° and line 2 large rimmed baking sheets with foil. Remove the hens from the marinade and transfer them to the baking sheets. Strain the marinade into a medium saucepan and bring to a boil, then simmer over moderately high heat for 5 minutes, stirring occasionally.

3. Roast the hens in the upper and lower thirds of the oven for about 10 minutes, or until they are lightly browned. Reduce the oven temperature to 375°. Roast the hens for about 50 minutes longer, basting with the reserved marinade every 15 minutes and shifting the pans from front to back and top to bottom halfway through roasting. The hens are done when the cavity juices run clear and an instant-read thermometer inserted in the inner thigh registers 160°. Transfer the hens to a platter and let rest for about 10 minutes before serving. —*Maria Helm Sinskey*

WINE Full-bodied, appley Loire white: 2012 Domaine du Closel La Jalousie Savennières.

● HEALTHY ● MAKE AHEAD ○ VEGETARIAN ● STAFF FAVORITE

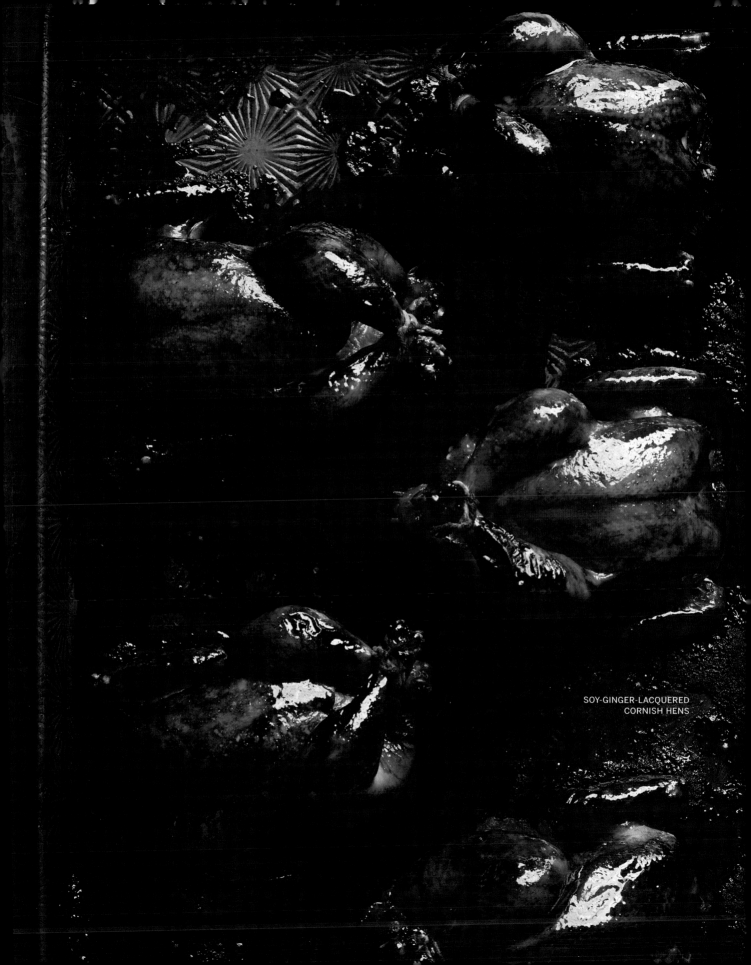

SOY-GINGER-LACQUERED
CORNISH HENS

Sour-Cherry-Stuffed Duck Breasts with Thyme

TOTAL: 1 HR 20 MIN • 8 TO 10 SERVINGS ●

Four 1- to 1¼-pound whole boneless
    Muscovy duck breasts, skin scored
    in a crosshatch pattern
Kosher salt
  2 tablespoons unsalted butter
  1 small shallot, minced
  1 cup dried sour cherries (6 ounces)
  2 tablespoons sugar
  2 tablespoons balsamic vinegar
  ¼ cup finely chopped parsley
1½ tablespoons chopped thyme
Freshly ground pepper

1. Lightly season the duck breasts all over with salt and set them skin side down on a large baking sheet. Refrigerate uncovered until the meat looks shiny, about 30 minutes.
2. Meanwhile, in a skillet, melt the butter. Add the shallot; cook over moderate heat, stirring, until just starting to brown, 4 minutes. Add the cherries and sugar; cook, stirring, until the sugar is dissolved and just starting to caramelize, 5 minutes. Add the vinegar and ¼ cup of water and cook, stirring, until the liquid is absorbed, 3 minutes. Fold in the parsley and thyme and season the stuffing with salt and pepper. Let cool.
3. Preheat the oven to 400°. Set the duck skin side down on a work surface. Spread the stuffing over the breasts. Fold over one side of each breast to enclose the stuffing; tie in 5 places with twine to make 4 roasts.
4. Heat a large ovenproof skillet. Season the roasts all over with pepper; cook over moderate heat, turning occasionally, until the skin is browned and nearly crisp, 10 to 12 minutes; spoon off the excess fat as needed.
5. Transfer the skillet to the oven; roast the duck until an instant-read thermometer inserted in the thickest part of each breast registers 118° to 120°, 12 minutes. Transfer to a carving board; let rest for 5 minutes. Snip off the twine. Thinly slice the roasts crosswise and serve. —*Maria Helm Sinskey*
WINE Medium-bodied Santa Barbara Pinot Noir: 2010 Cambria Julia's Vineyard.

Leg of a Neighbor's Duck

ACTIVE: 45 MIN; TOTAL: 2 HR 15 MIN
4 SERVINGS

Eight ½-pound Muscovy or
    Pekin duck legs
Kosher salt and freshly ground pepper
  2 tablespoons extra-virgin olive oil
  1 onion, finely chopped
  ½ fennel bulb, finely chopped
  3 garlic cloves, crushed
  1 bay leaf
  2 teaspoons finely chopped marjoram
  1 cup plus 2 tablespoons dry red wine
2 to 3 cups chicken stock or
    low-sodium broth
  2 tablespoons unsalted butter,
    softened
  1 tablespoon all-purpose flour

1. Preheat the oven to 325°. Season the duck with salt and pepper. In a large enameled cast-iron casserole, heat the oil. Add the vegetables and bay leaf; cook over moderate heat, stirring, until the vegetables are softened and just starting to brown, 10 minutes. Add 1 teaspoon of the marjoram and cook until fragrant, 1 minute. Add 1 cup of the wine and 2 cups of the chicken stock; bring just to a simmer. Nestle the duck in the casserole, skin side up; add additional stock if necessary to cover by two-thirds. Cover and braise the duck in the oven for 1½ hours, until tender.
2. Preheat the broiler. Transfer the duck legs to a rimmed baking sheet. In a small bowl, blend the butter with the flour until smooth.
3. Strain the braising liquid through a sieve set into a fat separator, pressing on the solids. Pour off the fat. Transfer the remaining liquid to a medium saucepan. Add the remaining marjoram; boil the sauce until reduced to 1¼ cups. Whisk in the butter paste; simmer over moderately high heat until the sauce is thickened, 2 minutes. Whisk in the remaining wine and season with salt and pepper; keep warm.
4. Broil the duck 8 inches from the heat until the skin is browned, 3 minutes. Transfer to plates; serve with the sauce. —*Daniel DeLong*
WINE Earthy California Pinot Noir: 2011 Banshee Sonoma Coast.

Roast Goose with Pork, Prune and Chestnut Stuffing

ACTIVE: 45 MIN; TOTAL: 5 HR
8 SERVINGS ●

  1 cup pitted prunes
  1 cup brandy
  7 tablespoons unsalted butter
  1 cup minced onion
One 12-pound goose, liver chopped
  ¼ cup ruby port
  1 pound fatty ground pork
  2 large eggs, lightly beaten
Generous pinch of ground allspice
  1 teaspoon chopped thyme
  1 garlic clove, minced
Kosher salt and freshly ground pepper
15 ounces cooked and peeled
    chestnuts, coarsely chopped
Boiling water
  3 cups chicken stock

1. In a bowl, cover the prunes with the brandy; let stand for 30 minutes. Strain and coarsely chop the prunes; reserve the prune brandy.
2. In a small skillet, melt 3 tablespoons of the butter. Cook the onion over moderate heat, stirring, until softened, 5 minutes. Add the liver; cook until no longer pink, 2 minutes. Add the port and boil, scraping up any browned bits, until almost evaporated, 2 minutes.
3. Scrape the mixture into the bowl of a stand mixer fitted with the paddle; let cool slightly. Add the pork, eggs, allspice, thyme and garlic; season with salt and pepper. Beat at low speed until combined, scraping down the side of the bowl. Stir in the chestnuts and prunes.
4. Preheat the oven to 425°. Set a rack in a roasting pan. Season the goose cavity with salt and fill loosely with the stuffing; secure the skin with toothpicks. Using a paring knife, prick the skin all over. Truss the goose; set it breast side up on the rack. Roast for 15 minutes, then reduce the oven temperature to 350° and roast for 3½ hours, until an instant-read thermometer inserted into the stuffing registers 160° and the thigh registers 165°. Baste the breast every 15 minutes with ¼ cup of boiling water; transfer the goose to a board and let rest for 15 minutes.

5. Pour the pan juices into a measuring cup; skim off the fat. Return the juices to the pan; add the prune brandy and the stock. Boil the sauce, scraping up any browned bits stuck to the bottom of the pan, until it is slightly thickened, 10 minutes. Remove from the heat; whisk in the remaining 4 tablespoons of butter. Season the sauce with salt and pepper.

6. Discard the toothpicks and string. Spoon the stuffing into a bowl. Carve the goose; serve with the stuffing and sauce. —*Kay Chun*

WINE Floral red Burgundy: 2010 Domaine Louis Boillot & Fils Pommard.

Bourbon-Glazed Turkey with Pearl Onion Giblet Gravy

ACTIVE: 1 HR; TOTAL: 4 HR 30 MIN PLUS OVERNIGHT BRINING • 12 SERVINGS ●

Brining the bird and basting it with a bourbon and brown sugar glaze as it roasts ensures juicy meat and beautifully lacquered skin.

One 15-pound turkey—heart, gizzard and
    liver chopped and reserved
  2 cups apple cider
1½ cups kosher salt
  2 cups dark brown sugar
  3 rosemary sprigs
  1 bunch of thyme
  1 bunch of sage
  3 pounds ice cubes
  1 medium onion, finely chopped
  2 celery ribs, finely chopped
  1 large carrot, thinly sliced
10 garlic cloves
  1 stick plus 2 tablespoons
    unsalted butter, softened
  1 cup bourbon
  2 tablespoons canola oil
One 12-ounce bag frozen pearl onions,
    thawed
  3 cups turkey stock or low-sodium
    chicken broth
  2 tablespoons all-purpose flour
  ¼ cup Mashed Roasted Garlic
    (page 262)

1. Put the turkey in a brining bag set in a tub or very large pot. In a large saucepan, combine the cider with the salt, 1 cup of the brown sugar and the rosemary, thyme and sage and bring to a simmer, stirring to dissolve the salt and sugar. Add 6 quarts of cold water to the brine and pour over the turkey. Add the ice to the brine and refrigerate the turkey overnight.

2. Preheat the oven to 450°; set a rack on the lowest shelf of the oven. Drain the turkey and pat dry. Discard the brine. Fill the turkey cavity with half of the onion, celery, carrot and garlic cloves; scatter the remaining vegetables in a large roasting pan. Set a V-shaped rack in the pan. Tie the turkey legs with butcher's twine and transfer the bird to the rack, breast side up. Add 2 cups of water to the pan and roast the turkey for 30 minutes.

3. Meanwhile, in a small saucepan, combine the remaining 1 cup of brown sugar with the 1 stick of butter and the bourbon and heat just until the sugar and butter melt.

4. Reduce the oven temperature to 350° and brush the turkey with some of the glaze. Continue roasting the turkey, brushing it every 15 minutes, for about 3 hours, until an instant-read thermometer inserted in the thigh registers 165°; add another 2 cups of water and tent the turkey with foil halfway through roasting. Transfer the turkey to a carving board and let rest for 30 minutes.

5. Strain the pan juices into a heatproof bowl and skim off the fat. (You should have about 1 cup.) Discard the vegetables.

6. In a large saucepan, heat the oil. Add the chopped turkey giblets and cook over moderate heat until lightly browned, about 5 minutes. Add the pearl onions and cook until lightly browned in spots, about 5 minutes longer. Add the turkey stock and the reserved turkey pan juices and bring to a boil, scraping up any browned bits from the bottom of the saucepan.

7. In a small bowl, mash the remaining 2 tablespoons of butter with the flour and whisk it into the gravy. Bring to a boil and simmer until the gravy thickens, about 5 minutes. Whisk in the roasted garlic. Carve the turkey and serve with the gravy.
—*Tanya Holland*

WINE Juicy, berried California red blend: NV Marietta Cellars Lot 59 Old Vine Red.

Pimentón-Roasted Whole Turkey Breast with Chorizo

ACTIVE: 45 MIN; TOTAL: 3 HR 30 MIN
12 TO 14 SERVINGS ●

  ½ pound Spanish chorizo,
    cut into ¼-inch dice
  3 onions, halved lengthwise and
    cut into ¼-inch wedges
Kosher salt
  2 tablespoons sherry vinegar
  ¼ cup finely chopped parsley
One 6-pound boneless whole turkey
    breast with skin
  1 lemon, thinly sliced
Extra-virgin olive oil, for brushing
  1 tablespoon pimentón de la Vera

1. In a large skillet, cook the chorizo over moderate heat, stirring, until the fat starts to render, 3 minutes. Add two-thirds of the onion; season with salt. Cook, stirring occasionally, until the onions are softened and browned, 10 minutes. Add the vinegar; cook for 1 minute. Stir in the parsley; let cool completely.

2. Set the turkey skin side down on a work surface; season with salt. Spread the onion mixture over the breast meat and under the tenderloins. Evenly space 5 foot-long pieces of kitchen twine under the breast. Fold the sides of the breast into the center, then tie up the turkey breast to make a neat roast.

3. Spread the lemon slices and the remaining onion wedges in the center of a roasting pan. Set the turkey breast skin side up on the onions and lemons and let stand at room temperature for 1 hour.

4. Preheat the oven to 425°. Brush the turkey breast with oil and season generously with salt. Sprinkle the pimentón all over the top and side. Roast for about 1 hour and 10 minutes, basting occasionally with any pan juices, until an instant-read thermometer inserted in the thickest part of the meat registers 160°; tent the roast with foil if it browns too quickly. Transfer the turkey breast to a carving board and let stand for 20 minutes. Thinly slice crosswise and serve. —*Maria Helm Sinskey*

WINE Earthy Spanish red: 2006 Ramirez de la Piscina Reserva Rioja.

PERFECTING TURKEY

Brined, deconstructed, deep-fried or dry-brined: Chefs **KEN ORINGER, CHRIS COSENTINO, MARCUS SAMUELSSON** and **FRANK STITT** share their techniques for a phenomenal bird.

APPLE-BRINED
TURKEY

BRINED TURKEY

Apple-Brined Turkey
ACTIVE: 1 HR; TOTAL: 3 HR 45 MIN PLUS 25 HR BRINING
AND DRYING • 8 SERVINGS

BRINE
- 3 cups apple juice
- 1 green apple, quartered
- ½ navel orange
- 2 tablespoons each coriander and fennel seeds and Old Bay Seasoning
- 4 tarragon sprigs
- 1 medium bunch of thyme
- 2 garlic cloves, crushed
- 8 sage leaves
- 1 tablespoon each whole allspice berries and black peppercorns
- 2 whole cloves
- 2 cups light brown sugar
- 1 cup kosher salt
- One 15-pound turkey, legs and breast separated (see Note)

HERB BUTTER
- 6 sticks unsalted butter (1½ pounds), at room temperature
- 3 tablespoons each chopped thyme and parsley
- 2 tablespoons each chopped chives and sage
- Salt and freshly ground pepper

1. BRINE THE TURKEY In a pot, combine all of the ingredients except the turkey and add 4 cups of water. Bring to a boil, stirring to dissolve the sugar. Remove from the heat and add 12 cups of cold water. Let stand until cool. Add the turkey and refrigerate for 12 hours.
2. Set a rack over a rimmed baking sheet. Remove the turkey from the brine and transfer it to the rack; pat the turkey dry with paper towels and refrigerate it uncovered for 12 hours.
3. MAKE THE HERB BUTTER In a medium bowl, blend all of the ingredients except the salt and pepper.
4. Set a clean rack over a clean baking sheet and set a large rack in a large roasting pan. Gently separate the turkey skin from the breast meat. Rub half of the herb butter over the breast meat under the skin. Spread the remaining herb butter all over the skin of the breast and legs; season with salt and pepper. Set the breast in the prepared roasting pan and tuck the wings under it. Transfer the legs to the rack on the baking sheet. Let stand at room temperature for 1 hour.
5. Preheat the oven to 400°. Roast the turkey for about 2 hours, basting every 15 minutes with the melted herb butter and tenting the breast with foil after 30 minutes, until an instant-read thermometer registers 165° in the thickest part of the breast and 180° in the inner thigh. Let rest for 30 minutes. Carve and serve. —*Ken Oringer*
NOTE Ask your butcher to separate the legs from the turkey.
WINE Spiced Pinot Noir: 2011 DeLoach Russian River Valley.

DECONSTRUCTED TURKEY

Herbed Turkey with Crispy Skin

ACTIVE: 30 MIN; TOTAL: 4 HR 15 MIN PLUS
OVERNIGHT DRY-BRINING • 10 SERVINGS

- 2 carrots, 2 onions and 3 celery ribs, chopped
- 4 Granny Smith apples, quartered
- 1 bunch each of thyme and rosemary, plus 2 tablespoons minced thyme and 2 teaspoons minced rosemary
- One 18-pound organic turkey, legs and breast separated
- ¼ cup apple cider vinegar
- Kosher salt and freshly ground pepper
- 2 cups cold rendered duck fat or softened butter
- 2 tablespoons minced sage
- 1 fresh bay leaf, minced
- 2 teaspoons finely grated lemon zest
- 1 teaspoon coarse sea salt

1. In a bowl, toss the vegetables, apples and thyme and rosemary bunches. Rub the turkey inside and out with the vinegar; season with kosher salt and pepper. Add one-third of the vegetable mixture to a large pot. Top with the legs and half of the remaining vegetable mixture. Set the turkey breast on top; scatter the remaining vegetables over the breast. Cover and refrigerate overnight.
2. In a medium bowl, combine the duck fat, minced herbs, lemon zest, sea salt and 1 teaspoon of pepper and mix well. Keep chilled but still spreadable.
3. Remove the turkey from the pot. Spread half of the vegetable mixture in a roasting pan and the other half on a rimmed baking sheet. Set the turkey breast on the vegetables in the roasting pan and the legs on the baking sheet. Let stand at room temperature for 1 hour.
4. Preheat the oven to 350°. Separate the skin from the breast meat; spread the herbed fat under the skin. Tuck the wings under the breast. Roast the legs for 2 hours and the breast for 2 hours and 15 minutes, basting occasionally, until an instant-read thermometer registers 165° in the inner thigh and 160° in the thickest part of the breast. Let rest 30 minutes. Carve and serve. —*Chris Cosentino*
WINE Fruit-dense, full-bodied Chardonnay: 2012 Chamisal Stainless.

DEEP-FRIED TURKEY

Deep-Fried Turkey with Berbere Spices

ACTIVE: 30 MIN; TOTAL: 2 HR 15 MIN
6 SERVINGS ●

- Canola oil, for deep frying
- 1 head of garlic, halved crosswise
- 2 rosemary sprigs
- One 10- to 12-pound turkey, rinsed
- 1 tablespoon garlic powder
- 1 tablespoon smoked paprika
- 2 teaspoons kosher salt
- 2 teaspoons celery salt
- 2 teaspoons ground cumin
- 2 teaspoons freshly ground black pepper
- 1 teaspoon ground ginger
- ½ teaspoon cayenne pepper

1. In a turkey deep fryer, heat the oil with the garlic halves and rosemary to 350°, following the manufacturer's instructions; discard the garlic and rosemary. Put the turkey on a rack set over a rimmed baking sheet and thoroughly dry it inside and out with paper towels.
2. In a small bowl, mix all of the remaining seasonings. Gently separate the turkey skin from the breast meat and rub some of the spice mix under the skin. Rub the remaining spice mix all over the outside of the turkey.
3. Following the manufacturer's instructions, carefully lower the turkey into the hot oil. Fry the turkey for about 3½ minutes per pound, until an instant-read thermometer inserted in the thickest part of the breast registers 160°. Carefully transfer the fried turkey to a clean rack set over a rimmed baking sheet and let rest for 1 hour. Carve and serve.
—*Marcus Samuelsson*
WINE Fragrant, berry-rich Oregon Pinot Noir: 2011 Cristom Mt. Jefferson Cuvée.

BEST FRYER *The F&W Test Kitchen loves Waring Pro's TF200 turkey fryer: With a built-in rotisserie and safety catches, it's much less likely to splash or spill hot oil—a big risk with other setups. Plus, it can sit on a countertop.* $166; amazon.com.

DRY-BRINED TURKEY

Slow-Roasted Turkey with Herb Salt

ACTIVE: 30 MIN; TOTAL: 5 HR 45 MIN
PLUS 2 DAYS DRY-BRINING • 8 SERVINGS ●

- 2 tablespoons kosher salt
- 1 tablespoon freshly ground pepper
- ½ tablespoon dried thyme
- ½ tablespoon dried savory
- 1 teaspoon dried sage
- ½ teaspoon dried rosemary
- ½ teaspoon dried marjoram
- 2 teaspoons finely grated lemon zest
- One 14-pound organic turkey, rinsed and patted dry
- 1 onion, quartered
- 1 celery rib, cut into 2-inch pieces
- 4 garlic cloves, crushed
- 1 stick unsalted butter, melted

1. Set a rack over a rimmed baking sheet. In a small bowl, mix the salt, pepper, herbs and zest. Rub the herb salt all over the turkey cavity. Transfer the turkey to the baking sheet and refrigerate uncovered for 2 days.
2. Transfer the turkey to a clean rack set over a clean baking sheet; let stand at room temperature for 1 hour.
3. Preheat the oven to 400°. Stuff the turkey with the vegetables. Tuck the wings under the breast; tie the legs together with kitchen twine. Brush all over with the butter. Put it in the oven and immediately reduce the temperature to 275°. Roast for about 3 hours and 15 minutes, basting occasionally, until an instant-read thermometer inserted in the inner thigh registers 165°. Cover the turkey with foil and let rest for 1 hour. Carve and serve. —*Frank Stitt*
WINE Rhone-style red blend: 2009 Terre Rouge Tête-à-Tête.

Turkey Kibbe Kebabs with Two Sauces

ACTIVE: 45 MIN; TOTAL: 1 HR 30 MIN
MAKES 6 KEBABS ● ● ●

PARSLEY, LEMON AND WALNUT SAUCE

2 lemons
¾ cup finely chopped flat-leaf parsley
⅓ cup coarsely chopped fresh mint
⅓ cup coarsely chopped walnuts
1 garlic clove, finely chopped
2 tablespoons extra-virgin olive oil
¼ teaspoon kosher salt
Pinch each of freshly ground black pepper and Aleppo pepper

YOGURT-GARLIC SAUCE

2 cups plain low-fat Greek yogurt
½ cup finely chopped flat-leaf parsley
2 garlic cloves, finely chopped
¼ teaspoon kosher salt

TURKEY KEBABS

1 pound ground turkey, dark meat
2 tablespoons extra-virgin olive oil, plus more for brushing
1 cup medium-grade bulgur, rinsed and drained well
1 small onion, coarsely chopped
1½ tablespoons all-purpose flour
2 teaspoons kosher salt
½ teaspoon freshly ground black pepper
½ teaspoon ground allspice
½ teaspoon ground cumin
¼ teaspoon Aleppo pepper

1. MAKE THE PARSLEY, LEMON AND WALNUT SAUCE Using a sharp knife, cut the lemons into eighths; discard any seeds. Cut the lemon flesh from the peel and coarsely chop the flesh. Transfer to a small bowl; add the remaining ingredients along with 2 tablespoons of water. Let stand for 1 hour.
2. MEANWHILE, MAKE THE YOGURT-GARLIC SAUCE In a small bowl, whisk the yogurt with ½ cup of water. Whisk in the parsley, garlic and salt. Let stand for 1 hour.
3. MAKE THE KEBABS Light a grill or preheat the broiler. In a food processor, combine the turkey with the 2 tablespoons of olive oil.

Add the remaining kebab ingredients and process to a paste, about 30 seconds. Form into six 7-by-1½-inch logs on metal skewers.
4. Brush the kebabs with olive oil and grill over moderately high heat, turning once, until golden brown and cooked through, about 5 minutes. Serve the kebabs with the two sauces. —*Paula Wolfert*
SERVE WITH Warm pita.
WINE Cranberry-scented, medium-bodied Pinot Noir: 2010 Chalone Monterey.

Roast Turkey with Chestnut-Apple Stuffing

ACTIVE: 1 HR 15 MIN; TOTAL: 5 HR 30 MIN
PLUS OVERNIGHT SALTING
10 TO 12 SERVINGS

TURKEY

One 13- to 15-pound turkey, neck and giblets reserved
Kosher salt
2 sticks unsalted butter, softened
2 tablespoons finely chopped sage
1 small shallot, minced
Freshly ground pepper
3 celery ribs, sliced ¼ inch thick
2 medium carrots, sliced ¼ inch thick
1 small onion, thinly sliced
2 cups turkey or chicken stock or low-sodium broth, for roasting

STUFFING

1 pound country bread, crusts removed and bread cut into 1-inch cubes (12 cups)
2 tablespoons extra-virgin olive oil
3 celery ribs, finely chopped
1 medium onion, finely chopped
3 Fuji apples—peeled, cored, quartered and thinly sliced crosswise
Reserved turkey giblets, finely chopped
¼ cup finely chopped parsley
2 tablespoons finely chopped sage
1 tablespoon chopped thyme
2 teaspoons finely chopped rosemary
2 cups peeled roasted chestnuts, crumbled (14 ounces)
2 cups turkey or chicken stock or low-sodium broth, warmed
Salt and freshly ground pepper

1. PREPARE THE TURKEY Rinse the turkey inside and out under cold water; pat dry with paper towels. Season inside with 1 tablespoon of kosher salt, outside with 3 tablespoons. Cover and refrigerate overnight.
2. Remove the turkey from the refrigerator and pat dry with paper towels. In a bowl, blend the butter, sage and shallot and season with salt and pepper. Starting at the cavity end of the bird, slip your hand between the skin and meat, loosening the skin over the breast and around the legs. Spread the shallot-sage butter under the skin, covering as much of the breasts and legs as possible. Scatter the celery, carrots, onion and turkey neck in a large roasting pan and set the turkey on top; let stand at room temperature for 1 hour.
3. MAKE THE STUFFING Preheat the oven to 375°. Bake the bread cubes on a large rimmed baking sheet until golden, 20 to 25 minutes. Let cool slightly, then transfer to a large bowl.
4. Increase the oven temperature to 425°. In a skillet, heat the oil. Add the celery and onion; cook over moderately high heat, stirring occasionally, until softened and barely browned, 7 minutes. Add the apples and giblets; cook, stirring occasionally, until the apples are just tender and the giblets are cooked, 5 minutes. Stir in the herbs and cook until fragrant, 1 minute. Add to the bread along with the chestnuts and the warm stock. Toss well and season the stuffing with salt and pepper; let cool.
5. Pack the turkey cavity and neck with the stuffing, then tie the legs together with kitchen twine. Roast until richly browned, 45 minutes. Baste with any accumulated pan juices and tent the breast with foil. Pour the remaining 2 cups of stock into the roasting pan. Turn the oven temperature down to 325° and roast for 2 to 2½ hours longer, basting every 30 minutes; remove the foil for the last 30 minutes of roasting. The turkey is done when an instant-read thermometer inserted in an inner thigh registers 165°. Transfer to a carving board; let rest for at least 30 minutes.
6. Scoop the stuffing into a bowl. Strain the pan juices into a heatproof bowl; skim off the fat. Carve the turkey; serve with the stuffing and the pan juices. —*Maria Helm Sinksey*
WINE Beaujolais: 2011 Guy Breton Morgon.

● HEALTHY ● MAKE AHEAD ● VEGETARIAN ● STAFF FAVORITE

ROAST TURKEY WITH
CHESTNUT-APPLE STUFFING

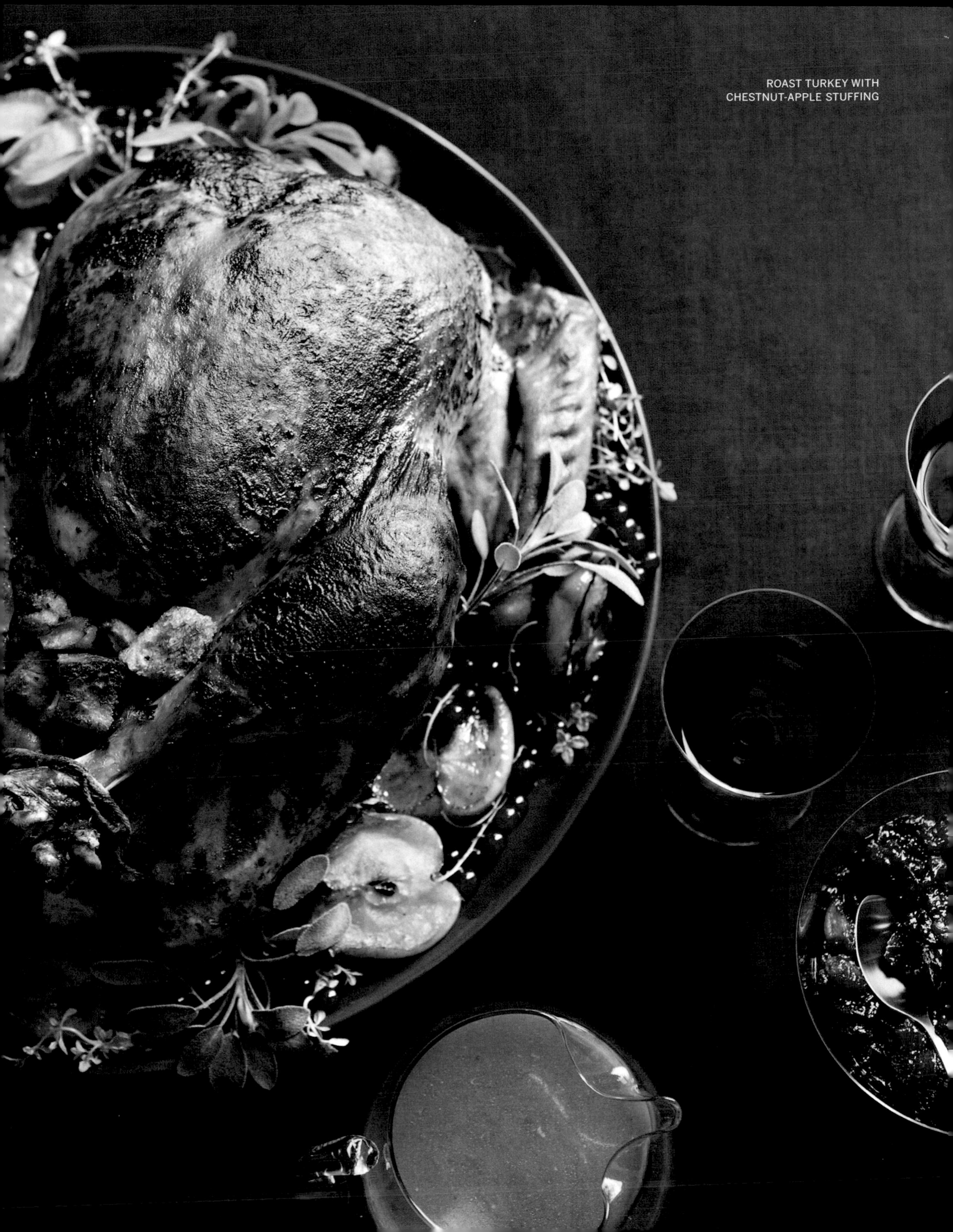

Yvonne Cadiz Kim presents a tray of food for a grill party hosted with her husband, chef Bill Kim (far left) of Chicago's Urbanbelly empire.

Opposite: recipe, page 185.
TRIPLE PORK BURGERS WITH QUICK CUCUMBER KIMCHI

PORK & VEAL

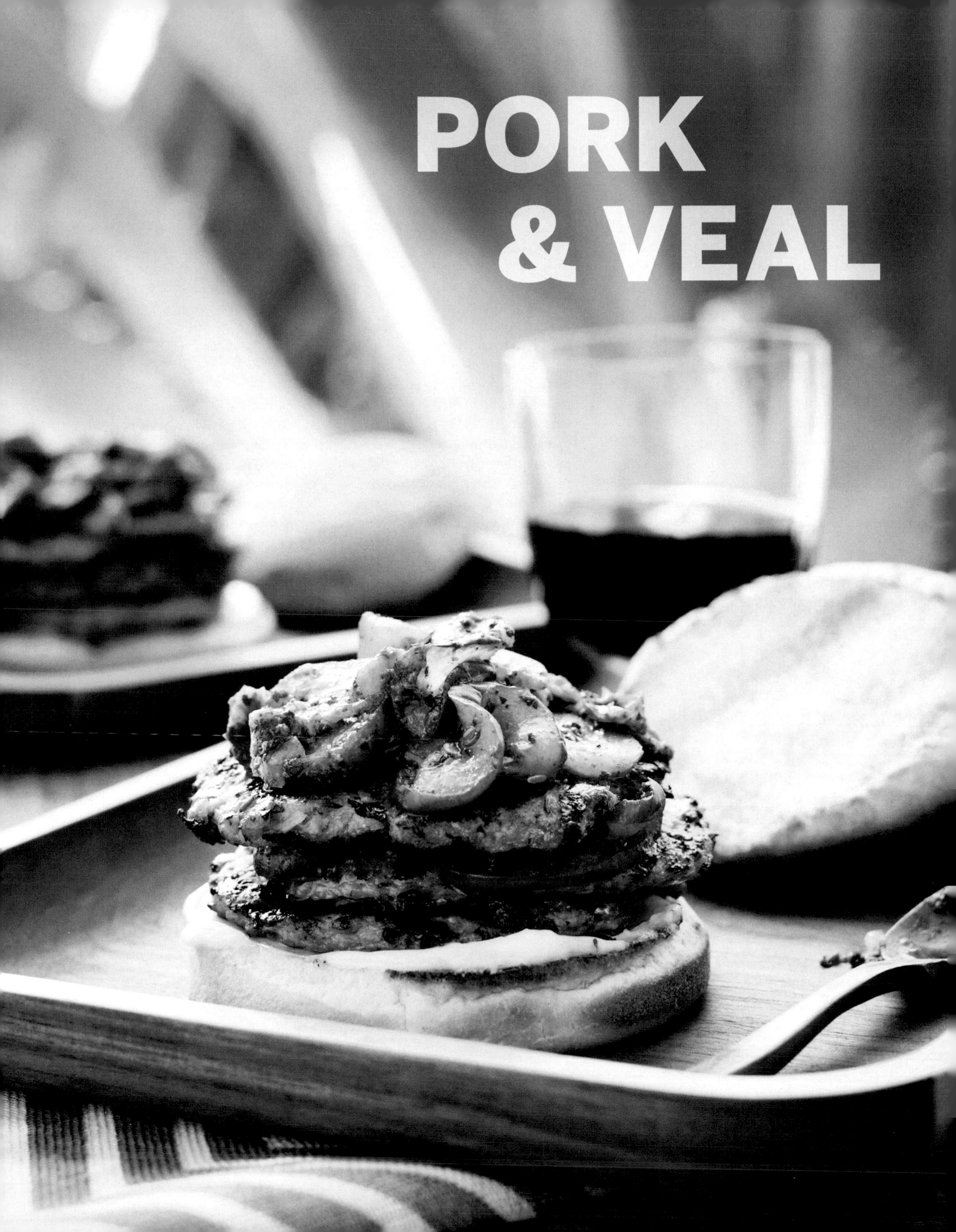

Skillet Pork Chops with Warm Escarole Caesar

TOTAL: 15 MIN • 2 SERVINGS ●

This dish is super-fast because while the pork chops finish cooking in the oven, you can make two side dishes in one pan: wilted escarole and sautéed radishes. The escarole is flavored with anchovies, Parmigiano, garlic and lemon juice, giving it an instant dressing that's reminiscent of Caesar salad.

- 3 tablespoons extra-virgin olive oil
- Two ¾-inch-thick rib pork chops (1 pound)
- Kosher salt and freshly ground black pepper
- 1 tablespoon unsalted butter
- 3 oil-packed anchovy fillets, drained
- 3 garlic cloves, finely chopped
- 1 head of escarole (12 ounces), rinsed and halved lengthwise
- 12 radishes, halved if large
- Freshly grated Parmigiano-Reggiano cheese and lemon wedges, for serving

1. Preheat the oven to 450°. Place a baking sheet in the oven to heat. In a large cast-iron skillet, heat 2 tablespoons of the olive oil. Season the pork chops with salt and pepper and cook over moderately high heat until golden on both sides, about 3 minutes. Transfer the chops to the hot baking sheet and roast for about 6 minutes, until just cooked through.

2. Meanwhile, in the same skillet, melt the butter in the remaining 1 tablespoon of olive oil. Add the anchovies and garlic and cook over moderate heat, stirring, for 30 seconds. Add the escarole, radishes and 2 tablespoons of water and season with pepper. Cook over moderate heat, turning occasionally, until the escarole is charred in spots and just wilted, about 3 minutes. Transfer the pork, escarole and radishes to plates and serve with grated cheese and lemon wedges. —*Kay Chun*

WINE Medium-bodied Italian red: 2010 Lohsa Morellino di Scansano.

Pork Chops with Smoky Mole-Style Rub

TOTAL: 30 MIN • 4 SERVINGS

This Mexican-inspired spice rub is also delicious on steak and chicken legs. The combination of paprika and ancho chile powder enhances the grilled meat's smoky flavor.

- 1 tablespoon cumin seeds
- 2 tablespoons smoked sweet paprika
- 1 tablespoon muscovado or dark brown sugar
- 1 tablespoon ancho chile powder
- 1 tablespoon dried oregano
- 1 teaspoon granulated garlic
- 1 teaspoon unsweetened cocoa powder
- 1 teaspoon toasted sesame seeds
- Four 1-inch-thick pork rib chops (about 2¾ pounds)
- Kosher salt and freshly ground black pepper

1. In a small skillet, toast the cumin seeds over moderate heat until fragrant, about 1 minute. Transfer to a spice grinder and let cool, then finely grind.

2. In a small bowl, whisk the ground cumin with the smoked paprika, brown sugar, chile powder, oregano, garlic, cocoa powder and sesame seeds.

3. Light a grill or preheat a grill pan. Season the pork chops with salt and pepper and rub 1 tablespoon of the spice mixture all over each chop.

4. Grill the pork chops over moderate heat, turning occasionally, until they are lightly charred and an instant-read thermometer inserted near the bone registers 135°, about 12 minutes. Transfer the pork chops to a carving board or platter and let them rest for 5 minutes before serving.
—*Jamie Bissonnette*

SERVE WITH Bissonnette's Creamy Cucumber and Grilled Potato Salad (page 259).

MAKE AHEAD The spice rub can be stored in an airtight container for up to 3 months.

WINE Chocolate-inflected Merlot from Washington state: 2011 Canoe Ridge The Expedition series.

Asian-Brined Pork Loin

ACTIVE: 30 MIN; TOTAL: 2 HR PLUS OVERNIGHT BRINING
8 TO 10 SERVINGS ●

The brine for this deliciously spicy pork loin takes only minutes to make and gives the meat plenty of flavor—no seasoning or sauce needed. The recipe calls for a bone-in pork loin roast, which includes the rib rack. You can serve the ribs along with the roast or reserve them for the Hoisin-Glazed Ribs on page 190.

- 1½ cups mirin
- 1½ cups low-sodium soy sauce
- 4 ounces fresh ginger, thinly sliced
- 10 small dried red chiles or 2 tablespoons crushed red pepper
- 1 orange, thinly sliced
- 2 tablespoons toasted sesame oil
- One 6-pound bone-in pork loin roast
- 1 tablespoon vegetable oil

1. In a large pot, combine the mirin, soy sauce, ginger, chiles, orange slices and sesame oil with 8 cups of cold water. Add the pork roast, cover and refrigerate overnight.

2. Preheat the oven to 350°. Drain the pork roast and let it come to room temperature. Pat dry. In a medium flameproof roasting pan, heat the vegetable oil. Add the pork roast and cook over moderate heat, turning occasionally, until it is browned all over, about 10 minutes. Transfer the roast to the oven, meaty side up, and roast for about 1 hour and 10 minutes, or until an instant-read thermometer inserted in the thickest part of the meat registers 135°. Cover the pork very loosely with aluminum foil and let it rest for 15 minutes.

3. Using a long, sharp knife and using the bones as your guide, carefully carve the pork roast off the bones in one piece. Slice it thinly before serving. Reserve the rib rack for another meal (see page 190) or cut into individual ribs and serve them alongside the roast. —*Grace Parisi*

WINE Smooth, fruit-forward Nero d'Avola: 2010 Valle dell'Acate Case Ibidini.

● HEALTHY ● MAKE AHEAD ● VEGETARIAN ● STAFF FAVORITE

SKILLET PORK CHOPS WITH
WARM ESCAROLE CAESAR

Maple-Brined Pork Tenderloin

**ACTIVE: 40 MIN; TOTAL: 1 HR 30 MIN PLUS
6 HR BRINING • 10 TO 12 SERVINGS** ●

Scott Boggs, the chef at Rose Bakery in New York City, soaks pork tenderloins in a spiced maple-cider brine to season them throughout and keep them extra-juicy; the sugars in the maple syrup caramelize as the meat roasts.

- 1 teaspoon whole black peppercorns, plus freshly ground black pepper for seasoning
- 6 whole cloves
- 4 allspice berries
- 3 juniper berries
- ⅓ cup kosher salt, plus more for seasoning
- 2 cups apple cider
- ½ cup pure Grade A dark amber maple syrup
- ⅓ cup maple sugar (see Note on page 50)
- 6 garlic cloves, peeled
- 6 thyme sprigs

Four 1¼-pound pork tenderloins
- ¼ cup canola oil

1. In a medium saucepan, toast the 1 teaspoon of black peppercorns with the cloves, allspice berries and juniper berries over moderate heat until fragrant, 2 minutes. Add the ⅓ cup of salt and the apple cider, maple syrup, maple sugar, garlic and thyme sprigs to the saucepan and bring just to a simmer, stirring. Add 3 cups of cold water and pour the brine into a small roasting pan; let cool. Add the pork tenderloins, cover and refrigerate for 6 to 8 hours.

2. Preheat the oven to 350°. Drain the pork, discarding the brine. Pat the pork dry and season lightly with salt and pepper. In a very large skillet, heat 2 tablespoons of the canola oil until shimmering. Add 2 of the pork tenderloins and cook over moderately high heat, turning, until browned all over, about 8 minutes. Transfer the pork to a rimmed baking sheet. Wipe out the skillet and repeat with the remaining 2 tablespoons of oil and 2 tenderloins.

3. Roast the pork tenderloins in the oven for about 18 minutes, turning twice, until an instant-read thermometer inserted in the thickest part of the meat registers 140°. Transfer the pork to a cutting board and let rest for 10 minutes. Slice the pork and serve. —*Scott Boggs*

WINE Spicy, dark-berried Italian red: 2010 Barberani Polago.

Three-Pepper Pork Tenderloin with Peach-Cucumber Salad

⏲ **TOTAL: 40 MIN • 6 TO 8 SERVINGS** ●

- ¼ cup extra-virgin olive oil, plus more for grilling and rubbing
- 2 teaspoons ground black pepper
- ½ teaspoon ground white pepper
- ¼ teaspoon cayenne pepper

Kosher salt
- 2 pork tenderloins (about 1½ pounds each), butterflied and lightly pounded
- 2 tablespoons fresh lime juice
- 2 tablespoons minced shallots
- 1 very large peach, diced
- ¾ pound Persian cucumbers, diced
- ½ cup coarsely chopped mint
- ½ cup coarsely chopped cilantro

Plain yogurt and grilled naan, for serving

1. Light a grill or preheat a grill pan; oil the grates or pan. In a small bowl, combine the black, white and cayenne pepper with 2 teaspoons of salt. Rub the pork with olive oil and pat the spice mixture all over it. Grill over moderately high heat, turning occasionally, until lightly charred and an instant-read thermometer inserted in the thickest part registers 135°, 8 to 10 minutes. Transfer the pork to a work surface and let rest for 10 minutes.

2. Meanwhile, in a bowl, whisk the lime juice with the ¼ cup of oil; season with salt. Add the shallots and let stand for 5 minutes. Add the peach, cucumbers, mint and cilantro; season with salt. Slice the pork and serve with the salad, yogurt and naan. —*Grace Parisi*

WINE Ripe, white peach–inflected German Riesling: 2011 Gunderloch Jean-Baptiste Kabinett.

Garlic and Rosemary Roast Pork Loin

**ACTIVE: 20 MIN; TOTAL: 1 HR 45 MIN
PLUS OVERNIGHT MARINATING
4 SERVINGS**

Instead of using lean pork tenderloin, Ethan Stowell, the chef at Tavolàta in Seattle (and an F&W Best New Chef 2008), likes to cook the fattier chuck loin, which is the last six inches of the cut where the shoulder wraps around the loin. "It's marbled and almost like pork rib eye," he says. Marinating the pork overnight allows the garlic and rosemary flavor to permeate the meat.

- ¼ cup plus 2 tablespoons extra-virgin olive oil
- 8 large garlic cloves, chopped

Leaves from 1 bunch of rosemary, coarsely chopped (½ cup)
- 2 teaspoons kosher salt
- ½ teaspoon freshly ground black pepper
- 2 pounds pork loin

Roasted potatoes, for serving

1. In a small bowl, stir ¼ cup of the olive oil with the garlic, rosemary, salt and pepper. Rub the mixture all over the pork. Transfer the pork and marinade to a large resealable plastic bag and refrigerate overnight.

2. Preheat the oven to 400°. Let the pork loin stand at room temperature for 30 minutes, then brush off as much of the marinade as possible.

3. In a large ovenproof skillet, heat the remaining 2 tablespoons of olive oil until shimmering. Add the pork loin to the skillet and cook over moderately high heat until it is browned all over, about 5 minutes. Transfer the pork loin to the oven and roast for 40 to 45 minutes, until the outside is golden and a thermometer inserted in the thickest part of the meat registers 135°. Transfer the pork roast to a work surface or carving board and let it rest for about 15 minutes before thinly slicing and serving with roasted potatoes. —*Ethan Stowell*

WINE Herb-scented Washington state red blend: 2010 Waters Interlude.

● HEALTHY ● MAKE AHEAD ● VEGETARIAN ● STAFF FAVORITE

GARLIC AND ROSEMARY
ROAST PORK LOIN

Mustard-Roasted Pork Loin with Squash Polenta

ACTIVE: 45 MIN; TOTAL: 2 HR
4 SERVINGS

SQUASH

One 3-pound butternut squash, halved lengthwise and seeded
3 tablespoons olive oil
Salt and freshly ground pepper
½ cup polenta (not instant)
¼ cup honey
2 tablespoons red wine vinegar
1 garlic clove, smashed
PORK
One 3½-pound bone-in pork loin (4 ribs)
Salt
3 tablespoons Dijon mustard
Freshly ground coarse pepper
HAZELNUT PICADA
½ cup hazelnuts
1 small garlic clove
6 sage leaves
Salt

1. **PREPARE THE SQUASH** Preheat the oven to 425°. Rub the cut side of one squash half with 1 tablespoon of the olive oil, then sprinkle with a generous pinch each of salt and freshly ground pepper. Set the squash half cut side down on a baking sheet and roast for 40 to 50 minutes, until tender. Scoop the flesh into a bowl and coarsely mash it.

2. In a medium saucepan, bring 2½ cups of water to a boil and whisk in the polenta. Bring to a simmer and cook over moderate heat, stirring occasionally, until soft and thick, about 20 minutes. Fold in the mashed squash and season with salt and pepper.

3. Meanwhile, peel the remaining squash half and cut it into ¾-inch cubes. On a rimmed baking sheet, toss the squash cubes with the remaining 2 tablespoons of olive oil and ½ teaspoon of salt. Roast for 30 to 35 minutes, until tender. Remove and reduce the oven temperature to 400°.

4. **ROAST THE PORK** In a small roasting pan, season the pork loin with ½ teaspoon of salt, then coat the meat with the Dijon mustard.

Sprinkle the pork with ½ teaspoon of pepper and roast for 45 to 55 minutes, until an instant-read thermometer inserted in the center registers 120°. Transfer the roast to a cutting board and let stand for 20 minutes. Reduce the oven temperature to 325°.

5. **MAKE THE HAZELNUT PICADA** Spread the hazelnuts in a pie pan and toast for about 10 minutes, until golden. Transfer to a towel and rub to remove the skins. In a mortar, pound the garlic to a paste with the sage and a pinch of salt. Add the hazelnuts and coarsely crush them in with the pestle.

6. In a skillet, cook the roasted squash cubes with the honey, vinegar and smashed garlic over moderate heat until simmering; discard the garlic. Slice the pork between the ribs. Mound the polenta on plates and top with the pork, squash cubes and hazelnut *picada* and serve. —*Ignacio Mattos*

WINE Full-bodied, fruity sparkling rosé: NV Fleury Pere & Fils Rosé de Saignée Brut.

Grilled Pork with Coconut Rice and Lemongrass Sambal

ACTIVE: 1 HR 45 MIN; TOTAL: 2 HR PLUS
6 HR SOAKING • 6 SERVINGS ●

After eating *sambal* (an Asian, chile-spiked condiment) in Bali, chef Suzanne Goin created a version to serve with pork that's fragrant with lemongrass and kaffir lime.

PORK
1 cup packed cilantro leaves
2 garlic cloves, crushed
2 jalapeños, seeded and chopped
¼ cup extra-virgin olive oil
Two 1-pound pork tenderloins
½ cup roasted peanuts
2 lemongrass stalks, tender inner white bulbs only, thinly sliced
2 fresh kaffir lime leaves, thinly sliced
2 Thai bird chiles, thinly sliced
4 shallots, very thinly sliced and separated into rings
1 tablespoon finely grated peeled fresh ginger
¼ cup fresh lime juice
½ cup grapeseed or canola oil
Kosher salt

RICE
2 cups jasmine rice
One 13.5-ounce can unsweetened coconut milk
2 ounces grated palm sugar (⅓ cup) or ¼ cup granulated sugar
2 heads of baby bok choy, halved and thinly sliced through the core
2 scallions, thinly sliced

1. **PREPARE THE PORK** In a food processor, combine ¾ cup of the cilantro with the garlic and jalapeños. With the machine on, drizzle in the olive oil until a loose paste forms. Coat the pork evenly with the cilantro paste and refrigerate for at least 4 hours or overnight.

2. Meanwhile, preheat the oven to 350°. Toast the peanuts in a pie plate for about 5 minutes, until fragrant. Finely chop the peanuts.

3. In a bowl, combine the lemongrass, lime leaves, chiles, shallots, ginger, lime juice and grapeseed oil. Season the *sambal* with salt.

4. **PREPARE THE RICE** In a bowl, cover the rice with water and let soak for 6 hours. Drain and rinse 3 times, until the water runs clear.

5. Bring a pot of water to a boil; line a steamer insert with a double layer of cheesecloth. Evenly spread the rice on the cloth. Set the steamer 3 inches over the water; cover. Steam the rice until almost tender, 45 minutes.

6. In a saucepan, cook the coconut milk and sugar over moderate heat, stirring, until the sugar is dissolved. Remove the steamer from the pot and drain. Spread the rice evenly in the pot. Pour the hot coconut mixture evenly over the rice; do not stir. Cover and let stand for 10 minutes. Stir and season with salt.

7. Light a grill; lightly oil the grate. Wipe off most of the marinade from the pork. Grill over moderate heat for 20 minutes, turning, until an instant-read thermometer inserted in the center registers 140°. Let rest for 15 minutes.

8. Toss the bok choy with half of the *sambal*, the remaining cilantro and the scallions. Spoon the rice onto a platter; scatter the bok choy on top. Thinly slice the pork; arrange on the rice with the remaining *sambal*. Garnish with the peanuts and serve. —*Suzanne Goin*

WINE Fruit-driven Rhône red: 2010 Holus Bolus Santa Barbara County Syrah.

● HEALTHY ● MAKE AHEAD ● VEGETARIAN ● STAFF FAVORITE

Pork Tenderloin Marinated in Amber Ale

ACTIVE: 40 MIN; TOTAL: 1 HR 30 MIN
PLUS 12 HR MARINATING • 6 SERVINGS ●

This recipe makes good use of a beer-and-vegetable marinade: The pork takes on a subtly delicious beer flavor, then the vegetables are simmered in the ale until tender and pureed into a simple sauce.

- 2 cups Belgian-style amber ale
- 1 small carrot, cut into ½-inch pieces
- 1 celery rib, cut into ½-inch pieces
- 1 small onion, cut into ½-inch pieces
Two 1¼-pound pork tenderloins
Kosher salt and freshly ground pepper
- 2 tablespoons canola oil

1. In a large resealable plastic bag, combine the ale, carrot, celery and onion. Add the pork tenderloins, close the bag and refrigerate for at least 12 hours or overnight.
2. Remove the pork from the marinade and let return to room temperature, reserving the marinade. Preheat the oven to 375°. Transfer the marinade and vegetables to a saucepan and simmer over moderately low heat, stirring, until the vegetables are tender, 20 minutes. Transfer the marinade and vegetables to a blender and puree to form a smooth sauce. Return the sauce to the saucepan and season with salt and pepper. Keep warm.
3. Pat the pork dry with paper towels and season with salt and pepper. In a very large ovenproof skillet, heat the oil until shimmering. Add the pork and cook over moderately high heat, turning occasionally, until browned all over, 10 minutes. Transfer the skillet to the oven and roast the pork for 10 minutes, until an instant-read thermometer inserted in the thickest part of the meat registers 140°.
4. Transfer the pork to a cutting board and let rest for about 10 minutes. Slice the pork crosswise and transfer to plates. Spoon the beer sauce over the pork and serve.
—Luca Cerato
SERVE WITH Roasted artichoke hearts and mashed or roasted potatoes.
BEER Belgian-style amber ale: Ommegang Rare Vos.

Sautéed Pork with Onion Marmalade

⏱ **ACTIVE: 30 MIN; TOTAL: 45 MIN**
8 SERVINGS ●

This dish features juicy seared pork medallions wrapped in pancetta and served with a marmalade of buttery caramelized onions.

- 2 medium white onions, minced
- 6 tablespoons unsalted butter
- ⅔ cup sugar
- ¾ cup plus ⅓ cup dry red wine
- ¾ cup raspberry vinegar
Salt
Eight 4-ounce pork tenderloin medallions
Freshly ground pepper
- 1 teaspoon minced rosemary
- 8 very thin slices of pancetta
- 2 tablespoons pure olive oil
- 8 garlic cloves
- ¼ cup balsamic vinegar
- 1½ cups beef stock

1. In a saucepan, cook the onions over low heat with the butter and sugar until caramelized, 30 minutes. Add ¾ cup of the wine along with the raspberry vinegar and boil until the liquid is syrupy, 8 minutes. Season with salt.
2. Meanwhile, season the pork with salt and pepper; sprinkle with the rosemary. Top each medallion with a slice of pancetta and tie together with string. In a skillet, heat the oil and garlic. Add the pork, pancetta side down, and cook over moderately high heat until browned, 3 minutes. Reduce the heat to moderate, turn the medallions and cook until just cooked through, 3 minutes. Transfer to a platter and tent with foil. Discard the garlic.
3. Add the remaining ⅓ cup of wine and the balsamic vinegar to the skillet and boil, scraping up the browned bits, until reduced by half, 2 minutes. Add the stock and simmer until reduced to ⅔ cup, 5 minutes. Stir in any pork juices and season with salt and pepper. Remove the strings and transfer the pork to plates. Serve with the onion marmalade and sauce. *—Massimo Bottura*
WINE Bright, medium-bodied Chianti Classico: 2009 Badia a Coltibuono.

Citrus and Garlic Pork Shoulder

ACTIVE: 1 HR 30 MIN; TOTAL: 6 HR
PLUS OVERNIGHT MARINATING
6 SERVINGS

- 1 tablespoon extra-virgin olive oil, plus more for brushing
- 4 garlic cloves, crushed
- 1 tablespoon fresh oregano leaves
- 1 teaspoon ground cumin
Kosher salt and freshly ground pepper
- 1 cup fresh lime juice (about 6 limes)
- ¼ cup fresh orange juice
- 1 onion, thinly sliced
One 6-pound skinless, bone-in pork shoulder
30 to 40 pounds hardwood charcoal

1. In a mortar, combine the 1 tablespoon of oil with the garlic, oregano, cumin, 1 tablespoon of salt and 1½ teaspoons of pepper; pound to a paste and scrape into a small bowl. Whisk in the lime and orange juices. Pour the marinade into a very large resealable plastic bag; add the onion and pork. Seal the bag, pressing out any air, and turn to coat the pork. Put the bag in a large baking dish; refrigerate overnight, turning occasionally.
2. Remove the pork from the bag; strain the marinade into a bowl. Pat the pork dry; let stand at room temperature for 45 minutes.
3. Light a hardwood charcoal fire and set up the grill for indirect cooking; you'll need to replenish the hot coals periodically to maintain the heat. Brush the pork with olive oil and season generously with salt and pepper. Grill the pork over indirect heat for 4 to 5 hours, turning and basting with the reserved marinade every 30 minutes, until the roast is almost done; move the roast farther from or closer to the fire as needed to keep it cooking at a constant heat. The roast is done when an instant-read thermometer inserted in the thickest part near the bone registers 160°.
4. Transfer the pork to a carving board, tent with foil and let rest for 30 minutes. Carve into thin slices and serve. *—Michael Chiarello*
WINE Grenache-based Rhône red: 2011 Chateau Pesquié Terrasses Ventoux.

Honey-Soy-Roasted Pork with Braised Vegetables

ACTIVE: 1 HR; TOTAL: 2 HR 30 MIN
6 TO 8 SERVINGS ●

One 4¼-pound boneless pork
    shoulder roast, tied
Kosher salt and freshly ground
    black pepper
 2 tablespoons vegetable oil
½ cup honey
¼ cup soy sauce
 1 cup veal demiglace
 1 cup chicken stock or
    low-sodium broth
 1 pound baby carrots (about 20),
    scrubbed
 1 pound medium turnips
    (about 5), peeled and cut
    into 1-inch wedges
¾ pound brussels sprouts,
    halved through the core

1. Preheat the oven to 400°. Season the pork all over with salt and pepper. In a large skillet, heat the oil until shimmering. Add the pork roast and cook over moderately high heat, turning, until browned all over, about 12 minutes. Transfer the pork to a 12-by-14-inch roasting pan.

2. Pour off all of the fat from the skillet. Add the honey and cook over moderate heat, stirring, until it turns a deep amber, 3 to 5 minutes. Stir in the soy sauce, then add the demiglace and chicken stock and bring to a boil. Pour the liquid over the pork and roast for about 50 minutes, basting every 10 minutes, until an instant-read thermometer inserted in the thickest part of the meat registers 120°; add ¼ cup of stock or water to the roasting pan if the juices evaporate too quickly.

3. Scatter the carrots, turnips and brussels sprouts around the pork and roast for about 25 minutes longer, basting occasionally, until the pork is glazed and an instant-read thermometer inserted in the thickest part of the meat registers 150°. Transfer the pork roast to a carving board, tent it with foil and let it rest.

4. Return the roasting pan to the oven and roast the vegetables for 20 to 25 minutes longer, until tender. Using a slotted spoon, transfer the vegetables to a medium bowl. Pour the pan juices into another smaller bowl or a gravy boat.

5. Thinly slice the pork and serve with the pan juices and vegetables. —*Tetsu Yahagi*
WINE German *spätlese:* 2012 Selbach-Oster Zeltinger Schlossberg.

Korean Garlic and Chile Pork

TOTAL: 30 MIN PLUS OVERNIGHT
MARINATING • 4 TO 6 SERVINGS ●
This sweet-spicy marinade is perfect on lean pork shoulder or fattier pork belly.

¼ cup *gochujang* (Korean chile paste)
 3 tablespoons sugar
 3 tablespoons minced garlic
 1 tablespoon minced peeled ginger
 1 tablespoon dry sake
 1 tablespoon mirin
 2 tablespoons toasted sesame oil
 2 tablespoons *gochugaru* (Korean
    chile powder)
½ small onion, thinly sliced
 2 pounds pork shoulder or pork belly,
    cut into 4-by-⅛-inch strips
Canola oil, for frying
Thinly sliced scallions, for garnish
Lettuce leaves and steamed
    short-grain rice, for serving

1. In a bowl, combine all of the ingredients except the pork, canola oil, scallions, lettuce and rice. Add the pork and turn to coat. Cover with plastic wrap and refrigerate overnight.

2. In a large nonstick skillet, heat 1 tablespoon of canola oil. Add the pork in batches, taking care not to crowd the pan, and stir-fry over moderately high heat until cooked through and browned in spots, about 2 minutes per batch. Add more oil to the skillet as necessary. 3. Transfer the pork to a platter and garnish with scallions. Serve with lettuce leaves and steamed rice. —*Hooni Kim*
WINE Slightly off-dry German Riesling: 2011 Hexamer Meddersheimer Altenberg Kabinett.

Sausage Burgers with Sriracha-Honey-Mustard Sauce

⏱ TOTAL: 40 MIN • 8 SERVINGS ●
These pork burgers are just as easy to make as plain beef burgers, but so much more flavorful. One trick is using both sweet and hot Italian sausages, which are already boldly seasoned. The other is creating an almost-instant glaze with honey, Sriracha and two types of prepared mustard.

1½ pounds ground pork
1½ pounds sweet and hot Italian
    sausages, casings removed
¼ cup honey
 3 tablespoons Sriracha
¼ cup Dijon mustard
¼ cup whole-grain mustard
 8 burger buns, split and toasted
Mayonnaise, coleslaw and pickles,
    for serving

1. In a large bowl, combine the ground pork with the sweet and hot sausage meat. Form the meat mixture into eight 4-inch patties about ¾ inch thick.

2. In a small saucepan, combine the honey, Sriracha and both mustards; bring to a boil. Simmer over moderate heat until a slightly glossy sauce forms, about 3 minutes; reserve half of the sauce in a bowl for serving.

3. Light a grill and oil the grates. Grill the burgers over moderately high heat for 5 minutes, turning once, until lightly charred and barely cooked through; brush with some of the sauce and grill, turning and brushing, until the burgers are cooked through and the sauce has caramelized to a glaze, about 5 minutes longer.

4. Spread the bottom halves of the buns with mayonnaise and top with the burgers. Spoon a little of the reserved sauce on top, followed by coleslaw and pickles. Close the burgers, cut in half and serve right away.
—*Grace Parisi*

MAKE AHEAD The uncooked sausage burgers can be refrigerated overnight. The sauce can be refrigerated for up to 5 days.
WINE Fragrant, fruit-forward Grenache: 2011 Beckmen Vineyards Estate.

● HEALTHY ● MAKE AHEAD ● VEGETARIAN ● STAFF FAVORITE

KOREAN GARLIC AND CHILE PORK

Yucatán Pork with Annatto and Ancho Chile

ACTIVE: 1 HR; TOTAL: 6 HR PLUS
OVERNIGHT MARINATING
6 SERVINGS

This classic Mexican dish of pork shoulder and spices uses a double layer of banana leaves as a flavorful pouch for cooking, but the thick, fibrous leaves are not edible.

¼ cup annatto (or achiote) seeds
½ cup pure ancho chile powder
2 tablespoons dried oregano
2 tablespoons kosher salt
2 tablespoons freshly ground
   black pepper
1 tablespoon ground allspice
1 onion, quartered
4 garlic cloves, sliced
1 cup freshly squeezed
   orange juice
¼ cup apple cider vinegar
2 tablespoons fresh lime juice
4 pounds trimmed boneless pork
   shoulder, cut into 1½-inch cubes
Twenty-four 18-inch frozen banana
   leaves (from two 1-pound
   packages)—thawed, rinsed and
   dried (see Note)
Twelve ¼-inch-thick lime slices
   (from 2 limes)
Twelve ¼-inch-thick jalapeño slices
   (from about 2 jalapeños)
Roasted Tomato and Árbol Chile Salsa
   (recipe follows), for serving

1. In a medium saucepan, bring 3 cups of water to a boil. Add the annatto seeds and simmer for 10 minutes. Cover, remove from the heat and let stand for 2 hours. Drain the seeds and transfer them to a blender. Add the chile powder, oregano, salt, black pepper, allspice, onion, garlic, orange juice, vinegar and lime juice. Puree until smooth. Transfer the marinade to a large bowl, add the pork and toss to coat thoroughly. Cover and refrigerate overnight.

2. Using a slotted spoon, transfer the pork cubes to another bowl. Add ¼ cup of the marinade and toss to coat.

3. Light a hardwood charcoal or gas grill and set it up for indirect grilling. Cut the fibrous string off the edge of each banana leaf and reserve. On a work surface, arrange 2 banana leaves in a cross pattern. Spoon ¾ cup of the pork in the center and top with a slice each of lime and jalapeño. Fold up the top leaf like an envelope to enclose the filling, then wrap the packet in the bottom leaf. Tie up the packet with the reserved banana string. Repeat with the remaining leaves and filling.

4. When the grill temperature reaches 300°, arrange the packets on the grate away from the heat source and grill, covered, for about 3 hours, until the pork is very tender; replenish the coals as necessary. Serve the pork with the tomato and árbol chile salsa.
—Andrew Zimmern

SERVE WITH Steamed rice, fried sweet plantains and cilantro leaves.

NOTE Banana leaves are available at specialty food stores or *gourmetsleuth.com*. A pound should be sufficient for this recipe, but buy extras in case any are cracked.

WINE Berry-rich Oregon Pinot Noir: 2012 Willamette Valley Vineyards Whole Cluster.

ROASTED TOMATO AND ÁRBOL CHILE SALSA

TOTAL: 20 MIN
MAKES ABOUT 2 CUPS ● ● ○

5 plum tomatoes,
   cored and halved lengthwise
3 tablespoons corn oil
5 garlic cloves, coarsely chopped
12 dried árbol chiles,
   stems discarded
1 teaspoon ground cumin
1 teaspoon dried oregano
Salt

1. Preheat the broiler and set a rack 8 inches from the heat. Arrange the tomato halves on a rimmed baking sheet, cut side down. Broil the tomatoes until the skins are charred and blistered, about 5 minutes. Turn the tomatoes cut side up and broil until charred in spots, about 5 minutes longer. Discard the tomato skins.

2. Meanwhile, in a medium skillet, heat the oil. Add the garlic and cook over moderately low heat until golden, about 3 minutes. Add the árbol chiles to the skillet and cook until softened slightly, about 2 minutes.

3. Scrape the chiles, garlic and oil into a food processor. Add 3 tablespoons of water and pulse, scraping down the sides as necessary, until a chunky puree forms, about 2 minutes. Add the tomatoes, cumin and oregano and pulse until a chunky salsa forms. Season with salt and serve. —AZ

Crispy Pork Belly with Kimchi Rice Grits and Peanuts

ACTIVE: 1 HR; TOTAL: 2 HR 45 MIN
4 SERVINGS ●

At Empire State South in Atlanta, chef Hugh Acheson punches up traditional Southern dishes with ingredients from around the globe. Here he adds slivers of kimchi to creamy rice grits to go with fried pork belly.

3 tablespoons vegetable oil
Two 8-ounce meaty pieces of pork belly,
   about 1 inch thick
Kosher salt and freshly ground pepper
1 small onion, chopped
2 small carrots, chopped
1 bay leaf
½ teaspoon coriander seeds
4 cups chicken stock or
   low-sodium broth
½ teaspoon sugar
¼ cup unseasoned rice vinegar
½ cup thinly sliced radishes
2 scallions, thinly sliced on the bias
½ cup rice grits, preferably
   Carolina Gold (see Note)
½ cup finely chopped kimchi
½ cup heavy cream
Crushed roasted peanuts, for garnish

1. Preheat the oven to 325°. In a large, deep ovenproof skillet, heat 2 tablespoons of the oil until shimmering. Season the pork with salt and pepper and add to the skillet, fatty side down. Cook over moderate heat, turning, until crisp and browned all over, about 20 minutes. Transfer to a plate.

2. Pour off all but 2 tablespoons of fat from the skillet. Add the onion, carrots, bay leaf and coriander seeds and cook over moderate heat, stirring occasionally, until the carrots just start to soften, about 5 minutes. Add 2 cups of the chicken stock and bring to a boil. Return the pork to the skillet. Cover and braise in the oven for about 2 hours, until the meat is very tender. Transfer the pork belly to a work surface and let cool slightly, then cut each piece in half crosswise. Discard the braising liquid and vegetables and wipe out the skillet.

3. Meanwhile, in a shallow bowl, whisk the sugar with the vinegar until dissolved. Add the radishes and scallions and refrigerate until chilled, about 15 minutes.

4. In a large saucepan, combine the rice grits and the remaining 2 cups of chicken stock and bring to a boil. Add a generous pinch of salt, cover partially and cook over moderately low heat, stirring, until the grits are tender and become suspended in a creamy porridge, 20 to 25 minutes. Stir in the chopped kimchi and heavy cream and season with salt and pepper. Keep warm over very low heat, adding 1 or 2 tablespoons of water if the grits become too thick.

5. In the large skillet, heat the remaining 1 tablespoon of oil until shimmering. Add the pork belly and cook over moderately high heat, turning once, until crispy, about 4 minutes. Spoon the grits into 4 shallow bowls and top with the crispy pork belly. Garnish with crushed peanuts and the pickled radishes and scallions and serve right away.
—*Hugh Acheson*

NOTE Rice grits are available at *ansonmills. com*, but they can also be made at home. In batches, pulse long-grain white rice in a spice grinder or blender just until the grains are very coarsely cracked, about one-third of the original size.

MAKE AHEAD The braised pork can be refrigerated for up to 2 days in the braising liquid. Pat the meat dry and bring it to room temperature before proceeding with Step 3 of the recipe.

WINE Peach-scented, full-bodied, dry Riesling: 2011 Knebel Trocken.

Triple Pork Burgers with Quick Cucumber Kimchi
📷 PAGE 175
ACTIVE: 1 HR; TOTAL: 3 HR
10 SERVINGS ●

Chicago chef Bill Kim's thin, triple-stacked burgers, loaded with ginger, lemongrass and herbs, are inspired by a lemongrass pork sausage he often serves at BellyQ. Instead of pickles, Kim serves the burgers with spicy cucumber kimchi.

  5 **pounds ground pork**
  1 **cup finely chopped napa cabbage**
  ½ **cup Thai sweet chile sauce, such as Mae Ploy**
  ¼ **cup minced fresh ginger (4 ounces)**
  2 **stalks of fresh lemongrass, tender inner bulbs only, minced (¼ cup)**
  5 **garlic cloves, minced**
  ¼ **cup finely chopped cilantro**
  ¼ **cup finely chopped Thai or sweet basil**
  2 **tablespoons Asian fish sauce**
  2 **tablespoons untoasted sesame oil or peanut oil**
  2 **teaspoons finely grated lemon zest**
  2 **teaspoons finely grated lime zest**
Kosher salt
 10 **brioche hamburger buns, split**
Mayonnaise and Quick Cucumber Kimchi (recipe follows), for serving

1. In a large bowl, mix the pork with the cabbage, chile sauce, ginger, lemongrass, garlic, cilantro, basil, fish sauce, sesame oil and lemon and lime zests. Using lightly moistened hands, form the pork mixture into thirty 5-inch patties, each about ⅓ inch thick.
2. Light a grill or preheat a grill pan. Season the patties very lightly with salt. Working in batches, grill the patties over high heat, turning once, until they are lightly charred and just cooked through, about 4 minutes total per batch. Transfer the cooked burgers to a platter and tent with foil while you grill the remaining patties.
3. Grill the hamburger buns, cut side down, until they are lightly toasted, about 20 seconds. Transfer to a platter.

4. Spread the buns with mayonnaise and layer three cooked patties on each. Top with some of the Quick Cucumber Kimchi. Close the burgers and serve them immediately.
—*Bill Kim*

WINE Robustly juicy, full-bodied rosé: 2012 Kir-Yianni Akakies.

QUICK CUCUMBER KIMCHI
ACTIVE: 20 MIN; TOTAL: 2 HR 30 MIN
MAKES ABOUT 2½ CUPS ● ● ●

Making traditional Korean kimchi usually involves tossing vegetables with garlic, salt, chiles and other flavorings and letting them stand for days until they ferment. Kim marinates these cucumbers for just two hours, so they're still crisp.

  2 **pounds Kirby cucumbers, halved lengthwise and sliced crosswise ¼ inch thick**
Kosher salt
  ¼ **cup untoasted sesame oil**
  ½ **small onion, thinly sliced**
  2 **tablespoons finely chopped Thai or sweet basil**
  2 **tablespoons *gochugaru* (Korean chile powder; see Note)**
  1 **tablespoon minced garlic**
  1 **tablespoon minced peeled fresh ginger**
  1 **teaspoon finely grated lime zest**
  ½ **teaspoon Asian fish sauce**

1. In a colander, toss the sliced cucumbers with 1 tablespoon of kosher salt and let stand for 20 minutes. Rinse the cucumbers and drain well.
2. In a large bowl, toss the rinsed and drained cucumbers with all of the remaining ingredients and let stand at room temperature for about 2 hours, stirring occasionally. Season the Quick Cucumber Kimchi with salt and serve. —*BK*

NOTE *Gochugaru* is available at Korean markets and online at *hmart.com*.

MAKE AHEAD The cucumber kimchi can be refrigerated for up to 3 days.

Chinese-Style Ribs with Guava Barbecue Sauce

ACTIVE: 45 MIN; TOTAL: 2 HR
4 SERVINGS ●

These smoky ribs from grilling maverick Steven Raichlen stand out for their sensational sticky barbecue sauce made with guava paste and rum—flavors inspired by Raichlen's hometown of Miami.

2 tablespoons sugar
1 tablespoon kosher salt
1 tablespoon dry mustard
1 teaspoon Chinese five-spice powder
½ teaspoon freshly ground pepper
½ teaspoon cinnamon
¼ teaspoon ground cloves
5 pounds baby back ribs
½ cup medium-dry sherry
Guava Barbecue Sauce (recipe follows), for glazing and serving

1. Light a charcoal grill. When the coals are covered with a light gray ash, push them to opposite sides of the grill and set a disposable drip pan in the center. Alternatively, if you're using a gas grill, turn off the center burners.
2. In a bowl, combine the sugar, salt, dry mustard, Chinese five-spice powder, pepper, cinnamon and cloves. Sprinkle the mixture over the ribs. Pour the sherry into a spray bottle.
3. Place the ribs on the hot grate above the drip pan and away from the coals, bony side down. Cover and grill for 30 minutes. Spray the ribs with sherry. Cover and grill for another 30 minutes. Shift the ribs around (but keep them bony side down) and spray once more with sherry. Cover and grill for 30 minutes longer, until the meat is tender. Replenish the coals as necessary.
4. Take the ribs off the grill and spread the coals out evenly. Brush the guava sauce on both sides of the ribs; grill directly over the fire (high heat on a gas grill) for about 1 minute per side, until glazed. Transfer the ribs to a work surface and let rest for 5 minutes. Cut down between the bones; arrange the ribs on a platter. Pass the remaining sauce at the table. —*Steven Raichlen*
BEER Hoppy, floral IPA: Southern Tier.

GUAVA BARBECUE SAUCE
⏱ **TOTAL: 25 MIN • MAKES 1¼ CUPS** ●

8 ounces canned guava paste (see Note), cut into ½-inch pieces (1 cup)
⅓ cup apple cider vinegar
¼ cup dark rum
3 tablespoons tomato paste
3 tablespoons fresh lime juice
1 tablespoon soy sauce
1 tablespoon Worcestershire sauce
2 teaspoons minced fresh ginger
1 scallion, white part only, minced
1 garlic clove, minced
Salt and freshly ground pepper

In a small saucepan, combine the guava paste with the vinegar, rum, tomato paste, lime juice, soy sauce, Worcestershire sauce, ginger, scallion, garlic and ¼ cup of water and bring to a boil. Simmer over low heat, stirring occasionally, until reduced to 1¼ cups, about 15 minutes. Season the sauce with salt and pepper. —*SR*
NOTE Guava paste is usually sold in flat metal cans. It is available at many supermarkets as well as Latin markets.
MAKE AHEAD The barbecue sauce can be refrigerated for up to 5 days.

Molasses-Smoked Baby Back Ribs

ACTIVE: 45 MIN; TOTAL: 2 HR 30 MIN
4 SERVINGS ●

MOP
One 12-ounce bottle lager
1 cup packed dark brown sugar
1 cup unsulfured molasses
1 stick unsalted butter, melted
⅓ cup white wine vinegar
¼ cup Creole or brown mustard
¼ cup chile powder
¼ cup smoked paprika
1 tablespoon tomato paste
½ tablespoon garlic powder
½ tablespoon onion powder
1 teaspoon cayenne pepper
Pinch of ground allspice

RIBS
Two 3-pound racks baby back ribs— membranes removed and racks halved
Kosher salt and freshly ground black pepper
3 cups hardwood chips, such as hickory or applewood, soaked in water for 1 hour and drained

1. **MAKE THE MOP** Light a grill. In a large bowl, combine all of the mop ingredients and whisk until smooth.
2. **PREPARE THE RIBS** Season the ribs all over with salt and black pepper. Layer two 18-inch sheets of heavy-duty aluminum foil on a work surface and set a half rack of ribs in the center; pull the edges of foil up around the ribs. Spoon ¾ cup of the mop over the rack and seal tightly in the foil. Repeat with the remaining 3 racks of ribs. Grill the rib packets over moderate heat, covered, for 45 minutes. Using tongs, transfer the rib packets to a baking sheet and let them cool slightly.
3. Meanwhile, transfer the remaining mop to a medium saucepan and bring to a boil. Simmer over moderately low heat, stirring constantly, until reduced to 1 cup, 12 to 15 minutes; let cool completely.
4. Wrap the wood chips in a double layer of foil and poke holes in the top of the packet. Remove the grill grate. Turn the heat off on half of the grill or rake the coals to one side. Set the wood chip packet directly on the flames or on the coals and replace the grill grate. When the chips are smoking, carefully open the rib packets and arrange the racks on the grill over indirect heat. Discard the foil and juices. Cover the grill and smoke the ribs until the meat is very tender, 1 hour. Brush the ribs with the reduced mop, transfer to a platter and serve.
—*Tim Byres*
MAKE AHEAD The finished ribs and the reduced mop can be refrigerated separately for up to 2 days.
BEER Crisp farmhouse-style ale: Jester King Le Petit Prince.

● HEALTHY ● MAKE AHEAD ○ VEGETARIAN ● STAFF FAVORITE

MOLASSES-SMOKED BABY BACK RIBS

Smoked Pork Sausage with Hard-Cider Sauce

TOTAL: 1 HR 30 MIN • 4 SERVINGS

1 dried chipotle chile

2 Granny Smith apples, halved and cored, plus ½ apple cut into matchsticks for garnish (optional)

2 ounces rye bread, crusts removed and bread torn into bite-size pieces

½ cup hard cider

¼ cup apple cider vinegar

2 tablespoons light brown sugar

Kosher salt

Four 4-ounce smoked pork sausages or cheddar wursts

1 tablespoon extra-virgin olive oil

1 pound broccoli, cut into 1-inch florets

1 tablespoon Dijon mustard

½ teaspoon caraway seeds

1½ tablespoons unsalted butter, cubed

1. Preheat the oven to 325°. In a bowl, cover the chipotle with hot water and let stand until softened, 30 minutes. Bake the halved apples cut side down on a rimmed baking sheet for 30 minutes, until tender. Let cool. Scoop the apple pulp into a food processor and discard the skins. Stem, seed and chop the chipotle; add it to the food processor and puree.

2. Meanwhile, spread the bread in a pie plate; bake until golden, about 10 minutes.

3. In a saucepan, boil the hard cider with the vinegar, sugar and apple puree. Simmer, stirring, until reduced to ¾ cup, 10 minutes. Remove from the heat and season with salt.

4. Light a grill. Grill the sausages over moderate heat, turning, until lightly charred on both sides and cooked through, 12 minutes. Transfer to a plate and tent with foil.

5. In a skillet, heat the oil. Add the broccoli; season with salt. Cover and cook until browned, 2 minutes. Stir in the mustard, caraway, cider sauce and ½ cup of water; bring to a boil. Remove from the heat. Stir in the butter; season with salt. Serve the sausages with the broccoli and sauce; garnish with the crumbs and apple matchsticks. —*Jack Riebel*

BEER Spicy, hoppy ale: Two Brothers Cane & Ebel Red Rye.

Bratwurst with Mustardy Fried Potatoes and Braised Cabbage

TOTAL: 2 HR 30 MIN PLUS 1 HR FOR MARINATING THE CABBAGE
6 TO 8 SERVINGS ●

¼ cup diced shallots

¼ cup red wine vinegar

¼ cup whole-grain mustard

¼ cup Dijon mustard

¾ cup plus 2 tablespoons extra-virgin olive oil

Kosher salt and freshly ground pepper

1½ pounds Yukon Gold potatoes

6 bratwursts

1 teaspoon thyme leaves

2 tablespoons chopped parsley

Citrus-Spiced Red Cabbage (page 228)

1 bunch of watercress, thick stems discarded

1. In a bowl, combine the shallots and vinegar and let stand for 5 minutes; stir in both mustards. Whisk in ¾ cup of the oil and season the vinaigrette with salt and pepper.

2. In a pot of salted boiling water, cook the potatoes until tender, 30 minutes. Drain and let cool slightly, then slip off the skins. Break the potatoes into 1½-inch chunks.

3. Light a grill or preheat a grill pan. Grill the bratwursts over moderate heat, turning, until heated through, 10 to 15 minutes.

4. In a large nonstick skillet, heat the remaining 2 tablespoons of oil. Add the potatoes and thyme and season with salt and pepper. Cook over moderately high heat, turning, until golden and crisp, 6 to 7 minutes. Remove the pan from the heat and add ½ cup of the vinaigrette and the parsley. Season with salt and pepper and toss to coat evenly.

5. Arrange half of the Citrus-Spiced Red Cabbage on a serving platter. Scatter the potatoes and three-fourths of the watercress over the cabbage and top with half of the bratwursts. Repeat with the remaining cabbage, watercress and bratwursts. Pass the remaining vinaigrette at the table.
—*Suzanne Goin*

WINE Powerful, savory red from the Loire: 2010 Philippe Alliet Chinon.

Mixed Grill with Roasted-Garlic-and-Pepper Salsa

TOTAL: 1 HR 30 MIN • 8 SERVINGS

2 tablespoons dried oregano

1 tablespoon crushed red pepper

½ cup extra-virgin olive oil, plus more for drizzling

5 tablespoons fresh lime juice

1 pound large shrimp, shelled and deveined

Kosher salt and freshly ground black pepper

6 pounds bone-in chicken parts

3 heads of garlic, halved crosswise

6 ounces mixed small sweet and hot peppers, thinly sliced (2 cups)

⅓ cup coarsely chopped cilantro

8 half-sour pickles, halved lengthwise

3 pounds assorted sausages

Lime wedges, for serving

1. Light a grill. In a very large bowl, whisk the oregano and crushed red pepper with the ½ cup of olive oil and 2 tablespoons of the lime juice. In a medium bowl, toss the shrimp with a few tablespoons of the mixture; season with salt and black pepper. Add the chicken to the large bowl and toss to coat.

2. On a sheet of heavy-duty foil, drizzle the garlic with oil; wrap tightly. Remove the chicken from the marinade. Grill the chicken and garlic packet over moderate heat, turning, until the chicken is cooked through and the garlic is tender, 40 minutes. Transfer the chicken to a platter; keep warm.

3. Unwrap the garlic and let cool slightly, then squeeze the cloves into a medium bowl. Stir in the peppers, cilantro and the remaining 3 tablespoons of lime juice.

4. Brush the grill grates with oil. Arrange the shrimp, pickles and sausages on the grill. Grill until the pickles are lightly charred and the shrimp are pink, 3 to 4 minutes; transfer to the platter. Grill the sausages for 10 minutes, turning, until well browned and cooked through. Add to the platter. Serve with the salsa and lime wedges. —*Kay Chun*

WINE Medium-bodied Spanish red: 2011 Bodegas Nekeas Vega Sindoa El Chaparral.

● HEALTHY ● MAKE AHEAD ● VEGETARIAN ● STAFF FAVORITE

SMOKED PORK SAUSAGE
WITH HARD-CIDER SAUCE

Osso Buco with Horseradish Gremolata

ACTIVE: 35 MIN; TOTAL: 3 HR 30 MIN
4 TO 6 SERVINGS ● ●

When he hosts dinner parties, Mario Batali often makes braised dishes. "They let me walk away from the kitchen and talk to my guests," says the star chef. "And the most remarkable fragrance fills my house." Here, he deeply browns veal shanks on the stove before braising them in the oven. The recipe calls for four large shanks, but there's plenty of meat to serve six people.

4　meaty veal shanks, cut 3 inches
　　thick (5¼ pounds)
Kosher salt and freshly ground pepper
¼　cup extra-virgin olive oil
½　Spanish onion, chopped
1　medium carrot, sliced ¼ inch thick
1　celery rib, sliced ¼ inch thick
2　tablespoons chopped thyme
2　cups dry white wine
2　cups Mario Batali's Essential
　　Tomato Sauce (page 364) or jarred
　　tomato sauce
2　cups chicken stock
1　cup lightly packed parsley, minced
1½ tablespoons finely grated
　　fresh horseradish
1　tablespoon finely grated lemon zest
Saffron Orzo (page 102), for serving

1. Preheat the oven to 375°. Season the veal with salt and pepper. In a large enameled cast-iron casserole, heat the oil until shimmering. Add the veal and cook over moderately high heat, turning, until browned all over, 12 minutes. Transfer the veal to a plate.

MARIO BATALI'S OSSO BUCO TIP

Before the veal goes in the oven, sear it well on the stove. "Let the meat go; you want a deep, dark caramelization before you even think of taking it off the heat."

2. Spoon off all but 2 tablespoons of the fat from the casserole. Add the onion, carrot, celery and thyme and cook over moderate heat, stirring occasionally, until softened. Add the wine and bring to a boil, scraping up any browned bits from the bottom of the casserole. Simmer until the wine is reduced by half, 4 minutes. Add the tomato sauce and chicken stock and bring to a boil. Return the shanks to the casserole, cover and braise in the oven for 2 hours and 15 minutes, until the meat is very tender and nearly falling off the bones. Let stand covered for 10 minutes.

3. Meanwhile, in a small bowl, toss the parsley with the horseradish and lemon zest; season the gremolata with salt and pepper.

4. Transfer the veal shanks to a platter (see Note). Season the sauce with salt and pepper and spoon it over the veal. Sprinkle some gremolata over the osso buco and serve with the Saffron Orzo, passing additional gremolata at the table. —*Mario Batali*

NOTE If serving 6 people, cut the veal off the bone into large chunks.

MAKE AHEAD The osso buco can be refrigerated for up to 2 days.

WINE Rich California Chardonnay: 2008 Au Bon Climat Nuits-Blanches au Bouge.

Hoisin-Glazed Ribs

☼ **TOTAL: 10 MIN • 2 SERVINGS**

This recipe can be made with the roasted and reserved rib rack from the Asian-Brined Pork Loin on page 176 or any other cooked pork ribs. The sticky-sweet glaze is also delicious on other cuts of prepared pork.

2　tablespoons hoisin sauce
½　teaspoon *sambal oelek*
½　teaspoon toasted sesame oil
Rack of roast ribs from Asian-Brined
　　Pork Loin (page 176) or other
　　cooked pork ribs

Light the broiler. In a bowl, combine the hoisin, *sambal oelek* and sesame oil. Brush the mixture all over the ribs and broil 8 inches from the heat for about 6 minutes, turning once, until browned and glazed. Cut into individual ribs and serve. —*Grace Parisi*

Honey-Bourbon-Glazed Ham

ACTIVE: 45 MIN; TOTAL: 3 HR 30 MIN
16 TO 20 SERVINGS

One 18-pound bone-in whole or
　　spiral-cut smoked ham,
　　at room temperature
1　cup sugar
1　tablespoon fennel seeds
1　tablespoon coriander seeds
4　star anise pods
4　bay leaves
2　cinnamon sticks
2　garlic cloves
One 1-inch piece of ginger, thinly sliced
1　dried red chile
1　teaspoon finely grated orange zest
2　cups bourbon
2　tablespoons low-sodium soy sauce
2　tablespoons honey

1. Preheat the oven to 325°. Place the ham in a large roasting pan and add 1 cup of water. Cover the pan with foil and bake the ham for about 2 hours and 45 minutes, basting occasionally with any accumulated juices, until an instant-read thermometer inserted in the thickest part registers 120°.

2. Meanwhile, in a medium saucepan, combine the sugar with 2 tablespoons of water and cook over moderately high heat, swirling the pan occasionally, until a light golden caramel forms, 8 to 10 minutes. Remove from the heat and quickly add the fennel seeds, coriander seeds, star anise, bay leaves, cinnamon, garlic, ginger, chile and orange zest; let stand for about 20 seconds, until fragrant. Carefully add the bourbon, soy sauce and honey. Return the glaze to a simmer and cook over moderate heat, stirring occasionally, until slightly thickened, about 10 minutes.

3. Remove the foil and brush the ham with the glaze. Roast for 30 minutes longer, glazing every 10 minutes, until the top is lightly caramelized. Transfer the ham to a platter; let rest for 15 minutes. Skim the fat from the pan juices; transfer them to a bowl. Serve the ham with the pan juices. —*Nicholas Wilber*

WINE Robust, affordable Napa Cabernet Sauvignon: 2010 Avalon Napa Valley.

Sustainable-food guru Anya Fernald of Belcampo at her California ranch, where she cooks a locavore lunch of beef, lamb and rabbit dishes.

Opposite: recipe, page 211.
GRILLED LAMB RIBS WITH CHIMICHURRI

BEEF, LAMB & GAME

Baby Kale and Steak Salad

⏱ TOTAL: 25 MIN • 4 SERVINGS ●

Top Chef Season 9 winner Paul Qui came up with this sugarless version of *nuoc cham,* the classic Vietnamese dipping sauce, for his father-in-law, who has diabetes. Coconut water replaces the sugar; shallot, garlic and jalapeño add bold flavor. Qui uses the sauce here to dress a kale and steak salad.

NUOC CHAM DRESSING

1½ tablespoons fish sauce,
    preferably Red Boat
¼ cup coconut water
1 tablespoon freshly squeezed
    lime juice
1½ teaspoons coconut vinegar or
    cider vinegar
1 tablespoon minced shallot
1 garlic clove, sliced
½ jalapeño, minced, with seeds

SALAD

One 12-ounce trimmed boneless
    rib eye steak, cut 1 inch thick
1 teaspoon canola oil
Salt and freshly ground pepper
1 tablespoon unsalted butter
1 garlic clove
1 thyme sprig
1 tablespoon Maggi liquid seasoning
    (a vegetable-based seasoning sauce)
5 ounces baby kale
½ small red onion, thinly sliced
1 small Japanese cucumber,
    peeled and thinly sliced
1 tomato, cut into wedges

1. MAKE THE NUOC CHAM DRESSING Combine all of the ingredients in a medium bowl and let stand for 15 minutes.

2. MEANWHILE, MAKE THE SALAD Rub the steak all over with the oil and season with salt and pepper. Heat a small cast-iron skillet until very hot. Add the steak and cook over moderately high heat for 2 minutes, until browned and crusty. Add the butter, garlic and thyme to the skillet and spoon the melted butter over the steak. Flip the steak and cook for 2 minutes longer, spooning the butter on top. Add the Maggi seasoning,

cover and let stand off the heat for 2 minutes. Transfer the steak to a paper towel–lined work surface, cover loosely with foil and let rest for 5 minutes.

3. Thinly slice the steak and place in a large serving bowl. Add the kale, onion, cucumber, tomato and *nuoc cham* dressing, toss the salad well and serve. —*Paul Qui*

MAKE AHEAD The *nuoc cham* dressing can be refrigerated for up to 1 week.

WINE Toasty, full-bodied Champagne: NV Bollinger Special Cuvée.

Steak au Poivre

ACTIVE: 30 MIN; TOTAL: 1 HR 15 MIN
6 SERVINGS

Three 1-pound bone-in rib eye steaks,
    cut ¾ inch thick
Kosher salt
Coarsely crushed black peppercorns
4 tablespoons unsalted butter
2 tablespoons extra-virgin olive oil
2 shallots, minced
⅓ cup brandy
¾ cup chicken stock
¼ cup heavy cream

1. Season the steaks with salt and black peppercorns and let stand for 45 minutes.

2. In a cast-iron skillet, melt 2 tablespoons of the butter in the oil. Working in batches, cook the steaks over moderately high heat, turning once, until medium-rare, 7 minutes per batch; transfer to a board and let rest.

3. Pour off all but 2 tablespoons of fat from the skillet. Add the shallots and cook over moderate heat, stirring, until softened, 2 minutes. Add the brandy and cook until most of the liquid has evaporated. Add the stock and cook, scraping up any browned bits, until slightly reduced, 3 minutes. Stir in the heavy cream and simmer until slightly thickened, 1 minute. Remove from the heat and stir in the remaining 2 tablespoons of butter. Season the sauce with salt. Slice the steaks and transfer to plates or a platter. Spoon the sauce on top and serve. —*Clint Simonson*

WINE Peppery, berry-dense Chilean Syrah: 2009 Chono Reserva.

Grilled Rib Steak with Brandy-Peppercorn Sauce

TOTAL: 2 HR • 4 SERVINGS

One 38-ounce bone-in rib eye steak
Kosher salt and coarsely ground pepper
3 thyme sprigs
2 tablespoons unsalted butter
2 tablespoons minced shallot
3 large garlic cloves, minced
2 teaspoons crushed brined
    green peppercorns
1 tablespoon Dijon mustard
½ cup Armagnac or other brandy
2 cups dry red wine
1 cup veal demiglace
½ cup heavy cream
1 tablespoon extra-virgin olive oil

1. Coat the steak with 2 tablespoons each of salt and pepper. Press 1 thyme sprig onto each side of the steak and let stand at room temperature for 1 hour.

2. Preheat the oven to 350°. In a small saucepan, melt the butter. Add the minced shallot and garlic and cook over low heat until softened. Add the crushed green peppercorns, the remaining thyme sprig, the mustard and 1 teaspoon of pepper and cook for 1 minute, stirring. Add the Armagnac and cook over moderate heat until reduced by half, about 5 minutes. Add the red wine and simmer until reduced by half, about 15 minutes. Stir in the demiglace and simmer until slightly reduced, about 5 minutes. Add the cream and simmer until the sauce is reduced to 1½ cups, about 10 minutes. Discard the thyme sprig.

3. Heat the oil in a large cast-iron skillet. Add the steak; cook over moderately high heat, turning once, until crusty and browned, 7 minutes total. Transfer the steak to the oven; roast, turning once, until cooked to 125°, 18 to 20 minutes. Transfer to a cutting board and let stand for 10 minutes, then carve the meat from the bone and slice it. Serve with the brandy-peppercorn sauce. —*Lee Hefter*

SERVE WITH Steamed spinach and Hefter's The Cheesiest Mashed Potatoes (page 264).

WINE Cherry-rich, herb-scented Cabernet Sauvignon: 2011 Foxglove Paso Robles.

● HEALTHY ● MAKE AHEAD ● VEGETARIAN ● STAFF FAVORITE

STEAK AU POIVRE

Coffee-Rubbed Strip Steaks with Chimichurri Sauce

ACTIVE: 50 MIN; TOTAL: 1 HR 30 MIN
4 SERVINGS ●

CHIMICHURRI
¼ cup sherry vinegar
¼ cup red wine vinegar
2 tablespoons extra-virgin olive oil
½ teaspoon sugar
1 small shallot, minced
¼ cup finely chopped parsley
1 tablespoon finely chopped cilantro
1 tablespoon finely chopped chives
1 teaspoon dried oregano
Kosher salt and freshly ground pepper
STEAKS
2 tablespoons finely ground
  dark-roast coffee beans
2 tablespoons chile powder
2 tablespoons dark brown sugar
1 tablespoon smoked paprika
1½ teaspoons ground cumin
1 tablespoon kosher salt
Four 10-ounce strip steaks
SALAD
1½ cups cilantro leaves
1 cup flat-leaf parsley leaves
½ cup snipped chives
1 small shallot, halved lengthwise and
  thinly sliced crosswise
Kosher salt and freshly ground pepper

1. MAKE THE CHIMICHURRI In a medium bowl, whisk both vinegars with the olive oil and sugar. Stir in the shallot, parsley, cilantro, chives and oregano and season with salt and pepper. Let the chimichurri stand for at least 20 minutes and up to 2 hours.

2. MEANWHILE, PREPARE THE STEAKS In a small bowl, mix all of the ingredients except the steaks. Pat the steaks all over with the coffee-chile rub and let stand at room temperature for 30 minutes.

3. Light a grill or preheat a grill pan; oil the grates or pan. Grill the steaks over moderate heat, turning once, until they're nicely charred outside and medium-rare within, 11 to 13 minutes. Transfer to a platter and let rest for 10 minutes.

4. MAKE THE SALAD In a large bowl, toss the cilantro, parsley, chives and shallot. Add 3 tablespoons of the chimichurri, season with salt and pepper and toss to coat the herbs.

5. Thinly slice the steaks and arrange on the platter; spoon some of the chimichurri on the meat. Serve with the herb salad and pass the remaining chimichurri on the side.
—*Tim Byres*
WINE Full-bodied, berry-rich, concentrated red: 2011 Crios Malbec.

Grilled Rib Eye Brochettes with Charmoula

ACTIVE: 45 MIN; TOTAL: 2 HR 30 MIN
15 SERVINGS ●

One 4-ounce bunch of flat-leaf parsley,
  stemmed and coarsely chopped
One 4-ounce bunch of cilantro,
  coarsely chopped with stems
3 garlic cloves, minced
2 tablespoons ground cumin
1 tablespoon ground coriander
2 tablespoons sweet paprika
1 teaspoon smoked paprika
1 teaspoon cayenne pepper
Pinch of saffron threads
¼ cup freshly squeezed
  lemon juice
1 cup extra-virgin olive oil,
  plus more for grilling
Kosher salt
Six 1½-inch-thick boneless rib eye
  steaks (7½ pounds)—excess fat
  trimmed, steaks cut into 1½- to
  2-inch cubes
2 small red onions,
  cut into 1½-inch pieces
2 large red bell peppers,
  cut into 1½-inch pieces

1. In a food processor, combine the parsley with the cilantro, garlic, cumin, coriander, sweet and smoked paprikas, cayenne and saffron and pulse until the herbs are finely chopped. Add the lemon juice and the 1 cup of olive oil and pulse to incorporate. Add 1 tablespoon of salt. Scrape half of the *charmoula* into a small bowl and refrigerate.

2. Scrape the remaining *charmoula* into a very large bowl. Add the steak cubes and turn to coat with the *charmoula*. Let stand at room temperature for 2 hours or refrigerate for up to 4 hours.

3. Light a grill. Thread 3 chunks of rib eye onto a long skewer, adding a piece of onion and bell pepper between each piece of meat. Oil the grill grates and grill the skewers over high heat, turning, until the meat and vegetables are lightly charred in spots and the meat is medium-rare to medium, about 15 minutes. Serve with the reserved *charmoula*.
—*Tim McKee*
WINE Spicy, berry-rich Côtes du Rhône: 2011 Domaine le Garrigon.

Turkish Lettuce Wraps

:) TOTAL: 30 MIN • 6 SERVINGS ●

8 ounces plain Greek yogurt
2 tablespoons tahini
2 garlic cloves, minced
1 tablespoon plus 2 teaspoons fresh
  lemon juice
¼ cup extra-virgin olive oil
Kosher salt
2 cups shredded carrots
¼ cup chopped cilantro
2 teaspoons ground cumin
1 teaspoon sweet paprika
2 heads of Bibb lettuce,
  leaves separated
1 pound very thinly sliced leftover
  Grilled Rib Eye (recipe above)
  or deli roast beef

1. In a small bowl, whisk the yogurt with the tahini, half of the garlic and 1 tablespoon of the lemon juice. Whisk in 2 tablespoons of the olive oil and season with salt.

2. In a medium bowl, toss the carrots with the cilantro, cumin, paprika and the remaining garlic, 2 teaspoons of lemon juice and 2 tablespoons of olive oil. Season with salt.

3. Arrange the lettuce leaves on a large platter and dollop some of the sesame yogurt in the center of each. Top with the beef and the carrot slaw and serve. —*Tim McKee*
BEER Refreshing German pilsner: Bitburger.

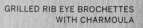

Cola-Marinated Flank Steak with Frito Chilaquiles

⏱ **TOTAL: 45 MIN • 4 TO 6 SERVINGS** ●

To make his version of *chilaquiles* (fried tortilla chips lightly cooked in salsa), Boston chef Jamie Bissonnette unabashedly opts for Fritos. "They have great corn flavor, and they are crunchier than I could ever get tortillas by frying them myself."

 4 **cups cola, preferably made with cane sugar**
 2 **teaspoons jarred Thai green curry paste**
 2 **Fresno chiles or jalapeños, thinly sliced crosswise**
One 1½-pound flank steak, **cut lengthwise and crosswise to make 4 steaks**
 1 **tablespoon canola oil, plus more for brushing**
Kosher salt and freshly ground **black pepper**
One 16-ounce jar salsa verde
 8 **ounces Fritos**
 ½ **cup chopped cilantro**
 2 **Hass avocados, diced**
 3 **tablespoons freshly grated Cotija cheese**
Lime wedges, for serving

1. In a 9-by-13-inch glass or ceramic baking dish, whisk the cola with the green curry paste and sliced Fresno chiles. Add the flank steaks and turn to coat thoroughly. Let the steaks stand at room temperature for 15 minutes, turning occasionally.
2. Light a grill or preheat a grill pan and oil the grate. Remove the flank steaks from the marinade and pat them dry. Brush the steaks with canola oil and season generously with salt and pepper. Grill over moderately high heat, turning once, until the steaks are medium-rare, about 8 minutes total. Transfer the steaks to a work surface and let rest for 10 minutes.
3. Meanwhile, in a large skillet, heat the 1 tablespoon of canola oil. Add the salsa verde and bring to a simmer. Cook over moderate heat, stirring, until slightly reduced and

thickened, about 4 minutes. Add the Fritos to the salsa and cook, stirring, until the chips are soft with some crunchy bits but not falling apart, about 2 minutes. Stir in ¼ cup of the cilantro and transfer the *chilaquiles* to a platter.
4. Thinly slice the steaks across the grain. Top the *chilaquiles* with the sliced steak and any accumulated meat juices. Scatter the diced avocados, Cotija cheese and remaining ¼ cup of chopped cilantro on top and serve immediately, with lime wedges.
—*Jamie Bissonnette*

WINE Bold, lively Tempranillo-based Rioja red: 2010 CVNE Cune Crianza.

Marinated Skirt Steak Tacos with Pecan-Chipotle Salsa

TOTAL: 45 MIN PLUS 3 HR MARINATING
4 TO 6 SERVINGS ●

At her Manhattan restaurant Salvation Taco, chef April Bloomfield serves admittedly inauthentic but delicious and creative Mexican-inspired food like this amazing steak taco.

 ⅓ **cup chopped cilantro, plus more for garnish**
 ½ **small red onion, chopped**
 ½ **medium serrano chile, with seeds**
 1 **garlic clove, crushed**
 1 **tablespoon fresh lime juice**
 1 **tablespoon Worcestershire sauce**
 1 **teaspoon Dijon mustard**
 1 **tablespoon extra-virgin olive oil, plus more for brushing**
Kosher salt and freshly ground pepper
 2 **pounds trimmed skirt steak, cut into 4- to 5-inch-long pieces**
 12 **warmed corn tortillas, for serving**
Shredded carrots, pickled jalapeños and **chopped white onion, for garnish**
Pecan-Chipotle Salsa (recipe follows) **and lime wedges, for serving**

1. In a food processor, combine the ⅓ cup of cilantro with the red onion, serrano chile, garlic, lime juice, Worcestershire sauce, mustard, 1 tablespoon of olive oil and a generous pinch each of salt and pepper. Puree until nearly smooth. Scrape the marinade into a

large resealable plastic bag. Add the steak pieces and turn until coated. Seal the bag and refrigerate for at least 3 hours or overnight.
2. Remove the steak from the marinade and let stand at room temperature for 15 minutes.
3. Light a grill or preheat a grill pan. Brush the steak with olive oil and season with salt and pepper. Oil the grill grates and grill the steak over high heat, turning once or twice, until the meat is lightly charred outside and medium-rare within, 5 to 6 minutes. Transfer the steak to a carving board, let rest for 5 minutes and slice across the grain; serve the steak with the tortillas, garnishes, Pecan-Chipotle Salsa and lime wedges.
—*April Bloomfield*

WINE Juicy Spanish Garnacha: 2011 Zestos.

PECAN-CHIPOTLE SALSA
TOTAL: 30 MIN PLUS COOLING
MAKES ABOUT 1 CUP ● ●

 3 **dried chipotle *morita* chiles, stemmed (see Note)**
 ½ **cup pecans, coarsely chopped**
 2 **tablespoons extra-virgin olive oil**
 ½ **cup finely chopped white onion**
 1 **garlic clove, finely chopped**
Kosher salt

1. In a medium skillet, toast the chipotles over moderate heat, turning, until pliable and fragrant, 1 to 2 minutes. Transfer the chiles to a food processor, add ½ cup of hot water and let stand until softened, about 10 minutes.
2. Meanwhile, in the same skillet, toast the pecans over moderate heat, tossing, until browned in spots, 6 minutes. Add the toasted pecans to the food processor and let cool slightly, then puree the salsa until smooth.
3. In the skillet, heat the olive oil until shimmering. Add the onion and garlic and cook over moderate heat, stirring, until softened and just starting to brown, 3 to 5 minutes. Add the pecan-chipotle puree and cook, stirring, until hot, about 2 minutes. Season with salt and transfer the salsa to a bowl. Let cool completely before serving. —*AB*

NOTE The purplish *morita* is the most common variety of dried chipotle in the US.

● HEALTHY ● MAKE AHEAD ● VEGETARIAN ● STAFF FAVORITE

MARINATED SKIRT STEAK TACOS
WITH PECAN-CHIPOTLE SALSA

Churrasco with Chimichurri

ACTIVE: 30 MIN; TOTAL: 2 HR 30 MIN
8 SERVINGS

At his Churrascos restaurants in Houston, chef Michael Cordúa serves a Nicaraguan version of *churrasco* (grilled meat), a recipe that originated in Argentina. When Argentinean gauchos in Nicaragua couldn't find the traditional skirt steak, they butterflied tenderloin to mimic the cut. The result is exquisitely tender and flavorful.

- 2 bunches of curly parsley (8 ounces), thick stems discarded
- 1/3 cup garlic cloves, crushed
- 3/4 cup plus 3 tablespoons extra-virgin olive oil
- 3 tablespoons white wine vinegar
- 2 pounds trimmed center-cut beef tenderloin

Kosher salt and freshly ground pepper

1. In a food processor, combine the parsley and garlic with 3/4 cup of the olive oil and the vinegar; pulse until smooth. Refrigerate the chimichurri for at least 2 hours and up to 8 hours.
2. Using a sharp chef's knife, make a 1/4-inch-deep cut down the length of the beef tenderloin. Turning the tenderloin and rolling it out as you go, spiral-cut the meat until you have a long, rectangular piece that's about 1/4 inch thick.
3. Light a grill. Season both sides of the tenderloin with salt and pepper. Rub two-thirds of the chimichurri over the meat and grill over moderately high heat, turning once, for about 4 minutes for medium-rare meat. Let rest for 15 minutes before slicing.
4. Meanwhile, in a small bowl, mix the remaining chimichurri and olive oil. Season with salt and pepper and serve with the steak. —*Michael Cordúa*

VARIATION In Step 2, cut the tenderloin lengthwise almost all the way through and open it up like a book, about 1 1/2 inches thick. Grill the steak over moderate heat for 7 to 8 minutes per side for medium-rare.

WINE Berry-dense, concentrated Syrah: 2011 Barrel 27 Right Hand Man.

Beef Brisket with Lemon-Oregano Sauce

ACTIVE: 40 MIN; TOTAL: 5 HR
PLUS OVERNIGHT CURING
10 SERVINGS ●

BRISKET

- 3 tablespoons extra-virgin olive oil
- 12 garlic cloves, minced
- 1/3 cup chopped oregano (about 2 bunches)
- 1 tablespoon kosher salt
- 2 tablespoons coarsely cracked black peppercorns
- 1 tablespoon juniper berries, crushed

One 6-pound first-cut brisket, with fat cap attached (see Note)
- 2 quarts chicken stock or low-sodium broth

SAUCE

- 3 tablespoons fresh lemon juice
- 3 garlic cloves, finely chopped
- 1/2 cup chopped oregano
- 1/2 cup plus 3 tablespoons extra-virgin olive oil

Kosher salt and freshly ground black pepper

1. **PREPARE THE BRISKET** In a large enameled cast-iron casserole, combine the olive oil with the garlic, oregano, salt, peppercorns and juniper berries. Put the brisket in the casserole, fat side up, and rub the garlic-oregano mixture all over it. Cover the casserole and refrigerate overnight.
2. Add the broth and 2 quarts of water to the casserole; the brisket should be submerged. Bring to a boil. Cover, reduce the heat to moderately low and simmer for about 3 1/2 hours, turning the brisket halfway, until the meat is very tender. Transfer the brisket fat side up to a rack set over a rimmed baking sheet and cover loosely with foil. Skim the fat from the surface of the broth; boil until reduced to 2 cups, about 30 minutes.
3. **MAKE THE SAUCE** In a food processor, puree the lemon juice, garlic, 1/4 cup of the oregano and the oil until emulsified. Season with salt and pepper. Transfer to a bowl. Stir in the remaining oregano.

4. Preheat the oven to 450°. Roast the brisket on the top shelf of the oven for 15 minutes, until deeply golden and crispy on top. Transfer to a cutting board; let rest for 15 minutes.
5. Thinly slice the brisket and drizzle with some of the reduced cooking liquid. Serve with the lemon-oregano sauce. —*Kay Chun*

NOTE The first-cut (or flat-cut) is a lean one, so leaving the fat cap attached is crucial: It keeps the brisket moist during braising.

WINE Herbal, full-bodied Italian red: 2011 Tormaresca Neprica.

Grilled Skirt Steak with Smoky Almond Sauce

TOTAL: 30 MIN • 4 SERVINGS

- 1 ounce ancho chiles, stemmed and seeded

Boiling water
- 2 large garlic cloves, sliced
- 1/2 cup toasted pumpkin seeds
- 1/4 cup almond butter
- 1 tablespoon sherry vinegar
- 1/2 cup extra-virgin olive oil, plus more for the pan

Salt and freshly ground pepper
- 1 1/2 pounds skirt steak, cut into 5-inch lengths

1. In a heatproof bowl, cover the anchos with boiling water and let stand for 15 minutes. Drain the chiles and coarsely chop. In a food processor, pulse the chiles and garlic until finely chopped. Add the pumpkin seeds, almond butter, vinegar and 1/2 cup of warm water; pulse to a coarse paste. With the machine on, add the 1/2 cup of oil in a steady stream. Season with salt and pepper. Scrape the almond sauce into a bowl; don't worry if the oil separates.
2. Preheat a grill pan and oil the pan. Season the steak with salt and pepper and grill over high heat for about 6 minutes, turning once, until lightly charred. Let the steak rest, then thinly slice across the grain and serve with the almond sauce. —*Grace Parisi*

MAKE AHEAD The almond sauce can be refrigerated for up to 1 week.

WINE Robust, smoky Shiraz: 2011 Paringa.

DIY GRILLING IN LEAVES

Grilling meat inside a leaf wrap is an ancient way to keep it moist while creating nutty flavors. Host of TV's *Bizarre Foods* and F&W contributing editor **ANDREW ZIMMERN** teaches the technique.

Grilled Beef Rolls with Nuoc Cham Dipping Sauce

ACTIVE: 1 HR; TOTAL: 5 HR • MAKES 40 ROLLS ● ● ●

Grilled beef rolls, called *bo la lot* in Vietnam, are wrapped in *lolot* leaves. Zimmern uses more accessible grape leaves.

This recipe uses two types of leaves: The grape-leaf bundles are grilled, then wrapped in fresh lettuce leaves.

BEEF ROLLS

- 2 pounds ground sirloin
- 3 garlic cloves, minced
- 3 tablespoons tomato paste
- 2 tablespoons each of soy sauce, cornstarch and rice wine (or sherry)
- 1 tablespoon each of Asian fish sauce, sugar and *sambal oelek* (or other Asian chile sauce)
- 1 teaspoon freshly ground black pepper
- 40 jarred brined grape leaves—drained, rinsed and patted dry
- Vegetable oil, for grilling

NUOC CHAM

- ¼ cup sugar
- ⅓ cup hot water
- ⅓ cup Asian fish sauce
- 3 tablespoons fresh lime juice
- 3 garlic cloves, minced
- 1 tablespoon minced jalapeño
- 1 tablespoon finely grated fresh ginger
- 3 tablespoons unsalted roasted peanuts, finely chopped
- Chopped cilantro and whole mint leaves, for garnish
- Lettuce leaves, for wrapping

1. MAKE THE BEEF ROLLS In a bowl, combine the ground beef with all the remaining ingredients except the grape leaves. Cover with plastic wrap and refrigerate for at least 4 hours or overnight.

2. Snip off any stems from the grape leaves. Spread 4 leaves on a work surface. Form a 1-tablespoon-size log of the beef filling at the stem end of each leaf. Fold the sides of each leaf over the filling, then tightly roll up the leaves to form 4 cylinders. Repeat with the remaining grape leaves and filling.

> **A WRAP HOW-TO**
> *Place the seasoned filling near the stem end of the brined grape leaf. Fold the sides of each leaf over the filling, then tightly roll up the leaf to form a cylinder.*

3. MAKE THE NUOC CHAM In a bowl, whisk the sugar into the hot water until dissolved. Whisk in the remaining ingredients, except the garnishes. Transfer the *nuoc cham* to a serving bowl.

4. Light a grill. Lightly brush the grill and beef rolls with oil. Arrange the rolls on the grill and cook over moderate heat, turning often to prevent burning, until firm and just cooked through, about 8 minutes. Sprinkle the rolls with cilantro and mint. Serve warm with lettuce leaves for wrapping and the *nuoc cham* for dipping.

WINE Spicy, blackberry-inflected Malbec: 2011 The Show.

Beef Burgers with Sweet-n-Smoky Ketchup

ACTIVE: 45 MIN; TOTAL: 1 HR 30 MIN
4 SERVINGS

- 4 dried pasilla or ancho chiles, stemmed and seeded
- 2 plum tomatoes, halved
- 4 unpeeled garlic cloves
- 1 jalapeño, halved and seeded
- ½ small onion
- 1 tablespoon extra-virgin olive oil, plus more for brushing

Kosher salt and freshly ground pepper

- ¼ cup apple cider vinegar
- 3 tablespoons unsulfured molasses
- 1 medium eggplant, cut crosswise ¼ inch thick
- 1 large beefsteak tomato, sliced crosswise ½ inch thick
- 1½ pounds ground beef chuck
- 4 brioche hamburger buns, split and toasted

Butter lettuce, for serving

1. Preheat the oven to 350°. In a medium skillet, toast the chiles over moderately high heat, pressing them with a spatula and turning once, until they are fragrant, about 1 minute. Transfer the chiles to a heatproof bowl and cover with very hot water. Let stand for about 30 minutes, until the chiles are completely rehydrated.

2. Meanwhile, on a large rimmed baking sheet, toss the plum tomatoes, garlic, jalapeño and onion with the 1 tablespoon of olive oil and season with salt and pepper. Bake for about 20 minutes, until the vegetables are just soft; let cool slightly. Peel the garlic.

3. Drain the pasilla chiles and transfer to a blender. Add the plum tomatoes, garlic, jalapeño, onion, vinegar and molasses and puree. Season the ketchup with salt and pepper and transfer to a bowl. Refrigerate until chilled, about 30 minutes.

4. Light a grill or preheat a grill pan. Brush the eggplant and beefsteak tomato slices with oil and season with salt and pepper. Grill over moderately high heat, turning once, until lightly charred. Transfer to a plate.

5. Form the ground beef into 4 burgers, each ½ inch thick; brush with olive oil and season with salt and pepper. Grill over moderately high heat, turning once, until the burgers are lightly charred and medium-rare, 7 minutes.

6. Spread the ketchup on the buns and top with the lettuce, burgers and grilled eggplant and tomato. Serve, passing any additional ketchup at the table. —*Tim Byres*

WINE Smoky, meaty Syrah from Washington state: 2009 McCrea Yakima Valley.

Sirloin with Piquillo Peppers and Capers

TOTAL: 30 MIN • 4 SERVINGS ●

- 2 teaspoons sweet paprika
- 1 teaspoon dark brown sugar

Kosher salt and freshly ground pepper

One 1½-pound sirloin steak (about 1¼ inches thick)

- ¼ cup extra-virgin olive oil
- 3 garlic cloves, thinly sliced
- 2 medium shallots, thinly sliced
- 1 tablespoon drained capers
- 1 teaspoon chopped fresh sage
- 8 piquillo peppers (Spanish roasted peppers), seeded and chopped
- 1 teaspoon Dijon mustard
- ½ teaspoon Worcestershire sauce

1. In a bowl, mix the paprika, brown sugar, 2 teaspoons of kosher salt and 1 teaspoon of pepper. Pat the mixture all over the meat.

2. In a small skillet, heat the olive oil over moderate heat. Add the garlic, shallots and capers and cook until softened, about 3 minutes. Stir in the sage and cook for 1 minute. Add the piquillos, mustard and Worcestershire; simmer over moderate heat for 15 minutes, stirring occasionally.

3. Meanwhile, light a grill or preheat a grill pan. Grill the steak over moderately high heat for about 12 minutes, turning once, until an instant-read thermometer inserted in the thickest part registers 130° for medium-rare meat. Let rest for 5 minutes, then slice and serve with the piquillo-pepper sauce. —*Bruce Aidells*

WINE Smooth, spicy Malbec: 2011 Alamos.

Nacho Burgers

TOTAL: 35 MIN • 4 SERVINGS ●

Of all the burger recipes F&W has run (more than 100), this one from star chef Bobby Flay is the over-the-top best, with juicy meat, gooey cheese, salsa and tortilla chips.

SALSA

- 3 tablespoons red wine vinegar
- 1 tablespoon vegetable oil
- 1 chipotle chile in adobo, seeded and minced
- 3 plum tomatoes, finely diced
- 2 tablespoons red onion, finely diced
- 3 tablespoons chopped cilantro

Salt

CHEESE SAUCE

- 1 tablespoon unsalted butter
- 1 tablespoon all-purpose flour
- 1½ cups milk
- ½ pound Monterey Jack cheese, shredded
- 2 tablespoons grated pecorino cheese

Salt and freshly ground pepper

BURGERS

- 1½ pounds ground beef chuck

Vegetable oil, for brushing

Salt and freshly ground pepper

- 4 hamburger buns, split and toasted

Sliced pickled jalapeños and blue corn tortilla chips, for topping

1. MAKE THE SALSA In a bowl, combine all of the ingredients and season with salt.

2. MAKE THE CHEESE SAUCE In a saucepan, melt the butter. Stir in the flour and cook over moderate heat for 30 seconds. Whisk in the milk and cook, whisking, until thickened, 5 minutes. Stir in the Jack cheese until melted, then stir in the pecorino; season with salt and pepper. Let cool until spreadable.

3. MAKE THE BURGERS Light a grill. Form the beef into 4 patties and brush with oil; season with salt and pepper. Grill over moderately high heat until browned outside and medium within, 4 minutes per side. Place on the buns, top with the cheese sauce, salsa, jalapeños and chips, and serve. —*Bobby Flay*

WINE Bold, berry-rich Zinfandel: 2011 Ravenswood Vintner's Blend.

● HEALTHY ● MAKE AHEAD ● VEGETARIAN ● STAFF FAVORITE

Double Cheeseburgers, Los Angeles–Style

⏱ **TOTAL: 45 MIN • 4 SERVINGS** ●

L.A. chef Roy Choi gives his otherwise classic American cheeseburger an Asian twist with sesame seeds and minty shiso leaves.

- ⅓ cup mayonnaise
- 1 tablespoon toasted sesame seeds
- 4 tablespoons unsalted butter, at room temperature
- 4 brioche hamburger buns, split
- 2 pounds ground chuck, shaped into eight ¼-inch-thick patties

Kosher salt and freshly ground pepper

- 2 tablespoons olive oil
- 8 slices of cheddar cheese
- 4 butter lettuce leaves
- 4 shiso or sesame (perilla) leaves (see Note)
- 4 thin slices of tomato
- 4 thin slices of red onion

Hot sauce, preferably Tapatío, for serving

1. In a small bowl, mix the mayonnaise with the sesame seeds.

2. Heat a large nonstick griddle or 2 nonstick skillets over moderate heat. Butter the cut sides of the hamburger buns and toast them on the griddle until golden, 4 to 5 minutes. Transfer to a platter.

3. Season the patties with salt and pepper. Brush the griddle with the oil, add the patties and cook over high heat for 2 minutes. Flip the patties and cook for 2 minutes longer; top each one with a slice of cheddar. Cook just until the cheese has melted, 1 minute.

4. Stack 2 burgers on each bun. Top with the lettuce, shiso, tomato and onion, then drizzle with hot sauce. Spread the top halves of the buns with the sesame mayo, close the burgers and serve. —*Roy Choi*

NOTE Fresh shiso, a plant in the mint family, is available at Japanese markets. Milder-flavored sesame leaves (sometimes called *perilla*) are available at Korean markets.

WINE Juicy, peppery Zinfandel: 2011 Sobon Estate Old Vines.

Free-Form Fennel Seed Meat Loaf

ACTIVE: 40 MIN; TOTAL: 2 HR

8 SERVINGS ●

- 1 cup fresh bread crumbs
- ½ cup whole milk
- ⅓ cup extra-virgin olive oil
- 1 large onion, finely chopped
- 2 medium carrots, finely chopped
- 1 celery rib, finely chopped
- 2 garlic cloves, minced

Kosher salt and freshly ground black pepper

- 3 tablespoons tomato paste
- 2 large eggs
- 2 teaspoons ground fennel seeds
- 2 teaspoons dried oregano
- 2 teaspoons celery seeds
- 1 teaspoon crushed red pepper
- 2¾ pounds ground beef chuck (80 percent lean)

1. Preheat the oven to 425° and line the bottom of a roasting pan with parchment paper. In a bowl, soak the bread crumbs in the milk.

2. In a large skillet, heat the olive oil until shimmering. Add the onion, carrots, celery, garlic and a generous pinch each of salt and black pepper and cook over moderate heat, stirring occasionally, until the vegetables are very soft and golden, about 15 minutes. Scrape the vegetables into a large bowl and let them cool. Add the tomato paste, eggs, milk-soaked bread crumbs, ground fennel seeds, oregano, celery seeds, crushed red pepper, 2 teaspoons of salt and ½ teaspoon of black pepper and stir to form a paste. Using your hands, gently work in the ground beef until combined; be careful not to overmix.

3. Transfer the meat mixture to the roasting pan and shape it into an oval loaf about 10 inches long. Bake the meat loaf for 50 to 60 minutes, until browned and an instant-read thermometer inserted in the center registers 150°. Let the meat loaf rest for 15 minutes, then cut into thick slices and serve. —*Anya Fernald*

WINE Herbal California Cabernet Franc: 2010 Lang & Reed North Coast.

Agrodolce Meatballs

⏱ **TOTAL: 45 MIN**

MAKES 18 MEATBALLS ● ●

Even in southern Italy, not every meatball is drenched in tomato sauce. These are cooked in a sweet-and-tart mixture of balsamic vinegar and chicken broth.

- ¾ pound ground sirloin
- ¾ pound ground pork
- 2 large eggs
- ¼ cup plain dry bread crumbs
- ¼ cup dried currants or raisins
- ¼ cup pine nuts
- 1 tablespoon drained capers
- 4 large scallions, white and tender green parts only, thinly sliced

Kosher salt and freshly ground black pepper

All-purpose flour, for dusting

- ½ cup extra-virgin olive oil
- 2 cups low-sodium chicken broth
- ¼ cup balsamic vinegar
- 1 tablespoon sugar

Crusty bread, for serving

1. In a large bowl, combine the meats with the eggs, bread crumbs, currants, pine nuts, capers and three-fourths of the scallions. Add 1 tablespoon of salt and ½ teaspoon of pepper and knead gently to combine. Roll the mixture into 18 meatballs and dust with flour.

2. In a large skillet, heat the olive oil until shimmering. Add the meatballs in a single layer and cook over moderate heat, turning once or twice, until browned and nearly cooked through, 7 to 8 minutes. Tilt the skillet and spoon off as much fat as possible.

3. Add the remaining scallions to the skillet and cook for 1 minute. Add the broth, vinegar and sugar and season lightly with salt and pepper. Cover partially and cook over moderately low heat, stirring, until the sauce is reduced to ½ cup and the meatballs are fully cooked, 8 minutes. Serve with crusty bread. —*Grace Parisi*

MAKE AHEAD The cooked meatballs and sauce can be refrigerated overnight.

WINE Smooth, cherry-scented Spanish red: 2008 Conde de Valdemar Crianza.

Cheesy Burgers with Soy-Spiked Ketchup

☼ TOTAL: 35 MIN • MAKES 6 BURGERS

"I love meat loaf, but I hate that it's cooked all the way through," says Jamie Bissonnette, a chef at Boston's Coppa and Toro. For these burgers, served medium-rare, he mixes ground beef with ingredients you might use for meat loaf, like ketchup, pickles and bread crumbs. On top: more ketchup that he doctors with hoisin (for sweetness), fresh lime juice (for tang) and soy sauce (for umami).

½ cup plus 2 tablespoons ketchup
1½ tablespoons soy sauce
1 tablespoon hoisin sauce
1 tablespoon freshly squeezed
    lime juice
1½ teaspoons ancho chile powder
1½ pounds ground beef chuck,
    preferably 80 or 85 percent lean
½ cup shredded Colby cheese
¼ cup minced red onion
2 tablespoons minced kosher pickles
2 tablespoons plain dry bread crumbs
3 garlic cloves, minced
½ teaspoon Tabasco
Canola oil, for brushing
Kosher salt and freshly ground
    black pepper
6 potato hamburger buns,
    split and toasted
Mayonnaise, lettuce and sliced red
    onion, for serving

1. In a medium bowl, whisk ½ cup of the ketchup with the soy sauce, hoisin, lime juice and ancho chile powder.
2. In a large bowl, combine the ground beef with the cheese, minced red onion, pickles, bread crumbs, garlic, Tabasco and the remaining 2 tablespoons of ketchup. Knead gently until thoroughly mixed. Form the meat into six 4-inch patties, about ½ inch thick.
3. Light a grill or preheat a grill pan. Brush the burgers with canola oil and season with salt and freshly ground pepper. Grill over moderately high heat, turning once, until lightly charred outside and medium-rare within, about 3 minutes.

4. Spread the cut sides of the buns with mayonnaise. Place lettuce on the buns, then top with the burgers. Spread some of the spiked ketchup on the patties and top with sliced onion. Close the burgers and serve, passing additional spiked ketchup at the table.
—Jamie Bissonnette

WINE Fruit-forward California Zinfandel: 2010 Peachy Canyon Westside.

Cheddar-Stuffed Burgers with Pickled Slaw and Fried Shallots

ACTIVE: 1 HR; TOTAL: 2 HR 30 MIN
MAKES 4 BURGERS ●

At the Bluejacket brewery's Arsenal restaurant in Washington, DC, chef Kyle Bailey makes these cheese-stuffed "Juicy Lucy" burgers with a custom blend of ground rib eye steak and pork fatback, and serves them on house-made herb-butter rolls. This streamlined version calls for ground beef chuck and store-bought brioche buns.

Kosher salt
8 cups finely shredded green cabbage
    (from a 1½-pound head)
1 cup distilled white vinegar
1 tablespoon sugar
2 tablespoons yellow mustard seeds
Vegetable oil, for frying
5 large shallots, very thinly sliced
    crosswise and separated into rings
¼ cup Wondra flour (see Note)
1½ pounds ground beef chuck,
    preferably 85 percent lean
1 teaspoon onion powder
1 teaspoon garlic powder
1 teaspoon sweet smoked paprika
1 tablespoon Worcestershire sauce
Freshly ground pepper
6 ounces extra-sharp cheddar cheese,
    shredded
2 cups baby arugula
4 brioche buns, split and toasted

1. In a large bowl, toss 1 tablespoon of kosher salt with the cabbage and massage it until it softens and releases its liquid, about 4 minutes. Drain the cabbage in a colander and rinse it.

2. Wipe out the bowl. Add the vinegar, sugar, mustard seeds, 1 cup of water and 1 tablespoon of salt. Add the cabbage to the vinegar mixture, toss to coat and place a plate on top to keep the cabbage submerged. Let the pickled cabbage stand at room temperature for 2 hours.
3. Meanwhile, in a large saucepan, heat 1½ inches of vegetable oil to 325°. In a medium bowl, toss the shallots with the Wondra flour. Fry the shallots all at once, stirring gently, until golden, about 7 minutes. Using a slotted spoon, transfer the shallots to a paper towel–lined plate to drain. Season the shallots with salt. Reserve the cooking oil.
4. In a medium bowl, combine the ground beef with the onion powder, garlic powder, smoked paprika, Worcestershire sauce and 2 teaspoons each of kosher salt and freshly ground pepper. Knead gently until thoroughly mixed. Form the beef into eight 4-inch patties. Press the shredded cheese into four 2½-inch disks. Sandwich the cheese disks between the patties. Pinch the edges together to seal.
5. Heat a grill pan or griddle. Brush the burgers with some of the shallot cooking oil and cook over moderate heat until browned on the bottom, about 3 minutes. Flip the burgers, invert a large heatproof bowl over them and cook the burgers until they are medium within and the cheese is melted, about 3 minutes longer.
6. Mound the arugula on the bun bottoms and top with the burgers. Drain the pickled cabbage and mound some of it on the burgers; reserve the rest of the pickled cabbage for another use. Top with the fried shallots and the bun tops and serve.
—Kyle Bailey

NOTE Wondra flour, which is more granular than regular all-purpose flour, is available at most supermarkets.

MAKE AHEAD The pickled cabbage can be refrigerated in its brine and the fried shallots can be stored at room temperature in an airtight container for up to 4 days. Drain the pickled cabbage before serving.

WINE Robust Cabernet from Washington state: 2011 Owen Roe Sharecropper's.

● HEALTHY ● MAKE AHEAD ● VEGETARIAN ● STAFF FAVORITE

CHEDDAR-STUFFED BURGERS WITH
PICKLED SLAW AND FRIED SHALLOTS

Prime Rib Roast with Horseradish Cream

ACTIVE: 30 MIN; TOTAL: 4 HR 30 MIN
10 SERVINGS ●

Basting with garlic-thyme butter gives this roast extra flavor. Don't worry if the garlic gets very dark—it will taste delicious.

ROAST

One 10-pound bone-in prime rib roast (about 4 bones), tied
Sea salt and freshly ground pepper
¼ cup extra-virgin olive oil
4 tablespoons unsalted butter
2 heads of garlic, halved crosswise
8 thyme sprigs

SAUCE

2 cups crème fraîche (16 ounces)
½ cup grated peeled fresh horseradish
1 tablespoon Champagne vinegar
1 tablespoon minced chives
1 tablespoon minced scallion
1 teaspoon salt
1 teaspoon cracked black pepper
¼ teaspoon piment d'Espelette or cayenne pepper (see Note)

1. PREPARE THE ROAST Preheat the oven to 325°. Using a sharp paring knife, make 1-inch-deep slits all over the surface of the meat; rub salt and pepper all over the outside and in the slits. Heat the olive oil in a very large skillet. Add the roast, meaty side down, and cook over high heat until browned, about 10 minutes. Add the butter, garlic and thyme and cook over moderate heat for 5 minutes, basting the roast with the butter.
2. Transfer the roast to a medium roasting pan, bone side down, and press the cut side of the garlic halves and the thyme sprigs onto the surface of the meat. Roast, turning the pan occasionally, for about 3½ hours; the meat is done when an instant-read thermometer inserted in the center registers 125°. Let rest for 15 minutes.
3. MEANWHILE, MAKE THE SAUCE Combine all of the ingredients in a bowl.
4. Carve the roast off the bone, then thinly slice. Serve with the horseradish cream.
—*Michael Tusk*

NOTE Piment d'Espelette, a Basque red chile powder, is available at specialty food stores and online at *vannsspices.com*.
WINE Substantial red with a tannic backbone: 2009 Paolo Scavino Barolo.

Asian-Spiced Short Ribs

ACTIVE: 30 MIN; TOTAL: 4 HR 30 MIN
6 SERVINGS ● ●

Chef Jean-Georges Vongerichten sprinkles short ribs with ground fennel before braising them in an East-West blend of Asian fish sauce, soy sauce and dry red wine.

Six 12-ounce bone-in beef short ribs
Kosher salt
Ground fennel, for seasoning
1 cup ketchup
1 cup dry red wine, such as Syrah
⅓ cup red wine vinegar
½ cup unsulfured molasses
3 tablespoons dried onion flakes
2 tablespoons Asian fish sauce
1 tablespoon soy sauce
1 tablespoon garlic powder
1 tablespoon seeded and minced chipotle chile in adobo
1 teaspoon toasted sesame oil

1. Preheat the oven to 325°. Light a grill. Season the ribs with salt and fennel. Grill over high heat, turning, until charred all over, 12 minutes. Transfer to a flameproof roasting pan.
2. In a large bowl, mix the ketchup, wine, vinegar, molasses, onion flakes, fish sauce, soy sauce, garlic powder, chipotle, sesame oil and 1 tablespoon of kosher salt. Whisk in 3 quarts of water. Pour the sauce over the ribs and bring to a simmer over 2 burners.
3. Cover the pan and braise in the oven, turning the ribs once, until very tender, 2½ hours.
4. Transfer the sauce to a large saucepan and boil over high heat until reduced to 4 cups, 1 hour; cover. Keep the ribs warm in a 200° oven.
5. Increase the oven temperature to 350°. Pour the sauce over the ribs and roast until the ribs are glazed, about 15 minutes, then serve. —*Jean-Georges Vongerichten*
WINE Spicy, juicy California red blend: 2008 Buena Vista The Count.

Beef Shank Sauce Over Polenta

ACTIVE: 1 HR; TOTAL: 4 HR
MAKES 10 CUPS ●

Beef shank is an economical cut with bones that create a rich broth when braised. The result is a tangy, velvety sauce to ladle over pasta or polenta.

5 pounds trimmed beef shanks, cut 2 inches thick
Kosher salt and freshly ground pepper
3 tablespoons extra-virgin olive oil
2 onions, cut into ½-inch dice
4 celery ribs, cut into ½-inch dice
2 carrots, cut into ½-inch dice
2 cups dry red wine
One 28-ounce can crushed tomatoes
2 cups low-sodium vegetable broth or water
Cooked polenta or pasta, for serving

1. Preheat the oven to 325°. Season the shanks with salt and pepper. In a large enameled cast-iron casserole, heat the oil until shimmering. Add half of the shanks and cook over moderately high heat, turning once, until browned, about 7 minutes. Transfer to a plate. Repeat with the remaining shanks.
2. Pour off all but 2 tablespoons of fat from the casserole. Add the onions, celery, carrots and a generous pinch of salt and cook over moderate heat, stirring, until the vegetables are very soft and golden, 15 minutes. Add the wine and bring to a boil. Simmer over moderate heat for 2 minutes. Add the tomatoes and broth and bring to a boil. Return the shanks and any accumulated juices to the casserole. Cover and braise in the oven for 3 hours, until the meat is very tender.
3. Using tongs or a slotted spoon, transfer the shanks to a plate and let cool slightly. Using 2 forks, shred the meat and scrape out marrow from the bones. Add the meat and marrow to the sauce and rewarm over moderately low heat. Season the sauce with salt and pepper and serve with polenta or pasta.
—*Anya Fernald*
WINE Lively, medium-bodied red: 2010 Vietti Tre Vigne Barbera d'Asti.

Skirt Steak with Bloody Mary Tomato Salad

⏱ TOTAL: 40 MIN • 4 SERVINGS ●

¼ cup drained bottled horseradish
2 tablespoons fresh lemon juice
2 teaspoons Worcestershire sauce
½ teaspoon celery seeds
Coarsely ground black pepper
¼ cup plus 2 tablespoons canola oil
Kosher salt
2 pounds heirloom tomatoes, chopped
2 small celery ribs, thinly sliced, plus ¼ cup celery leaves
⅓ cup sour cream
1 pound skirt steak, in 2 pieces

1. In a large bowl, stir 2 tablespoons of the horseradish with the lemon juice, Worcestershire, celery seeds and ½ teaspoon of black pepper. Whisk in ¼ cup of the canola oil in a steady stream; season with salt. Add the tomatoes and celery ribs and leaves, season with salt and pepper and toss.
2. In a small bowl, stir the sour cream with the remaining 2 tablespoons of horseradish.
3. Light a grill or preheat a grill pan. Rub the remaining 2 tablespoons of canola oil all over the steak and season with salt and black pepper. Grill the steak over moderately high heat, turning once, until nicely charred, 3 to 4 minutes per side for medium-rare. Transfer the steak to a work surface and let rest for 5 minutes. Slice the steak across the grain and serve with the tomato salad and horseradish cream. —*Kay Chun*
WINE Smooth, robust Washington state red blend: 2011 Hedges CMS.

Beef Hand Pies

TOTAL: 50 MIN • 6 SERVINGS ●

Two 14-ounce packages all-butter puff pastry, thawed
1½ cups chopped leftover Short Rib Stew (page 86) or other leftover beef stew (beef and vegetables cut into ¼-inch dice)
1 large egg, lightly beaten

1. Preheat the oven to 400°. On a lightly floured work surface, using a lightly floured rolling pin, roll out each sheet of puff pastry to a 13-by-9-inch rectangle. Stamp out six 4-inch rounds from each sheet. Transfer 6 rounds to a parchment paper–lined baking sheet. Roll out the remaining 6 rounds so they are slightly larger, about 4½ inches in diameter.
2. Mound ¼ cup of the filling in the center of each smaller pastry round. Brush the edges with some of the beaten egg and top with the larger pastry rounds; press to seal. Crimp the edges with the tines of a fork (recut with a ring cutter if a clean edge is desired). Brush with the remaining beaten egg and cut a small steam vent in the top of each pie. Bake for 25 to 30 minutes, until the pies are golden and puffed. Serve warm. —*Kay Chun*
BEER Toasty brown ale: Samuel Smith's Nut Brown.

Stupid-Simple Roast Beef with Horseradish Cream

ACTIVE: 15 MIN; TOTAL: 5 HR PLUS 2 DAYS CURING • 8 TO 10 SERVINGS ● ● ●

1 cup plus 1 tablespoon kosher salt
One 7- to 8-pound top round beef roast, tied with the full fat cap on the roast
1 tablespoon freshly ground pepper, plus more for seasoning
1 cup sour cream
½ cup prepared horseradish

1. Set a rack over a baking sheet. Rub ½ cup of the salt all over the roast and let stand for 10 minutes. Repeat with another ½ cup of the salt. Transfer the roast to the rack and refrigerate uncovered for 2 days. Bring to room temperature 3 hours before roasting.
2. Preheat the oven to 450°. Season the meat with pepper and roast for 20 minutes. Reduce the oven temperature to 225° and roast for about 1 hour and 30 minutes longer, until an instant-read thermometer inserted in the center of the roast registers 120°. Let the meat rest for 30 minutes.

3. In a bowl, mix the sour cream with the horseradish and the remaining 1 tablespoon of salt and pepper. Slice the roast and serve with the horseradish cream. —*Tom Mylan*
WINE Berry-rich California Cabernet Sauvignon: 2011 Ghost Pines.

Mixed Grill with Fresh Tomato-and-Pepper Salsa

📷 COVER

TOTAL: 1 HR PLUS OVERNIGHT MARINATING • 6 SERVINGS ●

1 medium red onion, cut into ⅓-inch dice
1 medium tomato—halved, seeded and cut into ⅓-inch dice
½ each of red, green and yellow bell peppers, cut into ⅓-inch dice
¾ cup extra-virgin olive oil
3 tablespoons fresh lemon juice
Kosher salt and freshly ground pepper
1½ pounds boneless leg of lamb roast
1½ pounds flanken-cut beef short ribs (cut across the bones), about ½ inch thick
1½ pounds fresh chorizo or hot Italian sausage

1. In a large bowl, combine the onion with the tomato, bell peppers, olive oil and lemon juice. Add a large pinch each of salt and pepper and mix well. Cover and refrigerate overnight. Bring to room temperature before serving.
2. Light a grill. Season the lamb and short ribs with salt and pepper and let stand for 10 minutes. Grill all of the meats over moderate heat, turning occasionally, until the short ribs are browned and cooked through, about 12 minutes; the chorizo is cooked through, about 15 minutes; and an instant-read thermometer inserted in the thickest part of the lamb registers 130° for medium-rare, 25 to 35 minutes, depending on thickness. Transfer the meats to a platter to rest for 5 minutes.
3. Season the salsa once more with salt and pepper. Carve the grilled meats and serve the salsa alongside. —*Marcelo Betancourt*
WINE Dark-berried Chilean Cabernet Sauvignon: 2010 Cono Sur Visión Cabernet.

Ribs with Hot-Pepper-Jelly Glaze

ACTIVE: 30 MIN; TOTAL: 3 HR PLUS
OVERNIGHT MARINATING
10 TO 12 SERVINGS ●

- 2 tablespoons coriander seeds
- 1 teaspoon dried orange peel
- ¼ cup dark brown sugar
- 2 tablespoons chile powder
- 1 tablespoon garlic powder
- 1 tablespoon onion powder
- Kosher salt and freshly ground pepper
- 4 English-cut beef short ribs, about 6 inches long (3 pounds)
- 2 racks baby back ribs (6 pounds), membranes removed
- 2 racks spareribs (4 pounds), membranes removed
- 1½ cups hot red pepper jelly
- ¼ cup white miso
- ¼ cup fresh lemon juice
- 2 tablespoons Sriracha (or to taste)
- Sesame seeds and chopped scallions, for garnish

1. In a spice grinder, grind the coriander and orange peel. Add the brown sugar, chile powder, garlic powder, onion powder and 1 tablespoon each of salt and pepper; pulse to combine. Rub the spice mix over all of the ribs and place in a large roasting pan. Cover and refrigerate overnight.
2. Preheat the oven to 325°. Put the short ribs in a small baking dish and cover with foil. Roast for 30 minutes.
3. Put the baby back ribs and spareribs on 2 rimmed baking sheets and cover with foil. Roast all of the ribs until tender, about 2 hours longer. Carefully pour the pan drippings into a medium bowl and skim off the fat. Reserve 1½ cups of the drippings and discard the rest.
4. In a medium saucepan, combine the pepper jelly with the miso, lemon juice, Sriracha and the reserved pan juices. Simmer the glaze for 5 minutes, whisking.
5. Light a grill. Arrange all of the ribs on the grill; cook over moderately high heat, turning and brushing with half of the glaze, until they are nicely caramelized, about 15 minutes.

Transfer the ribs to a work surface. Cut the baby back and spareribs in between the bones and slice the short ribs. Garnish with sesame seeds and scallions and serve the ribs with the remaining glaze on the side. —Grace Parisi

BEER Perfectly hoppy beer: Anchor Steam.

Grilled Lamb Chops with Marjoram Butter and Zucchini

ACTIVE: 25 MIN; TOTAL: 1 HR
4 TO 6 SERVINGS ●

Sweet, floral marjoram is celebrity Irish cook Rachel Allen's favorite herb to pair with grilled lamb, but this infused butter is just as delicious with steak or meaty fish.

- 1 stick unsalted butter, softened
- 1 scant tablespoon minced marjoram
- 1 medium garlic clove, finely grated
- ¾ teaspoon fresh lemon juice
- Kosher salt and freshly ground pepper
- Twelve 4- to 6-ounce lamb rib chops
- Extra-virgin olive oil, for brushing
- 2 medium zucchini—halved lengthwise, seeded and cut crosswise ½ inch thick

1. In a small bowl, mix 6 tablespoons of the butter with the marjoram, garlic and lemon juice. Season the butter with salt and pepper. Wrap the butter in a sheet of plastic wrap and shape into a log. Twist the ends to seal and refrigerate until firm, 30 minutes.
2. Light a grill or preheat a grill pan. Brush the lamb chops with olive oil and season with salt and pepper. Grill over high heat, turning once or twice, until nicely charred outside and medium-rare within, 6 minutes total. Transfer the chops to a platter and immediately top each one with a slice of the marjoram butter.
3. In a large skillet, melt the remaining 2 tablespoons of plain butter. Add the zucchini and a generous pinch each of salt and pepper and cook over high heat, tossing, until crisp-tender, 3 to 4 minutes. Serve the lamb chops with the zucchini and the remaining marjoram butter. —Rachel Allen

WINE Berried Cabernet Franc: 2011 Domaine Bernard Baudry Les Granges Chinon.

Grilled Lamb Chops with Peperonata

🕑 TOTAL: 40 MIN • 4 SERVINGS

Tender baby lamb chops are served with the rustic Italian sweet-and-savory pepper mixture called peperonata. Made with a hearty mix of stewed bell peppers, onions, raisins and anchovies, this peperonata is more of a side dish than a condiment.

- ⅓ cup extra-virgin olive oil, plus more for brushing
- 6 oil-packed anchovies, finely chopped
- 3 red and/or yellow bell peppers (about 1¼ pounds), thinly sliced
- 1 small sweet onion, thinly sliced
- 3 garlic cloves, thinly sliced
- Scant ½ cup golden raisins
- 2 tablespoons drained capers
- 1 tablespoon sugar
- ¼ cup white wine vinegar mixed with ¾ cup of water
- Kosher salt and freshly ground black pepper
- 8 small lamb chops (5 to 6 ounces each)

1. Preheat the oven to 375°. In a large, deep skillet, heat the ⅓ cup of olive oil until shimmering. Add the anchovies and cook over high heat, stirring, until dissolved, about 1 minute. Add the peppers, onion and garlic and cook, stirring, until softened and lightly browned, about 10 minutes. Stir in the raisins, capers and sugar. Add the vinegar mixture and simmer over low heat until the peppers are very tender and the liquid is slightly reduced, about 5 minutes. Season with salt and pepper and keep warm.
2. Heat a cast-iron grill pan until very hot. Brush the lamb chops with olive oil and season with salt and pepper. Grill the chops over high heat until they are lightly charred, about 1 minute per side. Transfer the grill pan to the oven and roast the chops for 3 minutes for medium meat. Serve the lamb chops with the peperonata. —Grace Parisi

WINE Ripe southern French red blend: 2010 Hecht & Bannier Saint Chinian.

● HEALTHY ● MAKE AHEAD ● VEGETARIAN ● STAFF FAVORITE

Sichuan Racks of Lamb with Cumin and Chile Peppers

ACTIVE: 45 MIN; TOTAL: 1 HR 45 MIN
12 SERVINGS

SPICED LAMB

¼ cup cumin seeds
1 tablespoon whole black peppercorns
2 tablespoons Sichuan peppercorns
4 Chinese dried red chiles
1 tablespoon plus ½ teaspoon
    fennel seeds
2 star anise pods
1 tablespoon each of onion powder,
    garlic powder and ground ginger
Five 3½- to 4-pound frenched racks of
    lamb, excess fat trimmed
2 tablespoons canola or peanut oil,
    plus more for brushing
Chinese dark soy sauce, for brushing
    (see Note)

SAUCE

2 cups veal stock or 1 cup veal
    demiglace mixed with 1 cup of water
1 tablespoon finely grated fresh ginger
1 garlic clove, crushed
1 teaspoon *tobanjan* (spicy fermented
    broadbean paste; see Note)
One 3-inch cinnamon stick
1 teaspoon sugar
½ teaspoon whole cloves
½ teaspoon black cardamom pods
½ teaspoon Sichuan peppercorns
1 Chinese dried red chile
½ star anise pod
½ teaspoon fennel seeds
1 tablespoon unsalted butter, cubed
Kosher salt
Thinly sliced scallions, thinly sliced red
    Fresno chiles and crispy fried
    shallots (see Note), for garnish

1. MAKE THE SPICED LAMB Preheat the oven to 400°. In a skillet, toast the cumin, black peppercorns, Sichuan peppercorns, dried chiles, fennel seeds and star anise over moderate heat, stirring, until fragrant, 3 minutes. Let cool, then finely grind in a spice grinder. Transfer to a bowl and mix with the onion and garlic powders and ginger.

2. Set a rack over each of 2 rimmed baking sheets. Lightly brush the lamb all over with oil and then soy sauce. Rub the spice mixture all over. In a large skillet, heat the 2 tablespoons of oil. In batches, sear the lamb over moderate heat until browned on both sides, 2 minutes per batch. Transfer to the racks.

3. Roast the lamb for 45 minutes, until an instant-read thermometer inserted in the center registers 135°. Let rest for 15 minutes.

4. MEANWHILE, MAKE THE SAUCE In a saucepan, combine the veal stock, ginger, garlic, *tobanjan*, cinnamon, sugar, cloves, cardamom, Sichuan peppercorns, dried chile, star anise and fennel seeds. Simmer over moderate heat until reduced to 1 cup, 15 minutes. Whisk in the butter and season with salt; strain into a bowl and keep warm.

5. Carve the lamb into chops; drizzle with the sauce. Garnish with scallions, sliced red chiles and crispy shallots and serve. —*Sang Yoon*

NOTE Chinese dark soy sauce and *tobanjan* are available at Asian food stores. For crispy fried shallots, very thinly slice shallots into rings and dust with Wondra flour; fry in 1½ inches of 325° vegetable oil until golden and crisp. Drain on paper towels.

WINE Sturdy, rich rosé Champagne: NV Camille Savès Brut Rosé.

Spicy Sichuan-Style Lamb with Cumin

TOTAL: 30 MIN • 4 SERVINGS ●

3 tablespoons canola oil
2 tablespoons ground cumin
1½ teaspoons crushed red pepper
1 tablespoon low-sodium soy sauce
1 tablespoon cornstarch
2 teaspoons toasted sesame oil
1 teaspoon sugar
Kosher salt and freshly ground
    black pepper
1¼ pounds trimmed boneless
    lamb shoulder, thinly sliced
1 large white onion,
    cut into 1½-inch pieces
2 scallions, thinly sliced
½ cup cilantro leaves
¼ cup low-sodium chicken broth

1. In a large bowl, combine 2 tablespoons of the canola oil with the cumin, crushed red pepper, soy sauce, cornstarch, sesame oil, sugar and 1 teaspoon each of salt and pepper. Add the lamb and onion and turn to coat. Let stand for 10 minutes.

2. Heat a large cast-iron skillet until very hot. Add the remaining 1 tablespoon of canola oil and swirl to coat. Add the lamb and onion and cook, stirring occasionally, until browned, 10 minutes. Stir in the scallions and cilantro. Add the broth and cook, stirring and scraping up any bits stuck to the bottom of the skillet, until the broth is evaporated, about 2 minutes. Serve. —*Grace Parisi*

SERVE WITH Steamed rice.

WINE Aromatic, concentrated Syrah from Chile: 2009 Chono Reserva.

Grilled Lamb Skewers with Mustard Onions

TOTAL: 30 MIN • 4 SERVINGS

½ cup distilled white vinegar
½ cup Dijon mustard
½ tablespoon agave nectar
1 yellow onion, thinly sliced
    (1½ cups)
Kosher salt and freshly ground
    white pepper
1 tablespoon peanut oil,
    plus more for grilling
2 pounds trimmed leg of lamb,
    cut into 1-inch pieces
Freshly ground black pepper

1. In a medium bowl, combine the vinegar, mustard and agave nectar. Stir in the onion and season with salt and white pepper.

2. Light a grill or preheat a grill pan and oil the grates. In a large bowl, toss the lamb with the 1 tablespoon of peanut oil and season generously with salt and black pepper. Thread the lamb pieces onto 8 skewers and grill over moderate heat, turning occasionally, until charred in spots, 6 to 7 minutes for medium meat. Transfer the lamb skewers to a platter and serve with the mustard onions. —*Sean Brock*

BEER Nutty amber ale: Abita Amber.

● HEALTHY ● MAKE AHEAD ● VEGETARIAN ● STAFF FAVORITE

Herb-and-Honey-Mustard-Crusted Leg of Lamb

ACTIVE: 30 MIN; TOTAL: 2 HR 30 MIN

8 SERVINGS ●

For this recipe, you can ask your butcher to debone the lamb, leaving in the decorative shin bone to make carving easy.

One 7- to 8-pound leg of lamb—
   aitch bone and femur removed,
   shin bone left intact
½ cup rosemary leaves, minced
1 teaspoon thyme leaves
3 garlic cloves, finely chopped
2 tablespoons Dijon mustard
⅓ cup extra-virgin olive oil
½ cup lavender honey
Salt and freshly ground black pepper

1. Preheat the oven to 500° for 30 minutes. Let the leg of lamb stand at room temperature while the oven heats. In a mini food processor, pulse the rosemary, thyme and garlic until minced. Add the mustard, olive oil and honey and pulse to blend. Season the herb mustard with salt and freshly ground black pepper.
2. On a work surface, open up the leg of lamb and season it generously with salt and pepper, rubbing them into the meat. Spread 1 tablespoon of the herb mustard all over the inside of the lamb. Roll up the meat and tie at 1-inch intervals with kitchen string. Generously season the outside of the lamb roast with salt, rubbing it into the meat, then rub the lamb roast with the remaining herb mustard.
3. Set the lamb on a wire rack in a roasting pan. Add 1 cup of water to the pan. Turn down the oven to 375° and roast the lamb for about 1½ hours, until an instant-read thermometer inserted in the center of the meat registers 130°; it should register 150° near the bone. Let the lamb rest for 15 minutes, then remove the string, slice and serve. —Danika Boyle

MAKE AHEAD The herb mustard can be refrigerated overnight.

WINE Ripe, dark-berried Washington state red: 2011 Owen Roe Sinister Hand.

Grilled Lamb Ribs with Chimichurri

📷 PAGE 193

ACTIVE: 50 MIN; TOTAL: 1 HR 35 MIN

8 SERVINGS

Grilling lamb ribs gives them a great char on the outside. The tangy, extra-herby chimichurri is a perfect partner for the rich meat.

RIBS
2 cups sherry vinegar
½ cup fresh lemon juice
½ cup chopped rosemary sprigs
6 garlic cloves, thinly sliced
4 racks well-trimmed meaty lamb
   spareribs (about 5½ pounds),
   cut in half
Olive oil, for brushing
Kosher salt and freshly ground pepper
CHIMICHURRI
1½ cups packed parsley leaves
4 garlic cloves, coarsely chopped
2 tablespoons packed oregano leaves
1½ tablespoons packed
   rosemary leaves
1 tablespoon packed thyme leaves
1 fresh bay leaf
1 teaspoon crushed red pepper
¾ cup extra-virgin olive oil
⅓ cup sherry vinegar
Kosher salt and freshly ground pepper

1. PREPARE THE RIBS In a medium bowl, whisk the sherry vinegar with the lemon juice, rosemary sprigs and sliced garlic. Pour the marinade into 2 large resealable plastic bags. Add the lamb ribs, seal the bags and turn to coat the ribs. Let the ribs marinate at room temperature for 1 hour, turning the bags over halfway through.
2. MEANWHILE, MAKE THE CHIMICHURRI In a food processor, combine all of the ingredients except the olive oil, vinegar, salt and pepper. Pulse until the herbs are finely chopped. Add the olive oil and vinegar and pulse to combine. Season the chimichurri with salt and pepper and transfer to a bowl.
3. Light a grill. Remove the ribs from the marinade. Scrape off the garlic and rosemary and pat the ribs dry with paper towels.

Brush the ribs with olive oil and season with salt and pepper. Grill the ribs over moderately high heat, turning, until nicely charred outside and medium-rare within, 10 to 12 minutes. Transfer to a platter and serve with the chimichurri. —Santiago Garat

WINE Dense, rustic Uruguayan red: 2011 Marichal Reserve Tannat.

Yogurt-Marinated Lamb Skewers

TOTAL: 40 MIN PLUS OVERNIGHT

MARINATING • 4 TO 6 SERVINGS ●

1 quart plain whole-milk yogurt
¼ cup canned or jarred brined
   green peppercorns—rinsed,
   drained and finely chopped
¼ cup minced shallots
5 garlic cloves, minced
3 tablespoons fresh lemon juice
2 teaspoons sugar
1 teaspoon ground cumin
½ cup finely chopped cilantro
½ cup finely chopped mint
Kosher salt and freshly ground pepper
3 pounds trimmed boneless leg
   of lamb, cut into 1½-inch cubes
18 skewers, soaked in water for 1 hour

1. In a large bowl, whisk the yogurt with the green peppercorns, shallots, garlic, lemon juice, sugar and cumin. Stir in the cilantro and mint and season lightly with salt and pepper.
2. Transfer 1 cup of the yogurt sauce to a bowl; cover and refrigerate. Pour the remaining yogurt sauce into a large resealable plastic bag. Add the lamb and turn to coat thoroughly. Seal the bag and refrigerate overnight.
3. Light a grill or preheat a grill pan. Remove the lamb from the marinade and thread the meat onto the skewers. Season with salt and pepper. Grill the lamb over high heat, turning, until charred in spots, about 7 minutes for medium meat. Transfer the skewers to a platter and serve with the reserved yogurt sauce. —Tim Byres

WINE Slightly herbal Cabernet Franc from France's Loire Valley: 2011 Chais St. Laurent La Vigne en Véron Chinon.

Lamb Chops Milanese with Sun-Dried Tomato Pesto

TOTAL: 1 HR • 4 SERVINGS ●

In this twist on the classic Italian dish veal Milanese (a pounded, breaded and fried veal cutlet), double-cut lamb chops are pounded thin, then fried until golden and crisp.

4 ounces drained oil-packed
 sun-dried tomatoes (½ cup)
Eight double-cut baby lamb chops,
 bones frenched (3 pounds)
Kosher salt and freshly ground pepper
2½ cups plain dry bread crumbs
6 large eggs
¼ cup finely chopped flat-leaf parsley
3 garlic cloves, minced
½ cup extra-virgin olive oil
2 tablespoons freshly grated
 Parmigiano-Reggiano cheese
Vegetable oil, for frying

1. In a medium bowl, cover the sun-dried tomatoes with water and let stand until plumped, about 30 minutes.
2. Meanwhile, on a work surface, lightly pound each lamb chop to a ½-inch thickness. Season the lamb with salt and pepper. Spread the bread crumbs in a shallow bowl and season them lightly with salt and pepper. In another shallow bowl, beat the eggs with the parsley, garlic and a pinch each of salt and pepper.
3. Transfer the sun-dried tomatoes and ¼ cup of the soaking liquid to a food processor and puree until a paste forms. With the machine on, drizzle in the olive oil until incorporated. Add the grated cheese and pulse. Season the sun-dried tomato pesto with salt and pepper and transfer to a bowl.
4. Dredge a lamb chop in the bread crumbs, tapping off the excess. Dip the lamb in the beaten egg, letting any excess drip back into the bowl, then dredge again in the bread crumbs. Transfer to a baking sheet. Repeat with the remaining lamb chops.
5. In a large, deep skillet, heat 2½ inches of vegetable oil to 350°. Set a rack on a baking sheet. Add 2 or 3 chops to the oil and fry over moderately high heat, turning, until the crust

is golden and the meat is medium, 3 minutes; using tongs, submerge the bones of each chop in the hot oil for at least 15 seconds. Transfer the lamb chops to the rack and fry the remaining chops. Serve with the pesto. —*Marcelo Betancourt*

MAKE AHEAD The sun-dried tomato pesto can be refrigerated for up to 3 days. Return to room temperature before serving.

WINE Robust Chilean Cabernet blend: 2010 Veramonte Primus.

Pomegranate-Glazed Lamb Chops

ACTIVE: 25 MIN; TOTAL: 1 HR
6 SERVINGS

This dish is a variation on *shashlik po karsky*, a Turkish-style lamb riblet kebab that was popular in the USSR. For the marinade, Russian cookbook author Anya von Bremzen whisks in pomegranate molasses, which also acts as a sweet-tangy glaze.

¾ cup extra-virgin olive oil
10 garlic cloves, minced
⅓ cup pomegranate molasses
3 tablespoons dried mint, crushed
2 tablespoons dried rosemary, crushed
Kosher salt and freshly ground pepper
Three 2¼-pound frenched racks of lamb,
 cut into individual chops
Herbed and Spiced Plum Compote
 (page 358), for serving

1. In a large bowl, whisk the olive oil with the garlic, pomegranate molasses, mint, rosemary, 2 teaspoons of salt and a generous pinch of pepper. Add the lamb chops and turn to coat with the pomegranate glaze; let stand at room temperature for 30 minutes.
2. Meanwhile, light a grill or preheat a grill pan. Lightly season the lamb chops with salt and pepper; grill over moderately high heat, turning, until they are lightly charred outside and medium-rare within, 4 to 6 minutes. Serve the lamb chops with the Plum Compote. —*Anya von Bremzen*

WINE Red cherry–scented, medium-bodied red: 2011 Domaine de la Bastide Côtes du Rhône.

Braised Lamb with Herb-Scented Jus

ACTIVE: 30 MIN; TOTAL: 4 HR
8 SERVINGS ●

This tender braised leg of lamb yields plenty of meat. Any leftovers are great sliced and served in a sandwich the next day.

1 large onion, quartered
1 leek, halved lengthwise
1 fennel bulb, quartered
1 large carrot, quartered
1 garlic head, halved horizontally
3 thyme sprigs
3 parsley sprigs
3 rosemary sprigs
1 fresh bay leaf
1 tablespoon whole
 black peppercorns
One 8-pound semi-boneless leg of lamb
 (aitch bone removed)
Salt
2 quarts chicken stock or
 low-sodium broth

1. Preheat the oven to 500°. In a roasting pan that's large enough to hold the lamb, spread out the vegetables, herbs and peppercorns. Season the lamb generously with salt. Set the lamb on top of the vegetables and roast for about 25 minutes, until the lamb is lightly browned.
2. Add the chicken stock to the pan and cover the pan with aluminum foil. Reduce the oven temperature to 300° and braise the lamb for 2 hours. Uncover the lamb and cook for 1 hour longer, until the meat is deeply browned on top and very tender. Let the lamb rest in the juices for 15 minutes, then transfer it to a carving board. Strain the cooking juices, discarding the solids, and spoon off the fat. Slice the lamb ¼ inch thick and serve with some of the cooking juices. —*David Mawhinney*

MAKE AHEAD The whole roasted lamb can be refrigerated overnight and served cold or covered and reheated in its cooking juices in a 300° oven.

WINE Dark, concentrated Syrah from Washington state: 2010 Owen Roe Ex Umbris.

● HEALTHY ● MAKE AHEAD ● VEGETARIAN ● STAFF FAVORITE

LAMB CHOPS MILANESE WITH
SUN-DRIED TOMATO PESTO

Lamb Roast with Mustard Pan Sauce

ACTIVE: 50 MIN; TOTAL: 2 HR 30 MIN
8 TO 10 SERVINGS

1 tablespoon fennel seeds
3 fennel bulbs—halved, cored and chopped
12 garlic cloves, smashed and peeled
5 tablespoons extra-virgin olive oil
2 tablespoons minced rosemary, plus 2 rosemary sprigs
1 teaspoon crushed red pepper
1 tablespoon coarsely cracked black peppercorns
Kosher salt
1 pound ground lamb
One 5½- to 6-pound boneless saddle of lamb (ordered from a butcher)
Freshly ground black pepper
1½ cups chicken stock or low-sodium broth
2 tablespoons unsalted butter
1 teaspoon Dijon mustard

1. In a medium skillet, toast the fennel seeds over moderate heat for 2 minutes; crush and transfer to a large bowl. In a food processor, finely chop the fresh fennel and garlic.
2. In the medium skillet, heat 3 tablespoons of the olive oil. Add the fennel-garlic mixture and cook over moderately low heat until softened, about 10 minutes. Add to the large bowl along with the minced rosemary, crushed red pepper, cracked peppercorns and 1 tablespoon of salt. Let cool and then mix in the ground lamb.
3. Preheat the oven to 425°. Spread the saddle of lamb on a work surface, fat side up. Using a knife, lightly score the fat crosswise at ½-inch intervals. Turn the saddle over and season with salt and black pepper. Spread all but 2 cups of the lamb filling over the meat; reserve the rest for another use, such as the Lamb-and-Fennel Meatballs recipe that follows. Roll up the roast, wrapping the flaps of fat around the outside and forming a neat cylinder, then tie at 1-inch intervals with kitchen string. Season the roast with salt and black pepper.
4. In a large ovenproof skillet, heat the remaining 2 tablespoons of oil. Add the roast; cook over moderately high heat until browned, 10 minutes. Add the rosemary sprigs to the skillet. Transfer the lamb to the oven and roast for 1 hour 15 minutes, or until an instant-read thermometer inserted in the center of the lamb (not the filling) registers 130°. Transfer to a carving board. Let rest for 15 minutes.
5. Meanwhile, pour off the fat in the skillet. Add the stock and simmer over moderately high heat for 3 minutes. Add the butter and simmer for 2 minutes. Strain the sauce into a bowl; whisk in the mustard. Season with salt and pepper.
6. Discard the strings from the roast. Slice the roast crosswise and serve with the mustard pan sauce. —Kay Chun

WINE Fruit-forward Italian red: 2011 Fattoria Le Pupille Morellino di Scansano.

Lamb-and-Fennel Meatballs

TOTAL: 40 MIN • 4 SERVINGS

2 cups lamb filling left over from Lamb Roast with Mustard Pan Sauce (recipe above) or 1 pound lamb-and-fennel sausage
¾ cup fresh ricotta cheese
2 tablespoons extra-virgin olive oil
One 24-ounce jar marinara sauce
2 basil sprigs
Kosher salt and freshly ground pepper
Freshly grated Parmigiano-Reggiano cheese, for serving

1. In a medium bowl, mix the lamb filling with the ricotta. Form the mixture into 2-inch balls. In a large skillet, heat the olive oil and cook the meatballs over moderate heat until browned all over, about 5 minutes.
2. Stir the marinara sauce into the meatballs and bring to a simmer. Add the basil sprigs, cover and simmer over moderate heat, stirring occasionally, until the meatballs are cooked through, about 15 minutes. Season with salt and pepper. Serve with grated cheese. —Kay Chun

WINE Fragrant, medium-bodied Chianti: 2010 Querciabella.

Cornmeal-Crusted Chicken-Fried Rabbit

ACTIVE: 35 MIN; TOTAL: 1 HR 30 MIN
4 SERVINGS

Rabbit is one of the most sustainable meats around, which is why Anya Fernald, CEO of the artisanal food–and–agritourism company called Belcampo, loves it so much. Because rabbit, like chicken, is delicate-tasting, Fernald likes to fry it with a crisp, lightly spiced coating. To add a little extra crunch, throw a bit more cornmeal into the mix.

2 cups cold buttermilk
Kosher salt
One 2½-pound rabbit—cut into 10 pieces, hind legs split
1½ cups all-purpose flour
¼ cup stone-ground cornmeal
1 teaspoon dried sage
½ teaspoon cayenne pepper
4 cups canola oil
1 cup pure olive oil
Coarse sea salt

1. In a large bowl, combine the buttermilk with 2½ teaspoons of kosher salt. Add the rabbit pieces and turn to coat. Let stand at room temperature for 1 hour.
2. Set a wire rack over a baking sheet. In a large resealable plastic bag, mix the flour with the cornmeal, dried sage, cayenne pepper and 1 teaspoon of kosher salt. Shake to blend. Remove the rabbit from the buttermilk, letting the excess drip back into the bowl, then add the rabbit to the cornmeal mixture in the bag; shake to coat thoroughly. Transfer the coated rabbit pieces to the wire rack.
3. In a large saucepan, combine the canola and olive oils and heat to 365°. Add the coated rabbit pieces and fry them, keeping the heat steady and turning the pieces once, until they are deeply golden on the outside and white throughout, 8 to 10 minutes. Transfer the fried rabbit to paper towels to drain and sprinkle with coarse sea salt. Let the fried rabbit stand for 5 minutes before serving. —Anya Fernald

WINE Fruit-forward California sparkling white: NV Scharffenberger Brut Excellence.

● HEALTHY ● MAKE AHEAD ● VEGETARIAN ● STAFF FAVORITE

LAMB-AND-FENNEL MEATBALLS

Star chef Tom Colicchio and his wife, filmmaker Lori Silverbush (with their son Mateo), set the table for a meal showcasing the best local vegetables.

Opposite: recipe, page 218.

ZUCCHINI WITH NIÇOISE OLIVES AND BURRATA

VEGETABLES & TOFU

Braised Peas with Prosciutto, Pepper and Pecorino

☺ TOTAL: 30 MIN • 10 TO 12 SERVINGS ●

⅓ cup extra-virgin olive oil
1 red onion, finely chopped
½ cup finely chopped prosciutto
(2 ounces)
Kosher salt
6 cups fresh peas (1 pound)
2 teaspoons freshly ground pepper
¼ cup freshly grated Pecorino Romano
cheese, plus more for serving

1. In a large, deep skillet, heat the olive oil until shimmering. Add the red onion, prosciutto and a pinch of salt and cook over moderate heat, stirring occasionally, until the onion is softened, 5 to 7 minutes.
2. Stir in the peas and 3 cups of water and bring to a boil. Simmer over moderately low heat, stirring occasionally, until the peas are tender and almost all of the water has evaporated, 15 to 20 minutes. Stir in the pepper and ¼ cup of cheese and season with salt. Transfer to a large bowl and serve, passing more cheese at the table. —*Ryan Hardy*

Slow-Cooked Green and Yellow Beans

TOTAL: 1 HR 15 MIN • 12 SERVINGS ● ●
A long, slow simmer over low heat is an especially good way to cook overgrown, slightly woody beans.

½ cup extra-virgin olive oil
1 very large yellow onion, minced
4 large garlic cloves, minced
3 medium tomatoes, chopped
Two 2-ounce cans anchovies in oil,
drained and chopped
½ cup capers, drained and rinsed
3½ pounds mixed green and
yellow beans, such as romano,
yellow wax and green beans
1 teaspoon finely grated lemon zest
3 tablespoons fresh lemon juice
½ cup coarsely chopped
flat-leaf parsley
Salt and freshly ground pepper

In a very large pot, heat the olive oil. Add the onion and garlic, cover and cook over moderate heat, stirring occasionally, until the onion is softened, about 4 minutes. Add the tomatoes, anchovies and capers, cover and cook over moderate heat until the tomatoes just begin to break down, about 5 minutes. Add the mixed beans and lemon zest, cover and cook for 5 minutes, stirring frequently. Add ½ cup of water, cover and cook over low heat, stirring frequently, until the beans are very tender and beginning to fall apart, about 45 minutes; add more water if the beans become too dry. Stir in the lemon juice and chopped parsley, season with salt and pepper and serve. —*Traci Des Jardins*
MAKE AHEAD The beans can be refrigerated for up to 2 days.

Chinese Long Beans with Cracked Black Pepper

☺ TOTAL: 25 MIN • 4 SERVINGS ● ● ●
This recipe from superchef Jean-Georges Vongerichten is a great example of how adding a few pantry staples (like sugar and soy sauce) can revitalize a simple vegetable dish.

1 tablespoon vegetable oil
½ small onion, thinly sliced
1 pound Chinese long beans or green
beans, cut into 3-inch lengths
½ red bell pepper, peeled and
cut into ⅓-inch dice
½ teaspoon sugar
2 tablespoons soy sauce
1 teaspoon cracked black pepper

Heat the vegetable oil in a large skillet. Add the onion and cook over moderately high heat, stirring occasionally, until lightly browned, about 3 minutes. Add the long beans and red pepper and stir-fry until the beans are slightly softened and browned in spots, about 5 minutes. Stir in the sugar. Add ¼ cup of water, cover and cook over moderately low heat until it has evaporated and the beans are tender, about 5 minutes. Add the soy sauce and pepper and cook for 1 minute. Transfer to a platter and serve.
—*Jean-Georges Vongerichten*

Zucchini with Niçoise Olives and Burrata

📷 PAGE 217
☺ TOTAL: 45 MIN • 8 TO 10 SERVINGS ●
When he was the chef at Manhattan's Gramercy Tavern in the 1990s, Tom Colicchio came up with this method of stewing tiny pieces of zucchini in just enough water to cover them. "You create a kind of zucchini broth, and what you get in the end is the essence of zucchini," he says.

¼ cup plus 2 tablespoons
extra-virgin olive oil
8 medium zucchini (about 3¼
pounds)—halved lengthwise,
seeded and cut into ⅓-inch dice
3 lemon thyme sprigs
Kosher salt
1 teaspoon finely grated
lemon zest
1 tablespoon fresh lemon juice
½ cup pitted Niçoise olives, chopped
Freshly ground pepper
¾ pound burrata or buffalo
mozzarella, sliced
Thinly sliced squash blossoms,
for garnish (optional)

1. In a very large skillet, heat 2 tablespoons of the olive oil. Add one-third of the zucchini, 1 lemon thyme sprig, a generous pinch of salt and ¼ cup of water and cook over moderately high heat, stirring occasionally, until the zucchini is barely tender and the water has evaporated, about 5 minutes; add more water if the zucchini starts to brown. Transfer the zucchini to a baking sheet to cool; discard the thyme sprig. Wipe out the skillet and repeat twice more with the remaining olive oil, lemon thyme and zucchini, adding a generous pinch of salt and ¼ cup of water to each batch.
2. In a large bowl, toss the cooled zucchini with the grated lemon zest, lemon juice and chopped olives. Season with salt and pepper and transfer to a serving platter. Arrange the burrata over the zucchini, garnish with thinly sliced squash blossoms and serve.
—*Tom Colicchio*

● HEALTHY ● MAKE AHEAD ● VEGETARIAN ● STAFF FAVORITE

ASPARAGUS

VINAIGRETTE

In a pot of salted boiling water, blanch 1 lb asparagus; transfer to an ice water bath to cool. Drain and chop. In a food processor, pulse the asparagus with 1 tbsp each of Dijon mustard, fresh lemon juice and chopped chives. Blend in ¾ cup canola oil. Season with salt and pepper. Strain through a sieve; discard the solids.

ROASTED

On a baking sheet, toss 2 lb asparagus with 2 tbsp olive oil; season with salt and pepper. Roast at 425° for 20 minutes, or until tender. In a skillet, stir ⅓ cup olive oil with 7 anchovy fillets over moderate heat until the anchovies dissolve. Add 2 minced garlic cloves; cook for 1 minute. Stir in 1 cup panko and cook until golden. Stir in 1 tbsp chopped parsley and 2 tsp lemon zest. Transfer the asparagus to a platter. Top with lemon juice and the panko.

PICKLES

Combine 2 lb asparagus and 6 dill sprigs in 2 large jars. In a large saucepan, combine 1 quart distilled white vinegar with 1 quart water, ¼ cup kosher salt, 2 tbsp sugar, 12 dried red chiles, 12 crushed garlic cloves and 2 tbsp each of black peppercorns and mustard seeds. Simmer for 10 minutes, stirring to dissolve the salt and sugar; let cool until lukewarm. Pour over the asparagus, cover and chill overnight for fresh pickles or 3 days for stronger pickles.

PESTO

In a pot of salted boiling water, cook ¾ lb spaghetti until al dente; drain, reserving ¼ cup pasta cooking water. Meanwhile, in a food processor, finely chop 1 lb asparagus; transfer to a bowl. Stir in ½ cup olive oil, ¼ cup grated Parmesan cheese, ½ cup basil leaves and 1 tbsp lemon juice; season with salt and pepper. Add the hot pasta and cooking water and toss. Season with salt and pepper. Drizzle with olive oil.

TABBOULEH

In a pot of salted boiling water, blanch 1 lb asparagus and transfer to an ice water bath to cool. Drain and chop. In a food processor, finely chop the asparagus; transfer to a bowl. Stir in 1 cup cooked bulgur wheat, 1 chopped tomato, ¼ cup chopped parsley, 2 sliced scallions, 2 tbsp chopped mint, 2 tbsp olive oil and 1 tbsp fresh lemon juice. Season with salt and pepper. —*Kay Chun*

ASPARAGUS
VINAIGRETTE

Summer Succotash Gratin

ACTIVE: 40 MIN; TOTAL: 1 HR 15 MIN
10 SERVINGS ● ●

2 tablespoons unsalted butter
¼ cup extra-virgin olive oil
1 small white onion, finely chopped
3 large garlic cloves, minced
1 large red bell pepper, finely chopped
3 cups fresh corn kernels
    (from 4 large ears)
½ pound green beans,
    cut into 1-inch lengths
3 cups cooked fava beans or thawed
    frozen baby lima beans
1 teaspoon Aleppo pepper
Salt and freshly ground black pepper
½ cup vegetable stock
2 tablespoons chopped basil
2 tablespoons finely chopped chives
1 cup heavy cream
2 large eggs, beaten
¾ cup panko (Japanese bread crumbs)
4 ounces Gruyère cheese, shredded
    (1 cup)

1. Preheat the oven to 425° and position a rack in the center. In a large, deep skillet, melt the butter in 2 tablespoons of the oil. Add the onion and garlic; cook over moderate heat, stirring, until softened, 5 minutes. Add the bell pepper, corn, green beans, favas and Aleppo pepper, season with salt and black pepper and cook, stirring, until the green beans are crisp-tender, 3 minutes. Add the stock; simmer until evaporated, 3 minutes.
2. Transfer the vegetables to a large baking dish and let cool slightly. Stir in the basil, chives, cream and eggs.
3. In a small bowl, toss the panko with the shredded cheese and the remaining 2 tablespoons of oil. Season the topping with salt and pepper; sprinkle over the succotash and bake for 10 minutes, until heated through.
4. Turn on the broiler and broil in the center of the oven for about 3 minutes, just until the top is golden. Let the gratin stand for 10 minutes, then serve. —Michael Romano
WINE Full-bodied white: 2011 Kermit Lynch Sunflower Cuvée Côtes du Rhône Blanc.

Green Beans with Parsley-Lemon Pesto

⏱ TOTAL: 40 MIN
10 TO 12 SERVINGS ● ● ● ●

½ cup pine nuts
2 cups flat-leaf parsley leaves
1 garlic clove, crushed
1 teaspoon finely grated lemon zest
1 tablespoon fresh lemon juice
¼ cup extra-virgin olive oil
Kosher salt and freshly ground pepper
4 pounds green beans, trimmed
Lemon wedges, for serving

1. In a small skillet, toast the pine nuts over moderate heat, tossing, until golden, about 5 minutes; transfer to a food processor and let cool completely.
2. Add the parsley, garlic, lemon zest and lemon juice to the food processor and pulse until the parsley is very finely chopped. With the machine on, gradually add the olive oil and process until the pesto is nearly smooth. Season with salt and pepper and scrape the pesto into a large bowl.
3. Put a steamer basket in the bottom of a pot. Fill the pot with 1 inch of water, add salt and bring to a boil. Add the green beans, cover and steam until the beans are bright green and crisp-tender, 8 to 10 minutes. Drain the beans and transfer to the large bowl. Toss with the pesto and season with salt and pepper; serve with lemon wedges. —Maria Helm Sinskey

Honey-Buttered Grilled Corn

⏱ TOTAL: 30 MIN • 4 SERVINGS ●
To accompany his barbecue, Dallas chef turned pit master Tim Byres grills corn on the cob in the husk with honey and cayenne for corn that's sweet with a hint of heat.

4 large ears of corn
1 stick unsalted butter, softened
2 tablespoons plus
    2 teaspoons honey
Kosher salt
Cayenne pepper
4 oregano or thyme sprigs

1. Pull the husks back from each ear of corn, leaving them attached to the stem. Holding an ear of corn in one hand, gather the husk together so that it covers the stem, forming a sort of handle. Remove all of the corn silk.
2. Light a grill or preheat a grill pan. In a bowl, blend the butter and honey. Working with 1 ear of corn at a time, using the husk as a handle, spread about 2 tablespoons of honey butter over the kernels. Season with salt and cayenne; press a sprig of oregano onto the kernels. Pull the husks back over the corn and tie with kitchen string. Repeat with the remaining 3 ears of corn.
3. Grill the corn over moderate heat, turning, until the husks are lightly charred and the corn kernels are just tender, about 15 minutes. Transfer the corn to a platter, remove the kitchen string and serve. —Tim Byres

Corn Queso Fundido

⏱ TOTAL: 30 MIN • 8 SERVINGS ● ●

1 pound frozen sweet corn kernels
    (3 cups), thawed
2 tablespoons extra-virgin olive oil
1 poblano chile—stemmed, seeded
    and finely diced
1 small onion, finely diced
Kosher salt
1 large garlic clove, minced
½ pound Monterey Jack cheese,
    shredded
Cilantro, radish matchsticks and thinly
    sliced jalapeños, for garnish

1. In a blender, puree half of the corn with ½ cup of water until smooth. Strain the puree through a fine sieve into a medium bowl.
2. In a cast-iron skillet, heat the oil. Add the poblano, onion, remaining corn and a pinch of salt and cook over moderate heat, stirring, until softened and barely browned, 10 minutes. Add the garlic and cook until fragrant, 2 minutes. Add the corn puree and cook, stirring, until bubbling, 2 minutes. Add the cheese and cook over low heat, stirring, until melted. Season with salt and garnish with cilantro, radish and jalapeño. Serve. —Justin Chapple
SERVE WITH Tortilla chips.

● HEALTHY ● MAKE AHEAD ● VEGETARIAN ● STAFF FAVORITE

Creamed Corn with Bacon

ACTIVE: 40 MIN; TOTAL: 1 HR 20 MIN

4 TO 6 SERVINGS ●

Lighter than standard creamed corn, this bacon-flecked version gets a little tang from sour cream and a bright kick from lime zest. A simple corn stock made from the cobs boosts the sweet corn flavor.

- 5 ears of corn—shucked, kernels cut off (5 cups) and cobs reserved
- 3 garlic cloves, 1 minced
- ½ onion, cut into 4 wedges, plus 1 cup minced onion
- 1 tablespoon coriander seeds
- 1 bay leaf

Kosher salt
- 1 teaspoon extra-virgin olive oil
- ¼ pound thick-cut bacon, cut into ¼-inch-thick lardons
- ½ cup sour cream
- 1 tablespoon unsalted butter
- ½ cup chopped cilantro

Finely grated zest of 1 lime

1. In a large pot, combine the corn cobs, whole garlic cloves, onion wedges, coriander seeds, bay leaf, 1 teaspoon of salt and 2 quarts of water. Bring to a boil and simmer briskly until the liquid has reduced to 2 cups, about 30 minutes. Strain the corn stock and discard the solids; keep the stock warm.

2. In a large skillet, heat the olive oil. Add the bacon and cook over moderate heat, stirring occasionally, until the fat has rendered and the bacon has browned, about 5 minutes. Add the minced onion and cook for 5 minutes, stirring occasionally. Add the minced garlic and cook for 1 minute. Stir in the corn kernels and 1 teaspoon of salt and cook for 2 minutes. Add the warm corn stock and bring to a simmer. Cook until the stock has reduced to ⅔ cup, about 10 minutes. Add the sour cream and simmer until the sauce begins to thicken, about 5 minutes. Stir in the butter. Remove the skillet from the heat and stir in the chopped cilantro and lime zest. Season the creamed corn with salt and serve warm. —Michael Symon

Corn on the Cob with Curry Mayonnaise and Chile Salt

⏱ TOTAL: 45 MIN • 10 SERVINGS ● ●

For his Asian take on *elote,* the grilled corn on the cob sold on the streets of Mexico, Chicago chef Bill Kim seasons mayonnaise with a curry-chile paste. In place of the cheese that's commonly sprinkled on top, he dusts the corn with a mix of lime zest, lemon zest, Thai chile and salt.

- 1 Thai chile, stemmed
- 1 teaspoon finely grated lemon zest
- 2 teaspoons finely grated lime zest

Kosher salt
- 1 cup mayonnaise
- 1 tablespoon curry powder
- 1½ tablespoons fresh lime juice
- 1 tablespoon Asian fish sauce
- 1 teaspoon *sambal oelek*
- 1 teaspoon ground turmeric
- 2 medium garlic cloves, minced
- 1½ tablespoons finely chopped cilantro, plus more for garnish
- 10 ears of corn

1. In a food processor, combine the Thai chile with the lemon zest, 1 teaspoon of the lime zest and ¼ cup of salt and pulse until the chile is finely chopped and incorporated. Transfer the chile-lime salt to a bowl.

2. In a medium bowl, whisk the mayonnaise with the curry powder, lime juice, fish sauce, *sambal oelek,* turmeric, garlic, the 1½ tablespoons of cilantro and the remaining 1 teaspoon of lime zest.

3. Peel back the corn husks, keeping them attached. Discard the silk. Fold the husks back over the corn and tie the tops with kitchen string. Transfer the corn to a very large bowl, cover with water and let soak for 10 minutes. Remove the corn from the water and blot dry.

4. Light a grill. Grill the corn in the husks over high heat, turning, until the kernels are crisp-tender, about 15 minutes. Let cool slightly, then carefully remove the husks and transfer the corn to a platter. Spread the curry mayonnaise all over the corn, sprinkle with the chile-lime salt and chopped cilantro and serve. —Bill Kim

Sweet and Tangy Corn with Roasted Peppers

TOTAL: 1 HR • 8 TO 10 SERVINGS ● ● ○

Star chef Tom Colicchio serves this mix of corn kernels and roasted red peppers as a salad, but it also makes a terrific relish for grilled fish or poultry.

- 3 red bell peppers
- ½ cup sugar
- ½ cup plus 2 tablespoons white wine vinegar
- 10 ears of corn, shucked and kernels cut off the cobs (about 10 cups)
- 3 medium leeks, white and light green parts only, halved lengthwise and thinly sliced crosswise
- 1 cup thinly sliced scallions, preferably red (about 8 scallions)

Kosher salt and freshly ground black pepper

1. Roast the bell peppers directly over a gas flame or under a preheated broiler, turning frequently, until they are charred all over. Transfer the peppers to a large bowl, cover tightly with plastic and let cool completely. Peel, seed and stem the peppers, then cut them into ⅓-inch dice.

2. Meanwhile, in a small saucepan, combine the sugar with 1 tablespoon of water and cook over moderate heat without stirring until lightly golden in color, 3 to 5 minutes. Add the vinegar and cook until the caramel dissolves, about 1 minute; let the dressing cool completely.

3. In a large saucepan of salted boiling water, blanch the corn kernels and sliced leeks until crisp-tender, 3 to 5 minutes; drain well and let cool completely.

4. In a large bowl, toss the corn and leeks with the roasted peppers, scallions and sweet-tart dressing. Season the corn with salt and pepper, transfer to a platter and serve.
—Tom Colicchio

MAKE AHEAD The recipe can be prepared through Step 3 one day ahead; refrigerate the roasted peppers, dressing and blanched corn and leeks separately.

● HEALTHY ● MAKE AHEAD ○ VEGETARIAN ● STAFF FAVORITE

Sautéed Collard Greens with Roasted Peanuts

⏱ **TOTAL: 30 MIN • 4 SERVINGS** ● ● ○

¼ cup extra-virgin olive oil

2 garlic cloves, thinly sliced

2 bunches of tender young collard greens (1½ pounds)—stems and ribs discarded, leaves thinly sliced

2 cups packed baby arugula (2 ounces), finely chopped

2 teaspoons finely grated lemon zest

2 tablespoons fresh lemon juice

4 dried árbol chiles, crumbled (2 teaspoons)

Kosher salt

½ cup roasted peanuts, chopped

In a very large skillet, heat 2 tablespoons of the olive oil. Add the garlic and cook over moderate heat, stirring, until fragrant, about 30 seconds. Add the collards and arugula in large handfuls, letting each batch wilt slightly before adding more. Cook, tossing frequently, until the collards start to soften, 5 to 7 minutes. Add the lemon zest, lemon juice and crumbled chiles, season with salt and toss to evenly coat the greens. Remove the skillet from the heat and stir in the remaining 2 tablespoons of olive oil. Transfer the greens to a serving platter, top with the peanuts and serve. —*Sean Brock*

Sautéed Spring Greens with Bacon and Mustard Seeds

⏱ **TOTAL: 20 MIN • 4 SERVINGS** ● ● ○

2 ounces thick-cut bacon, finely diced

2 tablespoons extra-virgin olive oil

1 large shallot, thinly sliced

1 hot red chile, seeded and minced

1 tablespoon yellow mustard seeds

1¼ pounds mixed young spring greens, such as dandelion, mustard, collards, Tuscan kale and spinach—stems and inner ribs trimmed, leaves cut into ribbons

Salt and freshly ground pepper

1 tablespoon white wine vinegar

In a large skillet, cook the diced bacon in the olive oil over moderate heat, stirring, until golden, about 3 minutes. Add the shallot, chile and mustard seeds and cook until softened, 2 to 3 minutes. Add the greens, season with salt and pepper and cook, tossing frequently, until wilted and tender, 5 to 6 minutes. Stir in the vinegar and serve. —*Grace Parisi*

MAKE AHEAD The cooked greens can be refrigerated overnight.

Sautéed Spring Greens and Manchego Frittata

⏱ **TOTAL: 35 MIN • 6 SERVINGS** ●

8 large eggs, beaten

2 ounces Manchego cheese, shredded (¾ cup)

Sautéed Spring Greens with Bacon and Mustard Seeds (recipe above)

Salt and freshly ground pepper

2 tablespoons canola oil

1. Preheat the broiler and position a rack 6 inches from the heat. In a large bowl, whisk the eggs with the Manchego and fold in the greens. Season with salt and pepper.

2. In a large nonstick ovenproof skillet, heat the oil. Add the eggs and cook over moderate heat until they're lightly browned and nearly set on the bottom and side, about 3 minutes. Broil for 1 to 2 minutes, until the eggs are set and lightly browned on top. Slide the frittata onto a large plate, cut into wedges and serve hot or warm. —*Grace Parisi*

Sautéed Spinach with Pancetta and Dried Cranberries

⏱ **TOTAL: 30 MIN**

10 TO 12 SERVINGS ●

½ pound thinly sliced pancetta, cut into thin strips

1 tablespoon extra-virgin olive oil

1 cup dried cranberries, chopped

1 small shallot, minced

2½ pounds baby spinach

Kosher salt and freshly ground pepper

In a large saucepan, cook the pancetta in the oil over moderately high heat until browned, 6 minutes. Add the dried cranberries and shallot and cook, stirring, until the shallot just starts to brown, 4 minutes. Stir in the spinach in large handfuls; let each batch wilt slightly before adding more. Cook, tossing, until all of the spinach is wilted, 3 to 5 minutes. Season with salt and pepper, transfer to a bowl and serve. —*Maria Helm Sinksey*

Almond-Milk Creamed Spinach

ACTIVE: 30 MIN; TOTAL: 1 HR

6 SERVINGS ● ○ ○

This silky spinach dish is simmered with unsweetened almond milk to give it a light creaminess.

Four 5-ounce bags baby spinach

4 tablespoons unsalted butter

2 shallots, thinly sliced

3 tablespoons all-purpose flour

2 cups unsweetened almond milk

½ cup grated Parmigiano-Reggiano or Cotija cheese

Salt and freshly ground pepper

¾ cup panko (Japanese bread crumbs)

2 tablespoons finely chopped marcona almonds

1. Preheat the oven to 425°. In a large saucepan, heat 1 inch of water. Add the spinach by the handful; allow each handful to wilt before adding more. When the spinach is wilted, drain it, pressing out as much water as possible. Wipe out the pot.

2. Melt 2 tablespoons of the butter in the pot. Add the shallots; cook over moderate heat until softened. Stir in the flour; cook for 1 minute. Add the almond milk; simmer until very thick, whisking occasionally, 5 minutes. Stir in the cheese and spinach. Season with salt and pepper. Spoon into a baking dish.

3. In a microwave-safe bowl, heat the remaining 2 tablespoons of butter until melted. Stir in the panko and almonds and sprinkle over the creamed spinach. Bake for 15 minutes, until golden. Serve. —*Grace Parisi*

MAKE AHEAD The recipe can be prepared through Step 2 and refrigerated overnight.

● HEALTHY ● MAKE AHEAD ○ VEGETARIAN ● STAFF FAVORITE

SAUTÉED COLLARD GREENS
WITH ROASTED PEANUTS

Asian Stir-Fried Spinach

⏲ TOTAL: 10 MIN • 4 SERVINGS ● ●

With the addition of unsweetened coconut milk, this dairy-free dish is like an Asian version of creamed spinach.

- 2 tablespoons grapeseed oil
- 3 garlic cloves, minced
- 10 ounces baby spinach
- ¼ cup unsweetened coconut milk
- 1 tablespoon fish sauce
- Fried onions (preferably Thai) or Durkee dehydrated onions, for serving

In a large skillet, heat the grapeseed oil until shimmering. Add the garlic and cook over high heat, stirring, for 30 seconds. Add the spinach all at once and toss until nearly wilted. Add the coconut milk and fish sauce and cook until the spinach is tender and the coconut milk has reduced, about 3 minutes. Top with fried onions and serve. —*Paul Qui*

Saag Paneer

⏲ TOTAL: 40 MIN • 2 SERVINGS ●

For this easy take on the classic Indian dish, you can replace the usual *paneer* with halloumi, a salty, firm Greek cheese.

- 3 tablespoons canola oil
- 8 ounces halloumi cheese or *paneer,* cut into ¾-inch cubes
- ¾ cup finely chopped white onion
- 3 garlic cloves, minced
- 2 teaspoons finely grated peeled fresh ginger
- 1 tablespoon unsalted butter
- 1½ teaspoons garam masala
- ¼ teaspoon freshly grated nutmeg
- Two 10-ounce bags leafy spinach, stemmed
- Kosher salt and freshly ground pepper
- 2 tablespoons heavy cream
- 2 teaspoons fresh lemon juice

1. In a large nonstick skillet, heat 2 tablespoons of the oil. Add the cheese and cook over moderate heat, turning frequently, until golden on all sides, 3 minutes. Using a slotted spoon, transfer the cheese to a plate.

2. Add the remaining 1 tablespoon of oil to the skillet along with the onion, garlic and ginger and cook over moderately low heat until the onion is softened, 5 minutes. Add the butter, garam masala and nutmeg and cook, stirring, for 1 minute. Add the spinach in batches, stirring often, until it wilts. Season with salt and pepper. Add ½ cup of water, cover and simmer until the spinach is very tender, about 5 minutes. Uncover and cook until most of the liquid has evaporated, about 5 minutes. Stir in the cream, lemon juice and cheese and serve. —*Kay Chun*

SERVE WITH Steamed basmati rice.

Spinach Spoon Bread

ACTIVE: 15 MIN; TOTAL: 1 HR

12 SERVINGS ● ● ●

Spoon bread, a Southern dish, is like a cross between corn bread and a savory pudding. Whipped egg whites give this spinach spoon bread an airy, soufflé-like texture.

- 3 tablespoons unsalted butter, melted, plus more for greasing the dish
- 10 ounces baby spinach
- 3 cups buttermilk
- 3 large eggs, separated
- 1 cup medium-grind yellow cornmeal
- ¼ cup plus 2 tablespoons all-purpose flour
- 1 tablespoon sugar
- 1½ teaspoons baking soda
- Scant 1 teaspoon kosher salt
- Pinch of freshly grated nutmeg
- Pinch of freshly ground white pepper

1. Preheat the oven to 350° and butter a 9-by-13-inch baking dish or very large enameled cast-iron skillet. In a saucepan of boiling water, cook the spinach just until wilted, about 30 seconds. Drain and cool under running water, then squeeze out as much water as possible. Finely chop the spinach.

2. In a large bowl, whisk the buttermilk with the egg yolks, cornmeal, flour, sugar, baking soda, salt, nutmeg, white pepper and the 3 tablespoons of melted butter. Fold in the chopped spinach.

3. In a clean bowl, using a handheld electric mixer, beat the egg whites until soft peaks form. Fold the whites into the batter and scrape it into the prepared baking dish.

4. Bake the spoon bread in the center of the oven for about 45 minutes, until golden. Let cool slightly, then serve. —*Tanya Holland*

MAKE AHEAD The spoon bread can be made earlier in the day and kept at room temperature; reheat in a 325° oven.

Swiss Chard with Sweet Garlic

⏲ TOTAL: 45 MIN • 8 SERVINGS ● ●

New York City chef Michael White transforms four ingredients into a great vegetable side: He simmers garlic in milk, so it's especially sweet, and combines it with sautéed greens.

- 1 head of garlic, cloves peeled and lightly smashed
- 2 cups milk
- ¼ cup extra-virgin olive oil
- 3 pounds Swiss chard, stems cut into ½-inch pieces and leaves cut into wide ribbons
- Salt and freshly ground pepper

1. In a saucepan, boil the garlic and 1 cup of the milk. Simmer over moderate heat for 5 minutes. Drain and return the garlic to the saucepan. Add the remaining 1 cup of milk and bring to a boil. Simmer over moderate heat until the garlic is just softened and the milk is reduced to ¼ cup, 10 minutes. Transfer the garlic to a mini processor with 2 tablespoons of the infused milk and 1 tablespoon of the oil; puree. Discard the remaining milk.

2. In a large saucepan of salted boiling water, cook the chard stems until crisptender, 5 minutes. Add the chard leaves and cook until tender, 2 minutes. Drain, shaking and pressing out the excess water.

3. In a large skillet, heat the remaining 3 tablespoons of oil until shimmering. Add the chard and cook over moderately high heat, stirring, for 2 minutes. Add the garlic cream and cook, stirring occasionally, until the cream coats the leaves, 4 minutes longer. Season with salt and pepper and serve.

—*Michael White*

Kale, Chard and Soppressata Pie

ACTIVE: 45 MIN; TOTAL: 3 HR
MAKES ONE 9-BY-13-INCH PIE ● ●

DOUGH

- 3 cups all-purpose flour
- ½ cup freshly grated Parmigiano-Reggiano cheese
- ½ teaspoon kosher salt
- 2½ sticks unsalted butter, cubed and chilled
- ⅓ cup ice water

FILLING

- 2 tablespoons extra-virgin olive oil
- 2 bunches of Swiss chard (1 pound), stems cut into ½-inch pieces and leaves chopped
- 2 bunches of Tuscan kale (1 pound), stems discarded and leaves chopped
- 2 garlic cloves, minced

Kosher salt and freshly ground pepper

- 4 ounces *ricotta salata* cheese, crumbled
- 2 ounces sliced soppressata, finely chopped
- 4 large eggs—3 lightly beaten, 1 beaten with 1 tablespoon water
- 2 tablespoons all-purpose flour

1. MAKE THE DOUGH In a food processor, pulse the flour, cheese and salt. Pulse in the butter until the mixture resembles small peas. Sprinkle with the ice water and pulse until the dough is evenly moistened and just starts to come together. Scrape the dough out onto a work surface and gather it into a ball; divide in half and pat each half into a 6-inch disk. Wrap the disks in plastic and refrigerate until well chilled, about 1 hour.

2. MEANWHILE, MAKE THE FILLING In a large skillet, heat the olive oil. Add the Swiss chard stems and cook over moderate heat, stirring occasionally, until tender, 8 to 10 minutes. Add the kale and garlic and cook until the kale is wilted, about 3 minutes. Stir in the Swiss chard leaves and season with salt and pepper; cover and cook until wilted, about 3 minutes. Drain the greens in a colander and let cool to lukewarm.

3. In a bowl, mix the greens, *ricotta salata* and soppressata. Season the filling with salt and pepper, then stir in the beaten eggs.

4. Preheat the oven to 400°. On a lightly floured work surface and using a lightly floured rolling pin, roll out 1 piece of the dough to an 11-by-15-inch rectangle, a scant ⅛ inch thick. Ease the dough into a 9-by-13-inch baking pan, pressing the dough into the corners. Refrigerate the bottom crust until chilled, about 15 minutes.

5. Sprinkle the flour over the chilled crust and scatter the filling evenly over the bottom. Trim any dough that's more than ½ inch above the filling. Roll out the remaining dough to an 11-by-15-inch rectangle, a scant ⅛ inch thick. Ease the dough over the filling and trim the overhang to ½ inch, then fold the rim over onto itself and pinch to seal. Cut a few slits in the top of the pie and brush with the egg wash.

6. Bake the pie until just starting to brown, 20 minutes. Reduce the oven temperature to 375°; bake for 30 to 35 minutes longer, until golden. Let the pie cool for 15 minutes before cutting it into squares; serve warm or at room temperature. —*Susan Spungen*

Tuscan Kale alla Parmigiana

TOTAL: 45 MIN • 10 SERVINGS ● ●

- 3 pounds Tuscan kale, stems discarded and leaves coarsely shredded
- 1 quart heavy cream

Pinch of finely grated nutmeg

Salt and freshly ground pepper

- 1 cup freshly grated Parmigiano-Reggiano cheese

1. In a pot of salted boiling water, cook the kale until tender, 5 minutes. Drain and rinse under cold water. Squeeze the kale very dry.

2. In a saucepan, bring the cream to a boil. Simmer over moderate heat until nearly reduced by half, 25 minutes. Stir in the nutmeg and season with salt and pepper. Add the kale and simmer until it is coated in a thick, creamy sauce, 7 minutes. Stir in the grated cheese, transfer to a bowl and serve. —*Michael Tusk*

Fiery Stir-Fried Iceberg Lettuce with Basil

TOTAL: 20 MIN • 4 SERVINGS ● ●

Iceberg lettuce, the 1970s salad bar mainstay, is cooked until it's juicy, spicy, crunchy and aromatic.

- 1 tablespoon canola oil
- 3 oil-packed anchovy fillets, drained and chopped
- 2 garlic cloves, finely chopped
- 1 head of iceberg lettuce (1 pound), leaves torn into large pieces
- 1 Thai bird chile, thinly sliced
- 1 teaspoon Asian fish sauce
- 2 teaspoons fresh lemon juice

Kosher salt and freshly ground pepper

- ¼ cup coarsely chopped Thai basil

In a large skillet, heat the canola oil. Add the anchovies and garlic and stir-fry over moderately low heat until the anchovies dissolve, about 2 minutes. Add the lettuce, chile and fish sauce and stir-fry until the lettuce is just wilted and coated in the sauce, about 2 minutes longer. Stir in the lemon juice and season with salt and pepper. Stir in half of the basil and transfer the stir-fried lettuce to a large platter. Garnish with the remaining basil and serve. —*Kay Chun*

OKRA TRICK

Chef Suvir Saran turns okra doubters into okra lovers with his method of frying thin strips until crunchy, then tossing them with the spice blend garam masala, onion, lemon juice, tomato and cilantro.

Sichuan-Style Hot-and-Sour Cabbage

TOTAL: 1 HR • 12 SERVINGS ●

- ¼ cup plus 2 tablespoons chicken stock or low-sodium broth
- 2 tablespoons Chinese light soy sauce (see Note)
- 2 tablespoons Chinese mushroom soy sauce (see Note)
- ¼ cup Chinese black vinegar (see Note)
- 1 tablespoon dark palm sugar
- ¾ teaspoon finely grated fresh ginger
- ½ teaspoon minced garlic
- 1½ teaspoons cornstarch
- 2 medium heads of green cabbage (4 pounds)—quartered, cored and cut into 1½-inch pieces
- ¼ cup canola or peanut oil
- 4 whole dried Chinese red chiles, broken in half, plus more crumbled for garnish
- 2 teaspoons whole Sichuan peppercorns
- Salt

1. In a small bowl, combine the chicken stock, soy sauces, vinegar, sugar, ginger, garlic and cornstarch; whisk to blend.
2. In a pot of salted boiling water, cook the thickest pieces of cabbage for 1 minute; add the remaining cabbage and cook for 30 seconds longer. Drain and transfer to a bowl of ice water to cool; drain and pat dry.
3. In a wok or very large skillet, heat 2 tablespoons of the oil until shimmering. Add half of the broken dried red chiles and 1 teaspoon of the Sichuan peppercorns and stir until fragrant, 10 seconds. Add half of the cabbage and stir-fry over high heat until charred in spots, 5 minutes. Add 3 tablespoons of the soy sauce mixture and cook, tossing, until all of the liquid has been absorbed, 1 minute. Add 2 more tablespoons of the soy sauce mixture and stir-fry until absorbed; repeat one last time, then transfer the cabbage to a large bowl. Repeat with the remaining 2 tablespoons of oil, dried chiles, Sichuan peppercorns, cabbage and soy sauce mixture.

4. Return the first batch of cabbage to the wok and cook until all of the cabbage is nicely glazed. Season with salt, transfer to a platter and garnish with crumbled dried chile peppers. Serve. —*Sang Yoon*

NOTE Light and mushroom soy sauces and black vinegar are available at Asian markets.

Sautéed Brussels Sprout Slaw with Sweet Peppers

TOTAL: 30 MIN • 12 SERVINGS ● ●

- 2½ pounds brussels sprouts, thinly sliced
- 1 large yellow bell pepper, thinly sliced
- 1 large red bell pepper, thinly sliced
- 1 large Spanish onion, thinly sliced
- ½ cup extra-virgin olive oil
- Salt and freshly ground pepper
- 1 tablespoon finely chopped flat-leaf parsley

1. In a large bowl, toss the brussels sprouts with the bell peppers and onion.
2. In each of 2 large skillets, heat ¼ cup of the olive oil until shimmering. Add the vegetables, season with salt and pepper and cook over high heat, stirring, until browned in spots and crisp-tender, about 4 minutes. Transfer the vegetables to a large bowl and garnish with the parsley. Serve right away. —*Tanya Holland*

Citrus-Spiced Red Cabbage

TOTAL: 50 MIN PLUS 1 HR MARINATING
6 SERVINGS ●

- One 1-pound red cabbage—halved, cored and sliced ⅛ inch thick
- ½ cup fresh lemon juice
- ½ cup fresh orange juice
- ⅓ cup sugar
- ¼ cup duck fat or unsalted butter
- 1 large onion, thinly sliced
- 2 teaspoons thyme leaves
- 1 árbol chile with seeds, crumbled
- ½ teaspoon ground allspice
- Kosher salt and freshly ground pepper
- 1½ cups dry red wine
- ½ cup port

1. In a large bowl, toss the cabbage, lemon juice and orange juice. Let stand at room temperature for 1 hour, tossing occasionally.
2. Set a large enameled cast-iron casserole over moderate heat for 1 minute. Add the sugar in an even layer and cook without stirring until melted and starting to caramelize, 3 minutes. Stir in the duck fat. Add the onion, thyme, chile, allspice, 1 teaspoon of salt and ¼ teaspoon of pepper. Cook over moderate heat, stirring often, until the onion is lightly caramelized, 7 minutes. Stir in the wine and port and cook over moderately high heat until the liquid is reduced to ⅔ cup, 5 minutes. Add the cabbage and accumulated juices and 1 teaspoon of salt. Cook over moderate heat, stirring often, until the cabbage is tender and glazed, 20 minutes. Season with salt and pepper. Serve hot or warm. —*Suzanne Goin*

Roasted Brussels Sprouts with Toasted Pecans and Avocado

ACTIVE: 20 MIN; TOTAL: 40 MIN
8 SERVINGS ● ● ●

- ½ cup pecans
- 2½ pounds brussels sprouts
- ¼ cup extra-virgin olive oil
- Salt and freshly ground pepper
- 1 Hass avocado, cut into ½-inch dice
- 1 teaspoon chopped thyme
- 2 tablespoons balsamic vinegar

1. Preheat the oven to 400°. Spread the pecans in a pie plate and bake for 5 minutes, until toasted. Let cool, then coarsely chop.
2. In a large saucepan of salted boiling water, blanch the brussels sprouts until bright green, 3 minutes. Drain well, cut in half and pat dry.
3. On 2 large rimmed baking sheets, toss the brussels sprouts with the olive oil. Season with salt and pepper and turn them cut side down. Roast in the upper and lower thirds of the oven for 20 minutes, until just tender and nicely browned on the bottom; switch the baking sheets halfway through roasting.
4. In a bowl, toss the brussels sprouts with the pecans, avocado and thyme. Season with salt and pepper, drizzle with the vinegar and serve. —*Jean-Georges Vongerichten*

Crushed Beets with Herbs and Arugula

ACTIVE: 20 MIN; TOTAL: 1 HR

4 SERVINGS ● ● ●

In this unusual dish from Uruguayan chef Marcelo Betancourt, beets are boiled in their skins until cooked through, then lightly flattened and pan-seared until crispy. Crushing the beets gives them an excellent, extra-tender texture. If you accidentally break a beet into pieces while flattening it, don't worry; it'll still work in the recipe.

- 1 head of garlic
- 4 medium beets (1¼ pounds)

Kosher salt

- 2 tablespoons unsalted butter
- 2 tablespoons extra-virgin olive oil
- ½ small onion, thinly sliced
- 4 thyme sprigs
- 4 small rosemary sprigs

Freshly ground pepper

- 2 ounces baby arugula (2 cups)

1. Preheat the oven to 375°. Cut off the top ½ inch of the head of garlic. Wrap the garlic in aluminum foil and bake for about 45 minutes, until very soft.

2. Meanwhile, in a medium saucepan, cover the beets with cold water and add a generous pinch of salt. Simmer the beets over moderately low heat until tender, 30 minutes. Drain and let cool slightly, then peel the beets.

3. On a work surface, using a mug or the bottom of a small bowl, gradually press down on the beets until they are about ¾ inch thick and cracked around the edges; try to keep the beets whole.

4. In a large cast-iron skillet, melt the butter in the olive oil. Add the beets and cook over moderately high heat until crusty on the bottom, about 4 minutes. Turn the beets and scatter the onion, thyme, rosemary and roasted head of garlic all around. Season with salt and pepper. Cook over moderately high heat, gently stirring the onion and herbs, until the onion is just soft and the beets are crusty, about 4 minutes longer.

5. Transfer the beets, onion and herbs to plates or a serving platter and scatter the baby arugula over the top. Squeeze the roasted garlic cloves from their skins and scatter them over the top. Spoon the pan juices over the arugula and serve.

—Marcelo Betancourt

MAKE AHEAD The roasted garlic and boiled beets can be refrigerated separately for up to 2 days; let return to room temperature before proceeding.

Grilled Radicchio with Lemon-Hazelnut Dressing

☺ TOTAL: 35 MIN • 6 SERVINGS ● ● ●

Radicchio can be intensely bitter; grilling it mellows the bitterness and gives it a smoky, almost meaty flavor.

- ¼ cup plus 2 tablespoons hazelnuts
- ¼ cup freshly squeezed lemon juice
- ¼ cup extra-virgin olive oil, plus more for brushing
- 2 tablespoons freshly grated Parmigiano-Reggiano cheese

Kosher salt and freshly ground black pepper

Three 6-ounce heads of radicchio, halved through the core

1. In a skillet, toast the hazelnuts over moderate heat, shaking the pan, until fragrant, 5 minutes. Transfer the nuts to a clean towel and rub off the skins. Coarsely chop ¼ cup of the hazelnuts; finely grind the remaining 2 tablespoons of hazelnuts.

2. In a medium bowl, whisk the lemon juice with the ¼ cup of olive oil, the cheese and the 2 tablespoons of finely ground hazelnuts. Season the lemon-hazelnut dressing with salt and freshly ground pepper.

3. Light a grill. Brush the radicchio halves with olive oil and season with salt and pepper. Grill over moderately high heat, turning, until the edges are lightly charred, about 4 minutes. Transfer to a platter and let cool slightly. Spoon the dressing on top, sprinkle with the chopped hazelnuts and serve.

—Linda Aldredge

Braised Root Vegetables and Cabbage with Fall Fruit

ACTIVE: 25 MIN; TOTAL: 1 HR

6 SERVINGS ● ● ●

When F&W editors first saw the recipe for this simple braised vegetable dish from legendary French chef Alain Ducasse, we were skeptical; the combination of ingredients just seemed so odd. But gently cooking the fruit and vegetables in chicken broth makes them surprisingly delicious. The dish has since become our favorite cold-weather side for chicken, pork and duck.

- 2 tablespoons unsalted butter
- 2 tablespoons extra-virgin olive oil
- 1 small white onion, thinly sliced
- 4 carrots, sliced ⅓ inch thick
- 4 large radishes, quartered
- 4 baby turnips, peeled and quartered
- ¾ pound Savoy cabbage, cored and coarsely chopped
- 1 Golden Delicious apple— peeled, cored and cut into 1-inch pieces
- 2 garlic cloves, thinly sliced

Kosher salt and freshly ground black pepper

- ½ cup low-sodium chicken broth
- 1 Bosc pear—peeled, cored and cut into 1-inch pieces

1. Preheat the oven to 350°. In a large, deep ovenproof skillet, melt the butter in the olive oil. When the foam subsides, add the onion, carrots, radishes, turnips, cabbage, apple and garlic. Season with salt and freshly ground black pepper and cook over high heat, stirring, until the vegetables are lightly browned in spots, about 6 minutes. Add the chicken broth and bring to a boil. Cover the skillet and braise in the oven for 25 to 30 minutes, until tender.

2. Remove from the oven, stir in the pear pieces and cook over high heat until the liquid is evaporated and the pear is tender, about 5 minutes. Transfer the braised fruits and vegetables to a bowl and serve.

—Alain Ducasse

● HEALTHY ● MAKE AHEAD ● VEGETARIAN ● STAFF FAVORITE

BEETS

PICKLES

Wrap 4 small red beets in foil and roast for 1 hour at 450°. Peel and quarter the beets. In a saucepan, simmer 1 cup raw unfiltered apple cider vinegar with 1 cup water, 3 crushed garlic cloves, 3 tbsp sugar, 2 tsp black peppercorns and 1 tbsp kosher salt until the sugar is dissolved. Let cool for 15 minutes. In a 1-quart glass jar, layer the beets with 1 small red onion cut into wedges, 4 hard-boiled eggs and 6 dill sprigs. Cover with the pickling liquid and let stand for 2 hours, then refrigerate overnight.

LATKES

Using a mandoline or julienne peeler, shred 1 large peeled baking potato and pat it dry. Shred 2 medium peeled beets and pat dry. Toss both in a bowl with ¼ cup all-purpose flour, 1 tbsp thyme leaves and 2 large eggs; season with salt and pepper. Heat 1 tbsp canola oil in a large nonstick skillet and add three ½-cup mounds of the latke mixture; press to flatten. Fry for about 7 minutes. Turn, add another 1 tbsp oil and fry for about 7 minutes longer, until crisp. Repeat to fry 3 more latkes. Drain and serve with sour cream.

SALAD

Wrap 2 medium golden beets in foil and roast for 1 hour at 450°. Peel and cut the beets into wedges. Reserve the beet greens and tear into bite-size pieces. In a saucepan of boiling water, cook 1 cup green du Puy lentils for 20 minutes; drain and cool under running water. In a large bowl, whisk 6 tbsp olive oil with 2 tbsp each of Dijon mustard and lemon juice. Add the beets, beet greens, lentils and 2 thinly sliced scallions and toss. Season with salt and pepper.

RELISH

On the large holes of a box grater, grate 2 medium peeled beets and put in a bowl. Stir in ½ cup chopped pitted kalamata olives, ¼ cup each of chopped parsley, chopped basil and olive oil and 1 tbsp fresh lemon juice.

HORS D'OEUVRES

In a bowl, mix 4 cups kosher salt with 2 tbsp caraway seeds, ¼ cup chopped sage leaves and 5 sage sprigs. Spread 1 cup in a large baking dish and top with 15 scrubbed baby beets. Top with the remaining salt and bake at 350° for 40 minutes. Crack the salt crust, dust off the beets and serve with yogurt. —*Kay Chun*

PICKLED BEETS
AND EGGS

Carrots with Caraway Yogurt and Wheat Berries

ACTIVE: 30 MIN; TOTAL: 1 HR
6 TO 8 SERVINGS ● ● ○

Tender, young carrots are best in this hearty, room-temperature vegetarian dish. The carrots are simply cooked with onion, garlic and sweet paprika; the resulting vegetable broth can be used later on as a flavorful base for a soup or stew.

- ¼ cup extra-virgin olive oil
- 1 large red onion, finely chopped
- 4 garlic cloves, finely chopped
- 1 tablespoon sweet Hungarian paprika, plus more for garnish

Sea salt

- 1½ pounds young carrots, scrubbed

Freshly ground black pepper

- 2 tablespoons chopped chives
- ¾ cup plain whole-milk Greek yogurt
- ¼ teaspoon caraway seeds
- 4 cups cooked wheat berries

1. In a medium saucepan, heat 3 tablespoons of the olive oil until shimmering. Add the onion and garlic and cook over moderate heat until softened, about 6 minutes. Add the 1 tablespoon of paprika and a generous pinch of salt and cook for 1 minute, stirring. Add 4 cups of water and the carrots and bring to a simmer. Cover and cook over low heat until tender, about 20 minutes. Season with salt and pepper.

2. Drain the carrots (reserving the vegetable broth for another use, if desired) and transfer to a platter. Sprinkle with 1 tablespoon of the chopped chives.

3. In a small bowl, mix the yogurt with the remaining 1 tablespoon of chives and season with salt and pepper. In a small skillet, heat the remaining 1 tablespoon of olive oil. Add the caraway seeds and toast over moderate heat until fragrant, about 1 minute. Drizzle the caraway oil over the yogurt and sprinkle with paprika. Serve the carrots with the yogurt and wheat berries. —*Sarah Copeland*

MAKE AHEAD The cooked carrots, caraway yogurt and wheat berries can be refrigerated separately for up to 3 days.

Roasted Carrots with Caraway and Coriander

TOTAL: 1 HR • 4 SERVINGS ● ● ●

This lovely dish combines a trio of ingredients from the same family—sweet roasted carrots, coriander and caraway—all served with a tangy buttermilk dressing.

- 1 teaspoon ground caraway
- 1 teaspoon ground coriander
- 2 tablespoons honey
- ½ teaspoon whole caraway seeds
- ½ cup cold buttermilk
- ½ cup cold plain whole-milk Greek yogurt
- ½ serrano chile, seeded and minced

Kosher salt

- 24 thin baby carrots (1 pound), tops discarded and carrots scrubbed
- 2 tablespoons unsalted butter, cubed
- ¼ cup sprouted mung beans or sprouted lentils
- ¼ cup salted roasted sunflower seeds
- ½ cup cilantro leaves

Lime wedges, for serving

1. Preheat the oven to 350°. In a small skillet, toast the ground caraway and coriander over low heat, stirring, until fragrant, about 2 minutes. Remove from the heat and stir in the honey.

2. In another small skillet, toast the whole caraway seeds over low heat, stirring, until fragrant, about 3 minutes. Transfer the toasted seeds to a small bowl and stir in the buttermilk, yogurt, serrano chile and half of the honey mixture. Season the dressing with salt and refrigerate.

3. Spread the carrots on a large baking sheet and season with salt. Toss with the remaining honey mixture and top with the butter. Roast for about 30 minutes, stirring occasionally, until the carrots are tender and slightly charred on the bottom.

4. Pour the buttermilk dressing onto a platter in a thin layer. Arrange the carrots on the dressing and top with the sprouted beans, sunflower seeds and cilantro. Serve with lime wedges. —*Nicolaus Balla*

Triple-Cheese Curried Cauliflower Gratin

ACTIVE: 45 MIN; TOTAL: 3 HR 30 MIN
12 SERVINGS ● ● ●

- 3 cups heavy cream
- ¼ cup *vadouvan* (see Note)
- 3 tablespoons finely chopped fresh curry leaves (½ ounce; see Note)
- 1 teaspoon chopped garlic

Salt and freshly ground white pepper

- 6 ounces Cantal cheese, shredded
- 6 ounces Emmental cheese, shredded
- ¾ cup freshly grated Parmigiano-Reggiano cheese (2½ ounces)

Extra-virgin olive oil, for brushing

- 2 pounds Yukon Gold potatoes, peeled and sliced ⅛ inch thick
- 1 head of cauliflower (2½ pounds)— halved lengthwise, cored and sliced ⅛ inch thick, crumbled pieces reserved
- 1 large white onion, very thinly sliced

1. In a medium saucepan, combine the cream with the *vadouvan,* curry leaves and garlic and bring to a simmer. Let stand off the heat for 15 minutes to infuse. Generously season the cream with salt and white pepper.

2. Preheat the oven to 350°. In a bowl, mix together all three cheeses. Lightly brush a 7-quart enameled cast-iron casserole with olive oil. Arrange one slightly overlapping layer of potatoes in it followed by one layer of the cauliflower (including the crumbles). Scatter some of the onion on top and sprinkle with ¾ cup of the cheese. Drizzle with ½ cup of the *vadouvan* cream. Repeat this layering 3 more times with the remaining potatoes, cauliflower, onion, cheese and cream. Pour the remaining cream mixture all over the top.

3. Cover with foil and poke a few holes in it. Bake the gratin for 1½ hours, until tender. Uncover and cook for 30 minutes longer, until the cream has been absorbed and the gratin is golden brown on top. Transfer to a rack and let stand for 20 minutes before serving. —*Sang Yoon*

NOTE Both curry leaves and *vadouvan* are available at *spicehouse.com.*

CARROTS

CARROT-PEAR SHRUB

In a blender, combine 3 packed cups grated carrots, 2 cups chopped ripe peeled Anjou pears, 2 tbsp finely grated ginger, 3 tbsp fresh lime juice, 1 tbsp raw unfiltered apple cider vinegar and ½ tsp kosher salt with ½ cup water; puree until smooth. Strain the shrub through a sieve lined with 3 layers of cheesecloth, pressing on the solids. Serve in 2 glasses over ice.

CARROT SALAD

In a bowl, whisk ¼ cup olive oil, ¼ cup lemon juice and 2 tbsp each of chopped chives and parsley; season with salt and pepper. Toss in ½ lb thinly sliced carrots and 2 thinly sliced golden beets; let stand for 15 minutes. Spread 6 oz thinly sliced mushrooms on a platter; top with the carrots and beets. Drizzle with more oil, garnish with shaved Parmesan and chopped chives and parsley; serve.

ROASTED CARROTS

Toss 3 bunches small carrots on a baking sheet with 2 sliced shallots, 3 tbsp olive oil and 2 tsp curry powder; season with salt and pepper. Roast at 425° for 20 minutes. Drizzle with 2 tbsp lemon juice; transfer to a platter. In a bowl, combine ¼ cup chopped cilantro, 1 tsp grated lemon zest, ½ minced jalapeño and ½ cup minced carrot tops; sprinkle over the dish.

CARROT BREAD

In a bowl, whisk 2 cups all-purpose flour, ¾ tsp salt and ½ tsp each of baking powder and baking soda. In another bowl, whisk 2 large eggs, ½ cup canola oil, ¾ cup light brown sugar and ½ cup granulated sugar. Stir in 1 packed cup grated carrots, 1 packed cup grated zucchini and ¾ cup shredded sweetened coconut; fold in the dry ingredients. Scrape into an oiled 8-by-4-inch loaf pan; sprinkle with ½ cup coconut. Tent the pan with foil and bake at 375° for 90 minutes, until a tester comes out clean. Let cool.

CARROT PILAF

In a saucepan, heat 2 tbsp olive oil. Cook 2 cups chopped carrots and 1 minced shallot over moderately high heat for 3 minutes. Stir in 1½ cups basmati rice, ¾ tsp caraway seeds and 2½ cups water; bring to a boil. Cover and cook over low heat for 15 minutes. Let stand for 10 minutes, then fluff the rice. Stir in ¼ cup chopped parsley; season with salt and pepper. Sprinkle with ⅓ cup each of salted roasted *pepitas* and chopped roasted almonds. Serve with lemon wedges.
—*Kay Chun*

CARROT-PEAR
SHRUB

Broccoli Rabe with Sausage

⏱ TOTAL: 30 MIN • 4 SERVINGS

Broccoli rabe and sausage are classic partners in an Italian sandwich. Chef Gabe Thompson of L'Apicio in New York City turns that filling into a spicy side dish.

- 1 pound broccoli rabe
- ¼ cup extra-virgin olive oil
- 4 ounces hot Italian sausage— casings removed, meat crumbled
- 2 garlic cloves, thinly sliced

Pinch of crushed red pepper

Salt

- 2 tablespoons fresh lemon juice
- ¼ cup grated pecorino cheese

1. In a pot of salted boiling water, cook the broccoli rabe until nearly tender, 4 minutes. Drain and cool under cold water. Squeeze and pat dry, then chop.
2. In a large skillet, heat 1 tablespoon of the oil. Add the sausage and cook over moderately high heat, breaking it up into small pieces, until browned. Add the remaining 3 tablespoons of oil, the garlic and crushed red pepper to the skillet and cook for 1 minute. Add the broccoli rabe and cook, stirring, until tender, about 3 minutes. Season with salt. Add the lemon juice and toss. Serve with the grated pecorino. —Gabe Thompson

INGREDIENT TIP

GOCHUJANG This Korean chile paste is fermented, so it has a deep flavor. It's great mixed into condiments, as a thickener for stews or turned into a sweet-spicy glaze on fried foods such as chicken wings or the Korean-Style Fried Cauliflower at right.

Korean-Style Fried Cauliflower

TOTAL: 1 HR • 6 SERVINGS ● ●

This ultra-crispy cauliflower, a.k.a. KFC, is a signature dish at Yardbird in Hong Kong. After being battered and fried, the cauliflower florets are tossed with a sweet and fiery sauce made with *gochujang*, the chile paste that is a staple of Korean cooking.

- 2 tablespoons *gochujang* (see Note)
- ⅔ cup sugar
- 6 garlic cloves
- 2 tablespoons mirin
- 2 tablespoons red yuzu *kosho* (see Note)
- 1 cup tempura batter mix (see Note)
- 1 large egg yolk
- 1 cup Asian whole wheat flour (see Note)
- ⅔ cup potato starch
- 1 head of cauliflower (1½ pounds), cut into 1½-inch florets

Canola oil, for frying

Toasted sesame seeds and lime wedges, for serving

1. In a blender, combine the *gochujang* with the sugar, garlic and mirin. Add 1 cup of water and blend until smooth. Add the yuzu *kosho* and 1 cup of water and pulse to combine. Transfer the mixture to a medium saucepan and bring to a boil. Simmer over moderate heat, stirring occasionally, until the sauce is reduced to 1½ cups, about 15 minutes. Transfer the *gochujang* sauce to a large bowl and let cool.
2. Meanwhile, in a large bowl, whisk the tempura flour with the egg yolk and 1 cup of ice water until smooth. Add the wheat flour, potato starch and 1 cup plus 2 tablespoons of ice water and whisk until smooth; the consistency should be that of thin pancake batter. Add the cauliflower, stirring to coat.
3. In a large saucepan, heat 2 inches of canola oil to 385°. Working in batches, lift the cauliflower florets from the batter, allowing the excess to drip back into the bowl. Fry the cauliflower, stirring occasionally, until the coating is golden and the florets are tender but not soft, about 6 minutes. Drain

the cauliflower on paper towels and immediately add to the sauce; toss to coat. Using a slotted spoon, transfer the cauliflower to a plate. Repeat with the remaining cauliflower. Serve each batch as it's finished cooking. Sprinkle the fried cauliflower with sesame seeds and serve with lime wedges. —Matt Abergel

NOTE *Gochujang* is a spicy Korean chile pepper paste. Red yuzu *kosho* is a Japanese condiment made with yuzu, red chiles and salt. Tempura batter mix, such as Nisshin, is a combination of soft flours, usually containing wheat and corn. These ingredients are all available at *amazon.com*. Asian whole wheat flour, such as Yi Feng, is available at *onlinefoodgrocery.com*.

BEER Crisp, refreshing, lightly hoppy pilsner: Oskar Blues Brewery Mama's Little Yella Pils.

Spicy Cauliflower Puree

⏱ ACTIVE: 15 MIN; TOTAL: 45 MIN

4 SERVINGS ● ●

- 1 tablespoon vegetable oil
- 1 large onion, sliced
- 2½ pounds cauliflower, core and stems discarded
- 1 dried chipotle, stemmed and seeded
- 1 bay leaf
- 1 quart unsweetened almond milk

Salt

1. In a large saucepan, heat the oil. Add the onion and cook over moderate heat until softened but not colored, about 5 minutes. Add the cauliflower, chipotle, bay leaf and almond milk and bring to a boil. Cover and simmer over low heat until the cauliflower is very tender, about 15 minutes. Discard the bay leaf and chipotle.
2. Boil the cauliflower until the liquid is reduced by half, about 10 minutes. Drain the cauliflower and onion and transfer to a blender. Puree until smooth. Season with salt and serve. —Grace Parisi

MAKE AHEAD The cauliflower puree can be refrigerated overnight. Reheat gently before serving.

● HEALTHY   ● MAKE AHEAD   ○ VEGETARIAN   ● STAFF FAVORITE

Spicy Jerk Vegetables with Yogurt-Scallion Sauce

TOTAL: 1 HR • 12 SERVINGS ●

- 1 tablespoon ground allspice
- 1 tablespoon onion powder
- 1 teaspoon freshly grated nutmeg
- 1 teaspoon dried powdered ginger
- 1 teaspoon garlic powder
- ½ teaspoon cayenne pepper
- 1½ tablespoons dried thyme

Kosher salt and freshly ground pepper

- 1¾ cups extra-virgin olive oil
- 3 large portobello mushrooms— gills scraped out with a spoon, mushrooms thickly sliced
- 1 pound oyster mushrooms, thickly sliced
- ½ pound shiitake mushrooms, stemmed
- 1 fennel bulb, sliced ¼ inch thick through the core
- 2 red bell peppers, quartered
- 1½ pounds thin eggplant, sliced ½ inch thick
- 1 pound medium asparagus
- 8 whole scallions, plus ½ cup minced scallions
- 1 sweet onion, sliced ½ inch thick
- 2 cups plain fat-free Greek yogurt
- ¼ cup fresh lime juice

Grilled bread, for serving

1. In a medium bowl, mix the spices, thyme and 1 tablespoon each of salt and pepper with 1½ cups of the oil. In a very large bowl, combine the mushrooms, fennel, peppers, eggplant, asparagus and whole scallions; gently toss with most of the seasoned oil. Brush the onion slabs with the remaining seasoned oil. **2.** Light a grill and oil the grate. Working in batches, grill the vegetables over moderately high heat, turning, until tender and charred, 10 minutes per batch. Arrange the vegetables on a platter and keep warm. **3.** In a bowl, whisk the yogurt with the minced scallions, lime juice and remaining ¼ cup of oil. Serve the vegetables with the yogurt sauce and grilled bread. —*Grace Parisi*
WINE Robustly fruity rosé: 2011 Jelu.

Aloo Gobi

🕐 TOTAL: 45 MIN • 4 SERVINGS ● ●

This is a light, fresh-tasting version of the popular Indian dish of potatoes, cauliflower and a blend of spices.

- 2 tablespoons canola oil
- 3 baking potatoes (1½ pounds), peeled and cut into 1-inch pieces
- 1 small head of cauliflower (1 pound), cut into 1-inch florets
- 3 large garlic cloves, minced
- 2 teaspoons finely grated peeled fresh ginger
- ½ teaspoon cumin seeds
- ½ teaspoon brown mustard seeds
- ½ teaspoon ground coriander
- 12 curry leaves (optional)

Kosher salt and freshly ground pepper

- 1 large tomato, chopped
- ⅓ cup frozen peas, thawed
- 1 tablespoon unsalted butter

Chopped cilantro, for garnish

In a large skillet, heat the oil. Add the potatoes and cauliflower; cook over moderate heat, stirring, until golden in spots, 7 to 8 minutes. Stir in the garlic, ginger, cumin seeds, mustard seeds, coriander and curry leaves and cook until fragrant, 1 minute. Season with salt and pepper; add 1½ cups of water. Cover and simmer over moderately low heat, stirring occasionally, until the vegetables are tender, 15 to 20 minutes. Stir in the tomato, peas and butter; cook for 2 minutes longer. Transfer the *aloo gobi* to a platter, garnish with the cilantro and serve. —*Kay Chun*

Charred and Smoky Belgian Endives

TOTAL: 20 MIN PLUS COOLING

6 SERVINGS ● ● ●

These olive oil–dressed grilled endives are terrific at room temperature or chilled.

- 6 red and white Belgian endives, halved lengthwise

Extra-virgin olive oil, for brushing and drizzling

Kosher salt and freshly ground pepper

Light a hardwood charcoal fire. Brush the endive halves with olive oil and season with salt and pepper. Grill over moderate heat, turning occasionally, until lightly charred and just tender, about 15 minutes. Transfer the endives to a platter, tent with foil and let steam for 5 minutes. Remove the foil and let the endives cool to room temperature. Refrigerate if desired. Generously drizzle with olive oil and serve. —*Michael Chiarello*

Kabocha Squash Puree with Balsamic and Sage

ACTIVE: 30 MIN; TOTAL: 1 HR 30 MIN

10 SERVINGS ● ● ●

- 2 kabocha squash (about 3 pounds each), halved and seeded
- 1 stick unsalted butter, softened
- 8 sage leaves

Salt and freshly ground pepper

- 2 tablespoons fresh lemon juice

Aged balsamic vinegar, for drizzling

1. Preheat the oven to 425° and line a large roasting pan with parchment paper. Rub the inside of each squash half with 1 tablespoon of the butter and press a sage leaf onto each one. Season the squash with salt and pepper and place cut side down in the roasting pan. Add 1 cup of water to the pan. Cover with foil and roast for about 1 hour, until the squash is tender. Let cool slightly. Discard the sage and scoop the flesh into a large bowl.
2. In a small skillet, melt the remaining 4 tablespoons of butter. Add the remaining 4 sage leaves and cook over moderate heat until the sage is crispy and the butter is lightly browned, about 5 minutes. Transfer the fried sage leaves to a plate.
3. Add the browned butter and lemon juice to the squash and mash to a puree. Season with salt and pepper. Transfer the squash to a serving bowl, drizzle with balsamic vinegar and garnish with the fried sage leaves. —*Michael Tusk*
MAKE AHEAD The squash puree can be refrigerated overnight. Reheat in a microwave before garnishing.

No-Bake Vegetarian Enchiladas

ACTIVE: 30 MIN; TOTAL: 2 HR

4 TO 6 SERVINGS ● ●

Tex-Mex food inspired Josef Centeno's Los Angeles restaurant Bar Amá. The recipe here is based on a dish created by his great-grandmother, who raised 12 kids. Because meat was expensive, she often made enchiladas using only vegetables, like carrots and potatoes. For his enchiladas, Centeno makes a *sofrito,* cooking carrots low and slow in olive oil with garlic and tomatoes.

CARROT SOFRITO

1¼ pounds carrots, coarsely chopped
1 small yellow onion, chopped
5 garlic cloves, peeled
½ pound tomatoes, chopped
½ cup extra-virgin olive oil
Kosher salt

ENCHILADAS

9 ounces *queso fresco,* crumbled
   (about 2 cups)
1 cup finely chopped cilantro
¾ cup finely chopped red onion
Canola oil, for warming
12 corn tortillas
Smoky Tomatillo Salsa (recipe follows)
Mexican *crema* or sour cream,
   for drizzling

1. MAKE THE CARROT SOFRITO Preheat the oven to 225°. In a food processor, pulse the carrots, onion and garlic until very finely chopped. Scrape the mixture into a medium bowl. Add the tomatoes to the food processor and pulse until nearly smooth.
2. In a medium, deep ovenproof skillet, heat 2 tablespoons of the olive oil until shimmering. Add the carrot mixture and a generous pinch of salt and cook over moderate heat, stirring occasionally, until softened slightly and nearly dry, 5 to 7 minutes. Add the tomato puree and cook, stirring occasionally, until most of the liquid has evaporated, 5 minutes. Stir in the remaining 6 tablespoons of olive oil. Transfer the skillet to the oven and bake for 1½ hours until the carrot *sofrito* is very soft. Season with salt, cover and keep warm over low heat, stirring occasionally.

3. ASSEMBLE THE ENCHILADAS In a medium bowl, toss the crumbled *queso fresco* with the cilantro and red onion.
4. In a small skillet, heat ½ inch of canola oil over moderately low heat. Add 1 tortilla to the skillet and cook until just pliable, about 20 seconds. Using tongs, transfer the tortilla to a baking sheet. Repeat with the remaining tortillas.
5. Working quickly, roll a scant ¼ cup of the cheese mixture in each tortilla and arrange them on a large platter, seam side down. Spoon the hot *sofrito* over the enchiladas and scatter the remaining cheese mixture on top; drizzle some of the Smoky Tomatillo Salsa and *crema* over them and serve, passing additional salsa and *crema* at the table. —*Josef Centeno*

WINE Minerally German Riesling: 2011 Joh. Jos. Prüm Bernkasteler Badstube Kabinett.

SMOKY TOMATILLO SALSA

TOTAL: 35 MIN • MAKES 1¼ CUPS ● ●

2 tomatillos, husked and rinsed
1 medium tomato
½ medium onion
1 serrano chile, stemmed
1 tablespoon extra-virgin olive oil
2 large dried chipotle chiles, stemmed
   and seeded
1 cup lightly packed cilantro
3 tablespoons fresh lime juice
Kosher salt

1. Preheat the oven to 500°. On a baking sheet, toss the tomatillos, tomato, onion and serrano with the oil. Roast for 10 minutes, until the vegetables are browned in spots and softened slightly. Let cool, then chop.
2. Meanwhile, in a small bowl, cover the chipotle chiles with hot water and let stand until softened, about 15 minutes. Transfer the chiles and ¼ cup of their soaking liquid to a food processor and puree.
3. Add the chopped vegetables to the processor and pulse until the salsa is nearly smooth. Add the cilantro and lime juice and pulse until the cilantro is minced. Season the salsa with salt, transfer to a bowl and serve. —*JC*

Curried Vegetables with Griddled Biscuit Roti

TOTAL: 40 MIN • 4 SERVINGS ●

Buss-Up-Shut is a Caribbean-Indian specialty of curry and the griddled flatbread called roti; the roti here resembles a torn shirt, hence the name. The coconut-curried vegetables (from leftover Spicy Jerk Vegetables on the previous page) in this version are perfect with the griddled biscuit dough.

2 tablespoons canola oil
1½ teaspoons minced fresh ginger
1 garlic clove, minced
2 teaspoons mild curry powder
1 cup shredded carrots
One 15-ounce can chickpeas, drained
1 cup unsweetened coconut milk
4 cups coarsely chopped vegetables,
   plus leftover sauce for serving, from
   Spicy Jerk Vegetables (previous page)
¼ cup chopped cilantro,
   plus cilantro sprigs for garnish
Salt and freshly ground pepper
All-purpose flour, for dusting
1 tube Pillsbury Grands Homestyle
   Buttermilk Biscuits
4 tablespoons unsalted butter, melted

1. In a large saucepan, combine the canola oil, ginger, garlic and curry powder and cook over moderate heat, stirring frequently, until the garlic is softened, about 1 minute. Add the carrots, chickpeas, coconut milk and Spicy Jerk Vegetables and simmer for 10 minutes. Stir in the chopped cilantro and season the curry with salt and pepper.
2. On a lightly floured work surface, roll out each biscuit a scant ¼ inch thick. Brush the dough with the butter. Heat a large griddle. Add 2 or 3 pieces of the rolled-out dough at a time and cook over high heat, turning, until golden, 3 minutes. Fold each griddled roti in half and coarsely chop or tear it. Repeat with the remaining biscuits.
3. Spoon the curry into bowls or plates; garnish with cilantro sprigs. Serve with the roti and yogurt-scallion sauce. —*Grace Parisi*
WINE Juicy, full-bodied Chenin Blanc from South Africa: 2012 Simonsig.

● HEALTHY ● MAKE AHEAD ● VEGETARIAN ● STAFF FAVORITE

Crabless Cakes with Hearts of Palm and Corn

⏱ TOTAL: 45 MIN • 6 SERVINGS ● ●

1 tablespoon extra-virgin olive oil, plus more for frying
2½ cups fresh corn kernels (from 4 ears of corn)
¼ cup minced onion
¼ cup minced green bell pepper
One 15-ounce can whole hearts of palm—drained, thinly sliced lengthwise and cut crosswise into ¾-inch lengths
2 teaspoons Old Bay Seasoning
2 tablespoons chopped flat-leaf parsley
¼ cup vegan mayonnaise
2 teaspoons Dijon mustard
¼ cup plus 2 tablespoons plain dry bread crumbs, plus more for coating
Salt and freshly ground pepper

1. In a nonstick skillet, heat the 1 tablespoon of oil. Add the corn, onion and bell pepper and cook over high heat until crisp-tender, 4 minutes. Scrape 1 cup of the mixture into a food processor and pulse to a coarse puree.
2. In a bowl, squeeze the hearts of palm to break them into shards. Add the puree and the remaining sautéed vegetables to the bowl along with the Old Bay, parsley, mayonnaise, mustard and the ¼ cup plus 2 tablespoons of bread crumbs. Season lightly with salt and pepper and stir until evenly moistened.
3. Line a baking sheet with parchment paper and fill a pie plate with bread crumbs. Scoop scant ¼-cup mounds of the hearts of palm mixture into the bread crumbs and roll to coat. Form the mounds into eighteen 2-inch cakes and transfer to the baking sheet.
4. Wipe out the nonstick skillet, then add a scant ⅛ inch of oil. Fry half of the cakes over moderate heat, turning once, until crispy, 2 minutes per side. Wipe out the skillet and add clean oil before frying the remaining cakes. Serve the cakes hot.
—*Richard Landau*

WINE Ripe Chardonnay from California's Russian River Valley: 2011 MacMurray Ranch.

Individual Mushroom Potpies with Parker House Crust

ACTIVE: 1 HR 30 MIN; TOTAL: 4 HR
MAKES 8 POTPIES ● ●

You can also make this recipe as one large potpie in a 9-by-13-inch baking dish, rolling out the dough to an 11-by-15-inch rectangle. Baking time will be about the same.

1 large baking potato, cut into ½-inch dice
One 1½-pound butternut squash, neck only, cut into ¾-inch dice (about 2 cups)
1 cup frozen pearl onions, thawed
2 carrots, thinly sliced
1 stick unsalted butter, melted
Salt and freshly ground pepper
1 large onion, diced
1 tablespoon chopped sage
1 teaspoon chopped thyme
1 teaspoon chopped rosemary
1½ pounds mixed mushrooms, such as shiitake and cremini, stemmed and thinly sliced (8 cups)
½ cup Marsala
½ cup all-purpose flour
6 cups Rich Mushroom Stock (recipe follows) or vegetable stock
Parker House Roll Dough (page 270)

1. Preheat the oven to 400°. In a medium bowl, toss the potato, squash, pearl onions and carrots with 3 tablespoons of the butter. Season with salt and pepper. Spread the vegetables on a baking sheet and roast for about 30 minutes, stirring once, until tender. Lower the oven temperature to 350°.
2. Meanwhile, in a large, deep skillet, heat 3 tablespoons of the butter. Add the diced onion, sage, thyme and rosemary and cook over moderately high heat, stirring, until the onion is softened, about 5 minutes. Add the mushrooms and cook until tender, about 10 minutes. Add the Marsala and cook until evaporated, about 5 minutes. Stir in the flour and cook until blended into the mushrooms, 1 minute. Add the Rich Mushroom Stock and bring to a boil, scraping up any browned bits from the bottom of the skillet. Simmer until thickened, about 5 minutes. Add the roasted vegetables and season with salt and pepper.
3. Spoon the potpie filling into eight 1-cup ramekins. Divide the Parker House Roll Dough into 8 equal balls. Working with one ball at a time, roll out the dough to a round that's 2 inches bigger than the rim of the ramekin. Drape the dough over the rim so there's a 1-inch overhang all around; trim any excess dough. Brush the dough rounds with the remaining 2 tablespoons of melted butter and arrange the ramekins on 2 baking sheets.
4. Bake the potpies for about 30 minutes, until the crust is deeply golden and risen; switch the sheets halfway through baking. Let the pies rest for 5 minutes before serving.
—*Michael White*

WINE Spiced, balanced, cool-climate Pinot Noir: 2010 Breggo Anderson Valley.

RICH MUSHROOM STOCK
TOTAL: 2 HR 30 MIN
MAKES ABOUT 6 CUPS ● ● ●

3 tablespoons extra-virgin olive oil
1 pound white mushrooms, chopped
1 large onion, chopped
2 medium carrots, chopped
1 celery rib, chopped
4 garlic cloves, chopped
1 thyme sprig
1 rosemary sprig
1 bay leaf
½ teaspoon whole black peppercorns
½ cup Marsala

In a large pot, heat the oil. Add the mushrooms, onion, carrots, celery, garlic, thyme, rosemary, bay leaf and peppercorns and cook over high heat until the vegetables are softened, 15 minutes. Add the Marsala and cook until evaporated, about 5 minutes. Add 2 quarts of water and bring to a boil. Simmer over moderate heat until reduced to 6 cups, 2 hours. Strain the stock, pressing down on the solids. —*MW*

MAKE AHEAD The stock can be refrigerated for up to 5 days or frozen for up to 1 month.

● HEALTHY ● MAKE AHEAD ● VEGETARIAN ● STAFF FAVORITE

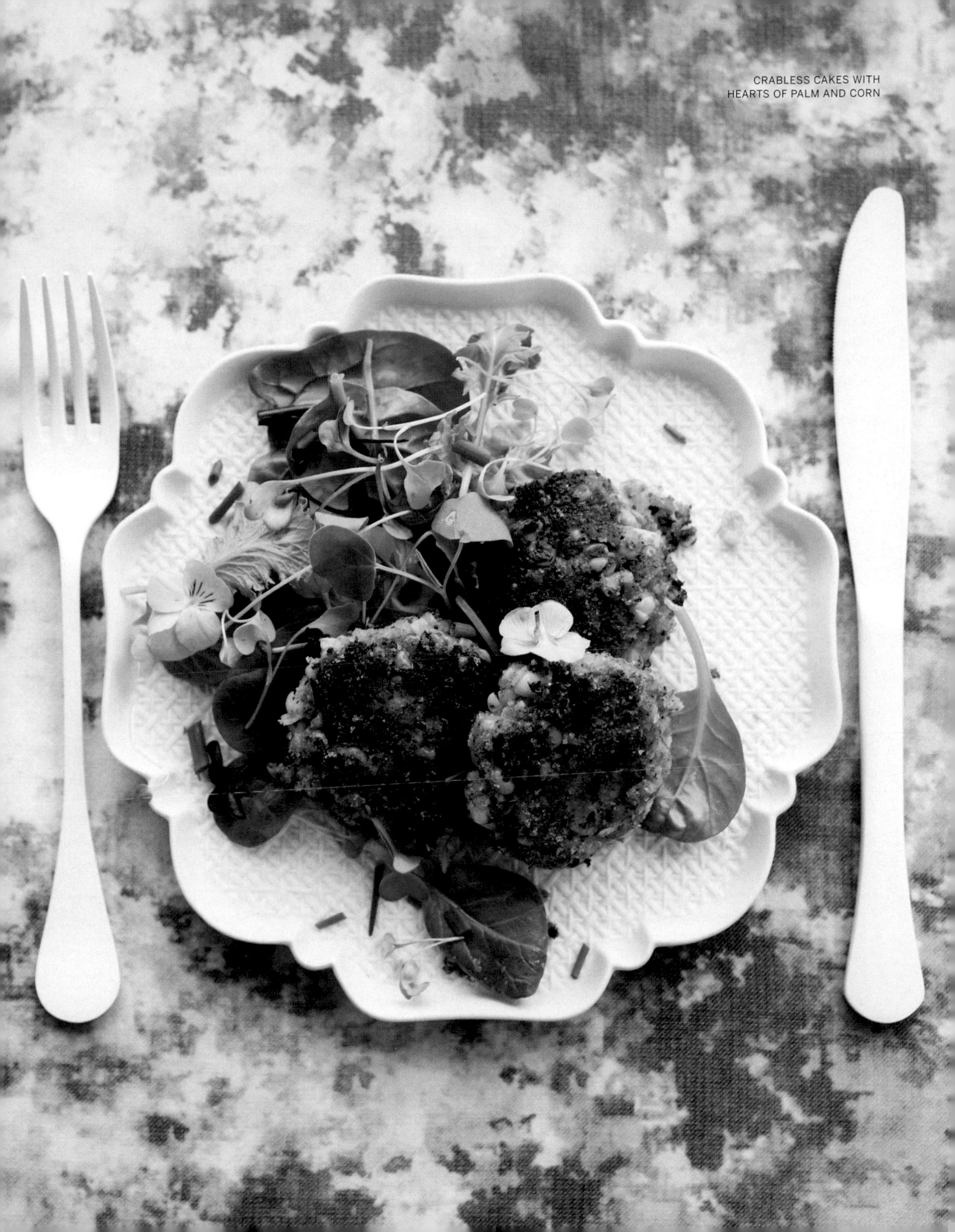

CRABLESS CAKES WITH
HEARTS OF PALM AND CORN

Ratatouille Spirals

ACTIVE: 1 HR; TOTAL: 3 HR
10 SERVINGS ● ●

- 3 pounds beefsteak tomatoes, scored with an "X" on the bottoms
- 3 tablespoons extra-virgin olive oil, plus more for brushing
- 2 large garlic cloves, finely chopped
- ½ teaspoon crushed red pepper
- Kosher salt
- 2 cups cubed country bread
- 2½ pounds firm medium zucchini, cut lengthwise into ⅛-inch-thick strips
- 2½ pounds small eggplant, preferably Japanese, cut lengthwise into ⅛-inch-thick strips
- 3 roasted red bell peppers, cut into ½-inch strips
- 18 oil-packed anchovies, cut into thin strips
- ¾ pound fresh mozzarella, cut into 2-by-½-inch sticks

1. In a medium pot of boiling water, blanch the tomatoes for 30 seconds; drain. Slip off the skins and halve the tomatoes crosswise. Coarsely chop the tomatoes, keeping the juices and seeds.

2. Preheat the oven to 375°. In a large, deep skillet, heat 2 tablespoons of the oil. Add the garlic and crushed pepper and cook over moderate heat for 1 minute. Add the tomatoes and juices and season lightly with salt. Cook, stirring frequently, until the sauce has thickened, about 25 minutes.

3. Meanwhile, on a baking sheet, toss the bread with the remaining 1 tablespoon of olive oil. Toast for about 15 minutes, stirring once, until golden.

4. In 2 separate colanders, toss the zucchini and eggplant strips with 1 tablespoon of salt each and let drain for 15 minutes. Shake out the excess liquid and pat the strips dry.

5. Spoon the tomato sauce into a shallow 2½-quart baking dish and scatter the bread cubes on top. On a work surface, top each zucchini strip with a strip of eggplant; blot dry if necessary. Place a strip of roasted pepper and anchovy and a stick of mozzarella at one end of each stack and roll up. Stand the rolls in the baking dish and brush with oil.

6. Cover with parchment paper. Bake for about 1 hour and 15 minutes, until the vegetables are just tender and the ratatouille is bubbling; remove the parchment halfway through baking. Let rest for 15 minutes before serving. —*Grace Parisi*

WINE Fruit-forward, light-bodied northern Italian red: 2012 Prunotto Dolcetto d'Alba.

Grilled Eggplant Parmesan

TOTAL: 45 MIN • 4 SERVINGS ● ●

- 1 large eggplant (1½ pounds), peeled and sliced crosswise ¼ inch thick
- 4 large plum tomatoes, sliced crosswise ¼ inch thick
- Extra-virgin olive oil, for brushing
- Salt
- ⅓ cup chopped green olives
- 1 to 2 tablespoons chopped oil-packed Calabrian chiles or other hot chiles
- ¼ cup finely shredded basil, plus whole basil leaves for garnish
- 6 ounces Fontina cheese, thinly sliced

1. Preheat the oven to 450° and heat a grill pan. Brush the eggplant and tomato slices with olive oil and season lightly with salt. Grill the eggplant in batches over moderately high heat, turning once, until softened and lightly charred, about 4 minutes. Grill the tomatoes, turning once, until lightly charred but still intact, about 2 minutes.

2. In a bowl, combine the olives, chiles and shredded basil. Line a large rimmed baking sheet with parchment paper. In the center, arrange half of the eggplant in a 9-inch square, overlapping the slices slightly. Top with half of the grilled tomatoes, olive mixture and Fontina. Repeat with the remaining ingredients, ending with the cheese.

3. Bake in the center of the oven for about 15 minutes, until bubbling and golden. Let stand for 10 minutes. Garnish with basil leaves and serve. —*Grace Parisi*

SERVE WITH Crusty bread.

WINE Light, berry-rich Piedmontese red: 2011 D'Oh! Dolcetto.

Sautéed Mushrooms with Red Wine

TOTAL: 1 HR 15 MIN • 6 SERVINGS ● ●

- 1 pound portobello mushrooms
- 6 tablespoons extra-virgin olive oil
- Kosher salt and freshly ground pepper
- 2 leeks, white and light green parts only, halved lengthwise and thinly sliced crosswise
- 2 garlic cloves, minced
- 2 pounds mixed white button and cremini mushrooms, halved
- 2 thyme sprigs
- ½ cup dry red wine
- 1¼ cups vegetable broth
- ½ teaspoon finely grated lemon zest
- 1 tablespoon fresh lemon juice
- 1 tablespoon dry Marsala
- 1 tablespoon unsalted butter
- 1 cup packed baby arugula

1. Preheat the oven to 350°. On a baking sheet, brush the portobellos with 1 tablespoon of the olive oil and season with salt and pepper. Bake for about 25 minutes, until tender; let cool slightly, then slice ½ inch thick.

2. Meanwhile, in a large, deep skillet, heat 1 tablespoon of the oil. Add the leeks, garlic and a big pinch of salt and pepper. Cook over moderate heat until the leeks are just starting to brown, 7 minutes; transfer to a bowl.

3. Heat 2 tablespoons of oil in the skillet. Add half of the button and cremini mushrooms and a thyme sprig, season with salt and pepper and cook over moderately high heat, stirring occasionally, until tender and browned, 8 minutes. Transfer to the bowl. Repeat with the remaining 2 tablespoons of oil, mushrooms and thyme sprig.

4. Combine all of the cooked mushrooms in the skillet. Add the red wine; cook until evaporated. Add the broth, zest and juice; cook over moderate heat, stirring, until the mushrooms are coated in a light sauce, 4 minutes. Stir in the Marsala; cook for 1 minute. Off the heat, stir in the butter and arugula; season with salt and pepper. —*Alex Guarnaschelli*

WINE Herbal Cabernet Franc: 2011 Domaine Fabrice Gasnier Les Graves Chinon.

● HEALTHY ● MAKE AHEAD ● VEGETARIAN ● STAFF FAVORITE

CRISPY TOFU BIBIMBAP WITH
MUSTARD GREENS AND ZUCCHINI

At Brawn in London, chef
Owen Kenworthy (right)
updates classics like steak
tartare and risotto.

Opposite: recipe, page 258.
FAVA BEAN AND
CAULIFLOWER RISOTTO

POTATOES, GRAINS & BEANS

Wheat Berry Salad with Tuscan Kale and Butternut Squash

ACTIVE: 20 MIN; TOTAL: 50 MIN
6 SERVINGS ● ● ●

- 1 pound peeled butternut squash, cut into ½-inch dice (3 cups)
- 6 tablespoons extra-virgin olive oil
- Salt and freshly ground pepper
- 2 cups whole einka (see Note) or other wheat berries
- 10 ounces Tuscan kale, stemmed, leaves sliced crosswise ¼ inch wide (4 cups)
- 2 tablespoons sherry vinegar
- ½ cup minced shallots
- 1 tablespoon finely chopped sage
- 2 garlic cloves, minced
- ⅓ cup dry white wine
- ¼ cup chopped flat-leaf parsley

1. Preheat the oven to 400°. On a rimmed baking sheet, toss the squash with 2 tablespoons of the olive oil and season with salt and pepper. Roast the squash for 20 to 25 minutes, until tender. Transfer to a large bowl.
2. Meanwhile, in a medium saucepan, cover the wheat berries with 5 cups of water and ¼ teaspoon of salt and bring to a boil. Simmer over moderate heat until tender, 25 minutes.
3. Add the kale to the wheat berries, cover and remove from the heat; let stand until the kale is wilted, 5 minutes. Drain well and add the wheat and kale to the squash. Add the vinegar and 2 tablespoons of the oil to the salad, season with salt and pepper and toss.
4. In a skillet, heat the remaining 2 tablespoons of oil. Add the shallots and a pinch of salt; cook over moderately high heat until just starting to brown, 3 to 4 minutes. Add the sage; cook for 1 minute, until fragrant. Add the garlic and cook, stirring, for 1 minute. Add the wine and simmer, stirring, until evaporated. Scrape the shallot and garlic into the salad and toss. Season with salt and pepper, garnish with parsley and serve. —*Stewart Dietz*
NOTE Protein-rich einka, or einkorn, is a tiny variety of wheat berry popular in Germany.
WINE Zesty, fruit-forward Sauvignon Blanc: 2012 Jean Reverdy Sancerre.

Toasted Farro and Scallions with Cauliflower and Eggs

TOTAL: 1 HR • 4 SERVINGS ●

This dish is inspired by a Moroccan porridge called *herbel*, which San Francisco chef Mourad Lahlou's mother and grandmother used to cook for him. It's traditionally made with barley, milk, butter and cinnamon, but Lahlou likes doing it his own way, substituting other grains such as farro for the barley.

- 5 tablespoons unsalted butter
- 4 scallions, white and tender green parts only, sliced
- 8 ounces farro (1 cup plus 2 tablespoons)
- Salt and freshly ground pepper
- 1 quart vegetable stock
- 2 tablespoons extra-virgin olive oil
- 3 cups 1-inch cauliflower florets
- 1 tablespoon sherry vinegar
- 4 large eggs

1. In a large saucepan, melt 3 tablespoons of the butter. Add the scallions and cook over moderate heat until softened, about 2 minutes. Add the farro, season with salt and pepper and cook for 1 minute, stirring. Add ½ cup of the stock and cook over moderate heat, stirring, until absorbed. Continue adding the stock ½ cup at a time, stirring frequently until it is absorbed before adding more. The farro is done when it's al dente, about 30 minutes.
2. In a medium skillet, heat the olive oil. Add the cauliflower, season with salt and pepper and cook over high heat until tender and browned in spots, about 5 minutes. Add the cauliflower to the farro along with the vinegar and the remaining 2 tablespoons of butter. Season with salt and keep warm.
3. Bring a saucepan of water to a boil. Add the eggs and cook for 4 minutes. Drain and rinse under cold water. Spoon the farro into 4 bowls. Peel the eggs and carefully remove the egg whites to keep the yolks whole. Carefully place the intact yolks in the center of each bowl of farro; discard the whites. Serve right away.
—*Mourad Lahlou*
WINE Full-bodied Loire Chenin Blanc: 2010 François Pinon Cuvée Tradition Vouvray.

Farro and Green Olive Salad with Walnuts and Raisins

🕐 TOTAL: 40 MIN
6 TO 8 SERVINGS ● ● ● ●

Heidi Swanson, creator of the culinary blog 101 Cookbooks (*101cookbooks.com*), loads this salad with so many olives that there's a piece in every single bite. It's worth seeking out bright green Castelvetrano olives (available at most olive bars), which have a meaty texture and mild, buttery flavor.

- 1¼ cups farro (½ pound)
- Fine sea salt
- 1 cup walnuts (3½ ounces)
- 2½ cups pitted green olives, preferably Castelvetrano, chopped (11 ounces)
- 4 scallions, white and light green parts only, finely chopped
- ⅓ cup snipped chives
- 2 tablespoons golden raisins
- ½ teaspoon crushed red pepper
- ¼ cup extra-virgin olive oil
- 3 tablespoons freshly squeezed lemon juice
- 1 tablespoon honey
- Shaved Pecorino cheese, for serving

1. Preheat the oven to 375°. In a medium saucepan, combine the farro with 4 cups of water and ½ teaspoon of salt. Bring to a boil and simmer, partially covered, until the farro is tender, about 20 minutes. Drain the farro and spread it on a baking sheet to cool.
2. Meanwhile, place the walnuts in a pie plate and toast for 5 to 7 minutes, until lightly golden and fragrant. Let cool, then coarsely chop.
3. In a large bowl, combine the farro, walnuts, olives, scallions, chives, raisins, crushed red pepper, olive oil, lemon juice and honey and season with salt. Toss well. Transfer the salad to a platter, garnish with cheese and serve.
—*Heidi Swanson*
MAKE AHEAD The salad can be refrigerated overnight. Bring the salad to room temperature before serving.
WINE Ripe peach–scented Sauvignon Blanc from California: 2012 Dry Creek Vineyard Fumé Blanc.

● HEALTHY ● MAKE AHEAD ● VEGETARIAN ● STAFF FAVORITE

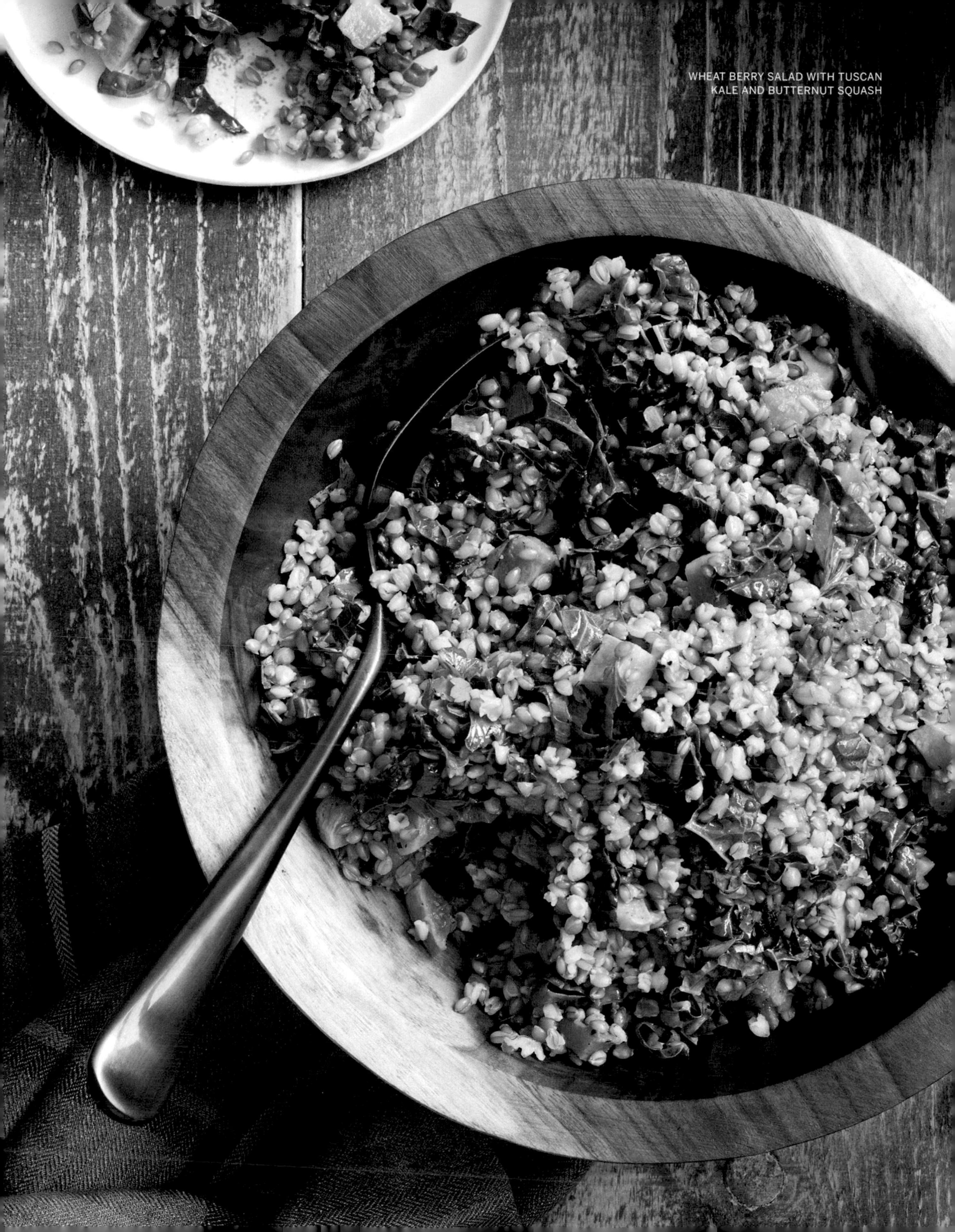

WHEAT BERRY SALAD WITH TUSCAN KALE AND BUTTERNUT SQUASH

Sunchoke-Kale Hash with Farro

ACTIVE: 40 MIN; TOTAL: 1 HR 15 MIN
10 SERVINGS ● ● ●

Comfort food is rarely healthy, or vegetarian. This soul-satisfying winter hash is both. The recipe from F&W Best New Chefs 2009 Jon Shook and Vinny Dotolo, of Animal and Son of a Gun in Los Angeles, combines crunchy sunchokes, silky oyster mushrooms, tender kale and chewy farro. It's wonderful served with grilled steak or on its own as a meatless main course.

¾ cup farro
2½ pounds large sunchokes,
   peeled and cut into 2-inch pieces
Salt
1 pound Tuscan kale,
   tough stems discarded
3 tablespoons extra-virgin olive oil
   blended with 3 tablespoons
   vegetable oil
1 small red onion, sliced ¼ inch thick
1 tablespoon unsalted butter
½ pound oyster mushrooms,
   halved if large
Freshly ground pepper

1. In a medium saucepan, cover the farro with 2 inches of water. Bring to a boil, cover and cook over low heat until the farro is tender, about 25 minutes. Drain the farro.
2. Meanwhile, in a large saucepan, cover the sunchokes with water and add a pinch of salt. Boil until the sunchokes are tender, 10 minutes; drain. Slice the sunchokes ¼ inch thick.
3. Fill the large saucepan with water and bring to a boil. Add the Tuscan kale and cook until just tender, about 3 minutes. Drain the kale and let cool slightly. Squeeze out any excess liquid from the leaves, then coarsely chop them.
4. In a small skillet, heat 2 tablespoons of the blended oil. Add the red onion and a pinch of salt and cook over moderately low heat, stirring occasionally, until the onion is browned, about 12 minutes.
5. In a nonstick skillet, melt the butter in 2 tablespoons of the blended oil. Add the

sunchokes in an even layer and cook over high heat until browned on the bottom, about 3 minutes. Turn the sunchokes, reduce the heat to moderately high and continue cooking until starting to brown, about 2 minutes. Push the sunchokes to the side of the skillet.
6. Add 1 more tablespoon of the oil and the oyster mushrooms. Season with salt and pepper and cook over moderately high heat until browned, 3 minutes. Add the remaining 1 tablespoon of oil along with the farro, kale and onion and cook, stirring, until hot. Season with salt and pepper and serve.
—Vinny Dotolo and Jon Shook
WINE Melon-scented South African Chenin Blanc: 2011 Teddy Hall Summer Moments.

Ratatouille Tabbouleh

TOTAL: 45 MIN • 4 SERVINGS ● ●

This hearty take on tabbouleh includes cooked vegetables in the mix, along with the traditional bulgur, fresh tomatoes, scallions and parsley.

1 cup medium-grade bulgur
   (5 ounces)
Boiling water
2 cups chopped or quartered
   tomatoes and cherry tomatoes
2 scallions, thinly sliced
½ cup coarsely chopped flat-leaf
   parsley
2½ cups chopped leftover Ratatouille
   Spirals (page 240) or roasted
   summer vegetables, such as
   eggplant, tomatoes and zucchini
2 tablespoons fresh lemon juice
¼ cup extra-virgin olive oil
Salt and freshly ground pepper

1. In a large heatproof bowl, cover the bulgur with 2 inches of boiling water and let stand until softened, about 20 minutes. Drain and press out the excess water; let cool. Return the bulgur to the bowl and add the tomatoes, scallions, parsley and ratatouille vegetables.
2. In a small bowl, whisk the lemon juice with the olive oil and season with salt and pepper. Pour the dressing over the tabbouleh and toss well. *—Grace Parisi*

Grain Salad with Scallion Dressing

TOTAL: 40 MIN • 4 SERVINGS ●

This vegetarian recipe combines a variety of textures: chewy grains, crunchy nuts, creamy chickpeas and a smooth roasted-scallion dressing. You can easily substitute any leftover cooked grains you have on hand.

2 large bunches of scallions
   (about 7 ounces)
½ cup plus 2 tablespoons
   extra-virgin olive oil
1 cup quinoa, rinsed and drained
½ cup bulgur wheat
3 tablespoons fresh lemon juice
Kosher salt and freshly ground
   black pepper
¼ cup unsalted roasted almonds,
   chopped
One 15-ounce can chickpeas—drained,
   rinsed and patted dry
½ small red onion, finely chopped
½ cup chopped flat-leaf parsley

1. Preheat the oven to 450°. Chop all but 2 of the scallions. On a rimmed baking sheet, toss the chopped scallions with 2 tablespoons of the olive oil. Roast for about 10 minutes, stirring occasionally, until the scallions are tender and lightly charred in spots.
2. Meanwhile, in a large saucepan of boiling water, cook the quinoa and bulgur together until just tender, 10 to 12 minutes. Drain well and then spread the grains on a rimmed baking sheet to cool.
3. Transfer the roasted scallions to a food processor. With the machine on, drizzle in the remaining ½ cup of olive oil. Add 1 tablespoon of the lemon juice and season the dressing with salt and pepper.
4. In a large bowl, combine the quinoa, bulgur, almonds, chickpeas, red onion and parsley. Add the roasted-scallion dressing and the remaining 2 tablespoons of lemon juice and toss well. Season with salt and pepper. Thinly slice the remaining 2 scallions, scatter on top and serve. *—Kay Chun*
MAKE AHEAD The dressing can be refrigerated overnight.

● HEALTHY ● MAKE AHEAD ● VEGETARIAN ● STAFF FAVORITE

Crispy Quinoa Sliders

TOTAL: 1 HR • MAKES 12 SLIDERS ● ●

Instead of quinoa, these mini vegetarian burgers can also be made with 2 cups of cooked medium cracked wheat or millet.

⅔ cup quinoa
Boiling water
Two 1-inch-thick slices of wheat bread, crusts removed and bread cubed
2 large eggs
1 zucchini, coarsely grated (about 1 cup)
½ cup freshly grated Parmigiano-Reggiano cheese
¼ cup chopped chives
3 small garlic cloves, minced
½ teaspoon kosher salt
¼ teaspoon freshly ground pepper
¼ cup extra-virgin olive oil
Mini burger buns, lettuce and sliced tomatoes, onion and pickles, for serving

1. In a medium saucepan, cook the quinoa in boiling water until just tender, about 10 minutes. Drain and spread on a baking sheet to cool; you should have about 2 cups.

2. In a food processor, pulse the bread cubes until coarse crumbs form; you should have about 1 cup. In a medium bowl, whisk the eggs. Squeeze the liquid from the zucchini and add the zucchini to the eggs. Stir in the Parmigiano-Reggiano cheese, chives, garlic, salt and freshly ground pepper. Mix in the quinoa and bread crumbs. Let the mixture stand for 10 minutes.

3. Using a ¼-cup measure, scoop 12 mounds and form each one into a ½-inch-thick patty. In a large nonstick skillet, heat 1 tablespoon of the olive oil. Add 6 patties and cook until golden on the bottom, about 3 minutes. Add another 1 tablespoon of the olive oil to the skillet, flip the patties and cook for about 3 minutes longer, until crisp. Repeat with the remaining patties and oil. Serve with mini burger buns, lettuce, tomatoes, onion and pickles. —*Kay Chun*

WINE Lively southern Italian white: 2011 Librandi Cirò Bianco.

Three-Mushroom-and-Quinoa Salad

TOTAL: 1 HR • 16 SERVINGS ● ● ●

Use this recipe as a template for any mixed-mushroom-and-grain salad. Some excellent options include brown rice, wild rice, black or white barley, farro or couscous.

½ cup pine nuts
2 teaspoons finely grated lemon zest
¼ cup fresh lemon juice
1 cup plus 2 tablespoons extra-virgin olive oil
Kosher salt and freshly ground black pepper
1 small onion, very finely chopped
3 cups quinoa
1 quart vegetable broth
1 pound cremini mushrooms, thinly sliced
1 pound portobello mushrooms—stems discarded, caps thinly sliced
1 pound hen-of-the-woods mushrooms, torn into large pieces
3 cups coarsely chopped flat-leaf parsley

1. Preheat the oven to 375°. On a small baking sheet, toast the pine nuts for 7 minutes, until they are lightly golden. Transfer the pine nuts to a very large bowl.

2. In a small bowl, combine the lemon zest and lemon juice. Whisk in ½ cup of the olive oil and season with salt and pepper.

3. In a large saucepan, heat 2 tablespoons of the olive oil. Add the onion and cook over moderate heat, stirring, until the onion is golden, about 5 minutes. Add the quinoa, broth and 1 cup of water and bring to a boil. Cover and simmer over low heat until the quinoa is tender and all of the liquid has been absorbed, 15 minutes; transfer to a baking sheet and let cool.

4. In a large skillet, heat 2 tablespoons of the olive oil. Add the cremini mushrooms, season with salt and pepper and cook over moderate heat, stirring occasionally, until the mushrooms are golden, about 8 minutes. Transfer the mushrooms to the bowl with the toasted pine nuts. Add another 2 tablespoons of oil

to the skillet. Add half of the portobellos, season with salt and pepper and cook, stirring occasionally, until golden, 4 to 5 minutes; transfer to the bowl. Repeat with 2 more tablespoons of oil and the remaining portobellos; transfer to the bowl. Add the remaining 2 tablespoons of oil and the hen-of-the-woods mushrooms to the skillet, season with salt and pepper and cook until golden, 7 to 8 minutes; add to the bowl.

5. Stir the cooled quinoa, lemon dressing and chopped parsley into the mushrooms and toss well. Season the salad with salt and pepper and serve. —*Nicholas Wilber*

MAKE AHEAD The salad can be kept at room temperature for up to 6 hours.

WINE Light-bodied red: 2012 Jean-Paul Brun Terres Dorées L'Ancien Beaujolais.

NEW GRAIN MILLS

TRIBEST WOLFGANG GRAIN MILL (above) An easy-to-use model that can produce any flour texture, allowing you to make everything from cakes to grits. *$599; amazon.com.*

VICTORIO HAND-OPERATED This machine is a low-commitment way to explore DIY milling. *$56; amazon.com.*

WONDERMILL ELECTRIC Works quickly, with three basic settings (pastry, bread and coarse) that make grinding simple and fail-safe. *$240; the wondermill.com.*

L'EQUIP NUTRIMILL This powerhouse has a huge capacity and offers the most control, but it has a learning curve. *$240; pleasanthillgrain.com.*

Soft Polenta with Mixed Mushrooms and Gremolata

TOTAL: 1 HR • 6 TO 8 FIRST-COURSE SERVINGS OR 4 MAIN-COURSE SERVINGS ●

Chef Suzanne Goin of A.O.C. in Los Angeles adores the straightforward flavors in this vegetarian dish: the sautéed mushrooms and greens and the tangy mascarpone cheese that melts into the silky polenta. She tops each dish with a vibrant gremolata, a condiment made of minced parsley, garlic and plenty of lemon zest.

POLENTA
8 cups water
1½ cups medium-grain polenta
Kosher salt
4 tablespoons unsalted butter
Freshly ground pepper

GREMOLATA
½ cup chopped flat-leaf parsley
1 teaspoon chopped garlic
1 tablespoon finely grated lemon zest

POLENTA TOPPINGS

For polenta parties at home, chef Michael Chiarello serves his luscious polenta (far right) with a trio of classic toppings.

SAUSAGE AND PEPPERS In a very large bowl, toss 3 thinly sliced bell peppers, 12 ounces cherry tomatoes, 3 thinly sliced onions, 2 seeded and thinly sliced serrano chiles, 5 thinly sliced garlic cloves, ½ cup olive oil and ¼ cup balsamic vinegar. Season with salt and freshly ground pepper. Roast on 2 large rimmed baking sheets until just softened, 15 minutes. Arrange 3 pounds sweet and/or spicy Italian sausages on the vegetables; roast until fully cooked and lightly browned. Transfer to a platter, scatter ¼ cup torn basil leaves on top and serve.

BOLOGNESE SAUCE OR PESTO
Serve homemade or good-quality store-bought versions in separate bowls.

MUSHROOMS AND GREENS
2 tablespoons unsalted butter
¼ cup extra-virgin olive oil
1½ pounds mixed mushrooms, such as cremini, oyster and stemmed shiitake, thickly sliced or quartered
Kosher salt and freshly ground pepper
4 ounces young greens, such as spinach, Russian kale or pea shoots, coarsely chopped (4 cups packed)
½ cup mascarpone cheese

1. MAKE THE POLENTA In a large saucepan, bring the water to a boil. Whisk in the polenta in a slow, steady stream. Add 1 tablespoon of kosher salt and cook over moderately low heat, whisking frequently, until the polenta is thickened and tender, about 30 minutes. Whisk in the butter and season the polenta with salt and freshly ground pepper. Press plastic wrap directly on the surface of the polenta to prevent a film from forming; cover and keep warm.

2. MEANWHILE, MAKE THE GREMOLATA On a work surface, mince the parsley and garlic with the lemon zest. Transfer the gremolata to a small bowl.

3. PREPARE THE MUSHROOMS AND GREENS In a large skillet, melt 1 tablespoon of the butter in 2 tablespoons of the olive oil. Add half of the mushrooms and season with salt and pepper. Cook over moderately high heat, stirring occasionally, until the mushrooms are golden and tender, about 5 minutes. Stir in half of the chopped greens and cook for 1 minute; transfer the mixture to a large bowl. Repeat with the remaining butter, oil, mushrooms and chopped greens.

4. Pour the polenta onto a large platter; if the polenta is very thick, reheat with ½ cup of water before serving. Spoon the mushrooms and greens on top and garnish with the mascarpone. Sprinkle the gremolata over the polenta and serve warm.
—*Suzanne Goin*

MAKE AHEAD The cooked polenta can be refrigerated overnight. Rewarm with a little water before serving.

WINE Rich Rhône white: 2010 Gilles Robin Les Marelles Crozes Hermitage Blanc.

Polenta by the Yard

TOTAL: 1 HR • 16 SERVINGS ● ●

In ancient Tuscany, polenta was served on a wooden board on the dining table. Chef Michael Chiarello of Bottega in Napa Valley takes inspiration from that tradition for this communal-eating experience. He pours a river of impossibly creamy, molten polenta along a holiday buffet table lined with butcher paper. Guests can then scoop up the polenta onto plates along with a variety of toppings. To achieve the luxurious texture of his polenta, be sure to use a variety made from finely milled cornmeal.

18 cups water
6 cups heavy cream
Kosher salt
4 cups fine-ground polenta (not instant; see Note)
2 cups shredded imported Fontina cheese (6 ounces)
1 cup freshly grated Parmigiano-Reggiano cheese, plus more for serving
½ teaspoon freshly grated nutmeg
Freshly ground pepper

1. Line a heatproof table with butcher paper. In a very large pot, combine the water with the heavy cream, season with salt and bring to a boil. Gradually whisk in the polenta and bring the mixture to a boil over moderately high heat, whisking constantly. Cook the polenta over moderate heat, stirring occasionally, until thick, creamy and no longer gritty, about 30 minutes.

2. Stir both cheeses into the polenta until melted, then stir in the nutmeg and season with salt and pepper. Immediately pour the polenta onto the butcher paper and invite guests to grab spoons and forks, add toppings and dive in. Pass additional grated Parmigiano-Reggiano at the table.
—*Michael Chiarello*

SERVE WITH Sausage and peppers, Bolognese sauce or pesto (see Polenta Toppings, far left).

NOTE Fine-ground polenta, such as Moretti's, is available at specialty food shops.

● HEALTHY   ● MAKE AHEAD   ● VEGETARIAN   ● STAFF FAVORITE

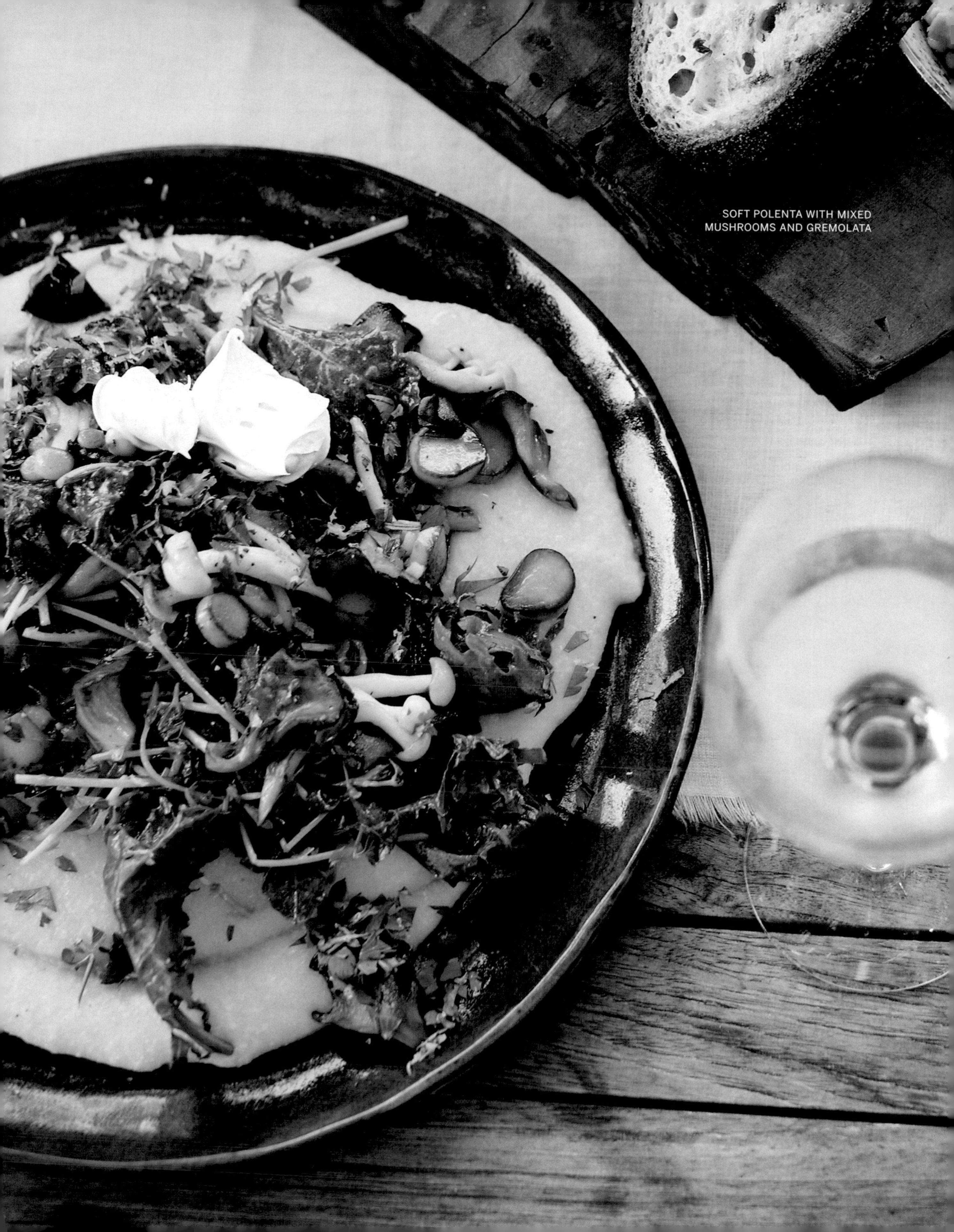

SOFT POLENTA WITH MIXED
MUSHROOMS AND GREMOLATA

Stewed Cannellini Beans with Tomatoes and Guanciale

ACTIVE: 40 MIN; TOTAL: 1 HR 40 MIN
PLUS OVERNIGHT SOAKING
8 SERVINGS ● ●

"As a poor student in Tuscany, I ate a ton of beans," says star sommelier Richard Betts. Here, he spikes cannellini beans with chiles and *guanciale* (pig jowl bacon).

- 2 cups dried cannellini beans (¾ pound), soaked overnight and drained
- 1 small onion, halved, plus 1 large onion, finely chopped

Kosher salt

- 1 tablespoon extra-virgin olive oil
- ½ pound *guanciale* or pancetta, finely chopped
- 3 garlic cloves, thinly sliced
- 3 dried hot red chiles
- 1 teaspoon finely chopped rosemary
- 1 teaspoon finely chopped sage

One 28-ounce can peeled whole Italian tomatoes in puree, crushed by hand

- 1 teaspoon finely chopped marjoram

Freshly ground pepper

1. In a saucepan, cover the beans and halved onion with water and bring to a boil. Simmer over moderate heat until tender, about 1 hour. Remove from the heat, add a generous pinch of salt and let stand for 10 minutes. Drain the beans and spread them on a baking sheet to cool slightly; discard the onion.

2. Meanwhile, in a large skillet, heat the oil. Add the *guanciale* and cook over moderately high heat, stirring, until translucent and the fat is just rendered, about 5 minutes. Add the chopped onion, garlic and chiles and cook over moderate heat, stirring, until the onion is softened and just starting to brown, 8 minutes. Stir in the rosemary and sage and cook until fragrant, 1 minute. Add the tomatoes with their juices and bring just to a simmer.

3. Add the beans to the skillet and cook over moderate heat, stirring, until coated in a light sauce, about 7 minutes. Stir in the marjoram, season with salt and pepper and serve.
—*Richard Betts*

Spicy Maple Baked Beans

ACTIVE: 45 MIN; TOTAL: 2 HR 30 MIN
8 TO 10 SERVINGS ●

Pittsburgh chef Kevin Sousa uses leftover franks from his Station Street Hot Dogs in the smoky, intense baked beans he serves at Union Pig & Chicken, a few blocks away. The dark porter ale adds a bitter kick that helps balance the sweetness of the beans.

- 1 cup ketchup
- 1 cup pure maple syrup
- 1 cup porter or other dark ale
- ½ cup molasses
- ½ cup Dijon mustard
- ½ cup powdered mustard
- ¼ cup red wine vinegar
- ¼ cup Worcestershire sauce
- ¼ cup packed light brown sugar
- 1 tablespoon chile powder
- ½ teaspoon cinnamon
- ½ teaspoon cayenne pepper
- ½ teaspoon granulated onion
- ½ teaspoon granulated garlic

Kosher salt

- 4 slices of bacon, finely chopped
- 1 onion, finely chopped

Four 15-ounce cans navy beans, rinsed and drained

- 10 all-beef hot dogs, halved lengthwise and thinly sliced crosswise

1. In a medium saucepan, combine the ketchup, maple syrup, ale, molasses, mustards, vinegar, Worcestershire sauce, brown sugar and spices. Bring the maple sauce to a boil, whisking to dissolve the sugar. Reduce the heat to moderately low and simmer the sauce until reduced by one-third, about 20 minutes. Season with salt.

2. Preheat the oven to 325°. In a large enameled cast-iron casserole, cook the bacon over moderate heat, stirring occasionally, until the fat has rendered, about 5 minutes. Add the onion and cook until softened and lightly browned, about 8 minutes. Stir in the beans, hot dogs and sauce, cover partially and bake for about 1 hour, until the beans are glazed. Season the baked beans with salt. Ladle into bowls and serve. —*Kevin Sousa*

New Orleans Red Beans and Rice with Pickled Peppers

⏱ TOTAL: 30 MIN • 4 SERVINGS ● ●

- 4 ounces thick-cut bacon, cut into ¼-inch dice
- 1 medium onion, finely chopped
- 1 inner celery rib, finely chopped
- 2 garlic cloves, minced
- 1 pickled jalapeño, finely chopped
- ¼ cup chopped Peppadew peppers, plus more for garnish

Two 15-ounce cans red kidney beans

- 1 cup low-sodium chicken broth

Salt and freshly ground pepper
Steamed white rice, for serving

1. In a large saucepan, cook the bacon over moderately high heat, stirring, until golden and crisp, about 5 minutes. Add the onion, celery, garlic, pickled jalapeño and ¼ cup of Peppadews and cook, stirring, until softened, 5 to 6 minutes. Add the beans with their liquid and the chicken broth and bring to a boil. Simmer over moderate heat until the liquid is slightly reduced, 8 minutes. Season the beans with salt and pepper.

2. Ladle the beans into bowls and top with a mound of rice. Garnish with more Peppadews and serve right away. —*Grace Parisi*
WINE Lively, berry-rich Beaujolais: 2011 Château Thivin Côte de Brouilly.

Ginger Rice

⏱ ACTIVE: 5 MIN; TOTAL: 35 MIN
6 SERVINGS ● ●

- 2 cups short-grain sushi rice, rinsed well and drained
- 1 tablespoon minced peeled fresh ginger
- 1 teaspoon grapeseed oil

In a medium saucepan, combine the rice, ginger and oil with 2 cups of water and bring to a boil. Cover and cook over very low heat until the water is absorbed and the rice is tender, about 25 minutes. Let stand off the heat for 5 minutes, then fluff the rice with a fork and serve. —*Paul Qui*

● HEALTHY ● MAKE AHEAD ● VEGETARIAN ● STAFF FAVORITE

Eggplant Dirty Rice

ACTIVE: 30 MIN; TOTAL: 1 HR 30 MIN
8 TO 10 SERVINGS ● ● ○

This spicy vegetarian take on classic New Orleans dirty rice swaps in eggplant for the usual chicken livers.

¼ cup canola oil
3 celery ribs, finely chopped
2 medium green bell peppers, seeded and finely chopped
1 medium onion, finely chopped
Salt
1 medium eggplant (about 1 pound), cut into ¾-inch cubes
1 tablespoon dried thyme
½ teaspoon finely ground black pepper
¼ teaspoon finely ground white pepper
¼ teaspoon cayenne pepper
3 garlic cloves, finely chopped
1 tablespoon tomato paste
¼ cup soy sauce
1½ cups medium-grain white rice
2½ cups vegetable broth
Hot sauce, for serving

1. Preheat the oven to 350°. In a large, deep casserole, heat the oil until shimmering. Add the celery, bell peppers and onion and season with salt. Cover and cook over low heat until the onion is translucent, about 5 minutes. Uncover and cook over moderate heat until the vegetables are lightly browned, about 10 minutes.

2. Add the eggplant, thyme, black and white peppers and cayenne and season with salt. Cook over moderate heat until the eggplant is softened, about 8 minutes. Stir in the garlic and tomato paste and cook for 1 minute. Add the soy sauce and scrape up any bits stuck to the bottom of the casserole. Stir in the rice and broth and bring to a boil.

3. Cover and bake for 17 minutes, until the rice is just tender. Remove from the oven and let stand, covered, for 10 minutes. Fluff the rice; serve with hot sauce. —*David Kinch*
WINE Fruit-forward, light-bodied red: 2011 Bruno Giacosa Dolcetto d'Alba.

Glossy Mushroom Rice

TOTAL: 1 HR 30 MIN PLUS OVERNIGHT SOAKING • 6 SERVINGS ● ● ○

Six kinds of dried and fresh mushrooms give this sticky vegetarian rice dish amazing flavor.

8 ounces pearl rice, rinsed well (see Ingredient Tip, below right)
One 6-inch square of kombu (see Note)
1 ounce dried shiitake mushrooms
½ ounce dried porcini mushrooms
¼ ounce dried matsutake mushrooms
Salt
¾ pound fresh king oyster mushrooms, thinly sliced lengthwise
6 ounces fresh maitake mushrooms
4 ounces fresh shiitake mushrooms, stemmed
6 tablespoons unsalted butter, 3 tablespoons melted
2 tablespoons low-sodium soy sauce
½ cup sake
1 small white onion, finely chopped
Freshly ground pepper
¼ cup snipped chives

1. Soak the rice in a large bowl of water overnight. In a large pot, combine the kombu with all the dried mushrooms and 3 quarts of water; cover and let stand overnight.

2. Bring the pot of kombu and mushrooms to a simmer over moderately high heat. Immediately remove the kombu and discard. Simmer the stock until reduced to 4 cups, about 1 hour. Strain the stock and discard the mushrooms (or reserve them for another use). Season lightly with salt.

3. Meanwhile, drain the rice and shake out the water. Let the rice air dry for 30 minutes, shaking it in the strainer occasionally.

4. Preheat the oven to 450°. On a rimmed baking sheet, toss all the fresh mushrooms with the 3 tablespoons of melted butter and the soy sauce. Roast for about 20 minutes, stirring once or twice, until the mushrooms are tender and browned in spots. Let cool slightly, then coarsely chop the mushrooms.

5. Line a large bamboo steamer with cheesecloth. Spread the rice over the cloth in a 1-inch-thick layer. In a small bowl, combine ¼ cup of the sake with ½ teaspoon of salt. Sprinkle the mixture over the rice. Set the steamer over a pot of boiling water and steam the rice over high heat until the grains are al dente and translucent, 8 minutes. Let cool slightly, then break up any clumps.

6. In a large, deep skillet, heat the remaining 3 tablespoons of butter. Add the onion and cook over moderately high heat, stirring occasionally, until softened, about 5 minutes. Add the chopped mushrooms and cook for 2 minutes, until sizzling. Stir in the steamed rice. Add the remaining ¼ cup of sake, season with salt and pepper and cook until the sake is absorbed, about 1 minute. Add ½ cup of the mushroom stock and cook over moderate heat, stirring, until absorbed. Add another ½ cup of the stock and cook, stirring, until the rice is tender but not mushy, about 10 minutes; you will have stock left over for another use. Stir in the chives and serve right away. —*Matt Abergel*
NOTE Kombu (dried kelp) is available at Asian markets and *amazon.com*.
WINE Earthy, spicy Oregon Pinot Noir: 2010 Cristom Mt. Jefferson Cuvée.

INGREDIENT TIP: RICE

More types of rice are available to home cooks than ever. Here, four varieties to try.

PEARL This strain of short-grain glutinous rice becomes very sticky when cooked. Available in Asian markets, it's used whole in the Glossy Mushroom Rice above or ground into the base for many Asian sweets.

CAROLINA GOLD Delicate in flavor, this versatile rice is the grandfather of long-grain rice in the Americas. Fantastic in Hoppin' John with Smoked Oysters (page 256), it's available at *ansonmills.com*.

CALASPARRA AND BOMBA Groomed for paella, these two types of Spanish rice can absorb more flavorful broth, as in the Iberian Ham and Artichoke Rice (page 256). They are available at specialty food shops.

Iberian Ham and Artichoke Rice

ACTIVE: 1 HR; TOTAL: 1 HR 45 MIN
6 SERVINGS ●

- 1 lemon, halved
- 3 large artichokes
- ½ cup plus 1 tablespoon extra-virgin olive oil

Kosher salt

- 2 tablespoons hazelnuts
- 1 cup finely chopped onion
- 6 ounces very thinly sliced dry-cured ham, such as *jamón Ibérico* or serrano, 4 ounces finely chopped
- 2 medium tomatoes—halved, seeded and finely chopped
- 4 cups chicken stock or low-sodium broth
- 2 cups Bomba or Calasparra rice (see Note)
- ½ cup lightly packed parsley
- ½ small garlic clove

1. Preheat the oven to 400°. Squeeze some of the juice from the lemon halves into a large bowl of water. Working with 1 artichoke at a time, snap off the dark green outer leaves. Holding the artichoke on its side, using a serrated knife, cut off all but ¾ inch of the remaining leaves. Peel and trim the bottom and stem of the artichoke. Halve the artichoke and scoop out the furry choke with a spoon. Cut the artichoke hearts in half again, rub with the lemon and add to the bowl of lemon water. Repeat with the remaining artichokes. Drain the artichokes and pat dry.

2. In a large ovenproof skillet, heat 1 tablespoon of the olive oil. Add the artichokes and a generous pinch of salt. Cook over moderate heat, tossing occasionally, until just starting to brown, about 4 minutes. Add ½ cup of water, cover and steam the artichokes until just tender, about 12 minutes. Transfer the artichokes to a plate and wipe out the skillet.

3. Spread the hazelnuts in a pie plate and toast for about 7 minutes, until fragrant. Let cool slightly, transfer the nuts to a kitchen towel and rub off the skins.

4. In the large skillet, heat 2 tablespoons of the olive oil until shimmering. Add the onion

and cook over moderate heat, stirring occasionally, until just softened, 5 minutes. Add the chopped ham and tomatoes and cook, stirring occasionally, until the tomatoes break down and the mixture thickens, 15 minutes. Meanwhile, in a medium saucepan, bring the chicken stock to a simmer; keep hot.

5. Add the rice to the skillet and stir to coat with the tomato mixture. Stir in the hot stock, spread the rice in an even layer and bring to a boil. Nestle the artichokes in the rice. Cover and bake for about 20 minutes, until most of the stock is absorbed. Uncover the skillet and bake for about 10 minutes longer, until the stock is completely absorbed and the rice is tender but moist. Remove the skillet from the oven, cover and let stand for 10 minutes.

6. Meanwhile, in a blender, combine the parsley, hazelnuts and garlic and pulse until finely chopped. Add the remaining 6 tablespoons of oil and puree until nearly smooth. Season the parsley sauce with salt. Serve the rice straight from the skillet, drizzled with the parsley sauce and topped with the sliced ham. —*Pablo Montero*

NOTE Bomba and Calasparra rice are available at specialty food stores and *tienda.com*.
WINE Bold, berry-rich Spanish red: 2009 Pago de los Capellanes Tinto Reserva.

Hoppin' John with Smoked Oysters

ACTIVE: 30 MIN; TOTAL: 1 HR 30 MIN
PLUS OVERNIGHT SOAKING • 4 SERVINGS

PEAS AND GRAVY

- 2 quarts chicken stock or low-sodium broth
- 1 cup Sea Island Red Peas, soaked overnight and drained (see Note)
- 1 medium onion, quartered
- 1 small carrot, halved
- 3 celery ribs, halved
- 1 small jalapeño, halved lengthwise
- 2 garlic cloves, lightly crushed
- 10 thyme sprigs
- 1 bay leaf

Kosher salt

- 2 tablespoons apple cider vinegar
- 1 tablespoon unsalted butter

RICE

Kosher salt

- ¼ teaspoon cayenne pepper
- 1 cup Carolina Gold rice, preferably Anson Mills Carolina Gold (see Note)
- 4 tablespoons unsalted butter, cubed

Two 3-ounce cans smoked oysters, drained

Thinly sliced scallions, for garnish

1. PREPARE THE PEAS AND GRAVY In a large pot, bring the chicken stock to a boil. Add the peas, onion, carrot, celery, jalapeño, garlic, thyme sprigs and bay leaf and cook over moderate heat, partially covered, until the peas are tender, about 1 hour. Season with salt. Drain the peas, reserving the broth. Pick out and discard the vegetables, thyme sprigs and bay leaf.

2. Transfer 1½ cups of the peas to a blender, reserving the rest. Add 2 cups of the broth, the vinegar and the butter and puree until smooth. Transfer the gravy to a bowl and keep warm. Reserve the remaining broth for another use.

3. MEANWHILE, MAKE THE RICE Preheat the oven to 300°. In a medium pot, bring 7 cups of water to a boil with 1 teaspoon of salt and the cayenne. Add the rice and simmer over moderate heat, stirring occasionally, until the rice is al dente, about 12 minutes. Drain and rinse the rice under cold water; drain again.

4. Spread the rice on a baking sheet and bake for about 10 minutes, stirring occasionally. Dot the butter evenly over the rice and bake for about 15 minutes longer, stirring occasionally, until the grains are almost dry and separated. Transfer the rice to a large bowl and stir in the reserved peas. Serve the rice and peas in bowls, topped with the pea gravy, smoked oysters and scallions.
—*Sean Brock*

NOTE Sea Island Red Peas are slightly sweet, creamy-textured field peas. Carolina Gold is a variety of long-grain rice with a sweet, clean flavor. Both the peas and rice are available at *ansonmills.com*.
BEER Crisp pilsner: Stoudts Pils.

● HEALTHY ● MAKE AHEAD ● VEGETARIAN ● STAFF FAVORITE

IBERIAN HAM AND
ARTICHOKE RICE

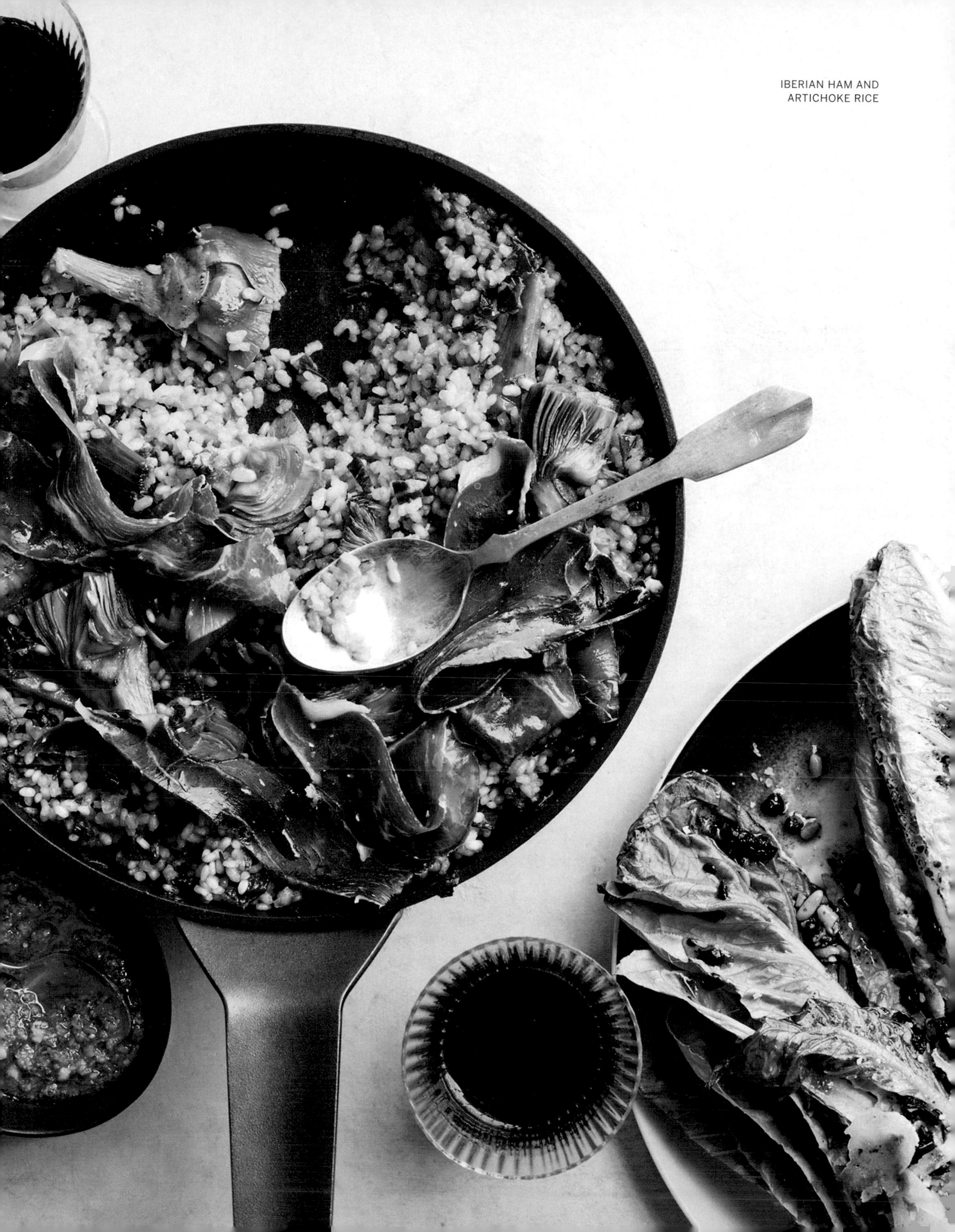

Fava Bean and Cauliflower Risotto

📷 PAGE 247
TOTAL: 1 HR 30 MIN • 6 SERVINGS ●

- 4 pounds fresh fava beans, shelled
- 5 tablespoons unsalted butter
- 1 small cauliflower, cut into small florets (3 cups)
- 1 large shallot, minced
- 2 garlic cloves, minced
- 1 bay leaf
- 1½ cups arborio or carnaroli rice
- ½ cup dry white wine
- 5 cups low-sodium chicken broth, warmed
- 1 tablespoon fresh lemon juice
- Freshly grated Parmigiano-Reggiano cheese
- Kosher salt and freshly ground pepper
- Extra-virgin olive oil, for drizzling

1. Bring a saucepan of water to a boil. Add the fava beans and blanch for 30 seconds. Drain and let cool under running water. Slip off the tough outer skins and transfer the beans to a bowl; you should have about 2 cups.

2. In the same saucepan, melt 2 tablespoons of the butter. Add half each of the fava beans and cauliflower and cook over moderately low heat, stirring, until the cauliflower is crisp-tender, 5 minutes. Add ½ cup of water, cover and simmer until the vegetables are tender, 5 minutes. Transfer to a food processor and puree until smooth, adding more water by the tablespoonful, if necessary.

3. Wipe out the saucepan and melt 2 tablespoons of the butter in it. Add the shallot, garlic and bay leaf and cook over moderate heat, stirring, until softened, 5 minutes. Add the rice and cook, stirring, until coated, 1 minute. Add the wine and cook, stirring, until it is absorbed. Add 1 cup of the warm broth and cook, stirring, until nearly absorbed; continue adding it 1 cup at a time, stirring until nearly absorbed between additions, until the rice is al dente, 20 minutes total. Halfway through cooking, stir in the remaining cauliflower.

4. Stir the fava-cauliflower puree into the risotto with the lemon juice, ½ cup of grated cheese and the remaining favas and 1 tablespoon of butter. Season with salt and pepper. Transfer to bowls, drizzle with oil and serve with more cheese. —*Owen Kenworthy*
WINE Minerally Loire white: 2011 Clos du Tue-Boeuf Frileuse Cheverny Blanc.

Fresh Carrot Risotto

🕐 **TOTAL: 40 MIN • 6 SERVINGS**
This clever risotto—made with carrot juice, chicken broth and baby peas—is a fun take on peas and carrots.

- 4 cups chicken stock, preferably homemade
- 2 cups fresh carrot juice
- 2 tablespoons extra-virgin olive oil
- 1 large shallot, finely chopped
- 1½ cups arborio rice (10 ounces)
- ½ cup dry white wine
- 2½ tablespoons white wine vinegar
- ½ cup freshly grated Parmigiano-Reggiano cheese
- 2 tablespoons unsalted butter
- Salt and freshly ground pepper
- 1 cup frozen baby peas

1. In a medium saucepan, bring the stock and carrot juice to a simmer; keep warm.

2. In a large saucepan, heat the olive oil. Add the shallot and cook over moderate heat, stirring, until softened, about 4 minutes. Add the rice and cook, stirring, until slightly milky-colored, about 1 minute. Add the wine and 2 tablespoons of the vinegar and cook, stirring, until the liquid is absorbed. Stir in the hot stock mixture, 1 cup at a time, stirring constantly and adding more stock once it has been absorbed, about 20 minutes total; the rice should be al dente and suspended in a thick, creamy sauce. Add the cheese and 1 tablespoon of the butter, season with salt and pepper and stir until creamy.

3. In a medium skillet, melt the remaining 1 tablespoon of butter. Add the peas, season with salt and pepper and cook over moderately high heat until warmed through, about 1 minute. Add the remaining ½ tablespoon of vinegar to the peas, then fold into the risotto. Serve immediately. —*Grace Parisi*

Fennel Risotto with Crispy Lamb Sausage

TOTAL: 1 HR • 4 SERVINGS
A homemade lamb sausage, prepared with store-bought ground lamb, fennel seeds and fresh fennel, amps up the flavor of this fennel risotto.

- 4 cups chicken broth mixed with 4 cups of water
- ¼ cup extra-virgin olive oil
- ½ small fennel bulb, cored and minced
- 1 small shallot, minced (¼ cup)
- 2 cups carnaroli or arborio rice
- ½ cup dry white wine
- One 1-inch-thick slice of white bread, cubed
- 3 tablespoons whole milk
- 2 cups lamb filling from Lamb Roast with Mustard Pan Sauce (page 214), or store-bought lamb sausages, casings removed
- 2 tablespoons unsalted butter
- 2 ounces *ricotta salata* cheese, grated (½ cup)
- Kosher salt and freshly ground pepper

1. Bring the chicken broth and water to a simmer; keep hot.

2. In a large saucepan, heat 2 tablespoons of the oil. Add the fennel and shallot and cook over moderate heat, stirring, until golden, about 5 minutes. Stir in the rice. Add the wine and simmer, stirring, until absorbed. Add 1 cup of the hot broth and cook, stirring, until absorbed. Continue adding the broth 1 cup at a time and stirring until it is nearly absorbed before adding more. The risotto is done when the rice is tender, 20 to 25 minutes.

3. In a large bowl, combine the bread and milk. Mix in the lamb filling; form into four 1-inch-thick logs. In a nonstick skillet, heat the remaining oil. Cook the sausages until browned and cooked through, 7 to 8 minutes, then slice.

4. Stir the butter and cheese into the risotto; season with salt and pepper. Serve with the sliced sausages. —*Kay Chun*
WINE Light-bodied northern Italian red: 2011 J. Hofstätter Lagrein.

● HEALTHY ● MAKE AHEAD ● VEGETARIAN ● STAFF FAVORITE

Potato Salad with Olive Vinaigrette

⏱ **TOTAL: 35 MIN • 6 SERVINGS** ● ● ○ ○

This bold potato salad is a lighter take on the mayo-rich standard. It's filled with the bright, piquant flavors typical of the Mediterranean. The kalamata olives contribute to a high fat content, but it's the heart-healthy, monounsaturated kind.

1½ pounds small potatoes, such as
     red or Yukon Gold, scrubbed
½ garlic clove
½ cup pitted kalamata olives
¼ cup flat-leaf parsley leaves
2 teaspoons capers
¼ cup extra-virgin olive oil
2 tablespoons fresh lemon juice,
     plus more for seasoning
Salt and freshly ground pepper
1 bunch of scallions, thinly sliced
½ cup mixed fresh herbs,
     such as tarragon, parsley
     and chives, chopped

1. In a large saucepan fitted with a steamer basket, bring 1 inch of water to a boil. Add the potatoes to the basket, cover and steam until tender, 25 to 30 minutes. Transfer the steamed potatoes to a plate and let cool until slightly warm.

2. Meanwhile, in the bowl of a mini food processor, finely chop the garlic. Add the olives, parsley and capers and pulse to a chunky paste. Add the olive oil and 2 tablespoons of lemon juice and process until the mixture is almost smooth. Season the olive vinaigrette with salt and pepper.

3. Halve the potatoes, then slice them ¼ inch thick. In a large bowl, toss the potatoes, scallions and chopped herbs with the olive vinaigrette and mix until coated. Season with salt, pepper and lemon juice. Let the salad stand for a few minutes to blend the flavors before serving. —*Jennifer Newens*

NOTE For a crunchy texture and peppery flavor, stir in thinly sliced radishes.

VARIATION Substitute pimiento-stuffed green olives for the kalamatas and chopped fresh dill for the parsley.

Creamy Cucumber and Grilled Potato Salad

⏱ **TOTAL: 45 MIN • 4 SERVINGS** ○

"When I was a kid, my mom would marinate cucumbers, red onions and canned potatoes in jarred creamy Italian dressing," says Boston chef Jamie Bissonnette. "I'm not saying she was a great cook, but creamy Italian dressing is still my favorite. I make a version of it for this salad."

2 pounds small to medium Red Bliss
     potatoes (about 12)
Kosher salt
⅓ cup crème fraîche or mayonnaise
2 tablespoons red wine vinegar
1 tablespoon light corn syrup or
     2 teaspoons sugar
1 teaspoon Dijon mustard
1 teaspoon celery seeds
1 small garlic clove, minced
¼ cup canola oil, plus more for
     brushing
Pinch of crushed red pepper
1 teaspoon finely chopped
     fresh oregano
½ cup chopped parsley plus
     1 teaspoon minced parsley
Freshly ground pepper
1 English cucumber, thinly sliced
⅓ cup thinly sliced red onion

1. In a large saucepan, cover the potatoes with water and bring to a boil. Add a generous pinch of salt and simmer over moderately low heat until just tender, about 15 minutes. Drain the potatoes and let cool completely, then cut them in half lengthwise.

2. Meanwhile, in a large bowl, whisk the crème fraîche, vinegar, corn syrup, mustard, celery seeds and garlic. Gradually whisk in the ¼ cup of oil. Stir in the crushed red pepper, oregano and 1 teaspoon of minced parsley and season the dressing with salt and pepper.

3. Light a grill or preheat a grill pan. Generously brush the potatoes with oil and season with salt and freshly ground pepper; grill, cut side down, over moderately high heat, turning once, until lightly charred and hot, 5 minutes. Transfer to a plate and let cool slightly.

4. Toss the potatoes with the dressing and season them with salt and freshly ground pepper. Fold in the cucumber, red onion and the ½ cup of chopped parsley and serve. —*Jamie Bissonnette*

Steamed New Potatoes with Dandelion Salsa Verde

⏱ **ACTIVE: 20 MIN; TOTAL: 40 MIN**
4 SERVINGS ● ● ●

1 shallot, minced
2 tablespoons Champagne or
     white wine vinegar
1 pound small new potatoes
1 bunch of dandelion greens
     (¾ pound), stems discarded
2 stemmed caperberries or
     1 tablespoon drained capers,
     minced
1 tablespoon freshly squeezed
     lemon juice
½ cup fruity extra-virgin olive oil,
     plus more for drizzling
Sea salt and freshly ground black
     pepper
Thinly sliced radishes, for garnish

1. In a medium bowl, combine the minced shallot and Champagne vinegar; let stand for 20 minutes.

2. Meanwhile, in a medium saucepan of boiling water, cook the potatoes until they are tender, about 15 minutes. Drain the potatoes and slice them ⅓ inch thick; keep warm.

3. Prepare a bowl of ice water. In a medium saucepan of salted boiling water, cook the dandelion greens until tender, 7 to 8 minutes. Drain and transfer the greens to the ice bath to cool. Drain and squeeze dry.

4. Finely chop the greens and add them to the bowl with the vinegared shallot. Stir in the minced caperberries, lemon juice and ½ cup of olive oil. Season the dandelion salsa verde with sea salt and black pepper.

5. Spoon some of the dandelion salsa verde onto plates. Top with the warm potato slices and season with sea salt. Garnish with radish slices, drizzle olive oil on top and serve. —*Daniel Patterson*

Fingerling Papas Bravas with Smoky Aioli

⏱ TOTAL: 40 MIN • 8 SERVINGS ● ●

Every tapas bar in Spain seems to serve these crisp potatoes. This version uses fingerlings, which become especially creamy when fried. The lemony aioli gets its deep flavor from smoked paprika.

3 pounds fingerling potatoes
Kosher salt
2 large egg yolks
1 small garlic clove, mashed to a
   paste or very finely grated
2 tablespoons fresh lemon juice
½ teaspoon finely grated lemon zest
1 cup vegetable oil,
   plus more for frying
1 teaspoon sweet smoked paprika,
   preferably pimentón de la Vera
2 tablespoons finely chopped
   flat-leaf parsley
Maldon sea salt or other flaky salt

1. In a very large saucepan, cover the potatoes with water. Generously season with kosher salt and bring to a boil. Simmer the potatoes until nearly tender, about 10 minutes. Drain and let the potatoes dry on paper towels. Transfer to a work surface and halve each potato lengthwise.
2. Meanwhile, in a medium bowl, whisk the egg yolks with the garlic, lemon juice and zest. Gradually add the 1 cup of oil in a very thin stream, whisking constantly, until a thick, creamy sauce forms. Whisk in the paprika and season the aioli with kosher salt.
3. In a large saucepan, heat 2 inches of oil until it reaches 350° on a deep-fry thermometer; line a baking sheet with paper towels. Working in batches, fry the potatoes until completely tender and lightly browned in spots, 5 minutes. Using a slotted spoon, transfer the potatoes to the paper towels. Sprinkle with parsley and Maldon salt and transfer to a bowl. Serve right away, with the smoky aioli. —*David Mawhinney*
WINE Green apple–inflected Spanish sparkling wine: 2009 Raventós i Blanc Brut L'Hereu.

Louisiana Cheese Fries with Crayfish and Gravy

ACTIVE: 1 HR; TOTAL: 3 HR
4 SERVINGS

PIMENTO CHEESE
1 red bell pepper
1 jalapeño
1 pound white cheddar cheese,
   shredded (3¼ cups)
¼ cup mayonnaise
2 tablespoons sour cream
½ tablespoon chopped cilantro
½ tablespoon fresh lemon juice
⅛ teaspoon cayenne pepper
Kosher salt and freshly ground
   black pepper
ANDOUILLE GRAVY
1 tablespoon canola oil
½ pound andouille sausage,
   cut into ¼-inch dice
¾ cup minced onion
⅓ cup minced green bell pepper
½ tablespoon minced garlic
1 tablespoon all-purpose flour
¼ cup chopped tomato
1½ cups chicken stock or
   low-sodium broth
¼ cup thinly sliced scallion
Kosher salt
POUTINE
4 cups cooked french fries
½ pound cooked and shelled crayfish
   tails, jumbo lump crabmeat or
   chopped shrimp

1. **MAKE THE PIMENTO CHEESE** Roast the red pepper and jalapeño directly over a gas flame or under a preheated broiler, turning, until charred all over. Transfer to a large bowl, cover tightly with plastic and let cool for 15 minutes. Peel, seed and stem the red pepper and jalapeño, then cut them into ¼-inch dice.
2. In a large bowl, mix half of the red pepper with half of the jalapeño; reserve the rest for another use. Add the cheese, mayonnaise, sour cream, cilantro, lemon juice and cayenne and mix well; season with salt and black pepper. Chill for at least 2 hours.

3. **MEANWHILE, MAKE THE GRAVY** In a medium cast-iron skillet, heat the oil. Add the andouille; cook over moderate heat, stirring, until the fat is rendered and the sausage is crispy, 8 minutes. Add the onion; cook, stirring, until translucent, 3 minutes. Stir in the green pepper and garlic; cook, stirring, until the garlic is fragrant, 2 minutes. Sprinkle in the flour; stir until incorporated. Add the tomato; cook over moderately low heat, stirring, until it starts to break down, 3 minutes. Add the stock; bring to a simmer. Cook until the gravy is thick enough to coat the back of a spoon, 5 minutes. Stir in the scallions; season with salt.
4. **MAKE THE POUTINE** Preheat the oven to 450°. Spread the fries on a heatproof serving platter. Spoon the gravy all over the fries; top with the crayfish. Dollop 1 cup of the pimento cheese all over the fries; reserve the rest for another use. Bake the poutine until the cheese is bubbly and melted, 5 minutes. Serve immediately. —*Kelly English*

Hash Browns

⏱ TOTAL: 30 MIN • 2 SERVINGS ● ●

1 pound Yukon Gold potatoes, peeled
   and cut into ½-inch pieces
Salt
2 tablespoons vegetable oil
2 tablespoons unsalted butter
Freshly ground pepper

1. Put the potatoes in a medium saucepan, add 4 cups of water and 1 teaspoon of salt and bring to a boil. Simmer, partially covered, until almost tender. Drain and pat dry.
2. Heat a 10-inch nonstick skillet. Add the vegetable oil and 1 tablespoon of the butter. When the foam subsides, add the potatoes and cook over moderately high heat, tossing, until lightly golden. Season with salt and pepper and roughly mash the potatoes with a spatula. Dot the remaining 1 tablespoon of butter over the potatoes, cover and cook until crusty on the bottom, about 3 minutes. Slide the potatoes onto a plate and invert them back into the pan. Cook until the underside is nice and crusty. Slide the potatoes onto a platter and serve. —*Julia Child*

● HEALTHY ● MAKE AHEAD ● VEGETARIAN ● STAFF FAVORITE

POTATOES

ACCORDION POTATOES

Slice 1 pound fingerling potatoes at ⅛-inch intervals, cutting down but not through the potatoes; transfer to a baking sheet. Whisk 6 tablespoons olive oil with 1 tablespoon pimentón or sweet paprika. Drizzle the potatoes with 5 tablespoons of the oil. Roast at 375° for 20 minutes. Insert a small bay leaf into each potato and roast 20 minutes longer. Discard the bay leaves, drizzle with the remaining oil and serve.

POTATO, SNAP PEA & PICKLE SALAD

Boil 1 pound new potatoes until tender; cool, peel and thinly slice them. In a skillet, cook 1 sliced red onion and 3 sliced scallions in 3 tablespoons olive oil over moderate heat until softened. In a bowl, whisk 3 tablespoons olive oil with 1 tablespoon each Dijon mustard and lemon juice, then add to the skillet. Fold in the potatoes, 2 chopped half-sour pickles and ½ cup sliced sugar snap peas. Season with salt and pepper, toss and serve.

GRILLED POTATOES WITH TOMATO DIP

Grate 3 tomatoes into a bowl; discard the skins. Add ½ cup jarred marinara sauce and 1 tablespoon of Sriracha or hot sauce; season with salt. Cut 1 pound fingerling potatoes into ⅛-inch-thick slices; toss with ¼ cup olive oil and season with salt. Grill over moderate heat, turning, until golden, about 10 minutes. Serve with the tomato dip.

BOILED POTATOES WITH SAGE BUTTER

Boil 1 pound new potatoes until tender. Drain and halve. Meanwhile, melt ½ stick unsalted butter in a skillet. Add ¼ cup small sage leaves and cook over moderate heat for 2 minutes. Add 2 thinly sliced scallions and cook for 2 minutes. Add the potatoes, season with salt and pepper and cook to warm them through. Serve the potatoes with breakfast sausages.

SMASHED POTATOES WITH CARAWAY

In a small saucepan, melt 2 tablespoons unsalted butter. Add 3 crushed garlic cloves and cook for 2 minutes. Discard the garlic and stir in 1 teaspoon caraway seeds. On a rimmed baking sheet, toss 1 pound new potatoes with 2 tablespoons olive oil and season with salt and pepper. Roast at 375° for 20 minutes. Using the back of a spoon, press down on each potato until it cracks. Spoon the caraway butter over the potatoes and roast for 20 minutes longer, until crispy. Serve with chopped chives.
—*Kay Chun*

ACCORDION POTATOES

Roasted-Garlic Mashed Potatoes

ACTIVE: 15 MIN; TOTAL: 1 HR 15 MIN
12 SERVINGS ● ●

Sweet roasted garlic and a generous amount of spicy Tabasco sauce make these creamy mashed potatoes deeply flavorful.

- 5 pounds Yukon Gold potatoes, peeled and cut into 2-inch chunks
- 1 stick unsalted butter, cut into tablespoons
- 1 cup heavy cream
- 2 tablespoons Mashed Roasted Garlic (recipe follows)
- 2 teaspoons Tabasco

Salt and freshly ground white pepper
- 1 tablespoon chopped flat-leaf parsley

1. In a large pot, cover the potatoes with water and bring to a boil. Simmer over moderate heat, uncovered, until tender, 20 minutes. Drain the potatoes and return them to the pot. Cook over low heat, gently tossing, until the potatoes are dry, 2 minutes.
2. Add the butter, cream and roasted garlic to the potatoes; mash over low heat until creamy and heated through. Add the Tabasco; season with salt and pepper. Transfer the mashed potatoes to a bowl, garnish with the parsley and serve. —*Tanya Holland*

MASHED ROASTED GARLIC

ACTIVE: 5 MIN; TOTAL: 1 HR 10 MIN
MAKES ABOUT ½ CUP ● ● ●

- 2 large heads of garlic, halved horizontally
- 1 teaspoon extra-virgin olive oil

Salt and freshly ground black pepper

Preheat the oven to 300°. Arrange the garlic cut side up on a sheet of foil and drizzle with the olive oil. Season the garlic with salt and pepper and wrap it in the foil. Roast the garlic for about 1 hour, until very soft. Let cool, then squeeze the garlic cloves out of the skins and mash. —*TH*

Mashed Potatoes with Bacon and Mustard

TOTAL: 1 HR • 10 TO 12 SERVINGS ●

Mashed potatoes meet potato salad in this recipe from F&W's Justin Chapple. The creamy and chunky potato dish is packed with tangy whole-grain mustard, fresh herbs and smoky, thick-cut bacon.

- 4 pounds Yukon Gold potatoes, peeled and cut into 1-inch pieces

Kosher salt
- ½ pound thick-cut meaty bacon, finely diced
- 1 large red onion, finely chopped
- ¼ cup apple cider vinegar
- 2 tablespoons whole-grain mustard
- 1 teaspoon celery seeds
- 1½ sticks unsalted butter
- 1¼ cups whole milk
- 1 cup mayonnaise
- ¼ cup finely chopped parsley

Freshly ground white pepper

1. In a large saucepan, cover the potatoes with water and bring to a boil. Add a generous pinch of salt and simmer over moderate heat until tender, about 20 minutes. Drain the potatoes in a colander, shaking off any excess water.
2. Meanwhile, in a large skillet, cook the diced bacon over moderately high heat, stirring occasionally, until crisp, about 8 minutes. Using a slotted spoon, transfer the bacon to paper towels to drain. Pour off all but 2 tablespoons of the bacon fat from the skillet. Add the chopped onion to the skillet and cook over moderate heat, stirring, until just starting to brown, about 6 to 8 minutes. Add the apple cider vinegar, whole-grain mustard and celery seeds and cook, stirring, until most of the liquid has been absorbed, about 2 minutes.
3. In the large saucepan, melt the butter in the milk over moderately low heat. Press the potatoes through a ricer into the saucepan and mix well. Fold in the mayonnaise, bacon, onion mixture and parsley, season with salt and white pepper and serve.
—*Justin Chapple*

MAKE AHEAD If you're not serving the potatoes right away, let them cool, then transfer to a bowl or large resealable plastic bag and refrigerate for up to 3 days. Rewarm the potatoes in the microwave in 2-minute intervals, stirring each time, until hot.

Whipped Sweet Potatoes with Coconut and Ginger

ACTIVE: 20 MIN; TOTAL: 1 HR 20 MIN
10 TO 12 SERVINGS ● ●

These fluffy pureed sweet potatoes are upgraded with luxurious coconut cream, zesty fresh ginger and a topping of nutty shredded coconut.

- 6 pounds sweet potatoes (6 large)
- 1 stick unsalted butter, melted
- ¾ cup unsweetened coconut cream (see Note)
- 1½ tablespoons finely grated peeled fresh ginger

Kosher salt and freshly ground white pepper

Unsweetened finely shredded coconut, for garnish

1. Preheat the oven to 400°. Poke the sweet potatoes several times with a fork and bake on a baking sheet for about 1 hour, until tender. Let cool slightly.
2. Peel the sweet potatoes and transfer to a food processor. Add the butter, coconut cream and ginger and puree until smooth. Season with salt and white pepper, garnish with shredded coconut and serve.
—*Justin Chapple*

NOTE Unsweetened coconut cream is available in cans at most supermarkets and health food stores. If you can't find it, you can also purchase canned unsweetened coconut milk and let the milk stand, then spoon the thick cream off the top.

MAKE AHEAD If you're not serving the sweet potatoes right away, let them cool, then transfer to a bowl or large resealable plastic bag and refrigerate for up to 3 days. Rewarm the sweet potatoes in the microwave in 2-minute intervals, stirring each time, until they are hot.

● HEALTHY ● MAKE AHEAD ● VEGETARIAN ● STAFF FAVORITE

WHIPPED SWEET POTATOES
WITH COCONUT AND GINGER

MASHED POTATOES WITH
BACON AND MUSTARD

The Cheesiest Mashed Potatoes

⏱ **ACTIVE: 15 MIN; TOTAL: 45 MIN**
4 SERVINGS ● ●

This mashed-potato dish from chef Lee Hefter of Beverly Hills's renowned Spago is so packed with cheese—mozzarella and Comté—it's almost like fondue.

- 2 large baking potatoes
- 6 tablespoons unsalted butter
- 1½ cups heavy cream
- 1 large garlic clove, minced
- 2 cups each of shredded mozzarella and imported Comté or Fontina cheese (6 ounces each)
- Salt

1. In a large saucepan, cover the potatoes with 2 inches of water. Bring to a boil and simmer until tender, about 30 minutes. Drain and peel the potatoes. Pass them through a ricer into the saucepan. Stir in the butter and ½ cup of the cream until incorporated.

2. In a small saucepan, combine the remaining 1 cup of cream with the minced garlic and bring to a boil. Stir the garlic cream into the potatoes and cook over low heat until smooth and creamy. Add the cheese by the handful, stirring it in until melted before adding more. Season with salt and serve hot. If necessary, add a few drops of hot water to loosen the potatoes. —*Lee Hefter*

Rich and Creamy Mashed Potatoes

⏱ **TOTAL: 40 MIN**
10 TO 12 SERVINGS ● ● ●

Reheated cold mashed potatoes are rarely as good as fresh, but this is a foolproof make-ahead dish. The secret to the velvety texture is mayonnaise.

- 4 pounds Yukon Gold potatoes, peeled and cut into 1-inch pieces
- Kosher salt
- 1½ sticks unsalted butter
- 1¼ cups whole milk
- 1 cup mayonnaise
- Freshly ground white pepper

1. In a large saucepan, cover the potatoes with water and bring to a boil. Add a generous pinch of salt and simmer over moderate heat until tender, about 20 minutes. Drain the potatoes in a colander, shaking off any excess water.

2. In the same saucepan, melt the butter in the milk over moderately low heat. Remove from the heat. Press the potatoes through a ricer into the saucepan and mix well. Fold in the mayonnaise, season with salt and white pepper and serve. —*Justin Chapple*

MAKE AHEAD If you're not serving the potatoes right away, let them cool, then transfer to a bowl or large resealable plastic bag and refrigerate for up to 3 days. Rewarm the potatoes in the microwave in 2-minute intervals, stirring each time, until hot.

Mashed Potatoes with Jalapeño and Cheddar

⏱ **TOTAL: 40 MIN**
10 TO 12 SERVINGS ● ●

- 4 pounds Yukon Gold potatoes, peeled and cut into 1-inch pieces
- Kosher salt
- 1½ sticks unsalted butter
- 1¼ cups whole milk
- ½ pound white cheddar cheese, shredded (2⅔ cups)
- 1 cup mayonnaise
- 1 large jalapeño—stemmed, seeded and minced
- Freshly ground white pepper

1. In a large saucepan, cover the potatoes with water and bring to a boil. Add a generous pinch of salt and simmer over moderate heat until tender, about 20 minutes. Drain the potatoes in a colander, shaking off any excess water.

2. In the same saucepan, melt the butter in the milk over moderately low heat. Remove from the heat and stir in the cheese. Press the potatoes through a ricer into the saucepan and mix well. Fold the mayonnaise and jalapeño into the potatoes and season with salt and white pepper. Serve right away. —*Justin Chapple*

Whipped Sweet Potatoes

ACTIVE: 20 MIN; TOTAL: 1 HR 20 MIN
10 TO 12 SERVINGS ● ●

- 6 pounds sweet potatoes (6 large)
- 1 stick unsalted butter, melted
- ½ cup sour cream
- Kosher salt and freshly ground white pepper

1. Preheat the oven to 400°. Poke the sweet potatoes several times with a fork and bake on a baking sheet for about 1 hour, until tender. Let cool slightly.

2. Peel the sweet potatoes and transfer them to a food processor. Add the butter and sour cream and puree until smooth. Season with salt and white pepper and serve. —*Justin Chapple*

Harissa-Whipped Sweet Potatoes

ACTIVE: 20 MIN; TOTAL: 1 HR 20 MIN
10 TO 12 SERVINGS ● ● ●

Harissa adds smoky heat to these silky make-ahead mashed sweet potatoes.

- 6 pounds sweet potatoes (6 large)
- 1 stick unsalted butter, melted
- ½ cup sour cream
- ¼ cup harissa
- Kosher salt and freshly ground white pepper

1. Preheat the oven to 400°. Poke the sweet potatoes several times with a fork and bake on a baking sheet for about 1 hour, until tender. Let cool slightly.

2. Peel the sweet potatoes and transfer them to a food processor. Add the butter, sour cream and harissa and puree until smooth. Season with salt and white pepper and serve. —*Justin Chapple*

MAKE AHEAD If you're not serving the sweet potatoes right away, let them cool, then transfer to a bowl or large resealable plastic bag and refrigerate for up to 3 days. Rewarm them in the microwave in 2-minute intervals, stirring each time, until hot.

Sweet Potato and Goat Cheese Gratin

ACTIVE: 30 MIN; TOTAL: 2 HR 45 MIN
8 TO 10 SERVINGS ● ○ ○

Goat cheese whisked into the cream adds a fantastic tang to this sweet and luscious gratin. Buttery bread crumbs get baked on top for a crispy, golden crust.

- 4 tablespoons unsalted butter, melted
- ¾ cup milk
- ¾ cup heavy cream
- 2 tablespoons honey
- 1 small garlic clove, minced
- 8 ounces fresh goat cheese, softened
- Salt and freshly ground pepper
- 3 pounds sweet potatoes, peeled and sliced lengthwise ⅛ inch thick
- ½ cup dry bread crumbs

1. Preheat the oven to 275° and brush a large baking dish with 2 tablespoons of the melted butter. In a medium saucepan, combine the milk, heavy cream, honey and minced garlic and bring just to a simmer. Remove the saucepan from the heat. Whisk in the goat cheese and season generously with salt and freshly ground pepper.

2. Line the bottom of the baking dish with a slightly overlapping layer of sweet potatoes. Top with ¼ cup of the goat cheese cream and spread evenly over the sweet potatoes. Repeat the layering with the remaining sweet potatoes and goat cheese cream, pouring any excess cream on top; you should have about 5 layers.

3. In a small bowl, combine the bread crumbs with the remaining 2 tablespoons of melted butter and scatter over the sweet potatoes. Cover the casserole with a sheet of buttered aluminum foil and bake for 1 hour. Remove the aluminum foil and bake for about 1 hour longer, until the sweet potatoes are tender and the top is golden. Let the gratin stand for 15 minutes before serving.
—*David Kinch*

MAKE AHEAD The Sweet Potato and Goat Cheese Gratin can be baked earlier in the day and reheated.

Roasted Sweet Potato Salad with Miso-Dijon Dressing

⊙ TOTAL: 45 MIN • 4 TO 6 SERVINGS ● ●

F&W's Kay Chun prefers Japanese white sweet potatoes for this dish. They have a mild, chestnut-like flavor and fluffy texture when roasted.

- 2 tablespoons white miso
- 2 tablespoons Dijon mustard
- ¼ cup plus 3 tablespoons canola oil
- ½ pound wild mushrooms, coarsely chopped
- 2 medium sweet potatoes (1½ pounds), preferably Japanese white, scrubbed and cut into 1½-inch pieces
- Kosher salt and freshly ground pepper
- Chopped chives, for garnish

1. Preheat the oven to 425°. In a small bowl, whisk the miso with the mustard, ¼ cup of the canola oil and 2 tablespoons of water.

2. In a large bowl, toss the mushrooms and sweet potatoes with the remaining 3 tablespoons of canola oil and season with salt and pepper. Spread the potatoes on a baking sheet. Roast for 15 minutes; turn them and add the mushrooms. Roast for 10 minutes longer, until the potatoes are tender and golden and the mushrooms are browned. Transfer the potatoes and mushrooms to a platter and drizzle with the dressing. Garnish with chives and serve warm. —*Kay Chun*

MAKE AHEAD The dressing can be refrigerated for up to 1 week.

Sweet Potato Wedges with Roasted-Almond Pesto

⊙ TOTAL: 40 MIN • 6 TO 8 SERVINGS ● ● ●

This chunky basil-almond pesto is excellent as a dip for roasted sweet potato wedges. It's also fabulous on pasta.

SWEET POTATOES

- 2 medium sweet potatoes (1½ pounds), scrubbed and cut into ½-inch-thick wedges
- 2 tablespoons extra-virgin olive oil
- Kosher salt and freshly ground pepper

PESTO

- 1 cup sliced almonds
- 1 cup packed basil leaves
- 1 small garlic clove, crushed
- ¾ cup extra-virgin olive oil
- ¼ cup freshly grated Parmigiano-Reggiano cheese
- 2 tablespoons fresh lemon juice
- Kosher salt and freshly ground pepper

1. MAKE THE SWEET POTATOES Preheat the oven to 425°. On a baking sheet, toss the sweet potatoes with the 2 tablespoons of oil; season with salt and pepper. Roast for 25 to 30 minutes, turning occasionally, until tender.

2. MEANWHILE, MAKE THE PESTO In a pie plate, toast the almonds for 3 minutes, until lightly golden; let cool completely. In a food processor, pulse the almonds, basil and garlic until finely chopped. With the machine on, drizzle in the ¾ cup of olive oil. Transfer to a bowl, stir in the cheese and lemon juice and season with salt and pepper. Serve the sweet potatoes with the pesto. —*Kay Chun*

BUILD-YOUR-OWN SWEET POTATO

Sweet potatoes are packed with vitamins and are far less starchy than regular potatoes—yet they are just as versatile. Here, the humble sweet potato is baked, split open and elevated with three different inventive toppings.

HEARTY CHILI Add a generous scoop of beef, turkey or bean chili; garnish with sharp cheddar cheese, sour cream, snipped chives and diced avocado.

PARMESAN-HERB Top with sautéed onion and garlic, fresh rosemary, thyme and shaved Parmigiano-Reggiano.

SWEET POTATO PIE Sprinkle with light brown sugar and cinnamon, chopped toasted pecans and crushed graham crackers. Garnish with mini marshmallows and pop under the broiler until bubbling.

Bakers are tackling all kinds of breads, while chefs put those loaves to good use. Here, crisp-chewy Persian flatbread (recipe, page 270).

BREADS, PIZZAS & SANDWICHES

ASIAN SLOPPY JOE
SLIDERS, PAGE 282

BREADS, PIZZAS & SANDWICHES

Layman's Rye Bread

ACTIVE: 45 MIN; TOTAL: 6 HR
MAKES ONE 9-BY-5-INCH LOAF ● ● ○ ○

At Runner & Stone, a bakery and restaurant in Brooklyn, New York, Peter Endriss makes his rye with a wild yeast starter that gives the bread a wonderfully tangy and complex flavor and aroma. For home cooks, he suggests using cornichon or pickle juice instead.

1¾ cups stone-ground dark rye flour, preferably Bob's Red Mill brand
2¼ cups bread flour, plus more for dusting
  1 cup strained juice from a jar of cornichons or dill pickles, at room temperature
2¼ teaspoons active dry yeast (1 packet)
  2 teaspoons sugar
  1 teaspoon salt
Vegetable oil, for greasing

1. Preheat the oven to 350°. On a rimmed baking sheet lined with parchment paper, thinly spread the rye flour. Toast for about 16 minutes, stirring every 4 minutes, until fragrant and just slightly darkened. Let cool.
2. In the bowl of a standing mixer fitted with the dough hook, combine the toasted rye flour with the 2¼ cups of bread flour, 1 cup plus 1 tablespoon of lukewarm water and the cornichon juice, yeast, sugar and salt. Mix at low speed until well combined, about 1 minute. Increase the speed to medium and mix until the dough just starts to pull away from the side and bottom of the bowl, about 3 minutes; it will still be sticky and shaggy.
3. Meanwhile, lightly oil a large bowl. With oiled hands, shape the dough into a ball and transfer to the oiled bowl. Cover loosely with plastic wrap and let rise in a warm place for 1 hour; the dough will rise only slightly.
4. Invert the dough onto a lightly floured work surface. Flatten gently and fold the edge into the center. Invert and return the dough to the oiled bowl. Cover and let rise in a draft-free place until puffy, about 1 hour.
5. Lightly oil a 9-by-5-inch loaf pan. Invert the dough onto a lightly floured work surface

and flatten into a 10-inch square. Roll up the dough to form a 10-inch log. Fit the loaf into the prepared pan, seam side down, tucking the ends underneath. Press the dough gently into the corners of the pan. Cover loosely and let rise in a warm place until the dough is just above the rim of the pan and no longer springs back to the touch, about 2½ hours.
6. Set a pizza stone on the second-lowest rack in the oven and a cast-iron skillet on the bottom of the oven. Preheat the oven to 400° for at least 30 minutes. Place the loaf pan on the pizza stone. Add 1 cup of ice to the skillet and shut the oven. Bake for about 55 minutes, until the bread is lightly browned on top and the bottom of the pan sounds hollow when tapped; remove the skillet halfway through baking. Unmold the loaf onto a rack and let the bread cool before slicing. —Peter Endriss

Homemade Bagels

ACTIVE: 45 MIN; TOTAL: 3 HR 30 MIN
PLUS OVERNIGHT PROOFING
MAKES 1 DOZEN BAGELS ● ● ○ ○

The trick to these crisp, chewy bagels is the *poolish,* a fermentation starter (also known as a mother dough) made with bread flour, yeast and water. It is quickly assembled the night before the bagels are made.

POOLISH
1⅓ cups bread flour
  ¼ teaspoon active dry yeast
DOUGH
  1 teaspoon active dry yeast
  ¼ cup honey
5⅓ cups bread flour
  1 cup plus 2 tablespoons whole-wheat flour
  1 tablespoon salt
  1 tablespoon baking soda
Poppy seeds, sesame seeds and coarse sea salt, for sprinkling

1. **MAKE THE POOLISH** In a medium bowl, using a wooden spoon, stir the bread flour with the yeast and 1 cup of lukewarm water until combined. Cover with plastic wrap and refrigerate overnight.

2. **MAKE THE DOUGH** In the bowl of a standing mixer fitted with the dough hook, combine the yeast and honey with 1⅔ cups of lukewarm water. Mix in the *poolish.* Add the bread flour, whole-wheat flour and salt and beat at medium speed until a smooth, stiff dough forms, 5 to 7 minutes. Transfer the dough to a lightly floured work surface and knead for 1 minute. Form the dough into a ball and transfer to a large, oiled bowl. Cover with plastic wrap and let stand in a draft-free spot until doubled in volume, about 1 hour.
3. Line a baking sheet with parchment paper and brush or spray generously with vegetable oil. Divide the dough into 12 pieces and form into tight balls; transfer to the baking sheet. Cover loosely with sprayed plastic wrap and let stand for 30 minutes.
4. To form the bagels, poke your finger in the center of each ball to make a ½-inch hole. Return the bagels to the baking sheet, cover and let stand until risen, about 1 hour. Add 1 bagel to a bowl of cold water. If it floats, the bagels have risen sufficiently.
5. Preheat the oven to 475° and position racks in the lower and middle thirds. Line 1 baking sheet with a clean, lightly moistened kitchen towel and line 2 others with parchment paper; spray the paper with oil. Bring 2 large, deep pots of water to a boil. Add ½ tablespoon of baking soda to each pot. Add 2 or 3 bagels to each pot, without crowding (the bagels will swell in the water), and simmer for 1½ minutes. Flip the bagels and simmer for 1½ minutes longer. Using a slotted spoon, transfer the bagels to the kitchen towel–lined sheet to drain. Before they dry, sprinkle the bagels generously with toppings, then immediately transfer them to the parchment paper–lined baking sheets. Repeat with the remaining bagels.
6. Bake the bagels for 18 to 20 minutes, shifting the pans from top to bottom and front to back halfway through, until deeply browned. Let cool slightly, then serve. —Zoe Nathan

MAKE AHEAD The bagels can be stored in an airtight container for up to 3 days. Sprinkle with water and reheat in a 350° oven until crusty and warm.

268

HEALTHY   MAKE AHEAD   VEGETARIAN   STAFF FAVORITE

HOMEMADE BAGELS

Persian Flatbread

📷 PAGE 266

ACTIVE: 30 MIN; TOTAL: 4 HR
MAKES 2 LARGE LOAVES ● ● ○

2¼ teaspoons active dry yeast
     (1 packet)
  4 cups bread flour, plus more
     for kneading
Salt
  1 teaspoon vegetable oil, plus
     more for greasing
  1 tablespoon all-purpose flour
  1 teaspoon sugar
Semolina or cornmeal, for sprinkling
  1 tablespoon nigella seeds
     (see Note)
  1 tablespoon sesame seeds

1. In the bowl of a standing mixer fitted with the dough hook, combine 2 cups of luke-warm water with the yeast and let stand for 5 minutes. Add the 4 cups of bread flour and 2 teaspoons of salt and mix at medium speed until a loose dough forms. Increase the speed to medium-high and mix until the dough is supple and smooth, about 6 minutes. Transfer the dough to a lightly floured work surface and knead for 1 minute. Transfer the dough to an oiled bowl, cover with plastic wrap and let stand in a draft-free spot until doubled in volume, about 1 hour.
2. Punch down the dough and form into 2 ovals. Transfer the ovals to an oiled baking sheet, cover with a sheet of oiled plastic wrap and let rise for 1 hour.
3. Meanwhile, in a small saucepan, combine the all-purpose flour with the sugar, 1 teaspoon of vegetable oil and ½ cup of water. Cook the flour paste over moderate heat, whisking, until thickened, about 2 minutes. Let the flour paste cool.
4. Preheat the oven to 450° and set a pizza stone on the lowest rack. Let the stone heat for at least 30 minutes. Generously sprinkle a pizza peel with semolina. Punch down 1 piece of the dough and transfer it to a lightly floured work surface. Press the dough into a 14-by-5-inch rectangle, then transfer to the peel; shake the peel lightly to make

sure the dough doesn't stick, adding more semolina if necessary. Using your fingers, press 5 deep lengthwise ridges into the dough. Rub about one-third of the flour paste over the surface and sprinkle with half of the nigella and sesame seeds. Slide the dough onto the hot stone and bake for about 18 minutes, until golden and risen. Repeat to make the second loaf (there will be some paste left over). Serve warm.
—*Jessamyn Rodriguez*

NOTE Nutty, peppery nigella seeds (also called black onion seeds) are avalable at specialty food stores.

Parker House Roll Dough

ACTIVE: 15 MIN; TOTAL: 1 HR 30 MIN
MAKES ENOUGH DOUGH FOR 8 INDIVIDUAL
POTPIES ○

This fluffy dough makes a splendid biscuit-like topping for chef Michael White's individual mushroom potpies (page 238).

  3 cups all-purpose flour,
     plus more for dusting
  1 cup instant potato flakes
  2 teaspoons salt
1½ cups milk
  3 tablespoons unsalted butter
2½ tablespoons sugar
  2 packets instant dry yeast
  1 large egg

1. In the bowl of a standing mixer fitted with the dough hook, combine the 3 cups of flour with the potato flakes and salt. In a small microwave-safe bowl, heat the milk, butter and sugar just until warm. Stir in the yeast and let stand until foamy, about 5 minutes. Add the yeast mixture and egg to the mixing bowl and beat at medium speed until smooth, about 5 minutes. Scrape the dough out onto a lightly floured work surface and knead until supple and silky, about 3 minutes.
2. Spray the mixing bowl with vegetable oil spray and add the dough. Cover and let rise until doubled in size, about 1 hour. Punch down the dough and transfer to a floured work surface. Let rest for 5 minutes before using.
—*Michael White*

Sweet Potato Biscuits

TOTAL: 30 MIN PLUS TIME FOR COOKING
THE SWEET POTATO • MAKES ABOUT
FOURTEEN 2-INCH BISCUITS ● ○

These buttery, super-tender biscuits are great with a drizzle of honey.

  1 cup chilled sweet potato puree
     (see Note)
  ¾ cup chilled buttermilk
2¼ cups all-purpose flour
  2 tablespoons light brown sugar
2½ teaspoons baking powder
  ½ teaspoon baking soda
  1 teaspoon kosher salt
  1 stick cold unsalted butter, cut into
     cubes, plus 1 tablespoon melted
     butter for brushing

1. Preheat the oven to 450°. Line a baking sheet with parchment paper. In a small bowl, whisk the sweet potato puree with the buttermilk. In a large bowl, whisk the flour with the brown sugar, baking powder, baking soda and salt. Sprinkle the cubed butter over the dry ingredients; using a pastry blender or 2 table knives, cut the butter into the flour until the mixture resembles very coarse crumbs, with some pea-size pieces of butter remaining. Stir in the sweet potato mixture just until a soft dough forms.
2. Turn the dough out onto a floured work surface and pat it into a 1-inch-thick round. Using a 2-inch round biscuit cutter, stamp out as many biscuits as you can. Gently press the scraps together and stamp out more biscuits. Arrange the biscuits on the prepared baking sheet and bake for about 15 minutes, until golden brown. Brush with the melted butter; serve warm. —*Tanya Holland*

NOTE To make the sweet potato puree: Pierce one 12-ounce sweet potato in a few spots with a fork and microwave at high power for about 10 minutes or roast at 350° for about 1 hour, until tender. Let the sweet potato cool slightly, then peel and puree in a food processor. Measure out 1 cup of puree and refrigerate until chilled.

MAKE AHEAD The sweet potato biscuits can be reheated in a 350° oven.

● HEALTHY ● MAKE AHEAD ○ VEGETARIAN ● STAFF FAVORITE

SWEET POTATO BISCUITS

Salt-and-Pepper Crème Fraîche Biscuits

ACTIVE: 25 MIN; TOTAL: 2 HR

MAKES 2 DOZEN 2-INCH BISCUITS ● ●

Pastry chef Tiffany MacIsaac serves these biscuits at GBD, the fried-chicken-and-doughnut restaurant she opened in Washington, DC, with her husband, chef Kyle Bailey. Seasoned with freshly ground black pepper and a sprinkling of Maldon sea salt, the warm biscuits are delicious sandwiching a fried egg or simply spread with butter.

 1 large egg
 1 large egg yolk
 ¾ cup crème fraîche
 ¼ cup milk
 2½ cups all-purpose flour,
      plus more for dusting
 2 tablespoons plus 2 teaspoons sugar
 1 tablespoon plus ¼ teaspoon
      baking powder
 2 teaspoons table salt
 1½ teaspoons freshly ground
      black pepper
 1½ sticks unsalted butter, cut into
      ¼-inch dice and chilled
 ¼ cup heavy cream
Maldon salt, for sprinkling

1. In a small bowl, whisk the egg with the egg yolk, crème fraîche and milk. In a large bowl, combine the 2½ cups of flour with the sugar, baking powder, table salt and pepper. Using a pastry blender or 2 butter knives, cut the butter into the flour mixture until it resembles coarse meal. Add the egg mixture and stir with a wooden spoon until the dough is evenly moistened. Gather the dough into a ball and knead 2 or 3 times, just until it comes together.

2. Line 2 large baking sheets with parchment paper and dust them with flour. Transfer the dough to one of the baking sheets and press it into an 8-by-10-inch rectangle. Cover with plastic wrap and refrigerate for 1 hour.

3. Preheat the oven to 400°. Transfer the dough to a floured work surface and roll it out to an 11-inch square. Fold the square in half and roll it out again to an 11-inch square.

Repeat the folding and rolling once more. Using a 2-inch round biscuit cutter, stamp out as many biscuits as possible. Gather the scraps, reroll and stamp out more biscuits.

4. Evenly space the biscuits on the prepared baking sheets. Brush the tops with the cream and sprinkle with Maldon salt. Bake the biscuits in the upper and lower thirds of the oven for about 20 minutes, until golden; shift the baking sheets from top to bottom and front to back halfway through. Serve the biscuits warm. *—Tiffany MacIsaac*

MAKE AHEAD The biscuits can be baked and rewarmed in the oven.

Whole-Wheat Buttermilk Biscuits

ACTIVE: 15 MIN; TOTAL: 50 MIN

MAKES 9 BISCUITS ● ● ●

Lance Gummere, co-owner of Bantam + Biddy in Atlanta, makes these incredible biscuits with just a bit of cheddar to give them a savory edge.

 2 cups whole-wheat flour (see Note)
 1 tablespoon turbinado sugar
 1 tablespoon baking powder
 1 teaspoon salt
 ⅓ cup shredded sharp cheddar cheese
 1 stick cold unsalted butter, cubed
 ½ cup plus 2 tablespoons buttermilk

1. Preheat the oven to 450°. In a large bowl, whisk the flour, sugar, baking powder and salt. Whisk in the cheddar cheese. Using your fingers or a pastry blender, rub or cut in the butter until the mixture resembles coarse meal with some pea-size pieces remaining. Mix in the buttermilk, stirring, just until the dough holds together.

2. On a lightly floured work surface, roll out the dough to a 7½-inch square that's ¾ inch thick. Cut the dough into nine 2½-inch squares and transfer the squares to an ungreased baking sheet. Bake the biscuits for about 12 minutes, until golden brown on top. Let the biscuits cool slightly and serve. *—Lance Gummere*

NOTE Gummere loves the fresh flavors of Carolina Ground flour (*carolinaground.com*).

Corn Bread for Khrushchev

ACTIVE: 20 MIN; TOTAL: 1 HR 15 MIN

6 TO 8 SERVINGS ● ●

In the US, Nikita Khrushchev is best known for his shoe-banging at the United Nations. In Russia, the eccentric former premier is mostly remembered for his obsession with planting corn everywhere—which earned him the nickname of Kukuruznik (Corn Man). As a comical tribute to Khrushchev, food writer Anya von Bremzen often makes this moist, fluffy Moldovan corn bread with feta and sour cream. It's fantastic for dunking into sauces and dips.

 1 stick unsalted butter,
      melted and cooled slightly,
      plus more for the pan
 2 large eggs, lightly beaten
 2 cups milk
 ½ cup sour cream
 2 cups fine yellow cornmeal,
      preferably stone-ground
 ¾ cup all-purpose flour
 2 teaspoons baking powder
 1 teaspoon salt
 1 teaspoon sugar
 ½ teaspoon baking soda
 ¾ pound feta cheese, crumbled
Thinly sliced jarred roasted red peppers,
      for serving (optional)

1. Preheat the oven to 400° and butter a 9-inch square baking pan. In a large bowl, beat the eggs with the milk, sour cream and melted butter. In a medium bowl, whisk the cornmeal with the flour, baking powder, salt, sugar and baking soda. Whisk the dry ingredients into the wet ingredients until smooth, then fold in the crumbled feta.

2. Scrape the batter into the prepared pan and bake for about 40 minutes, until the cornbread is golden on top and a toothpick inserted in the center comes out clean. Let the corn bread cool slightly, then cut into squares and serve with roasted peppers. *—Anya von Bremzen*

MAKE AHEAD The corn bread can be stored in an airtight container overnight; serve at room temperature.

● HEALTHY ● MAKE AHEAD ● VEGETARIAN ● STAFF FAVORITE

Bacon-and-Egg Pizza
⏱ TOTAL: 45 MIN
MAKES ONE 12-INCH PIZZA ●
Crisp bacon, custardy scrambled eggs and two cheeses—Brie and mozzarella—push this breakfast pizza over the top.

- 6 ounces thick-sliced bacon, cut crosswise into ⅓-inch lardons
- 4 large eggs
- 1 tablespoon heavy cream
- Kosher salt
- 2 tablespoons unsalted butter
- All-purpose flour, for dusting
- 1 pound pizza dough
- ⅓ cup crème fraîche
- 3 ounces Brie, thinly sliced (with rind, if desired)
- 2 ounces fresh mozzarella, shredded
- Snipped chives, for garnish

1. Set a pizza stone in the oven and preheat the oven to 500°. Spread the bacon in a pie plate and bake for 15 minutes, stirring once, until nearly crisp. Using a slotted spoon, transfer the bacon to paper towels to drain.
2. Meanwhile, in a bowl, whisk the eggs with the cream and a pinch of salt. In a medium nonstick skillet, cook the eggs and 1 tablespoon of the butter over low heat, whisking frequently, until small curds form and the eggs are creamy, about 12 minutes. Remove the eggs from the heat. Stir in the remaining 1 tablespoon of butter and season with salt.
3. On a lightly floured work surface, stretch out the pizza dough to a 12-inch round and transfer to a lightly floured pizza peel. Spread the crème fraîche evenly over the dough, leaving a 1-inch border all around. Top with the bacon, Brie and mozzarella.
4. Slide the pizza onto the hot stone and bake for about 7 minutes, until lightly golden and bubbling. Remove the pizza from the oven and spoon the scrambled eggs on top. Slide the pizza back onto the stone and bake for 2 minutes longer, until the eggs are hot. Garnish with chives, cut into wedges and serve. —*Jesse Sutton*
WINE Lively, lightly sweet Washington state Riesling: 2011 Eroica.

Sausage Lovers' Grilled Pizza
⏱ TOTAL: 45 MIN
MAKES ONE 14-INCH PIZZA

- 1 pound summer squash (about 2), grated on the large holes of a box grater
- Kosher salt
- 2 tablespoons extra-virgin olive oil, plus more for brushing
- One 14-ounce can diced tomatoes, drained
- Pinch of sugar
- One 1-pound ball of pizza dough, thawed if frozen
- One 8-ounce ball of fresh mozzarella, thinly sliced
- 2 cooked sausages, thinly sliced
- 4 peperoncini, stemmed and thinly sliced
- Basil leaves, for garnish

1. Light a grill. In a colander set over a bowl, toss the squash with ½ teaspoon of salt; let stand for 15 minutes, then squeeze out the excess liquid.
2. In a large nonstick skillet, heat the 2 tablespoons of olive oil until shimmering. Add the squash and cook over moderately high heat just until golden in spots, 3 minutes.
3. In a food processor, pulse the tomatoes until almost smooth; season the tomato sauce with salt and the sugar.
4. On a lightly floured work surface, roll out the pizza dough to a ¼-inch-thick round or oval. Brush the dough with olive oil and oil the hot grill grate. Drape the dough, oiled side down, onto the hot grate. Grill over moderate heat until marks appear on the bottom and the dough is slightly firm and puffed, 3 minutes. Turn the dough over onto a cookie sheet and brush with oil. Spread the tomato sauce over the dough, leaving a 1-inch border. Scatter the squash over the pizza and top with the sliced mozzarella and sausages.
5. Slide the pizza back onto the grill. Cover the grill and cook until the crust is done and the cheese is melted, 5 minutes. Transfer the pizza to a platter, garnish with the peperoncini and basil and serve. —*Kay Chun*

WINE Bold southern Italian red: 2011 Tormaresca Neprica.

Coppa-and-Gorgonzola Piadine
ACTIVE: 35 MIN; TOTAL: 1 HR
MAKES 1 DOZEN PIADINE ●
Star chef Mario Batali's terrific flatbread sandwiches are topped with slices of creamy Gorgonzola *dolce* and *coppa* (cured pork) as soon as they're taken off the griddle.

DOUGH
- 3½ cups all-purpose flour
- ½ teaspoon baking soda
- 2 teaspoons kosher salt
- ¼ cup lard or solid vegetable shortening, at room temperature

TOPPINGS
- 1½ pounds Gorgonzola *dolce*, thinly sliced
- ½ pound sliced spicy *coppa*
- 2 thinly sliced Bartlett pears

1. MAKE THE DOUGH In a standing mixer fitted with the dough hook, blend the flour, baking soda, salt and lard at medium-low speed until the mixture resembles coarse meal. With the machine on, add 1 cup of water in a thin stream and mix until the dough forms a ball. Increase the speed to medium and knead for 5 minutes.
2. Roll the dough into an 8-inch log and cut into 12 pieces. Roll each piece into a ball and arrange on a baking sheet. Cover the dough with plastic wrap and let stand at room temperature for 30 minutes.
3. Heat a cast-iron griddle over moderate heat. On an unfloured work surface, roll out each ball of dough to a thin 7-inch round. Working in batches, griddle the *piadine* just until lightly browned on the bottom, 1 to 2 minutes. Turn and brown the other side, 1 minute more. Keep the *piadine* warm in foil in a preheated oven while you cook the rest.
4. ADD THE TOPPINGS Arrange the *piadine* on a platter or plates. Top with the Gorgonzola, *coppa* and pears and serve. —*Mario Batali*
WINE Sparkling red from Emilia-Romagna: 2011 Fiorini Corte degli Attimi Lambrusco di Sorbara.

DIY THIN-CRUST PIZZA

THOMAS MCNAUGHTON, the chef and dough master at San Francisco's Flour + Water, Salumeria and Central Kitchen, is renowned for his ethereal, Neapolitan-style pies. Here, he shares his recipe for pizza dough that bakes up tender inside and crisp outside, even in a standard home oven.

STEP 1 MAKE THE DOUGH

"Flour, salt, water and yeast—that's it," says McNaughton about this super-simple dough recipe. It's the same one he uses to make his amazing restaurant pies.

Slow-Rising Pizza Dough
ACTIVE: 1 HR 15 MIN; TOTAL: 3 DAYS
MAKES FIVE 10-INCH PIZZAS ● ○ ○

1¾ pounds "00" flour (5½ cups; see Note), plus more for dusting
0.75 grams active dry yeast (½ teaspoon; see Note)
27 grams salt (3 tablespoons)

1. Lightly dust a very large bowl with flour. In a small bowl, whisk the yeast with ¼ cup of warm water and let stand until foamy, about 5 minutes.
2. In the bowl of a standing mixer fitted with the dough hook, combine the 1¾ pounds of flour with the yeast mixture and 1¾ cups of warm water and mix at low speed for 1 minute. Increase the speed to medium and mix until all of the flour is incorporated, about 4 minutes. Add the salt and mix at medium speed until a soft, smooth dough forms, about 5 minutes longer.
3. Scrape the dough out onto a lightly floured work surface and form it into a large ball. Transfer the dough to the prepared bowl and cover the bowl securely with plastic wrap so that it's airtight. Let the dough stand in a warm place until it has doubled in bulk, about 8 hours. Refrigerate the dough for at least 8 hours or overnight.
4. Let the pizza dough return to room temperature in the bowl, about 2 hours.
5. Lightly dust 2 large baking sheets with flour. Scrape the dough out onto a lightly floured work surface and punch it down. Using a sharp knife, cut the dough into 5 equal pieces. Form the pieces into balls and transfer them to the prepared baking sheets. Using the tip of a paring knife, gently pop any air bubbles on the surface of each ball. Securely cover the dough balls by sliding each baking sheet into a clean 13-gallon plastic kitchen bag and tying them closed. Let the dough stand in a warm place until it has a little more than doubled in bulk, about 8 hours. Refrigerate the dough for at least 8 hours or overnight.
NOTE Doppio zero, or "00," flour is a fine Italian flour available at specialty food shops and online at *amazon.com*. To accurately weigh small quantities, use a scale that counts in 0.01-gram increments, such as one from American Weigh ($25; *amazon.com*).

SIX KEY MOVES

1 FORM BALLS After the first rise and an overnight rest, punch down the pizza dough and portion it into 5 equal pieces. Shape each portion into a ball.

2 LET RISE Transfer the dough balls to lightly floured baking sheets, making sure to leave plenty of space between them. Wrap securely in a large plastic bag.

3 PROOF FULLY When the dough balls have more than doubled in size and then rested overnight again, they are ready to be formed into pizzas.

4 FORM ROUNDS Using your fingers, press and stretch a dough ball out to a 10-inch round, working from the center of the ball toward the edge.

5 TRANSFER ROUNDS Move the dough round to a lightly floured peel before adding any toppings.

6 ADD TOPPINGS Top with sauce, cheese, herbs or any ingredients you choose. Less is more, especially with sauce.

STEP 2 SHAPE & ASSEMBLE

Shape the dough into a disk on a counter, transfer to a peel, then add the toppings of your choice. McNaughton insists on using canned San Marzano tomatoes for the sauce on his red pies. "You aren't going to make consistently good sauce using fresh tomatoes."

1. Set a pizza stone in the top third of the oven. Preheat the oven to 500° for at least 45 minutes. Meanwhile, remove the baking sheets from the refrigerator and let the dough stand for 20 minutes.
2. Working on a well-floured surface and using your fingers, press and stretch a dough ball out to a 10-inch round, working from the center toward the edge; avoid pressing on the outermost edge. Transfer the dough round to a lightly floured pizza peel. Add toppings to the dough round as desired, making sure to leave a 1-inch border around the edge.

STEP 3 BAKE THE PIZZA

Turn the oven to broil for 5 minutes, then return it to 500°. Slide the pizza onto the pizza stone, opening and closing the oven door as quickly as possible. Bake until the bottom is lightly charred, 6 minutes for a chewier crust, 8 minutes for a crispier one. Avoid opening the oven door during baking.

BAKING TOOL Nathan Myhrvold's *Modernist Cuisine* recommends a steel slab instead of a pizza stone because it retains heat better. *$72; bakingsteel.com.*

When topping pies like this Margherita, less is more, especially with sauce.

PIZZA TOPPINGS

PERFECT PIZZA SAUCE Pass one 28-ounce can whole San Marzano tomatoes through a food mill. Blend the puree with 1 tablespoon extra-virgin olive oil and season with salt.

MARGHERITA Spread ½ cup Perfect Pizza Sauce evenly onto the dough and top with ¼ pound sliced fresh mozzarella cheese, about 10 fresh basil leaves, a drizzle of extra-virgin olive oil and a light grating of Parmigiano-Reggiano cheese.

SAUSAGE AND OLIVE Spread ⅓ cup Perfect Pizza Sauce onto the dough and top with 2 ounces uncooked crumbled Italian sausage, ¼ cup pitted and halved Gaeta olives, 1 teaspoon chopped capers, ½ teaspoon chopped oregano and ¼ cup shaved pecorino *sardo* cheese.

SQUASH AND ARUGULA Grate Parmigiano-Reggiano over the dough and top with ¾ cup shredded Fontina, 2 ounces thinly sliced summer squash (about ½ small squash), 1 teaspoon chopped rosemary and 1 or 2 chopped Calabrian red chiles, then top with ½ cup arugula leaves after baking.

Portobello, Cheese and Arugula-Pesto Panini

⏱ **TOTAL: 45 MIN • 6 SERVINGS** ●

In the evening, chef Mike Isabella offers a four-course tasting menu at G, his dual-concept restaurant in Washington, DC. During the day, he offers more casual foods like this hot pressed mushroom sandwich spread with peppery arugula pesto and tangy pickled-cherry-pepper mayonnaise.

- 2 tablespoons pine nuts
- 4 ounces baby arugula (2 packed cups)
- ¼ cup freshly grated Parmigiano-Reggiano cheese
- 1 garlic clove, minced
- ½ cup extra-virgin olive oil
- Kosher salt
- 6 portobello mushrooms (about 2 pounds), stems discarded
- 3 store-bought pickled red cherry peppers, seeded and minced
- ½ cup mayonnaise
- 6 ciabatta rolls, split
- 10 ounces Taleggio cheese, rind removed, cheese sliced ⅓ inch thick

1. Preheat the oven to 400°. In a small skillet, toast the pine nuts over moderate heat, shaking the pan, until golden, about 4 minutes. Transfer the pine nuts to a mini food processor and let cool. Add the arugula, Parmigiano-Reggiano, garlic and ¼ cup of the olive oil and process until smooth. Season the pesto with salt.

2. Using a spoon, scrape the brown gills from the underside of the portobello mushroom caps. Place the mushrooms on a baking sheet, top side up, and brush them with the remaining ¼ cup of olive oil. Season the mushrooms with salt and roast for about 20 minutes, turning once, until tender. Let cool. Transfer the mushrooms to a work surface and thinly slice them.

3. Heat a panini press or griddle. In a small bowl, stir the cherry peppers into the mayonnaise, then spread the mayonnaise on the bottom halves of the ciabatta rolls. Top with the Taleggio, portobello and pesto and close the sandwiches. Cook the panini until golden and crisp outside and the cheese is melted within: 3 minutes in a press or 3 minutes per side on a griddle. Cut the panini in half and serve. —*Mike Isabella*

MAKE AHEAD The sliced roasted portobellos can be refrigerated overnight. The arugula pesto can be made earlier in the day and refrigerated with a piece of plastic wrap pressed against its surface.

WINE Robust Syrah: 2009 3CV.

Inside-Out Grilled Ham-and-Cheese Sandwiches

⏱ **TOTAL: 10 MIN**

MAKES 4 SANDWICHES

The best way to improve on a great grilled cheese is to add ham and dill pickles, then sprinkle some grated cheese on the outside of the bread for an extra-crispy crust.

- 4 tablespoons unsalted butter, softened
- 8 slices of bakery Pullman bread
- ½ cup freshly grated Parmigiano-Reggiano cheese
- ½ pound sliced Swiss cheese, preferably Gruyère
- 8 ounces thinly sliced ham
- Dill pickle slices (optional)
- 2 tablespoons Dijon mustard
- ¼ cup apricot preserves

1. Butter one side of each slice of bread and sprinkle with Parmigiano-Reggiano, pressing to help the grated cheese adhere.

2. Invert the bread slices onto a work surface, cheese side down. Top 4 of the slices with the Swiss cheese, ham and pickles.

3. Mix the Dijon mustard and apricot preserves and spread on the remaining 4 slices of bread. Close the sandwiches.

4. Preheat a griddle over moderate heat. Griddle the sandwiches, turning, until they are golden and crisp on the outside and melted inside, about 3 minutes. Cut the sandwiches in half and serve right away. —*Grace Parisi*

WINE Ripe, spicy Argentinean Malbec: 2011 Nieto Senetiner Reserva.

Steamed Bacon Buns with Hoisin

⏱ **TOTAL: 40 MIN • 4 SERVINGS** ●

- ½ pound thick-cut smoky bacon, cut into 2-inch pieces
- Sixteen ⅛-inch-thick coins of peeled fresh ginger
- 1 cup low-sodium chicken broth
- ¼ cup mirin
- ¼ cup unseasoned rice vinegar
- 2 tablespoons sugar
- 1 tablespoon soy sauce
- One 16.3-ounce tube of buttermilk biscuit dough (8 biscuits), such as Pillsbury Grands
- Hoisin sauce, Sriracha, sliced scallions, sliced radishes and bread-and-butter pickles, for serving

1. In a large skillet, cook the bacon and ginger over moderately high heat, turning the bacon once, until lightly browned, about 5 minutes. Spoon off all of the fat in the skillet. Add the chicken broth, mirin, vinegar, sugar and soy sauce to the skillet and simmer over very low heat, turning the bacon occasionally, until it is tender and the liquid is reduced to a syrupy glaze, about 10 minutes. Cover and keep warm.

2. Meanwhile, fill a roasting pan with 2 inches of water and set 4 ramekins in the corners of the pan. Line a 9-by-13-inch baking pan with parchment paper and spray with vegetable oil spray. Arrange the biscuits in the baking pan and set it on top of the ramekins in the roasting pan, over the water. Cover the roasting pan very tightly with foil and bring to a boil over high heat. Steam the biscuits until fluffy and cooked through, about 8 minutes.

3. Carefully split each biscuit with your fingers and arrange them on a platter; spread the bottoms with hoisin sauce and Sriracha and top with the glazed bacon. Drizzle each bun with some of the glaze and garnish with sliced scallions, radishes and pickles. Close the buns and serve right away. —*Grace Parisi*

WINE Medium-bodied, berry-rich California Pinot Noir: 2010 Rickshaw.

● HEALTHY ● MAKE AHEAD ● VEGETARIAN ● STAFF FAVORITE

INSIDE-OUT GRILLED HAM-AND-
CHEESE SANDWICHES

Nashville Hot and Crispy Chicken Sandwiches

TOTAL: 45 MIN PLUS 8 HR MARINATING
MAKES 4 SANDWICHES

The chicken in this delightful sandwich is brined in spicy dill pickle juice, then fried and brushed with schmaltz (chicken fat) and Korean chile powder.

2½ cups brine from jarred spicy dill pickles, plus sliced spicy dill pickles for serving
Eight 4- to 5-ounce boneless chicken thighs with skin, pounded ½ inch thick
¼ cup schmaltz (rendered chicken fat; see Note), melted
½ cup *gochugaru* (Korean chile powder)
1 tablespoon sugar
½ teaspoon garlic powder
2 teaspoons cayenne pepper
Kosher salt
1 cup all-purpose flour
1 tablespoon ground white pepper
2 teaspoons sweet paprika
Canola oil, for frying
8 slices of white sandwich bread

1. In a large resealable plastic bag, combine the pickle brine and chicken thighs. Seal the bag and refrigerate the chicken for at least 8 hours or overnight.
2. Meanwhile, in a small bowl, whisk the schmaltz with the *gochugaru,* sugar, garlic powder, 1 teaspoon of the cayenne and 1 teaspoon of salt.
3. Remove the chicken thighs from the marinade and pat them dry. In a shallow bowl, whisk the flour with the white pepper, paprika, 1 tablespoon of salt and the remaining 1 teaspoon of cayenne.
4. Set a rack over a baking sheet. In a large, deep skillet, heat ⅓ inch of oil until shimmering. Dredge half of the chicken in the seasoned flour, shaking off any excess. Fry the chicken thighs skin side down over moderate heat until well browned and crisp, 4 minutes. Turn the chicken and cook until no trace of pink remains, 4 minutes. Transfer to the rack. Repeat with the remaining chicken.

5. Generously brush the fried chicken all over with the *gochugaru* paste. Put 4 slices of bread on a work surface; arrange 2 thighs on each. Top with sliced pickles, close the sandwiches and serve. —*Jared Van Camp*
NOTE Schmaltz is available in the refrigerated section of most supermarkets.
BEER Frothy, lightly hoppy pilsner: North Coast Brewing Scrimshaw.

Hippie-Style Egg Salad Sandwiches

TOTAL: 40 MIN
MAKES 4 SANDWICHES ● ○

This outstanding egg salad has a number of surprise ingredients, including roasted sunflower seeds, sunflower sprouts, grated carrots and plenty of fresh herbs.

½ cup mayonnaise
2 tablespoons finely grated carrot
1 tablespoon apple cider vinegar
2 teaspoons Dijon mustard
10 large hard-cooked eggs, coarsely chopped
2 tablespoons minced celery
1 tablespoon minced green bell pepper
1 tablespoon finely chopped parsley
1 tablespoon finely chopped tarragon
1 tablespoon snipped chives
3 tablespoons salted roasted sunflower seeds or toasted pine nuts, plus more for garnish
Kosher salt and freshly ground pepper
Tabasco
8 slices of Pullman bread, toasted
Sunflower sprouts, for garnish

1. In a large bowl, whisk the mayonnaise with the carrot, vinegar and mustard. Fold in the chopped eggs, celery, bell pepper, herbs and the 3 tablespoons of sunflower seeds. Season with salt, pepper and Tabasco.
2. Spoon the egg salad on half of the toasts. Garnish with sunflower sprouts and sunflower seeds, close the sandwiches and serve. —*Aimee Olexy*
MAKE AHEAD The egg salad can be refrigerated overnight. Fold in the herbs and seeds shortly before serving.

King Oyster Mushroom "BLT" with Basil Mayonnaise

TOTAL: 30 MIN • 2 SERVINGS ● ● ●

At Vedge, a vegan restaurant in Philadelphia, chef Richard Landau skips the creepy packaged faux bacon in favor of king oyster mushrooms, also known as king trumpets or royal trumpets. These have a firm, meaty texture and flavor that can mimic bacon on a BLT. While the texture of king oysters is unique, other wild mushrooms, like shiitake, would also be tasty on this sandwich.

2 tablespoons extra-virgin olive oil
½ pound king oyster mushrooms (see Note), trimmed and very thinly sliced lengthwise
Salt and freshly ground pepper
¼ cup vegan mayonnaise
2 tablespoons finely shredded basil, plus more for garnish
4 slices of country bread, lightly toasted
4 small romaine lettuce leaves, whole or shredded
1 large red tomato, thinly sliced

1. In a large skillet, heat 1 tablespoon of the olive oil until shimmering. Add half of the mushroom slices in a single layer and cook, turning once, until golden, about 6 minutes. Drain the mushrooms on paper towels and season them with salt and pepper. Repeat with the remaining 1 tablespoon of olive oil and mushrooms.
2. In a small bowl, combine the mayonnaise with the 2 tablespoons of shredded basil and season with salt and pepper. Spread 1 tablespoon of the basil mayonnaise on each slice of bread and top with lettuce. Arrange the sliced tomato on the lettuce, followed by the mushrooms. Sprinkle the sandwiches with salt and pepper and garnish with basil. Serve the sandwiches open-face or closed. —*Richard Landau*
NOTE King oyster mushrooms are available at farmers' markets and specialty shops.
WINE Light Beaujolais: 2011 Domaine Dubost Brouilly.

● HEALTHY ● MAKE AHEAD ● VEGETARIAN ● STAFF FAVORITE

KING OYSTER MUSHROOM "BLT"
WITH BASIL MAYONNAISE

DIY VEGGIE BURGERS

Constructing a delicious meat-free burger takes creativity and experimentation. Chicago chef **JIMMY BANNOS, JR.,** of The Purple Pig shows how to turn a long list of ingredients into a fantastic patty.

Fresh and Juicy Veggie Burgers
TOTAL: 1 HR 20 MIN • MAKES 8 BURGERS ● ● ●

- 1 head of garlic, halved horizontally
- 2 tablespoons extra-virgin olive oil, plus more for drizzling and brushing
- ¼ cup thinly sliced asparagus
- ⅓ cup fregola
- One 15-ounce can chickpeas, drained
- ¼ cup chopped marinated artichokes
- 2 tablespoons chopped pitted Gaeta olives
- 2 tablespoons chopped scallions
- 2 tablespoons plain full-fat Greek yogurt
- 1 tablespoon fresh lemon juice
- 1 teaspoon each of chopped basil, mint and parsley
- 2¼ cups cooked red or white quinoa
- Salt and freshly ground pepper
- 8 slices of scamorza cheese
- 8 burger buns, toasted

1. Preheat the oven to 375°. Set the garlic cut side up on foil, drizzle with oil and wrap tightly. Roast until very tender, 1 hour. Let cool. Squeeze the cloves out of their skins into a bowl; mash to a paste.

2. Bring a saucepan of salted water to a boil. Put the asparagus in a strainer, submerge it in the water and cook just until crisp-tender, 2 minutes. Cool the asparagus under running water and pat dry.

3. Return the water to a boil. Add the fregola and cook until very tender, about 20 minutes. Drain well and let cool slightly. In a food processor, puree the garlic paste, fregola, chickpeas and the 2 tablespoons of olive oil; transfer the mixture to a bowl. Stir in the asparagus, artichokes, olives, scallions, yogurt, lemon juice, herbs and quinoa. Season with salt and pepper.

4. Heat a large cast-iron griddle; brush with oil. Form the mixture into eight 3-inch patties. Brush with oil; cook over high heat until golden, 4 minutes. Flip and top each patty with a slice of cheese. Reduce the heat to moderate, cover and cook until the patties are heated through and the cheese is melted. Set the burgers on the buns.

SERVE WITH Sun-dried-tomato spread, marinated mushrooms and sliced fresh tomatoes.

WINE Bright, cherry-scented Austrian red: 2011 Heinrich.

BUILDING A GREAT VEGGIE BURGER

Bannos matches the essential qualities of a great veggie burger to the ingredients in his recipe, offering easy substitutions.

HEFT

FREGOLA
"I love the nuttiness of fregola—a toasted pasta from Sardinia—but you could substitute orzo, couscous or another pasta."

CHICKPEAS
"I use chickpeas, but you could swap them out for lentils or almost any bean."

FLAVOR

SCALLIONS
"They're delicious in the burger, but you could also substitute onions."

ROASTED GARLIC
"It's like the salt and pepper of my kitchen; I just love it. It adds so much complexity."

TEXTURE

ASPARAGUS
"Barely cooked, it adds a pop of texture, along with freshness. You could try corn, carrots or snap peas instead."

QUINOA
"Without something grainy to simulate the texture of beef, your burger will taste like a bean cake. Also try farro instead of quinoa."

FRESHNESS

BASIL, PARSLEY AND MINT
"These herbs add so much brightness to the veggie burger. In place of basil, parsley and mint, you could use almost any fresh herb: sage, oregano, thyme, tarragon, chervil or chives."

ACIDITY

MARINATED ARTICHOKES
"Artichokes add acidity and earthy flavor. Or replace them with pickled fennel, celery or chard stems."

LEMON JUICE
"Acidity is as essential to a dish as salt. Lime juice or vinegar are other good options."

MOISTURE

GREEK YOGURT
"Yogurt helps bind the burgers while keeping them from becoming dry; it also contributes a lot of tanginess and fresh flavor. Good, real Greek yogurt is a beautiful thing, but you could also switch it out for crème fraîche or sour cream."

FRESH AND JUICY
VEGGIE BURGER

BLT Hot Dogs with Caraway Remoulade

⏱ **TOTAL: 30 MIN • 8 SERVINGS**

In this riff on a BLT, hot dogs are topped with a crunchy lettuce-and-basil slaw dressed with a caraway remoulade—a tangy pickle mayo flecked with toasted caraway seeds.

½ cup mayonnaise
1 tablespoon minced shallot
2 teaspoons chopped capers
1 tablespoon chopped dill pickle
1 tablespoon caraway seeds, toasted
8 hot dogs, cooked
8 hot dog buns, toasted
8 slices of crisp, cooked applewood-smoked bacon
1 cup chopped tomatoes
4 cups shredded iceberg lettuce
⅓ cup small basil leaves

1. In a medium bowl, whisk the mayonnaise with the shallot, capers, pickle and toasted caraway seeds.
2. Put the cooked hot dogs in the buns; top with the bacon and tomatoes. Toss the lettuce and basil with some of the caraway remoulade. Top the dogs with the slaw. Serve any remaining remoulade on the side.
—*Kay Chun*

Jerk Vegetable Cubano

⏱ **TOTAL: 15 MIN • 4 SERVINGS** ● ●

Spicy grilled vegetables plus dill pickles and melted cheese make the perfect vegetarian alternative to a Cubano sandwich.

¼ cup mayonnaise
4 hoagie rolls, split
4 cups coarsely chopped vegetables, plus leftover sauce for serving, from Spicy Jerk Vegetables (page 235)
1 cup sliced dill pickles
½ pound sliced Gruyère or Swiss cheese

1. Spread the mayonnaise on the cut sides of the rolls and top with the vegetables, pickles and cheese.

2. Close the sandwiches and toast in a panini press or griddle until the rolls are crusty and the cheese is melted. Cut in half and serve with the yogurt sauce. —*Grace Parisi*

Blue Ribbon Barbecue Chicken Cheeseburgers

⏱ **TOTAL: 40 MIN • 4 SERVINGS**

Inspired by a best-selling dish at their Blue Ribbon restaurants in New York City, owners Eric and Bruce Bromberg opened Bromberg Bros. Blue Ribbon Fried Chicken. The menu includes a knockout chicken burger: "We'll pit our chicken burger against your beef burger any day," they say.

8 thick-cut strips of bacon (½ pound)
1½ pounds ground chicken
Kosher salt and freshly ground black pepper
4 slices of aged cheddar cheese
Barbecue sauce, for brushing
4 sesame seed hamburger buns, split and toasted
Thinly sliced red onion and tomato and shredded iceberg lettuce, for serving

1. In a large cast-iron skillet, cook the bacon over moderate heat, turning once, until browned and crisp, 8 to 10 minutes. Transfer the bacon to paper towels to drain and cut the strips in half. Pour off all but 2 tablespoons of fat from the skillet.
2. Form the chicken into four ½-inch-thick patties and season generously with salt and pepper. Add the patties to the skillet and cook over moderately high heat until browned on the bottom, about 4 minutes. Flip the burgers, top with the cheese and crisp bacon and cook until the cheese is melted and the burgers are just cooked through, about 8 minutes.
3. Spread barbecue sauce on the bottom buns and top with the cheeseburgers, sliced onion, tomato and lettuce. Close the burgers and serve right away.
—*Bruce Bromberg and Eric Bromberg*
WINE Juicy, medium-bodied Garnacha from Spain: 2010 Celler de Capçanes Mas Donís.

Asian Sloppy Joe Sliders

📷 **PAGE 267**

TOTAL: 1 HR • MAKES 20 SLIDERS ●

Star chef Ming Tsai serves these spicy, gingery sliders at his Boston gastropub, Blue Dragon. They're based on a recipe his mother made for him when he was young: She'd fill his thermos with the ground meat and tuck the slider buns into his lunchbox. "Everyone at school wanted them, so I'd usually trade a little slider for a complete lunch," says Tsai.

2 tablespoons canola oil
2 medium red onions, finely chopped
1 cup finely chopped celery
3 tablespoons *sambal oelek* or other Asian chile sauce
2½ tablespoons minced garlic
1 tablespoon minced fresh ginger
Kosher salt and freshly ground pepper
1 pound ground chicken thighs
1 pound ground pork
1 cup hoisin sauce
1 cup drained canned diced tomatoes
¼ cup fresh lime juice
20 brioche dinner rolls, split and toasted
Shredded iceberg lettuce and spicy pickles (optional), for serving

1. In a large, deep skillet, heat the canola oil until shimmering. Add the onions, celery, *sambal oelek*, garlic, ginger and a generous pinch each of salt and pepper and cook over moderate heat, stirring occasionally, until the vegetables are softened, about 8 minutes. Add the ground chicken and pork and cook, stirring occasionally to break up the meat, until no pink remains, about 5 minutes. Stir in the hoisin, tomatoes and lime juice and bring to a boil. Simmer over moderately low heat, stirring occasionally, until thickened, about 20 minutes. Season with salt and pepper.
2. Spoon about ¼ cup of the sloppy joe filling on the bottom half of each roll. Top with shredded lettuce and pickles and serve.
—*Ming Tsai*

MAKE AHEAD The sloppy joe filling can be refrigerated for up to 3 days.

BEER Bold, hoppy California pale ale: Sierra Nevada.

● HEALTHY ● MAKE AHEAD ● VEGETARIAN ● STAFF FAVORITE

BLT HOT DOGS WITH
CARAWAY REMOULADE

At Lafayette, his French-inspired café in Manhattan, chef Andrew Carmellini serves stellar coffee and luxurious egg dishes.

Opposite: recipe, page 290.

SOFT-SCRAMBLED EGGS WITH
SMOKED SABLEFISH AND TROUT ROE

BREAKFAST & BRUNCH

Mushroom Hash with Poached Eggs

TOTAL: 1 HR • 4 SERVINGS

- 4   slices of rye bread (4 ounces), torn into ¼-inch pieces
- ½   cup extra-virgin olive oil
- Kosher salt and freshly ground black pepper
- ¼   pound shiitake mushrooms, stems discarded and caps thinly sliced
- ¼   pound cremini mushrooms, thinly sliced
- ¼   teaspoon baking powder
- 1   teaspoon finely chopped thyme
- 1   small onion, very finely chopped
- 1   garlic clove, minced
- ½   teaspoon crushed red pepper
- ¾   pound Italian sausage, casings removed and sausage broken into pieces
- 8   large eggs
- Fleur de sel and snipped chives, for garnish
- Hot sauce, for serving

1. Preheat the oven to 450°. On a rimmed baking sheet, toss the rye bread pieces with 2 tablespoons of the olive oil and season with salt and black pepper. Bake for about 5 minutes, until the crumbs are light golden but not completely dry.
2. In a large skillet, heat 2 tablespoons of the olive oil until shimmering. Add the mushrooms, baking powder and ½ teaspoon of the thyme and season with salt and black pepper. Cook over moderately high heat, stirring occasionally, until the mushrooms are tender and browned, about 8 minutes. Transfer the mushrooms to a plate.
3. Wipe out the skillet. Add the remaining ¼ cup of olive oil and heat until shimmering. Add the onion, garlic, crushed red pepper and the remaining ½ teaspoon of chopped thyme. Cook over moderate heat, stirring occasionally, until softened and just starting to brown, about 8 minutes. Add the sausage pieces and cook over moderately high heat, breaking up the meat with a spoon, until browned, about 7 minutes. Stir in the rye bread crumbs, mushrooms and ½ cup of water and season with salt and black pepper. Keep the mushroom hash warm over very low heat, stirring occasionally.
4. Meanwhile, bring a very large, deep skillet of water to a simmer over moderate heat. Working with 1 egg at a time, crack the eggs into a small bowl and carefully add to the simmering water. Poach the eggs over moderate heat until the whites are set but the yolks are still slightly runny, about 5 minutes.
5. Using a slotted spoon, carefully lift the poached eggs out of the water; blot them dry with paper towels. Spoon the hash onto 4 plates and top with the eggs. Garnish the hash with fleur de sel and snipped chives and serve with hot sauce. —*Zoe Nathan*

Crispy Sweet Potato Hash Browns with Charred Poblanos

TOTAL: 45 MIN • 4 SERVINGS ●

- 3   poblano chiles
- 2   tablespoons extra-virgin olive oil
- 1   small red onion, thinly sliced
- 2   tablespoons unsalted butter
- 2   medium sweet potatoes (1½ pounds), peeled and cut into ¼-inch dice
- 3   garlic cloves, thinly sliced
- 1   rosemary sprig
- 2   tablespoons fresh lemon juice
- Kosher salt and freshly ground pepper

1. Roast the poblanos directly over a gas flame or under a preheated broiler, turning, until charred all over. Transfer to a bowl, cover tightly with plastic wrap and let cool. Peel, seed and stem the poblanos, then thinly slice them.
2. In a large skillet, heat the olive oil. Add the onion and cook, stirring, until golden, about 5 minutes. Add the butter, sweet potatoes, garlic and rosemary and cook over moderate heat, stirring occasionally, until the potatoes are tender and lightly browned, about 10 minutes. Stir in the poblanos and lemon juice and season with salt and pepper. Discard the rosemary sprig and serve. —*Kay Chun*
SERVE WITH Fried eggs.

Smothered Cauliflower with Eggs

TOTAL: 40 MIN • 4 SERVINGS ● ● ○

Heidi Swanson, the author of *Super Natural Every Day* and the blogger behind 101 Cookbooks (*101cookbooks.com*), creates a stunning twist on the Italian breakfast dish called Eggs in Purgatory: She poaches eggs in a yellow-tomato sauce simmered with sweet, caramelized cauliflower steaks.

- One 10-ounce head of cauliflower— leaves removed, head cut into slabs
- ½   cup all-purpose flour
- ¼   cup extra-virgin olive oil
- 1   pound yellow tomatoes, cored and finely chopped (3 cups)
- ¼   teaspoon crushed red pepper
- ½   teaspoon finely grated lemon zest
- Salt
- 2   tablespoons sliced almonds
- 4   large eggs
- Marjoram leaves and herb flowers (optional), for garnish
- Crusty bread, for serving

1. In a large saucepan of boiling salted water, cook the cauliflower until crisp-tender, 3 minutes. Drain and pat dry. Transfer to a bowl and toss with the flour, tapping off the excess.
2. In a large, deep skillet, heat the olive oil until shimmering. Add the cauliflower and cook over moderately high heat, turning, until browned. Add the tomatoes, crushed red pepper and lemon zest to the skillet and season with salt. Cook over moderate heat until the tomatoes have broken down, 5 minutes.
3. Meanwhile, toast the almonds in a small, dry skillet over moderate heat, stirring, until lightly browned, 5 minutes. Let cool.
4. Using a spoon, make 4 wells in the tomato sauce. Crack the eggs into the wells, cover and cook over moderately low heat until the eggs are just set, 3 minutes. Garnish the eggs with the almonds, marjoram leaves and flowers and serve right away, with crusty bread. —*Heidi Swanson*
WINE Full-bodied, fruity white from Oregon's Willamette Valley: 2012 Bethel Heights Pinot Gris.

● HEALTHY ● MAKE AHEAD ○ VEGETARIAN ● STAFF FAVORITE

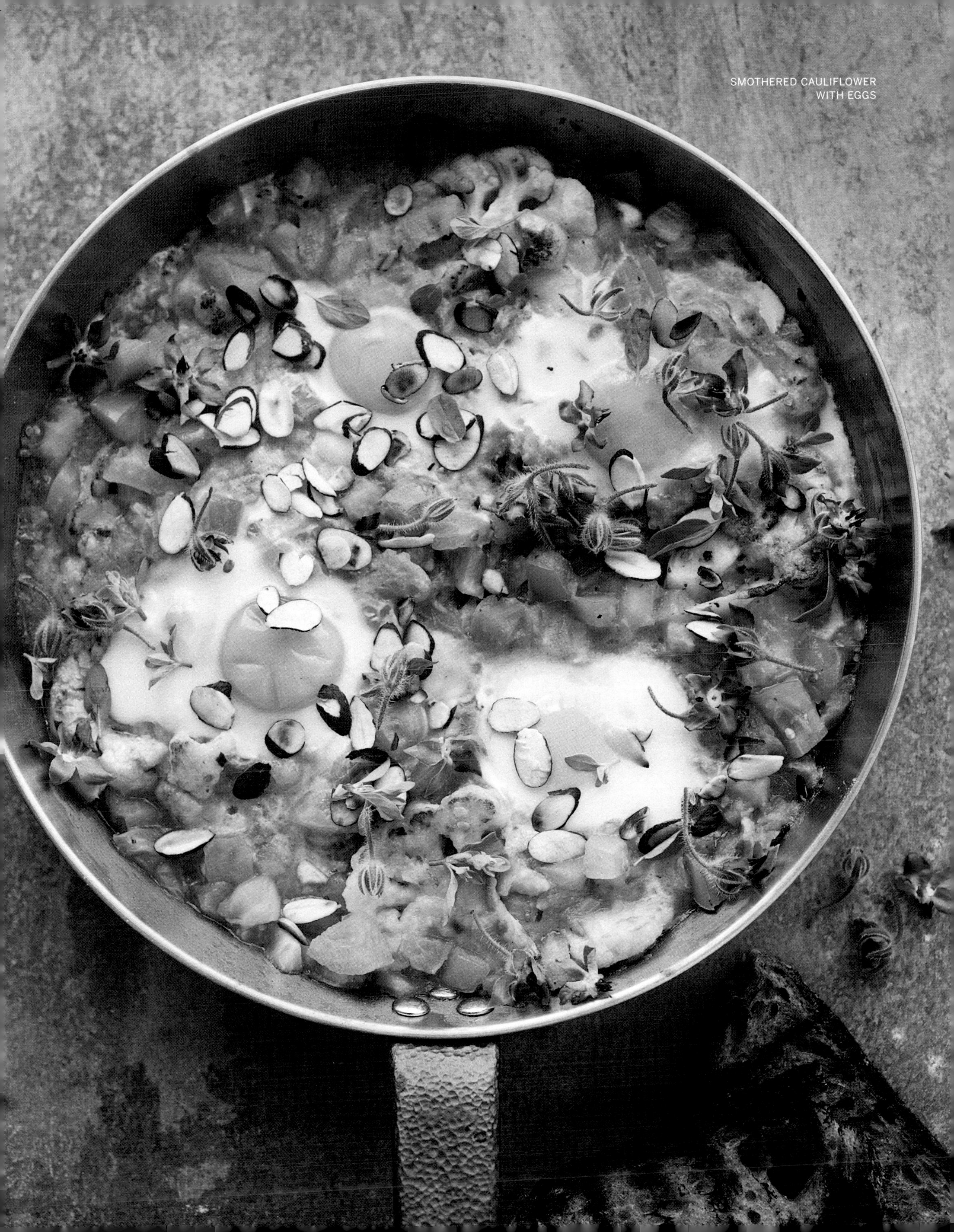

SMOTHERED CAULIFLOWER
WITH EGGS

Three-Cheese-and-Herb Frittata Sandwiches

⏱ TOTAL: 45 MIN • 6 SERVINGS ●

Adding parsley, chives and cheese to eggs creates a fresh-tasting, creamy frittata that is terrific warm, chilled or at room temperature. Zoe Nathan, chef at Milo and Olive in Los Angeles, layers the frittata with prosciutto, arugula and tomatoes on her own homemade bagels (page 268), but the sandwich is also delicious on store-bought bagels.

- 2 tablespoons unsalted butter
- 2 tablespoons extra-virgin olive oil
- 2 small onions, finely chopped
- ½ teaspoon finely chopped thyme
- Pinch of crushed red pepper
- 1 bay leaf
- Kosher salt and freshly ground black pepper
- 10 large eggs
- 4 ounces fresh goat cheese, crumbled
- ½ cup finely grated Parmigiano-Reggiano cheese
- ⅓ cup finely chopped parsley
- ⅓ cup finely chopped chives
- 3 ounces Gruyère cheese, shredded (1 cup)
- 3 cups baby arugula
- 1½ tablespoons red wine vinegar
- 6 bagels, homemade (page 268) or store-bought, split and lightly toasted
- Softened butter, for brushing
- 2 medium tomatoes, thinly sliced
- 12 thin slices of prosciutto (6 ounces)
- 12 large basil leaves, torn

1. Preheat the oven to 475°. In a 12-inch ovenproof nonstick skillet, melt the butter in the olive oil. Add the onions, thyme, crushed red pepper, bay leaf and a generous pinch each of salt and black pepper. Cover and cook over moderate heat, stirring occasionally, until the onions are very soft and browned, about 20 minutes. Discard the bay leaf.

2. In a large bowl, whisk the eggs with the goat cheese, Parmigiano-Reggiano, parsley, chives, ½ cup of the Gruyère, 1 teaspoon of salt and ¼ teaspoon of freshly ground black pepper. Pour the egg mixture into the skillet and cook over moderately low heat, stirring gently, until the eggs start to set, about 5 minutes. Sprinkle the frittata with the remaining ½ cup of Gruyère cheese. Transfer the skillet to the oven and bake the frittata for 8 to 10 minutes, until the center is just set. Run a rubber spatula around the edge of the frittata and slide it onto a work surface. Let the frittata cool slightly, then cut it into 6 pieces.

3. In a medium bowl, toss the arugula with the vinegar and season with salt and freshly ground black pepper. Brush the cut sides of the bagels with butter and fill with the frittata, arugula, sliced tomatoes, prosciutto and basil. Close the bagels, cut in half and serve. —Zoe Nathan

MAKE AHEAD The frittata can be refrigerated overnight. Bring to room temperature before slicing and proceeding with Step 3.

Ratatouille Toasts with Fried Eggs

ACTIVE: 1 HR; TOTAL: 1 HR 20 MIN
6 SERVINGS ● ●

This dish is better when it's made a day in advance, so the ratatouille flavors have time to meld. Then the toasts can be assembled in just a few minutes.

RATATOUILLE

- ½ cup plus 2 tablespoons extra-virgin olive oil
- 3 medium tomatoes, seeded and cut into ½-inch dice (2 cups)
- 5 garlic cloves
- 1¼ teaspoons crushed red pepper
- Kosher salt
- One 12-ounce eggplant, seeds removed and flesh cut into ½-inch dice (2 cups)
- 2 small zucchini, cut into ½-inch dice (2 cups)
- 2 large red onions, cut into ½-inch dice
- 1 red bell pepper, cut into ½-inch dice
- 1 bay leaf
- 1 cup chopped basil
- Freshly ground black pepper

EGGS AND TOASTS

- 2 tablespoons extra-virgin olive oil, plus more for drizzling
- 6 large eggs
- Kosher salt and freshly ground black pepper
- Six ½-inch-thick slices of sourdough bread, toasted
- Chopped basil, for garnish

1. MAKE THE RATATOUILLE In a large skillet, heat 2 tablespoons of the olive oil. Add the tomatoes, 1 garlic clove and ¼ teaspoon of the crushed red pepper and season with salt. Cook the tomatoes over moderate heat, stirring occasionally, until just softened, about 5 minutes. Scrape the tomatoes into a medium saucepan and discard the garlic clove. Wipe out the skillet. Repeat with the eggplant, zucchini, onions and red bell pepper, cooking each vegetable separately in 2 tablespoons of oil with 1 garlic clove, ¼ teaspoon of crushed red pepper and a generous pinch of salt until just tender and lightly browned, about 7 minutes per vegetable. Add the cooked vegetables to the tomatoes in the saucepan.

2. Add the bay leaf, ½ cup of the basil and ⅓ cup of water to the saucepan with the vegetables. Cover and cook over moderately low heat, stirring occasionally, until the vegetables are very tender, about 20 minutes. Discard the bay leaf and stir in the remaining ½ cup of basil. Season the ratatouille with salt and black pepper and let cool slightly.

3. MEANWHILE, FRY THE EGGS In a large nonstick skillet, heat the 2 tablespoons of olive oil over moderate heat. Crack 3 of the eggs into the skillet and fry until the whites are firm and the yolks are runny, 3 to 5 minutes. Transfer to a plate, season with salt and black pepper and keep warm. Repeat with the remaining 3 eggs.

4. To serve, spoon the ratatouille onto the toasts and top with the eggs. Drizzle with olive oil and chopped basil and serve. —Zoe Nathan

MAKE AHEAD The ratatouille can be refrigerated for up to 3 days. Reheat gently and serve warm or at room temperature.

● HEALTHY   ● MAKE AHEAD   ● VEGETARIAN   ● STAFF FAVORITE

RATATOUILLE TOAST
WITH FRIED EGG

Poached Eggs with Bacon Crumbs and Spinach

⏱ **TOTAL: 35 MIN • 4 SERVINGS**

These lovely poached eggs, served on a bed of sautéed spinach and sprinkled with bacon-flavored bread crumbs, make an elegant brunch dish or first course.

- 2 ounces day-old baguette, cut into ½-inch pieces
- ¼ pound bacon, minced (1¼ cups)

Kosher salt and freshly ground black pepper

- 1 tablespoon extra-virgin olive oil
- 10 ounces baby spinach
- 1 tablespoon distilled white vinegar
- 4 large eggs

Freshly grated nutmeg, for garnish

1. In a food processor, pulse the baguette pieces until coarse crumbs form. In a medium skillet, toast the crumbs over moderate heat, stirring occasionally, until golden, 8 minutes. Transfer the bread crumbs to a medium bowl. **2.** Wipe out the skillet. Add the bacon and cook over moderate heat, stirring occasionally, until browned and crisp, about 8 minutes. Using a slotted spoon, transfer the bacon to paper towels to drain, then stir the bacon into the bread crumbs. Season the bacon crumbs with salt and pepper. **3.** In a large skillet, heat the olive oil until shimmering. Add the spinach and 3 tablespoons of water and cook over moderately high heat, stirring, until just wilted, about 3 minutes. Using tongs, transfer the spinach to a bowl and season with salt and pepper; keep warm. **4.** Meanwhile, bring a large, deep skillet of water to a simmer over moderate heat. Add the white vinegar and a generous pinch of salt. Working with 1 egg at a time, crack the eggs into a small bowl and carefully slide into the simmering water. Poach the eggs over moderate heat until the whites are set but the yolks are still slightly runny, about 4 minutes. Drain the poached eggs on paper towels. **5.** Transfer the spinach to plates. Top with the eggs, a sprinkle of bacon crumbs and a pinch of nutmeg. Serve right away. —*Marcelo Betancourt*

Soft-Scrambled Eggs with Smoked Sablefish and Trout Roe

📷 PAGE 285

⏱ **TOTAL 20 MIN • 2 SERVINGS** ○

- 6 large eggs, beaten
- ¼ cup plus 2 tablespoons heavy cream
- 1 tablespoon unsalted butter

Kosher salt

- 4 ounces smoked sablefish, sliced ¼ inch thick (see Note)

Trout roe (see Note), sliced scallions and sour cream, for garnish

Toasted sesame, everything or plain bagels, for serving

1. In a medium nonstick skillet, combine the beaten eggs with the cream and ½ tablespoon of the butter. Cook the eggs over moderately low heat, stirring them constantly, until small curds form and the eggs are creamy, 5 to 7 minutes. Remove the skillet from the heat. **2.** Gently stir the remaining ½ tablespoon of butter into the eggs and season them lightly with salt. Spoon the eggs onto plates and top with the sliced sablefish. Garnish with trout roe, sliced scallions and a dollop of sour cream. Serve right away, with toasted bagels. —*Andrew Carmellini*

NOTE If smoked sablefish and trout roe are unavailable, smoked salmon and salmon roe can be substituted.

Breakfast Fried Rice

ACTIVE: 15 MIN; TOTAL: 50 MIN

2 SERVINGS ● ● ○

- 1 tablespoon untoasted sesame oil or peanut oil
- 4 scallions, thinly sliced
- 3½ cups cold cooked brown rice
- 1 tablespoon unseasoned rice vinegar
- 1 tablespoon soy sauce, plus more for serving
- 2 cups chopped fresh spinach
- 2 eggs, lightly beaten

Salt and freshly ground pepper

Hot sauce, for serving

1. In a large nonstick skillet, heat the sesame oil until it is shimmering. Add the sliced scallions and cook over moderate heat until they are tender, 2 to 3 minutes. Add the cooked brown rice, rice vinegar and 1 tablespoon of soy sauce and stir-fry until the rice is heated through, about 3 minutes. Add the chopped spinach and stir-fry until it is wilted, 2 to 3 minutes longer. **2.** Push the cooked rice to the side of the skillet and add the lightly beaten eggs to the middle; stir until cooked, 1 minute. Mix the eggs into the rice. Season with salt and pepper and serve with soy sauce and hot sauce. —*Erin Alderson*

Scrambled Egg and Swiss Chard Tacos

⏱ **TOTAL: 35 MIN • 6 SERVINGS** ● ● ●

- 2 tablespoons extra-virgin olive oil
- ½ cup plus 2 tablespoons minced white onion
- 2 serrano chiles, seeded and minced

Kosher salt

- 1¼ pounds rainbow Swiss chard, leaves and stems thinly sliced
- 6 large eggs, lightly beaten
- 2 plum tomatoes, seeded and finely chopped
- 3 tablespoons minced cilantro

Freshly ground pepper

Warmed corn tortillas, for serving

In a large skillet, heat the olive oil until shimmering. Add ½ cup of the minced onion, the chiles and a generous pinch of salt and cook over moderate heat, stirring occasionally, until the onion is just starting to brown, about 8 minutes. Add the Swiss chard and cook, stirring, until softened, about 5 minutes. Stir in the eggs and tomatoes and cook over moderately low heat, stirring constantly, until the eggs are just cooked, about 5 minutes. Stir in the remaining 2 tablespoons of minced onion and the cilantro and season with salt and pepper. Serve the eggs in warm corn tortillas. —*Kelly Myers*

SERVE WITH Salsa verde and Mexican *crema* or sour cream.

● HEALTHY ● MAKE AHEAD ○ VEGETARIAN ● STAFF FAVORITE

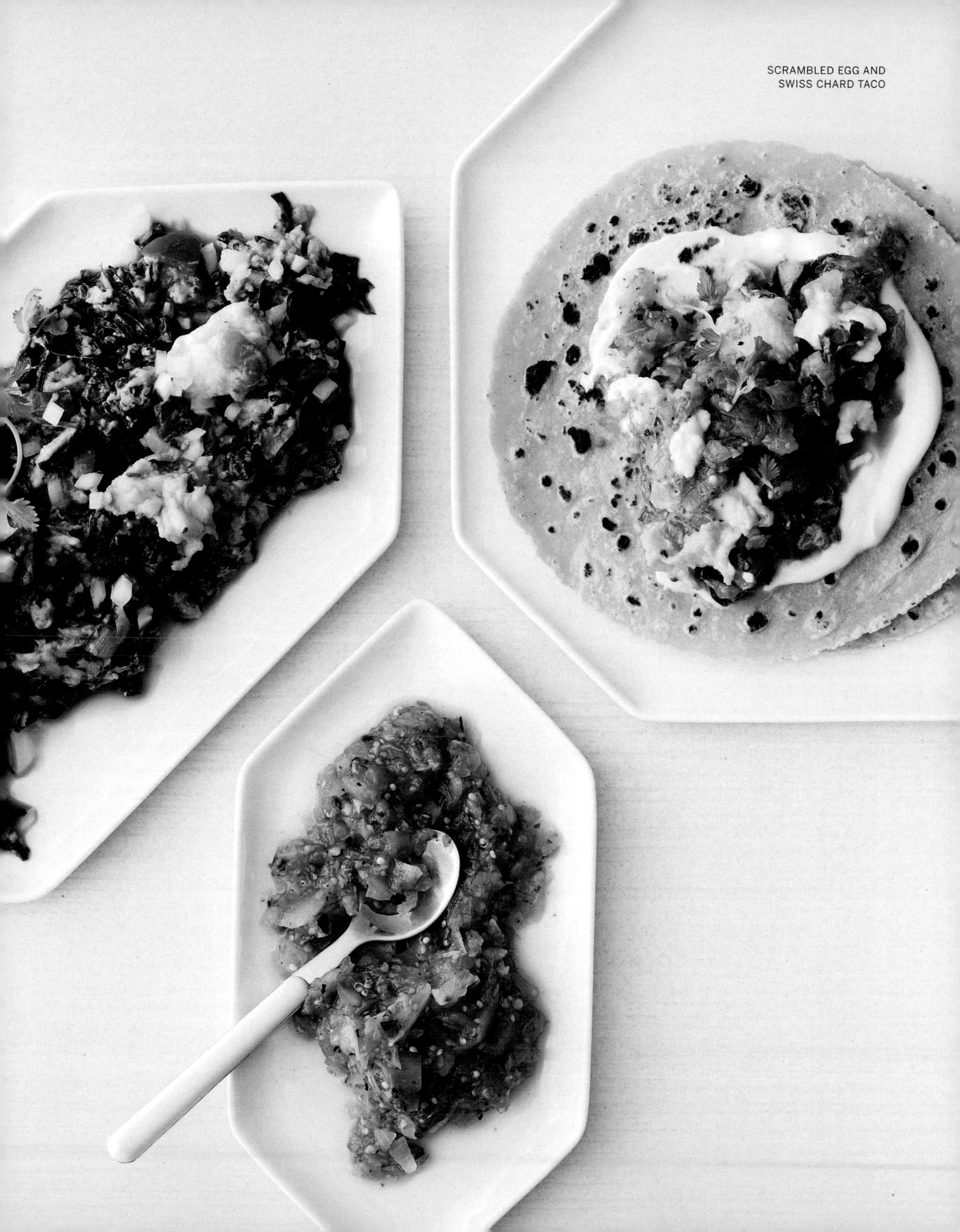

SCRAMBLED EGG AND
SWISS CHARD TACO

Shakshuka with Swiss Chard

TOTAL: 1 HR • 4 SERVINGS

Cooks throughout the Middle East poach eggs in tomato sauce for *shakshuka*. This version includes bacon and Swiss chard.

    3 tablespoons extra-virgin olive oil
    4 ounces meaty bacon, minced
    1 medium onion, minced
    4 garlic cloves, minced
    1 large bunch of Swiss chard, stems
       minced and leaves reserved
   32 ounces (4 cups) prepared
       tomato sauce
    1 teaspoon dried basil
Pinch of crushed red pepper
Kosher salt and freshly ground
       black pepper
    8 large eggs
    3 tablespoons freshly grated
       Parmigiano-Reggiano cheese
   ¼ cup thinly sliced basil leaves

1. Preheat the oven to 350°. In a large oven-proof skillet, heat the olive oil. Add the bacon, onion, garlic and chard stems and cook over moderate heat, stirring occasionally, until the stems are softened, about 5 minutes. Add the tomato sauce, dried basil and crushed red pepper and simmer until the sauce is thickened, about 15 minutes. Season with salt and black pepper.

2. Meanwhile, in a large pot of salted boiling water, blanch the chard leaves for 3 minutes. Drain and let cool slightly. Squeeze out the excess water. Form the chard leaves into 8 small piles and arrange them in the sauce around the side of the skillet.

3. Crack the eggs into the skillet between the piles of chard. Transfer the pan to the oven and bake the eggs for 12 to 15 minutes, until the egg whites are just set and the yolks are still runny.

4. Transfer the skillet to a rack and sprinkle the cheese on top. Let stand for 5 minutes. Garnish the *shakshuka* with the sliced basil and serve immediately. —*Michael Anthony*

SERVE WITH Crusty bread.

WINE Lively, light-bodied red: 2012 Domaine Dupeuble Beaujolais Rouge.

Brioche with Prosciutto, Gruyère and Egg

⏱ **TOTAL: 40 MIN • 6 SERVINGS** ●

"I love a good frisée salad," says L.A. chef Suzanne Goin. "And of course I love toasted, buttery bread, with big slabs of melted cheese and prosciutto and an egg on top." Her towering, sumptuous open-face sandwich, a staple at her A.O.C. wine bar since it opened over 10 years ago, combines all of her favorite things.

  Six 1-inch-thick slices of brioche
    2 tablespoons unsalted butter, plus
       softened butter for brushing
    6 ounces frisée, torn into bite-size
       pieces (3 cups)
   ¼ cup lightly packed parsley leaves
    2 scallions, thinly sliced
    2 tablespoons fresh lemon juice
    2 tablespoons extra-virgin olive oil
Kosher salt and freshly ground pepper
    6 large eggs
   ½ pound Gruyère cheese, thinly sliced
   12 thin slices of prosciutto (6 ounces)

1. Preheat the broiler. Brush both sides of the brioche slices with softened butter and arrange in a single layer on a large rimmed baking sheet. Broil the brioche 8 inches from the heat, turning once, until lightly toasted, about 2 minutes total. Leave the broiler on.

2. In a medium bowl, toss the frisée with the parsley, scallions, lemon juice and olive oil. Season the salad with salt and pepper.

3. Melt 1 tablespoon of butter in each of 2 large nonstick skillets. Crack 3 eggs into each skillet and cook sunny side up over moderate heat until the whites are firm and the yolks runny, about 5 minutes. Transfer to a plate and season with salt and pepper.

4. Top the brioche with the Gruyère, covering as much of the toasts as possible with the cheese. Broil 8 inches from the heat for about 3 minutes, until the cheese is melted. Transfer the cheesy brioche toasts to plates. Top with the frisée salad, prosciutto and fried eggs and serve at once. —*Suzanne Goin*

WINE Bright, berry-scented sparkling rosé: 2009 Llopart Brut Rosé Cava.

Custardy Baked Orzo with Spinach, Bacon and Feta

ACTIVE: 30 MIN; TOTAL: 1 HR 30 MIN
6 SERVINGS ●

Not many Americans eat pasta for breakfast, but this Greek-inspired recipe with orzo, leeks, spinach and bacon aims to make a few converts. It's from the brunch menu at chef Mike Isabella's Kapnos restaurant in Washington, DC.

Salt
    1 cup orzo
   12 ounces thick-cut bacon,
       cut into ½-inch pieces
  1½ pounds leeks, white and tender
       green parts only, thinly sliced
   10 ounces baby spinach
    8 ounces feta cheese, crumbled
Freshly ground pepper
    4 large eggs
   ½ cup plain Greek yogurt
   ½ cup milk

1. Preheat the oven to 375°. In a large saucepan of salted boiling water, cook the orzo until al dente. Drain the orzo and transfer to a medium bowl.

2. In a large, deep skillet, cook the bacon over moderate heat until browned but not crisp, about 8 minutes. Add the leeks and cook until tender, about 8 minutes. Add the bacon-and-leek mixture to the orzo, leaving about 1 tablespoon of fat in the skillet. Add the spinach to the skillet and cook until wilted; transfer to a colander and press out the excess liquid. Add the spinach to the orzo, fold in the feta and season with salt and pepper.

3. In a bowl, whisk the eggs with the yogurt and milk, season with pepper and stir into the orzo. Scrape the mixture into an oiled 12-by-8-inch baking dish and bake for about 45 minutes, until the eggs are set and the top is browned. Let stand for 10 minutes before serving. —*Mika Isabella*

MAKE AHEAD The fully assembled dish can be refrigerated overnight and baked the following day.

WINE Vibrant, fresh white from the Greek Peloponnese region: 2011 Gai'a Notios White.

● HEALTHY ● MAKE AHEAD ○ VEGETARIAN ● STAFF FAVORITE

BRING BACK THE QUICHE BY JULIA CHILD

What lovely little luncheons and suppers we used to have in the '60s, when real people ate quiche. Maybe you weren't around during its glory days, or you may not remember what a quiche is—it's all so long ago. To begin with, a quiche is an open-face savory pie with a custard filling. The original, quiche Lorraine, came to us from Alsace-Lorraine, that beautiful region of France bordering the Rhine, Germany and Switzerland. The custard for that rich and famous mother of the quiche was simply heavy cream, eggs and bits of bacon. Delicious!

Later versions substituted milk for cream, added lobster, crab, broccoli, mushrooms, spinach and so forth. During its vogue in this country, the creative quiche was rampant, with fanciful fillings. Quiche was everywhere, and cheap, careless versions eventually ruined the appeal. The passion and the fashion dissipated.

But what an easy, pleasant way to entertain. You'd have a guest or two for lunch and serve them a quiche hot out of the oven. What a welcome when you enter a home that's filled with the aroma of buttery pastry baking.

THE PARIS YEARS *While living in Paris in the 1950s, Julia began taking cooking classes and trying out recipes in her small apartment kitchen on the Rue de l'Université.*

HOW TO GO ABOUT THE QUICHE
Of course you could use a raw, store-bought pie shell, and some that I've tried recently have been perfectly acceptable. (During quiche's heyday, my nice neighbor, who didn't do much cooking, wanted to serve a quiche but trembled at the thought of making dough. I suggested a brand of pie shell and the custard proportions. The next day she rushed up to me all beaming and happy: "I made a quiche! I bought the shell, and I made quiche! It was so beautiful. I'm so proud of myself!")

If you are not buying a preformed frozen shell, I shall assume you are already familiar with making pie dough. Use your own recipe, or try my formula of 2½ sticks of unsalted butter and 4 tablespoons of shortening for 3½ cups of unbleached flour, 2 teaspoons of salt and ⅔ to 1 cup of ice water. It makes enough dough for two 9-inch quiches plus leftovers for appetizers, since the dough freezes perfectly for months.

PREBAKING THE SHELL Whatever raw shell you plan to use, homemade or store-bought, you want to prebake it briefly to prevent a soggy bottom. Set a buttered pie pan in the frozen store-bought shell or press a sheet of buttered foil against the bottom and sides of a homemade shell and weigh it down with dried beans. Bake for about 10 minutes at 450° to set the crust, then remove the pie pan or foil and beans and bake for 7 to 8 minutes longer to brown it very lightly. Now you are ready to fill the quiche.

MAKING THE CUSTARD The proportions never vary. Every ½ cup of liquid includes 1 egg. For example, for a 9-inch quiche, whisk 3 large eggs in a 4-cup measure and when blended, pour in enough milk to reach the 1½-cup mark. If, in the midst of battle, you find you need more custard, whisk 1 egg in a measure and pour in milk to the ½-cup mark. As to liquid, that's up to you—skim, 1 percent, 2 percent or regular milk; or cream, from half-and-half to heavy; or part sour cream and part milk or cream. Season nicely with salt, white pepper and a pinch or two of nutmeg.

Heat the oven to 375°. Spread ½ cup of cheese in the crust and strew with 3 crumbled bacon strips. Pour in enough custard to reach within ¼ inch of the lowest part of the shell rim and strew 2 tablespoons of cheese on top. Slide the quiche onto the middle rack of the oven and bake for 30 minutes, or until the top is nicely browned. Let cool for 5 minutes before serving.

Butternut Squash and Kale Strata with Multigrain Bread

ACTIVE: 1 HR; TOTAL: 3 HR
8 TO 10 SERVINGS ● ● ●

2½ tablespoons unsalted butter, plus more for greasing
2 pounds butternut squash—peeled, seeded and cut into ½-inch dice
¼ cup plus 1 tablespoon extra-virgin olive oil
Kosher salt and freshly ground black pepper
2 medium onions, thinly sliced, plus ½ small onion, finely chopped
¾ pound kale, ribs discarded and leaves chopped
2 garlic cloves, minced
Pinch of crushed red pepper
2 teaspoons finely chopped thyme
¼ cup all-purpose flour
2½ cups milk
1 cup heavy cream
½ cup crème fraîche
1 teaspoon sugar
8 large eggs
One ¾-pound multigrain baguette, cut into 1-inch pieces
⅓ cup freshly grated Parmigiano-Reggiano cheese

1. Preheat the oven to 425° and butter a 9-by-13-inch baking dish. On a large rimmed baking sheet, toss the squash with 2 tablespoons of the olive oil and season with salt and black pepper. Bake for about 25 minutes, tossing once, until the squash is just tender. Reduce the oven temperature to 325°.
2. Meanwhile, in a large skillet, heat 2 tablespoons of the oil. Add the sliced onions, season with salt and cook over moderately low heat, stirring occasionally, until golden, about 25 minutes. Scrape the onions into a bowl.
3. In the same skillet, heat the remaining 1 tablespoon of oil until shimmering. Add the kale, garlic, crushed red pepper and 1 teaspoon of the thyme and season with salt. Cook over moderately high heat, tossing, until the kale is wilted and just tender, 5 minutes; scrape into the bowl with the cooked onions.
4. In a medium saucepan, melt the 2½ tablespoons of butter. Add the chopped onion and the remaining 1 teaspoon of thyme and cook over moderately low heat, stirring, until softened, 5 minutes. Add the flour and cook over moderate heat, whisking constantly, until a light golden paste forms, 3 minutes. Whisk in 1 cup of the milk and cook, whisking, until very thick and no floury taste remains, 8 to 10 minutes. Remove from the heat and whisk in the cream, crème fraîche, sugar, 2 teaspoons of salt, ½ teaspoon of black pepper and the remaining 1½ cups of milk. Let the béchamel cool.
5. Beat the eggs into the cooled béchamel in the saucepan. Pour into a large bowl, add the bread and the vegetables and mix well. Pour the strata mixture into the prepared baking dish and let stand for 30 minutes, pressing down the bread occasionally.
6. Bake the strata for 55 minutes to 1 hour, until almost set. Increase the oven temperature to 475°. Sprinkle the Parmigiano on the strata and bake for about 10 minutes more, until the top is lightly browned. Let the strata stand for 15 minutes before serving. —*Zoe Nathan*
MAKE AHEAD The recipe can be prepared through Step 5 and refrigerated overnight.

Mashed Banana and Whole-Grain Porridge

TOTAL: 15 MIN • 4 SERVINGS ● ● ●

2 cups low-fat milk
¾ cup mashed bananas
Pinch of cinnamon
Kosher salt
4 cups frozen mixed chewy grains (20 ounces), such as wheat berries, Kamut, barley and farro
2 tablespoons quick-cooking oats
Fresh fruit, toasted almonds and pure maple syrup, for serving

In a medium saucepan, whisk the milk with the bananas, cinnamon and a generous pinch of salt. Cook over moderate heat, stirring, until thickened slightly, about 3 minutes. Add the frozen grains and oats and cook, stirring, until the grains are heated through and the porridge is creamy, about 5 minutes. Spoon into bowls and top with fruit, almonds and maple syrup. —*Justin Chapple*
MAKE AHEAD The porridge can be refrigerated overnight. Reheat gently, adding milk as needed to thin out the porridge.

Cranberry–Pumpkin Seed Energy Bars

ACTIVE: 20 MIN; TOTAL: 2 HR 40 MIN
MAKES 1 DOZEN BARS ● ● ● ●

1 cup pecans, crushed
1 cup rolled oats
⅓ cup pumpkin seeds
¼ cup flaxseeds
⅔ cup muscovado or dark brown sugar
½ cup honey
4 tablespoons unsalted butter
½ teaspoon salt
2 teaspoons pure vanilla extract
2 cups puffed rice cereal
½ cup dried cranberries

1. Preheat the oven to 350° and line a large rimmed baking sheet with parchment paper. Spread the pecans, oats, pumpkin seeds and flaxseeds on the prepared baking sheet and bake until fragrant, about 8 minutes. Transfer the mixture to a large bowl.
2. In a small saucepan, bring the sugar, honey, butter and salt to a boil over moderate heat. Simmer until the sugar is dissolved and a light brown caramel forms, 5 minutes. Remove from the heat and stir in the vanilla.
3. Drizzle the hot caramel all over the nut-and-oat mixture. Stir in the puffed rice and dried cranberries until evenly coated.
4. Line an 8-inch square baking dish with parchment paper, extending the paper over the sides of the pan. Scrape the cereal mixture into the baking dish and spread it in an even layer. Cover the mixture with a second sheet of parchment and press down to compress it. Let stand until firm, about 2 hours.
5. Discard the top piece of parchment. Using the overhanging paper, lift out the cereal square and transfer it to a work surface. Cut into 12 bars and serve. —*Lara Ferroni*

● HEALTHY ● MAKE AHEAD ● VEGETARIAN ● STAFF FAVORITE

BUTTERNUT SQUASH AND KALE STRATA
WITH MULTIGRAIN BREAD

Blueberry Muffins with Banana Butter

⏱ TOTAL: 45 MIN

MAKES 1 DOZEN MUFFINS ● ●

Crisp on top, with light, fluffy centers and plenty of big juicy blueberries, these are the ultimate blueberry muffins. The sweet, creamy banana butter that accompanies them would also be terrific on pancakes or even plain toast.

MUFFINS

- 2 cups all-purpose flour
- 2 teaspoons baking powder
- ¼ teaspoon kosher salt
- 1 stick unsalted butter, melted and cooled
- ½ cup whole milk
- ¾ cup granulated sugar
- ¼ cup light brown sugar
- 1 teaspoon finely grated lemon zest
- 2 large eggs
- 1½ cups blueberries

BANANA BUTTER

- 6 tablespoons unsalted butter, at room temperature
- 1 very ripe banana, sliced
- ½ teaspoon fresh lemon juice

Pinch of kosher salt

1. MAKE THE MUFFINS Preheat the oven to 375° and fill 12 muffin cups with paper liners.
2. In a large bowl, whisk the flour with the baking powder and salt. In a medium bowl, whisk the butter with the milk, both sugars, the lemon zest and eggs. Add the wet ingredients to the dry ingredients and whisk just until combined. Fold in the blueberries. Spoon the batter into the muffin cups and bake for 20 to 25 minutes, until the muffins are golden. Let cool for 5 minutes. Unmold the muffins and let cool on a rack.
3. MAKE THE BANANA BUTTER In a food processor, puree the butter, banana, lemon juice and salt. Serve with the muffins.
—*Kay Chun*

MAKE AHEAD The muffins can be stored in an airtight container for up to 2 days. The banana butter can be kept in a jar and refrigerated for up to 1 week.

Vegan Banana-Walnut Muffins

ACTIVE: 15 MIN; TOTAL: 1 HR

MAKES 9 MUFFINS ● ●

Mashed banana and applesauce make these gluten-free muffins incredibly moist, while xanthan gum, an industrial powder beloved by molecular chefs, gives them a fluffy rise.

- ¾ cup all-purpose gluten-free flour, preferably Bob's Red Mill (see Note)
- ½ teaspoon baking soda
- ½ teaspoon baking powder
- ¼ teaspoon xanthan gum, preferably Bob's Red Mill (see Note)
- ¼ teaspoon cinnamon
- ⅛ teaspoon kosher salt
- ¾ cup mashed banana (from 1 large banana)
- ¼ cup unsweetened applesauce
- ½ cup light brown sugar
- 2½ tablespoons canola oil
- 1 teaspoon pure vanilla extract
- 1 tablespoon light agave nectar
- ¾ cup chopped walnuts (3 ounces)

1. Preheat the oven to 350°. Line 9 muffin cups with paper liners.
2. In a small bowl, whisk the flour with the baking soda, baking powder, xanthan gum, cinnamon and salt. In a medium bowl, whisk the mashed banana and applesauce with the brown sugar, canola oil, vanilla extract and agave nectar. Stir in the dry ingredients just until incorporated, then stir in half of the walnuts.
3. Spoon the batter into the muffin cups, filling each one three-quarters full. Top with the remaining walnuts. Bake for 30 to 35 minutes, until the muffins are golden and a tester inserted in the center comes out clean. Transfer the muffins to a rack to cool slightly before serving.
—*Tully Phillips and Jennifer Wells*

NOTE Xanthan gum is used to add volume to baked goods. Like gluten-free flour, it is available at natural food shops and supermarkets or online at *bobsredmill.com*.

MAKE AHEAD The muffins can be stored at room temperature for 2 days.

Skillet Monkey Bread Biscuits with Berry Dunk

⏱ TOTAL: 40 MIN • MAKES ABOUT

3 DOZEN SMALL BISCUITS ●

- 2 cups all-purpose flour, plus more for dusting
- 1 cup plus 3 tablespoons sugar
- 1 tablespoon baking powder
- ¼ teaspoon kosher salt
- 1 stick cold unsalted butter, cut into ½-inch cubes, plus 4 tablespoons unsalted butter, melted and cooled
- 1 teaspoon finely grated lemon zest
- 1 cup heavy cream

Scant ½ teaspoon ground cardamom

- 6 cups mixed fresh berries

1. Preheat the oven to 425° and lightly butter a 12-inch cast-iron skillet. In a large bowl, combine the 2 cups of flour with 3 tablespoons of the sugar and the baking powder and salt. Using a pastry blender, cut in the cubed butter until it is the size of small peas. Stir in the lemon zest, then stir in the cream just until the dough is evenly moistened.
2. Turn the dough out onto a lightly floured work surface and knead several times, until it just comes together. Roll out the dough ¾ inch thick. Using a 1¼-inch round cutter, stamp out as many biscuits as you can. Gently press the scraps together and stamp out more biscuits.
3. Mix the remaining 1 cup of sugar with the cardamom. Spread half of the cardamom sugar in a pie plate. Brush the biscuits with the melted butter and coat them all over in the cardamom sugar. Arrange the biscuits in the buttered skillet in a single layer. Drizzle any remaining butter on top and sprinkle with any cardamom sugar left in the pie plate. Bake in the lower third of the oven for about 25 minutes, until the biscuits are golden and risen. Let cool slightly.
4. In a medium saucepan, combine the remaining cardamom sugar with the berries. Bring to a boil, crushing the berries, and cook until thickened, about 5 minutes. Spoon the berry dunk into small bowls and serve with the monkey bread biscuits. —*Grace Parisi*

● HEALTHY ● MAKE AHEAD ● VEGETARIAN ● STAFF FAVORITE

Brown Butter–Sour Cream Crumb Cake

**ACTIVE: 30 MIN; TOTAL: 1 HR 30 MIN
PLUS COOLING • 10 TO 12 SERVINGS ● ●**

CRUMB TOPPING
- 1 stick unsalted butter, cubed and chilled
- ¼ cup plus 2 tablespoons sugar
- 1 cup all-purpose flour
- ½ teaspoon baking soda
- Scant ½ teaspoon salt

CAKE
- 1½ sticks unsalted butter
- 2 cups all-purpose flour
- 1½ teaspoons baking powder
- ¼ teaspoon baking soda
- ½ teaspoon salt
- Scant ½ teaspoon freshly grated nutmeg
- 1 cup sugar
- 2 large eggs
- 1½ teaspoons pure vanilla extract
- ½ cup sour cream

1. MAKE THE CRUMB TOPPING In a food processor, combine the butter with the sugar, flour, baking soda and salt and process until the mixture forms small crumbs. Transfer to a plate and press into ½-inch clumps. Refrigerate the crumb topping for 15 minutes, until firm.

2. MAKE THE CAKE In a small saucepan, cook the butter over moderate heat until the solids turn brown, 5 minutes. Immediately scrape the butter and solids into a shallow bowl and freeze until firm but not hard, 15 minutes.

3. Preheat the oven to 350°. Spray a 9-inch springform pan with baking spray and line the bottom with parchment paper. Spray the paper. In a large bowl, whisk the flour with the baking powder, baking soda, salt and nutmeg. Scrape the firmed brown butter into the bowl of a standing mixer fitted with the paddle. Add the sugar and beat at moderate speed until light and fluffy, 5 minutes. Add the eggs and vanilla and beat until smooth. Working in 3 alternating additions, beat in the dry ingredients and the sour cream, scraping down the bowl occasionally.

4. Scrape the cake batter into the prepared pan and scatter the crumbs on top. Bake in the middle of the oven for 45 minutes, until the cake is golden and a skewer inserted in the center comes out clean. Let cool.

5. Remove the ring and transfer the cake to a plate. Peel the paper off the bottom of the cake before serving. —*Grace Parisi*

Glazed Lemon-Ginger Scones

**ACTIVE: 20 MIN; TOTAL: 1 HR
MAKES 8 SCONES ● ● ●**

To Aimee Olexy of Talula's Daily in Philadelphia, scones are a less sweet, more civilized option in the breakfast-pastry world. Her lemony scones are light, crumbly and laced with pieces of chewy candied ginger.

- 2¼ cups all-purpose flour
- ¼ cup granulated sugar
- 1 tablespoon baking powder
- 2 teaspoons finely grated lemon zest
- ½ teaspoon salt
- 1½ cups heavy cream
- ¼ cup plus 2 teaspoons fresh lemon juice
- ¼ cup finely chopped candied ginger
- 2 cups confectioners' sugar

1. Preheat the oven to 375° and line a baking sheet with parchment paper. In a bowl, whisk the flour with the granulated sugar, baking powder, lemon zest and salt. Using a wooden spoon, stir in the cream and 2 tablespoons of the lemon juice; fold in the candied ginger.

2. On a lightly floured work surface, gently knead the dough just until it comes together. Pat into a 9-inch round, a scant ½ inch thick. Cut the dough into 8 wedges and arrange them 1 inch apart on the prepared baking sheet. Bake the scones for 20 to 25 minutes, until slightly firm and lightly browned on the bottom, pale on top. Let cool for 5 minutes, then transfer to a rack to cool completely.

3. In a medium bowl, whisk the confectioners' sugar with the remaining 2 tablespoons plus 2 teaspoons of lemon juice until the glaze is smooth. Drizzle the lemon glaze over the scones and let stand for 15 minutes before serving. —*Aimee Olexy*

Maple-Bacon Bread Pudding

**ACTIVE: 30 MIN; TOTAL: 3 HR
8 TO 10 SERVINGS ● ●**

- 1 pound thick-cut bacon
- Unsalted butter, for greasing
- 17 large eggs
- 1 cup crème fraîche
- ¾ cup sugar
- 1 vanilla bean, split and seeds scraped
- 1 teaspoon kosher salt
- 3¾ cups half-and-half
- ¾ cup pure maple syrup, plus more for serving
- 1½ pounds brioche (3 small loaves), crusts discarded and loaves sliced 1 inch thick (see Note)
- Chopped toasted pecans, for serving

1. Preheat the oven to 350°. Line a large rimmed baking sheet with aluminum foil and arrange the bacon on it in a single layer. Bake the bacon for 25 to 30 minutes, until it is browned and nearly crisp. Transfer the bacon to paper towels to drain and cool, then coarsely chop it.

2. Meanwhile, butter a 9-by-13-inch ceramic baking dish. In a large bowl, beat the eggs with the crème fraîche, sugar, vanilla seeds and salt, then beat in the half-and-half and the ¾ cup of maple syrup.

3. Layer half of the brioche slices in the prepared baking dish and sprinkle with half of the chopped bacon. Repeat the layering with the remaining brioche and bacon. Pour the custard over the brioche and gently press the bread into the custard. Cover and refrigerate for at least 1 hour.

4. Preheat the oven to 325°. Uncover the bread pudding; bake until puffed and just set in the center, about 1 hour 10 minutes. Let stand for 15 minutes. Serve with chopped pecans and maple syrup. —*Zoe Nathan*

NOTE Leftover bread crusts, such as those from the brioche here, can be lightly toasted, then chopped in a food processor to use as bread crumbs.

MAKE AHEAD The recipe can be prepared through Step 3 and refrigerated overnight.

● HEALTHY ● MAKE AHEAD ● VEGETARIAN ● STAFF FAVORITE

GLAZED LEMON-GINGER SCONES

Brioche French Toast with Brown Sugar–Cranberry Sauce

⏲ TOTAL: 35 MIN • 6 SERVINGS ●

CRANBERRY SAUCE

- 2 cups fresh or thawed frozen cranberries, chopped
- ½ cup plus 2 tablespoons packed light brown sugar
- 4 large strips of orange zest
- ½ teaspoon salt
- 6 tablespoons unsalted butter, cubed
- ¼ cup heavy cream

FRENCH TOAST

- 6 large eggs
- ¾ cup heavy cream
- 1½ tablespoons packed light brown sugar
- ¼ teaspoon pure vanilla extract
- ¼ teaspoon salt

Unsalted butter, for greasing

Twelve 1-inch-thick slices of brioche (1 pound)

Lightly sweetened whipped cream, for serving

1. MAKE THE CRANBERRY SAUCE In a medium saucepan, combine the chopped cranberries with the light brown sugar, orange zest, salt and 2 tablespoons of water and bring to a boil. Simmer over moderately high heat, stirring occasionally, until the cranberries are soft and the sauce is ruby-colored, 3 to 5 minutes. Remove the cranberry mixture from the heat and whisk in the butter and heavy cream. Cook over moderately low heat, whisking, until the butter is completely melted and the sauce is hot, about 3 minutes. Discard the orange zest. Keep the cranberry sauce warm over very low heat.

2. MAKE THE FRENCH TOAST Preheat the oven to 225°. In a large baking dish, whisk the eggs with the heavy cream, light brown sugar, vanilla extract and salt. Heat a large cast-iron griddle and lightly butter it. Working in batches, dip half of the brioche slices in the egg mixture, turning them, until they are well moistened. Transfer the soaked brioche to the griddle and cook over moderate heat, turning once, until the French toast is golden and cooked through, about 4 minutes. Transfer the French toast to a baking sheet, cover loosely with aluminum foil and keep warm in the oven. Repeat with the remaining brioche slices. Serve the French toast with the cranberry sauce and whipped cream. —*Zoe Nathan*

Lemon–Poppy Seed Buttermilk Pancakes

⏲ TOTAL: 30 MIN

MAKES FIFTEEN 3-INCH PANCAKES ● ●

These luscious gluten-free pancakes are made with both lemon zest and juice; poppy seeds add a nice crunch.

- 1½ cups Silvana's Kitchen Gluten-Free All-Purpose Flour (recipe follows)
- 2 tablespoons sugar
- 2 teaspoons baking powder
- ½ teaspoon baking soda
- ½ teaspoon salt
- 1½ cups buttermilk
- 2 large eggs, at room temperature
- 2 teaspoons pure vanilla extract

Finely grated zest of 2 lemons

- 2 tablespoons fresh lemon juice
- 1 tablespoon poppy seeds
- 6 tablespoons unsalted butter, melted and cooled, plus more for the griddle

Warm pure maple syrup, for serving

1. In a large bowl, whisk the flour with the sugar, baking powder, baking soda and salt. In a medium bowl, whisk the buttermilk with the eggs, vanilla, lemon zest, lemon juice, poppy seeds and the 6 tablespoons of melted butter. Using a wooden spoon, stir the wet ingredients into the dry ingredients just until combined.

2. Heat a large nonstick skillet or griddle and brush lightly with melted butter. Scoop ¼-cup mounds of batter into the skillet and spread to 3-inch rounds. Cook over moderate heat until the pancakes are golden on the bottom, about 2 minutes. Flip each pancake; cook until fluffy and cooked through, about 2 minutes longer. Transfer the pancakes to plates and serve with syrup. —*Silvana Nardone*

SILVANA'S KITCHEN GLUTEN-FREE ALL-PURPOSE FLOUR

⏲ TOTAL: 15 MIN • MAKES 11 CUPS ● ●

- 6 cups white rice flour
- 3 cups tapioca flour
- 1½ cups potato starch
- 2 tablespoons xanthan gum
- 1 tablespoon salt

In a large bowl, whisk together all of the ingredients. Store the flour in an airtight container at room temperature for up to 1 year. —*SN*

Almond-Butter-and-Jelly French Toast

⏲ TOTAL: 30 MIN • 4 SERVINGS ●

- 3 cups frozen mixed berries
- ¼ cup sugar
- 3 large eggs
- 1½ cups milk
- 8 slices of good-quality white bread
- ½ cup salted almond butter
- ¼ cup roasted, salted, chopped almonds, plus more for garnish
- ¼ cup seedless raspberry preserves
- 2 tablespoons unsalted butter

1. In a saucepan, combine the berries, sugar and ½ cup of water and bring to a boil. Simmer over moderately low heat, stirring and crushing occasionally, until the sauce is slightly thickened, about 10 minutes.

2. Meanwhile, in a large baking dish, beat the eggs with the milk. Arrange the bread on a work surface; spread 4 of the slices evenly with the almond butter. Sprinkle the ¼ cup of almonds on top. Spread the raspberry preserves evenly on the remaining slices of bread and close the sandwiches.

3. Heat a large griddle and add 1 tablespoon of the butter. Dip the sandwiches in the egg mixture, pressing to soak. Cook over moderate heat until browned, 3 minutes. Add the remaining butter and flip the sandwiches; cook until golden, 3 minutes longer. Transfer the French toast to plates and spoon the berry sauce on top. Garnish with almonds and serve right away. —*Grace Parisi*

BRIOCHE FRENCH TOAST WITH
BROWN SUGAR–CRANBERRY SAUCE

With produce from his favorite farm stands, star chef and *Top Chef* head judge Tom Colicchio cooks dinner—from salads to dessert—at his summer home on Long Island.

Opposite: recipe, page 320.
POACHED PEACHES WITH BAKED RICOTTA

TARTS, PIES & FRUIT DESSERTS

Granny Smith Apple Crisp

ACTIVE: 30 MIN; TOTAL: 1 HR 15 MIN
PLUS COOLING • 12 SERVINGS ● ●
Granny Smiths are the key to this delicious crisp from California chef Tanya Holland; the apples' tartness complements the sweet, crunchy oat-flecked crumb topping.

>   3   pounds Granny Smith
>   apples—peeled, cored and
>   thinly sliced
>   2   tablespoons freshly squeezed
>   lemon juice
>   ½   cup granulated sugar
>   1   stick unsalted butter, finely
>   diced and chilled, plus
>   2 tablespoons
>   1½   cups all-purpose flour
>   1½   cups light brown sugar
>   ¾   cup rolled oats
>   (not quick-cooking)
>   1   teaspoon cinnamon
>   ½   teaspoon fine sea salt
> Scant ½ teaspoon ground
>   cardamom
> Crème fraîche or vanilla ice cream,
>   for serving

1. Preheat the oven to 350°. In a large bowl, toss the apples with the lemon juice and granulated sugar. In a very large skillet, melt the 2 tablespoons of butter. Add the apples and cook over moderate heat, stirring occasionally, until softened but not browned, about 5 minutes. Scrape the apples into a large baking dish.

2. Wipe out the bowl. Add the flour, brown sugar, oats, cinnamon, salt, cardamom and the 1 stick of diced butter and, using your fingers, rub the butter into the dry ingredients until the mixture resembles coarse meal. Press the topping into clumps and scatter it over the apples.

3. Bake the crisp for 45 to 50 minutes, until the apples are bubbling and the topping is golden. Let the crisp cool, then serve warm with crème fraîche or ice cream.
—*Tanya Holland*

MAKE AHEAD The apple crisp can be made earlier in the day and reheated.

Caramelized-Pear Crisp with Dried Cranberries

ACTIVE: 1 HR; TOTAL: 2 HR
10 SERVINGS ● ●
In her *A.O.C. Cookbook,* Los Angeles chef Suzanne Goin makes this crisp with a compote of fresh and dried cranberries. The simpler version here layers dried cranberries with caramelized pear wedges that are baked beneath a crumbly, buttery topping.

>   1½   sticks cold unsalted butter,
>   cut into tablespoons, plus more
>   for buttering the dish
>   ¼   cup plus 2 tablespoons dark
>   brown sugar
>   ⅓   cup plus 2 tablespoons
>   granulated sugar
>   1¼   cups all-purpose flour
>   ½   teaspoon kosher salt
>   ¼   teaspoon cinnamon
> Pinch of freshly grated nutmeg
>   5   pounds ripe but firm Anjou or
>   Bartlett pears—peeled, halved
>   lengthwise, cored and cut into
>   1-inch wedges
>   1   cup dried cranberries (5 ounces)
> Vanilla ice cream, for serving

1. Preheat the oven to 375°. Butter an 8-by-12-inch ceramic baking dish, then sprinkle 2 tablespoons of the brown sugar over the bottom. In a food processor, pulse ⅓ cup of the granulated sugar with the flour, salt, cinnamon, nutmeg and remaining ¼ cup of brown sugar. Add 8 tablespoons of the butter and pulse until the mixture resembles coarse meal; transfer to a bowl and pinch into clumps. Refrigerate the topping until chilled, about 30 minutes.

2. Meanwhile, melt 1 tablespoon of the butter in a cast-iron skillet. Add ½ tablespoon of the granulated sugar and cook over high heat, swirling, until dissolved, 1 minute. Add one-fourth of the pears, cut side down, and cook, turning once, until browned on the cut sides, 6 to 8 minutes. Transfer the pears to a baking sheet and wipe out the skillet. Repeat three more times with the remaining butter, granulated sugar and pears.

3. Arrange half of the pears in a single layer in the baking dish and sprinkle with half of the cranberries. Top with the remaining pears and cranberries. Sprinkle the topping over the fruit and bake for 35 to 40 minutes, until the crisp is bubbling and golden brown. Let cool for 10 minutes; serve with ice cream.
—*Suzanne Goin*

Flaugnarde with Pears

ACTIVE: 30 MIN; TOTAL: 4 HR 15 MIN
6 TO 8 SERVINGS ● ●
This not-too-sweet fallen pear pancake is from Paula Wolfert's 1983 classic, *The Cooking of Southwest France. Flaugnarde* (flow-NYARD) is a sibling of the more familiar baked fruit dessert called clafoutis. It's just as good for brunch as it is for dessert, served puffed and hot, right out of the oven.

>   3   large eggs
>   ¾   cup cake flour
>   ¼   cup all-purpose flour
> Pinch of salt
>   1   cup warm milk
>   1   tablespoon dark rum
>   3   tablespoons superfine sugar
>   2½   tablespoons unsalted butter,
>   softened
>   2   ripe medium Bartlett pears—
>   peeled, cored and thinly sliced

1. In a medium bowl, whisk together the eggs, cake and all-purpose flours, salt and ¼ cup of the milk until smooth. Whisk in the remaining ¾ cup of milk, the rum and 1½ tablespoons of the sugar. Cover with plastic wrap and let stand at room temperature for 3 hours.

2. Preheat the oven to 450° and coat a deep 9-inch cake pan with half of the butter. Pour the batter into the pan and arrange the pear slices on top. Dot with the remaining butter and bake in the lower third of the oven for 15 minutes. Reduce the oven temperature to 400° and bake for about 30 minutes longer, or until the *flaugnarde* is puffed and deeply golden. Let cool for 2 minutes, then sprinkle with the remaining 1½ tablespoons of sugar and serve. —*Paula Wolfert*

FLAUGNARDE WITH PEARS

Apple Pie Bars

ACTIVE: 1 HR; TOTAL: 2 HR
MAKES 4 DOZEN BARS ● ○ ○

CRUST
- 3 sticks unsalted butter, softened
- ¾ cup granulated sugar
- 3 cups all-purpose flour
- ½ teaspoon kosher salt

FILLING
- 6 tablespoons unsalted butter
- ½ cup light brown sugar
- 12 Granny Smith apples (about 6 pounds)—peeled, cored and thinly sliced
- 1 tablespoon cinnamon
- ¼ teaspoon freshly grated nutmeg

TOPPING
- ¾ cup walnuts
- 3 cups quick-cooking oats
- 2 cups all-purpose flour
- 1½ cups light brown sugar
- 1¼ teaspoons cinnamon
- ½ teaspoon baking soda
- ½ teaspoon kosher salt
- 3 sticks cold unsalted butter, cut into ½-inch cubes

1. MAKE THE CRUST Preheat the oven to 375°. Line a 15-by-17-inch rimmed baking sheet with parchment paper. In a standing mixer fitted with the paddle attachment, beat the butter with the granulated sugar at medium speed until light and fluffy, 2 minutes. At low speed, beat in the flour and salt until a soft dough forms. Press the dough over the bottom of the prepared baking sheet and ½ inch up the sides. Bake in the center of the oven for 20 minutes, until the crust is golden. Let cool on a rack.

2. MAKE THE FILLING In each of 2 large skillets, melt 3 tablespoons of the butter with ¼ cup of the brown sugar. Add the apples to the skillets; cook over high heat, stirring occasionally, until softened, 10 minutes. Stir half of the cinnamon and nutmeg into each skillet. Cook until the apples are caramelized and very tender and the liquid is evaporated, 10 minutes longer; scrape up any bits stuck to the bottom of the skillets

and add up to ½ cup of water to each pan to prevent scorching. Let cool.

3. MAKE THE TOPPING Spread the walnuts in a pie plate; toast until golden and fragrant, 8 minutes. Let cool, then coarsely chop the walnuts. In a large bowl, mix the oats with the flour, light brown sugar, cinnamon, baking soda and salt. Using a pastry blender or 2 knives, cut in the butter until the mixture resembles coarse meal. Stir in the walnuts and press the mixture into clumps.

4. Spread the apple filling over the crust. Scatter the crumbs on top, pressing them lightly into an even layer. Bake in the center of the oven for about 1 hour, until the topping is golden; rotate the pan halfway through baking. Let cool completely on a rack before cutting into 2-inch bars. —*Cathy Johnson*

Caramelized-Apple Custard Tart with a Rye Crust

ACTIVE: 1 HR; TOTAL: 6 HR
MAKES ONE 9-INCH DEEP-DISH PIE ● ○ ○

CUSTARD
- 2¼ cups heavy cream
- 2 large eggs plus 4 large egg yolks
- 1 teaspoon pure vanilla extract
- ½ cup sugar
- 2 tablespoons all-purpose flour
- ½ vanilla bean, chopped

Pinch of kosher salt

PASTRY
- 1¼ cups light rye flour, preferably Bob's Red Mill
- 1¼ cups all-purpose flour
- 2 tablespoons sugar
- 1 teaspoon kosher salt
- 1 stick plus 2 tablespoons cold unsalted butter, cubed
- 6 tablespoons ice water

CARAMELIZED APPLES
- 3 tablespoons unsalted butter
- ⅓ cup sugar
- 1 Granny Smith apple—peeled, cored, quartered and sliced ⅛ inch thick
- ½ vanilla bean—split lengthwise and seeds scraped, pod reserved for another use
- 2 tablespoons Champagne vinegar

1. MAKE THE CUSTARD In a blender, puree all of the ingredients until smooth. Transfer to a bowl, cover and refrigerate for 3 hours, until completely chilled.

2. MEANWHILE, MAKE THE PASTRY In a food processor, pulse the light rye flour with the all-purpose flour, sugar and salt to blend. Add the butter and pulse until it is the size of small peas. Drizzle in the ice water and pulse until the pastry just starts to come together. Turn the pastry out onto a work surface and gather into a ball. Flatten to a 1-inch-thick disk, wrap in plastic and refrigerate for 1 hour.

3. On a lightly floured work surface, using a lightly floured rolling pin, roll out the pastry ⅛ inch thick. Place a 9-inch deep-dish glass pie plate upside down on the pastry as a template and cut out a round that is 1½ inches wider than the dish. Transfer to the pie plate; fold the edge under itself and crimp decoratively. Refrigerate for 30 minutes.

4. Preheat the oven to 350°. Line the pastry with parchment paper and fill the pie dish with pie weights. Bake for about 1 hour and 15 minutes, until the shell is golden brown all over and cooked through. Cover the pie rim with foil if it gets too dark. Transfer the pie to a rack and let cool completely, about 1 hour.

5. MEANWHILE, MAKE THE CARAMELIZED APPLES In a large skillet, cook the butter with the sugar over moderate heat until bubbling and caramelized, about 3 minutes. Add the apple and vanilla seeds and cook, stirring occasionally, until the apples are very tender and caramelized, about 5 minutes. Carefully add the vinegar and simmer until the caramel is slightly thickened, about 3 minutes.

6. Preheat the oven to 325°. Scatter half of the apples in the shell. Strain the custard into a bowl and pour it into the shell. Cover the crust with foil to prevent it from burning.

7. Bake the tart for about 1 hour and 15 minutes, until the custard is golden and just set. Spoon the remaining caramelized apples on top. Transfer the tart to a rack and let cool to room temperature. The tart can be served at room temperature but is best chilled. —*Kim Boyce*

MAKE AHEAD The tart can be refrigerated for up to 2 days.

● HEALTHY ● MAKE AHEAD ○ VEGETARIAN ● STAFF FAVORITE

Guest-at-the-Doorstep Apple-Berry Charlotte

ACTIVE: 30 MIN; TOTAL: 1 HR 30 MIN
PLUS COOLING • 6 SERVINGS ● ○

Classic Soviet cuisine abounded in nifty quick recipes for unexpected guests. This puffy dessert from Anya von Bremzen, author of *Mastering the Art of Soviet Cooking,* requires only sliced tart apples, a few handfuls of berries and a simple batter.

- 6 tablespoons unsalted butter, melted and cooled, plus more for the pan
- 2 tablespoons plain dry bread crumbs
- 3 large eggs
- ¼ cup milk
- ¼ teaspoon pure vanilla extract
- 1¼ cups granulated sugar
- 1½ cups all-purpose flour
- 1 cup blackberries, plus 8 to 12 berries for garnish
- 4 large Granny Smith or other firm tart apples—peeled, quartered, cored and thinly sliced crosswise
- 1 cup blueberries
- ½ teaspoon cinnamon
- Confectioners' sugar, for dusting

1. Preheat the oven to 375°. Butter a 10-inch cast-iron skillet and dust the bottom with the bread crumbs. In a large bowl, using an electric mixer, beat the eggs with the milk, vanilla and 1 cup of the granulated sugar. Beat in the 6 tablespoons of melted butter until incorporated, then beat in the flour until a thick batter forms.

2. In another large bowl, toss the 1 cup of blackberries with the sliced apples, blueberries, cinnamon and the remaining ¼ cup of granulated sugar.

3. Spread one-fourth of the batter in the prepared skillet and top with the apples and berries. Using an offset spatula, spread the remaining batter over the fruit in an even layer. Scatter the remaining 8 to 12 blackberries on top and gently press them into the batter. Bake in the center of the oven for about 1 hour, until lightly golden and a toothpick inserted in the center comes out with a few moist crumbs attached. Let cool completely, then dust with confectioners' sugar. Slice into wedges and serve.
—*Anya von Bremzen*

SERVE WITH A dollop of crème fraîche or vanilla ice cream.

MAKE AHEAD The charlotte can be baked earlier in the day; let the dessert stand at room temperature.

Quince Tarte Tatin

ACTIVE: 45 MIN; TOTAL: 2 HR
10 SERVINGS ○ ●

For this stunning twist on the classic French upside-down tart, San Francisco chef Michael Tusk adds slices of fresh quince instead of the usual wedges of apple. Quince is more dense than apple, so it retains a bit of firmness even after it's cooked.

- 2 cups sugar
- ½ cup light corn syrup
- 1 vanilla bean, split and seeds scraped
- 1 stick unsalted butter, cut into tablespoons
- 3½ pounds quinces (about 10)—peeled, sliced lengthwise ¼ inch thick, cores discarded
- 1 pound all-butter puff pastry, chilled
- Crème fraîche, for serving

1. Preheat the oven to 350°. In a heavy 14-inch skillet, combine the sugar, light corn syrup and vanilla bean and seeds with ½ cup of water and bring to a boil, stirring to dissolve the sugar. Cook over moderate heat without stirring, gently swirling the syrup in the skillet occasionally and washing down the side of the skillet with a wet pastry brush, until a medium-light amber caramel forms, about 10 minutes. Off the heat, stir in the butter. Add the quince slices and cook over moderately low heat, stirring occasionally with a nonstick rubber spatula, until softened, about 5 minutes. Let the quince cool slightly. Evenly distribute the quince slices over the bottom of the skillet or, for a neater appearance, carefully arrange them in concentric circles.

2. On a lightly floured work surface, roll out the puff pastry to a 14-inch square. Using the skillet lid as a template, cut out a 14-inch round. Cut eight 1-inch-long steam vents in the pastry round and lay it over the fruit. Bake the tart in the center of the oven for about 55 minutes, until golden brown and cooked through. Let stand for 15 minutes.

3. Cover the tart with a large plate and very carefully invert the tart onto the plate. Cut into wedges and serve with crème fraîche.
—*Michael Tusk*

WINE Honeyed, dried fruit–scented vin santo: 2006 Badia a Coltibuono.

Dark Chocolate Cremoso with Cornflakes and Fresh Fruit

TOTAL: 40 MIN PLUS 4 HR CHILLING
6 SERVINGS ● ○

Thicker than a chocolate mousse, this ganache-like *cremoso* is fabulous for entertaining because it can be made in advance. Plus, the fruit salad and clever cornflake garnish take very little time to prepare.

- 1 cup whole milk
- 3 large egg yolks
- 2 tablespoons heavy cream
- 2 tablespoons sugar
- 7 ounces dark chocolate (70 percent), finely chopped
- 1 kiwi, finely diced
- 5 strawberries, finely diced
- 1 Bosc pear, finely diced
- ¾ cup cornflakes, finely crushed

1. In a saucepan, whisk the milk, egg yolks, cream and sugar. Whisking constantly, bring the mixture just to a simmer over moderate heat, then reduce the heat to moderately low and cook until thickened, 15 minutes. Off the heat, stir in the chocolate until melted.

2. Pour the mixture into a heatproof bowl and let cool slightly. Press a sheet of plastic wrap onto the surface of the *cremoso* and refrigerate for at least 4 hours, until chilled and set.

3. In a medium bowl, toss the fruit, spoon it onto plates and mound the cereal alongside. Scoop the *cremoso* on top of the fruit and serve. —*Marcelo Betancourt*

INSTEAD OF PIE, MAKE PIE BARS

There's nothing wrong with the usual pecan, pumpkin or fruit pies, but pastry chef **SARAH JORDAN** of Chicago's Boka serves the classic fillings as pie bars. It's fun, surprising and a much easier way to feed a crowd. You don't even have to roll out the dough; you simply press it into the baking dish.

Pecan Pie Bars

ACTIVE: 40 MIN; TOTAL: 1 HR 45 MIN PLUS
COOLING • MAKES ONE 9-BY-13-INCH PAN

 4 tablespoons unsalted
    butter
 1 cup light corn syrup
 1 cup dark brown sugar
 5 large eggs
1½ teaspoons pure vanilla extract
1½ teaspoons salt
 2 cups pecan halves (see Note)
Baked Press-In Crust (recipe below)

1. Preheat the oven to 350°. In a medium saucepan, melt the butter over moderate heat. Remove the saucepan from the heat and whisk in the light corn syrup and dark brown sugar, then whisk in the eggs until they are thoroughly blended. Whisk in the vanilla extract and salt and stir in the pecan halves until combined.
2. Pour the pecan filling into the prebaked pie bar crust and bake for about 35 minutes, until the filling is set. Transfer the pan to a rack and let cool completely. Cut into bars and serve.
NOTE The largest pecans, called mammoth, make a striking presentation. Look for them (approximately 200 to 250 halves per pound) in specialty food shops.

Lemon-Cranberry Pie Bars

ACTIVE: 1 HR; TOTAL: 1 HR 45 MIN PLUS
COOLING • MAKES ONE 9-BY-13-INCH PAN

 1 cup cranberries
2¾ cups granulated sugar
Pinch of ground cloves
 4 large eggs plus 2 egg yolks
 1 teaspoon finely grated lemon zest
 ½ cup fresh lemon juice
 ¾ cup all purpose flour
Baked Press-In Crust (recipe below)
Confectioners' sugar, for dusting

1. Preheat the oven to 350°. In a saucepan, simmer the cranberries with ¼ cup of the sugar, the cloves and ¼ cup of water over moderately low heat until the berries pop and the liquid thickens, about 8 minutes. Transfer to a blender and puree until smooth. Strain and press the puree through a fine sieve set over a bowl and let cool completely.
2. In a medium bowl, whisk the remaining 2½ cups of sugar with the eggs, egg yolks, lemon zest, lemon juice and flour.
3. Mix 1 cup of the lemon filling into the cranberry puree; pour the rest of the lemon filling into the crust. Swirl in the cranberry-lemon mixture. Bake for 35 minutes, or until set. Transfer the pan to a rack; let cool. Dust with confectioners' sugar and serve.

Pumpkin Pie Bars

ACTIVE: 45 MIN; TOTAL: 1 HR 45 MIN PLUS
COOLING • MAKES ONE 9-BY-13-INCH PAN

 ¼ cup dark brown sugar
 ½ cup granulated sugar
 1 teaspoon cinnamon
 ¼ teaspoon ground cloves
 ¼ teaspoon ground ginger
 ¼ teaspoon ground cardamom
 ¼ teaspoon salt
 2 large eggs
One 15-ounce can pure
    pumpkin puree
One 12-ounce can evaporated milk
Baked Press-In Crust (recipe below)
Crème fraîche, for serving

1. Preheat the oven to 425°. In a bowl, whisk the sugars with the spices and salt. In another bowl, whisk the eggs. Whisk in the sugar mixture, then whisk in the pumpkin puree and evaporated milk until smooth.
2. Pour the filling into the crust and bake for 10 minutes. Lower the oven temperature to 350° and bake for about 25 minutes longer, until the filling is fully set. Transfer the pan to a rack and let cool completely. Cut into bars and serve with crème fraîche.
MAKE AHEAD The pumpkin pie bars can be refrigerated for up to 2 days.

BAKED PRESS-IN CRUST

TOTAL: 1 HR PLUS COOLING • MAKES ONE 9-BY-13-INCH CRUST

2½ sticks cold unsalted butter, cut into cubes
 ¼ cup plus 2 tablespoons light brown sugar
 ¼ cup plus 2 tablespoons granulated sugar
2½ cups all-purpose flour sifted with ½ teaspoon kosher salt

1. In the bowl of a stand mixer fitted with the paddle, cream the butter with the sugars at medium speed for 2 minutes. With the mixer at low speed, beat in the sifted flour-and-salt mixture.

2. Preheat the oven to 350°. Line a 9-by-13-inch baking pan with parchment paper, allowing 2 inches of overhang on the 2 long sides. Transfer the dough to the pan and press it over the bottom and 1¼ inches up the sides all around. (You can cover the dough with plastic wrap and press with the bottom of a measuring cup.) Be sure the corners are not too thick. Refrigerate until firm.

3. Bake the crust for 30 to 35 minutes, until golden brown; halfway through baking, use the back of a spoon to smooth the sides and corners of the crust. Transfer the pan to a wire rack and let the crust cool before filling.

PECAN PIE BARS

LEMON-CRANBERRY
PIE BARS

PUMPKIN PIE BARS

Cranberry Granita

ACTIVE: 30 MIN; TOTAL: 7 HR

MAKES 4 CUPS ● ● ○

2 cups cranberries
½ cup sugar
Finely grated zest of 1 orange
½ cup fresh orange juice
Sweetened whipped cream, for serving

1. In a saucepan, combine the cranberries, sugar and orange zest with 1½ cups of water and bring to a boil. Reduce the heat and simmer until the cranberries pop and soften, about 15 minutes.
2. Transfer the cranberry mixture to a blender and puree at high speed for 2 minutes. Strain the puree through a fine sieve into a bowl and let cool completely.
3. Stir the orange juice into the puree and pour it into a 9-by-13-inch metal baking dish. Freeze the granita for 1 hour. Scrape the frozen edges into the center and freeze for about 3 hours longer, scraping hourly, until the granita is icy and flaky. Freeze for at least 2 hours longer, or preferably overnight.
4. Scrape the granita into glasses, top with sweetened whipped cream and serve.
—Sarah Jordan

Lemon Curd Parfaits

ACTIVE: 1 HR; TOTAL: 6 HR

8 SERVINGS ● ○

MERINGUE
1 teaspoon distilled white vinegar
½ teaspoon cornstarch
4 large egg whites
1 cup sugar
LEMON CURD
9 large egg yolks
⅔ cup fresh lemon juice
1 cup plus 2 tablespoons sugar
1 stick unsalted butter,
  cut into ½-inch cubes
WHIPPED CREAM
2 cups heavy cream
2 tablespoons sugar
1 teaspoon pure vanilla extract
2 pints raspberries

1. MAKE THE MERINGUE Preheat the oven to 200°. Line a baking sheet with parchment paper. In a small bowl, stir the vinegar with the cornstarch to form a slurry.
2. In the bowl of a stand mixer fitted with the whisk, beat the egg whites at medium speed until soft, frothy peaks form. Increase the speed to medium-high and gradually add ⅓ cup of the sugar; beat for 2 minutes. Repeat with the remaining sugar in 2 batches, beating for 2 minutes between additions. Continue to beat until the meringue is stiff and glossy, 7 to 8 minutes. Sprinkle the slurry over the meringue and fold it in.
3. Using a large spoon, dollop the meringue onto the prepared baking sheet. Using an offset spatula, spread the meringue 1½ inches thick. Bake for about 3 hours, until firm and white; turn off the oven and keep the oven door slightly ajar. Leave the meringue in the oven for 2 hours, until mostly dry but still slightly chewy.
4. MEANWHILE, MAKE THE LEMON CURD In a glass bowl, combine the egg yolks, lemon juice and sugar and whisk until smooth. Place the bowl over a saucepan of simmering water (do not let the bowl touch the water) and cook, whisking constantly, until the curd has thickened to the consistency of cake batter, about 20 minutes. Remove the bowl from the heat and whisk in the butter, a few cubes at a time, until incorporated. Press plastic wrap directly onto the surface of the lemon curd and let cool to room temperature. Refrigerate for 1 hour, or until cold.
5. MAKE THE WHIPPED CREAM In a large bowl, combine the cream, sugar and vanilla and beat with an electric handheld mixer until soft peaks form. Refrigerate.
6. To serve, break the meringue into small pieces. Spoon half of the meringue and ¼ cup of lemon curd into each of 8 parfait glasses. Top with ½ cup of whipped cream and a few raspberries. Repeat with the remaining meringue, lemon curd, whipped cream and raspberries. Serve immediately.
—Sarah Jordan

MAKE AHEAD The lemon curd can be refrigerated for up to 2 days. The meringue can be stored in an airtight container overnight.

Layered Citrus Salad

⏱ TOTAL: 45 MIN • 10 SERVINGS ● ● ○ ○

¼ cup Champagne vinegar
¼ cup extra-virgin olive oil
2 tablespoons sugar
Pinch of salt
1 tablespoon chopped mint and/or tarragon, plus more for garnish
3 Ruby Red grapefruits
4 oranges
6 tangerines or 3 tangerines and 3 blood oranges
½ cup toasted unsalted pistachios, chopped
Sliced candied kumquats and fresh kumquats, for garnish

1. In a small bowl, whisk the vinegar and olive oil with the sugar, salt and the 1 tablespoon of chopped mint until the sugar is dissolved.
2. Using a very sharp knife, peel all of the citrus fruits, being sure to remove any bitter white pith. Thinly slice the citrus crosswise and pick out and discard any pits. Layer the citrus on a platter or in glasses and drizzle evenly with the dressing. Garnish with the pistachios, kumquats and mint and serve.
—Sarah Jordan

Honey-Broiled Figs with Ricotta

⏱ TOTAL: 15 MIN • 8 SERVINGS ○

1 cup fresh ricotta cheese
2 tablespoons honey, plus more for drizzling
12 large Black Mission figs, halved

1. Preheat the broiler and position a rack 6 inches from the heat. In a food processor, combine the ricotta with the 2 tablespoons of honey and puree until very smooth.
2. Arrange the figs cut side up on a rimmed baking sheet. Dollop 2 teaspoons of the ricotta puree on each fig; lightly drizzle with honey. Broil for 2 minutes, until just browned in spots and the ricotta is barely melted; serve warm or at room temperature.
—Richard Betts

● HEALTHY ● MAKE AHEAD ○ VEGETARIAN ○ STAFF FAVORITE

CRANBERRY
GRANITA

LEMON CURD
PARFAIT

LAYERED
CITRUS SALAD

Bittersweet Chocolate-Truffle Tart with Candied Oranges

ACTIVE: 1 HR 30 MIN; TOTAL: 5 HR 15 MIN
MAKES ONE 10-INCH TART ● ● ●

Joanne Chang of Flour Bakery + Café in Boston is a master of desserts. Here, she makes an elegant French-style chocolate tart crowned with thin slices of candied orange. Because the rinds will be eaten, it's best to use organic or unsprayed oranges.

CRUST
- 1 stick unsalted butter, at room temperature
- ¼ cup sugar
- ½ teaspoon kosher salt
- 1 cup all-purpose flour
- 1 large egg yolk

CANDIED ORANGES
- 2 cups sugar
- 2 navel oranges, preferably organic or unsprayed—scrubbed, cut crosswise into ⅛-inch-thick slices and seeded
- 1 cup water

FILLING
- ¾ cup heavy cream
- ½ cup whole milk
- 1 tablespoon grated orange zest
- ½ pound bittersweet chocolate, finely chopped
- 2 large egg yolks
- 4 tablespoons unsalted butter, softened
- ¼ teaspoon kosher salt

Unsweetened whipped cream or crème fraîche, for serving

GRILLED-FRUIT TIP

For his berry crostini (at far right), chef Michael Chiarello grills strawberries, blackberries and blueberries over high heat until they burst, then uses them as a topping for buttery, caramelized toasts. A perforated grill sheet or basket prevents berries from falling through the grate.

1. MAKE THE CRUST In a standing mixer fitted with the paddle attachment, cream the butter with the sugar and salt at medium speed until pale and fluffy, about 2 minutes. Scrape down the side of the bowl. Beat in the flour at low speed until the mixture resembles wet sand, then beat in the egg yolk until the dough just comes together. Scrape the dough out onto a work surface, gather up any crumbs and pat the dough into a disk. Wrap the dough in plastic and refrigerate until well chilled, at least 1 hour.

2. MEANWHILE, MAKE THE CANDIED ORANGES In a medium saucepan, combine the sugar, oranges and water and bring just to a simmer, stirring to dissolve the sugar. Cook over moderately low heat, stirring occasionally, until the orange slices are very tender and suspended in a slightly thick syrup, about 1 hour and 15 minutes; let cool completely.

3. On a lightly floured work surface, roll out the dough to a 12-inch round. Without stretching it, fit the dough into a 10-inch fluted tart pan with a removable bottom. Trim the overhang and use it to patch any holes. Refrigerate the tart shell for 30 minutes.

4. Preheat the oven to 350°. Bake the tart shell for 35 minutes, until golden. Let cool.

5. MEANWHILE, MAKE THE FILLING In a small saucepan, combine the cream, milk and zest and bring just to a simmer. Remove from the heat and let stand for 30 minutes. Return the mixture just to a simmer, then strain it through a fine sieve into a heatproof bowl. Add the chocolate; let stand for 2 minutes, then whisk until the chocolate is melted and the mixture is smooth. Whisk in the egg yolks, then whisk in the butter and salt.

6. Put the tart shell on a rimmed baking sheet. Pour the filling into the shell and bake for about 15 minutes, until the filling at the edge is just set and the center is nearly set. Let stand at room temperature for 2 hours.

7. Drain the candied oranges well, then arrange them on the tart. Cut the tart into wedges and serve with whipped cream or crème fraîche. —*Joanne Chang*

MAKE AHEAD The recipe can be prepared through step 6 one day ahead and kept at room temperature, uncovered.

Fire-Roasted Berry Crostini with Honey Crème Fraîche

☺ **TOTAL: 30 MIN • 6 SERVINGS** ● ●

Michael Chiarello, the chef at Napa Valley's Bottega restaurant and author of *Live Fire*, likes to cook every course on the grill. "Just like trying to get more miles per gallon, you want to get more meals per log out of your grill," he says. These super-simple crostini, which take just 30 minutes, can be prepared at the end of a grilling session.

- ½ cup crème fraîche
- 1 tablespoon honey

Three ½-inch-thick slices of country bread, halved crosswise

Softened unsalted butter, for brushing

- ¼ cup sugar, plus more for sprinkling
- 4 cups mixed fresh berries, such as raspberries, blueberries, blackberries and halved strawberries

Pinch of kosher salt

1. Light a hardwood charcoal fire.

2. In a small bowl, whisk the crème fraîche with the honey.

3. Brush both sides of the bread slices with butter and generously sprinkle with sugar. Grill the bread over moderately high heat, turning once, until crisp and caramelized, about 3 minutes. Transfer the crostini to a platter and let cool.

4. In a medium bowl, toss the berries with the ¼ cup of sugar and the salt. Spread the berries on a perforated grill sheet or in a grill basket and grill over moderately high heat, tossing, until juicy and starting to burst, about 4 minutes. Transfer the berries to a bowl and let cool slightly.

5. Spoon the grilled berries on the crostini and top with dollops of the honey crème fraîche. Transfer to plates and serve right away. —*Michael Chiarello*

MAKE AHEAD The honey crème fraîche can be refrigerated overnight.

WINE Lightly sweet sparkling red: NV Cascina Ca' Rossa Birbét Brachetto d'Acqui.

● HEALTHY ● MAKE AHEAD ● VEGETARIAN ● STAFF FAVORITE

FIRE-ROASTED BERRY CROSTINI
WITH HONEY CRÈME FRAÎCHE

Strawberry Meringue Roulade with Raspberry Sauce

TOTAL: 1 HR PLUS CHILLING

8 SERVINGS ● ○ ○

This fantastic meringue from the Irish cookbook writer and television chef Rachel Allen is baked and rolled around strawberries and cherry brandy–spiked whipped cream. It's a fixture on the dessert menu at Ballymaloe House, the Allen family's famed country hotel on Ireland's southern coast. "I love the contrast of the white meringue with the brilliant red from the strawberries and the raspberry sauce," says Allen.

Vegetable oil, for brushing

4 large egg whites

1¼ cups superfine sugar

¾ pound fresh raspberries

2 tablespoons fresh lemon juice

1½ cups heavy cream

2 tablespoons confectioners' sugar

2 tablespoons kirsch

½ pound strawberries, hulled and thinly sliced

1. Preheat the oven to 350°. Line a 9-by-13-inch baking pan with foil, leaving a 1-inch overhang on the long sides. Lightly brush the foil and sides of the pan with vegetable oil.

2. In the bowl of a stand mixer fitted with the whisk, beat the egg whites at medium-high speed to soft peaks. Beat in 1 cup of the superfine sugar at high speed until the whites are stiff and glossy, about 2 to 3 minutes. Using an offset spatula, spread the meringue in the prepared pan in an even layer. Bake the meringue in the center of the oven for about 15 minutes, until very lightly colored and springy. Using the overhanging foil, transfer the meringue to a rack to cool.

3. Meanwhile, in a food processor, puree the raspberries, lemon juice and remaining ¼ cup of superfine sugar until smooth; strain the puree through a fine sieve into a bowl. Cover the raspberry sauce and refrigerate until chilled, about 30 minutes.

4. Wipe out the bowl of the mixer. Add the heavy cream, confectioners' sugar and kirsch and beat until the cream forms soft peaks.

5. Turn the meringue so a long side is facing you. Spread the whipped cream over the meringue, leaving a 1½-inch border on the long side nearest you. Arrange the sliced strawberries on top, pressing them gently into the whipped cream. Starting at the long side nearest you, and using the foil, carefully roll up the meringue jelly roll–style; the top will crack. Wrap the roulade in the foil and refrigerate until chilled, at least 45 minutes or up to 5 hours. Unwrap the roulade and cut into 1-inch-thick slices. Serve with the raspberry sauce. —*Rachel Allen*

Blueberries with Rhubarb Syrup and Maple Cream

ACTIVE: 20 MIN; TOTAL: 1 HR 15 MIN

6 SERVINGS ● ○

Linda Aldredge, founder of the beauty company Lulu Organics, loves to cook at her 100-square-foot tree house in New York's Catskill Mountains. In August, when the property is covered with wild berries, she usually harvests enough for jars of jam and for easy desserts like this one.

¾ pound rhubarb stalks, cut into ½-inch pieces

1 cup sugar

Pinch of salt

2 tablespoons fresh lemon juice

2 cups chilled heavy cream

1 tablespoon pure maple syrup

1 pint blueberries

1. In a saucepan, combine the rhubarb with the sugar, salt and 1 cup of water and bring to a boil. Simmer over moderately low heat, stirring occasionally, until the fruit is very soft, 20 minutes. Strain the syrup through a cheesecloth-lined sieve into a heatproof bowl, pressing on the solids. Stir in the lemon juice. Let the syrup cool, then refrigerate until chilled, about 45 minutes.

2. In a large bowl, beat the cream with the maple syrup until firm peaks form. Put the blueberries in bowls or glasses and top with the maple whipped cream. Spoon some of the rhubarb syrup on top and serve.

—*Linda Aldredge*

Skillet Biscuits with Berries

⏱ **TOTAL: 40 MIN** • **8 SERVINGS** ○

This tart and super-fruity summer dessert cooks mostly on the stovetop, with just a quick finish under the broiler to caramelize the biscuits.

1½ cups all-purpose flour

2 tablespoons light brown sugar

1½ teaspoons baking powder

½ teaspoon salt

1½ sticks cold unsalted butter, cut into ¼-inch pieces

¼ cup plus 2 tablespoons half-and-half

¾ cup granulated sugar, plus more for sprinkling

12 ounces raspberries

12 ounces blackberries

1½ teaspoons finely grated orange zest

1 cinnamon stick

Sweetened whipped cream, for serving

1. In a large bowl, combine the flour, brown sugar, baking powder and salt. Using a pastry blender, cut in the butter until the mixture resembles coarse meal. Add the half-and-half and stir until the dough is evenly moistened. Using an ice cream scoop or a large spoon, scoop the dough into 8 loose mounds and place on a wax paper–lined baking sheet.

2. Preheat the broiler and position a rack 6 inches from the heat. In a large, deep, ovenproof skillet, combine the ¾ cup of granulated sugar with the berries, orange zest, cinnamon stick and 1 cup of water and bring to a vigorous boil. Simmer over moderate heat, stirring occasionally, until the berries are juicy and just broken down, 10 minutes.

3. Arrange the mounds of dough on top of the fruit. Cover and simmer over very low heat until the biscuits are springy to the touch and cooked through, 15 minutes. Sprinkle the biscuits with granulated sugar and broil for 5 minutes, shifting the pan as necessary, until the biscuits are lightly browned in spots. Let cool slightly and discard the cinnamon stick. Serve the biscuits and berries with whipped cream.

—*Jenn Louis*

● HEALTHY ● MAKE AHEAD ○ VEGETARIAN ● STAFF FAVORITE

STRAWBERRY MERINGUE ROULADE
WITH RASPBERRY SAUCE

Plum Galette

📷 PAGE 378

ACTIVE: 30 MIN; TOTAL: 2 HR
8 SERVINGS ● ● ●

PASTRY

1½ cups all-purpose flour
1½ sticks cold unsalted butter,
     cut into ½-inch pieces
¼ teaspoon salt
⅓ cup ice water

FILLING

¼ cup plus ⅓ cup sugar
3 tablespoons ground almonds
3 tablespoons all-purpose flour
2½ pounds large plums—halved, pitted
     and cut into ½-inch wedges
3 tablespoons unsalted butter,
     cut into small bits
½ cup apricot jam, strained

1. **MAKE THE PASTRY** Put the flour, butter and salt in a food processor and process for 5 seconds. Add the ice water and process for 5 seconds longer, just until the dough comes together; the butter should still be visible.

2. Gather the dough into a ball. On a lightly floured surface, roll out the dough into a 16-by-18-inch oval ¹⁄₁₆ to ⅛ inch thick. Transfer it to a large, heavy baking sheet and chill until firm, about 20 minutes.

3. **MAKE THE FILLING** Preheat the oven to 400°. In a bowl, combine ¼ cup of the sugar with the ground almonds and flour; spread this mixture evenly over the dough to within 2 inches of the edge. Arrange the plums on top; dot with the butter. Sprinkle all but 1 teaspoon of the remaining ⅓ cup sugar over the fruit. Fold the edge of the dough up over the plums to create a 2-inch border. Sprinkle the border with the reserved 1 teaspoon of sugar.

4. Bake the galette in the middle of the oven for about 1 hour, until the fruit is very soft and the crust is richly browned. If any juices have leaked onto the baking sheet, slide a knife under the galette to release it from the sheet. Evenly brush the preserves over the hot fruit; brush some up onto the crust, too, if desired. Let the galette cool to room temperature before serving. —*Jacques Pépin*

Sour Cherry and Poppy Seed Strudels

ACTIVE: 45 MIN; TOTAL: 5 HR
8 SERVINGS ●

The older generation of Hungarian women hand-pull a flaky dough for strudel. This easy version uses a tender cream cheese dough.

4 ounces cream cheese,
     at room temperature
1 stick unsalted butter, at room
     temperature, plus 1 tablespoon
     melted butter for brushing
¼ cup plus 2 tablespoons
     granulated sugar
1 teaspoon pure vanilla extract
¼ teaspoon fine sea salt
2 cups all-purpose flour,
     plus more for dusting
2 tablespoons poppy seeds
2 tablespoons plain dry bread crumbs
2 cups drained pitted sour cherries
     (known as morello), packed in light
     syrup, patted dry
Confectioners' sugar, for dusting

1. In a food processor, combine the cream cheese with the 1 stick of butter, ¼ cup of the granulated sugar, the vanilla and salt and process until smooth. Add the 2 cups of flour and pulse just until a sticky dough forms. Scrape the dough onto a large sheet of plastic wrap and shape into a rectangle; wrap up the dough and refrigerate until firm, about 3 hours.

2. In a spice grinder, pulse the poppy seeds with the remaining 2 tablespoons of granulated sugar until the seeds are just cracked. Transfer the poppy seeds to a small bowl and stir in the bread crumbs.

3. Line a large rimmed baking sheet with parchment paper. On a floured work surface, dust the dough with flour. Roll out the dough to an 11-by-15-inch rectangle; carefully transfer it to the prepared baking sheet. Freeze the dough until firm, about 20 minutes.

4. Preheat the oven to 400°. Working on the baking sheet, cut the dough in half crosswise so you have two 11-by-7½-inch rectangles; brush off any excess flour. Spoon half of the poppy seed mixture in a lengthwise stripe down the middle of each piece of dough, then arrange the cherries on top. Fold one side of the dough up and over the filling and brush with some of the melted butter. Fold the opposite side of the dough up and over the filling and press gently to help it adhere. Cut 4 slits across the top of each strudel and freeze until well chilled, about 15 minutes.

5. Bake the 2 strudels in the center of the oven until the crust is browned and the filling is bubbling, 40 minutes. Let cool completely. Dust the strudels with confectioners' sugar, slice and serve. —*Sarah Copeland*

Cherry-Almond Clafoutis

TOTAL: 1 HR PLUS COOLING
8 SERVINGS ● ● ●

1 cup granulated sugar,
     plus more for dusting
5 large eggs
½ vanilla bean, split, seeds scraped
¾ cup all-purpose flour, sifted
¾ cup plus 2 tablespoons
     almond flour or almond meal
1 teaspoon kosher salt
1 cup whole milk
1 cup heavy cream
12 ounces sweet cherries, pitted
Confectioners' sugar, for dusting
Sweetened whipped cream, for serving

1. Preheat the oven to 350°. Butter a 10-inch round gratin dish and dust with granulated sugar. In a large bowl, whisk the 1 cup of granulated sugar with the eggs and vanilla seeds. Whisk in the all-purpose flour, almond flour and salt until just incorporated. Add the milk and cream and whisk until light and very smooth, 3 minutes. Pour into the prepared gratin dish and arrange the cherries on top.

2. Bake for 35 to 40 minutes, until the clafoutis is set. Let cool. Dust with confectioners' sugar and serve with whipped cream. —*Belinda Leong*

MAKE AHEAD The clafoutis can be refrigerated overnight. Serve at room temperature.

WINE Sweet sparkling red wine: 2011 Tenimenti Ca'Bianca Brachetto d'Acqui.

● HEALTHY   ● MAKE AHEAD   ● VEGETARIAN   ● STAFF FAVORITE

CHERRY-ALMOND
CLAFOUTIS

Nectarine Pavlovas

ACTIVE: 40 MIN; TOTAL: 2 HR 30 MIN
PLUS COOLING • 6 SERVINGS ●

MERINGUES

- 4 **large egg whites, at room temperature**
- ½ **teaspoon cream of tartar**
- ½ **cup plus 1 tablespoon superfine sugar**
- ½ **cup sifted confectioners' sugar**

FILLING

- 1 **cup plus 2 tablespoons milk**
- 1 **chamomile tea bag**
- 1 **large egg**
- ¼ **cup granulated sugar**
- 2 **tablespoons cornstarch**
- 2 **tablespoons unsalted butter, cubed**
- 3 **large nectarines, very thinly sliced**

1. MAKE THE MERINGUES Preheat the oven to 250° and line 2 medium baking sheets with parchment. Position racks in the lower and upper thirds of the oven. In the bowl of a standing mixer fitted with the whisk, beat the egg whites with the cream of tartar at medium speed until soft peaks form. Slowly pour in ½ cup of the superfine sugar and beat at high speed until the egg whites are stiff and glossy. In a small bowl, whisk the sifted confectioners' sugar with the remaining 1 tablespoon of superfine sugar. Using a rubber spatula, gently fold the sugar mixture into the meringue in 3 additions.

2. Spoon 3 rounded ½-cup mounds of meringue onto each baking sheet. Using the back of the spoon, form the meringues into 4-inch rounds with a well in the center. Place the meringues in the oven and immediately lower the temperature to 200°. Bake for 2 hours, or until crisp on the outside but still a bit chewy in the center; rotate the sheets halfway through baking. Let cool completely.

3. MEANWHILE, MAKE THE FILLING In a medium saucepan, heat the milk just until small bubbles appear around the edge. Add the tea bag, cover and let steep off the heat for 10 minutes, pressing the tea bag occasionally. Discard the tea bag.

4. In a medium heatproof bowl, whisk the egg with the granulated sugar and cornstarch. Gradually whisk in the warm milk. Transfer the mixture to the saucepan and cook over moderate heat, whisking vigorously, until very thick, smooth and shiny, 3 to 4 minutes. Scrape the pastry cream into a bowl and let cool slightly. Whisk in the cubed butter until incorporated. Place a sheet of plastic wrap directly onto the surface of the pastry cream and refrigerate for about 2 hours, until chilled.

5. Gently spread the pastry cream into the center of the meringues and arrange the nectarine slices on top in concentric circles, forming rosettes. Serve the Pavlovas right away. —*Caitlin Freeman*

Nectarine-Thyme Crumbles

ACTIVE: 20 MIN; TOTAL: 1 HR 30 MIN
6 SERVINGS ●

- 6 **nectarines, thinly sliced**
- 6 **tablespoons granulated sugar**
- 1½ **tablespoons fresh lemon juice**
- 6 **thyme sprigs**

Salt

- ¾ **cup all-purpose flour**
- 4 **tablespoons light brown sugar**
- 2 **tablespoons wheat germ**
- ¼ **cup unsalted butter, softened**

1. In a medium bowl, toss the nectarines with the granulated sugar, lemon juice, thyme and a pinch of salt; let stand for 1 hour.

2. Preheat the oven to 375°. In another bowl, combine the flour, brown sugar and wheat germ with a pinch of salt. Using your fingers, work in the butter until the mixture is sandy. Press the streusel into small clumps and scatter on a rimmed baking sheet.

3. Spoon the nectarines, thyme and any juices into 6 individual cast-iron baking dishes. Bake the nectarines for about 20 minutes, until the fruit is softened. Meanwhile, bake the streusel, stirring once, for about 10 minutes, until browned.

4. Sprinkle the streusel over the fruit, bake for 5 minutes longer and serve.
—*Grace Parisi*

Grilled Fruit with Honeyed Lemon Thyme Vinegar

TOTAL: 30 MIN PLUS 2 WEEKS FOR
INFUSING THE VINEGAR • 6 SERVINGS ● ●
For this elegant summer dessert, chef Dan Barber of Blue Hill at Stone Barns in Pocantico Hills, New York, infuses honey with his own lemon thyme vinegar, creating a tangy-sweet accompaniment to grilled stone fruit.

- 2 **tablespoons extra-virgin olive oil, plus more for the grill**
- ¼ **cup honey**
- 2 **tablespoons Lemon Thyme Vinegar (recipe follows)**
- 3 **medium apricots, halved**
- 2 **medium peaches and 2 medium nectarines, cut into thick wedges**
- 2 **medium plums, halved**

Vanilla ice cream, for serving

1. Light a grill or heat a grill pan and brush lightly with oil. In a small saucepan, bring the honey and Lemon Thyme Vinegar to a simmer. Cook over very low heat for 5 minutes.

2. In a bowl, toss the fruit with the 2 tablespoons of oil. Grill the fruit over high heat, turning, until lightly charred in spots, about 3 minutes. Transfer to bowls, drizzle with the honeyed vinegar and serve with ice cream.
—*Dan Barber*

WINE Frothy, berry-sweet Brachetto d'Acqui: 2012 Banfi Rosa Regale.

LEMON THYME VINEGAR

TOTAL: 5 MIN PLUS 2 WEEKS INFUSING
MAKES ABOUT 3 CUPS ● ● ●
This terrific herbal vinegar couldn't be easier: It basically makes itself as it stands for two weeks.

Three 1-ounce bunches of lemon thyme, thick stems discarded
1½ **bottles (26 ounces) Champagne vinegar**

In a 1-quart jar, combine the lemon thyme and vinegar. Cover tightly and let stand at room temperature for at least 2 weeks and up to 3 weeks. Discard the thyme sprigs. —*DB*

● HEALTHY ● MAKE AHEAD ● VEGETARIAN ● STAFF FAVORITE

GRILLED FRUIT WITH
HONEYED LEMON THYME VINEGAR

Poached Peaches with Baked Ricotta

📷 PAGE 303

ACTIVE: 30 MIN; TOTAL: 1 HR 15 MIN
PLUS 3 HR COOLING
8 TO 10 SERVINGS ● ○

BAKED RICOTTA

2¼ pounds fresh ricotta cheese
      (4½ cups)
  2 vanilla beans—halved lengthwise
      and seeds scraped, beans reserved
      for another use
1½ tablespoons finely grated
      lemon zest
  9 large eggs
¾ cup sugar
¼ cup plus 2 tablespoons
      all-purpose flour
½ teaspoon kosher salt

PEACHES

  1 cup sugar
½ cup honey
  4 cups water
  3 fresh lemon verbena sprigs or
      1 cup loosely packed dried leaves,
      plus additional fresh verbena sprigs
      for garnish (optional)
10 ripe but firm peaches (about 4½
      pounds), halved and pitted

1. MAKE THE BAKED RICOTTA Preheat the oven to 350°. Lightly coat a 2½-quart glass or ceramic baking dish with baking spray and set the dish in a roasting pan.
2. In a colander set over a large bowl, drain the ricotta, gently pressing out any excess liquid; discard the liquid. Transfer the ricotta to a large bowl and stir in the vanilla seeds and lemon zest.
3. In another large bowl, whisk the eggs and sugar until smooth. Whisk the egg mixture into the ricotta until smooth, then fold in the flour and salt. Pour the mixture into the baking dish. Add enough hot water to the roasting pan to reach halfway up the sides of the baking dish. Bake the ricotta for about 40 minutes, until lightly golden on top and just set in the center. Transfer the dish to a rack and let cool to room temperature, 3 hours.

4. MEANWHILE, PREPARE THE PEACHES In a large saucepan, combine the sugar, honey and water; bring to a simmer. If using dried verbena, wrap in a large square of cheesecloth and tie with kitchen string. Add the verbena and peaches to the pan. Bring just to a boil, then simmer gently over moderately low heat, turning the peaches occasionally, until just tender, 7 to 8 minutes. Using a slotted spoon, transfer the peaches to a baking sheet. Let cool slightly. Slip off the skins.
5. Discard the lemon verbena and simmer the poaching liquid over moderate heat until reduced to a light syrup, about 10 minutes. Strain the syrup into a bowl and let cool to room temperature, about 1 hour.
6. Cut the baked ricotta into squares and serve with the peaches and syrup. Garnish with lemon verbena sprigs. —*Tom Colicchio*

Sweet Peach Olive Oil Cake

ACTIVE: 20 MIN; TOTAL: 1 HR 30 MIN
12 SERVINGS ● ○

  3 ripe peaches, thinly sliced
1½ cups extra-virgin olive oil
  1 cup plus 2 tablespoons sugar
½ teaspoon kosher salt
  3 large eggs
  2 cups all-purpose flour
½ teaspoon baking powder
½ teaspoon baking soda

1. Preheat the oven to 350°. Line a 9-by-13-inch baking pan with parchment paper and coat with vegetable oil spray. In a bowl, toss the peaches with ¼ cup of the olive oil, ¼ cup plus 2 tablespoons of the sugar and the salt. Let stand until juicy, about 15 minutes.
2. In a bowl, whisk the eggs, the remaining ¾ cup of sugar and 1¼ cups of olive oil. In another bowl, whisk the flour, baking powder and baking soda. Whisk the dry ingredients into the egg mixture. Fold in the peaches and juices. Scrape the batter into the pan; bake for 35 minutes, until golden and a toothpick inserted into the center comes out clean. Let cool slightly before serving. —*Kristen Kish*
SERVE WITH Sweetened vanilla Greek yogurt or vanilla ice cream.

Coconut Tapioca Puddings with Mango and Lime

ACTIVE: 45 MIN; TOTAL: 4 HR
4 SERVINGS ● ● ○

This beautiful dessert layers creamy tapioca pudding with chunky mango-lime puree. Assembled in glasses ahead of time, the puddings would be ideal for a dinner party.

½ cup small pearl tapioca
2½ cups whole milk
½ vanilla bean, halved lengthwise
      and seeds scraped
Kosher salt
One 14-ounce can unsweetened
      coconut milk
  2 large egg yolks
  3 tablespoons sugar
  2 cups peeled and diced mango
  1 tablespoon finely grated lime zest
  2 tablespoons fresh lime juice

1. In a large saucepan, combine the tapioca, whole milk, vanilla bean and seeds and a pinch of salt. Bring to a simmer over moderate heat and cook, whisking occasionally, until the tapioca is translucent and tender, about 20 minutes. Whisk in the coconut milk.
2. In a small bowl, whisk the egg yolks with the sugar. Gradually whisk in half of the warm tapioca in a steady stream. Continue whisking and pour the egg yolk mixture back into the saucepan. Cook the pudding over moderate heat, stirring occasionally, until thickened, about 5 minutes. Transfer the pudding to a bowl and let cool to room temperature. Discard the vanilla bean.
3. In a medium bowl, combine the mango, lime zest and juice. Transfer half of the mango to a food processor and puree until smooth. Stir the puree into the remaining diced mango. Divide half of the fruit into 4 glasses, top with the tapioca pudding, then top with the remaining fruit. Cover the puddings and refrigerate for about 2 hours, or until chilled, before serving. —*Kay Chun*
MAKE AHEAD The assembled puddings can be refrigerated overnight. Let them stand at room temperature for about 30 minutes before serving.

● HEALTHY ● MAKE AHEAD ● VEGETARIAN ● STAFF FAVORITE

COCONUT TAPIOCA PUDDINGS
WITH MANGO AND LIME

Mojito-Watermelon Pops

ACTIVE: 40 MIN; TOTAL: 6 HR
MAKES 8 SMALL POPS ● ●

MOJITO LAYER
5 ounces Simple Syrup (page 374)
4 ounces water
2¼ ounces light rum
2 ounces fresh lime juice
3 tablespoons packed mint leaves
¼ ounce lime cordial
¼ teaspoon xanthan gum (see Note)

WATERMELON LAYER
10 ounces watermelon juice
2 ounces light agave nectar
2 ounces fresh lime juice
1½ ounces citron vodka
¼ ounce lime cordial
Pinch of kosher salt
¼ teaspoon xanthan gum

1. MAKE THE MOJITO LAYER In a blender, puree all of the ingredients except the xanthan gum on high speed until smooth and bright green, about 30 seconds. Pour into a bowl. Slowly sprinkle the xanthan gum over while quickly whisking, until slightly thickened and foamy. Let rest for 15 minutes, then skim any foam. Pour 1½ tablespoons of the mojito layer into each of eight 3-ounce popsicle molds or paper cups. Freeze until almost firm, about 1 hour. Poke a popsicle stick into the center of each.
2. MAKE THE WATERMELON LAYER In another bowl, combine all of the ingredients except the xanthan gum. Slowly sprinkle the xanthan gum over while quickly whisking, until slightly thickened. Let rest for 15 minutes, then skim any foam.
3. Carefully add 1½ tablespoons of the watermelon layer to the mojito layer in each of the molds. Freeze until almost firm, 1 hour. Pour the remaining mojito mixture on top and freeze until almost firm, 1 hour. Top with the remaining watermelon layer and freeze until firm, 2 hours. Unmold and serve.
—Patricia Richards
NOTE The thickening agent xanthan gum is available at many supermarkets and online at *amazon.com*.

Bubble Sundaes with Peach-Blueberry Compote

◴ TOTAL: 25 MIN • 10 SERVINGS ● ●

1 cup plus 1½ tablespoons fresh lemon juice
1¼ cups sugar
½ cup medium pearl tapioca
4 peaches, peeled and diced
2 cups blueberries
One ½-inch piece of fresh ginger, smashed
Pinch of salt
2½ pints vanilla ice cream, for serving

1. In a medium saucepan, combine 2 cups of water with 1 cup each of the lemon juice and sugar; bring to a boil, stirring to dissolve the sugar. Add the tapioca; cook over moderate heat, stirring often, until the pearls are plumped and tender, 3 to 5 minutes. Remove the tapioca from the heat; let cool to room temperature, stirring occasionally. Do not refrigerate.
2. Meanwhile, in another medium saucepan, combine the diced peaches, blueberries, smashed ginger and salt with the remaining 1½ tablespoons of lemon juice and ¼ cup of sugar; bring to a boil. Simmer over moderately low heat until the compote is deep purple and slightly thickened, 10 minutes. Scrape the compote into a heatproof bowl and let cool completely. Pick out the ginger.
3. Scoop ice cream into glasses or bowls and top with the compote. Garnish the sundaes with the tapioca and serve. —Bill Kim

Balsamic Strawberries with Strawberry Sorbet

◴ TOTAL: 40 MIN • 6 SERVINGS ● ●

1 pound strawberries, quartered
1½ tablespoons good-quality balsamic vinegar
Freshly ground pepper
Strawberry sorbet, for serving

In a large bowl, toss the strawberries with the vinegar and a generous pinch of pepper. Let stand at room temperature for 30 minutes. Serve over strawberry sorbet. —Mario Batali

Lemony Frozen-Yogurt Terrine with Blueberries and Mango

ACTIVE: 45 MIN; TOTAL: 1 HR 45 MIN
PLUS OVERNIGHT FREEZING
8 SERVINGS ● ● ● ● ●

This stunning frozen treat, made with fat-free yogurt and fresh fruit, is delightfully creamy.

1 quart plain fat-free Greek yogurt
1 cup turbinado sugar, preferably light golden
1½ tablespoons finely grated lemon zest
¾ cup fresh lemon juice
1 teaspoon kosher salt
2 mangoes—peeled, cut off the pit and coarsely chopped (3 cups)
¼ cup honey
2 tablespoons heavy cream
½ pint blueberries (1 cup)
¼ cup unsalted pistachios

1. Line an 8-by-4-inch metal or glass loaf pan with plastic wrap, leaving a few inches of overhang all around. In a medium bowl, combine the yogurt, sugar, lemon zest, lemon juice and salt and whisk until smooth. Transfer to an ice cream maker and freeze according to the manufacturer's instructions; the yogurt should be frozen but still spreadable.
2. Meanwhile, in a food processor, combine the mangoes, honey and cream and puree until smooth. Transfer half of the mango puree to a bowl and refrigerate.
3. Working quickly, spread a third of the frozen yogurt in the prepared loaf pan in a ½-inch-thick layer. Gently spread half of the unrefrigerated mango puree on top and scatter with some of the blueberries and pistachios; gently push them into the puree. Repeat with another third of frozen yogurt and the remaining unrefrigerated mango puree, blueberries and pistachios. Spread the remaining frozen yogurt on top. Cover and freeze the terrine until firm, at least 8 hours or up to 5 days.
4. Carefully unmold the terrine onto a platter; peel off the plastic wrap. Cut the terrine into ½-inch-thick slices, rinsing the knife under hot water and drying it between cuts. Serve with the chilled mango puree. —Kay Chun

● HEALTHY ● MAKE AHEAD ● VEGETARIAN ● STAFF FAVORITE

For a summer party at her Hungarian farmhouse, cookbook author Sarah Copeland prepares strudel and other classic eastern European desserts.

Opposite: recipe, page 330.

WALNUT CAKE WITH APRICOT PRESERVES

CAKES, COOKIES & MORE

Giant Black-and-White Layer Cake

ACTIVE: 1 HR 15 MIN; TOTAL: 2 HR PLUS
CHILLING • ABOUT 32 SERVINGS ● ●

CAKE

   6   cups cake flour (28 ounces
        or 800 grams)
   2   tablespoons baking powder
1½   teaspoons table salt
   2   cups milk
1½   tablespoons pure vanilla extract
   3   sticks unsalted butter, softened
   4   cups granulated sugar
   8   large eggs, at room temperature
Confectioners' sugar, for dusting

FROSTING AND FILLING

   1   quart heavy cream
   2   cups granulated sugar
1½   pounds extra-dark (75 to 85
        percent) chocolate, chopped
   4   sticks unsalted butter
        (1 pound), softened
   2   cups confectioners' sugar

1. MAKE THE CAKE Preheat the oven to 350°; arrange 3 racks in the oven. Line three 12-by-17-inch baking sheets with parchment paper and spray with vegetable oil.
2. In a large bowl, whisk the cake flour with the baking powder and salt. In a large measuring cup, combine the milk and vanilla extract. In the bowl of a stand mixer fitted with the paddle attachment, beat the softened butter until creamy. Add the granulated sugar and beat at medium speed until fluffy, about 5 minutes. Add the eggs, one at a time, beating well between additions. At low speed, beat in the dry and wet ingredients in three alternating batches.
3. Spread the batter (there will be about 14 cups) evenly on the 3 baking sheets. Bake for about 30 minutes, just until springy; shift the pans halfway through for even baking. Let the cakes cool completely in the pans.
4. Dust the cake tops generously with confectioners' sugar. Invert the cakes onto cutting boards or sturdy cardboard, remove the sheets and peel off the parchment. Shake the boards to make sure the cakes don't stick.

5. MAKE THE FROSTING AND FILLING In a very large saucepan, combine 3½ cups of the cream with the granulated sugar and bring to a boil. Simmer over low heat for 10 minutes, stirring, until slightly reduced. Remove from the heat. Add the chocolate. Let stand for 5 minutes, then whisk until smooth. Let the ganache cool.
6. Using an electric mixer at medium speed, beat the remaining ½ cup of cream into the ganache. Add the butter and beat until creamy, about 1 minute. Transfer half of the ganache (about 3½ cups) to a bowl and beat in the confectioners' sugar to make the filling.
7. Immediately spread half of the filling over the top of a cake layer. Top with a second layer and spread with the remaining filling. Top with the third cake layer. Chill for 20 minutes.
8. Trim the cake neatly. Slide parchment paper strips under the cake to catch frosting. Spread a thin layer of frosting around the sides of the cake, then top with the remaining frosting. Refrigerate until set, about 2 hours.
9. Remove the paper strips. Bring the cake to room temperature. Serve. —*Grace Parisi*

Double-Chocolate Layer Cake

ACTIVE: 40 MIN; TOTAL: 1 HR 30 MIN
PLUS CHILLING • MAKES ONE 8-INCH
LAYER CAKE ● ● ●

"This is the most fabulous chocolate cake that I've ever made," Ina Garten declared when F&W ran her recipe in 2007. The buttermilk keeps the cake moist and light, and the bit of coffee in the cake and frosting keeps the sweetness in check.

CAKE

1¾   cups all-purpose flour, plus more
        for dusting
   2   cups granulated sugar
   ¾   cup unsweetened cocoa powder
   2   teaspoons baking soda
   1   teaspoon baking powder
   1   teaspoon kosher salt
   1   cup buttermilk
   ½   cup vegetable oil
   2   large eggs
   1   teaspoon pure vanilla extract
   1   cup freshly brewed hot coffee

FROSTING

   6   ounces semisweet chocolate,
        coarsely chopped
   2   sticks (½ pound) unsalted butter,
        at room temperature
   1   large egg yolk
   1   teaspoon pure vanilla extract
   1   cup plus 1 tablespoon
        confectioners' sugar, sifted
   1   tablespoon instant coffee granules

1. MAKE THE CAKE Preheat the oven to 350°. Butter two 8-inch round cake pans and line them with parchment; butter the paper. Dust the pans with flour; tap out any excess.
2. In the bowl of a stand mixer fitted with the paddle, mix the flour with the sugar, cocoa powder, baking soda, baking powder and salt at low speed. In a bowl, whisk the buttermilk with the oil, eggs and vanilla. Slowly beat the buttermilk mixture into the dry ingredients until just incorporated, then slowly beat in the hot coffee until fully incorporated.
3. Pour the batter into the pans. Bake for 35 minutes, or until a toothpick inserted in the center of each cake comes out clean. Let cool in the pans for 30 minutes, then invert the cakes onto a rack to cool. Peel off the paper.
4. MAKE THE FROSTING In a microwave-safe bowl, heat the chocolate at high power in 30-second intervals, stirring, until most of the chocolate is melted. Stir until completely melted, then set aside to cool.
5. In the cleaned bowl of the stand mixer fitted with the paddle, beat the butter at medium speed until pale and fluffy. Add the egg yolk and vanilla and beat for 1 minute, scraping down the bowl. At low speed, slowly beat in the confectioners' sugar, about 1 minute. In a small bowl, dissolve the instant coffee in 2 teaspoons of hot water. Slowly beat the coffee and the cooled chocolate into the butter mixture until just combined.
6. Set a cake layer on a plate with the flat side facing up. Evenly spread one-third of the frosting over the cake to the edge. Top with the second cake layer, rounded side up. Spread the remaining frosting over the top and side of the cake. Refrigerate for at least 1 hour before slicing. —*Ina Garten*

DOUBLE-CHOCOLATE LAYER CAKE

Coconut Chiffon Bundt Cake with Coconut Frosting

ACTIVE: 30 MIN; TOTAL: 2 HR 30 MIN

MAKES ONE 10-INCH BUNDT CAKE ● ●

CAKE

1¾   cups cake flour, plus more
      for dusting
1   tablespoon baking powder
1   teaspoon kosher salt
1¼   cups granulated sugar
1   cup sweetened shredded
      coconut
7   large eggs, separated
¾   cup unsweetened coconut milk
½   cup vegetable oil
2   teaspoons pure vanilla extract

FROSTING

1¼   cups confectioners' sugar
¼   cup unsweetened coconut milk

Toasted shredded coconut,
      for garnish

1. MAKE THE CAKE Preheat the oven to 350°. Lightly grease a 10-inch Bundt pan and dust with flour. In a large bowl, sift the 1¾ cups of cake flour with the baking powder, salt and ¾ cup of the granulated sugar. Stir in the shredded coconut. In another large bowl, whisk the egg yolks with the coconut milk, vegetable oil and vanilla extract.

2. In the bowl of a stand mixer fitted with the whisk, beat the egg whites until frothy, 1 to 2 minutes. With the mixer on, gradually add the remaining ½ cup of sugar and beat until the whites are glossy and soft peaks form, 1 to 2 minutes.

3. Make a well in the center of the dry ingredients. Mix in the coconut milk mixture until incorporated. Stir one-fourth of the beaten egg whites into the batter, then carefully fold in the remaining beaten whites until no streaks remain. Scrape the batter into the prepared pan.

4. Bake the cake for 45 to 50 minutes, until golden and the edges start to pull away from the pan. Transfer to a rack and let cool for 1 hour. Run a paring knife around the side of the cake to loosen it, then invert the cake onto a plate.

5. MAKE THE FROSTING In a bowl, whisk the confectioners' sugar with the coconut milk until smooth. Spoon the frosting over the cake, allowing it to drip down the side. Garnish with toasted coconut. —*Joanne Chang*
WINE Madeira: Blandy's 5-Year-Old Malmsey.

Chocolate Blackout Cake

ACTIVE: 25 MIN; TOTAL: 2 HR 30 MIN

8 TO 10 SERVINGS ● ●

An old Brooklyn classic, Blackout Cake is an ultra-chocolaty, custardy, cake-crumb-coated dessert with somewhat mythic status. Chicago pastry chef Gale Gand began making the cake upon special request for birthdays; now it's become one of her most obsessed-over signature dishes. "I get all these calls—it's like a drug deal—and people say, 'I hear you do Blackout Cake.' If you Google *blackout cake,* my name pops up."

CAKE

1   stick unsalted butter, softened,
      plus more for the pan
2¼   cups cake flour, plus more for
      dusting
¼   cup solid vegetable shortening
2   cups sugar
3   large eggs
2   teaspoons pure vanilla extract
¾   cup unsweetened natural cocoa
      powder (see Note)
1   teaspoon baking powder
1   teaspoon baking soda
½   teaspoon salt
1   cup milk

FILLING

2½   cups sugar
1   tablespoon light corn syrup
1½   cups unsweetened natural cocoa
      powder
⅔   cup cornstarch
6   tablespoons unsalted butter,
      cut into small cubes
½   teaspoon pure vanilla extract

Pinch of salt

1. MAKE THE CAKE Preheat the oven to 375°. Butter two 9-inch round cake pans, coat lightly with flour and line the bottoms with parchment paper. In a stand mixer fitted with the whisk, beat the 1 stick of butter with the shortening until creamy. Add the sugar and beat at medium speed until fluffy, about 3 minutes. Add the eggs one at a time, beating well between additions. Add the vanilla. At very low speed, beat in the cocoa powder, baking powder, baking soda and salt. Add the 2¼ cups of cake flour and the milk in 3 separate alternating batches, scraping down the side and bottom of the bowl occasionally.

2. Divide the cake batter between the prepared pans and smooth the tops. Bake in the center of the oven for about 30 minutes, until a toothpick inserted in the centers comes out with a few moist crumbs attached. Let the cakes cool for 15 minutes, then invert them onto a rack and let cool completely.

3. MEANWHILE, MAKE THE FILLING In a large saucepan, combine 2½ cups of water with the sugar, corn syrup and cocoa powder and bring to a boil, whisking constantly. In a bowl, whisk the cornstarch with ½ cup of water until smooth, then whisk into the cocoa mixture. Cook over moderately high heat, whisking constantly, until very thick, 3 minutes. Off the heat, whisk in the butter, vanilla and salt. Scrape the filling into a bowl and press a sheet of plastic wrap onto the surface of the filling. Let cool, then refrigerate until firm, 45 minutes.

4. Using a serrated knife, halve each cake layer horizontally. Break up the less attractive top cake layer and transfer to a food processor; pulse into crumbs. Reserve the two cake bottoms and one smoother top.

5. Set one of the cake bottoms on a cake plate and spread with 1½ cups of the filling. Top with the second bottom layer and another 1½ cups of filling. Cover with the cake top and spread the remaining filling all over the top and side. Pat the crumbs all over the cake. Refrigerate for at least 1 hour before serving. —*Gale Gand*

NOTE Natural cocoa powder is one of two types of unsweetened cocoa. It's bitter and adds intense chocolate flavor to the cake. Don't use Dutch-process or other alkalized cocoa; when combined with baking soda, it can make a cake taste soapy.

Date Cake with Caramel Sauce

ACTIVE: 20 MIN; TOTAL: 1 HR 45 MIN
PLUS COOLING • 8 TO 10 SERVINGS ● ●

Light, moist and not overly sweet, this cake is topped with a creamy caramel sauce—making it almost like a sticky toffee pudding.

CAKE

12	ounces pitted plump Medjool dates
2	tablespoons dark rum
2	tablespoons brewed espresso
1	cup all-purpose flour
1	cup cake flour
1½	teaspoons baking soda
½	teaspoon cinnamon
¼	teaspoon freshly grated nutmeg
⅛	teaspoon ground cloves

Pinch of salt

1½	sticks unsalted butter, softened
¾	cup light brown sugar
4	large eggs

CARAMEL

¾	cup sugar
¾	cup plus 2 tablespoons heavy cream

1. MAKE THE CAKE Preheat the oven to 325°. Butter and flour a 9-by-3-inch round cake pan; line the bottom with parchment. Butter and flour the paper. In a medium microwave-safe bowl, cover the dates with the rum, espresso and ¾ cup of water and heat at high power for 2 minutes. Transfer to a food processor and let stand until the dates are softened. Puree until smooth.

2. In a medium bowl, whisk both flours with the baking soda, cinnamon, nutmeg, cloves and salt. In a large bowl, using a handheld electric mixer, beat the butter and brown sugar until fluffy. Beat in the eggs until incorporated, then beat in the date puree. Add the dry ingredients all at once and beat at low speed until incorporated.

3. Scrape the batter into the prepared pan and bake in the middle of the oven for 1 hour, until a toothpick inserted in the center comes out clean. Let cool for 15 minutes, then invert the cake onto a rack to cool completely.

4. MAKE THE CARAMEL In a medium saucepan, simmer the sugar and ¼ cup of water over moderate heat until a deep-amber caramel forms, 6 minutes. Remove from the heat; add the cream. Cook over low heat, stirring, until the hardened caramel is dissolved.

5. Cut the cake into wedges and serve with the caramel sauce. —*Mourad Lahlou*

Walnut Cake with Apricot Preserves

📷 PAGE 325

ACTIVE: 20 MIN; TOTAL: 1 HR
8 SERVINGS ● ● ● ●

Unsalted butter and all-purpose flour, for greasing and dusting the pan

3½	cups walnuts (about 10 ounces)
⅔	cup sugar
2	teaspoons baking powder
6	large eggs, separated
½	cup apricot preserves

Confectioners' sugar, for dusting

1. Preheat the oven to 325°. Butter and flour a 9-inch springform pan. In a food processor, pulse the walnuts with a pinch of the sugar until very finely ground. Add the baking powder and pulse to combine.

2. In a large bowl, using a handheld electric mixer, beat the egg whites at high speed until soft peaks form.

3. In another bowl, beat the egg yolks with the remaining sugar at medium-high speed until pale and thick, about 3 minutes. At low speed, beat in the walnuts, just to combine.

4. Stir one-third of the egg whites into the batter. Using a rubber spatula, fold in the remaining beaten whites in 2 batches, until no streaks remain.

5. Scrape the batter into the pan and bake for 40 minutes, until golden and springy. Transfer to a rack and let cool in the pan. Run the tip of a knife around the cake and unmold it.

6. Using a serrated knife, split the cake horizontally. Set the bottom layer on a cake plate and spread with the apricot preserves. Replace the top layer and dust with confectioners' sugar. Cut into wedges and serve. —*Sarah Copeland*

SERVE WITH Whipped cream and peaches.
WINE Golden, ripe Hungarian dessert wine: 2010 Royal Tokaji Mad Cuvée.

Baked Alaska Birthday Cake

TOTAL: 2 HR PLUS OVERNIGHT FREEZING
10 TO 14 SERVINGS ● ●

With moist chocolate cake, three flavors of ice cream, nutty ganache and fluffy meringue, this is the ultimate birthday cake. To simplify the recipe, skip the meringue and coat the cake with cookie crumbs instead.

½	cup pecans
12	ounces chocolate pound cake, cut lengthwise into ½-inch-thick slices
4	ounces bittersweet chocolate, chopped
½	cup heavy cream, at room temperature
1	pint firm coffee chocolate chip ice cream
1	pint firm chocolate ice cream
1	pint firm dulce de leche ice cream
1½	cups sugar
6	large egg whites, at room temperature

Pinch of salt
Pinch of cream of tartar

1. Preheat the oven to 350°. Spread the pecans in a pie plate and toast for 8 minutes, until fragrant. Let cool completely, then transfer to a food processor. Crumble one-third of the pound cake slices into the food processor and pulse with the pecans until coarsely chopped.

2. In a microwave-safe bowl, heat the chocolate at high power in 30-second bursts until it is nearly melted. Whisk until smooth, then whisk in the cream. Stir the pecan-cake crumbs into the ganache.

3. Line a 12-cup flat-bottomed vessel with strips of parchment paper, making sure the paper extends by 4 inches on all sides. Arrange half of the remaining pound cake slices neatly on the bottom of the vessel (you may have to cut them to fit). Remove the coffee chocolate chip ice cream from the carton and carefully slice it into slabs. Fit the slabs over the cake and press to an even layer. Spread with half of the nutty ganache and freeze until firm, about 1 hour.

4. Repeat the layering with the chocolate ice cream, the remaining nutty ganache and the dulce de leche ice cream. Top with the remaining pound cake slices. Fold the parchment paper over the cake and freeze overnight or until very firm.

5. Remove the cake from the vessel and place it on a cake plate. Remove the paper. Return the cake to the freezer.

6. In a medium saucepan, bring ¼ cup of water to a boil with the sugar, stirring until dissolved. Brush down any sugar crystals from the side of the pan with a wet pastry brush. Boil for 2 minutes. Meanwhile, in the bowl of a stand mixer fitted with the whisk attachment, beat the egg whites with the salt and cream of tartar until soft peaks form. With the machine at medium speed, carefully beat in the hot sugar syrup until incorporated. Increase the speed to high and beat until the meringue is stiff and glossy and no longer hot, 5 minutes.

7. Using a spatula, spread half of the meringue all over the cake. Fill a pastry bag fitted with a plain tip with the remaining meringue and pipe peaks on top. Using a pastry torch, toast the meringue until browned in spots. Return the cake to the freezer for 15 minutes. Cut the cake with a slightly moistened knife and serve right away. —*Grace Parisi*

MAKE AHEAD The cake can be prepared through Step 4 and frozen for up to 1 week. Let thaw slightly before proceeding.

Hot Chocolate Pudding Cakes

⏲ TOTAL: 40 MIN • 8 SERVINGS ●

1½ sticks unsalted butter, plus melted
     butter for brushing the ramekins
Unsweetened cocoa powder, for dusting
  ¾ pound bittersweet chocolate,
     chopped
  8 large egg yolks
  ½ cup sugar
  ½ cup all-purpose flour
  4 large egg whites
Pinch of kosher salt
Crème fraîche and chopped roasted
     pistachios, for serving

1. Preheat the oven to 425°. Brush eight 6-ounce ramekins with melted butter and dust with cocoa powder. In a microwave-safe bowl, melt the chocolate with the 1½ sticks of butter at high power in 30-second bursts. Whisk until smooth.

2. In a bowl, whisk the egg yolks with the sugar until thick. Whisk in the chocolate mixture and flour. In another bowl, using a handheld electric mixer, beat the egg whites with the salt at high speed until soft peaks form. Beat one-third of the egg whites into the chocolate batter. Using a rubber spatula, fold in the remaining egg whites until no white streaks remain. Divide the batter among the ramekins, filling them two-thirds full. Arrange the ramekins on a sturdy baking sheet.

3. Bake the cakes in the center of the oven until the tops and sides are set but the centers are still soft, 15 minutes. Let stand for 30 seconds, then run the tip of a knife around the rims and invert the cakes onto plates. Serve with crème fraîche and pistachios. —*Owen Kenworthy*

Hot Cocoa Cupcakes with Meringue Frosting

ACTIVE: 30 MIN; TOTAL: 1 HR PLUS COOLING

MAKES 12 CUPCAKES ● ● ●

These rich chocolate cupcakes mounded with a fluffy marshmallow-esque meringue frosting are gluten-free.

CUPCAKES

1½ cups Silvana's Kitchen Gluten-Free
     All-Purpose Flour (page 300)
  1 teaspoon baking powder
  ½ teaspoon baking soda
  ½ teaspoon kosher salt
  ½ cup natural cocoa powder
     (not Dutch-process)
  ½ cup semisweet chocolate chips
  ¾ cup boiling water
  1 cup sugar
  ¾ cup sour cream,
     at room temperature
  ½ cup canola oil
  2 large eggs, at room temperature
  1 tablespoon pure vanilla extract

FROSTING

  4 large egg whites, at room
     temperature
  1 cup sugar
Pinch of cream of tartar
  ¾ teaspoon pure vanilla extract

1. MAKE THE CUPCAKES Preheat the oven to 350°; line a 12-cup muffin pan with paper liners. In a bowl, whisk the flour, baking powder, baking soda and salt. In another bowl, whisk the cocoa, chocolate chips and boiling water until smooth. Add the sugar, sour cream, oil, eggs and vanilla; whisk until no streaks remain. Whisk in the dry ingredients.

2. Fill the muffin cups with the batter; bake until a toothpick inserted in the center of a cupcake comes out clean, about 20 minutes. Transfer to a rack and let cool completely.

3. MAKE THE FROSTING In a heatproof bowl set over a saucepan of simmering water (the bottom of the bowl shouldn't touch the water), whisk the egg whites with the sugar and cream of tartar until the sugar has dissolved, 3 minutes. Remove from the heat. Using a handheld electric mixer, beat the whites at high speed until stiff peaks form, about 6 minutes. Beat in the vanilla.

4. Transfer the meringue frosting to a piping bag fitted with a large round tip and frost the cupcakes. —*Silvana Nardone*

SUPEREASY DESSERT

Molecular godfather Ferran Adrià gave us the simplest, most satisfying dish ever: melted chocolate on toasts, topped with a little olive oil and sea salt.

Chocolate Cupcakes with Caramel Ganache and Coconut

ACTIVE: 40 MIN; TOTAL: 2 HR 15 MIN
MAKES 18 CUPCAKES ● ● ●

FROSTING

12 ounces milk chocolate, finely chopped
2 ounces bittersweet or semisweet chocolate, finely chopped
¼ cup granulated sugar
1 cup heavy cream

CUPCAKES

1 cup plus 2 tablespoons all-purpose flour
½ cup unsweetened Dutch-process cocoa powder
1 teaspoon baking powder
½ teaspoon baking soda
¼ teaspoon salt
¾ cup buttermilk
1½ sticks unsalted butter, at room temperature
¾ cup granulated sugar
¼ cup light brown sugar
1 large egg
1 teaspoon pure vanilla extract
One 12-ounce bag unsweetened large-flaked coconut

1. MAKE THE FROSTING Combine both chocolates in a large bowl. In a medium saucepan, combine the sugar and ¼ cup of water and cook over moderate heat until dissolved. Boil without stirring, brushing down the side of the pan with a wet pastry brush occasionally, until a deep-amber caramel forms, 8 to 10 minutes. Reduce the heat to low and carefully add the cream; it will bubble vigorously. Whisk until smooth, then pour the caramel over the chocolate. Let stand for 1 minute, then whisk until the frosting is smooth. Refrigerate until completely cool but spreadable, about 2 hours.

2. MEANWHILE, MAKE THE CUPCAKES Preheat the oven to 350°. Line 18 muffin cups with paper liners. In a medium bowl, whisk the flour, cocoa powder, baking powder, baking soda and salt. In a measuring cup, combine the buttermilk and ¼ cup of water. In a large bowl, using a handheld electric mixer, beat the butter with both sugars at medium speed until light and fluffy, about 3 minutes. Beat in the egg and vanilla. With the mixer on low speed, beat in the flour mixture in 3 additions, alternating with the buttermilk.

3. Spoon the batter into the cups, filling them three-quarters full. Bake for 20 minutes, until a tester inserted in the center of a cupcake comes out clean. Cool in the pan for 10 minutes; transfer to a rack to cool completely.

4. Meanwhile, spread the coconut on a rimmed baking sheet and toast for 2 to 3 minutes, until lightly golden. Let cool.

5. Frost the cupcakes, top with the toasted coconut and serve. —*Kay Chun*

Gluten-Free Pumpkin-Ginger Cupcakes

ACTIVE: 45 MIN; TOTAL: 2 HR
MAKES 16 CUPCAKES ● ● ●

When Mani Niall opened Mani's Bakery in Los Angeles in 1989, it was among the first places in the country to offer vegan and gluten-free sweets. Here, Niall tops super-moist gluten-free cupcakes with fluffy, creamy mascarpone frosting and salty caramel.

FROSTING

6 ounces mascarpone, at room temperature
6 ounces cream cheese, at room temperature
3¾ cups confectioners' sugar, sifted
1 tablespoon pure vanilla extract

CUPCAKES

1 cup white rice flour
½ cup tapioca flour
1 teaspoon baking powder
½ teaspoon baking soda
1 teaspoon kosher salt
1 teaspoon ground ginger
¾ teaspoon cinnamon
¼ teaspoon ground allspice
¼ teaspoon freshly grated nutmeg
¾ cup packed light brown sugar
¾ cup granulated sugar
¾ cup vegetable oil
3 large eggs, at room temperature
1¼ cups pure pumpkin puree

CARAMEL

½ cup granulated sugar
¾ cup heavy cream
½ teaspoon flaky sea salt, such as Maldon
¼ cup chopped or sliced crystallized ginger, for garnish (optional)

1. MAKE THE FROSTING In a medium bowl, using a handheld electric mixer, beat the mascarpone and cream cheese until smooth. Add the confectioners' sugar and beat until incorporated. Beat in the vanilla. Cover and refrigerate the frosting until it is firm enough to spread, about 1 hour.

2. MEANWHILE, MAKE THE CUPCAKES Preheat the oven to 350°. Line 16 muffin cups with paper liners. In a large bowl, whisk the rice flour with the tapioca flour, baking powder, baking soda, salt, ginger, cinnamon, allspice and nutmeg. In a medium bowl, whisk the brown sugar with the granulated sugar, vegetable oil and eggs. Add the wet ingredients to the dry ingredients and whisk until smooth; whisk in the pumpkin puree.

3. Spoon the batter into the prepared muffin cups. Bake for about 25 minutes, until the cupcakes spring back when gently pressed. Transfer the cupcakes to a rack and let cool completely.

4. MAKE THE CARAMEL In a medium saucepan, spread the sugar evenly and cook over moderately low heat, shaking the pan to keep the sugar in an even layer. Cook, swirling the saucepan occasionally, until the sugar is melted and a deep-amber caramel forms. Slowly add the cream (be careful, the caramel will boil vigorously) and cook, whisking, until smooth. Transfer the caramel to a heatproof bowl and stir in the salt. Let cool to room temperature.

5. Frost the pumpkin-ginger cupcakes and drizzle them with the caramel sauce. Garnish with the crystallized ginger and serve.
—*Mani Niall*

MAKE AHEAD The unfrosted cupcakes can be stored overnight in an airtight container at room temperature. The caramel can be refrigerated for up to 1 week; rewarm before using.

Triple-Cheese Cheesecake with Amaretti Crust

ACTIVE: 30 MIN; TOTAL: 3 HR 30 MIN
8 TO 10 SERVINGS ● ●

AMARETTI CRUST

- 3 ounces amaretti cookies (about 20)
- 2 ounces honey graham crackers (about 4 whole crackers), crushed

Pinch of kosher salt

- 5 tablespoons unsalted butter, melted

CHEESECAKE

- 1 teaspoon unflavored powdered gelatin
- ¾ cup heavy cream, chilled

Two 8-ounce packages cream cheese, softened

- ¾ cup fresh ricotta cheese
- ¾ cup sugar

Pinch of kosher salt

- ¼ cup mascarpone cheese or sour cream
- ¼ cup fresh lemon juice

HONEYED APRICOTS

- ¾ cup honey

Three 3-inch rosemary sprigs

- 6 ounces dried California apricots

1. MAKE THE CRUST Preheat the oven to 350°. In a food processor, pulse the amaretti with the graham crackers and salt until finely ground. Transfer the crumbs to a small bowl and stir in the butter. Press the crumbs evenly over the bottom and halfway up the side of an 8-inch springform pan. Bake for about 10 minutes, until the crust is set. Cool on a rack.

2. MAKE THE CHEESECAKE In a microwave-safe dish, sprinkle the gelatin over 2 tablespoons of cold water; let stand until the gelatin is softened, about 10 minutes. Meanwhile, in a small bowl, beat the heavy cream until soft peaks form; refrigerate.

3. In a bowl, beat the cream cheese, ricotta, sugar and salt with an electric mixer at high speed until light and fluffy, about 5 minutes. Beat in the mascarpone and lemon juice.

4. Microwave the gelatin until melted, 5 seconds; scrape into the cream cheese mixture and beat until incorporated, then fold in the whipped cream. Pour the mixture into the cooled crust and smooth the surface. Refrigerate the cake until firm and set, 3 hours.

5. MAKE THE HONEYED APRICOTS In a medium saucepan, combine the honey with 3 cups of water and the rosemary. Bring to a boil and cook over moderately high heat, stirring occasionally, until the honey is dissolved. Add the apricots and simmer until tender, 10 minutes. With a slotted spoon, transfer the apricots to a bowl. Boil the rosemary syrup until thickened, 20 to 25 minutes. Strain the syrup over the apricots and let cool.

6. Unmold the cheesecake and serve with the honeyed apricots. —*Kay Chun*

Ligurian Olive Oil Cake

ACTIVE: 20 MIN; TOTAL: 50 MIN
PLUS COOLING
MAKES ONE 10-INCH CAKE ● ●

- 7 tablespoons unsalted butter, melted, plus more for greasing
- 1¾ cups all-purpose flour, plus more for dusting
- 1½ teaspoons baking powder
- ¼ teaspoon salt
- ¾ cup extra-virgin olive oil
- 3 tablespoons whole milk, at room temperature
- 4 large eggs, at room temperature
- 1 cup sugar

Finely grated zest of 2 lemons or tangerines

1. Preheat the oven to 350°. Butter and flour a 10-inch round cake pan. Into a medium bowl, sift together the 1¾ cups of flour, the baking powder and the salt. In another medium bowl, whisk the melted butter with the olive oil and milk.

2. In a large bowl, using a handheld electric mixer, beat the eggs with the sugar and citrus zest until pale and thickened, about 3 minutes. Alternately beat in the dry and wet ingredients, starting and ending with the dry ingredients. Pour the batter into the prepared pan; bake for about 30 minutes, until the top is golden brown and the side pulls away from the pan. Transfer to a rack and let cool before serving. —*Anne Quatrano*

Goat Cheese Cakes with Rosemary and Lavender Honey

ACTIVE: 30 MIN; TOTAL: 1 HR 45 MIN
8 SERVINGS ● ●

Tangy goat cheese blends beautifully with smooth cream cheese in this luscious, ultra-sophisticated cheesecake.

CRUST

- 8 ounces gingersnaps, crushed
- 2½ tablespoons sugar
- 3½ tablespoons unsalted butter, melted and cooled

FILLING

- 12 ounces cream cheese, softened

One 11-ounce log of fresh goat cheese, at room temperature

- ¾ cup sugar
- 3 large eggs plus 3 large egg yolks
- 1½ teaspoons cornstarch
- 1 tablespoon minced rosemary

Lavender honey, for serving

1. MAKE THE CRUST Preheat the oven to 350° and line a large baking sheet with parchment paper. Spray eight 4-inch ring molds or 4-inch shallow ramekins with vegetable spray; line the bottoms of the ramekins with parchment disks. Set on the baking sheet.

2. In a food processor, pulse the gingersnaps with the sugar to fine crumbs. Add the butter and process until the crumbs are evenly moistened. Press the crumbs into the rings or ramekins in an even layer. Bake in the center of the oven for 12 minutes, until fragrant. Reduce the oven temperature to 300°.

3. MEANWHILE, MAKE THE FILLING In a bowl, using a handheld electric mixer, beat the cream cheese and goat cheese until smooth. Beat in the sugar at medium speed until creamy, 2 minutes. Beat in the eggs and yolks, one at a time, until smooth, then beat in the cornstarch and rosemary.

4. Pour the filling into the molds or ramekins and bake for 25 minutes, until just set. Let cool, then refrigerate until chilled, 1 hour.

5. To serve, unmold the cakes onto dessert plates and drizzle with honey. —*Sandi Reinlie*

WINE Honeyed, orange marmalade–scented Sauternes: 2010 Petit Guiraud.

● HEALTHY   ● MAKE AHEAD   ● VEGETARIAN   ● STAFF FAVORITE

TRIPLE-CHEESE CHEESECAKE
WITH AMARETTI CRUST

Chocolate–Peanut Butter Shortbread Sandwich Cookies

ACTIVE: 50 MIN; TOTAL: 3 HR PLUS CHILLING • MAKES 1 DOZEN SANDWICH COOKIES ● ●

At Craftsman and Wolves pâtisserie in San Francisco, William Werner makes his own peanut butter. Home cooks can buy pure peanut butter without added sugar, preferably from a shop where it's made on-site.

COOKIES

1⅔ cups all-purpose flour

3 tablespoons rice flour

⅓ cup Dutch-process unsweetened cocoa powder

1 teaspoon salt

2 sticks unsalted butter, softened

½ cup sugar, plus more for sprinkling

1 vanilla bean—split, seeds scraped

FILLING

½ cup creamy peanut butter

¼ cup confectioners' sugar

2 tablespoons unsalted butter, softened

1½ tablespoons heavy cream

1 teaspoon pure vanilla extract

½ teaspoon salt

1. MAKE THE COOKIES Sift both flours with the cocoa and salt into a bowl. In a stand mixer fitted with the paddle, beat the butter with the ½ cup of sugar and vanilla seeds at medium speed until smooth but not fluffy, 1 minute. Beat in the dry ingredients in two additions at low speed. Scrape the dough onto a work surface and shape it into a disk. Wrap in plastic and refrigerate until firm, at least 1 hour.

2. Roll out the dough between 2 large sheets of parchment paper to a 9-by-16-inch rectangle, about ¼ inch thick. Slide the dough onto a large baking sheet and refrigerate until firm, about 15 minutes.

3. Preheat the oven to 350°. Line 2 large baking sheets with parchment paper. Remove the top sheet of paper from the dough. Cut the dough into 4-by-1½-inch rectangles. Sprinkle both sides with sugar and transfer them to the prepared baking sheets. Bake for

14 minutes, until barely firm. Let the cookies cool on the baking sheets for 10 minutes, then transfer them to a rack to cool completely.

4. MAKE THE FILLING In a bowl, using an electric mixer, beat the peanut butter and confectioners' sugar until smooth. Beat in the butter, cream, vanilla and salt. Wrap with plastic; refrigerate until firmed up, 15 minutes.

5. Turn half of the cookies bottom side up and spread each one with 1 tablespoon of the filling. Top with the remaining cookies and press lightly. Refrigerate until firm before serving, storing or gifting. —*William Werner*

Maple-Bourbon Banana Pudding Cake

ACTIVE: 15 MIN; TOTAL: 1 HR

6 SERVINGS ● ●

As this cake bakes, the syrup seeps to the bottom, creating a sweet, rich sauce.

6 tablespoons unsalted butter

½ cup superfine sugar

1 overripe banana, mashed

1 large egg

1 cup whole milk, at room temperature

1 cup all-purpose flour

1 tablespoon baking powder

Pinch of salt

¾ cup pure maple syrup

½ cup light brown sugar

2 tablespoons bourbon

¼ cup finely chopped pecans

Vanilla ice cream, for serving

1. Preheat the oven to 375°. In a deep 2-quart baking or soufflé dish, melt the butter in the microwave. Whisk in the superfine sugar and banana, mashing until thoroughly combined. Whisk in the egg and milk.

2. In a bowl, whisk the flour, baking powder and salt; whisk into the baking dish until combined (the batter will be pretty loose).

3. In a microwave-safe cup, heat the maple syrup, light brown sugar and ½ cup of hot water at high power until hot, 1 minute. Add the bourbon. Drizzle the syrup mixture over the batter; it will seep to the bottom. Do not stir. Scatter the pecans on top.

4. Set the dish on a rimmed baking sheet and bake for 40 minutes, until the cake is golden. Let cool for 5 minutes, then scoop into bowls and serve with ice cream. —*Grace Parisi*

Brown Butter Pistachio Financiers

⏱ **TOTAL: 45 MIN**

MAKES 3 DOZEN FINANCIERS ● ● ●

"I've been making financiers for years," says Boston chef Kristen Kish about these French tea cakes. She often changes up the flavors, making them with pistachios instead of traditional almonds. To intensify the nuttiness, she adds brown butter to the batter.

1¾ sticks (7 ounces) unsalted butter, plus more for coating

1 cup all-purpose flour, plus more for coating

¾ cup light brown sugar

4 large egg whites

3 tablespoons granulated sugar

¼ teaspoon pure almond extract

1 cup toasted unsalted pistachios, finely ground

½ cup cake flour

Pinch of salt

Sweetened whipped crème fraîche and fresh berries, for serving

1. Preheat the oven to 400°. Butter and flour 36 mini muffin cups. In a saucepan, cook the 7 ounces of butter over moderate heat, shaking the pan, until the milk solids begin to brown, about 5 minutes. Scrape the butter and browned solids into a large bowl and let cool. Whisk in the brown sugar, egg whites, granulated sugar and almond extract.

2. In another bowl, whisk the pistachios with the 1 cup of all-purpose flour, the cake flour and the salt. Fold the dry ingredients into the brown butter mixture until combined.

3. Spoon the batter into the muffin cups and bake for about 15 minutes, until risen but still slightly soft in the center. Let cool slightly, then invert onto a rack to cool. Serve the financiers with crème fraîche and berries. —*Kristen Kish*

● HEALTHY   ● MAKE AHEAD   ● VEGETARIAN   ● STAFF FAVORITE

Big White Chocolate, Almond and Cranberry Cookies

ACTIVE: 30 MIN; TOTAL: 2 HR
PLUS COOLING
MAKES ABOUT 2 DOZEN COOKIES ● ○ ○

Almond flour and toasted almonds give these thin, crisp cookies a double dose of almond flavor.

- 1 cup slivered almonds
- 1 cup all-purpose flour
- 1 cup bread flour
- 2/3 cup almond flour
- 1 teaspoon baking soda
- 1/2 teaspoon kosher salt
- 14 ounces white chocolate, cut into small chunks (2½ cups)
- 1¼ cups dried cranberries
- 2 sticks unsalted butter, softened
- 3/4 cup granulated sugar
- 3/4 cup light brown sugar
- 2 large eggs
- 2 large egg yolks
- 1 teaspoon pure vanilla extract

1. Preheat the oven to 350°. Spread the slivered almonds in a pie plate and toast for about 8 minutes, until fragrant. Let cool.
2. In a medium bowl, whisk all three flours with the baking soda and salt. Add the white chocolate, cranberries and the cooled almonds and toss well.
3. In a stand mixer fitted with the paddle, beat the butter with both sugars at medium speed until light and fluffy, about 3 minutes. Scrape down the side of the bowl. Beat in the whole eggs, egg yolks and vanilla until incorporated, about 2 minutes. At low speed, beat in the dry ingredients. Cover the mixing bowl with plastic wrap and refrigerate the dough until it is well chilled, at least 1 hour or overnight.
4. Preheat the oven to 350° and line 2 baking sheets with parchment paper. Bake the cookies in two batches: Scoop ¼-cup balls of the dough onto the baking sheets, spacing them 2 inches apart; lightly press them down with your palm. Bake in the upper and lower thirds of the oven for about 17 minutes, until the cookies are golden around the edges but slightly soft in the center; shift the baking sheets from top to bottom and front to back halfway through. Let the cookies cool slightly, then transfer them to a rack to cool completely. Repeat with the remaining dough. —*Joanne Chang*

Cardamom Thumbprints

🕐 TOTAL: 45 MIN
MAKES 3 DOZEN COOKIES ● ○ ○

These adorable cookies have a crumbly almond sugar base. The thumbprints are filled with jam, but melted chocolate would also be wonderful.

- 1 cup fine almond flour
- 1 cup all-purpose flour
- 1/2 teaspoon ground cardamom
- 1/4 teaspoon kosher salt
- 1 stick unsalted butter, softened
- 1/2 cup sugar
- 1 large egg
- 1 teaspoon pure vanilla extract
- One 10-ounce jar apricot, seedless raspberry or strawberry jam

1. Preheat the oven to 350°. Line 2 baking sheets with parchment paper. In a small bowl, whisk both flours with the cardamom and salt. In a medium bowl, using a handheld electric mixer, beat the butter with the sugar at medium speed until light and fluffy, about 3 minutes. Beat in the egg and vanilla. At low speed, beat in the dry ingredients. Gather up the dough and knead a few times to form it into a ball.
2. Using a small ice cream scoop or a tablespoon measure, portion the dough into 36 rolled balls. Arrange the balls on the prepared baking sheets about 1 inch apart. Using the back of a teaspoon, make an indentation in the center of each ball. Bake the cookies for 10 minutes, until slightly firm. Remove the baking sheets from the oven and press the indentations again. Return the cookies to the oven and bake for 7 to 8 minutes longer, until lightly golden and dry but not hard. Transfer the cookies to racks to cool completely. Fill the thumbprints with jam and serve. —*Kay Chun*

Chocolate Amaretti Cookies

ACTIVE: 30 MIN; TOTAL: 1 HR 15 MIN
MAKES ABOUT 3½ DOZEN COOKIES
● ○ ○

There's no flour in this chocolaty take on the chewy Italian almond cookies called amaretti. Instead, the recipe calls for Pernigotti cocoa powder (available at *chefshop.com*), which has a higher fat content than most.

- One 7-ounce package pure almond paste, broken up
- 1 cup sugar
- 1/4 cup plus 2 tablespoons unsweetened cocoa powder, preferably Pernigotti
- Pinch of salt
- 3 large egg whites
- 1/2 cup mini chocolate chips
- Pearl sugar or Italian *pignoli* (see Note), for decorating

1. Preheat the oven to 375° and line 2 baking sheets with parchment paper. Arrange racks in the upper and lower thirds of the oven.
2. In a food processor, combine the almond paste, sugar, cocoa powder and salt and process until the almond paste is very finely chopped. Add the egg whites and process until smooth. Add the chocolate chips and pulse just until incorporated.
3. Transfer the batter to a pastry bag fitted with a ½-inch plain tip. Pipe half of the batter 2 inches apart on the prepared baking sheets in slightly rounded teaspoons (about 1 inch in diameter). Alternatively, use a spoon to dollop the batter. Generously sprinkle the cookies with pearl sugar or *pignoli*.
4. Bake the cookies for 13 to 14 minutes, until risen and lightly cracked but still soft, shifting the pans from top to bottom and front to back halfway through. Slide the paper onto racks; let the cookies cool completely on the paper. Let the baking sheets cool completely, line with fresh parchment paper and repeat with the remaining batter. Invert the parchment onto a work surface and peel it off the cookies. —*Grace Parisi*
NOTE Pearl sugar is available at *amazon.com*. Italian pine nuts (*pignoli*) have a more delicate flavor than Chinese pine nuts.

Gluten-Free Buckwheat Gingerbread Cookies

TOTAL: 40 MIN PLUS 4 HR CHILLING
MAKES 4 DOZEN COOKIES ● ●

This recipe is based on hermits, traditional American soft, spiced cookies. California baker Mani Niall uses buckwheat flour to add an earthy flavor and hearty texture—and to make the cookies gluten-free.

- 2¼ cups buckwheat flour
- ½ teaspoon baking powder
- ½ teaspoon baking soda
- ½ teaspoon cinnamon
- ½ teaspoon freshly grated nutmeg
- ½ teaspoon kosher salt
- ¼ teaspoon ground cloves
- 1 stick unsalted butter, at room temperature
- ¾ cup packed light brown sugar
- 2 large eggs, 1 at room temperature
- ⅓ cup buckwheat honey
- 2 tablespoons finely grated peeled fresh ginger

1. In a medium bowl, sift the buckwheat flour, baking powder, baking soda, cinnamon, nutmeg, salt and cloves. In a large bowl, using a handheld electric mixer, beat the butter at medium speed until creamy. Add the sugar and beat until fluffy, 3 minutes. Beat in the room-temperature egg and the honey and ginger. At low speed, beat in the dry ingredients in three additions just until combined. Turn the dough out onto a work surface and pat it into a 6-inch round. Wrap in plastic and refrigerate for 4 hours or overnight.

2. Preheat the oven to 375°. Line 2 baking sheets with parchment paper. Turn the dough out onto a lightly floured work surface. Divide it into 6 equal pieces. Form each piece into a 6-inch-long log; if the dough is sticky, wet your hands slightly. Transfer 3 logs to each baking sheet, spacing them 3 inches apart.

3. In a small bowl, beat the remaining egg and brush it all over the logs. Bake for 12 to 15 minutes, until the logs are springy to the touch. Transfer to a rack to cool completely. To serve, slice the logs on the diagonal into ½-inch-thick cookies. —*Mani Niall*

Chocolate Chip Cookies with Red Miso Buttercream

ACTIVE: 30 MIN; TOTAL: 1 HR 30 MIN
MAKES 3½ DOZEN COOKIES ● ●

These chewy-crisp chocolate chip cookies become a delicious sweet-savory revelation when paired with miso buttercream flecked with lemon verbena.

- 2 sticks unsalted butter, softened
- 1 cup granulated sugar
- 1 cup light brown sugar
- 2 large eggs
- 2 teaspoons pure vanilla extract
- 1 teaspoon baking soda
- 3 cups all-purpose flour
- ½ teaspoon salt
- 2 cups chopped bittersweet chocolate

Red Miso Buttercream (recipe follows)

1. Preheat the oven to 350° and line 3 baking sheets with parchment paper. In a stand mixer fitted with the paddle attachment, beat the butter until creamy, 1 minute. Add the granulated sugar and brown sugar and beat at medium speed until light and fluffy, 3 minutes. Beat in the eggs and vanilla. In a small bowl, dissolve the baking soda in 2 teaspoons of hot water and stir into the batter. At low speed, beat in the flour and salt until incorporated. Add the chocolate and beat just to distribute evenly.

2. Scoop 1½-inch balls of dough onto the lined baking sheets, spacing them 1½ inches apart. Bake in the center of the oven, one baking sheet at a time, for 16 minutes, until golden; shift the baking sheet from front to back halfway through. Let the cookies cool. Serve with the Red Miso Buttercream. —*Erik Bruner-Yang*

RED MISO BUTTERCREAM
TOTAL: 15 MIN • MAKES 1½ CUPS ● ●

- 1 stick unsalted butter, softened
- 1 tablespoon red miso
- ¼ cup confectioners' sugar
- ½ teaspoon pure vanilla extract
- 1 teaspoon very finely chopped fresh lemon verbena

In a medium bowl, using a handheld electric mixer, beat the butter with the red miso at medium speed until smooth. Beat in the confectioners' sugar and vanilla extract; stir in the lemon verbena and serve. —*EB*

Pepita-and-Mango Triangles

TOTAL: 45 MIN
MAKES 40 COOKIES ● ● ●

These thin, buttery almond cookies have just the right amount of salty *pepitas* (pumpkin seeds) and chewy bits of dried fruit.

- 1 cup fine almond flour
- 1 cup all-purpose flour
- ¼ teaspoon kosher salt
- 1 stick unsalted butter, at room temperature
- ½ cup sugar
- 1 large egg
- 1 teaspoon pure vanilla extract
- ½ cup salted toasted pumpkin seeds (*pepitas*)
- ½ cup finely chopped dried mango, apricots or cranberries

1. Preheat the oven to 350°. Line 2 baking sheets with parchment paper. In a small bowl, whisk both flours with the salt. In a medium bowl, using a handheld electric mixer, beat the butter with the sugar at medium speed until light and fluffy, about 3 minutes. Beat in the egg and vanilla. At low speed, beat in the dry ingredients, *pepitas* and mango. Gather up the dough and knead a few times to form it into a ball.

2. Transfer the dough to a work surface lined with parchment paper. Using a lightly floured rolling pin, roll out the dough to a 10-by-12-inch rectangle. Transfer the dough (on the paper) to a baking sheet and freeze for 15 minutes, until firm but not frozen.

3. Using a sharp knife, trim the edges of the dough. Cut the dough into twenty 2-by-3-inch rectangles, then cut each in half diagonally to form 40 triangles. Arrange the cookies on the prepared baking sheets, spacing them 1 inch apart. Bake for 10 to 12 minutes, until lightly golden and set. Transfer the cookies to racks to cool. —*Kay Chun*

● HEALTHY   ● MAKE AHEAD   ○ VEGETARIAN   ● STAFF FAVORITE

CHOCOLATE CHIP COOKIES WITH
RED MISO BUTTERCREAM

Chocolate-Pecan Shortbread Bars

ACTIVE: 30 MIN; TOTAL: 1 HR 30 MIN
PLUS CHILLING • MAKES 32 BARS ●●

SHORTBREAD

2 sticks unsalted butter, softened
½ cup confectioners' sugar
2 cups all-purpose flour
¼ teaspoon fine sea salt

TOPPING

3 sticks unsalted butter
¾ cup dark brown sugar
¼ cup light corn syrup
8 ounces bittersweet chocolate, finely chopped
2 tablespoons heavy cream
4 large eggs, beaten
3 cups pecan halves, chopped (10 ounces)

Flaky sea salt

1. MAKE THE SHORTBREAD Preheat the oven to 350° and line a 12-by-17-inch baking pan with foil, allowing it to extend ½ inch over the edge on all sides. Spray the foil with vegetable oil spray.

2. In a stand mixer or food processor, beat the butter with the confectioners' sugar, flour and salt until a soft dough forms. Transfer the dough to the prepared baking pan and, using a flat-bottomed glass, press the dough into an even layer. Freeze the dough for about 10 minutes, until firm.

3. Bake the shortbread in the center of the oven for 20 minutes, until lightly golden.

4. MEANWHILE, MAKE THE TOPPING In a saucepan, combine the butter, brown sugar, corn syrup, chocolate and cream and cook over low heat just until melted and smooth. Remove from the heat and let cool slightly. Whisk in the eggs, then fold in the pecans.

5. Spread the topping over the shortbread crust and sprinkle lightly with sea salt. Bake the shortbread bar for about 25 minutes, until the topping is set. Let cool to room temperature, then refrigerate until firm. Using the foil, carefully lift the bar out of the pan; discard the foil. Cut the shortbread into 32 triangles and serve. —*Tanya Holland*

Double Chocolate–Peanut Butter Chip Brownies

ACTIVE: 30 MIN; TOTAL: 1 HR 45 MIN
PLUS COOLING • MAKES 2 DOZEN
BROWNIES ●●●

It's hard to believe these rich, super-fudgy brownies are gluten-free. They're just as good cold as at room temperature.

3 sticks (¾ pound) unsalted butter, cut into tablespoons, plus more for greasing
¾ pound semisweet or dark chocolate, finely chopped
¾ cup plus 2 tablespoons white rice flour
¾ cup tapioca flour
½ teaspoon kosher salt
6 large eggs
3 cups sugar
1 tablespoon pure vanilla extract
1 cup peanut butter chips
½ cup semisweet chocolate chips

1. Preheat the oven to 350°. Lightly grease a 9-by-13-inch metal baking pan.

2. Place the 3 sticks of butter in a heatproof bowl and set the bowl over a saucepan of simmering water (the bottom of the bowl should not touch the water). Melt the butter, stirring occasionally. Add the chopped chocolate and stir until melted. Remove the bowl from the heat.

3. In a small bowl, whisk the rice flour with the tapioca flour and salt. In a large bowl, whisk the eggs with the sugar and vanilla until blended. Fold in the dry ingredients until incorporated, then fold in the peanut butter chips and chocolate chips. Fold in the melted chocolate mixture. Scrape the batter into the prepared dish.

4. Bake for about 1 hour and 15 minutes, until the brownie is slightly puffed and a tester inserted in the center comes out with a few moist crumbs attached. Transfer the pan to a rack and let cool completely before turning out the brownie and cutting it into bars. —*Tully Phillips and Jennifer Wells*

MAKE AHEAD The brownies can be stored in an airtight container for up to 3 days.

Creamy Peanut Butter Pie

ACTIVE: 30 MIN; TOTAL: 1 HR 30 MIN
MAKES ONE 9-INCH PIE ●●●

You'll find the perfect balance of sweet and salty flavors in this delicious whipped-cream-topped peanut butter pie.

8 ounces peanut butter sandwich cookies, such as Nutter Butters
Salt
4 tablespoons unsalted butter, melted
½ cup creamy peanut butter
4 ounces cream cheese, at room temperature
½ cup plus 2 tablespoons confectioners' sugar
1¾ cups heavy cream
1 teaspoon pure vanilla extract
¼ cup salted roasted peanuts, coarsely chopped

1. Preheat the oven to 350°. In a food processor, pulse the cookies with ¼ teaspoon of salt until finely ground. Scrape the cookies into a 9-inch pie plate. Stir in the melted butter, ½ tablespoon at a time, until the crumbs are the texture of wet sand; you may not need to use all of the butter. Using your fingers, press the crumbs evenly over the bottom and up the side of the pie plate. Freeze the crust for 15 minutes.

2. Bake the crust for about 10 minutes, until lightly golden. Let cool on a rack.

3. In a medium bowl, combine the peanut butter with the cream cheese, ½ cup of the confectioners' sugar and ¼ teaspoon of salt; mix until thoroughly blended. In another bowl, whip ¾ cup of the heavy cream until stiff. Whisk the whipped cream into the peanut butter mixture. Spread the peanut butter filling in the crust in an even layer. Refrigerate until chilled, about 30 minutes.

4. In the same whipped-cream bowl, whip the remaining 1 cup of heavy cream and 2 tablespoons of confectioners' sugar with the vanilla until stiff. Spread the whipped cream over the pie. Sprinkle the pie with the chopped peanuts, cut into slices and serve. —*Allison Kave and Keavy Landreth*

●HEALTHY ●MAKE AHEAD ●VEGETARIAN ●STAFF FAVORITE

Nanaimo Bars

TOTAL: 40 MIN PLUS 4 HR FREEZING

MAKES 8 BARS ● ○

These sweet-salty bars are said to be named after their place of origin, the Canadian town of Nanaimo in British Columbia. They're made here with a layer of ice cream instead of the traditional buttercream.

½ cup walnuts (2 ounces)

11 digestive biscuits, broken

2½ ounces salted pretzels (about 7 rods)

1 stick plus 2 tablespoons unsalted butter, cut into tablespoons

¼ cup packed dark brown sugar

¼ cup unsweetened Dutch-process cocoa powder

1 large egg, beaten

1 teaspoon pure vanilla extract

2 pints mint chocolate chip ice cream, slightly softened

5 ounces dark chocolate, chopped

2 tablespoons heavy cream

1 tablespoon corn syrup

1. Preheat the oven to 350°. Line an 8-by-8-inch baking dish with parchment paper, leaving a few inches of overhang all around.
2. Spread the walnuts on a baking sheet and bake for about 5 minutes, until lightly toasted. Cool, chop and transfer to a large bowl.
3. Meanwhile, in a food processor, pulse the biscuits until fine crumbs form; add to the walnuts. In a resealable plastic bag, crush the pretzels with a rolling pin until small chunks form; add the pretzels to the walnuts.
4. In a large saucepan, melt the stick of butter over very low heat. Add the brown sugar and cocoa powder and whisk until smooth. Slowly drizzle the egg and vanilla into the saucepan, whisking, until thickened, 2 minutes. Mix in the walnut mixture. Press the mixture into the prepared baking dish in an even layer and refrigerate the cookie base for 30 minutes.
5. Spread 1½ pints of the ice cream over the cookie base and freeze for 2 hours. Reserve the remaining ice cream for another use.
6. Meanwhile, in a medium heatproof bowl, combine the chocolate, heavy cream, corn syrup and the remaining 2 tablespoons of butter. Place the bowl over a saucepan of simmering water; make sure the bottom of the bowl does not touch the water. Stir until the chocolate is melted and the ganache is smooth. Let cool to room temperature.
7. Pour the chocolate ganache over the ice cream and spread it evenly. Freeze for 2 hours, until set. Cut into 8 bars and serve.
—Matt Lewis and Renato Poliafito

Chocolate-Coconut Bars

ACTIVE: 20 MIN; TOTAL: 1 HR

MAKES 18 BARS ● ○

1 cup fine almond flour

1 cup all-purpose flour

¼ teaspoon kosher salt

1 stick unsalted butter, softened

½ cup sugar

1 large egg

1 teaspoon pure vanilla extract

6 ounces finely chopped dark chocolate (¾ cup)

¼ cup unsweetened cocoa powder

One 7-ounce bag unsweetened large coconut flakes (4 cups)

¾ cup sweetened condensed milk

1. Preheat the oven to 375°. Lightly grease a 9-inch square baking pan and line the bottom with parchment paper. In a small bowl, whisk both flours with the salt. In a medium bowl, using a handheld electric mixer, beat the butter with the sugar at medium speed until light and fluffy, about 3 minutes. Beat in the egg and vanilla. At low speed, beat in the dry ingredients along with the chopped chocolate and cocoa powder. Press the dough evenly into the pan. Bake for about 15 minutes, until set.
2. In a medium bowl, mix the coconut flakes and condensed milk. Spoon the topping over the dough and bake for 15 minutes, until the flakes are golden. Transfer to a rack to cool for 5 minutes.
3. Run a knife around the edge of the pan to loosen the cookie. Carefully turn out the cookie and peel off the paper. Turn it coconut side up on the rack. Let cool completely before cutting into bars. —Kay Chun

Vanilla Ice Cream Bread Pudding with Whiskey Caramel

ACTIVE: 10 MIN; TOTAL: 1 HR

8 SERVINGS ○

Melted vanilla ice cream stands in for time-consuming custard in this luscious bread pudding—a brilliant shortcut.

BREAD PUDDING

Butter, for greasing

1 pound brioche, crust removed and bread torn into 1-inch pieces (6 cups)

1½ pints vanilla bean ice cream, preferably Jeni's Splendid Ice Creams' Ndali Estate or Häagen-Dazs

4 large eggs, beaten

1 cup sugar

CARAMEL SAUCE

⅔ cup sugar

½ cup heavy cream, at room temperature

1 tablespoon whiskey

Pinch of sea salt

1. MAKE THE BREAD PUDDING Preheat the oven to 350°. Butter a shallow 2-quart baking dish and spread the torn brioche in it. Scoop the ice cream into a glass bowl and warm in the microwave in 20-second bursts, stirring, just until melted. Whisk in the eggs, sugar and ¾ cup of water. Pour the custard over the brioche and let stand for 15 minutes, pressing to submerge the bread in the custard.
2. Bake the bread pudding for 30 to 35 minutes, until the top is browned. Let cool slightly.
3. MEANWHILE, MAKE THE CARAMEL SAUCE In a medium saucepan, combine the sugar with 2 tablespoons of water. Cook over moderate heat, swirling the pan and brushing down the side with a wet pastry brush, until the sugar dissolves. Cook undisturbed until a medium-amber caramel forms, about 5 minutes. Add the cream (be careful, it may boil vigorously) and simmer, whisking, until the caramel is smooth, 1 to 2 minutes. Let cool slightly, then stir in the whiskey and salt.
4. Serve the warm bread pudding with the caramel sauce. —Jeni Britton Bauer

DIY PASTRY PUFFS

Airy cream-puff dough *(pâte à choux)* is the base for gougères, éclairs and many other exquisite treats. Here, a step-by-step tutorial in mastering the classic from baker **ERIC KAYSER** of La Maison Kayser.

DON'T WAIT *"Eat your choux the same day, the sooner the better,"* advises Kayser.

CHOUQUETTES

Pâte à Choux
ACTIVE: 20 MIN; TOTAL: 1 HR 15 MIN
MAKES ABOUT 3 DOZEN CHOUX PUFFS ●

- 1 stick plus 1 tablespoon unsalted butter, cut into cubes
- 1 teaspoon sugar
- ½ teaspoon salt
- 200 grams all-purpose flour (about 1½ cups)
- 8 large eggs

1. Preheat the oven to 400°. Line 2 large baking sheets with parchment paper.

2. In a large saucepan, combine 1½ cups of water with the butter, sugar and salt and bring to a boil. Reduce the heat to moderate. Add the flour all at once and stir vigorously with a wooden spoon until a tight dough forms and pulls away from the side of the pan, 2 minutes. Remove the pan from the heat.

3. In a bowl, beat 7 eggs and add to the dough in four batches, stirring vigorously between additions until the eggs are completely incorporated and the pastry is smooth. The dough should be glossy and very slowly hang, stretch and fall from the spoon in thick ribbons. If necessary, beat in the remaining egg.

4. Transfer the dough to a piping bag fitted with a ½-inch plain tip. Pipe 1½-inch mounds onto the baking sheets, leaving 1 inch between them. Proceed as directed at right.

STEP-BY-STEP: MAKING PÂTE À CHOUX

1 COMBINE Bring the water, cubed butter, sugar and salt to a boil in a saucepan, then add the flour all at once.

2 STIR WELL Cook and dry the mixture, stirring briskly, until a tight dough forms and pulls away from the pan.

3 ADD EGGS Working in batches, add the beaten eggs to the dough, stirring vigorously between additions.

4 PIPE Use a pastry bag to pipe mounds of dough onto parchment-lined baking sheets, leaving 1 inch between them.

3 GREAT CHOUX RECIPES

1. CHOUQUETTES Sprinkle each mound with ½ teaspoon pearl sugar (decorating sugar). Bake for 30 minutes, until browned and puffed.

2. GOUGÈRES Sprinkle the mounds with 1 cup shredded Gruyère cheese. Bake for 30 minutes, until browned and puffed.

3. CREAM PUFFS Bake the choux for 30 minutes, until browned and puffed. Let cool completely. Using a serrated knife, halve each puff horizontally. Fill each one with 2 tablespoons sweetened whipped cream and 3 fresh raspberries, or 2 tablespoons chocolate pastry cream (see below). Replace the tops and dust with confectioners' sugar.

CHOCOLATE PASTRY CREAM In a bowl, whisk 6 egg yolks, 9 tablespoons sugar, 1½ tablespoons flour and 1½ teaspoons cornstarch. In a saucepan, bring 2⅔ cups milk and 1⅓ cups heavy cream to a simmer; whisk ½ cup into the eggs, then whisk the mixture into the saucepan. Cook over low heat, whisking, until thick. Off the heat, whisk in 1¼ cups chopped dark chocolate until melted. Transfer to a bowl, cover with plastic and refrigerate until cool.

New Orleans–Style Chicory Beignets

ACTIVE: 1 HR; TOTAL: 4 HR

MAKES ABOUT 3 DOZEN BEIGNETS ●

2 cups ground coffee-and-chicory blend (see Note)
About 3 cups milk
2¼ teaspoons active dry yeast
3 tablespoons granulated sugar
4½ cups bread flour, plus more for rolling
2 sticks chilled unsalted butter, cut into cubes
4 teaspoons kosher salt
Vegetable oil, for frying
Confectioners' sugar, for dusting

1. In a large jar, shake the coffee with 2 cups of the milk. Refrigerate for 1 hour. Strain the milk through a fine sieve into a measuring cup and add as much fresh milk as needed to make 1½ cups. Discard the coffee grounds.
2. In the bowl of a stand mixer fitted with the dough hook, combine ¼ cup of the coffee milk with the yeast and granulated sugar; let stand until foamy, 5 minutes. Add the remaining coffee milk, the 4½ cups of bread flour and the butter and salt. Mix at low speed until the dough just comes together, 2 minutes. Increase the speed to medium and mix until the dough is smooth, 5 minutes. Transfer to a greased bowl, cover and let stand in a warm place until slightly risen, 2 hours. Divide the dough into 4 pieces.
3. On a floured work surface, roll out one piece of dough a scant ⅓ inch thick. Cut into 2-inch squares, then cut each square into two triangles. Transfer to a floured baking sheet. Repeat with the remaining dough. Let stand for 20 minutes.
4. In a large saucepan, heat 2 inches of oil to 360°. Line a baking sheet with paper towels. Working in batches, fry 10 or 12 beignets at a time until browned and cooked through, 5 minutes. Drain on the paper towels; transfer to a bowl. Dust generously with confectioners' sugar and serve immediately. —David Kinch
SERVE WITH Vanilla ice cream and espresso.
NOTE This blend combines coffee with chicory, a root that is roasted and ground.

Fig Bars with Red Wine and Anise Seeds

ACTIVE: 1 HR; TOTAL: 2 HR 30 MIN

MAKES ABOUT 4 DOZEN BARS ● ○ ●

FILLING
1½ cups chopped stemmed dried black figs (10 ounces)
¾ cup dry red wine
⅓ cup sugar
¾ teaspoon grated lemon zest
¾ teaspoon anise seeds
DOUGH
1 stick unsalted butter, softened
½ cup sugar
1 teaspoon pure vanilla extract
1 teaspoon grated lemon zest
½ teaspoon kosher salt
1 large egg
1½ cups all-purpose flour

1. MAKE THE FILLING In a medium saucepan, combine the figs, wine, sugar, lemon zest and anise seeds with 1 cup of water and bring to a boil. Simmer over low heat until the figs are softened and the liquid is syrupy and reduced to ½ cup. Let the figs cool in their syrup, then puree in a food processor until smooth. Transfer the filling to a pastry bag fitted with a ½-inch plain tip.
2. MAKE THE DOUGH In a bowl, using a handheld electric mixer, beat the butter until creamy. Beat in the sugar, vanilla, lemon zest and salt at medium-high speed until fluffy, 3 minutes. Beat in the egg. At low speed, beat in the flour. Divide the dough in half, shape into rectangles and wrap in plastic. Freeze until firm, 20 minutes.
3. Preheat the oven to 350°. Roll out 1 piece of dough between 2 sheets of floured parchment to a 9-by-12-inch rectangle, dusting with flour as needed. Remove the top sheet of parchment. Cut the rectangle into three 3-by-12-inch strips through the parchment; transfer to a baking sheet. Pipe two ½-inch-wide ropes of filling down the middle of each dough strip. Refrigerate just until firm enough to fold, 5 minutes. Fold the dough lengthwise over the filling; turn onto a work surface, seam side down. Discard the parchment.
4. Cut each roll crosswise into 8 bars and arrange on a parchment-lined baking sheet. Bake for 20 minutes, until golden on the bottom. Let cool. Repeat with the remaining dough and filling. —Hedy Goldsmith

Mayan Chocolate Puddings

ACTIVE: 30 MIN; TOTAL: 1 HR 15 MIN

PLUS 4 HR CHILLING

12 SERVINGS ● ● ●

These simple chocolate pots de crème are spiced with cinnamon and allspice. A touch of ground habanero chiles gives them a slightly smoky flavor.

2 cups heavy cream
2 cups whole milk
12 ounces bittersweet chocolate, finely chopped
¼ teaspoon cinnamon
¼ teaspoon kosher salt
⅛ teaspoon ground habanero pepper or cayenne pepper
⅛ teaspoon ground allspice
12 large egg yolks
½ cup sugar
Sweetened whipped cream, for serving

1. Preheat the oven to 325°. In a medium saucepan, combine the heavy cream with the milk and bring to a boil over moderate heat. Remove from the heat and whisk in the chocolate until melted, then whisk in the cinnamon, salt, habanero and allspice.
2. In a large bowl, whisk the egg yolks with the sugar until pale, about 2 minutes. Gradually whisk in the hot chocolate mixture until smooth. Ladle the custard into twelve 5-ounce ramekins.
3. Set the ramekins in a large roasting pan or 2 deep baking pans and transfer to the middle of the oven. Fill the roasting pan or baking pans with enough boiling water to reach halfway up the sides of the ramekins. Bake for about 40 minutes, until the puddings are set but still slightly wobbly in the center. Using tongs, transfer the ramekins to a baking sheet and refrigerate until chilled, at least 4 hours. Top the puddings with whipped cream and serve. —Mara Jernigan

● HEALTHY ● MAKE AHEAD ○ VEGETARIAN ● STAFF FAVORITE

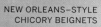

NEW ORLEANS–STYLE
CHICORY BEIGNETS

Gingerbread and White Chocolate Mousse Trifle

ACTIVE: 1 HR 15 MIN; TOTAL: 3 HR
8 SERVINGS ● ●

This dreamy trifle, with its layers of rich gingerbread cake and creamy chocolate mousse, can be assembled ahead of time and served straight from the refrigerator.

GINGERBREAD

1¼ cups all-purpose flour
1½ teaspoons ground ginger
 1 teaspoon baking soda
 ½ teaspoon kosher salt
 ¼ teaspoon ground cloves
 ¼ teaspoon freshly grated nutmeg
 ½ cup unsulfured molasses
 ½ cup sugar
 1 stick unsalted butter, melted
 1 large egg
1½ teaspoons finely grated fresh ginger
 1 tablespoon minced
    crystallized ginger

MOUSSE

 2 teaspoons unflavored
    powdered gelatin
 4 large egg yolks
 ¼ cup sugar
 3 cups heavy cream
 ½ cup whole milk
 2 teaspoons finely grated lemon zest
 ½ teaspoon kosher salt
10½ ounces white chocolate, chopped

CARAMEL

 ¾ cup sugar
 ½ cup pomegranate juice
 ½ teaspoon fresh lemon juice
 ½ cup fresh pomegranate seeds
 Slivered crystallized ginger, for garnish

1. MAKE THE GINGERBREAD Preheat the oven to 325°. Line the bottom of a 9-by-13-inch baking pan with parchment paper and lightly spray the bottom and sides of the pan with baking spray.
2. In a medium bowl, sift the flour with the ground ginger, baking soda, salt, cloves and nutmeg. In a large bowl, using a handheld electric mixer, beat the molasses with the sugar and butter at medium speed until

fluffy. Beat in the egg and the fresh and crystallized ginger. At low speed, beat in the dry ingredients. Gradually beat in ½ cup of water. Spread the batter in the prepared pan.
3. Bake the gingerbread for about 20 minutes, rotating the pan once, until a tester inserted in the center comes out clean. Transfer the gingerbread to a rack to cool for 30 minutes, then turn it out and let it cool completely, 1 hour. Refrigerate the gingerbread until firm, about 1 hour. Peel off the parchment paper and cut the gingerbread into 1-inch cubes.
4. MEANWHILE, MAKE THE MOUSSE In a small bowl, sprinkle the gelatin over 2 tablespoons of water and let stand for 5 minutes. In a medium bowl, beat the egg yolks with the sugar until fluffy.
5. In a medium saucepan, combine ½ cup of the cream with the milk, zest and salt and bring to a simmer. While whisking, drizzle the hot milk mixture into the egg yolks until incorporated. Transfer the mixture to the saucepan and cook over low heat, stirring, until the custard is thickened and coats the back of a spoon, about 10 minutes. Remove from the heat. Add the gelatin and white chocolate and stir until melted. Strain the custard into a medium metal bowl set in a bowl of ice water and cool to room temperature, stirring, about 2 minutes. Remove the bowl from the ice bath.
6. In a large bowl, beat the remaining 2½ cups of heavy cream until soft peaks form. Fold the whipped cream into the custard. Refrigerate the mousse until chilled, about 2 hours.
7. MAKE THE CARAMEL In a medium saucepan, combine the sugar with 3 tablespoons of water and cook over moderate heat, stirring, until the sugar dissolves; brush down the side of the pan with a wet pastry brush. Cook undisturbed until a medium-amber caramel forms, about 5 minutes. Carefully add the pomegranate juice and lemon juice and simmer until slightly thickened, about 5 minutes. Let cool to room temperature.
8. In an 8-inch, 2-quart trifle bowl, make 4 layers of the gingerbread, mousse and caramel. Garnish with the pomegranate seeds and crystallized ginger slices and serve.
—*Monica Glass*

Bittersweet Chocolate Crémeux

TOTAL: 30 MIN PLUS 6 HR CHILLING
8 SERVINGS ● ● ●

Crémeux (French for "creamy") is a dense, soft, classic pudding that's the new darling of many American pastry chefs. This super-chocolaty *crémeux* from Belinda Leong of B. Patisserie in San Francisco has a salty edge.

1½ cups heavy cream
1½ cups whole milk
 5 large egg yolks
 ½ cup sugar
 2 teaspoons kosher salt
 9 ounces dark chocolate (70 to 72
    percent cacao), such as Valrhona
    Guanaja (see Note), finely chopped
 Sweetened whipped cream and
    chocolate shavings, for serving

1. In a medium saucepan, bring the heavy cream and whole milk to a simmer over moderate heat. Remove the saucepan from the heat. In a medium bowl, whisk the egg yolks with the sugar and salt. Gradually whisk in the hot cream. Transfer the mixture to the saucepan and cook over moderately low heat, stirring constantly with a wooden spoon, until the custard is slightly thickened and coats the back of the spoon, about 5 minutes.
2. Strain the custard through a fine sieve into a medium heatproof bowl. Add the chopped chocolate and let stand until melted, about 2 minutes. Whisk vigorously until smooth, then pour the *crémeux* into a shallow glass or ceramic dish. Press a sheet of plastic wrap directly onto the surface of the *crémeux* and refrigerate until set, at least 6 hours or overnight. Spoon the *crémeux* into bowls, top with sweetened whipped cream and chocolate shavings and serve.
—*Belinda Leong*

NOTE Leong likes Valrhona Guanaja's balance of bitter and sweet. It's available at specialty food shops and online at *valrhona-chocolate.com*.

WINE Toffee-and-chocolate-scented Madeira: Broadbent 5-Year Reserve.

● HEALTHY ● MAKE AHEAD ● VEGETARIAN ● STAFF FAVORITE

Honey-and-Thyme Custards

ACTIVE: 20 MIN; TOTAL: 1 HR 30 MIN
4 SERVINGS ●

⅓ cup mild honey, such as clover,
plus more for serving
½ cup heavy cream
1½ cups milk
3 thyme sprigs
1 vanilla bean, seeds scraped
4 large egg yolks
2 tablespoons cornstarch
1 tablespoon sugar
¾ teaspoon unflavored gelatin
softened in 1 tablespoon water
Raspberries and sea salt, for serving

1. In a saucepan, cook the ⅓ cup of honey over moderately low heat for 2 minutes. Add the heavy cream, milk, thyme and vanilla bean and seeds and simmer over low heat for 4 minutes. Discard the thyme and vanilla bean.
2. In a heatproof bowl, whisk the egg yolks, cornstarch and sugar. Gradually whisk in the hot honey milk. Return to the saucepan; whisk over moderate heat until thickened and bubbling, 3 to 4 minutes. Off the heat, whisk in the softened gelatin. Strain into 4 small jars and refrigerate until chilled, 1 hour. Serve with berries, honey and a sprinkling of sea salt.
—Kristen Kish

Almond-Milk Rice Pudding

TOTAL: 30 MIN • 6 SERVINGS ● ● ●

1½ cups sushi rice, rinsed
⅓ cup sugar
Pinch of salt
7 cups unsweetened almond milk
Cherry preserves, for serving

In a large saucepan, combine the rice, sugar, salt and 1 cup of the almond milk. Cook over low heat, stirring, until the almond milk is absorbed, 5 minutes. Gradually add 5 more cups of almond milk, ½ cup at a time, stirring and cooking until the sauce is very thick, 25 minutes. Let cool, then stir in the remaining 1 cup of almond milk. Serve topped with cherry preserves. —Grace Parisi

Gluten-Free Gingersnap Ice Cream Sandwiches

ACTIVE: 30 MIN; TOTAL: 2 HR 30 MIN
MAKES 10 ICE CREAM SANDWICHES ● ●

½ cup light brown sugar
¼ cup grapeseed oil
3 tablespoons Lyle's Golden Syrup (see Note)
1 tablespoon molasses
1 large egg
1¾ cups almond meal, such as Bob's Red Mill
1½ teaspoons cinnamon
1 teaspoon baking soda
¾ teaspoon ground cloves
¾ teaspoon ground ginger
½ teaspoon freshly ground pepper
½ teaspoon ground cardamom
Demerara sugar, for rolling
2½ pints dairy- and gluten-free ice cream, such as Luna & Larry's Coconut Bliss chocolate-hazelnut fudge, softened slightly

1. In a bowl, thoroughly blend the brown sugar with the oil, Lyle's Golden Syrup and molasses. Beat in the egg. In another bowl, stir the almond meal with the cinnamon, baking soda, cloves, ginger, pepper and cardamom. Stir the dry ingredients into the brown sugar mixture until well blended. Refrigerate the dough for at least 1 hour or overnight.
2. Preheat the oven to 350° and line 2 baking sheets with Silpats or parchment paper. Scoop the dough into heaping 1-tablespoon mounds and roll into 20 balls, then roll the balls in the demerara sugar. Set the balls 2 inches apart on the prepared baking sheets. Bake the cookies for about 14 minutes, rotating the sheets halfway through baking, until they are slightly firm. Let stand for 5 minutes, then transfer the cookies to a rack to cool completely.
3. Scoop the ice cream onto the underside of half of the cookies and top with the remaining cookies. Press together slightly and serve.
—Coco Kislinger
NOTE Lyle's Golden Syrup is available online at kingarthurflour.com.

MAKE AHEAD The cookies can be kept in an airtight container at room temperature overnight. The ice cream sandwiches can be individually wrapped and frozen in an airtight container for up to 3 days.

Ice Cream Sundaes with Brown Butter Crumble

ACTIVE: 20 MIN; TOTAL: 1 HR 40 MIN
PLUS COOLING
MAKES ABOUT 3 CUPS ● ●

Brown butter, made by warming unsalted butter in a skillet until it's deeply golden, adds a wonderful nutty flavor to a chunky, streusel-like crumble. Sprinkle it on vanilla ice cream with chocolate and caramel sauces for outrageously good sundaes.

1 stick plus 6 tablespoons unsalted butter
½ cup granulated sugar
1½ cups all-purpose flour
¾ cup dark brown sugar
½ cup almond meal or almond flour
1¼ teaspoons fine sea salt
Vanilla ice cream, caramel sauce and chocolate sauce, for serving

1. In a small saucepan, cook the butter over moderate heat, shaking the pan occasionally, until it is nutty-smelling and golden and the foam subsides, about 5 minutes. Pour the brown butter into a heatproof bowl and stir in the granulated sugar. Let cool slightly.
2. Line a baking sheet with parchment paper. In a medium bowl, whisk the flour with the dark brown sugar, almond meal and fine sea salt. Stir in the brown butter mixture until evenly moistened crumbs form. Transfer to the prepared baking sheet and, using your hands, press the crumbs into an even layer a scant ⅓ inch thick. Cover the baking sheet with plastic wrap and refrigerate until well chilled, about 1 hour.
3. Preheat the oven to 350°. Break the dough into small chunks and bake until it is golden and slightly dry, about 20 minutes. Let the crumble cool, then serve it over vanilla ice cream with caramel and chocolate sauces.
—Belinda Leong

Butter-Pecan Blondie Sundaes with Creamy Caramel Sauce
ACTIVE: 35 MIN; TOTAL: 1 HR 30 MIN
8 SERVINGS PLUS LEFTOVER BLONDIES
● ●

Bob Truitt, pastry chef at The Butterfly in New York City, loves anything that includes caramel and ice cream. "But there always needs to be a crunch," he says. For these sundaes, he makes pecan-studded blondies as the base and a candied pecan topping.

- 2 cups all-purpose flour
- 1 teaspoon baking powder
- ¼ teaspoon baking soda
- ½ teaspoon salt
- 2 sticks unsalted butter, softened
- 1½ cups light brown sugar
- ½ cup granulated sugar
- 2 large eggs
- 1 teaspoon pure vanilla extract
- 1 cup pecan halves, chopped

Butter-pecan ice cream and candied pecans, for serving
Creamy Caramel Sauce (recipe follows)

1. Preheat the oven to 350° and spray a 9-by-13-inch baking pan with baking spray. In a small bowl, whisk the flour with the baking powder, baking soda and salt. In a standing mixer fitted with the paddle, beat the butter with the brown and granulated sugars at medium speed until fluffy. Add the eggs and vanilla and beat until smooth. Add the dry ingredients and beat at low speed until incorporated. Beat in the pecan halves. Spread the batter in the prepared pan; bake for about 30 minutes, until the top is shiny and lightly crackled and the edges pull away from the sides of the pan. Let cool completely.
2. Invert the blondie bar onto a board, cut into twelve 3-inch squares, then cut 8 of the squares into quarters (save the remaining squares for snacks). Divide half of the blondie pieces among 8 parfait glasses. Top with a scoop of ice cream and the remaining blondies. Sprinkle with candied pecans and drizzle with Creamy Caramel Sauce. Garnish with more candied pecans and serve. —*Bob Truitt*

CREAMY CARAMEL SAUCE
⟳ **TOTAL: 20 MIN**
MAKES ABOUT 1½ CUPS ● ○

- 1¼ cups sugar
- 1 cup heavy cream
- 1 tablespoon unsalted butter

Pinch of salt

In a small saucepan, combine the sugar and ¼ cup of water and cook over moderate heat, stirring, until the sugar dissolves. Cook without stirring until a medium-amber caramel forms, about 5 minutes. Add the cream, butter and salt and simmer until thickened, about 2 minutes; let cool. —*BT*

Ice Cream Bonbon Pops
TOTAL: 45 MIN PLUS FREEZING
MAKES 18 BONBONS ● ○

These ice cream pops, which were inspired by movie-theater snacks, are fantastic for parties; just roll ice cream in chopped candy, poke sticks in the balls and freeze. You will need a small, half-ounce ice cream scoop.

Crushed popcorn
- 1 pint vanilla ice cream, or your favorite flavor

About eighteen 4-inch lollipop sticks
Crushed candy, such as Sno-Caps, Whoppers, Skittles and M&M's

Place 2 large parchment paper–lined plates in the freezer for 15 minutes. Spread out crushed popcorn on a baking sheet. Using an ice cream scoop and working quickly, scoop out 9 ice cream balls and set them on top of the popcorn. Return the pint of ice cream to the freezer so it doesn't melt. Roll the balls in the popcorn to coat, pressing to help it adhere. Insert sticks into the centers of the balls, then transfer the bonbons to one of the frozen plates and place in the freezer. Repeat with the candy and remaining ice cream and plate. Freeze the bonbons until completely firm, about 30 minutes. —*Kay Chun*

MAKE AHEAD The ice cream bonbons can be refrigerated overnight.

Île Flottante for a Crowd
ACTIVE: 45 MIN; TOTAL: 2 HR 30 MIN
10 SERVINGS ● ○ ○

Île flottante ("floating island") perfectly describes the classic French dessert of a light round of meringue floating on a pool of crème anglaise. To make a more party-friendly version, pastry chef Alissa Frice of St. Jack in Portland, Oregon, cleverly molds a giant meringue in a Bundt pan, then slices it for individual servings.

- 9 eggs, separated
- 1 teaspoon cream of tartar
- ¾ teaspoon kosher salt
- 2 cups plus 2 tablespoons sugar
- 2 cups heavy cream
- 1 cup whole milk
- ½ vanilla bean, split, seeds scraped
- 2 tablespoons amaretto

Mixed berries, for garnish

1. Preheat the oven to 325°. Set a roasting pan in the center of the oven and add 1 inch of boiling water to it. Lightly spray a 15-cup Bundt pan with cooking spray.
2. Using a handheld mixer, beat the egg whites with the cream of tartar and ¼ teaspoon of salt at high speed until foamy. Beat in 1 cup plus 2 tablespoons of sugar, 1 tablespoon at a time, until the meringue holds stiff peaks.
3. Scoop the meringue into the Bundt pan and set in the roasting pan. Bake for 20 minutes, until just firm. Transfer to a rack for 20 minutes. Top the pan with an inverted plate and turn the meringue out onto it.
4. In a saucepan, simmer the cream, milk and vanilla bean. Meanwhile, in a heatproof bowl, whisk the yolks with the remaining sugar, salt and amaretto. Whisk half of the hot cream mixture into the yolks. Whisk the yolk mixture into the remaining cream in the saucepan. Cook over low heat, stirring, until the custard coats the back of a spoon, 8 minutes. Fine-strain the crème anglaise into a heatproof bowl and refrigerate until chilled, 1 hour.
5. To serve, ladle some of the chilled crème anglaise into a shallow bowl, top with a slice of the meringue and garnish with berries. —*Alissa Frice*

● HEALTHY ● MAKE AHEAD ○ VEGETARIAN ● STAFF FAVORITE

BUTTER-PECAN BLONDIE SUNDAE WITH
CREAMY CARAMEL SAUCE

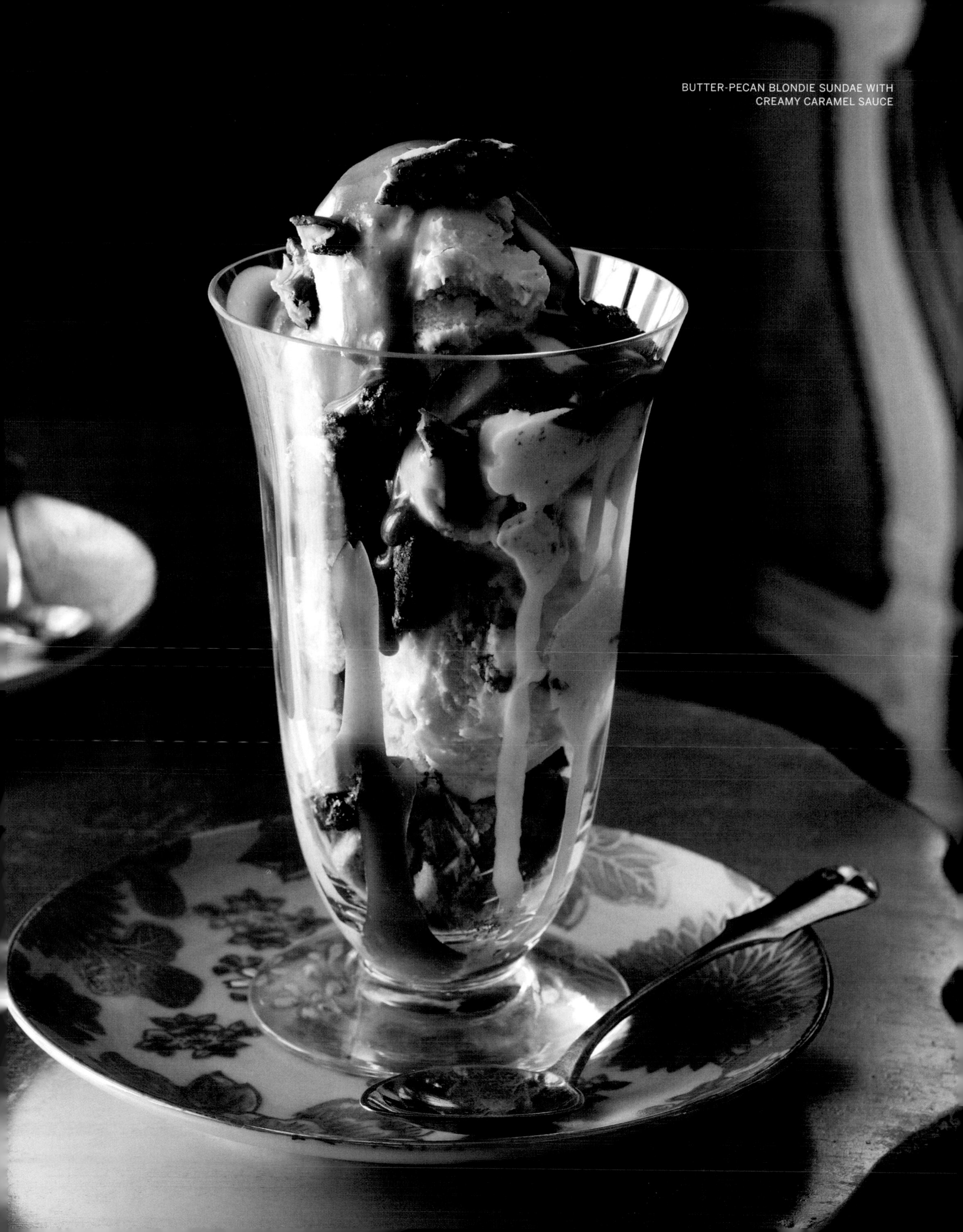

Peppermint Buttercrunch

TOTAL: 45 MIN PLUS 3 HR COOLING
MAKES 1½ POUNDS ● ● ●

At Dominique Ansel Bakery in New York City, bags of this chocolate-covered toffee come with a tiny hammer to break off pieces. "I love the idea of making something for people that can be shared," Ansel says.

  1 stick plus 6 tablespoons
     unsalted butter
  1 cup sugar
  ½ teaspoon salt
  ½ teaspoon pure vanilla extract
  ½ teaspoon natural
     peppermint extract
 12 ounces bittersweet chocolate,
     finely chopped
  1 cup crushed peppermint candies

1. Line a large rimmed baking sheet with a silicone baking mat or parchment paper.

2. In a medium saucepan, combine the butter, sugar and salt with 2 tablespoons of water and cook over moderate heat, stirring, until the temperature reaches 298° on a candy thermometer, 10 minutes. Remove the pan from the heat and stir in the vanilla and peppermint extracts. Immediately pour the buttercrunch onto the prepared baking sheet and, using an offset spatula, spread it in an even layer; let cool completely.

3. In a medium glass bowl, heat half of the chocolate in a microwave oven at high power in 30-second intervals, stirring between bursts, until just starting to melt. Stir in the remaining chopped chocolate until smooth.

4. Spread half of the melted chocolate on the cooled buttercrunch. Sprinkle half of the peppermint on top; let stand until set.

5. Gently set another large baking sheet on top of the buttercrunch and carefully invert the baking sheets; peel off the baking mat or parchment. Spread the remaining melted chocolate on the buttercrunch and sprinkle with the remaining crushed peppermint; let stand until the chocolate is completely set. Break the buttercrunch into pieces before serving, storing or gifting.
—*Dominique Ansel*

Roasted Cashew and Sesame Brittle

TOTAL: 45 MIN PLUS 1 HR COOLING
MAKES ABOUT 2 POUNDS ● ● ●

Yigit Pura creates a sweet brittle mosaic with cashews and sesame seeds. "The combination of white and black seeds together is very Turkish," says the Ankara-born pastry chef of Tout Sweet Pâtisserie in San Francisco.

2¾ cups raw cashews (12 ounces)
  ¼ cup white sesame seeds
  2 tablespoons black sesame seeds
1½ teaspoons vanilla bean paste
     (available at *nielsenmassey.com*) or
     2 teaspoons vanilla extract
  1 teaspoon Maldon salt or other
     flaky sea salt
  ½ teaspoon baking soda
  ¼ teaspoon freshly grated nutmeg
1¾ cups sugar
  ¼ cup light corn syrup
  2 sticks unsalted butter, cut into
     tablespoons and softened

1. Preheat the oven to 300°. Spread the cashews and sesame seeds on a rimmed baking sheet and bake for 12 to 15 minutes, until lightly golden. Let cool.

2. Line a large rimmed baking sheet with a silicone baking mat or parchment; lightly coat the parchment with nonstick cooking spray.

3. In a small bowl, whisk the vanilla bean paste with the salt, baking soda and nutmeg.

4. In a large saucepan, bring the sugar, corn syrup and ½ cup of water to a boil. Cook over moderately high heat, brushing down the side of the pan occasionally with a wet pastry brush, until the syrup reaches 250° on a candy thermometer, about 10 minutes. Remove the saucepan from the heat, then carefully whisk in the butter.

5. Bring the syrup back to a boil and cook over moderately high heat, stirring frequently, until golden brown, 5 to 7 minutes. Remove from the heat and carefully stir in the vanilla bean mixture, then the cashews and sesame seeds. Immediately scrape the brittle onto the prepared baking sheet and, working quickly, spread it in an even layer with an offset spatula. Lay another silicone baking mat or a sheet of sprayed parchment over the brittle and use a rolling pin to even it out. Remove the top baking mat and let the brittle cool completely, about 1 hour. Break the brittle into pieces before serving, storing or gifting. —*Yigit Pura*

Lemon and Fresh Sorrel Sherbet

TOTAL: 30 MIN PLUS 5 HR CHILLING AND
FREEZING • MAKES ABOUT 1 QUART ● ●

San Francisco pastry chef Belinda Leong started to incorporate wild greens and herbs into her desserts in 2009, during a foraging internship at the world-renowned Noma restaurant in Copenhagen. When sorrel's in season, she uses the tart, lemony green to flavor her tangy sherbet, but mint, thyme and basil are also terrific.

1¼ teaspoons unflavored
     powdered gelatin
  1 cup fresh lemon juice
1½ cups sugar
2¼ cups whole milk
  5 large sorrel leaves or ½ cup lightly
     packed mint leaves
  2 teaspoons finely grated
     lemon zest

1. In a small bowl, sprinkle the gelatin over the lemon juice and let stand until softened, about 5 minutes.

2. In a medium saucepan, combine the sugar with 1½ cups of water and bring to a boil. Simmer over moderate heat until the sugar is dissolved, 2 to 3 minutes. Remove from the heat and whisk in the lemon juice mixture. Let cool completely, then refrigerate until chilled, 2 hours.

3. In a blender, combine the lemon mixture with the milk and sorrel and puree until almost smooth, about 30 seconds. Strain the mixture through a fine sieve into a bowl and stir in the lemon zest.

4. Pour the sherbet mixture into an ice cream maker and freeze according to the manufacturer's instructions. Transfer to an airtight container, cover and freeze until firm, at least 2 hours, before serving. —*Belinda Leong*

● HEALTHY ● MAKE AHEAD ● VEGETARIAN ● STAFF FAVORITE

PEPPERMINT
BUTTERCRUNCH

Chef Wylie Dufresne at WD-50 in
Manhattan, where he creates brilliant
dishes with surprise ingredients,
like onions slow-cooked with cloves.

Opposite: recipe, page 359.

ONION-CLOVE COMPOTE

SNACKS, SAUCES & CONDIMENTS

Spiced Roasted Chickpeas

⏱ ACTIVE: 10 MIN; TOTAL: 40 MIN
MAKES 3½ CUPS ● ●

Susan Spungen, author of the manual *What's a Hostess to Do?*, loves to serve these crisp, spiced chickpeas at cocktail parties. Roasted in the oven with just a little oil, they're a healthy alternative to fried chips.

Two 15-ounce cans chickpeas—rinsed, drained and patted dry
2 tablespoons extra-virgin olive oil
1 teaspoon ground cumin
1 teaspoon ground coriander
1 teaspoon chile powder
Kosher salt and freshly ground pepper

Preheat the oven to 400°. In a medium bowl, toss the chickpeas with the olive oil, cumin, coriander and chile powder and season with salt and pepper. Spread the chickpeas on a rimmed baking sheet and roast for 30 minutes, or until slightly crisp and golden brown. Serve warm or at room temperature. —*Susan Spungen*

Baked Sweet Potato Chips

ACTIVE: 10 MIN; TOTAL: 1 HR 15 MIN
MAKES 3 CUPS ● ●

1 small sweet potato (8 ounces), peeled and thinly sliced on a mandoline ⅛ inch thick
3 tablespoons extra-virgin olive oil
Kosher salt and freshly ground pepper

1. Preheat the oven to 275°. Set a rack on each of 2 baking sheets.
2. In a large bowl, toss the sweet potato slices with the olive oil and season with salt and pepper; make sure that each slice is coated with oil.
3. Arrange the slices in a single layer on the racks. Bake for 45 to 50 minutes, rotating the sheets halfway through baking, until the chips are deeply golden. The chips will crisp as they cool. —*Kay Chun*
MAKE AHEAD The chips can be stored in an airtight container overnight. Recrisp in a 250° oven if necessary.

Dill Pickle Dust for Popcorn

⏱ TOTAL: 5 MIN
MAKES ABOUT ¼ CUP ● ●

This ingenious popcorn seasoning mix includes pickling spices along with a touch of citric acid, which adds the mouth-puckering tang of pickle brine in powder form.

1 tablespoon coriander seeds
1 tablespoon kosher salt
½ teaspoon mustard seeds
½ teaspoon garlic powder
½ teaspoon onion powder
½ teaspoon dill seed
½ teaspoon citric acid (see Note)
1 teaspoon dried dill

In a spice grinder, pulse all of the ingredients to a fine powder. —*Grace Parisi*
TOSS WITH Buttered popcorn.
NOTE Citric acid is available at vitamin shops and online at *williams-sonoma.com*.

Spicy Japanese Dust for Popcorn

⏱ TOTAL: 5 MIN
MAKES ABOUT ¼ CUP ● ●

2 sheets nori (dried seaweed), crumbled
2 tablespoons toasted sesame seeds
1 tablespoon *togarashi* (see Note)
1 tablespoon kosher salt

In a food processor, pulse all of the ingredients to a fine powder. —*Grace Parisi*
TOSS WITH Buttered popcorn.
NOTE *Togarashi*, a Japanese blend of chiles and sesame, is available at Asian markets.

Ranch Dust for Popcorn

⏱ TOTAL: 5 MIN
MAKES ABOUT ¾ CUP ● ●

¼ cup plus 2 tablespoons buttermilk powder (see Note)
¼ cup nutritional yeast (see Note)
1 tablespoon onion powder
1 tablespoon kosher salt
½ teaspoon freshly ground pepper

In a food processor, pulse all of the ingredients to a fine powder. —*Grace Parisi*
TOSS WITH Buttered popcorn.
NOTE Buttermilk powder is available at supermarkets and online at *kingarthurflour.com*. Nutritional yeast has a very savory, almost cheese-like flavor and is available at well-stocked specialty and natural food stores.

Chicken Crisps

ACTIVE: 30 MIN; TOTAL: 1 HR 20 MIN
4 SERVINGS ● ●

Crunchy chicken skins resemble *chicharrones* (fried pork rinds), but they're better: baked, not fried, and easier to make.

½ cup vegetable oil
5 garlic cloves, very thinly sliced
¾ pound chicken skin in large pieces (from 3 to 4 chickens), excess fat removed
Kosher salt and *togarashi* (see Note below left), for seasoning
Whole-grain mustard, for brushing
Honey, for drizzling
Finely grated lime zest, for garnish

1. Preheat the oven to 375° and line 2 baking sheets with parchment paper. In a small saucepan, combine the oil with the garlic and cook over moderate heat, stirring often, until the garlic is golden and crisp, about 8 minutes. Using a slotted spoon, transfer the garlic chips to paper towels to drain.
2. Spread out the chicken skin in a single layer on the prepared baking sheets and season lightly with salt and *togarashi*. Top the chicken skin with another sheet of parchment paper and another baking sheet to weigh it down. Bake for 40 to 50 minutes, until the skins are golden and crisp; rotate the baking sheets from front to back and top to bottom halfway through baking.
3. Transfer the crispy chicken skins to paper towels to drain. Lightly brush with whole-grain mustard and transfer to a serving bowl. Drizzle lightly with honey, garnish with the garlic chips and lime zest and serve. —*Matthias Merges*
BEER Citrusy wheat beer: Paulaner.

● HEALTHY ● MAKE AHEAD ● VEGETARIAN ● STAFF FAVORITE

SPICED ROASTED CHICKPEAS

DIY BATTER, PICKLES & FOAM

Modernist chef and *Top Chef* All-Star **RICHARD BLAIS** shares his trick (a siphon) for making super-crisp onion rings, truly quick pickles and extra-light sauces.

HOW TO MAKE THE CRISPIEST **ONION RINGS**

Sometimes, deep-fry batter recipes call for beating in beer or club soda (the little air bubbles lighten the mixture), or adding vodka (alcohol boils off more quickly than water, enhancing a batter's texture). Here, Blais uses both strategies and amplifies their effect by aerating the batter in a siphon—a canister charged with pressurized gas, commonly used to make seltzer and to whip cream. The results are some of the laciest, crunchiest onion rings you'll ever taste. This batter is equally good on all kinds of fried foods, like other vegetables, fish and pork cutlets.

Crisp and Lacy Onion Rings

⏲ **TOTAL: 30 MIN • 2 TO 4 SERVINGS** ● ●

- 1¾ cups all-purpose flour
- ½ cup plus 1 tablespoon rice flour
- Kosher salt
- ½ teaspoon baking soda
- 1 cup light ale or lager
- ½ cup vodka
- Vegetable oil, for frying
- 1 medium sweet onion, sliced crosswise ½ inch thick and separated into rings

1. In a bowl, whisk ¾ cup of the all-purpose flour with the rice flour, 1½ teaspoons of salt and the baking soda. Whisk in the beer and vodka until the batter is very smooth. Strain the batter, then pour it into the canister of a 1-pint iSi Gourmet Whip Plus siphon. Seal the siphon and charge it with one iSi cream (N₂O) cartridge according to the manufacturer's instructions. Shake the siphon to distribute the gas. Repeat with a second cream cartridge.

2. In a large saucepan, heat 2 inches of oil to 350°. Put the remaining 1 cup of all-purpose flour in a shallow bowl. Dredge the onion rings in the flour. Working in 3 or 4 batches, shake off the excess flour and transfer the rings to a large bowl. Holding the siphon upside down, carefully press the handle to dispense just enough batter to coat the rings. Using tongs, lift the onion rings from the batter, allowing any excess to drip off, and carefully transfer them to the hot oil. Fry the onion rings until they are golden brown and puffed, about 3 minutes per batch. Drain on paper towels and season lightly with salt. Repeat with the remaining onion rings and batter; serve hot.

SIPHON SOURCE
The 1-pint iSi Gourmet Whip Plus is sold at *amazon.com* for $83; 24 cream (N₂O) cartridges are $17.

SIPHON-BATTERED ONION RINGS, STEP-BY-STEP

1 DISPENSE With the siphon upside down, press the handle to dispense enough batter to coat the rings.

2 FRY Lift the onion rings from the batter, allowing any excess to drip off, then fry until crisp.

3 DRAIN Transfer the fried onion rings to paper towels and allow to drain. Season with salt and eat hot.

BLAIS ON THE JOY OF THE SIPHON

"YOU CAN TAKE HEAVY THINGS AND MAKE THEM LIGHTER."

Blais turns cucumbers into pickles in under two hours.

THE LIGHTEST **SAUCE**

Foams may seem passé, an overused chef trick. But their airy consistency can help make a good dish great. Consider the blue-cheese foam here, made by loading a home-made blue-cheese dressing into a siphon and charging it with gas. Whether you're serving the dressing with an iceberg-lettuce wedge that is all about cool crunch, or eating it with hot and crispy chicken wings, the light and frothy texture is a wonderful contrast.

Blue-Cheese Foam
ACTIVE: 10 MIN; TOTAL: 50 MIN
MAKES ABOUT 2½ CUPS OF FOAM ● ●

- ½ cup full-fat sour cream
- ½ cup buttermilk
- 1½ ounces blue cheese, crumbled (¼ cup)
- 1 tablespoon red wine vinegar

Kosher salt

1. Combine everything except the salt in a blender and puree until very smooth. Season the mixture with salt and pour it into the canister of a 1-pint iSi Gourmet Whip Plus siphon. Charge the siphon with one iSi cream (N₂O) cartridge according to the manufacturer's instructions. Shake the siphon and refrigerate until well chilled, 30 minutes.

2. To serve, hold the siphon upside down and shake it. Press the lever to release the blue-cheese foam.

SERVE WITH Sliced tomatoes, iceberg lettuce wedges, fresh figs or buffalo chicken wings.

THE QUICKEST **PICKLES** EVER

Even so-called quick pickles can take several hours or overnight to marinate. But fill a siphon with pickle ingredients and charge it with pressurized gas, and the brine penetrates deep into the vegetable in a matter of minutes. In addition to the cucumber in this bread-and-butter-pickle recipe, try the method with other thinly sliced vegetables, like red onion, radishes and okra.

Quick Bread-and-Butter Pickles
ACTIVE: 30 MIN; TOTAL: 1 HR 30 MIN
MAKES 2 CUPS ● ● ○

- ½ English cucumber (½ pound), sliced crosswise ⅛ inch thick
- ½ small onion, very thinly sliced
- 3 tablespoons kosher salt
- ½ cup apple cider vinegar
- ¼ cup sugar
- ½ small jalapeño, chopped
- ½ teaspoon celery seeds
- ½ teaspoon ground turmeric
- ¼ teaspoon jarred grated horseradish

1. In a large colander, toss the cucumber and onion with 2 tablespoons of the salt and let stand for 10 minutes. Rinse the cucumber and onion and drain well.

2. Meanwhile, in a medium saucepan, combine the remaining 1 tablespoon of kosher salt with 1 cup of water and the vinegar, sugar, jalapeño, celery seeds, turmeric and horseradish; bring just to a boil, stirring to dissolve the salt and sugar. Remove the brine from the heat. Add the cucumber and onion and let cool completely; you should have a total of 2 cups.

3. Transfer the cucumber and onion with the brine to the canister of a 1-pint iSi Gourmet Whip Plus siphon. Seal the siphon and charge it with one iSi cream (N₂O) cartridge according to the manufacturer's instructions. Shake the siphon to distribute the gas and refrigerate for 20 minutes.

4. Hold a measuring cup upside down over the nozzle to catch any liquid. With the siphon in an upright position, very gently press the handle to release the gas. When all of the gas has been released, unscrew the top. Pour the pickles into a bowl or jar and serve.

MAKE AHEAD The pickles can be refrigerated in their brine for up to 2 weeks.

Curried Puffed Grains

TOTAL: 25 MIN PLUS COOLING
4 SERVINGS ● ● ●

Crisp puffed grains seasoned with a home-made curry mix add a texture and flavor jolt to dishes. They make a fun topping for twice-baked sweet potatoes.

- ¼ cup extra-virgin olive oil
- ¼ cup pure maple syrup
- ¾ teaspoon Madras curry powder
- ¼ teaspoon cayenne pepper

Kosher salt
- 4 cups mixed puffed grains, such as rice, wheat, corn and millet

Preheat the oven to 325°. In a large bowl, combine the olive oil with the maple syrup, curry powder and cayenne and season with salt. Add the puffed grains and stir to coat. Spread in an even layer on a parchment paper–lined baking sheet and bake, stirring twice, until lightly browned, about 20 minutes; the mix will crisp as it cools. Break up any big clumps. —Grace Parisi

Quinoa Crispies

ACTIVE: 20 MIN; TOTAL: 1 HR
MAKES ½ CUP ● ● ●

Quinoa crisps up quickly in a pan, making it perfect for adding crunch to everything from roasted vegetables to deviled eggs.

- ¼ cup white or red quinoa

Vegetable oil, for frying
Kosher salt

1. In a medium saucepan of salted boiling water, cook the quinoa until just tender, 12 minutes. Drain well in a fine sieve; spread on a rimmed baking sheet. Let stand, tossing occasionally, until cooled and dry, 30 minutes.
2. Set a fine sieve over a heatproof bowl. In a medium skillet, heat ¼ inch of oil until shimmering. Add the quinoa and fry over moderate heat, stirring, until the sizzling subsides and the quinoa is crisp, about 2 minutes. Drain in the sieve and transfer to paper towels. Season with salt.
—Justin Chapple

Pickled Cucumbers with Sichuan Pepper and Chiles

TOTAL: 30 MIN PLUS OVERNIGHT
PICKLING • MAKES 1 QUART ● ● ●

- 1½ pounds Kirby cucumbers—peeled in stripes, halved lengthwise, seeded and sliced crosswise ¼ inch thick
- ½ cup unseasoned rice vinegar
- ¼ cup white soy sauce (see Note)
- 3 tablespoons fresh grapefruit juice
- 2 tablespoons fresh lime juice
- 2 tablespoons honey
- 1 tablespoon *sambal oelek*
- 3 dried hot chiles, such as Chinese
- 2 whole cloves
- ½ teaspoon Sichuan peppercorns
- 1 star anise pod
- ½ teaspoon coriander seeds

1. Fill a large heatproof jar with the cucumbers. Add the rice vinegar, white soy sauce, grapefruit juice, lime juice, honey, *sambal oelek* and 1 cup of water.
2. In a skillet, toast the chiles, cloves, Sichuan peppercorns, star anise and coriander seeds over moderate heat until fragrant, about 2 minutes. Add the hot spices to the jar, cover and shake until evenly distributed. Refrigerate overnight before serving.
—Erik Bruner-Yang

NOTE Look for white soy sauce, a lighter-colored soy sauce, at Asian markets.
MAKE AHEAD The pickles can be refrigerated for up to 1 week.

Raspberry Vinegar

ACTIVE: 5 MIN; TOTAL: 2 WEEKS
MAKES ABOUT 3 CUPS ● ● ●

- 24 ounces raspberries, rinsed and dried

One 17-ounce bottle Champagne vinegar

In a 1-quart jar, combine the berries with the vinegar. Cover tightly and let stand at room temperature for at least 2 weeks and up to 3 weeks. Strain the vinegar into a clean bottle. —Dan Barber

Spiced and Pickled Blackberries

TOTAL: 20 MIN PLUS 1 WEEK PICKLING
MAKES 4½ CUPS ● ● ●

These tart, plump pickled berries are terrific in salads or served alongside cured meats.

- 8 black peppercorns
- 3 allspice berries
- 2 juniper berries

One ½-inch piece of peeled fresh ginger, thinly sliced
- 1 small bay leaf
- 2 cups red wine vinegar
- 3 tablespoons kosher salt
- 6 tablespoons sugar
- 1 shallot, quartered lengthwise
- 1 thyme sprig
- 18 ounces blackberries

1. In a mortar, lightly crush the peppercorns, allspice, juniper, ginger and bay leaf. Transfer to a medium saucepan; add the vinegar, salt, sugar, shallot, thyme and 2 cups of water. Bring just to a boil, stirring to dissolve the sugar and salt. Let the brine cool completely.
2. Strain the brine into clean glass jars; add the berries. Cover and refrigerate for at least 1 week before serving. —Steven Satterfield

Herbed and Spiced Plum Compote

TOTAL: 45 MIN PLUS 2 HR CHILLING
MAKES ABOUT 4½ CUPS ● ● ●

- 2 pounds firm black or prune plums, pitted and chopped
- 2 tablespoons sugar
- 1 large garlic clove, finely grated
- 1 teaspoon dried savory or mint, crushed
- ¾ teaspoon ground coriander
- ½ teaspoon Aleppo pepper
- ¼ teaspoon ground fenugreek

Pinch of cinnamon
Kosher salt and freshly ground pepper
- ¼ cup packed cilantro, minced
- 2 scallions, thinly sliced
- 2 tablespoons minced parsley
- 2 tablespoons minced tarragon

● HEALTHY ● MAKE AHEAD ● VEGETARIAN ● STAFF FAVORITE

1. In a medium saucepan, combine the plums with ½ cup of water and bring to a boil. Simmer over moderate heat, stirring often, until the plums are falling apart, about 20 minutes. Add the sugar and garlic and cook, stirring, until the sugar is dissolved, about 2 minutes. Remove the compote from the heat and let cool.

2. Meanwhile, in a small skillet, combine the savory, coriander, Aleppo pepper, fenugreek and cinnamon. Toast the spices over moderate heat, shaking the pan, until fragrant, about 1 minute.

3. Stir the spices into the compote and season with salt and pepper. Scrape into a bowl, cover with plastic and refrigerate until well chilled, about 2 hours. Fold in the cilantro, scallions, parsley and tarragon just before serving. —*Anya von Bremzen*

Carrot Jam

TOTAL: 1 HR PLUS
OVERNIGHT MACERATING
MAKES NINE ½-PINT JARS ● ● ●

Cookbook author Eugenia Bone loves giving this beautiful, easy-to-make jam as a gift. "I write all over the jar," she says. "Great on a mozz sandwich! Eat me with pot roast!" The jam is also fantastic on a cheese plate or spooned on fresh ricotta for an unexpected and delicious hors d'oeuvre.

    4 pounds carrots, coarsely
       shredded (about 18 cups)
    6 cups sugar
    2 tablespoons finely grated
       lemon zest
    1 cup fresh lemon juice (8 lemons)
    2 teaspoons kosher salt
Three 3-inch cinnamon sticks
   12 whole cloves
Big pinch of freshly grated nutmeg

1. In a large enameled cast-iron casserole or heavy pot, combine the carrots, sugar, lemon zest, lemon juice and salt; mix well. Wrap the cinnamon sticks and cloves in a double layer of cheesecloth and tie into a bundle. Tuck the bundle into the carrots. Cover and refrigerate overnight.

2. Add the nutmeg and ½ cup of water to the carrots and bring to a boil. Cook over moderately high heat, stirring occasionally, until the carrots are shiny and the liquid is syrupy, about 40 minutes. Discard the spice bundle. Let the carrot jam cool to room temperature, then refrigerate. —*Eugenia Bone*

Onion-Clove Compote
📷 PAGE 353
TOTAL: 1 HR 30 MIN • MAKES 2 CUPS ● ● ○

    2 tablespoons unsalted butter
    3 yellow onions (2 pounds), thinly
       sliced crosswise
    5 whole cloves
Kosher salt

In a large, shallow pot, melt the butter. Add the onions and cloves and season with salt. Cook over low heat, stirring frequently, until the onions are very soft but not browned, 1 to 1½ hours. Add water by the tablespoon if the onions get too dry. Discard the cloves. Serve warm. —*Wylie Dufresne*

SERVE WITH Grilled steak or shrimp, poultry, sandwiches or soup.

Matcha-Dusted
Caramel Almonds
⏱ ACTIVE: 15 MIN; TOTAL: 45 MIN
MAKES ABOUT 3 CUPS ● ○

    ½ cup sugar
    1 tablespoon unsalted butter
Big pinch of salt
    ½ pound unsalted roasted almonds
       (1½ cups)
    3 tablespoons matcha green tea
       powder (see Note)

1. Line a baking sheet with parchment paper. In a small saucepan, combine the sugar with 2 tablespoons of water and cook over moderate heat, swirling the pan, until the sugar dissolves, about 3 minutes. Continue to cook, brushing down the side of the pan with a wet pastry brush, until a deep-amber caramel forms, 3 to 5 minutes. Remove the pan from the heat and whisk in the butter and salt. Add

the almonds and quickly stir to coat them in the caramel. Scrape the almonds onto the prepared baking sheet and, using a spatula, spread in a single layer; let cool.

2. Sift the matcha into a large bowl. Break the nut clusters into single nuts. In batches, toss the nuts in the matcha, then toss the nuts in a sieve to shake off any excess powder. Transfer to a bowl and serve. —*Kay Chun*
NOTE Matcha is available at Asian markets, tea shops and *amazon.com*.

Soft Vanilla Bean Caramels
TOTAL: 45 MIN PLUS 4 HR COOLING
MAKES ABOUT 2 POUNDS ● ○

  2½ cups sugar
    2 cups heavy cream
    ¾ cup light corn syrup
    1 vanilla bean, split lengthwise and
       seeds scraped
    1 stick unsalted butter, cut into
       tablespoons and softened
    ½ teaspoon kosher salt

1. Coat a 9-by-13-inch baking pan with non-stick cooking spray and line it with parchment paper, leaving 1 inch of overhang on each of the long sides.

2. In a large saucepan, combine the sugar with the cream, corn syrup and vanilla bean and seeds and bring to a boil. Cook over moderately high heat, stirring occasionally, until the temperature reaches 233° on a candy thermometer, about 13 minutes. Carefully whisk in the butter and salt and cook, stirring constantly, until the caramel is golden and reaches 244° on a candy thermometer, about 7 minutes longer. Carefully pick out and discard the vanilla bean. Immediately pour the hot caramel into the prepared pan and let cool at room temperature until set, at least 4 hours or overnight.

3. Holding the parchment paper overhang, transfer the cooled caramel to a work surface. Using a sharp knife, cut the firmed-up caramel into squares. Wrap each caramel in a square of parchment paper or a candy wrapper and twist the ends to seal. Serve, store or gift the caramels. —*Chris Hanmer*

DIY MARMALADE

Active: 2 hr; Total: 3 days · Makes ten ½-pint jars

In its complex balance of bitter and sweet, marmalade is the thinking man's jam. **RACHEL SAUNDERS** of Blue Chair Fruit Company shows how to make three flavors—all prepared with the same base.

This recipe takes 3 days to make, but the active time is minimal—about 2 hours. Follow the instructions below to know what steps to tackle on each of the 3 days.

PREPARE THE LEMON JELLY BASE

DAY 1 Cut 2 pounds of lemons into 8 wedges each. In a large nonreactive saucepan, cover them with 2 inches of water (about 8 cups) and let stand at room temperature overnight.

DAY 2 Bring the lemons to a boil. Simmer over moderate heat, stirring occasionally, until very tender and the liquid is reduced by half, about 2 hours and 15 minutes. Pour the lemons into a fine sieve set over a large heatproof bowl; let cool completely. Wrap the sieve and bowl with plastic and let drain overnight at room temperature; discard the lemon wedges.

CHOOSE YOUR MARMALADE FLAVOR

Meyer Lemon Marmalade

  2 pounds Meyer lemons—
    cut lengthwise into 8 wedges
    each, seeded and very
    thinly sliced crosswise
Lemon Jelly Base (recipe above)
7½ cups sugar (3¼ pounds)
  ¼ cup fresh lemon juice

DAY 2 In a large nonreactive saucepan, cover the Meyer lemon slices with 1 inch of water (about 4 cups) and let stand covered at room temperature overnight.

DAY 3 Bring the Meyer lemons to a boil. Simmer over moderate heat, stirring occasionally, until the lemons are very tender, about 40 minutes. Add the Lemon Jelly Base to the saucepan. Stir in the sugar and lemon juice and bring to a boil. Simmer over moderate heat, without stirring, until the marmalade darkens slightly, about 30 minutes; skim off any foam as necessary.

Lemon Marmalade

  2 pounds lemons—
    cut lengthwise into 8 wedges
    each, seeded and very
    thinly sliced crosswise
Lemon Jelly Base (recipe above)
8½ cups sugar (3¾ pounds)
  ¼ cup fresh lemon juice

DAY 2 In a large nonreactive saucepan, cover the lemons with 2 inches of water; bring to a boil. Simmer over moderately high heat for 5 minutes, stirring occasionally. Drain in a fine strainer; discard the cooking liquid. Return the lemons to the pan; cover with 1 inch of water. Bring to a boil; simmer over moderate heat, stirring occasionally, until the lemons are very tender, 40 minutes; let stand covered at room temperature overnight.

DAY 3 Add the jelly base to the lemons in the pan. Stir in the sugar and lemon juice; bring to a boil. Simmer over moderate heat, without stirring, until darkened slightly, 30 minutes; skim off any foam as necessary.

Valencia Orange Marmalade

  2 pounds Valencia oranges—
    cut lengthwise into 8 wedges
    each, seeded and very
    thinly sliced crosswise
Lemon Jelly Base (recipe above)
  8 cups sugar (3½ pounds)
  ¼ cup fresh lemon juice

DAY 1 In a large nonreactive saucepan, cover the oranges with 2 inches of water (about 8 cups). Let stand overnight.

DAY 2 Bring the oranges to a boil and simmer over moderate heat, stirring occasionally, until the oranges are very tender, about 40 minutes. Let stand covered at room temperature overnight.

DAY 3 Add the Lemon Jelly Base to the oranges in the saucepan. Stir in the sugar and lemon juice and bring to a boil. Simmer over moderate heat, without stirring, until the marmalade darkens slightly, about 30 minutes; skim off any foam as necessary.

FINISH & JAR

FINISH Spoon 1 tablespoon of the marmalade onto a chilled plate and refrigerate until it is room temperature, about 3 minutes; the marmalade is ready when it thickens like jelly. If it's not ready yet, continue simmering and testing every 10 minutes until it passes the test, up to 1 hour and 30 minutes.

JAR Spoon the marmalade into ten ½-pint canning jars, leaving ¼ inch of space at the top. Screw on the lids. Using canning tongs, lower the jars into a large pot of boiling water; boil for 15 minutes. Remove the jars with the tongs; let stand until the lids seal. Store the marmalade in a cool, dark place for up to 6 months.

LEMON JELLY BASE, STEP-BY-STEP

1 **SOAK** Cover the lemon wedges with water and let stand overnight.

2 **COOK** Simmer until very tender and the liquid is reduced by half.

3 **DRAIN** Drain the Lemon Jelly Base overnight on the countertop.

LEMON MARMALADE, STEP-BY-STEP

1 **IMMERSE** Cover the lemon slices with 2 inches of water.

2 **COOK** Bring the lemon slices to a boil and simmer for 5 minutes.

3 **DRAIN** Strain through a fine sieve, add fresh water and cook once more.

4 **BLEND** Add the Lemon Jelly Base, sugar and lemon juice and cook.

5 **TEST** Spoon the marmalade onto a chilled plate and let cool.

6 **FINISH** Stop cooking when the marmalade gels at room temperature.

No-Cook Strawberry Jam

ACTIVE: 30 MIN; TOTAL: 2 HR
MAKES 4½ CUPS ● ● ●

Made with instant pectin, this gingery strawberry jam is amazingly fresh-tasting. Instead of canning the jam in hot water, store it in the freezer to maintain its just-picked flavor.

1½ cups sugar
¼ cup plus 2 tablespoons
    Ball RealFruit Instant Pectin
2 pounds strawberries,
   hulled and quartered
2½ tablespoons fresh lemon juice
2½ tablespoons finely grated
    peeled fresh ginger
Pinch of kosher salt

1. In a large bowl, whisk the sugar with the pectin. In a food processor, pulse half of the strawberries until finely chopped, then transfer them to the sugar mixture. Repeat with the remaining strawberries. Add the lemon juice, ginger and salt and stir until the sugar is dissolved, 5 minutes.

2. Spoon the jam into clean glass jars or plastic containers, leaving ¾ inch of space at the top. Let the jam stand at room temperature until slightly thickened, 30 minutes. Refrigerate until the jam is chilled and set, 1 hour.
—Justin Chapple

Blue-Barb Jam

TOTAL: 40 MIN PLUS CHILLING
MAKES 4 CUPS ● ● ●

This lively blueberry-and-rhubarb jam has just the right balance of sweetness and tang.

1 pound rhubarb stalks,
   cut into 1-inch pieces
1 pound blueberries
3 cups sugar
2 tablespoons fresh lemon juice
Pinch of salt

1. In a large saucepan, combine all of the ingredients. Cook over moderately high heat, stirring constantly, skimming off any foam, until the berries have burst and the rhubarb is soft, 12 minutes. Remove from the heat.

2. Using a wooden spoon, mash the rhubarb and blueberries against the side of the saucepan. Simmer the jam over moderate heat, stirring occasionally, until thickened, about 10 minutes. Pour the jam into jars and let cool completely; refrigerate until well chilled.
—Jessica Koslow

Warm Chocolate-Almond Sauce

TOTAL: 10 MIN • MAKES 1¾ CUPS ● ●

A luscious chocolate sauce made with almond milk comes together in just 10 minutes. Drizzle it over ice cream and top with nuts for an indulgent but not-too-rich sundae.

1 cup sweetened almond milk
8 ounces bittersweet chocolate,
   chopped
⅛ teaspoon pure almond extract
Pinch of salt

In a small saucepan, heat the almond milk over moderate heat. When it is hot, remove from the heat and add the chocolate, almond extract and salt. Let stand until the chocolate is melted. Whisk until smooth. Serve warm.
—Grace Parisi

MAKE AHEAD The chocolate sauce can be refrigerated for up to 1 week. Reheat gently before serving.

Hazelnut-Chocolate Spread

TOTAL: 30 MIN • MAKES 3 CUPS ● ●

Creamy, nutty and chocolaty, this is what Nutella spread dreams of being. It's unbelievable in ice cream sandwiches or as a shortbread cookie frosting. Or use it in a more universally loved application: spread on hot buttered toast.

1 stick unsalted butter, softened
1 cup hazelnuts
7 ounces bittersweet chocolate,
   chopped
2 ounces unsweetened chocolate,
   chopped
1 can sweetened condensed milk
Pinch of salt
1 tablespoon boiling water

1. Preheat the oven to 350°. In a medium ovenproof skillet, melt 1 tablespoon of the butter. Add the hazelnuts and cook over moderate heat until just beginning to brown in spots, about 2 minutes. Transfer the skillet to the oven and roast the nuts for about 6 minutes, until the skins blister. Transfer the nuts to a clean kitchen towel and rub off the skins. Let the nuts cool.

2. In a food processor, combine the hazelnuts with both chocolates and process until the nuts are finely chopped and the chocolate just begins to melt, 4 minutes.

3. In a small saucepan, heat the sweetened condensed milk with the salt until hot. With the food processor on, add the hot condensed milk and process until incorporated. Add the remaining 7 tablespoons of butter and process until smooth, 2 minutes. Add the boiling water and process until creamy, 2 minutes longer. —Grace Parisi

Cranberry-Fig Chutney

TOTAL: 45 MIN PLUS COOLING
MAKES 2¾ CUPS ● ●

1 tablespoon extra-virgin olive oil
1 small red onion, chopped (¾ cup)
1 garlic clove, minced
¾ pound fresh Black Mission figs,
   stemmed and quartered
One 12-ounce bag fresh or
   frozen cranberries
6 tablespoons turbinado sugar
¼ cup red wine vinegar
1 teaspoon finely grated orange zest
½ cup fresh orange juice
½ star anise pod
One 4-inch cinnamon stick
Pinch of salt

In a large saucepan, heat the olive oil. Add the onion and garlic; cook over moderately high heat, stirring, until softened, 5 minutes. Add all of the remaining ingredients and ½ cup of water; bring to a boil. Simmer over low heat, stirring, until thick and jammy, 25 minutes. Let the chutney cool, then discard the star anise and cinnamon stick. —Tanya Holland
SERVE WITH Roast turkey or cheeses.

● HEALTHY ● MAKE AHEAD ○ VEGETARIAN ● STAFF FAVORITE

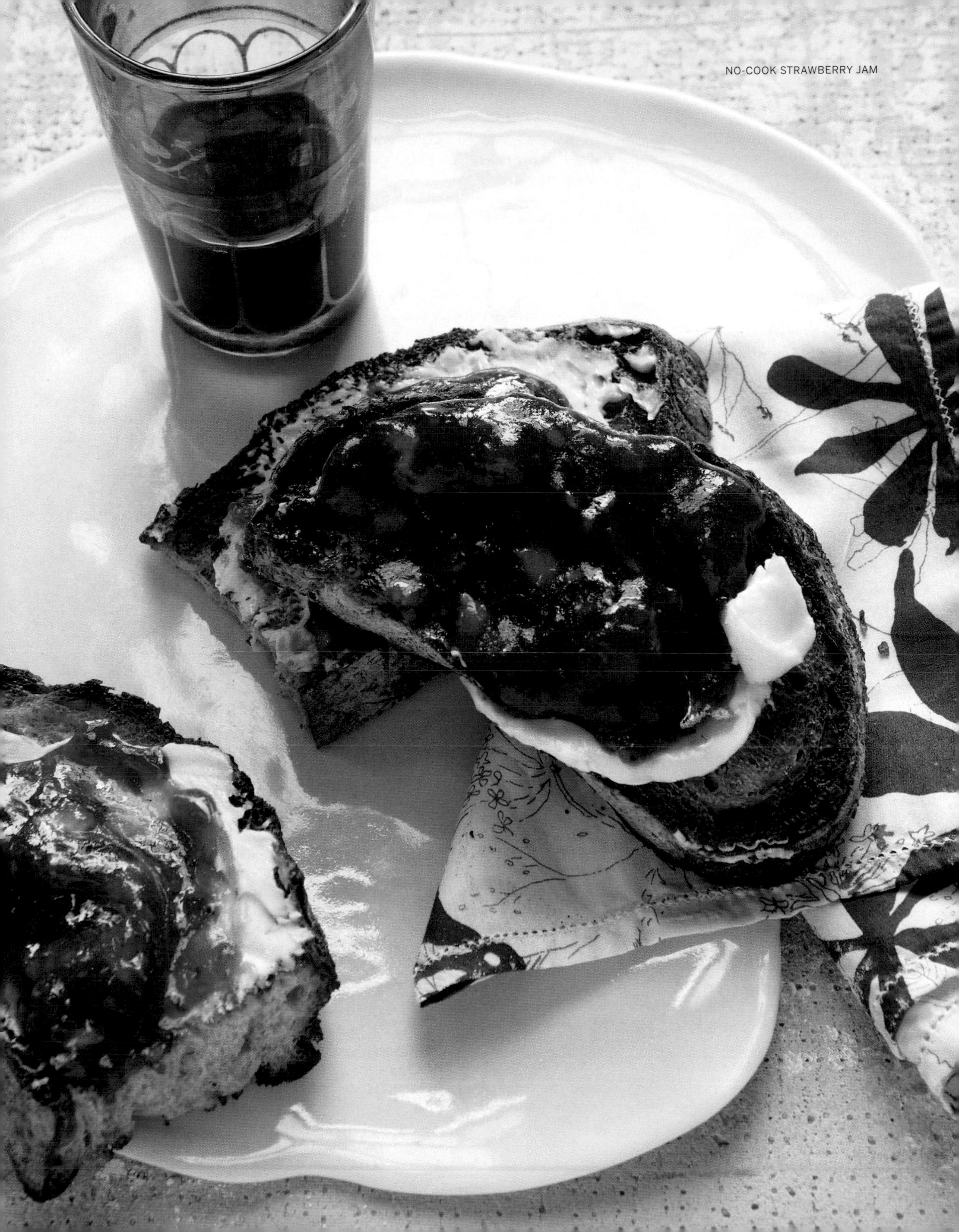

Cranberry-Apricot Chutney

TOTAL: 20 MIN PLUS COOLING
MAKES 2¼ CUPS ● ● ○

- 2 tablespoons vegetable oil
- 1 large shallot, finely chopped
- 1 garlic clove, minced
- ½ teaspoon cinnamon
- ¼ teaspoon ground cloves
- Pinch of freshly grated nutmeg
- 1 pound fresh or frozen cranberries
- ¾ cup dried apricots, finely chopped
- ¾ cup dark brown sugar
- ¼ cup apple cider vinegar
- 2 teaspoons fresh lemon juice
- Kosher salt and freshly ground pepper

In a medium saucepan, heat the oil. Add the shallot and garlic and cook over moderately high heat, stirring, until softened, 3 minutes. Add the cinnamon, cloves and nutmeg and cook, stirring, 2 minutes. Add the cranberries, apricots, sugar, vinegar and ¼ cup of water and cook, stirring, until the cranberries start to burst, 5 minutes. Mash some of the cranberries and cook, stirring, until the chutney thickens, about 5 minutes. Stir in the lemon juice; season with salt and pepper. Let cool before serving. —*Justin Chapple*

Smoky Turkey Gravy

TOTAL: 1 HR 45 MIN • MAKES 4 CUPS ● ●

- 2 tablespoons canola oil
- 2 turkey wings
- 1 turkey neck (optional)
- 1 pound chicken wings
- 1 smoked turkey leg
- 2 smoked turkey wings
- 1 small onion, chopped
- 2 carrots, chopped
- 1 head of garlic, halved
- 1 teaspoon whole black peppercorns
- 1 dried guajillo chile (optional)
- 2 quarts low-sodium chicken broth
- 2 tablespoons unsalted butter
- ¼ cup all-purpose flour
- 1 teaspoon pimentón de la Vera
    (sweet smoked Spanish paprika)
- Kosher salt and freshly ground pepper

1. In a large pot, heat the oil. Add the turkey wings, turkey neck (if using) and chicken wings and cook over moderately high heat until browned all over, 7 to 8 minutes; transfer to a baking sheet. Add the smoked turkey leg and wings to the pot and cook, turning, until lightly browned, 3 to 4 minutes; transfer to the baking sheet.
2. Add the onion, carrots, garlic, peppercorns and chile (if using) to the pot and cook over moderate heat, stirring, until the vegetables are golden, 5 minutes. Return all of the turkey and chicken to the pot along with any accumulated juices. Stir in the broth and 4 cups of water. Bring to a boil, cover partially and simmer until the stock is smoky and reduced to 5 cups, 1 hour. Strain the stock into a large bowl or measuring cup and discard the solids.
3. In a large saucepan, melt the butter. Whisk in the flour and cook over moderate heat, whisking, until the roux is tan, 3 minutes. Add the pimentón and cook, whisking, for 1 minute. Whisk in the strained stock and cook over moderate heat, whisking, until thickened, 5 minutes. Season the gravy with salt and pepper and serve warm. —*Kay Chun*

Tomato-Ginger Jelly

TOTAL: 45 MIN PLUS 12 HR CHILLING
MAKES FOUR ½-PINT JARS ● ●

A generous amount of ginger gives this bright tomato jelly its zing. Great with grilled white fish, roast pork or poached chicken, it can be refrigerated for three weeks.

- 6 medium tomatoes
- 2 cups white wine vinegar
- ¾ cup sugar
- 2 garlic cloves, minced
- 2 tablespoons minced fresh ginger
- Kosher salt and freshly ground pepper
- Low-sugar powdered pectin (see Note)

1. Bring a small saucepan of salted water to a boil. Using a sharp paring knife, score an "X" on the bottoms of the tomatoes. Blanch the tomatoes for 30 seconds, then drain. Slip off the skins and halve the tomatoes crosswise. Remove the seeds and coarsely chop the tomatoes.
2. In a medium saucepan, combine the vinegar and sugar and cook, stirring, until the sugar has dissolved. Add the tomatoes, garlic and ginger and cook over moderate heat for 5 minutes. Season with salt and pepper.
3. Working over a clean saucepan, pass the tomato mixture through a sieve, pressing on the solids. Bring to a boil. Add pectin according to the liquid ratios on the package and boil for 1 minute.
4. Funnel the hot jelly into 4 hot, sterilized ½-pint jars, leaving about ¼ inch of room on top. Screw on the lids securely. Using canning tongs, lower the jars into a pot of boiling water, making sure they are covered by at least 1 inch of water. Boil for 15 minutes, then transfer the jars to a rack to cool completely. Refrigerate until the jelly has set, at least 12 hours. —*Tom Colicchio*

NOTE Look for pectin (such as Sure-Jell or Pomona's) that is for use in less- or no-sugar-needed recipes at supermarkets.

Mario Batali's Essential Tomato Sauce

TOTAL: 1 HR • MAKES 5 CUPS ● ● ○

This excellent, all-purpose tomato sauce is flavored with a little shredded carrot and a good dose of caramelized garlic.

- ¼ cup extra-virgin olive oil
- 1 large onion, finely chopped
- 4 garlic cloves, thinly sliced
- ¼ cup finely shredded carrot
- 1 tablespoon finely chopped thyme
- Two 28-ounce cans whole peeled
    tomatoes with their juices, crushed
- Kosher salt

In a large saucepan, heat the oil until shimmering. Add the onion and garlic and cook over moderate heat, stirring occasionally, until softened and just starting to brown, 10 minutes. Add the carrot and thyme and cook, stirring, until the carrot is softened, about 5 minutes. Add the tomatoes and their juices and bring to a boil. Simmer over moderately low heat, stirring occasionally, until thickened and reduced to 5 cups, about 30 minutes. Season with salt. —*Mario Batali*

● HEALTHY ● MAKE AHEAD ○ VEGETARIAN ● STAFF FAVORITE

7-MINUTE SAUCES

CHIPOTLE

CHUTNEY

PEANUT

HARISSA

AIOLI

FOR CHICKEN
CHIPOTLE-MAPLE SAUCE

In a food processor, combine 2 seeded chipotles in adobo with ½ cup ketchup, 3 tablespoons cider vinegar, 1 tablespoon Worcestershire sauce, 2 tablespoons butter and ¼ cup pure maple syrup. Puree until smooth. Scrape the sauce into a small saucepan and simmer for 2 minutes, until glossy. Also good on beef and pork.

FOR RIBS
CHEATER'S CHUTNEY

In a small saucepan, simmer 2 tablespoons cider vinegar with 2 tablespoons small golden raisins and ½ teaspoon each of minced fresh ginger and curry powder over low heat until the vinegar is evaporated, 2 minutes. Stir in 1 minced scallion and ½ cup apricot preserves and season with salt. Also good on chicken and lamb.

FOR SHRIMP
SPICY PEANUT SAUCE

In a food processor or blender, combine ½ cup creamy peanut butter (preferably Skippy or Jif) with 2 tablespoons fresh lime juice, ½ cup unflavored coconut water, 1 tablespoon Asian fish sauce, 1 tablespoon *sambal oelek* or Sriracha, 1 garlic clove and 1 teaspoon minced fresh ginger. Puree until smooth. Also good on noodles, tofu and chicken.

FOR LAMB
HARISSA VINAIGRETTE

In a bowl, whisk 1 tablespoon *sambal oelek* or Sriracha with 1 tablespoon red wine vinegar, 1 teaspoon tomato paste and ½ teaspoon ground caraway seeds. Whisk in ¼ cup extra-virgin olive oil and season with salt and pepper. Also good on grilled chicken and fish.

FOR FISH
LEMON-CAPER AIOLI

In a small bowl, whisk ½ cup mayonnaise with 1 tablespoon fresh lemon juice, 1 tablespoon chopped capers, 2 teaspoons minced fresh tarragon and 1 minced garlic clove. Whisk in 2 tablespoons extra-virgin olive oil in a steady stream; season with salt and pepper. Also good on grilled pork and shellfish.
—*Grace Parisi*

Green Romesco

⏱ TOTAL: 45 MIN
MAKES 1½ CUPS ● ● ○ ○

This creamy Spanish almond sauce uses green bell and poblano peppers instead of the usual red peppers. It's lovely spread on corn or stirred into a fresh shell-bean stew.

- 1 medium green bell pepper, cored and cut into 2-inch chunks
- 1 large poblano chile, stemmed and cut into 2-inch pieces
- 2 garlic cloves, halved and peeled
- 1 tablespoon extra-virgin olive oil
- Salt and freshly ground black pepper
- ½ cup raw slivered almonds
- ½ cup cilantro leaves
- 1 teaspoon sherry vinegar

Preheat the oven to 400°. On a baking sheet, toss the bell pepper, poblano and garlic with the oil; season with salt and pepper. Roast for 25 minutes, until softened. Scatter the almonds on top and roast for 8 minutes, until lightly golden. Let cool slightly, then transfer to a food processor with the cilantro, vinegar and ½ cup of water; process to a chunky puree. Season the *romesco* with salt and pepper and serve. —*Richard Landau*

Miso Romesco

⏱ TOTAL: 30 MIN
MAKES ABOUT 1 CUP ● ● ○ ○ ○

- 3 roasted red bell peppers (6 ounces), drained and patted dry
- 1 tomato, cored and quartered
- ¼ cup plus 1 tablespoon olive oil
- 2 tablespoons *shiro* miso (light yellow)
- ¼ cup unsalted roasted almonds
- One 1-inch-thick slice of white bread, toasted and cut into 1-inch croutons
- 1 teaspoon red wine vinegar
- ¼ cup grapeseed or canola oil
- Kosher salt and freshly ground pepper

1. Preheat the oven to 450°. On a rimmed baking sheet, coat the bell peppers and tomato with 1 tablespoon of the olive oil and roast for 15 minutes.

2. In a blender, combine the roasted peppers, tomato, miso, almonds, croutons, vinegar and 2 tablespoons of water; puree until almost smooth. With the blender on, drizzle in the remaining olive oil and the grapeseed oil. Season with salt and pepper. —*Kay Chun*
SERVE WITH Roasted cauliflower.

Cajun Sofrito Ketchup

⏱ TOTAL: 25 MIN
MAKES 1½ CUPS ● ● ○

This doctored ketchup has a little extra kick, thanks to a hit of Cajun spices, and a chunky texture from sautéed vegetables (*sofrito*).

- 1 tablespoon extra-virgin olive oil
- ½ cup minced green bell pepper
- ½ cup minced onion
- 1 cup diced plum tomatoes
- 2 teaspoons Cajun spice blend
- 1 cup ketchup

In a skillet, heat the oil until shimmering. Add the pepper and onion; cook over moderately high heat, stirring, until lightly browned, 3 minutes. Add the tomatoes and Cajun spice and cook over moderate heat, stirring, until the tomatoes have broken down, 8 minutes. Off the heat, stir in the ketchup. Let cool, then transfer to a jar. —*Richard Landau*

Schmaltz Aioli

⏱ TOTAL: 20 MIN • MAKES ¾ CUP ●

Indispensable in Jewish cooking for generations, schmaltz (chicken fat) is a go-to fat for chefs like Evan Bloom of San Francisco's Wise Sons. He uses it to make this silky, rich aioli.

- 2 large egg yolks
- 2 teaspoons apple cider vinegar
- ½ small garlic clove, minced
- ½ cup vegetable oil
- ¼ cup schmaltz (chicken fat), melted and cooled slightly (see Note)
- 2 teaspoons minced tarragon
- 2 teaspoons minced parsley
- 1 teaspoon minced celery leaves (optional)
- ½ teaspoon minced savory or oregano
- Kosher salt and freshly ground pepper

In a medium bowl, whisk the egg yolks with the vinegar and garlic. Add a few drops of oil at a time, whisking constantly until the sauce starts to emulsify. When it starts to look creamy, gradually add the rest of the oil in a very thin stream, whisking constantly until a thick sauce forms. Whisk in the schmaltz in a thin stream until it is incorporated. Stir in the tarragon, parsley, celery leaves and savory. Season the aioli with salt and pepper. —*Evan Bloom*
SERVE WITH Fries or roasted vegetables.
NOTE Schmaltz is available in the refrigerated section of most supermarkets.

Mushroom XO Sauce

⏱ ACTIVE: 20 MIN; TOTAL: 45 MIN
MAKES 1 CUP ● ● ○

Instead of using the usual dried seafood to make this spicy, funky Chinese condiment, chef Richard Landau creates a vegan version with umami-rich shiitake mushrooms at Vedge in Philadelphia. It's terrific over simply cooked mild vegetables like zucchini or cauliflower.

- ½ pound shiitake mushrooms, stemmed and caps finely diced (4 cups)
- 1 tablespoon toasted sesame oil
- 1 teaspoon tamari
- 1 tablespoon fermented black beans, rinsed and mashed
- 2 teaspoons Sriracha
- 1 teaspoon rice vinegar
- 1 teaspoon sugar
- ¼ cup water

1. Preheat the oven to 450° and line a baking sheet with parchment paper. In a bowl, toss the mushrooms with the sesame oil. Spread the mushrooms out on the baking sheet and roast for 12 minutes, stirring once or twice, until dried and lightly browned.

2. Transfer the mushrooms to a bowl and stir in all of the remaining ingredients. Let stand for 30 minutes before serving. —*Richard Landau*
MAKE AHEAD The sauce can be refrigerated for up to 1 week.

● HEALTHY ● MAKE AHEAD ○ VEGETARIAN ● STAFF FAVORITE

FROM TOP: GREEN ROMESCO,
OLIVE BAGNA CAUDA (PAGE 12),
CAJUN SOFRITO KETCHUP

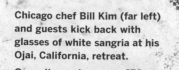

Chicago chef Bill Kim (far left) and guests kick back with glasses of white sangria at his Ojai, California, retreat.

Opposite: recipe, page 376.
RIESLING SANGRIA WITH LYCHEES

COCKTAILS,
PUNCHES
& MORE

Carpano and Soda

⏱ TOTAL: 5 MIN • MAKES 1 DRINK ● ●

Carpano Antica is a spicy, nutty, sweet Italian vermouth with a slightly bitter edge. Combine it with club soda and bitters for an ultra-refreshing aperitif.

Ice
1½ ounces Carpano Antica Formula or other sweet vermouth
3 ounces chilled club soda or seltzer
2 dashes of Angostura bitters
1 mint sprig, for garnish

Fill a rocks glass with ice. Pour the vermouth over the ice and top with the club soda. Stir, then garnish with the bitters and mint sprig. —Linda Aldredge

VARIATION For a boozier, more bitter drink, use the same amount of amaro (an Italian herbal liqueur) instead of Carpano Antica. Try an intensely bitter amaro, such as Luxardo Fernet; sweeter, earthy Amaro CioCiaro; or the minty S. Maria al Monte.

Kimchi Bloody Mary

ACTIVE: 30 MIN; TOTAL: 1 HR
MAKES 8 DRINKS ●

2 cups packed kimchi (16 ounces)
46 ounces tomato juice, such as Sacramento
¼ cup Sriracha
2 tablespoons Worcestershire sauce
2 tablespoons sherry vinegar
Salt and freshly ground pepper
16 ounces vodka
Ice
Mint sprigs or shiso leaves, for garnish

Working in batches, puree the kimchi with the tomato juice, Sriracha, Worcestershire and vinegar. Set a fine-mesh strainer over a bowl and strain the kimchi puree, pressing gently on the solids to extract as much juice as possible; you should have about 6 cups of kimchi-Mary mix. Discard the solids. Chill thoroughly, then season with salt and pepper and stir in the vodka. Serve over ice, garnished with mint or shiso. —Don Lee

My Clementine

TOTAL: 5 MIN PLUS 1 HR CHILLING
MAKES 8 DRINKS ●

Club soda adds fizz to this citrusy pitcher drink made with fresh-squeezed juice from clementines and limes.

14 ounces vodka
12 ounces fresh clementine juice
6 ounces fresh lime juice
6 ounces Aperol (bitter orange Italian aperitif)
4 ounces light agave nectar
Ice
12 ounces chilled club soda
8 lime wheels, for garnish

1. In a pitcher, combine the vodka, clementine and lime juices, Aperol and agave nectar; stir well. Refrigerate until chilled, 1 hour.
2. Working in batches, and filling with fresh ice each time, shake the drink in a cocktail shaker; strain into ice-filled collins glasses. Stir 1½ ounces of club soda into each glass and garnish. —Patricia Richards

Concord Grape Gin Fizz

⏱ TOTAL: 5 MIN • MAKES 1 DRINK ●

Frothy and not too sweet, this vibrant purple cocktail is like grape soda for grown-ups.

5 Concord grapes
2 ounces Concord grape juice
1½ ounces gin
1 ounce port
½ tablespoon fresh lemon juice
1 large egg white
1 teaspoon superfine sugar
Ice
Chilled soda water
1 lemon twist, for garnish

In a cocktail shaker, muddle the grapes until they've released a deep purple juice. Add the grape juice, gin, port, lemon juice, egg white and sugar and shake vigorously for 30 seconds. Add ice and shake for 1 more minute. Strain into a chilled collins glass, top with soda water and garnish with the lemon twist. —Allison Kave and Keavy Landreth

Evergreen Swizzle

TOTAL: 5 MIN PLUS 4 HR CHILLING
MAKES 12 DRINKS ● ●

18 ounces gin
6 ounces yellow Chartreuse
6 ounces Zirbenz (pine liqueur)
6 ounces strained fresh lime juice
12 small rosemary sprigs, for garnish

In a pitcher, combine the gin, Chartreuse, Zirbenz and lime juice with 18 ounces of water and stir well. Pour into 12 small bottles and chill for at least 4 hours, until very cold. Garnish each drink with a rosemary sprig. —Jamie Boudreau

Citrus Scandi

⏱ TOTAL: 5 MIN • MAKES 1 DRINK ●

1 orange wedge
1½ ounces vodka
¼ ounce aquavit
¼ ounce Cointreau or other triple sec
¾ ounce fresh grapefruit juice
Ice
1 orange twist

Squeeze the orange wedge into a cocktail shaker, drop it in, then add the vodka, aquavit, Cointreau and grapefruit juice. Fill the shaker with ice and shake well. Strain into a chilled coupe or 2 shot glasses; pinch the orange twist over the drink and discard. —Kathy Casey

12 Cases of Apples

TOTAL: 5 MIN PLUS 4 HR CHILLING
MAKES 12 DRINKS ● ●

12 ounces bonded apple brandy (preferably Laird's) or rum
12 ounces Lillet blanc
6 ounces Drambuie
24 dashes of Angostura bitters

In a pitcher, combine all of the ingredients with 18 ounces of water and stir well. Pour into 12 small bottles and chill for at least 4 hours, until very cold. —Jamie Boudreau

● HEALTHY ● MAKE AHEAD ● VEGETARIAN ● STAFF FAVORITE

CITRUS SCANDI

Smuggler's Coffee

TOTAL: 15 MIN • MAKES 1 DRINK ●

This hot coffee drink pays homage to the coffee beans and sugarcane that are grown at Belcampo Belize, an eco-lodge in southern Belize with its own distillery and sugarcane, coffee and cacao plantations.

½ cup hot strong coffee
2 teaspoons sugar
1 ounce gold rum
1 ounce dark rum
1 small cinnamon stick
1 long strip of orange zest, plus finely grated zest for garnish
Sweetened whipped cream and grated Mexican chocolate, for garnish

In a mug or heatproof glass, stir the coffee and sugar until the sugar dissolves. Stir in both rums, then add the cinnamon stick and the strip of orange zest. Garnish the drink with whipped cream, grated Mexican chocolate and grated orange zest.
—Matthew Runeare

Lady Marmalade

TOTAL: 5 MIN • MAKES 1 DRINK ●

Inspired by the Eat Real Festival in Oakland, California, a showcase for artisanal food products like jam, this rum cocktail includes orange marmalade, which lends a nicely sweet and bitter edge.

4 basil leaves
1½ teaspoons orange marmalade
1 teaspoon superfine sugar
2 ounces light rum, preferably Caliche
½ ounce fresh lime juice
¼ ounce Cointreau
Dash of orange bitters
Ice
1 ounce chilled club soda or seltzer

In a chilled collins glass, muddle the basil leaves with the orange marmalade and sugar. Stir in the rum, lime juice, Cointreau and bitters. Fill the glass with ice and stir well. Top with club soda and serve.
—Matthew Runeare

Mi Vida

TOTAL: 15 MIN PLUS 1 HR CHILLING
MAKES 8 DRINKS ●

10 ounces mezcal
10 ounces fresh grapefruit juice
8 ounces St-Germain elderflower liqueur
4 ounces fresh lime juice
2 ounces light agave nectar
3 tablespoons pink peppercorns, finely ground, mixed with ⅓ cup of superfine sugar
1 small lime wedge
Ice

1. In a pitcher, combine the mezcal, grapefruit juice, elderflower liqueur, lime juice and agave; stir well. Refrigerate until chilled, 1 hour.
2. Spread the peppercorn sugar on a small plate. Moisten the outer rim of 8 martini glasses or coupes with the lime wedge and coat lightly with the peppercorn sugar. Working in batches, and filling with fresh ice each time, shake the drink in a cocktail shaker, then strain into the prepared glasses.
—Patricia Richards

The Palomaesque Cocktail

TOTAL: 10 MIN • MAKES 1 DRINK ●

1 ounce smoky mezcal, such as Del Maguey Vida
1½ teaspoons honey
1½ ounces Cocchi Americano (Italian aperitif wine)
1 ounce fresh grapefruit juice
½ ounce fresh lime juice
Pinch of salt
Ice
1½ ounces chilled seltzer
½ grapefruit wheel

In a cocktail shaker, stir the mezcal with the honey until dissolved. Add the Cocchi Americano, grapefruit juice, lime juice and salt. Fill the shaker with ice and shake until well chilled. Fill a large glass with ice and add the seltzer and grapefruit wheel. Strain into the glass and serve. —Scott Baird

Amante Picante Margarita

TOTAL: 15 MIN PLUS 1 HR CHILLING
MAKES 8 DRINKS ●

Muddling in fresh jalapeño makes these cucumber-lime margaritas enticingly spicy.

½ large seedless English cucumber, thinly sliced, plus 8 slices for garnish
½ medium jalapeño, very thinly sliced
¼ cup cilantro, plus more for garnish
18 ounces silver tequila
8 ounces fresh lime juice
6 ounces light agave nectar
½ teaspoon celery bitters (optional)
1 lime wedge
¼ cup kosher salt mixed with 1 teaspoon finely grated lime zest
Ice

1. In a pitcher, muddle the ½ sliced cucumber with the jalapeño and ¼ cup of cilantro. Add the tequila, lime juice, agave and bitters and stir well. Refrigerate until chilled, 1 hour.
2. Moisten the rim of 8 rocks glasses with the lime wedge and coat with the lime salt. Working in batches, and filling with fresh ice each time, shake the drink in a cocktail shaker, then strain into the glasses. Garnish with cucumber and cilantro. —Patricia Richards

Black Dahlia

TOTAL: 5 MIN • MAKES 1 DRINK ●

Mezcal, the potent Mexican spirit made from roasted agave hearts, provides the smokiness for this terrific drink. Lemon juice and Grand Marnier give it a citrus kick.

1 ounce mezcal
¾ ounce Moscatel sherry
½ ounce Grand Marnier
½ ounce Zwack (spicy, herbal Hungarian liqueur)
¾ teaspoon fresh lemon juice
Ice
1 grapefruit twist, for garnish

In a mixing glass, combine all of the ingredients except ice and the garnish; fill with ice and stir well. Strain into a coupe and garnish with the grapefruit twist. —Leo Robitschek

● HEALTHY ● MAKE AHEAD ● VEGETARIAN ● STAFF FAVORITE

SMUGGLER'S COFFEE

The Blue Steel

⏱ TOTAL: 5 MIN • MAKES 1 DRINK ●

2   ounces gold rum
½   ounce Simple Syrup (recipe below)
½   ounce fresh lime juice
¼   ounce passion fruit juice
¼   ounce orgeat (almond-
       flavored syrup)
Dash of Angostura bitters
Crushed ice
½   ounce blue curaçao
Orange and lime wheels, for garnish

In a collins glass, combine the rum, Simple Syrup, lime and passion fruit juices, orgeat and bitters; stir well. Add crushed ice and stir with a swizzle stick or bar spoon, then pack more crushed ice on top. Pour the blue curaçao over the drink and garnish with orange and lime wheels. —*Kevin Diedrich*

Rhum and Funk

TOTAL: 10 MIN PLUS 4 HR STEEPING
MAKES 1 DRINK ●

This Cocoa Puffs–infused drink is the specialty at Miami's The Broken Shaker. "People go crazy for it," says co-owner Elad Zvi.

1   sugar cube
2   dashes of orange bitters
Dash of Angostura bitters
2½ ounces Cocoa Puffs Rhum
       (see Note)
Ice
1   spiral-cut orange twist, for garnish

SIMPLE SYRUP

A quick combination of sugar and water, this clear syrup is used to sweeten countless cocktails.

In a small saucepan, simmer 1 cup sugar with 1 cup water over moderate heat, stirring, until the sugar dissolves. Let the syrup cool completely, then refrigerate for up to 1 month. Makes about 12 ounces.

In a chilled rocks glass, muddle the sugar with both bitters and the Cocoa Puffs Rhum; fill with ice and and stir well. Garnish with the twist. —*Gabriel Orta and Elad Zvi*

NOTE To make Cocoa Puffs Rhum, combine 1½ cups Cocoa Puffs cereal and 8 ounces aged *rhum agricole* in a bowl; let stand at room temperature for 4 hours. Strain into a jar, cover and store at room temperature for up to 1 month. Makes about 8 ounces.

Orange-Scented Dark Rum and Dubonnet Aperitif

⏱ TOTAL: 5 MIN • MAKES 1 DRINK ●

Ice
2   ounces dark rum
1   ounce Dubonnet
¾   ounce dry French vermouth,
       such as Dolin
3   drops of orange flower water
Dash of orange bitters
1   orange twist

Fill a rocks glass with ice. In a mixing glass, stir the rum, Dubonnet, vermouth, orange flower water and orange bitters. Pour into the glass. Pinch the twist over the drink, rub it around the rim and add it to the cocktail. —*Daniel Gritzer*

Maple-Bourbon Smash

⏱ TOTAL: 5 MIN • MAKES 1 DRINK ●

½   ounce pure maple syrup, preferably
       Grade A dark amber
½   ounce fresh orange juice
¼   ounce fresh lemon juice
4   dashes of Angostura bitters
½   orange wheel
2   ounces bourbon
Ice
1½ ounces chilled seltzer

In a rocks glass, combine the maple syrup with the orange juice, lemon juice and bitters. Add the orange wheel and lightly muddle. Add the bourbon and stir well. Fill the glass with ice and top with the seltzer. —*Robb Turner*

Whiskey Chai

🕐 TOTAL: 25 MIN • 6 SERVINGS ●

This warm, boozy nightcap combines bourbon (or rye) with a mix of whole spices. For a shortcut, you can buy Chai Spice Blend from TeaSource (*teasource.com*).

2   cinnamon sticks, broken into pieces
20 black peppercorns
16 whole cloves
8   cardamom pods, seeds removed
       from the pods
1   teaspoon ground ginger
Pinch of freshly grated nutmeg
1   quart whole milk
¼   cup light brown sugar
1   tablespoon loose black tea
3   ounces bourbon or rye whiskey

1. In spice grinder, combine all of the spices and pulse to a powder.
2. In a saucepan, bring the milk to a simmer. Remove from the heat. Add the spices, sugar and tea and let stand for 10 minutes. Strain the chai into a bowl. Wipe out the saucepan.
3. Return the chai to the saucepan and rewarm over moderate heat. Stir in the whiskey and serve hot. —*Linda Aldredge*

Kenwood Flip

⏱ TOTAL: 5 MIN • MAKES 1 DRINK ●

This New Orleans–inspired bourbon cocktail is bold and pleasingly bitter, with an airy egg white foam on top.

3   strawberries, sliced
1   large egg
1   tablespoon fresh lime juice
1   teaspoon superfine sugar
2   ounces bourbon
½   ounce green Chartreuse
Ice
Dash of rhubarb bitters

In a cocktail shaker, muddle the strawberries with the egg, lime juice and sugar. Add the bourbon and Chartreuse and shake vigorously, until frothy. Add ice and shake until chilled. Strain into a martini glass and top with the bitters. —*David Kinch*

Brandy Old-Fashioneds

**ACTIVE: 20 MIN; TOTAL: 4 HR 30 MIN
PLUS OVERNIGHT MACERATING
MAKES 8 DRINKS PLUS EXTRA SYRUP** ●

- 1 cup sugar
- 5 navel oranges—zest strips cut from 3 of them, 8 wheels cut from the remaining 2 for garnish
- 8 maraschino cherries, plus 8 more for garnish

Ice

- 8 dashes of Bitter Truth Jerry Thomas' Own Decanter or Angostura bitters
- 16 ounces brandy
- 8 ounces chilled club soda

1. In a bowl, combine the sugar and zest. Rub between your fingers until the sugar is the texture of wet sand, 2 minutes. Cover and let stand for 4 hours, stirring occasionally. Stir in 8 cherries; refrigerate overnight.
2. Add 4 ounces of hot water to the orange-cherry sugar and stir to dissolve. Refrigerate the mixture until chilled. Strain the orange-cherry syrup into a jar.
3. Fill a large cocktail shaker with ice or work in batches with a regular shaker. Add 4 ounces of the orange-cherry syrup along with the bitters and brandy. Shake well, then strain into 8 ice-filled rocks glasses. Top each drink with 1 ounce of club soda and garnish with an orange wheel and a maraschino cherry.
—*Eben Freeman*

Maybelle Punch

**ACTIVE: 15 MIN; TOTAL: 30 MIN
MAKES 2 DRINKS** ●

Pernod, for rinsing

- 4 mint sprigs
- ½ ounce orange juice
- 3 dashes of celery bitters
- 1 ounce Ginger-Infused Simple Syrup (see Note)
- 2 ounces Cognac

Ice

- 2 ounces chilled ginger beer
- 2 fresh cherries and 2 strips of orange zest, for garnish

Rinse 2 Champagne coupes with Pernod; pour off the excess. In a cocktail shaker, muddle the mint with the orange juice, bitters and ginger syrup. Add the Cognac and ice and stir. Strain into the coupes and top with the ginger beer. Garnish each drink with a cherry and orange zest. —*David Kinch*
NOTE To make Ginger-Infused Simple Syrup, combine ½ cup each of water and sugar in a small saucepan and add ¼ cup shredded peeled fresh ginger. Simmer over low heat for 5 minutes. Let cool and strain.

Kansai Kick

TOTAL: 5 MIN • MAKES 1 DRINK ●
New York City mixologist John deBary makes this zippy drink with Japanese whisky, which is quite similar to Scotch.

- 1½ ounces Japanese whisky, preferably Yamazaki 12-year-old
- ¾ ounce Sercial Madeira
- ¾ ounce fresh lime juice

Scant ½ ounce orgeat (almond-flavored syrup)

Ice

In a cocktail shaker, combine the whisky, Madeira, lime juice and orgeat. Add ice; shake well. Strain into a chilled coupe. —*John deBary*

Sufferin' Sassafras!

**TOTAL: 5 MIN PLUS 4 HR CHILLING
MAKES 12 DRINKS** ●●
Instead of making cocktails one at a time, you can premix this drink in a large batch and serve it in small bottles.

- 12 ounces bonded rye
- 12 ounces Punt e Mes
- 3 ounces root-beer liqueur, preferably Art in the Age Root
- 1½ ounces allspice liqueur, preferably St. Elizabeth Allspice Dram
- 12 orange twists, for serving

In a pitcher, combine the rye, Punt e Mes, both liqueurs and 24 ounces water; stir well. Pour into 12 small bottles; chill for at least 4 hours. Serve with orange twists. —*Jamie Boudreau*

Georgia on My Mind

**TOTAL: 5 MIN PLUS 1 HR CHILLING
MAKES 8 DRINKS** ●●●

- ⅓ cup lightly packed mint leaves, plus small mint sprigs for garnish
- 12 ounces bourbon
- 4 ounces crème de pêche (peach liqueur)
- 4 ounces fresh lemon juice
- 2 ounces pure maple syrup
- 24 ounces chilled apricot or peach ale, such as Samuel Smith's Organic Apricot Ale

Ice

1. In a pitcher, combine all of the ingredients except the ale, ice and mint sprigs and stir until the maple syrup is dissolved. Refrigerate until chilled, about 1 hour.
2. Add the apricot ale to the pitcher; stir well. Pour into 8 ice-filled highball glasses and garnish with mint sprigs. —*Patricia Richards*

Aqua di Vida Spiced Sangria

**TOTAL: 15 MIN PLUS 1 HR CHILLING
8 SERVINGS** ●●

One 750-milliliter bottle dry red wine, preferably Tannat (see Note)

- 8 ounces brandy
- 6 ounces fresh orange juice
- 6 ounces fresh lemon juice
- ½ cup confectioners' sugar
- 1 orange, thinly sliced crosswise
- 1 Pink Lady apple, thinly sliced crosswise
- 6 whole cloves
- 2 star anise pods
- 12 ounces chilled dry sparkling wine, such as cava

Ice, for serving

In a large pitcher, combine all of the ingredients except the sparkling wine and ice. Refrigerate until well chilled, at least 1 hour. Add the sparkling wine and serve over ice. —*Matthew Runeare*
NOTE Tannat, Uruguay's primary red grape, makes big, burly red wines.

Grilled Citrus and Grape Sangria

ACTIVE: 20 MIN; TOTAL: 1 HR 45 MIN
6 TO 8 SERVINGS ● ○ ○

Grilled oranges, lemons and grapes add a wonderful, subtle smokiness to sangria.

- 3 cups stemmed seedless red grapes
- 2 oranges and 2 lemons, cut crosswise into ½-inch wheels
- Two 750-milliliter bottles rosé
- 8 ounces Simple Syrup (page 374)
- 8 ounces brandy
- Ice

1. Light a hardwood charcoal fire. Put the grapes on a perforated grill sheet or in a grill basket; grill over high heat, tossing occasionally, until they just start to burst, about 6 minutes. Transfer to a plate to cool completely.
2. Meanwhile, grill the orange and lemon wheels over high heat, turning once, until lightly charred, about 6 minutes. Transfer to a plate to cool completely.
3. In a large pitcher, combine the wine with the Simple Syrup, brandy and grilled fruit and stir well. Refrigerate until the sangria is chilled and the flavors are blended, at least 1 hour and up to 8 hours. Serve the sangria over ice. —Michael Chiarello

Riesling Sangria with Lychees

📷 PAGE 369
TOTAL: 20 MIN PLUS 1 HR CHILLING
10 SERVINGS ● ○

- 1 orange
- 1 cup raspberries, halved
- 1 Asian pear—peeled, cored and thinly sliced
- 4 ounces dry sake
- 4 ounces bourbon
- 4 ounces fresh lemon juice
- 4 ounces triple sec
- 2 tablespoons sugar
- One 20-ounce can lychees in syrup— lychees halved, syrup reserved
- 2 chilled 750-milliliter bottles slightly off-dry Riesling
- Ice

1. Using a knife, peel the orange, removing the bitter white pith. Working over a pitcher, cut in between the membranes to release the sections. Squeeze the juice from the membranes into the pitcher and discard the membranes. Add the raspberries, pear, sake, bourbon, lemon juice, triple sec, sugar and lychees with their syrup. Refrigerate until chilled, at least 1 hour.
2. Stir in the Riesling and serve the sangria in ice-filled wineglasses. —Bill Kim

Egg Creams with Spiced Chocolate Syrup

ACTIVE: 15 MIN; TOTAL: 1 HR
MAKES 7 EGG CREAMS ● ○

Inspired by the soda fountains of her mother's Brooklyn childhood, mixologist Gina Chersevani created this delicious egg cream soda, which starts with homemade chocolate syrup spiced with cardamom, black peppercorns and cinnamon. One old-school touch: a pinch of citric acid, for tartness.

- 5 green cardamom pods
- 2 tablespoons whole black peppercorns
- 1 cinnamon stick, cracked
- 1 cup sugar
- ½ cup unsweetened Dutch-process cocoa powder
- Ice
- Heavy cream, citric acid (optional, see Note) and seltzer, for serving

1. In a small saucepan, toast the cardamom, peppercorns and cinnamon over moderate heat until fragrant, 2 minutes. Add 1 cup of water and bring to a boil. Remove from the heat; let stand for 15 minutes. Stir in the sugar and cocoa; return to a simmer. Cook for 5 minutes over low heat. Cool the syrup, then strain into a jar or plastic container.
2. For each soda, in a tall ice-filled glass, stir ¼ cup of the syrup with 1 tablespoon of heavy cream and a pinch of citric acid. Top with seltzer, stir and serve. —Gina Chersevani
NOTE Citric acid is sold at vitamin shops, well-stocked grocery stores and online at williams-sonoma.com.

Frosty Strawberry-and-Cream Milk Shakes

⏱ TOTAL: 5 MIN • MAKES 4 SHAKES ● ●

- 1 pint vanilla ice cream, softened
- ½ cup whole milk
- 1 pound strawberries, hulled and quartered
- 2 teaspoons finely grated lemon zest

In a blender, puree the ice cream and milk until smooth. Pour into 4 glasses. Rinse out the blender. Add the strawberries and zest; puree. Top the milk shakes with some of the strawberry puree and serve. —Kay Chun

Horchata Milk Shakes

TOTAL: 30 MIN PLUS 3 HR SOAKING
MAKES 5 CUPS ○

- 1 cup long-grain white rice, rinsed well
- 4 medium cinnamon sticks, cracked
- ¼ cup sliced almonds
- 1 tablespoon plus ¼ teaspoon ground cinnamon
- 1 tablespoon sugar
- ¼ cup plus 2 tablespoons sweetened condensed milk
- ½ banana (2 ounces)
- 1 pint vanilla ice cream
- ½ cup ice

1. In a bowl, cover the rice with 3 cups of water. Add the cinnamon sticks; let stand at room temperature for at least 3 hours or overnight; discard the cinnamon sticks.
2. Meanwhile, in a skillet, toast the almonds over moderate heat, tossing, until fragrant, 3 minutes. In a bowl, blend 1 tablespoon of the ground cinnamon with the sugar.
3. Transfer the rice and its liquid to a blender. Add the almonds; puree for 2 minutes. Strain the horchata through a fine sieve into a bowl. Rinse out the blender.
4. Return the horchata to the blender. Add the condensed milk, banana and the remaining ¼ teaspoon of cinnamon and puree. Add the ice cream and ice and blend. Pour into glasses, sprinkle the cinnamon sugar on top and serve. —Rick Ortiz

● HEALTHY ● MAKE AHEAD ○ VEGETARIAN ● STAFF FAVORITE

PAGE NUMBERS IN **BOLD** INDICATE PHOTOGRAPHS

D

PAGE NUMBERS IN **BOLD** INDICATE PHOTOGRAPHS

PAGE NUMBERS IN **BOLD** INDICATE PHOTOGRAPHS

PAGE NUMBERS IN **BOLD** INDICATE PHOTOGRAPHS

PAGE NUMBERS IN **BOLD** INDICATE PHOTOGRAPHS

PAGE NUMBERS IN **BOLD** INDICATE PHOTOGRAPHS

CONTRIBUTORS

RECIPES

MATT ABERGEL is the chef and co-owner of Yardbird and Ronin in Hong Kong.

GRANT ACHATZ is the chef and co-owner of Alinea, Next and The Aviary cocktail bar, all in Chicago.

HUGH ACHESON is the chef and owner of Five & Ten in Athens, Georgia, and chef and co-owner of The National in Athens and Empire State South in Atlanta.

JODY ADAMS is the chef and owner of Rialto and the chef and co-owner of Trade, both in the Boston area.

FERRAN ADRIÀ, a pioneer of molecular gastronomy, was the chef at the now-closed El Bulli in Roses, Spain. His El Bulli Foundation created the forthcoming BulliPedia, a massive culinary wiki.

BRUCE AIDELLS, the founder of Aidells Sausage Co., has written numerous cookbooks, most recently *The Great Meat Cookbook.*

ERIN ALDERSON, a writer and photographer, founded the food blog Naturally Ella. She is also the author of *The Homemade Flour Cookbook.*

LINDA ALDREDGE owns Lulu Organics, an organic beauty products company.

RACHEL ALLEN is an Irish celebrity chef and cookbook author. Her most recent book is *Rachel's Everyday Kitchen.*

ERIK ANDERSON is the chef at The Catbird Seat in Nashville.

DOMINIQUE ANSEL is the chef and owner of Dominique Ansel Bakery in New York City.

MICHAEL ANTHONY is the chef and co-owner of Gramercy Tavern in New York City.

BANK ATCHARAWAN is the owner and wine director of Chada Thai & Wine in Las Vegas.

KYLE BAILEY is the chef at Birch & Barley, GBD and The Arsenal, all in Washington, DC.

SCOTT BAIRD is a bartender and co-owner of The Bon Vivants cocktail consulting firm and its flagship bar, Trick Dog, in San Francisco.

NICOLAUS BALLA is a co-chef at Bar Tartine in San Francisco.

JIMMY BANNOS, JR., is the chef and co-owner of The Purple Pig in Chicago.

DAN BARBER is the chef and co-owner of Blue Hill in Manhattan and Blue Hill at Stone Barns in Pocantico Hills, New York.

DARIO BARBONE is a co-founder and co-owner of Baia Pasta in Oakland, California.

AARON BARNETT is the chef and co-owner of St. Jack in Portland, Oregon.

MARIO BATALI is the chef and co-owner of more than a dozen restaurants in New York City, Las Vegas, L.A. and Singapore and a co-owner of Eataly, a market and restaurant complex in Manhattan and Chicago. He co-hosts *The Chew* and most recently published *Molto Batali.*

RICK BAYLESS is the chef and co-owner of several restaurants in the Chicago area and San Francisco, including Frontera Grill, Xoco and Topolobampo. He hosts PBS's *Mexico—One Plate at a Time* and most recently wrote *Frontera: Margaritas, Guacamoles, and Snacks.*

JOHN BESH is the chef and owner of the Besh Restaurant Group, which includes August and Domenica in New Orleans and Lüke in San Antonio.

MARCELO BETANCOURT is the chef at Vik Retreats in José Ignacio, Uruguay.

RICHARD BETTS is a Master Sommelier and co-founder of Betts & Scholl Wines, Scarpetta Wines and Sombra Mezcal.

JENNIFER BIESTY will be the chef at her forthcoming restaurant Shakewell Bar & Kitchen in Oakland, California.

JAMIE BISSONNETTE is a co-chef and co-owner of Coppa in Boston and Toro in Boston and New York City.

RICHARD BLAIS is the chef and co-owner of The Spence in Atlanta and chef at Flip Burger Boutique in Atlanta and Birmingham, Alabama.

EVAN BLOOM is a co-chef and co-owner of Wise Sons Jewish Delicatessen in San Francisco.

APRIL BLOOMFIELD is the chef and co-owner of The Spotted Pig, The Breslin, The John Dory Oyster Bar and Salvation Taco, all in New York City, and Tosca Cafe in San Francisco.

SCOTT BOGGS is the chef and manager of Rose Bakery in New York City.

EUGENIA BONE writes the *Denver Post* food blog Well-Preserved. Her most recent book is *Mycophilia,* about her love of fungi.

MASSIMO BOTTURA is the chef and owner of Osteria Francescana and Franceschetta 58 in Modena, Italy.

JAMIE BOUDREAU is the mixologist and owner of Canon in Seattle.

DANIEL BOULUD is the chef and owner of 14 restaurants, including Daniel and DB Bistro Moderne in Manhattan, Café Boulud in Toronto and Maison Boulud in Beijing.

KIM BOYCE is the baker and owner of Bakeshop in Portland, Oregon, and author of *Good to the Grain.*

DANIKA BOYLE owns Petite Pêche & Co., a culinary travel company in Austin.

STUART BRIOZA is the chef and co-owner of State Bird Provisions and the upcoming The Progress, both in San Francisco.

JENI BRITTON BAUER is the founder and owner of Jeni's Splendid Ice Creams, with shops in Ohio, Tennessee, Illinois and Georgia.

SEAN BROCK is the chef at McCrady's in Charleston, South Carolina, and Husk in Charleston and Nashville.

BRUCE BROMBERG and his brother **ERIC BROMBERG** are the co-chefs and co-owners of the Blue Ribbon Restaurant Group, with several Blue Ribbon restaurants in New York City and Blue Ribbon Sushi Bar & Grill in Las Vegas.

ERIK BRUNER-YANG is the chef and owner of Toki Underground in Washington, DC.

DANNY BUA is the sous chef at Lockeland Table in Nashville.

TIM BYRES is the chef and co-owner of Smoke, Chicken Scratch and Bar Belmont, all in Dallas.

JOSH CAPON is the chef and co-owner of B&B Winepub and El Toro Blanco and the chef at Lure Fishbar, all in New York City.

CONTRIBUTORS

ANDREW CARMELLINI is the chef and co-owner of Locanda Verde and Lafayette, both in New York City, and The Dutch in New York City and Miami.

VIC CASANOVA is the chef and owner of Gusto in Los Angeles.

KATHY CASEY is the owner of Kathy Casey Food Studios—Liquid Kitchen, a food and beverage consulting company; host of *Kathy Casey's Liquid Kitchen;* and author of nine cookbooks, most recently *Sips & Apps.*

JOSEPH CASSINELLI is the chef and owner of Posto and The Painted Burro in the Boston area.

FRANK CASTRONOVO is a co-chef and co-owner of several restaurants in New York City, including Frankies 457 and Prime Meats.

JOSEF CENTENO is the chef and owner of Bar Amá, Bäco Mercat and Orsa & Winston, all in L.A.

LUCA CERATO is the chef and co-owner of Bir'ostu, the restaurant at CitaBiunda brewpub in Neive, Italy.

JEFF CERCIELLO is the chef and owner of Farmshop, with locations in Santa Monica and Larkspur, California.

DAVID CHANG is the chef and founder of the Momofuku restaurant group, with restaurants in New York City, Sydney and Toronto, including Momofuku Noodle Bar and Momofuku Milk Bar.

JOANNE CHANG is the pastry chef and co-owner of Flour Bakery + Café, with locations in the Boston area, and chef and co-owner of Myers + Chang, also in Boston.

JUSTIN CHAPPLE is F&W's Test Kitchen associate editor.

GINA CHERSEVANI is a mixologist and co-owner of Buffalo & Bergen in Washington, DC.

MICHAEL CHIARELLO is the chef and owner of Bottega in Napa Valley and Coqueta in San Francisco; the host of Food Network's *Easy Entertaining with Michael Chiarello;* and the author of several cookbooks, most recently *Live Fire.*

JULIA CHILD, a former F&W contributor, authored numerous cookbooks, most famously *Mastering the Art of French Cooking,* and starred in many cooking shows, including *The French Chef.* She founded the Julia Child Foundation for Gastronomy and the Culinary Arts.

ROY CHOI is the chef and co-owner of Kogi BBQ food trucks as well as several brick-and-mortar restaurants in the L.A. area.

KAY CHUN is F&W's Test Kitchen senior editor.

JOE CICALA is the chef at Le Virtù in Philadelphia.

MICHAEL CIMARUSTI is the chef and co-owner of L.A.'s Providence and Connie & Ted's.

TOM COLICCHIO, the head judge on *Top Chef,* is the chef and owner of numerous restaurants, including Craft in Manhattan and L.A. and Craftsteak in Las Vegas.

SARAH COPELAND writes the culinary blog Edible Living and most recently authored the vegetarian cookbook *Feast.*

MICHAEL CORDÚA is the chef and co-owner of seven Houston-area restaurants, including Churrascos, Américas and Artista.

CHRIS COSENTINO, winner of *Top Chef Masters* Season 4, is the chef and co-owner of Incanto and owner of Boccalone Salumeria, both in San Francisco.

GERARD CRAFT is a co-chef and co-owner of Niche, Brasserie, Taste and Pastaria, all in the St. Louis area.

JESSE CRUZ is the chef and co-owner of Lucky Belly in Honolulu.

TIM CUSHMAN is the chef and co-owner of O Ya in Boston.

MATT DANZER is a co-chef and co-owner of Uncle Boon's in New York City and co-owner of Reddings Market on Shelter Island, New York.

JAIME DAVIS is the pastry chef at No. 9 Park in Boston.

JOHN DEBARY, the assistant editor and recipe tester for F&W *Cocktails 2013,* is bar director for the Momofuku restaurant group in New York City.

DANIEL DELONG is a co-chef and co-owner of Sir and Star at The Olema and Manka's Inverness Lodge, both in Marin County, California.

TRACI DES JARDINS is the chef and owner of Jardinière and Mijita Cocina Mexicana and chef and co-owner of Public House, all in San Francisco.

KEVIN DIEDRICH is the bar manager at Jasper's Corner Tap & Kitchen in San Francisco.

STEWART DIETZ is the chef and owner of Stewart Dietz Catering in Methow Valley, Washington.

VINNY DOTOLO is a co-chef and co-owner of Animal, Son of a Gun and Trois Mec, all in L.A.

SHAUN DOTY is the chef and co-owner of Bantam + Biddy and a co-owner of Chick-a-Biddy, both in Atlanta.

DANIEL DUANE is a San Francisco–based writer; his latest book is *How to Cook Like a Man.*

ALAIN DUCASSE is the chef and owner of more than 20 restaurants around the world, including Le Louis XV in Monaco, Plaza Athénée in Paris, Adour in New York City and Washington, DC, and Mix in Las Vegas.

WYLIE DUFRESNE is the chef and co-owner of WD-50 and Alder in New York City.

TARA DUGGAN is a cookbook author and food writer at the *San Francisco Chronicle.* Her most recent cookbook is *Root-to-Stalk Cooking.*

SERGIO DURANDO is the chef at Le Baladin in Piozzo, Italy.

CLOTILDE DUSOULIER is the blogger behind Chocolate & Zucchini and author of *The French Market Cookbook.*

GRAHAM ELLIOT, culinary director for the Lollapalooza music festival, is the chef and co-owner of Graham Elliot and Graham Elliot Bistro in Chicago and Primary Food & Drink in Greenwich, Connecticut.

PETER ENDRISS is the baker and co-owner of Runner & Stone in Brooklyn, New York.

KELLY ENGLISH is the chef and owner of Restaurant Iris and The Second Line in Memphis, and Kelly English Steakhouse in St. Louis.

RENEE ERICKSON is the chef and co-owner of several Seattle restaurants, including The Walrus and the Carpenter and Boat Street Café.

FRANK FALCINELLI is a co-chef and co-owner of several restaurants in New York City, including Frankies 457 and Prime Meats.

ANYA FERNALD is the CEO and co-founder of Belcampo, an artisanal food–and–agritourism company in California, Uruguay and Belize.

LARA FERRONI, a blogger, food photographer and writer, is the author of *Put an Egg on It.*

BOBBY FLAY is the chef and owner of many restaurants in the US and Bahamas, including Mesa Grill and Bar Americain. He is the host of *Brunch at Bobby's,* among other cooking shows.

TREY FOSHEE is the chef and co-owner of George's at the Cove in La Jolla, California.

CAITLIN FREEMAN is the pastry chef for Blue Bottle Coffee, with locations in New York City and the San Francisco Bay Area, and the author of *Modern Art Desserts.*

EBEN FREEMAN, director of bar operations and innovations for the Altamarea Group, runs the cocktails program at The Butterfly in Manhattan.

DAVID FRENKIEL, co-author of the cookbook *Vegetarian Everyday,* co-writes the blog Green Kitchen Stories.

ALISSA FRICE is the pastry chef at St. Jack in Portland, Oregon.

DYLAN FULTINEER is the chef at Rappahannock in Richmond, Virginia.

TERRENCE GALLIVAN is a co-chef and co-owner of The Pass & Provisions in Houston.

GALE GAND is the pastry chef and co-owner of Tru in Chicago. She has written several cookbooks, most recently *Gale Gand's Brunch!*

MATT GANDIN is the chef at Comal in Berkeley.

SANTIAGO GARAT owns Rolling Beat, a catering and food consulting company in Montevideo, Uruguay, and co-owns Sudestada restaurant in Buenos Aires.

COLBY GARRELTS is the chef and co-owner of Bluestem in Kansas City, Missouri, and Rye in Leawood, Kansas.

INA GARTEN is the host of Food Network's *Barefoot Contessa*. She has written eight *Barefoot Contessa* cookbooks.

MONICA GLASS is the pastry chef at Clio and Uni Sashimi Bar in Boston.

SUZANNE GOIN is the chef and co-owner of four Los Angeles restaurants, including Lucques and A.O.C.

HEDY GOLDSMITH is the pastry chef for The Genuine Hospitality Group restaurants in Miami and Grand Cayman, including Michael's Genuine Food & Drink. She is also the author of *Baking Out Loud*.

JOHN GORHAM is the chef and co-owner of Toro Bravo, Tasty n Sons and Tasty n Alder in Portland, Oregon, and a co-author of the cookbook *Toro Bravo*.

DANIEL GRITZER is an associate food editor at *Food & Wine*.

SARAH GRUENEBERG is the chef at Spiaggia in Chicago.

ALEX GUARNASCHELLI, a judge on Food Network's *Chopped* and winner of *The Next Iron Chef*, is the chef and co-owner of two Butter restaurants in New York City.

LANCE GUMMERE is a co-owner of Bantam + Biddy and Chick-a-Biddy in Atlanta.

JOSH HABIGER is the chef at Pinewood Social in Nashville.

CHRIS HANMER, winner of *Top Chef: Just Desserts* Season 2, is the pastry chef and owner of CH Pâtisserie in Sioux Falls, South Dakota, and founder and owner of The School of Pastry Design in Las Vegas.

RYAN HARDY is the chef and co-owner of Charlie Bird in New York City.

MARCELLA HAZAN was a renowned cookbook author and teacher of Italian cuisine. She wrote six acclaimed cookbooks, including *Essentials of Classic Italian Cooking*.

LEE HEFTER is a managing partner and executive corporate chef for the Wolfgang Puck fine dining and events groups, overseeing many restaurants globally, including Spago in Beverly Hills and Cut in London and Dubai.

MARIA HELM SINSKEY is the chef at Robert Sinskey Vineyards in Napa and author of *The Vineyard Kitchen*.

TANYA HOLLAND is the chef and owner of Brown Sugar Kitchen and B-Side BBQ in Oakland, California, and the author of *New Soul Cooking*.

JAMES HOLMES is the chef and owner of Olivia and Lucy's Fried Chicken in Austin.

LINTON HOPKINS is the chef and co-owner of Restaurant Eugene and Holeman & Finch Public House in Atlanta.

DANIEL HUMM is the chef and co-owner of Eleven Madison Park and The NoMad restaurant in New York City.

MIKE ISABELLA is the chef and owner of Graffiato, Kapnos and G in Washington, DC. He is also the author of *Crazy Good Italian*.

CHRISTOPHER ISRAEL is the chef and owner of Grüner in Portland, Oregon.

MARA JERNIGAN is the general manager of Belcampo Belize, an eco-lodge and farm in southern Belize's Toledo district.

CATHY JOHNSON is a baker and web designer for Big Sugar Bakeshop in Los Angeles.

SARAH JORDAN is the pastry chef at Boka and GT Fish & Oyster in Chicago.

ALLISON KAVE is the baker and founder of First Prize Pies and a co-baker and co-owner of Butter & Scotch in New York City.

ERIC KAYSER is the master baker and owner of La Maison Kayser artisan bakeries, with more than 100 locations worldwide. His most recent cookbook is *My Cupcakes and Crackers*.

JOSH KEELER is the chef and co-owner of Two Boroughs Larder in Charleston, South Carolina.

THOMAS KELLER is the chef and co-owner of The French Laundry and Ad Hoc in Napa Valley, Per Se in New York City and multiple locations of Bouchon Bakeries and Bistros. He is also the author of *The French Laundry Cookbook*.

OWEN KENWORTHY is the chef at Brawn in London.

MARCIA KIESEL, formerly F&W's Test Kitchen supervisor, co-authored *The Simple Art of Vietnamese Cooking*.

LAUREN KIINO is the chef and owner of Il Cane Rosso in San Francisco.

BILL KIM is the chef and co-owner of Urbanbelly, Belly Shack and BellyQ restaurants in Chicago.

HOONI KIM is the chef and co-owner of Danji and Hanjan in New York City.

DAVID KINCH is the chef and owner of Manresa in Los Gatos, California.

KRISTEN KISH, winner of *Top Chef* Season 10, is chef de cuisine at Menton in Boston.

COCO KISLINGER is the founder and owner of Coco Bakes, a gluten-free baking company in L.A.

JESSICA KOSLOW is the chef and owner of Sqirl in Los Angeles.

CHRISTOPHER KOSTOW is the chef at The Restaurant at Meadowood in St. Helena, California.

MOURAD LAHLOU is the chef and owner of Aziza in San Francisco.

RICHARD LANDAU is a co-chef and co-owner of Vedge in Philadelphia.

KEAVY LANDRETH is the baker and founder of Kumquat Cupcakery and a co-baker and co-owner of Butter & Scotch in New York City.

PHOEBE LAPINE, co-author of the cookbook *In the Small Kitchen*, writes the food blog Feed Me Phoebe.

DON LEE is the director of product development for Cocktail Kingdom, an online purveyor of professional and custom barware and artisanal bitters and syrups.

BELINDA LEONG is the pastry chef and co-owner of B. Patisserie in San Francisco.

MATT LEWIS, a co-founder of Baked in Brooklyn, New York, co-wrote *Baked Elements*.

PAUL LIEBRANDT is the chef at The Elm in Brooklyn and owner of Crumpet Consulting.

FELIP LLUFRIU is the chef at Roca Moo restaurant at Hotel Omm in Barcelona.

JENN LOUIS is the chef and co-owner of Sunshine Tavern and Lincoln and the chef and owner of Culinary Artistry, all in Portland, Oregon.

BARBARA LYNCH is the chef and owner of several Boston restaurants, including No. 9 Park, B&G Oysters, Sportello and Menton.

TIFFANY MACISAAC is the pastry chef for the Neighborhood Restaurant Group, with many locations in the DC metro area, including Birch & Barley and GBD.

DEBORAH MADISON writes an eponymous food blog and has authored several cookbooks, most recently *Vegetable Literacy*.

JOY MANNING is a food writer and editor and co-author of *Almost Meatless*.

DOMENICA MARCHETTI is an Italian home cook and food writer. She is the blogger behind Domenica Cooks and the author of *The Glorious Vegetables of Italy*.

ZARELA MARTINEZ is the former chef of the now-closed Zarela in New York City and author of *Zarela's Veracruz*.

NOBU MATSUHISA is the chef and co-owner of Nobu and Matsuhisa restaurants worldwide and co-owner of the Nobu Hotel in Las Vegas.

IGNACIO MATTOS is the chef and co-owner of Estela in New York City.

DAVID MAWHINNEY is the chef at Haven's Kitchen, a cooking school, specialty food shop and private event space in New York City.

TONY MAWS is the chef and owner of Craigie on Main and The Kirkland Tap & Trotter, both in the Boston area.

JOSHUA MCFADDEN is the chef at Ava Gene's and Roman Candle Baking Co. in Portland, Oregon.

TIM MCKEE is the chef and co-owner of La Belle Vie in Minneapolis.

THOMAS MCNAUGHTON is the chef and co-owner of Flour + Water, Central Kitchen and Salumeria, all in San Francisco.

STEVE MENTER is the chef at Pulqueria in New York City.

MATTHIAS MERGES is the chef and owner of Yusho and Billy Sunday cocktail bar in Chicago.

CARLO MIRARCHI is the chef and co-owner of Roberta's and Blanca in Brooklyn, New York.

JOHNNY MONIS is the chef and co-owner of Komi and Little Serow in Washington, DC.

PABLO MONTERO is the chef at Abadía Retuerta LeDomaine hotel and winery in Valladolid, Spain.

KELLY MYERS is the chef and co-owner of Xico in Portland, Oregon.

TOM MYLAN is a butcher and co-owner of The Meat Hook in Brooklyn, New York.

SILVANA NARDONE is the author of *Cooking for Isaiah* and the gluten-free-food blog Silvana's Kitchen. She is also the owner and editor-in-chief of the digital magazine Easy Eats.

ZOE NATHAN is the pastry chef and co-owner of Rustic Canyon, Huckleberry Café and Milo and Olive, all in Santa Monica, California.

MICHAEL NATKIN is the author of the *Herbivoracious* cookbook and website.

JENNIFER NEWENS is a cookbook author and editor. Her most recent book is *Cooking with Spice*.

JOE NG is the chef and co-owner of RedFarm in New York City.

MANI NIALL is the baker and owner of Sweet Bar Bakery in Oakland, California, and author of *Good Morning Baking!*

DIRK NIEPOORT is a winemaker and manager for his family's Niepoort wine company in the Douro Valley in Portugal.

NANCY OAKES is the chef and co-owner of Boulevard and Prospect, both in San Francisco, and a co-author of *Boulevard: The Cookbook*.

AIMEE OLEXY is the founder and co-owner of Talula's Garden restaurant and Talula's Daily market in Philadelphia.

JAMIE OLIVER is a TV personality and the chef and owner of several restaurants worldwide, including Jamie's Italian in the U.K., Dubai and Sydney. His most recent cookbook is *Jamie Oliver's Food Escapes*.

KEN ORINGER is the chef and co-owner of several restaurants, including Clio and Coppa in Boston and Toro in Boston and New York City.

IVAN ORKIN is the chef and owner of Ivan Ramen, with two locations each in Tokyo and Manhattan.

GABRIEL ORTA is a mixologist and co-owner of Bar Lab, a Miami-based beverage program consulting firm, and co-founder of The Broken Shaker bar at the Freehand Miami hostel.

RENE ORTIZ will be a co-owner of the forthcoming Launderette restaurant and grocery and Angry Bear Chinese takeout in Austin.

RICK ORTIZ is the chef and owner of Antique Taco in Chicago.

CHRIS PANDEL is the chef and co-owner of The Bristol and Balena in Chicago.

FRANCIS PANIEGO is the chef and co-owner of Tondeluna and chef at Echaurren and El Portal de Echaurren restaurants in Ezcaray, Spain.

GRACE PARISI is a former F&W Test Kitchen senior editor and the author of *Get Saucy*.

DAVE PASTERNACK is the chef and co-owner of Esca in New York City.

DANIEL PATTERSON is the chef and co-owner of Coi, Plum, Plum Bar, Haven and Alta CA all in the San Francisco Bay Area.

JACQUES PÉPIN, master chef and F&W contributing editor, is the dean of special programs at Manhattan's International Culinary Center and host of PBS's *Jacques Pépin: More Fast Food My Way*. His most recent cookbook is *Essential Pepin*.

TULLY PHILLIPS is the owner of Tu-Lu's Gluten-Free Bakery in New York City and Dallas.

RENATO POLIAFITO, a co-owner of Baked in Brooklyn, New York, co-wrote *Baked Elements*.

ZACH POLLACK is a co-chef and co-owner of Sotto in Los Angeles.

YIGIT PURA, winner of *Top Chef: Just Desserts* Season 1, is the pastry chef and co-owner of Tout Sweet Pâtisserie in San Francisco.

ANNE QUATRANO is a co-chef and co-owner of several restaurants in Atlanta, including Bacchanalia, Abattoir and Quinones Room.

PAUL QUI, winner of *Top Chef* Season 9, is the chef and co-owner of Qui and the East Side King restaurant and food trucks in Austin.

STEVEN RAICHLEN is the host of PBS's *Primal Grill* and author of numerous cookbooks, including *Planet Barbecue* and *How to Grill*.

SANDI REINLIE is the pastry chef at Vespaio in Austin and a pastry instructor for the culinary tours company Petite Pêche & Co.

JONAH RHODEHAMEL is the chef at Oliveto in Oakland, California.

PATRICIA RICHARDS, a master mixologist, runs the beverage program at Wynn Las Vegas and Encore Resort in Las Vegas.

JACK RIEBEL is the chef and co-owner of Butcher & The Boar in Minneapolis.

ERIC RIPERT is the chef and co-owner of Le Bernardin in New York City and chef-adviser for Blue by Eric Ripert in Grand Cayman.

LEO ROBITSCHEK is the bar manager at Eleven Madison Park and The NoMad Hotel in New York City.

JESSAMYN RODRIGUEZ is the founder and CEO of Hot Bread Kitchen, a New York City–based nonprofit that employs foreign-born and low-income people in an artisanal bread bakery.

MICHAEL ROMANO is the culinary director and co-owner of the Union Square Hospitality Group, presiding over its numerous restaurants, including Union Square Cafe and Gramercy Tavern in Manhattan.

GABRIEL RUCKER is the chef and co-owner of Le Pigeon and Little Bird in Portland, Oregon.

MATTHEW RUNEARE is the brand director for Belcampo Inc., an artisanal food–and–agritourism company in California, Belize and Uruguay.

STEVE SAMSON is a co-chef and co-owner of Sotto in Los Angeles.

MARCUS SAMUELSSON is the chef and co-owner of Red Rooster and American Table in New York City and American Table Brasserie and Bar in Stockholm. He is also the author of *Yes, Chef: A Memoir*.

SUVIR SARAN is the chairman of the Asian Studies Center at the Culinary Institute of America. He has co-authored several cookbooks, most recently *Masala Farm*.

RENATO SARDO is the president, co-founder and head pasta maker at Baia Pasta, an artisanal food company in Oakland, California.

STEVEN SATTERFIELD is the chef and co-owner of Miller Union in Atlanta.

RACHEL SAUNDERS founded the artisanal jam company Blue Chair Fruit.

MICHAEL SCHLOW is the chef and owner of several restaurants in the Boston area, including Via Matta and Alta Strada.

LISA SHIN is a co-owner of Wing Wings in San Francisco.

JON SHOOK is a co-chef and co-owner of Animal, Son of a Gun and Trois Mec, all in L.A.

SETH SIEGEL-GARDNER is a co-chef and co-owner of The Pass & Provisions in Houston.

NANCY SILVERTON is a co-founder of Campanile, founder of La Brea Bakery and co-chef and co-owner of Pizzeria Mozza and Osteria Mozza, all in the Los Angeles area.

CLINT SIMONSON owns the indie record label De Stijl Records.

KEVIN SOUSA is the chef and owner of several Pittsburgh restaurants, including Station Street.

JOHNNY SPERO is the sous chef at Minibar by José Andrés in Washington, DC.

SUSAN SPUNGEN is a food stylist, recipe developer and author of *What's a Hostess to Do?* and *Recipes: A Collection for the Modern Cook.*

FRANK STITT is the chef and co-owner of Highlands Bar and Grill, Bottega and Chez Fonfon in Birmingham, Alabama.

ETHAN STOWELL is the chef and co-owner of six Seattle restaurants, including How to Cook a Wolf, Staple & Fancy and Tavolàta.

ALEX STUPAK is the chef and co-owner of Empellón Taqueria and Empellón Cocina, both in New York City.

KRISTINE SUBIDO is the chef and co-owner of Pecking Order in Chicago.

JESSE SUTTON is the chef at Social Restaurant + Wine Bar in Charleston, South Carolina.

HEIDI SWANSON is the creator of the food blog 101 Cookbooks and author of three cookbooks, including *Super Natural Every Day.*

MICHAEL SYMON is the chef and co-owner of Lola, Lolita and B Spot in Cleveland. He co-hosts ABC's *The Chew.*

AMY THIELEN is the author of *The New Midwestern Table* and the blog Sourtooth. She also hosts Food Network's *Heartland Table.*

GABE THOMPSON is the chef at L'Apicio, Dell'anima, L'Artusi and Anfora in New York City.

MICHAEL TOSCANO is the chef and co-owner of Perla and Montmartre in New York City.

JEREMIAH TOWER, famed for his now-closed San Francisco restaurant Stars, is a food writer and architect. His books include *California Dish.*

BOB TRUITT is the pastry chef for the Altamarea Group's restaurants, including The Butterfly in New York City and Al Molo in Hong Kong.

MING TSAI is the chef and owner of Blue Ginger and Blue Dragon, both in the Boston area, and the

host of *Simply Ming.* His most recent cookbook is *Simply Ming in Your Kitchen.*

ROBB TURNER co-owns Madava Farms in Dutchess County, New York.

MICHAEL TUSK is the chef and co-owner of Quince and Cotogna in San Francisco.

JARED VAN CAMP is the chef at Old Town Social in Chicago.

MARC VETRI is the chef and co-owner of Vetri, Osteria, Amis and Alla Spina, all in Philadelphia.

LUISE VINDAHL, co-author of *Vegetarian Everyday,* co-writes the blog Green Kitchen Stories.

ANYA VON BREMZEN, an F&W contributor, is the author of several cookbooks, most recently *Mastering the Art of Soviet Cooking.*

JEAN-GEORGES VONGERICHTEN, an F&W contributing editor, is the chef and co-owner of dozens of restaurants around the world, including Jean Georges in Manhattan and Shanghai.

CATHY WATERMAN is the owner and designer of an eponymous custom jewelry and tableware design company.

JENNIFER WELLS is the chief operating officer of Tu-Lu's Gluten-Free Bakery in New York City and Dallas.

WILLIAM WERNER is the chef and co-owner of Craftsman and Wolves in San Francisco.

MICHAEL WHITE is the chef and co-owner of the Altamarea restaurant group, including The Butterfly, Marea and Ai Fiori in Manhattan and Al Molo in Hong Kong.

NICHOLAS WILBER is the chef at The East Pole in New York City.

PAULA WOLFERT is the author of numerous cookbooks known for bringing the authentic tastes of Mediterranean cuisine to home chefs, including *The Food of Morocco.*

KUNIKO YAGI is the chef at Hinoki & the Bird in Los Angeles.

TETSU YAHAGI is the chef de cuisine at Spago Beverly Hills.

SANG YOON is the chef and owner of Lukshon in Los Angeles and Father's Office gastropub in L.A. and Santa Monica and the chef and co-owner of Helms Bakery in L.A.

ANDREW ZIMMERN, an F&W contributing editor, writes the Kitchen Adventures column on *foodandwine.com.* He is also the host and creator of *Bizarre Foods with Andrew Zimmern* and the chef behind AZ Canteen food truck in Minneapolis.

ELAD ZVI is a mixologist and co-owner of Bar Lab, a Miami-based beverage program consulting firm, and co-founder of The Broken Shaker bar at the Freehand Miami hostel.

IMAGES

LUCAS ALLEN 17, 371

CEDRIC ANGELES 116, 117, 345

QUENTIN BACON 327

CHRIS COURT 53, 81, 89, 151, 177, 179, 223, 285, 353

TARA FISHER 183, 234, 315

JOHANNA FRENKEL 40

ETHAN HILL 352

CHRISTINA HOLMES 97, 170, 171, 189, 261, 297, 313, 317, 321, 360, 361

JODY HORTON 146, 147

FRANCES JANISCH 363

JULIA CHILD FOUNDATION FOR GASTRONOMY AND THE CULINARY ARTS 293

JOHN KERNICK 21–23, 35, 51, 67, 93, 126, 127, 141, 174, 175, 197, 209, 221, 233, 241, 246, 247, 271, 274, 275, 280, 281, 323, 333, 356 (food), 357, 365, 368, 369

LINE KLEIN 47, 135, 283

LISA LINDER 123

WENDY MACNAUGHTON 44, 63, 122, 227

JOHNNY MILLER 107, 215, 219, 335, 342, 343

MARTIN MORRELL 149

MARCUS NILSSON 139, 187, 205, 339

CON POULOS 11, 27, 31, 39, 41, 43, 59, 65, 73, 77, 85, 99, 103, 121, 129, 131, 155, 159, 163, 167, 173, 199, 229, 237, 239, 243, 245, 257, 263, 266, 267, 269, 277, 279, 287, 289, 295, 299, 301, 305, 309, 311, 319, 351, 367, 377

ANDREW PURCELL 291

ANDERS SCHONNEMANN 324, 325

ANSON SMART 356 (portrait)

FREDRIKA STJÄRNE 61, 68, 69, 192, 193, 195, 213, 225, 231, 373

ALICE TAIT 19

PETRINA TINSLAY 15, 119, 201, 329, 355

MICHAEL TUREK 55, 90, 91, 145, 191, 216, 217, 284, 302, 303

JONNY VALIANT 8, 9, 249, 349

PEGGY WONG 253

PRODUCT IMAGES George Paul Vinegar (57), Teroforma (64), Cuizinetoolz (140), Tribest Corporation (251)

MEASUREMENT GUIDE

BASIC MEASUREMENTS

GALLON	QUART	PINT	CUP	OUNCE	TBSP	TSP	DROPS
1 gal	4 qt	8 pt	16 c	128 fl oz			
½ gal	2 qt	4 pt	8 c	64 fl oz			
¼ gal	1 qt	2 pt	4 c	32 fl oz			
	½ qt	1 pt	2 c	16 fl oz			
	¼ qt	½ pt	1 c	8 fl oz	16 tbsp		
			⅞ c	7 fl oz	14 tbsp		
			¾ c	6 fl oz	12 tbsp		
			⅔ c	5⅓ fl oz	10⅔ tbsp		
			⅝ c	5 fl oz	10 tbsp		
			½ c	4 fl oz	8 tbsp		
			⅜ c	3 fl oz	6 tbsp		
			⅓ c	2⅔ fl oz	5⅓ tbsp	16 tsp	
			¼ c	2 fl oz	4 tbsp	12 tsp	
			⅛ c	1 fl oz	2 tbsp	6 tsp	
				½ fl oz	1 tbsp	3 tsp	
					½ tbsp	1½ tsp	
						1 tsp	60 drops
						½ tsp	30 drops

US TO METRIC CONVERSIONS

THE CONVERSIONS SHOWN HERE ARE APPROXIMATIONS. FOR MORE PRECISE CONVERSIONS, USE THE FORMULAS TO THE RIGHT.

VOLUME		WEIGHT		TEMPERATURE		CONVERSION FORMULAS
1 tsp = 5 mL		1 oz = 28 g		475°F = 246°C		$tsp \times 4.929 = mL$
1 tbsp = 15 mL		¼ lb (4 oz) = 113 g		450°F = 232°C		$tbsp \times 14.787 = mL$
1 fl oz = 30 mL		½ lb (8 oz) = 227 g		425°F = 218°C		$fl\ oz \times 29.574 = mL$
¼ c = 59 mL		¾ lb (12 oz) = 340 g		400°F = 204°C		$c \times 236.588 = mL$
½ c = 118 mL		1 lb (16 oz) = ½ kg		375°F = 191°C		$pt \times 0.473 = L$
¾ c = 177 mL				350°F = 177°C		$qt \times 0.946 = L$
1 c = 237 mL		**LENGTH**		325°F = 163°C		$oz \times 28.35 = g$
1 pt = ½ L		1 in = 2.5 cm		300°F = 149°C		$lb \times 0.453 = kg$
1 qt = 1 L		5 in = 12.7 cm		275°F = 135°C		$in \times 2.54 = cm$
1 gal = 4.4 L		9 in = 23 cm		250°F = 121°C		$(°F - 32) \times 0.556 = °C$